W9-BCU-794

THE SPECULATOR

THE SPECULATOR

BERNARD M. BARUCH IN WASHINGTON,

1917–1965

JORDAN A. SCHWARZ

THE UNIVERSITY OF NORTH CAROLINA PRESS

CHAPEL HILL

Library of Congress cataloging in Publication Data

Schwarz, Jordan A   1937–
The speculator, Bernard M. Baruch in Washington, 1917–1965.
Bibliography: p.
Includes index.
1. Baruch, Bernard Mannes, 1870–1965. 2. United
States—Politics and government—20th century.
3. Statesmen—United States—Biography.
4. Capitalists and financiers—United States—
Biography. I. Title.
E748.B32S3   973.9'092'4 [B]   80-17386
ISBN 0-8078-1396-6

Frontispiece by Barry Moser

To my son and daughter,
Orrin Nathaniel and Jessica Shiri,
and to all the sons and daughters of the
City College of New York

Many improvements have been made by the ingenuity of the makers of machines, when to make them became the business of a peculiar trade; and some by that of those who are called philosophers or men of speculation, whose trade it is not to do anything, but to observe everything; and who, upon that account, are often capable of combining together the powers of the most distant and dissimilar objects.

ADAM SMITH
*An Inquiry into the Nature and
Causes of the Wealth of Nations*

In reading the history of nations, we find that, like individuals, they have their whims and peculiarities; their seasons of excitement and recklessness, when they care not what they do. We find that whole communities suddenly fix their minds upon one object, and go mad in its pursuit; that millions of people become simultaneously impressed with one delusion, and run after it, till their attention is caught by some new folly more captivating than the first. We see one nation suddenly seized, from its highest to its lowest members, with a fierce desire of military glory; and neither of them recovering its senses until it had shed rivers of blood and sowed a harvest of groans and tears, to be reaped by its posterity. . . . Money, again, has often been a cause of the delusion of multitudes. Sober nations have all at once become desperate gamblers, and risked almost their existence upon the turn of a piece of paper.

CHARLES MACKAY
*Extraordinary Popular Delusions
and the Madness of Crowds,*
preface to the 1852 edition

The Circumlocution Office was (as everybody knows without being told) the most important Department under Government. No public business of any kind could possibly be done at any time, without the acquiescence of the Circumlocution Office. Its finger was in the largest public pie, and in the smallest public tart. It was equally impossible to do the plainest right and to undo the plainest wrong, without the express authority of the Circumlocution Office. . . . Whatever was required to be done, the Circumlocution Office was beforehand with all the public departments in the art of perceiving— HOW NOT TO DO IT.

Through this delicate perception, through the tact with which it invariably seized it, and through the genius with which it always acted on it, the Circumlocution Office had risen to overtop all the public departments and the public condition had risen to be—what it was.

It is true that How not to do it was the great study and object of all the public departments and professional politicians all round the Circumlocution Office. It is true that every new premier and every new government, coming in because they had upheld a certain thing as necessary to be done, were no sooner come in than they applied their utmost faculties to discovering How not to do it. It is true that from the moment when a general election was over, every returned man who had been raving on hustings because it hadn't been done, and who had been asking the friends of the honourable gentleman in the opposite interest on pain of impeachment to tell him why it hadn't been done, and who had been asserting that it must be done, and who had been pledging himself that it should be done, began to devise, How it was not to be done.

CHARLES DICKENS
Little Dorrit, Chapter 10

 CONTENTS

CONTENTS

CONTENTS

CONTENTS

ILLUSTRATIONS

 PREFACE

This is a book about Bernard M. Baruch, who transcended a career as a successful speculator in Wall Street finances to become a speculator in Washington politics from the First World War to the Vietnamese war. In Washington he promoted national economic policies intended to achieve market stabilization and social order through the considerable influence he wielded upon policy makers and public opinion. For nearly five decades, Baruch was a powerful and fascinating personage; his career is important for what it tells us about him and the politics of his time.

In writing about himself, Baruch insisted that his story relate the movements and events of which he was a part as a means of educating readers about their own times. Although that assertion was typically egotistical of Baruch, he was correct in interpreting his public career as a partial mirror of his milieu's quest for business stabilization. Baruch himself thus dictated this purpose—a rather large one for any book—by attaining influence and playing many roles as a shaper and reflector of major developments of his time. It is my task to reconstruct and understand him and those developments.

Considering the scope of Baruch's involvements, it is imperative that I include a disclaimer: this book in no way pretends to be a definitive study of the man. Baruch's business and personal activities are peripheral to this story, although some of them have been included because they impinged upon his public endeavors or because they reveal a private side of his public personality. This is an analytical study of Baruch and his varied political activities, and it is written with an acute awareness that his actions and insights are significant for our time.

Baruch is a significant figure in twentieth-century American political history because he was an astute observer of his own era, a speculator anticipating times to come, and an advocate of policies for dealing with future economic developments. His chief bête noire in his business and public careers was inflation. Seldom very articulate, Baruch could be eloquent on the dreaded social consequences of high prices. He was a conservative who believed that radical measures were sometimes imperative for stabilization. In war, which he considered an appropriate undertaking for the pursuit of national interests, he advocated comprehensive statist action that would assure order until the hostilities and their aftermath were concluded. In peace he prescribed cooperative arrangements that organized society for nonstatist planning. He was not always consistent or correct in his assessments, but in war or peace he usually recommended corporatist organization to maximize order in America's political economy. Although some historians have quoted Baruch's opinions as representative of business attitudes, it is evident that he frequently was an outsider both in business and in politics. His thinking was a variant on that of corporatist business philosophers who sought to organize a community of interests that could respond to internal and external pressures threatening price stabilization. In the twilight of his life, Baruch considered his mission a failure, and the history of our political economy since his passing in 1965 confirms that judgment. Yet his abortive quest bestows upon his career greater meaning for his times and our own.

In my research on Baruch and his activities, I generally avoided interviews with his surviving friends or acquaintances, most of whom remember him as either a saint or a rogue. Although I concentrated upon published or unpublished written materials contemporary to the events discussed, it did seem logical to discuss him with certain individuals. I am grateful to Harold Epstein, David Ginsburg, Samuel Lubell, Elizabeth Novarro, and Margaret Coit for graciously submitting in person to my questions. A few others chose to make themselves unavailable. John Kenneth Galbraith responded to questions by mail and, as always, was both very perceptive and quotable. Baruch was a memorable person whose contacts were as varied as his life was extensive; so it was almost inevitable that I would discover people whose work crossed his path and mine and who were willing to share with me impromptu remembrances of him. I appreciate the vignettes given me by Forrest Pogue, Sidney Skolsky, Eliot Janeway, Arthur S. Link, and David E. Lilienthal. Brooks Colcord gave me permission to quote from a letter written by Lincoln Colcord. There are too many archivists who have assisted me for mention here, but Nancy Bressler, Curator of Public Affairs Papers at the Seeley G. Mudd Library of Princeton University, is best representative of the patience and sense of service to historians that I have found in most depositories. I would like to thank also the staff of the Northern Illinois University Library, in particular the people at the Circulation, Interlibrary Loan, Government Documents, and Microforms departments.

I cannot forget those institutions and colleagues who gave encouragement and support in the making of this book. The American Philosophical Society helped out with a grant. Northern Illinois University assisted several times with faculty research stipends, council of deans grants, and two sabbatical leaves. Along the way three historians and friends heartened me: William E. Leuchtenburg of Columbia University, Frank Freidel of Harvard University, and Paul A. Carter of the University of Arizona. I have learned a great deal from my fellow historians, especially from the works of Ellis W. Hawley of the University of Iowa, and it has been my good fortune to have him read and comment upon my manuscript. Likewise, Arthur S. Link of Princeton University added measurably to my education on the Wilsonians, as did Carl Parrini and Martin David Dubin of Northern Illinois University. Robert W. Collins of North Carolina State University and Robert Dallek of the University of California at Los Angeles also gave me the benefit of their incisive comments. Robert D. Cuff of York University deserves special appreciation for the historical understandings I have gained from his writings, our conversations, and his criticisms of my manuscript. Of course, this book should in no way reflect upon him or the others who made suggestions and corrections.

My department chairman, J. Carroll Moody, has listened to more stories about Baruch than he cares to remember, which may be why he has so eagerly facilitated the typing of my manuscript. Credit for the typing goes to Laurel Davies, Elaine Kittleson, Cynthia Poortenga Phillips, and Jean Schiller of the Department of History office; Barbara Lauger of the Graduate School; and Zola Agranoff and Barbara Sherman. Another historian, James D. Norris, Dean of the College of Liberal Arts and Sciences, kept this book on schedule with grants for typing services. Lewis Bateman of The University of North Carolina Press has been a sympathetic editor whose "pitch" is worth heeding. Janis Bolster provided the finishing touches of a skilled copyeditor. Linda L. Schwarz has been a sharing wife, a loving mother, and a diligent career woman, conducting her own search for order in a home I often destabilized for the sake of this book. Finally, Orrin and Jessica deserve a share of the dedication because they give so much reassurance for the future.

THE SPECULATOR

 # CHAPTER ONE
IDENTIFYING BARUCH

Who was Bernard M. Baruch?

To the generations that lived through World War II that question would draw several responses. They remembered him as a very rich man who had made his fortune in Wall Street; an elder statesman who sat on park benches in Lafayette Square, opposite the White House, because President Roosevelt seldom would confer official positions upon him; and an unofficial advisor to presidents, from Wilson through Kennedy— a man whose sagacity and wisdom they dared not discount. Perhaps the man in the street would have known more about Baruch, perhaps less. But it is unlikely that the name would have been unfamiliar.

By the time Baruch died in 1965 he had been in the public eye for almost a half century. Of course there had been times when his fame swelled and then waned. He had first ventured upon the national scene in 1915 as a champion of American preparedness for involvement in World War I. Until then his reputation had not reached beyond Wall Street, where he was known as a very successful short seller with a penchant for inside deals on raw materials and railroad reorganizations. As a maverick trader he had acquired untold millions, enough to make him concerned more with wealth as a vehicle toward other objectives than as an end by itself. Politics had always attracted him, and his money and gracious personality drew powerful people to him. At a time when "malefactors of great wealth" in politics were suspect, his contributions to political campaigns and his apparently enlightened perspectives on social issues made him welcome to progressive Democrats and to President Woodrow Wilson. Before long this political dilettante was appointed to temporary government posts where a right-thinking businessman was most useful—

he was a member of the Allied Purchasing Commission and the raw materials expert on the Advisory Commission to the Council of National Defense. When the United States intervened in World War I, Baruch headed up the raw materials section of the War Industries Board until he became its chairman in 1918. In that position he effected a consolidation of its authority that earned him the sobriquet "czar" or "dictator" of America's war industries. By the end of the war only Herbert Hoover of the Food Administration among the civilian leaders rivaled Baruch's fame. He resigned shortly after the Armistice to become one of President Wilson's economic advisors to the Paris Peace Conference. By mid-1919 he was one of Wilson's most trusted compatriots. He could afford to decline Wilson's offer of the secretaryship of the Treasury and remain a prominent Democrat.

Baruch had an instinct for power, publicity, and prestige. Although his influence would never be as great with another president as with Wilson, no occupant of the White House could ever afford to slight him. Baruch's base of support lay with the Senate Democratic leadership, which, during its eclipse in the Republican twenties, looked to him as a source of economic wisdom and munificent campaign contributions. By the end of the decade few of them could remember which came first—his wisdom or his contributions. It is enough to say that both were valued highly. Furthermore, his public-spirited activity on behalf of agricultural parity with industry marked him as a Wall Streeter of eclectic and enlightened interests. All this he proved adept at publicizing either directly through his own devices or indirectly through admiring journalists like Arthur Krock, Mark Sullivan, Frank Kent, and the many reporters and editors whom he befriended on the *New York Times*, the Hearst papers, the Scripps-Howard chain, and other papers throughout the nation. Even if Baruch was a Democrat, Republican Presidents Harding, Coolidge, and Hoover found an invitation to him useful because of its newsworthiness and his influence with Senate Democrats.

The zenith of Baruch's congressional influence came during 1931–32. President Hoover, struggling to maintain a consensus in support of his voluntaristic strategy for combating the depression, turned to Baruch for aid in keeping Congress in line. Baruch did not fail him; but deteriorating events proved more powerful than Baruch. Franklin D. Roosevelt became the beneficiary of those circumstances. Like his predecessors, Roosevelt recognized the need to deal with Baruch and, albeit cautiously, did so.

Since 1918, Baruch had dreamed of being a power broker for a Democratic president. Twice he had been identified with abortive efforts to make William G. McAdoo the Democratic nominee for president. His strategy then became one of ostensible preconvention neutrality, lest he alienate the victor. Roosevelt's triumph in 1932 brought Baruch quickly to his side, but it was evident that the winner's formula for rewards, "For

Roosevelt before Chicago," placed Baruch outside the new president's circle of friends. Nevertheless, the depression crisis called for unity rather than exclusion.

The Baruch influence in the early New Deal was mixed. On the one hand, Roosevelt appointed two of Baruch's confidants—George N. Peek and Hugh Johnson—to head two key recovery agencies, the Agricultural Adjustment Administration and the National Recovery Administration. But Baruch himself received little recognition (certainly not the post of secretary of state he so ardently coveted), and Roosevelt's policy of monetary inflation went counter to Baruch's counsel. By 1935, Peek and Johnson were exiled from the New Deal and Baruch was counted among its conservative Democratic opponents. But Baruch proved to be too shrewd to be relegated to that curious list of Roosevelt antagonists. He never went public in his opposition, kept up his senatorial contacts, and made allies among White House workers such as Eleanor Roosevelt. Not until conservative opposition to Roosevelt had grown in strength did he dare to challenge Roosevelt openly, as he did on the tax bill of 1938. By that time the issue of preparedness for another war made Baruch's cultivated prominence on that subject a factor in the politics of a new era.

World War II saw a renaissance in Baruch's power. An outspoken critic of the administration's mobilization and stabilization policies, Baruch surrendered his ambition to lead another War Industries Board when it became evident that Roosevelt had no intention of ever allowing it. Instead, he turned to acting as a free-lance troubleshooter in the wartime bureaucracy and as a one-man pressure group *pro bono publico*. The prestige of the latter was conceded by Roosevelt when he appointed Baruch to head the Rubber Survey Committee in 1942 for the primary purpose of educating the public to accept gasoline rationing. In 1943, Baruch could have headed the top mobilization agencies if he had been willing to curb his unaccountable independent role. He did accept another temporary assignment that called for public education when he wrote an influential report on reconversion of war industry to civilian production.

When he was in his mid-seventies and hard of hearing, and known for his vanity and stubbornness, Baruch's image as an elder statesman worthy of public trust made him useful to President Truman. In 1946 he accepted the role of head of the American delegation to the United Nations Atomic Energy Commission for the purpose of winning Soviet acceptance and U.S. public approval of an American plan for international atomic control. Although he knew nothing about atomic energy, Baruch insisted upon making the plan tougher: the Soviets withheld approval even as the American people applauded it. But he was no longer the venerable institution he had been a few years before. In 1948, Truman staged a public quarrel with him, thereby condemning Baruch to the unhappy status of administration pariah. He still maintained public favor by appearing at congressional committee hearings, accepting organizational awards, throwing his political endorsement to Dwight Eisenhower in 1952, and commissioning his biography and his memoirs in the late 1950s. His opinions concerning economic policy were still sought by the press and by public officials. Seldom, however, were they heeded.

He was a failure in his principal public purpose: to educate the American people to accept planning for economic stabilization. He believed that the turmoil of capitalism demanded a strategy for public order that did not infringe upon the freedom of private ownership. Absolutely free enterprise engendered production chaos; and chaos was incompatible with a high standard of living and America's incipient greatness. Competition may have been salutary in the initial stages of America's development, but great economic units and capital requirements called for self-discipline. The philosophy of voluntary cooperation had been popularized among businessmen of the early twentieth century, but it had required an exigency like World War I to manufacture an excuse for experiencing it. Only government could execute comprehensive economic planning. It fell to Baruch to espouse quasi-cartelistic wartime business activity that preserved economic stability without abridging private enterprise. The stabilization lessons of the war, Baruch believed, ought not to be forgotten with the coming of peace.

The concept of voluntary cooperation for economic stabilization was assiduously promoted during the 1920s by, among others, Secretary of Commerce Hoover and private citizen Baruch. They did not prescribe government intervention in the market; they merely sought enlightened federal leadership of a self-disciplined private enterprise. To counter overproduction in certain overly competitive industries, stabilization advocates sought nothing less than cartelistic organization. Though they would not repeal the Sherman antitrust law or the principle of competition, they would modify them enough to allow cooperation that planned supply to conform with demand. Later, these were the underlying ideas behind the New Deal's initial attack upon low prices in the Great Depression. However, Baruch deplored the prominent role the New Deal assumed in the marketplace, preferring private initiative to government discipline. In other words, peacetime economic organization ought to be voluntaristic, but war demanded federal planning.

The problem inherent in a free-enterprise system at war was the essential incompatibility of a free market and war. Baruch considered a free market that depressed prices tolerable and potentially healthy; but a free market in war absurdly inflated prices, distorting the entire national economy and its place in world markets. National security required the economy's mobilization; national prosperity required its stabilization. To ensure domestic tranquility and social justice, Washington had no choice but to regiment the free market for the duration of war and the reconversion period. The experience of World War I had justified this radical doctrine.

Throughout the interwar period, Baruch had been the leading publicist for industrial planning for war. But the Roosevelt White House, responding to pressures from unions, farmers, and some businessmen, took dilatory incremental steps toward stabilization. Throughout 1940–45 a conflict of philosophies raged through the war administration between advocates of a broad economic expansion and partisans of stabilization. As the leading public proponent of stabilization, Baruch articulated the terms of the debate. But he prevailed only as long as the nation was mobilized for total war. Peace, along with the anticipation that it would bring widespread unemployment, shifted the balance in favor of expansionist policies. Innately a deflationist, Baruch was out of step with the postwar tolerance of higher prices. During the cold war, he argued, America ought to define limits regarding the extent of free enterprise. However, policy makers, reinforced by Keynesian analysis inspired in the Great Depression, accelerated spending in both the military and civilian sectors. This spending produced an anomalous contradiction: wartime demand amid peacetime supply. The cold war perpetuated inflation.

The Korean War occasioned renewed insistence by Baruch upon the need for comprehensive controls, but the Truman administration treated the crisis with partial stabilization measures. Baruch approved defense spending, but he came to realize that the lessons of stabilization learned during two world wars were being ignored or forgotten. The shibboleths of free enterprise had been buttressed by the 1950s growth-minded "new economics." More than ever the Old Man's deflationist economic concepts appeared illiberal and anachronistic.

Baruch was illiberal, but he was also relevant. Stabilization was eschewed by the Johnson administration during the Vietnam War, with consequences that still have not been fully appreciated. Events since Baruch's death in 1965 have inadvertently challenged notions that expansion brought manageable inflation, which offset unemployment. Americans have learned that inflation and unemployment are not alternatives, but are simultaneously possible; for that matter, one is not more socially acceptable than the other. Although presidents in the 1960s and 1970s repeated the doctrine of voluntarism Baruch had advanced in the 1920s, they never embraced the faith in social restraints he articulated in the 1940s. More than ever the American economy is noncompetitive but socially irresponsible. It is not so much a matter of no controls as it is one of no *public* controls. Social gains of the 1940s are being reversed by the lack of any societal commitment to a stabilization policy similar to one advanced by Baruch. This, then, is not solely Baruch's story; it is a history of America's abortive quest in the twentieth century for social justice through economic stabilization.

OF NEW YORK AND SOUTH CAROLINA

Like many Americans, Bernard M. Baruch had uncertain roots. He was not of one group or of one region. He led a dichotomous life, deliberately cultivating dual identities. His background encouraged this duality: although his parents were both Jews, their ancestors came from opposite ends of Europe—Poland and Iberia. They were Americans who combined contrasting American experiences: the new immigration and old-stock America, the urban and rural nations, New York City and South Carolina. Born on 19 August 1870 in Camden, South Carolina, Baruch lived his first decade as a "country boy"; then his father moved the family to New York City, where Bernard spent his adolescence. His father prospered in a Manhattan practice of medicine; his mother became a society matron; and Baruch found fame and fortune in that narrow corner at the southern tip of the island where wealth speculates on the lives of the rest of the island, the nation, and the world.

Baruch's activities made him a cosmopolitan. As a speculator he had to make his first residence in America's financial capital, New York City. But he maintained a second home in South Carolina suitable for entertaining the powerful from America's other capital, Washington, D.C. He understood America's deep suspicions of New York's parochialism of power. Two residences were imperative for advancing his ambitions. It could be said that New Yorkers with national ambitions need a second home to acquire another identity with which non-New Yorkers are more comfortable. Theodore Roosevelt played cowboy in South Dakota; Franklin Roosevelt played country gentleman in Hyde Park and in Georgia; poor Al Smith had only Rome. Away from his dealing in Wall Street, Baruch could claim that he was bound "by ties of blood and love" to the state of his birth, that he was "at heart, . . . a South Carolinean."[1] Nevertheless, he was a New Yorker. His South Carolina ties were symbolic and recreational; his New York City ties were real and material.

New York City contributed to Baruch's power while South Carolina made it respectable. The southern senators who took his advice and money treasured him as "a good old boy" who had beaten Wall Street at its own game. The public believed in him as an economic and political sage as long as it could be assured that neither New York nor Washington had corrupted him. Always attuned to the significance of symbols, Baruch in the Great Depression moved his business address from Wall Street to mid-town Manhattan to avert identification with "economic royalists."

Businessmen and politicians were often treated to the rustic gentility of Baruch's South Carolina estate, secure in the knowledge that the problems of the world they helped create would not intrude because their considerate host refused to install a telephone in his wilderness retreat. That is where he hunted as he might have in his country boyhood; that is what made his claim "I always remember that I was brought up on hogs and hominy" so convincing when he repeated it in his plush Fifth Avenue home.[2]

He was the most famous American Jew of his time. He exploited that reputation without ever permitting it to interfere with his secularism. Like his other roots, this ambivalence was an inheritance from his parents. His mother was a Daughter of the Confederacy and an observing Jew; his father was an immigrant who believed that he was an American rather than a Jew. Baruch, a loving son, kept faith with both parents. He married an Episcopalian, allowed her to raise their three children in her church, and, good cosmopolitan that he was, professed strongly that he could rid the world of bigotry by forsaking his peculiar heritage. However, partly out of love for his mother, he still closed his office and attended synagogue on the High Holy Days.

It was a mixed blessing to be the most famous Jew in America. He was both a convenient symbol for American Jews' successes and a target for hatred of them. He was everybody's favorite Jew when a token representation was required to demonstrate America's opportunities. At the same time, bigots, ranging from ordinary cranks to the extraordinary Henry Ford, heaped abuse upon him as a representative of the oldest continuous international conspiracy. Baruch's Jewishness was something he never flaunted and never, to his credit, denied. It followed him wherever he went and decidedly limited his attainments. Wealth, fame, and power did not enable him to escape anti-Semitism. Certain doors were always closed to him on the grounds of his heritage. He endured his share of the slurs most famous men attract and many others reserved only for Jews without wealth or fame.

Baruch considered himself an assimilated Jew. It was a paradox that made some Jews revere him while others, usually more familiar with Baruch's conception of his Jewishness, loathed him as an apostate. What sort of a Jew was he? A Jewish former associate answered the question by exclaiming, "A Jew? He was an anti-Semite!" This hyperbole was induced by Baruch's ambivalent attitudes toward other Jews. He disliked "professional Jews," those who proclaimed their heritage, publicly promoted Jewish causes, and in other ways called attention to the problems of Jews in America and in the world. In religion he was an agnostic. He gave generously to all religious philanthropies for no other conviction than his belief in the virtue of voluntary activity; although he claimed to give equally to the three major faiths, it is possible that a true accounting would reveal a bias in favor of Jewish charities. As the most prominent Jew in America, he was constantly involved by others in the quest for a homeland for the world's oppressed Jews. But he rejected Zionism, preferring in its stead a universal homeland for all refugees from persecution. Under no circumstances would he have such a refuge give Jews preferential treatment. He belonged to America and then to humanity. An American Jew has recalled, "I asked Mr. Baruch about Israel bonds and he replied, 'I buy American bonds!' "[3]

South Carolina is essentially irrelevant to an understanding of Baruch's significance—the role he played in shaping the twentieth-century American political economy. Yet he himself stressed the importance of his boyhood home to his manhood. He treasured very happy memories of growing up in a rural town of two thousand where the home folk made their own sugar and picked hickory nuts and walnuts, where the Baruch boys fished and swam in the factory pond and wore shoes only when the weather demanded it or on the Jewish sabbath. Such idyllic boyhood freedom could only have been sharpened in his memory by the contrast with New York City's confinements. He later claimed to have witnessed "the travail and bitterness of the reconstruction days" and "the end of the carpetbag period," and he conveyed the notion that the era had made an indelible impression upon him. These clichés went down well with southern friends and the press, but his first decade in South Carolina could have been little more than hazy representations or oft-told tales distorted by the retelling.

If Camden did not form the mature Baruch, his family did. His parents gave his life a direction in South Carolina and then in New York. Only when he entered the City College of New York and then, at age twenty-one, started to work on Wall Street, did an environment other than his home begin to influence him profoundly. Until then, he was largely a product of a purposeful parental upbringing.

Baruch did not consciously create myths of his beginnings, though he sometimes pretended to have had a disadvantaged youth. "Both you and I come from the wrong street, concerning [sic] which they say commences at the graveyard and ends at the river," he once told a friend.[4] But his memoirs told the truth: "We lived in a large, comfortable house and had about as much of material things as any of our neighbors." He had no reason to fabricate a struggle against humble origins because he was proud that his father, Dr. Simon Baruch, was a respected and prominent physician. In his later years he would claim that the two men who most influenced him were Woodrow Wilson and his father. Many people considered it a part of his charm that Baruch could bracket his father with a president of the United States. It was, to some degree, what made Baruch so beguiling and convincing: when his hair was white he still spoke lovingly and admiringly of his father. He spent much time and money commemorating his father's considerable attainments in public health. When Dr. Baruch was seventy-seven and Bernard was the forty-seven-year-old chairman of the War Industries Board, they lunched one afternoon in Washington with friends, one of whom observed that during a lull in the conversation the younger Baruch extended his hand toward his father, and Dr. Baruch put his hand out to meet his son's; the handclasp, thought Baruch's friend, was an act of spontaneous love with "no affectation about it."[5]

War figured as largely in Dr. Baruch's life as it would in his son's. At fifteen he fled from the threat of conscription in the Prussian army and his native Posen, a part of east central Europe that was sometimes Polish, sometimes German, leaving behind his father, Bernhard, and his mother, the former Theresa Gruen. Simon Baruch's destination was Camden, South Carolina; there Mannes Baum, a friend of the family in the Old Country, owned a small general store. The bright young Simon earned his keep as Baum's bookkeeper for a brief while, until his patron enrolled him at the South Carolina Medical College in Charleston and later at the Medical College in Virginia. He earned his medical degree almost a year after the Civil War erupted.

The erstwhile fugitive from the Prussian army, feeling the social pressures of watching other young Camden men enlist for the southern cause, declared his allegiance to his adopted state and became a Confederate army medical officer. Twice the Union army took him prisoner and twice it exchanged him for its own men. The exchanges were symptomatic of the rebel army's desperate need for medical officers: the inexperienced young doctor had already been pressed into service as a surgeon. This status even earned him special treatment as a Union prisoner, prompting him later to describe his second captivity as reminiscent of a "summer spent at a seaside resort," during which he wrote a medical paper, later published under the title "Two Penetrating Bayonet Wounds of the Chest." He witnessed the battle of Gettysburg and Sherman's march through the Carolinas.[6] The war had made him a Confederate for life. According to his eldest son, the playing of "Dixie" would bring a rebel yell from Dr. Baruch. Later the family uncovered a white hood and long robe with a crimson cross on its breast—the regalia of the Ku Klux Klan—tucked neatly next to the Confederate uniform in an attic trunk. Dr. Baruch's commitment to the lost cause exalted him in Bernard's eyes and suggests South Carolina's exaggerated prominence in the speculator's life.

In 1867, Dr. Baruch married Mannes Baum's niece, Isabella Wolfe, nearly ten years his junior. Belle was the daughter of a once wealthy slaveholder who claimed to have lost his property to Sherman's ravaging army, retaining several debt-burdened plantations and a wardrobe full of Confederate money. She traced her ancestry back to Spanish-Portuguese

Jews who had migrated to New York in the 1690s and was thus entitled to belong to the Daughters of the American Revolution as well as to the Daughters of the Confederacy; she maintained both memberships carefully. Thus, Bernard Mannes Baruch was both a new and an old American; at his convenience he could claim to be an immigrant's son or "bone-of-the-bone and blood-of-the-blood" of old South Carolina, the great-great-grandson of a Continental army soldier.

As a millionaire, Baruch maintained an even more gracious style of living than many of his wealthy friends. This manner he may have acquired from his mother, who, as a young girl, had become accustomed to being treated as a leisured lady. Although Dr. Baruch's practice in South Carolina was successful enough for his son to write later, "I cannot recall that our family ever suffered economic adversity," Belle wanted her talented husband to achieve greater recognition as a New York physician. In the winter of 1880 he gave in to her importuning and, with $18,000 from the sale of his practice and home and from savings, moved the Baruch family to New York City.

Apparently, Dr. Baruch was less concerned with money and status than his wife. He instilled in Bernard certain values that included service to society. While Belle plotted the careers of the four Baruch boys in professions with standing in any community, Simon impressed upon Bernard the idea that there was more to life than "merely making money." The doctor crusaded for public baths for the poor, a campaign leading to New York's erection of the Rivington Street baths on the lower East Side (which Bernard would later endow in return for their renaming in honor of his father). As a scholar of medicine he edited the *Journal of Baineology*, the *Dietetic and Hygiene Gazette*, and *Gailland's Medical Journal*. Because of an appendicitis attack suffered by a visiting friend, he became one of the first doctors to diagnose and remove a ruptured appendix successfully. Yet he was not a surgeon, but was principally known as a publicist of hydrotherapy and public hygiene.

When she was not engaged with the numerous social and charity organizations that occupied her, Belle Baruch spent much of her time plotting professional careers for the Baruch sons. Hartwig, two years older than Bernard, was named for her grandfather, a Charleston rabbi. Although she wanted Harty to follow in his namesake's footsteps, he turned out to be the family thespian and played the Broadway stage for many years before following Bernard to Wall Street. Herman, two years younger than Bernard, was her choice to become a lawyer, but he decided upon medicine and practiced for eight years before joining Bernard's Wall Street firm. Of the Baruch brothers, Herman seemed to benefit most from Bernard's fame and influence. A handsome and intelligent man, in 1918 he became a lifetime partner in H. Hentz and Company, and later he served as U.S. ambassador to Portugal and to the Netherlands on the strength of his older brother's contributions and connections. Sailing, the youngest of the four, was something of a problem: thrown out of a military academy as a youth, he went from job to job until Bernard gave him employment. Only Bernard and Herman achieved their mother's minimum ambition for the four boys—a college education.

Bernard entered the College of the City of New York at the age of fourteen. The city had no public high schools then, and the college, located at Lexington Avenue and Twenty-third Street, site of today's Baruch College of the City University of New York, combined an academy and a baccalaureate curriculum in a five-year program. City College had no tuition and charged only nominal fees. It had a rigid curriculum allowing few elective courses, with the general education program focused upon the classics, sciences, humanities, and political economy. Its faculty had to be versatile: one professor might teach biology, zoology, and geology; another might teach political economy, logic, philosophy, ethics, and psychology. Needless to say, the generalist was king and the specialist practically unknown. Both professors and students were expected to be universal men, an attitude Baruch assumed all his life in spite of the knowledge explosion attendant on an increasingly complex world. (When he became a trustee of City College, he remained a traditionalist and fought against electives as an easy route to evading a sound liberal arts education.) In the 1880s the City College student read and spoke Greek and Latin and every morning attended an assembly presided over by President Alexander Stewart Webb, a Union general in the Civil War. Each morning one student gave an oration. The practice did little for Baruch, as he remained frightened of public speaking until his fifties.

Baruch was not a good student. He had graduated second in his grammar school class, but CCNY was different. He performed poorly in the sciences and survived the classics only with the aid of a tutor. Judging by his inability to express himself well either orally or on paper, he lacked skill in his native English as well. He remained afraid even to commit his words to public scrutiny without a professional writer's assistance. Baruch was intelligent, but, as he confessed to the Harvard dean who told him many years later that Bernard, Jr., had failed economics, he tended to be "intellectually lazy."[7] For instance, although he enjoyed the theater, Shakespeare required too much attention. His memory always was sharp. He retained data with an ease that would impress later associates, but he possessed little creativity or appreciation for humanistic talents. Yet, unlike his son, he paid strict attention to political economy, taught at City College by George B. Newcomb, who, in Baruch's words, "plugged away at the law of supply and demand and taught us to believe in it." These lessons must have impressed Baruch: "Ten years later I became rich by remembering those words."[8]

What he lacked in academic achievement he made up in campus social, political, and athletic activities. The Greek-letter fraternities gave Baruch his first real taste of religious exclusion when they shunned him because he was a Jew. Nevertheless, he was personally popular enough to be elected senior class president. He stood six-feet-four inches tall, with a weight of 170 pounds spread over a broad chest and slender legs, and he was something of an athlete. He played lacrosse and baseball, suffering a damaged left eardrum in a brawl during a ball game; it hastened the deafness that many people later mistakenly attributed to advancing age. Following college he worked out at gymnasiums, boxed (he was always a great fight fan in that sport's heyday), and maintained a muscular physique through regular exercise. In his eighties he would send friends greetings cards with a photograph showing a trim Baruch diving into a swimming pool.

Though he preferred lifting weights to lifting books, Baruch was sensitive to his intellectual failings. He was ambivalent toward intellectuals. Later in life he became aware that worldly men read widely, dealt with profound ideas, and quoted the great writers. He read corporate reports, espoused the general education he had not absorbed, and quoted Thomas Macauley, Woodrow Wilson, nineteenth-century treatises, or one of the few books of current interest that had caught his fancy. His own writings were crafted by ghosts—hired journalists, lawyers, or the latest history honors student from CCNY. He envied articulate individuals. They had mastered the fundamentals that had eluded him.

All his life he dealt with the products of Harvard, Yale, and Princeton while maintaining a close public identification with the sons of immigrants who attended City College. He contributed generously to CCNY, and it, of course, honored him as the most famous alumnus. He held honorary degrees from Princeton and Johns Hopkins, but at an academic convocation he rebuffed the suggestion that he wear Princeton's colors instead of those of "my own college." City College, said Baruch, "comes closer to giving reality to the American dream than better known private colleges and universities." A free public education provided American youth with equal opportunities and assimilated newcomers: "We have made Americanization synonymous with expanded opportunity."[9] City College was where the industry and intellect of New York's proletariat earned an elite education that hastened its rise and absorption into the American system. From it, Bernard Mannes Baruch, immigrant's son and Son of the American Revolution, *sans* any special skills or the scholarship of learned men, entered the American marketplace.

As Baruch told it, his mother originally wanted him to follow his father as a doctor. When he was ten or eleven, she took him to a phrenologist who agreed that he would make a good doctor but asserted that bigger things awaited him in finance or politics. So Belle Baruch gave up the idea of her son becoming a doctor. Upon his graduation from City College at nineteen years of age, she told him to seek employment in business.

In this land of economic opportunity, Baruch was loath to start at the bottom. When he didn't find a job easily, he drew up a list of his father's wealthy patients and began to sound them out on available positions; it helped to have a good connection. He began by approaching copper magnate Daniel Guggenheim, who offered him a job as an ore buyer in Mexico. Belle Baruch welcomed any association for her sons with the Guggenheims, but she vetoed schemes that took Bernard far from her. Another of his father's patients, a wholesaler in glassware for druggists, hired him for three dollars a week. But mother and son were not satisfied with that position, and soon she found one more to their liking. Julius A. Kohn, a retired clothing merchant who invested in financial markets, needed a young man for office tasks, one who would be a diligent, apt student of speculation; Belle Baruch had just the lad. And so Bernard Baruch came to Wall Street.

Kohn taught his young clerk how to speculate on arbitrage, foreign exchange, and reorganizations. Baruch learned that one corporate security could sell at different prices on different markets, both domestic and foreign; a speculator could buy in New York and sell at a profit in London or vice versa, if the speculator had a memory that quickly retained the fluctuating values of varying currencies. Also, in an age when overexpansion had eroded the profitability of railroads, a canny speculator could reap his own profits on railroad reorganization securities. Baruch now formed the habit of a lifetime; "account books," the elder statesman recalled of the young clerk, "became my favorite reading."[10] He patiently studied the figures and drew significance from them.

Moreover, he wanted to gamble. He liked the racetrack or any situation that tested his nerve, knowledge, and audacity. Financial risks did not frighten him. In Wall Street and in life he was competitive with his peers and deferential to his elders. His penchant for winning never offended and his good nature made him a pleasant person in anybody's company. He made friends easily and listened well; ingratiating oneself with the right people often brought a speculator the right information. Baruch had the perfect (if there is such a thing) intelligence, temperament, and personality for late nineteenth-century Wall Street. Even his laziness was well suited for the financial district. Where else could a young clerk take an unapproved summer's vacation in Europe only two months after he began a job and expect to find it waiting for him upon his return?

Whatever his mother thought of it, he had an urge to roam. He soon left Kohn and with a college chum, Dick Lydon, went west to find a fortune in the gold and silver mines of Colorado. By day he worked in a mine and by night he played the roulette wheels of Cripple Creek. Neither the "San Francisco" mine nor the roulette wheels proved worth the time and effort. So he decided to head back to Wall Street and big-time gambling.

Once more his mother knew somebody who had a place for a young man willing to learn about finance. In 1891 he began at A. A. Houseman and Company as an office boy with his eye on the bookkeeper's tasks. Besides account books, he made the *Financial Chronicle* and *Poor's Manual* his favorite reading, becoming adept at disgorging a myriad of corporate information useful to his superiors. The brokers were gambling men who appreciated a knowledgeable subordinate who could find his way around a stock exchange as easily as a racetrack. Baruch knew both milieus, and it did not take long before his earnings at the brokerage found their way into an account in his name. Investing at 10 or 20 percent margin, Baruch had found a better outlet for his gambling instinct than the horse track or the gaming tables.

Even before he went with Houseman he had taken a flyer in the market. At twenty he had put a few hundred dollars of his own, together with eight thousand of his father's, into a trolley company that collapsed not long afterwards. It proved to be an early setback that taught him caution.

Fortunately for Baruch, the great depression of the 1890s hit when he was more an observing student than an active participant in the market. He had little equity and the initial decline in prices wiped him out. And so began his real education. Professor Newcomb's abstract world had become Baruch's real world. It was one in which men were part of an organic nature beyond their capacity to control but in which they might endure and prosper, if they had patience and perseverance. Even those qualities were not enough; the men who thrived were those who studied the behavior of their fellow men in their environment, who appreciated that the problem was "to balance the nature of things in this world in which we live with the nature of mankind." Baruch's experience taught him that the market economy indeed operated according to Professor Newcomb's revered law of supply and demand: "When prices go up two processes will set in—an increased production and a decreased consumption. The effect will be a gradual fall in prices. If prices get too low two processes will set in—decreased production because a man will not continue to produce at a loss and second, increased consumption. These two factors will tend to establish the normal balance."[11]

It was so incredibly simple that we have to marvel that, knowing this, the whole world did not prosper. Obviously the problem lay in recognizing when prices were too low or too high. Not all men could prosper because the market economy required that some men fail: without failure there could be no success. To achieve the latter a speculator needed more than good intuition or good instincts, though an abundance of them certainly helped; the speculator had to *study* the market's behavior and that of his fellow speculators carefully. He had to be abreast of the latest corporate developments, listen for the latest gossip, and then precisely weigh all this against his knowledge of the organism and its parts. Sometimes a speculator had to follow the crowd, but not too closely; it was better to anticipate or lead the rest.

Organic nature was cyclical: depression followed prosperity because low prices followed high because consumption did not follow production because men were not wise enough to know when they ought to sell and buy. Therefore, the speculator had to be a soothsayer, a maverick, a trend setter. He anticipated low prices, buying at their nadir, selling at their imminent apogee. In the latter phase he was known as a "bear," a pessimist who could create low prices simply by challenging euphoria with a transaction that signaled a lack of confidence.

Baruch was schooled on speculation in a bear market. The great depression of the nineties ruined many men, but Baruch was in his early twenties, a time when he had little wealth to lose and a great deal to learn. He carefully studied those men who reaped others' losses and listened well to their explanations of why they were the giants of finance. As prices plummeted they were buying and consolidating for strength; like the predatory creatures they were, they drew their might from the misfortune of less daring men. They seemed to know misery was approaching, even if they were not voicing their dismal anticipations. Baruch began to make his own forecasts based on what he read and heard in Wall Street. He counseled customers politely but assuredly on which particular bonds or securities to buy; when their prices began to rise, he had made customers. He gave them his cautious tips; he saved the long shots for his own account. When he was twenty-five, Houseman made him a junior partner in the small firm. Baruch self-indulgently bought a Prince Albert coat, a silk hat, and all the accessories that informed his customers that their salesman had done well enough to afford such fine attire.

Economics, Professor Newcomb had taught his young charges, could never be divorced from governmental activity; it was truly a political economy. Baruch enjoyed politics almost as much as finance. It too had a symmetry of winners and losers and required that victors be savants of crowd behavior. A good prognosticator in finance had to be equally farsighted in politics. More times than not, the two melded in ways not immediately apparent to the untrained observer. Baruch learned enough about their interaction to make his first big killing in Wall Street.

He had been watching American Sugar Refining Company's struggle against cheaper imported sugar in domestic markets. Western beet sugar growers had been campaigning for tariff protection in the House of Representatives, but other interests had prevailed. ASR, the refiner of three-quarters of the domestically grown sugar, needed the tariff to be competitive in its own market. Baruch studied the Senate debate and forecast that it would approve a lower tariff. The upper chamber did not disappoint him. By the time he finished parlaying his earnings in ASR and hastily sold out, he was $60,000 richer. Here was evidence that men made markets—not only where they produced, bought, and sold, but in their political forums as well.

That prices were set by market forces and statute defied too his faith in natural forces; the deistic Baruch was unprepared then to advocate man's control over nature. For if men transferred their struggles from the financial markets to the political markets, it was as yet uncertain who the victors, if any, would be. Government suggested control and popular government suggested an end to cycles, a reduction in the numbers of losers. A government responsive to all men could not tolerate any victims, but where there were no victims, would there be any victors? If the markets were controlled, would there be any incentive for speculation? Any gambler knew that nobody wages on a horse race when everybody knows its outcome. Uncertainty was a prerequisite for adventure. Attainment required the recognition of risk. Forces for control always challenged forces of nature. Indeed, the forces for order were a part of the natural organism and contributed to its complexity. But it was imperative that controls must never appear to dominate the marketplace. Speculation demanded both freedom and order, both victor and victim.

Baruch's generation confronted the conundrum of how much freedom and order, how many victors and victims. The depression of the nineties had an inordinate number of the latter. The losses of 1893–94 suggested an excess of freedom, an excess of competition, and an excess of disorder. No society could long tolerate such vicissitudes and suffering. The balance of forces was threatened by the diminution of winners. Consolidation brought about fewer competitors, less risk, and more control—not by government, but by victors like J. P. Morgan, John D. Rockefeller, and others who cared little for a balance of forces. Baruch's generation —the future leaders of the second and third decades of the twentieth century—would have to decide whether it would submit to these moguls' control or create alternative forces for controlling competition and bigness. It would have to define where freedom ended and order began.

Beginning in late 1897, as the first signs of substantive recovery from the great depression became apparent, Bernard Baruch, a young parvenu, was on the verge of making it. With $19,000 of his ASR profits he bought a seat on the New York Stock Exchange. On 20 October 1897 he took a wife, Annie Griffen, a statuesque woman only a few inches shorter than he, the daughter of a glass importer and the great-granddaughter of an Episcopalian minister. In August 1899 a daughter was born to the Baruchs and named for her father's mother. After Belle came Bernard, Jr., and then Renee. Baruch bought a brownstone on West Eighty-sixth Street, then a more spacious home on West Fifty-second Street off Fifth Avenue; eventually he would acquire a Fifth Avenue address across from Central Park at Eighty-sixth Street. He seemed never to need instruction on speculating or living on a grand scale.

Baruch cultivated two reputations that were typical of the partial truths he often purveyed: that he was the "Lone Wolf of Wall Street" and that he took daring but creative risks. One story he often related was intended to make both points, but it reveals him as a reluctant maverick who succeeded not by daring but by prudent study.

As Baruch told it, the only time he directly spoke with J. P. Morgan was in 1909. A representative of Wall Street's most powerful name sought him out with the request that Baruch investigate a sulfur dome for Morgan; if it proved worthy of their interest, the Morgans would provide the capital for development and split any profits 60–40 with Baruch. Two factors account for this sudden interest in collaboration with Baruch: the basic patent on the Frasch process had expired, making sulfur extraction more attractive to investment capital; also, Baruch had already made a considerable fortune and reputation through speculation in oil, copper, and gold extractions, thereby demonstrating a talent for effective use of mining engineers. With one of the best in the profession, Seeley W. Mudd, Baruch headed for Texas to explore the sulfur dome. Mudd's verdict was that the dome was rich, but he and Baruch calculated that, given the current world market for sulfur, its profitability had only an even chance. Such odds did not bother Baruch. Besides, he was eager for a partnership with the greatest name in the financial district. Enthusiastically, Baruch sought to coax Morgan into an arrangement by offering half of the capital needed for the "gamble." He unfortunately chose the wrong word for the venture. Morgan brusquely replied, "I never gamble," and the would-be partnership ended before it began.

Morgan invested; Baruch gambled. Morgan sought a sure return on his dollars; Baruch risked his. Morgan pyramided his money; Baruch sold short. Morgan created wealth, industry, and jobs; Baruch played for quick profits. Morgan was an institution; Baruch was a hustler. Morgan built corporations; Baruch depressed their capital markets. In the eyes of Wall Street, though both men took advantage of the system's weaknesses, Baruch's techniques were more asocial and disreputable.

Baruch's personal wealth did not win him respectability in the great houses of finance. Although they were eager to use his unquestioned talent for finding good investments, the moguls frowned upon any public association with him. Wall Street's other loners—for example, Eugene Meyer, Jr., and Joseph P. Kennedy—respected Baruch, as did the middle-class speculators who yearned to emulate his acquisitive feats. But the Morgans and the Warburgs would never rate Baruch as anything more than a plunger.[12]

When he was in his mid-forties and bent upon attaining the personal satisfaction and public respectability that governmental service could afford him, Baruch attempted to convert his notoriety as a "speculator" to his advantage. A determining circumstance occurred prior to American involvement in World War I. President Wilson had appointed Baruch in 1916 to the Advisory Commission of the Council of National Defense. Late in the year he sold short on steel after a speech by the British prime minister suggesting that peace talks with the Germans were imminent. It carried a hint that a break in America's war prosperity was at hand, and Baruch instinctively began to unload his high-priced holdings. Yet not many Americans had evaluated the situation as cogently as had Baruch. Another Wall Street maverick accused him of profiteering on the basis of privileged information. Soon the charges were carried in bold headlines by newspapers across the nation, and explanations were being demanded. Opponents of war preparedness had been saying that U.S. involvement in Europe's war would benefit Wall Street, and here was an example of an unholy advocate of preparedness using his position to gamble on peace. The House Rules Committee promised an investigation into Baruch's dealings. Though he sincerely claimed that he had sold short only on his interpretation of public knowledge, who would believe the word of a gambler?

Shortly before the Rules Committee investigation opened, Baruch counseled with his friend Eugene Meyer, Jr. The first question any committee asked its witness concerned his occupation. How should Baruch respond? His answer had to correspond with the subsequent explanation of his legitimate activities and public knowledge of them. With Meyer's encouragement, he decided to confront Congress with candor. And so, for all the world to hear, Baruch characterized himself before the committee as a "speculator and investor," thereby blending notoriety with integrity.[13]

Thereafter he never hesitated to use "speculator" to describe himself. In fact, he monotonously employed the word to bolster his claim to prophecy. He insisted that a speculator was not a gambler or a plunger; those pejorative words corrupted the original meaning and distorted the reality of what he did as a businessman and a public sage. Somewhat defensively, he reminded listeners that "speculator" was derived from the Latin *speculari*, meaning to view or to observe. Moreover, Baruch elevated the speculator from interpreter of events to manipulator of history. By his definition, the passive prophet became an active participant because of what he saw. The soothsayer had an obligation not merely to forecast disaster, but to take measures to prevent it. Like a social scientist, he culled all known and necessary information, interpreted it, and accordingly made recommendations for subsequent corrective behavior. No longer was he merely a Wall Street short seller and no longer were the exchanges merely "upper-class racetracks." Because Wall Street was "the total barometer for our civilization," Baruch projected himself as a total interpreter of that civilization's behavior. More than most men, the speculator had to be a generalist: he had to utilize his knowledge of economics, politics, society; had to be conversant in the sciences and technology and a patron of the arts. He was a scholar of human behavior who applied his insights.[14]

For decades he flaunted his public speculations and urged his audiences to respect and heed them. He had a reputation to build and to uphold. "People believe in me," an elderly Baruch asserted; "They think I'm honest and they listen to my advice. They think I'm always right." He did not consider them misguided. His legions of friends and admirers responded to his pronouncements by raising them to the status of wisdom. Whatever his defects, here was a man of unusual depth of perception. Robert Moses claimed that Baruch "had the classic open mind of a Greek philosopher, the insatiable curiosity of a Renaissance man, and the inventiveness of Benjamin Franklin." Even the vain Baruch, who had passed on by the time of Moses' acclaim, would have been embarrassed by such absurd hyperbolic comparisons. It was enough for him to be known simply as a public philosopher with a wide range of interests and perceptions—in the colloquialism of his time, a "broad-gauged" man. When an industrialist challenged his entrepreneurial acuity because Baruch had never managed any enterprise but his own portfolio, the speculator retorted that a generalist's knowledge enabled him to succeed in any undertaking.[15]

A speculator, he said, always "looked ahead." Without the least pretension of modesty, he asserted that he usually was "a little ahead of the event." When he made a prediction, he once told a writer, "you find a justification for this prediction—if not now, then in a very few months to come." He claimed to have trained himself to judge true circumstances dispassionately, to discover the real value of anything. His pronouncements were based upon extensive examination. He did not render a forecast until all evidence was available. "I can't get up in public and say the first thing that comes into my head. I have to study things out."[16] Yet the speculator could not afford to ponder at such length that his quest for all facts immobilized him. As an activist, he had to prescribe for himself and others quickly, lest events pass them by.

Of course he studied. But he also admitted that most of his information was gleaned from talking to the right people. What if he talked to the wrong people? In discerning and selecting the right fact from the wrong one, his experience and insight separated him from other men. He knew how to evaluate his sources because he was a perceptive judge of ideas and men. He was not above claiming that he possessed instincts superior to others'.

Instinct: what did that intuitive quality have to do with the facts Baruch claimed to study coolly? Among his peers, such inherent qualities mattered. Some men undoubtedly had better instincts, and benefited from them accordingly. Dwight Morrow, a Morgan partner, once postulated that "there were two types of men, one governed by instinct and 'hunches' and the other by knowledge of facts." Morrow believed that Herbert Hoover, whom he had been discussing, belonged to the first category.[17] If we subscribe to Morrow's simplistic formulation, then Baruch, who shared many of Hoover's characteristics, likewise was a man much moved by what he perceived. Thus, for all his vaunted claim to studying facts and performing as warranted by them, Baruch was the "hunch player" par excellence.

Even so, he was an extraordinary hunch player. Though he lacked an imposing intellect or any substantial originality of thought, he possessed a fairly coherent system of ideas and a reasonably good understanding of people. But the latter reflects his temperament and personality, rather than his powers of induction. He drew quick and correct conclusions from available statistics, but he distrusted the conclusions of more deductive men. His educated hunches were examples of what a friend classified as "that indefinable quality of perception, that curious combination of instinct and reason." How he arrived at decisions often puzzled associates who were left with the responsibility of verifying that they had been the right ones. Sometimes this self-proclaimed collector of facts treated information with only a cursory glance or discarded it altogether. Yet no matter how his brain functioned, the results tended to be convincing. "Baruch's brain is like a dolphin," wrote his factotum of the forties, Samuel Lubell, "diving at one point, coming up somewhere else. How he reaches his conclusions is never clear." Perhaps he was too inarticulate to analyze his thought processes for others. Raymond Moley concurred with most of his doctrines while admitting that "Baruch himself can scarcely rationalize or explain the processes of his judgments. No one has yet defined a hunch."[18]

That he was a hunch player should not detract from the quality of his judgments if we subscribe to the expediency that results justify processes. His hunches paid off handsomely for him in the stock market. Nor does this mean that the measure of the man is his wealth. Rather, to some degree, it suggests that the man's wealth is the measure of his judgment—

in the marketplace, in society, and in politics. In all markets he had to be perspicacious, and that required a greater comprehension of forces than other men possessed. At times he zealously oversold his wisdom in order to persuade the public of his sound judgment. Humility came more readily to him in his later years, when, by his own standards, he judged many of his ventures to be failures. Failure, too, was a part of being a speculator. When he no longer had to persuade admirers of his near infallibility, then he could acknowledge that some of his earlier enterprises had not worked out as he had intended.

OF BEAR MARKET FAME

Baruch had a special affinity with the professional gambler who earns his livelihood by betting on sports events or races or, to a lesser degree, roulette. After all, no gambler on a fight, a game, or a race ventures his money without first studying the participants' records. The more the gambler knows about them, the better his "edge" on less-informed gamblers whose bets manipulate the odds' prices to the advantage of the knowledgeable gambler. The informed gambler enjoys his edge because he might know that a horse runs poorly at a certain distance, dislikes a muddy track, or nurses a minor injury. Nevertheless, whatever the edge, he still risks his money—if the outcome is not controlled by outside forces who subject it to a "fix." Of course free competition and honest speculation are undermined by the fixer who reduces a probability to a certainty.

Baruch admired speculation that tested a gambler's nerve in a free market. He considered himself a man with a "sporting instinct." Unlike many modern gamblers, Baruch did not bet on team sports like baseball, football, and basketball because they had not become the professionalized big business institutions that mass media—radio beginning in the twenties and television in the late forties—made them. His outlets were card games, gaming tables, racetracks, and boxing matches. The crowd he knew at the old Waldorf-Astoria, a favorite watering hole for speculators, were notorious gamblers: Diamond Jim Brady, John "Bet-a-Million" Gates, Thomas W. Lawson, James R. Keene, and others. They were infamous for their gargantuan appetites for adventure, women, food, and money. They bought and sold anything. Baruch respected them as men who studied the markets, mined corporate information, and warily watched the politicians whose decisions influenced markets. He admired their courage and their sybaritic style, but his adulation fell short of embracing any unsystematic market behavior. Allegedly inside information often misled them because their tips, even if correct, ignored human behavior that influenced the markets. Thus, the gamblers leaned too heavily upon an "edge" and forgot that the market was not a race-track but a societal barometer.

According to Baruch, he disdained tips. It defied logic for him to base an investment upon an unsubstantiated shred of gossip unless it confirmed what he already knew and figured prominently in his larger perspective of business conditions. He certainly never rejected a tip that confirmed what he knew. Tips were pernicious: they either inflated a stock's price far in excess of its real value or touched off a selling panic that depressed prices. Either way the speculator without the privileged information was a loser.

Even so, a good deal of Baruch's money was made because he was privy to information unavailable to most buyers and sellers. His "first big deal," at the age of twenty-eight, developed because circumstances had brought him to the attention of Thomas Fortune Ryan, a Morgan rival in finance whose staunch Catholicism made him a Wall Street loner before Joseph P. Kennedy arrived. Ryan's Union Tobacco was one of the few tobacco producers not in the clutches of James B. Duke's tobacco trust. After running a few errands to St. Louis in behalf of Ryan's struggle for control of Ligget and Myers, Baruch was assigned the task of waging war against the market price of Duke's Continental Tobacco. It was the first time Baruch proved that he was a skillful bear operator. He bought up large lots of Continental, and by the time he was finished unloading them, not only was its price headed for lower levels, but Ryan had a handsome profit instead of the $200,000 loss he had anticipated. A. A. Houseman and Company, Baruch's employers, reaped a $150,000 commission from the transactions.

Baruch took his portion of the profits and bought his brother Harty a seat on the exchange. Then, on the basis of a tip, he bought a distillery stock due for combination with three other firms. However, it failed to attract enough speculation to achieve a higher price. Speculators wiser than Baruch recognized that consolidation did not assure strength. He took a big loss, which he had covered, as was his habit, with cash reserves.

Baruch learned from this setback that optimists could lose. It paid to be a pessimist. When others were bullish, be a bear. Sell when the market was buying and buy when the market was selling. Such philosophy or psychology did not win him friends. It meant that he made his millions when others confronted misery. Yet that was part of his genius—knowing when to end an investment commitment or avoid an involvement. Speculators who succeed are unavoidably Cassandras. Baruch would be one of the most famous speculators and one of the shrillest Cassandras.

By his thirty-second birthday, Baruch had accumulated a hundred thousand dollars for each of his years. Lest readers be taking notes on how to make fortunes in the stock market, they should be advised that the Securities and Exchange Commission has, since its inception in 1933, set rules against most of the market manipulations that allowed Baruch to make his millions.

Baruch used inside information, crowd psychology, and bearish selling to make his early fortune. When a promoter named Roswell P. Flower took over Brooklyn Rapid Transit in 1899, bullish buying pushed BRT from 20 to 137 before a heart attack killed Flower and threw the market into a small panic. The Morgan, Vanderbilt, and Rockefeller groups stepped in to steady the market and then, at the time when Baruch chose to unload his holdings in BRT, they got out. BRT's price plummeted, but Baruch escaped—$60,000 richer.

Another manipulation that added to Baruch's wealth involved the 1901 efforts of the Rockefeller group, led by Henry H. Rogers, to push copper prices higher. Its 20 to 25 percent share of the world market would benefit by the new price levels, but other American producers, notably the Guggenheim brothers, refused to cooperate in production restrictions. Wall Street, however, was impressed by the powerful people behind Amalgamated Copper, and next to United States Steel, it became the most sought-after stock on the exchange. Even if Amalgamated could not manipulate copper prices, at least it could inflate its own price beyond believability.[19] Baruch bought and watched. Again, as in the BRT episode, the price weakened, rose again, and then, upon President McKinley's assassination, collapsed. Once more Morgan stepped in to steady prices and again Baruch bailed out along with Amalgamated's promoters. How much the Amalgamated's manipulators made can only be imagined, but Baruch admitted to profits of about $700,000. Again he had been the beneficiary of price manipulation, inside information, and bear instincts.

He made millions as a plunger, but it would always be his fondest ambition to control some great enterprise, to be known as an "instrument of our national growth" like Morgan and Harriman. Never truly original, he claimed a romance with railroads that went back to the first train whistle he heard as a boy across the South Carolina countryside. Counting his profits in the wake of the 1901 panic, Baruch studied the rails situation with an eye toward control of a likely rail. He concluded that the Louisville and Nashville Railroad stock was underpriced and underappreciated for its growth possibilities. First he began to buy all the shares he could afford and to promote its virtues with his friends until only the Rothschilds owned more of L&N than Baruch. Lacking a corner on the railroad's stock, he persuaded "Bet-a-Million" Gates and Edwin C. Hawley to join his venture with other known railroad speculators. L&N's price rose swiftly, but his friends, Gates and Hawley, did not share Baruch's hankering for control of the corporation. They quickly sold their shares to J. P. Morgan for substantial profits. Morgan was intent on forming a Southern Securities Company to match his Northern Securities Company, a railroad holding company then under litigation in a test of the Sherman Antitrust Act; so Baruch too sold his holdings to Morgan, except for 6,666 shares. Having bought early and sold early, Baruch emerged from the L&N quest with a million dollar profit.

He claimed later that having failed to achieve operation of the railroad was one of his life's disappointments, but some skeptics in Wall Street suspected that the venture turned out the way Baruch planned. He had taken a property others had lost interest in, promoted it successfully, jacked up its price (a practice he disavowed because respectable investors frowned upon it), and in a few months had made himself rich. His operations had earned him Wall Street respect, consolation enough for his failure to achieve L&N control.

It must be repeated: market rules were lax in those days, long before the New Deal tightened the codes of speculation. Also, business information then lacked systematic accounting or distribution. Corporate reports were either unknown or unbelievable. Tip sheets were for gullible suckers who heeded market manipulators. C. W. Barron and John Moody published market information, but it was not until 8 July 1899 that Dow-Jones launched the *Wall Street Journal* (in his later years, Baruch claimed that he believed only *Journal* reports written by his cronies and otherwise ignored that prestigious financial newspaper). In the early twentieth century, gossip was a normal source of business information. Wall Street was a small community of strangers who met irregularly to exchange inside dope, form loose alliances, and even shape antagonisms that shifted with the circumstances; strong friendships and enduring enmities were unlikely in a tight environment where promoters "met each other at the lunch club or here or there somewhere."[20] Except for Morgan, Rockefeller, and the Guggenheims, the big investment houses were still in the making. At the time, then, Wall Street was a market where a lone wolf with a good stake could convert that stake into a substantial fortune to compare with that of Eugene Meyer or Joseph P. Kennedy—if he enjoyed the conviviality and connections of Bernard Baruch.

A Wall Street maxim went: "Remember a bear market always begins when everything is brightest and the public most bullish." Baruch deserved the reputation of a bear. In 1903, however, it paid to be a pessimist. In fact, given the cyclical behavior of the market economy, it always paid to expect a decline when prices were high. But that year, while Gates, Hawley, and other high-rolling friends of Baruch were buying, the new millionaire reasoned that prices were too high to be true and opted to sell most of his holdings. He was not one to follow the financial crowd: "A speculator should travel his road alone," was one of his many maxims. A "rich man's panic" ensued and some of Baruch's Waldorf buddies took heavy losses before Morgan again stepped in and used his prestige and power to ease the slide in prices. No wonder the big brokers disdained lone plungers whose speculative excesses recklessly inflated or deflated securities; the bears could create trends, but only Morgan could reverse them.

And so, while others were counting their losses, Baruch took his winnings and parted company with A. A. Houseman, opening his own firm at 111 Broadway. He no longer considered himself a high-risk operator; he would show the financial district's responsible institutions that he could engage in "constructive enterprise and development."[21]

OF INVESTMENT RESPECTABILITY

Following the panic of 1903, Baruch embarked upon a third phase as a speculator. From 1891 to 1897 he served his apprenticeship in a bear market, becoming a multimillionaire in the bull markets preceding 1903. Now he sought respectability as a financier in an era of consolidation, gradually cultivating his political connections en route to becoming a financial angel for Woodrow Wilson's campaign for president in 1912.

The speculator yearned to be known as a "creator of true wealth, not [of] money but of things useful." Personal wealth through speculation was not enough without the societal esteem attached to the man recognized as a builder. Great men did more than watch their millions multiply. We are told by Baruch that his father was surprisingly unimpressed by his son's wealth; he asked, "Now that you have money, what are you going to do with it?" The physician wanted to know how wealth could improve the speculator if the speculator could not improve the society. Baruch considered studying law or medicine, but he did not entertain them seriously. Politics captivated him, but this interest had a vocational relationship to his market activities. A friend, Garet Garrett, knowing of Baruch's fascination with politics, scolded him: "I keep telling you B.M., you don't belong in Wall Street; you should be in Washington."[22] But neither Washington nor Baruch was prepared for the switch; he knew little about electoral politics, lacked connections with the Republican majority in Washington, and, besides, still nurtured greater ambitions in Wall Street. Also, could anything surpass the excitement of speculation?

Later in life, when he embarked upon a public career, he announced a temporary retirement from Wall Street; but he never really forsook speculation. It was always an extension of his personality. He merely adjusted his speculation to suit other ambitions. His business habits were adjusted to popular taste. He did not resist fashion. In fact, Baruch caught the latest notions at their peak rather than at their ascendancy. Even his speculations were sometimes yesterday's hot interest. Rails were passé when Baruch caught the fever. He turned enthusiastically to raw material speculation while never divorcing himself from his old love, the rails.

Baruch's genius, or perhaps it was just his instinct for risk speculation, was well served in the copper, sulfur, gold, rubber, tungsten, zinc, and iron ore explorations of the early twentieth century. Millions could be lost in these ventures, and even greater millions could be gained. The shrewd investor armed himself with a capable geological engineer to minimize his risk. Technology developed new methods for ore extraction, and abundant cheap labor diminished the costs of operation. Problems arose when excessive producer competition overwhelmed the still un-developed demand for converting ores to consumer uses. Prices may have depended upon supply and demand, but supply and demand depended upon control through organization.

These speculations in ores satisfied Baruch because, he said, he was putting new resources at the disposal of mankind. He acted as a midwife in the birth of new industries. He considered himself no longer a Wall Street bear, but an industrial financier. But he did not stay with mature enterprises long: "Always restless by nature, as soon as one of these enterprises reached the dividend-paying stage, I usually got out and searched about for another."[23] He insisted that he abandoned only suc-cessful enterprises. Although he could afford some losses, if a speculation did not pan out as expected he protected other investors by staying with it until it produced or proved beyond redemption. His favorite example of his investor statesmanship was the Alaska Juneau Gold Company, a venture that promised much but paid little. Baruch and Eugene Meyer, Jr., were the principal stockholders in that fruitless speculation. For decades both men never tired of telling friends that mere exploiters would have cut their losses and left smaller speculators holding its nearly worth-less securities. However, they never succumbed to such irresponsible behavior.

Baruch's memoir account of his speculations during 1903–15 is cu-rious. He departs from a deal-by-deal narrative and, in a few chapters, charts an industry-by-industry association with the Guggenheim brothers in copper and rubber, the short-run interest in sulfur with Morgan, and the abortive long-run connection with Meyer in gold. His reticence in supplying greater detail is puzzling. Is it because the first $3.2 million is the most interesting and the other millions are merely redundant? He asserts both his "lone wolf" independence and his investment associa-tions with the statesmen of finance. He suggests that he had ceased imitating the plungers of a bygone era. Beset by "conflicting desires," he attempted to emulate rail speculator E. H. Harriman: "He bet on horses, races, prizefights, and elections—things I also liked to do." Like Harri-man, Baruch built a fortune from "scratch." Unlike Harriman, he never controlled a railroad. Harriman, twenty-two years Baruch's senior, belonged to a nineteenth-century materialistic generation; conscious of the progressive era's social awareness, Baruch insists, "My generation was less satisfied with money-making." Yet moneymaking seems to be all Baruch did in this period. And that chagrined him. The times were idealistic and he belonged to a profession without the redeeming social utility of his father's medical practice.[24]

During this period, Baruch was also a good deal less the lone wolf of Wall Street than his legend suggested. Though much of his speculation had been solo, beginning in 1905 his biggest deals developed when he was acting as part of a team of speculators led by the Guggenheim brothers. This transition coterie of investors bridged the time and social gaps between the Waldorf plungers and the esteemed financial houses. They were the makings of new brokerages, a new Wall Street. Within this group alliances were formed, items of information exchanged, deals made, and concepts of economic stabilization debated. Baruch was not unique, not in his speculating, his ambitions for investment respectability, his quest for a career in public service beyond mere moneygrubbing, or his developing concepts of political economy that called for the increased interest of young Wall Streeters in Washington's role. Young brokers reinforced one another's aspirations, ideas, and activities. The close environment at the southern tip of Manhattan Island encouraged their cooperation, rather than their competition. Often they would diverge, either because their investment interests changed or because the often strange ways of party politics, ambition, and personal jealousies inspired respectful rivalries. Yet their schemes for national economic stabilization showed a consensus of values that transcended political party or individual investment interests.

Eugene Meyer, Jr., was a young speculator with a background and a career remarkably similar to Baruch's; their antagonism seemed as inevitable as their alliance. Five years Baruch's junior, Meyer too had been born a Jew to an immigrant father (French) and raised far from Wall Street (California). Like Baruch, he came from a comfortable home (his father had a partnership in the international brokerage of Lazard Frères), gained his first big stake in arbitrage while working for an investment firm (Lazard Frères), and struck out on his own when he decided that he had little more to learn or earn from the firm. For a brief while, Meyer and Baruch even entertained the possibility of a partnership. Whatever decided them against it, it is doubtful that their matched egos would have allowed it to endure. And so they became merely good friends until about 1910, when their speculative interests required them to become business associates. Like Baruch, Meyer had a philosophy of speculation that stressed the importance of systematic investigation and a bearlike "practice of getting out of the market during cyclones of speculation and of then reentering in force when the heedless had been laid low." They joined the Guggenheims and John D. Ryan in copper ventures in Utah and Chile. By 1915, Meyer and Baruch had begun their collaboration in the Alaska Juneau gold mine. Like Baruch, Meyer used its failure to verify his investor statesmanship; like Baruch, Meyer "felt primarily American" and not at all Jewish, identified himself socially with the German Jews in financial circles, and married a tall, statuesque Gentile girl whose "qualities could be a passport to a broader, fuller life." Part of that enriched life meant public service by investing in a winning presidential candidate who would provide access to Washington. Both men depicted themselves as possessing an "unusual capacity to foresee approaching events," cultivated the charming art of good conversation, but were paralyzed by the prospect of public speaking.[25] Even their public careers had frequent collaborations and took parallel directions along different party routes.

Baruch and Meyer made their marks in speculation during Wall Street's golden age. From the first quarter of 1904 to the first quarter of 1906, the Dow-Jones average of stock prices doubled. Baruch sold out of American Smelting and Refining Company, the Guggenheim-controlled copper monopoly, and reaped a healthy profit. Despite fears of labor unions and antitrust suits, it was an age of corporate consolidation. Almost a half century later, Baruch nostalgically remembered the early 1900s as the only time of "normal" economic conditions.[26]

Baruch's vaunted farsightedness in raw materials appears to have failed in manufacturing. His memoirs are devoid of any mention of a speculation in anything but rails and raw materials. In a sense that omission indicates that Baruch followed the conventional speculative wisdom of the time. Big profits were to be found by tearing copper from the earth, not by assembling automobiles. Henry Ford had to be his own best investor; Morgan and other Wall Street moguls were timid and wanted no part of motors until after World War I. Baruch followed suit. But Baruch could be a romantic about certain investments. Southern corporations drew his attention, although many of them were not in good condition. "People are still foolish enough to believe I do not make any mistakes," he commented decades later. "Sometimes I am sorry I did not make public the many, many mistakes I made."[27]

If he included his Wabash Railroad speculations of 1911–15 among his mistakes, he did not say so. Several years after he had sought control of the Louisville and Nashville, he bought into the sick Wabash, knowing that it needed improvements but could not attract the capital for them. An early draft of his memoirs carried an account of this speculative disaster,[28] but the published version omitted it. In the midst of that venture he was moved to call it the most painful experience of his career. Instead of proving a glorious effort at controlling a vital rail system in the heartland of America, it cost him an undisclosed amount of capital and left him quite embarrassed. He blamed the failure on economic conditions and a "lack of team play in the management of the Road"; he even suggested that he had been duped by management's "gross misrepresentation of earnings."[29] No wonder Baruch tried to hide the Wabash venture; the speculator felt suckered by a gamble that had led to receivership and reorganization with little promise of profits for himself. Moreover, it came at a time in his life when he should have known better than to engage in youthful flights of fancy, and it came at a time in national economic development when individual control of a railroad had given way to multiple-investor consolidation of weak systems.

Undoubtedly his copper and sulfur ventures more than compensated for the Wabash folly. But it still hurt him. Railroads were his passion. In association with Meyer and the Kuhn, Loeb and Hayden, Stone brokerages he tried to buy a large chunk of Southern Pacific stock without success. A friend told a business reporter, "The market is down, and that is a sure sign 'Barney' Baruch is going hunting, as he usually does in November."[30] It was 1915 and Baruch could afford to be discouraged with Wall Street, for he had laid the groundwork for a transfer of his energies to Washington.

PERSONALITY AND PERSONAL QUALITIES

Baruch was gregarious. He enjoyed company and appeared to hate every minute he was alone. In part this was attributable to a theatrical quality that sent him in search of an informal audience. Besides, he did not read much and, if provided with knowledgeable company, learned through good conversation.

He could be a superb companion. He had a very masculine sense of humor, a raconteur's gift for telling stories, a newspaperman's nose for gossip. He flattered acquaintances by assuming they were authoritative sources who could yield significant information if he barraged them with questions. More erudite persons were often surprised to find that this speculator provided such pleasurable company. Otto Kahn, an intense investment banker and a learned art collector, wasted little time with most people, but he rated Baruch as one of the few men who put him at ease and never bored him.[31]

Baruch's charm was part southern, part Victorian. He was an old-fashioned, courtly, properly deferential gentleman who lived in a grand style that included a South Carolina estate, private railroad cars, suites in the finest hotels, and an abundance of invitations to friends and acquaintances to partake of his hospitality. His manliness appealed to men and women; gambling, boxing, and hunting made him a dashing figure. Lean, dark, and handsome, this cavalier was a natural ladies' man.

"Women were always attracted to him," one recalled. He was an "interesting conversationalist because of his knowledge of, and involvement in, the world of power and politics," and he never tired of reminding listeners of his wealth and proximity to great men and events. Even when he was aging, he maintained an erect carriage and proud bearing, thick white hair, a strong aquiline nose, crafty blue eyes. He was always the most distinguished-looking man in any group, and when dressed in a white tie, tails, and a high silk hat, he was splendidly impressive. He had a deep voice and a flattering grace of manner—his courtly old-school gentleman pose.[32] At any age he attracted women. He did not discourage their attentions even as he preserved his reputation as a family man. The extent of his liaisons, or their number, can only be conjectured, but it can safely be said that he never lacked opportunities.[33]

He could be a warm person. He was not a passionate man: enthusiasm could be interpreted as a sign of weakness. But he could commit himself to people and to causes, mostly the former. He wanted people to love him and love was something he offered to others in kind. He radiated a "sweetness" nearly unknown among powerful men in business and government. Although he could evoke both toughness and vulnerability, the credibility of his warmth challenges our cynicism because it seems so uncharacteristic of his milieu. His sincerity was always open to cynicism; yet there were many believers in his kindheartedness. His friends knew many moments of unrestrained expressions of affection. Thus, he needed to tell the daughter of an old friend who had just died, "I loved your father very much."[34] It never appeared to be affected love.

He cultivated his own "society." Pet names and endearments were part of being initiated into his circle. Once admitted to his friendship, a Baruch buddy became the object of intimacy, sophomoric humor, and camaraderie. He blended business and social friendships, rarely distinguishing between them. Once a person began to work closely with him, Baruch pursued that associate's company at all hours. He was forever extending invitations or soliciting them. He seems never to have eaten alone, except through default. Following an evening of gossip with a coworker that ended late, he could turn up at another's bedside the next morning fresh for a new day of chatter. Even his strolls across Washington and Wall Street rarely were without somebody's company. Luckily, he knew so many people that it was not long before he chanced upon an acquaintance wherever he went. Strangers from all levels of society were at ease in his presence. But he preferred useful people: the rich, aristocrats, politicians, artists, journalists, and various celebrities. Obsequious individuals were as welcome to his circle as contentious ones, just as long as they were civil and did not bore him.

Investment broker John Hancock called him "the kind of man people like to work with." He was reknowned for his "gaiety of spirit" and "capacity for affection and loyalty." These qualities often led people to misjudge him. He could be so straightforward as to suggest a simple, shallow character. That was disarming. Frequently he employed light banter as a prelude to persistent cajoling, for he was a determined man who wanted his way. He sought his objective with tolerance and a smile. He could be direct without being unpleasant. He could be indirect without being devious. He was an expert negotiator because he could charm an adversary. He bore grudges for many years without revealing them, as he would do with Jesse Jones. He set aside old antagonisms when it suited him, as he would do with Herbert Hoover. He unreasonably assailed an unforgivable few, as he would do with John Maynard Keynes. Frequently blunt, most of the time he averted confrontations. He was, according to one witness, "a master of charmingly indirect talk which suddenly opens to leave an inference the size of a bomb crater."[35]

Always, as James P. Warburg reminds us, "there were two feelings about Baruch." If his friends were legion, so were his detractors. Even his friends conceded that he was opinionated, egotistical, and obsessed with the appearance of power more than the assertion of principle. Certainly his success at making money and the right friends evoked the envy of competitors. He sought and attracted too much publicity for the comfort of his adversaries. He was tenacious in his pursuit of the role of an insider—the man in the know or at the center of the action. According to the disdainful Warburg, "How Baruch gets into anything always has the same answer—he wants to get in. He was scratching all the time." To his detractors there was little that was truly graceful or charming about this Wall Street Sammy Glick. Helen Lawrenson, an old flame who lived to tell it all, wrote: "He was an obsessive conniver and manipulator who liked to be described as a mysterious Richelieu-like figure behind the scenes, a secret string-puller. There has been no more widely publicized secret string-puller in our history. That this is so was partly due to his own knack for self-promotion. As a flower turns toward the sun, so Baruch sought the limelight. Even now, a magic glint still clings to his name." Less malevolently, but no more accurately, Jonathan Daniels labeled Baruch simply a "benign manipulator."[36]

It was difficult to quarrel with him—not because his judgments were correct, but because he was so certain they were. "Vain" is probably the adjective most often used in characterizing him. He considered himself an authority on many matters and withheld that fact from nobody. He was "a man of strong likes and dislikes," observed one acquaintance. "I rarely saw a man who was more *personal* in his political and economic judgments," noted David Lilienthal. These perspectives came twenty-eight years apart; so we know that it was not a characteristic confined to one stage of Baruch's life. Such self-certainty was often hard to take. His "conviction is sometimes tiresome, even oppressive to vaguer men," wrote *Time*.[37]

He did not discuss affairs of state; he pontificated upon them. To the caustic Colonel Edward M. House, he once "recommended himself as being perhaps the most suitable person living to give a comprehensive view of world trade. . . . His admiration for Baruch and his methods is wonderful to contemplate." Needless to say, some acquaintances considered him arrogant. Without subtlety he pursued power, prominence, acclaim, and admiration. It sometimes took a while before his likable qualities made themselves apparent to strangers, but his fame and wealth inspired patience with him. His friends accepted and rationalized his vanity; it was "that glad and innocuous kind which never takes on the tiresome affectation of square-jawness, so tiresome and common among financiers and industrial kings." Fans like Robert Moses learned to tolerate his "childlike, inoffensive egomania."[38] After all, he possessed numerous genuinely good qualities.

His generosity was his most lovable idiosyncracy. Because his wealth was such a prominent part of being Baruch, he displayed it as openly as his vanity. He showered numerous tokens of his esteem upon friends and acquaintances: flowers for ladies, quail (or whatever) from his most recent hunt for men. His closest circle of friends and preferred public men were treated to vacations at his South Carolina estate or a summer's cruise to England with a hunt in Scotland. "It is really a pleasure for me to know that people I like are enjoying the things which I have," he assured a friend. Benevolence was not without an ulterior motive, we can suppose, but it would be difficult to find one other than its appeal to his vanity and the small debt it incurred from powerful public figures and lesser types. And so he accumulated an impressive list of beneficiaries who were entertained in lavish Baruch style. When Winston Churchill was a frustrated political failure and visited the United States in 1931, Baruch picked up his New York hotel bill—brandy, cigars, and other amenities included. Upon hearing that the Democrats were short of funds during the 1918 congressional campaign, Baruch hastily grabbed War Industries Board stationery and wrote: "The Central Trust Company, New York City, please pay to the order of Wilbur M. Marsh twenty-five thousand dollars ($25,000.00) and charge the same to my account. Bernard M. Baruch." "That is Bernie's way," commented a Democrat when shown the letterhead. As will be discussed in detail later, Baruch bankrolled an untold number of political campaigns. During World War II everyone in Washington seemed to know that Baruch had paid for the party celebrating Harry Hopkins's marriage to Louise Macy, if only because Baruch spread the word himself. Word of his generosity invited numerous special pleaders with causes worthy of his beneficence. Eleanor

Roosevelt made him a philanthropist for her liberal projects. Once she advised some friends with good causes that Baruch had "devious ways" of contributing cash: "If you sigh a little and say you haven't enough to meet a specific need, I think you will find it forthcoming."[39] She had practiced her device almost as much as he had practiced his response.

His generosity was always forthcoming—but rarely without invisible strings attached. The speculator was never careless with his money. He used it to invest in friendships; to open doors politicians had closed to Wall Street plungers whose public associations with them were worrisome; to win access and fame as an advisor to presidents; to find a warm public reception for his ideas on the nation's political economy.

POLITICAL ENTRY

Among other things, Baruch speculated in friendships. He cultivated associations with the ardor and care of a man who appreciated that achievements often were a product not of his efforts but of the company he kept. Some of his investments in people paid off as quickly as the Louisville and Nashville, but many of them were held with hope for decades, like Alaska Juneau—and, except for demonstrating his character, were as unproductive.

But no association yielded as much for Baruch as that with Woodrow Wilson. Initially it had been a prudent speculation; Wilson was already the nominee of his party and given an excellent chance of becoming the first Democratic president in the twentieth century when Baruch became a major contributor. Later, he would demonstrate uncommon devotion to Wilson's historical legacy, a more daring political risk.

The story of Baruch's introduction to Wilson illustrates another of his ambivalences—loyalty to the Democratic party. When he endorsed the GOP's Eisenhower in the 1950s, the octogenarian Baruch asserted that he was breaking a lifelong habit of Democratic support that grew out of his southern birth (one more instance of how he used South Carolina for its political convenience). Yet in national politics prior to Wilson's emergence, he had been just another Wall Streeter for Republicans McKinley, Roosevelt, and Taft.[40] In 1912 he distinguished himself in the investment milieu by backing Wilson while associates like Eugene Meyer cautiously clung to Taft.

Nevertheless, his act was not quite as daring as Baruch later made it appear. Several Wall Street men were to be found in Wilson's camp. Henry Morgenthau, Sr., chaired the Democratic finance committee that year. The list of big contributors to Wilson's campaign includes some of the prominent German Jews in New York: Hy Goldman, Jacob Schiff, Samuel Untermeyer, Nathan Straus, and Charles S. Guggenheimer. Baruch gave $12,500, a figure matched only by Schiff and surpassed only by Cleveland H. Dodge.[41] William Jennings Bryan's party needed all the help of financiers it could muster. Indeed, Wilson wooed them in order to demonstrate his availability to businessmen and his need for their financial assistance.

William F. McCombs, a New York lawyer and a fellow trustee of City College, introduced Baruch to Wilson in 1912. A former student of Wilson's at Princeton, McCombs was an ambitious, chimerical political plunger whose erratic behavior proved to be his downfall not long after Baruch enrolled in the Wilson crusade. McCombs's political history was a tragedy of sorts. When Baruch first met McCombs in 1910, Wilson had been his long-shot presidential favorite; then, at the 1912 convention, McCombs panicked and nearly undermined the candidacy, a mistake that relegated him to a fund-raising task during the campaign, while promoter William Gibbs McAdoo achieved the prominence that had once been McCombs's. (Interestingly, Wilson, McAdoo, McCombs, and Baruch were all transplanted southerners.) And so Baruch, a friend of McAdoo and an enthusiastic bankroller for Wilson, gained access to a major party candidate for president. Baruch's only noteworthy previous contribution to a candidate went to William Jay Gayn
New York (and earned him Gaynor's offer of a City College trusteeship in 1910).

Wilson took time from the 1912 campaign in October to explain his New Freedom philosophy to Baruch. At New York's Plaza Hotel, with others present because Wilson "was doubtful" about conferring with a Wall Street broker without witnesses, they discussed the significance of corporate growth. As Baruch recalled it, the candidate was anxious for the speculator to understand that any concentration of economic power threatened the opportunities of a majority of businessmen. Pointing to the telephone, Wilson argued that "a reasonable monopoly" called for public regulation of concentrated capital. He assured Baruch, then heavily into copper ore speculation, that control of large quantities of raw materials like coal by one corporation was tolerable if it did not stifle competition.[42]

That explanation of Wilson's trust-busting rhetoric satisfied Baruch; and so did the subsequent New Freedom legislation. He found no contradictions between Wilson's program in theory and in its application. As Wilson had promised, he brought national legislation in line with emerging economic realities. "Wilson did not seek change for the sake of change," Baruch later wrote. "As with every true liberal there was a strong conservative instinct in him. His reforms were not intended to remake the American political and economic system, but to strengthen, preserve, and protect it (from itself, in many respects) by correcting and eliminating the abuses which had grown up about it."[43] Ever paternalistic, Baruch agreed with Wilson that Washington ought to save the corporate system *from itself*. It was a greedy and chaotic system that encouraged individual indifference to community welfare. From New York, Baruch viewed with enthusiasm the enactment of the Federal Reserve System, the Federal Trade Commission, the Clayton Antitrust Act, the Underwood Tariff, and the Federal Farm Loan Act.

During the early Wilson years he simply cultivated his connections with the New Freedom Democrats, performing whatever little errands they found or manufactured for him. It was Baruch who carried a message to Billy McCombs to forget public office for the time being and resume his law practice.[44] He bought and promoted government bond offerings on behalf of his friend, McAdoo, then the secretary of the Treasury. He championed a Democratic preparedness-for-war drive as an alternative to Theodore Roosevelt's own well-publicized efforts. Through these efforts he accumulated myriad obligations, awaiting the moment when he could convert them into an offer of a position within the administration. Then he would step forward as a celebrator of Wilsonian "practical idealism."

A WILSONIAN "PRACTICAL IDEALIST"

The big corporation was a twentieth-century fact of life: Wilson understood that and therefore Baruch could understand Wilson. It is doubtful that Baruch could have endorsed any Wilsonian trust-busting unless he had been opportunistic or had undergone a change of mind since 1909; then he had forecast that higher prices would return following the panic of that year because Washington would not "do anything to hurt our business which must be conducted in the shape of large corporations."[45] Wilson's task would be to develop a national economic policy that stressed both big business *and* competition for stability and growth. Yet Baruch seems to have been among the minority of contemporaries who interpreted Wilsonian speeches as approving big business. Only careful listeners and readers have understood a rhetoric that, an observer remarked, "is like a light which destroys the outlines of what it plays upon; there is much illumination, but you see very little."[46]

The object of Wilson's beacon of light was America's ill-understood political economy. He believed that not even its most prominent participants appreciated its workings and that even fewer could foresee its consequences. It was an evolving corporate capitalist system full of complexities that simplified themselves only when multiple units consolidated. Wilson used terms like "competition" and "trust" as symbols of good and evil to dramatize nuances overlooked by an unsophisticated public. Still, Wilson possessed an impressive capacity to clarify the operations of the system, forecast its tendencies, and translate its intricacies into direct, nondidactic treatises. Seldom have political leaders exhibited his economic intelligence or dared to educate the electorate in a political campaign as Wilson did in 1912. We can see why Baruch was so taken with Wilson; here were Professor Newcomb's lectures on the American political economy updated to 1912!

As every student of American history knows, Wilson discussed the trusts, big business, the concentration of capital. Although Wilson articulated "the politics of morality,"[47] it might be more accurate to label it "the politics of idealism." The former suggests a code that is both unreal and inflexible; though Wilson used it as a rhetorical device, it was incongruent with the "practical idealism" displayed in his analysis of the American political economy and in his own designated role within it. His idealism embraced big business while erecting organizational devices to improve upon it. He disdained the leveling utopias envisioned by moralizing "sentimentalists," a pejorative term in Wilson's lexicography, along with "socialists." He unflinchingly described a society that had abridged or forgotten its ideal of economic opportunity. The tendencies of modern American capitalism were wrongheaded, he said: "The truth is, we are all caught in a great economic system which is heartless."

Wilson accused the big corporation of abusing American society. It was a public institution that mistreated the public. It was a private form of cooperation among a limited number of individuals that excluded cooperation with the larger community. It fostered selfish indifference to its suppliers, its consumers, and its competitors. But he was as concerned with competition's excesses as he was with its erosion. What he feared most was monopoly, the concentration of wealth and power to the exclusion of opportunity. Monopoly was illiberal in that it limited the extension of opportunity to individuals and groups lacking the essential of American enterprise—capital.

However, Wilson did not want to rewrite history. He believed in coming to terms with the big corporations and the new conditions they had brought. Beginning with the "singular fact . . . that nothing is done in this country as it was done twenty years ago," Wilson exhorted Americans to accept the revolutionary reality of the big corporation and reorganize government and restructure laws to conform with contemporary circumstances. Conservative men had to recognize radical times: "We have changed our economic conditions, absolutely, from top to bottom; and, with our economic society, the organization of our life. The old political formulas do not fit the present problems; They read now like documents taken out of a forgotten age." The revolution in economic structure had made much of American government irrelevant in its organization and its interaction with social realities. Wilson sounded a call for action: "A new economic society has sprung up, and we must effect a new set of adjustments." This is hardly the atavism that some of Wilson's detractors saw in him. As boldly as TR, he dispensed with Bryanite mawkishness toward the Constitution and the Declaration of Independence; the practical idealist had determined to "reconstruct" government to conform with corporate reality.

"I am, therefore, forced to be a progressive." He begged Americans not to fear progressivism; the alternatives were acquiescence to insensitive monopoly or leveling socialism. He assailed the latter threat both because it sharpened his own progressivism and because he believed it was real. The socialist vote had doubled in recent years and would continue its rise unless Americans embraced his socially realistic progressivism, which was merely organizational change in conformity to economic facts. Americans endorsed change when it brought "improvement" instead of "variety for its own sake." He reassured Americans that his progressivism would "preserve the essentials of our institutions," while catering to the rhetoric of radicalism: "Progress, development, —these are modern words."[48] They were also the words of American business promoters.

But what about big business? How much more clearly could he define his position than this: "I am for big business, and I am against the trusts"? The test of a moral big business was whether it competed or monopolized in its markets. Big business competed with other big businesses, but trusts competed with nobody. With competition came opportunity, economy, and efficiency; with trusts came privileges, waste, and exploitation. The big corporation that competed for capital, suppliers, and customers justified its size.

Wilson accused monopoly of using political power illegitimately (e.g., for tariff making), hoarding capital resources, squandering raw materials, exploiting industrial labor, and charging exorbitant prices. To deal with the trusts, government would have to be modernized through an aroused "organized opinion" to assert the national interest. This necessitated cooperative action in behalf of community values, for "the whole stability of a democratic polity rests upon the fact that every interest is every man's interest." Thus, the prosperity of workers, farmers, and small businessmen was interlaced with that of competitive big business and publicly disciplined trusts.

Wilson was, as Baruch and historians have noted, devoted to states' rights, but that did not imply that he favored a weak, inactive federal government. To the contrary, he believed that Washington's dormant legislative authority and flaccid bureaucratic powers had allowed the trusts to flourish. He did not oppose big government if it, like big business, practiced economy and efficiency. He did not dogmatically insist upon different spheres for Washington and business, for public and private investment; "in the new order," he declared, "government and business must be associated closely."[49] The federal government he would preside over would play a more active role in its society.

Wilson's conceptions of political economy held a special appeal to a speculator. He wanted a carefully measured, orderly expansion of credit; he wanted price stability and predictability. Development, he suggested, had been stifled by a monopoly of capital that did not risk new enterprises or open new markets to larger numbers of promoters and entrepreneurs. He heralded an unshackling of "restrictions upon the prosperity of this country" from the "deadening aristocracy of privilege."

His primary target was steel. Its price was manipulated by the U.S. Steel "combination" put together by J. P. Morgan when he bought out Andrew Carnegie early in the century. Wilson accused Steel of fixing prices. Morgan's control of capital and Steel's monopoly of raw materials and its rigging of transportation rates all inhibited price movements in response to supply and demand. A free market was captive to interests of the Steel monopoly. A broad spectrum of businessmen would benefit by a federal assault upon Steel's stranglehold: the bankers who yearned to break Morgan's monopoly of steel capital, the ore producers in quest of competitive buyers, and the railroad operators in dire need of capital investment, cheaper steel rails, and competitive shippers. (Remember that at this time Baruch speculated heavily in ores, held the largest single bloc of stock in the underfinanced Wabash Railroad, and was involved in an unknown number of rail reorganizations.) Also, if U.S. trade barriers were lowered, then foreign barriers might reciprocally fall, permitting U.S. raw material producers in the mines and farms to find markets abroad; increased demand overseas would boost domestic production. And American manufacturers would take heart from their enhanced opportunities to sell in foreign markets instead of timidly staying home and complaining about the end of enterprise.[50]

Prices would decline. Baruch the bear welcomed lower prices: inflation was an anathema to the speculator and the system. Customers bought at lower prices and stayed home when they were high. High prices brought good profits only as long as a volume of trade could be sustained. When the turnover slackened, nobody benefited except the speculator who looked forward to depressed prices. Another man's excess inventory, reduced production, and slashed payroll made a speculator's promising market. As Wilson pointed out, artificially high prices dampened trade for everyone, including the price manipulators themselves. By removing the props from prices, Wilson bullishly believed that he would stimulate everyone's trade; the Steel conspirators would be blessed and would bless their governmental emancipators.

Finally, there lurked the international threat of capital itself against the nation. Although Baruch's investments took him into overseas markets like rubber in Africa and copper in Chile, he remained an unabashed nationalist, loathing foreign cartels in raw materials whose machinations distorted the U.S. cost of living. Like Wilson he distrusted aggrandized enterprises that extended beyond American shores and American control. Noting the highly centralized organization of business within a federalized political structure, Wilson believed that the time was at hand when only Washington could articulate the national interest in commerce. He emphasized that a head-to-head clash with a significant combination like U.S. Steel might be preferable to tolerating the cancerous growth of a "colossal 'community of interest' . . . that even the government of the nation itself might come to fear."[51] Thus, the government had to liberalize the capital system to save all Americans from an overbearing plutocratic hegemony of big finance.

To be sure, not all of what Wilson intended was clear in 1913–14, but the New Freedom legislation approximated his purposes. The Federal Reserve Act freed capital from its concentration in the hands of the moguls of finance, thereby permitting a liberalization of credit that benefited not only southern and western financiers but Wall Street competitors with Morgan as well. The Underwood Tariff enraged big steel before it became evident that lower prices would be translated into greater volume and rising profits. The Clayton Antitrust Act prohibited price manipulation by monopolies but, to Wilson's disappointment, did not approve industrial cooperation through trade associations. However, the Federal Trade Commission took care of that. The FTC would guard against monopoly, design rules of competition that tolerated cooperation, and, without any intended contradiction, encourage corporate combination in the export trade. If the New Freedom laws and agencies worked, more credit would be available for more entrepreneurs seeking expanded opportunities in domestic and foreign markets. And, significantly for speculators, American businessmen and consumers would enjoy lower prices through commercial expansion. Essentially, these laws provided what Wilson intended—better opportunities for most businessmen.[52]

But the depression of 1914 belied the promise of expansion. Most businessmen predictably blamed the Wilson administration's "excess of legislating" for the 1913–15 economic contraction. Wilson believed it politically wise to mollify his corporate antagonists with assurances of his understanding of their problems and with noninterference in their affairs. By the end of 1914 he proclaimed that "the regulation of business is now virtually complete" and that, thanks to the New Freedom, the future promised businessmen "ungrudged, unclouded success." Baruch was one businessman who shared Wilson's optimism. Although a Wall Street selling panic had led to the closing of the stock exchange in mid-year, Baruch eagerly awaited its reopening. Low prices, he believed, virtually guaranteed a surge in buying in 1915. Unlike other speculators who were frightened by the eruption of war in Europe in August 1914 and fearful of its portents for U.S. business, Baruch was confident that the new year would see not just a revival, but a boom.[53]

His confidence was well founded. At every chance the Wilson administration let businessmen know that it was not hostile to substantial profit making. In certain respects, the men who led the federal departments were a speculator's dream. They were not waiting for prosperity to germinate; they were out promoting it.

After some hesitation, business picked up briskly through the winter of 1915. Prodded by the Wilson administration, capital, steel, and raw materials flowed abroad. Baruch's sanguine prognostications found fulfillment. In March he exulted to Secretary of the Treasury William G. McAdoo, "I believe that this country is on the verge of a condition of prosperity such as the world has never witnessed." He veritably believed that the expansion would carry the United States to world economic domination:

> This is due to a number of causes. First, and of greatest importance, is
> the sounding of economic conditions of this country; it has thoroughly
> liquidated itself financially, and commercially. The passage of the
> Federal Reserve Law, an act which will not be appreciated to its fullest
> extent for some time to come, has helped to marshal the gold of the
> world at the centre of its greatest supply, the United States, for the
> benefit of the commercial interests. The regulation of . . . large
> businesses, railroads, etc., has, in my opinion, been started in the right
> direction and in most instances been finished. . . . The desire now to be
> fair with large interests, is a very important factor. The war,
> unfortunate from an [sic] humanitarian standpoint, is a factor that is
> causing an acceleration in the prosperity that will come to this country
> in any condition. With many of our farm products going out at high
> prices, with the sales of large commissions for war, large profits are
> being made in this country.

In other words, the war was good for business. Baruch later that year crudely linked the war to economic expansion: "Security values are being affected, and will be affected for some time to come by the demand for capital to continue the war and repair the war's damage; but if the uncertainty concerning our ability to defend our possessions were removed by the organization of an adequate defense, I believe this country would embark on one of the greatest eras of prosperity ever experienced."

Aside from a stabilized banking system, a new creditor status, fair regulatory laws, and cascading war orders, Baruch pointed to America's heightened self-sufficiency of production and a breakthrough in foreign trade as additional contributions to a new era of Wilsonian prosperity. For "once having started ourselves in the supply of this country and [other] countries of manufactured goods, it will continue even after the war." Some time later, McAdoo concurred that "an era of exceptional development and stable prospertiy" lay ahead. But McAdoo worried that the war might end before the United States had made the most of its opportunities.[54] Time was short; businessmen and the government had to cooperate in organizing the greatest economic expansion in history.

THE PREPAREDNESS MOVEMENT

As Baruch told it, the turning point in his search for a career in public service was World War I. When it broke out, he later wrote,"I certainly was no global thinker. Military strategy meant little or nothing to me; nor did I have any comprehension of what needed to be done to mobilize a nation's economy for a total war."[55] But he learned quickly. Few people were as adept as Baruch in translating a little information into complete familiarity with a problem and using it to develop a strategy for remedial action.

Prior to the eruption of war in Europe, Baruch's ties to the Wilson administration had been tenuous at best. He enjoyed friendships with Colonel Edward M. House, the president's closest advisor; McAdoo; and others in lower-level administration posts. He eagerly tried to be useful to them in the hope that they would be useful to him. When the war erupted, both the economy and Baruch were at low ebb. He was restless in Wall Street, where, according to Eugene Meyer, he had made "a lot of friends and a good many enemies."[56] Beginning in 1914–15 he began to develop his alliance with Colonel House and to take a serious interest in U.S. preparedness for war. Both would be avenues for an entry into the administration.

Perhaps Baruch had discovered that House was a nepotist, ever pushing relatives or others with close ties to him into key government positions. At any rate, acting as a trustee of CCNY, Baruch in October 1914 offered the college presidency to House's brother-in-law, Sidney Mezes, a former president of the University of Texas and teacher of the philosophy of religion. House was the first person Baruch informed of the Mezes appointment. With Mezes in the presidency, Baruch's value to House increased considerably. As a member of the board of trustees, he protected Mezes from the wrath of fellow trustee William F. McCombs, the erstwhile Wilson supporter whom the president had shunted aside. In 1916, Baruch considered leaving the board, but House vetoed the resignation "on Mezes' account," and Baruch remained to protect the brother-in-law. Ten months later, House asked Baruch to employ his influence with the board to win a leave of absence for Mezes, whom House wanted for a governmental role in expanding American world trade. However, an embittered McCombs threatened to block the arrangement, and the task of persuading his recalcitrant fellow trustee to accede to House's designs fell into Baruch's willing hands. Apparently, Baruch was successful, for Mezes would continue to draw his salary while a director of the Inquiry and later as a member of the U.S. delegation to the Paris Peace Conference.[57]

At the same time, Baruch dabbled in the preparedness movement. He rebuffed an invitation to join the New York Peace Society in 1915, explaining that as much as he espoused peace he saw "a great army and a great navy" as its prerequisite. As the issue grew in importance he urged friends to join preparedness organizations as a rebuke to the contemptuous "peace at any price" advocates. He followed his own advice by enlisting in the National Security League, a Wall Street group formed in December 1914 to investigate preparedness, spread "patriotic education," and promote universal military training. He also contributed thousands of dollars to General Leonard Wood's Plattsburgh Camp for the training of elite citizens for military leadership, to the *Army and Navy Journal*, and to the Navy League. During one of his many talks with Wood, a former army chief of staff, he offered to organize businessmen to assist the government in purchasing military equipment.[58] His preparedness role would be useful to the administration later because so many in the movement were Republicans or followers of the bellicose Theodore Roosevelt and so few were bona fide Wilsonian businessmen.

The high prices of 1915 made him more enthusiastic for a move to Washington. War orders had built an enormous bull market, and almost every economic index showed a healthy rise above 1914's figure. "We are living in a regular maelstrom of speculation in New York City," Baruch told a friend. "It makes an old-timer like me dizzy to look at it. I feel like grabbing all my money and putting it in a closet and running away with it." High prices made a bear like Baruch uneasy enough to take his winnings and get out—to Washington?

But the boom continued through 1916. In September he exclaimed to a friend, "You have no idea how prosperous things are in this country. Securities like Steel and Smelters are now earning at the rate of about forty dollars a share . . . and lots of lesser steel companies that were bankrupt at the beginning of the War have now become rich and powerful." The coincidence of war and prosperity contained a moral that could not be overlooked. Peace and pessimism were not too remote; speculators had to make the best of their opportunities. "Of course this cannot continue after the War but meanwhile they have fattened themselves considerably. Many new multi-millionaires have been made since the beginning of the War." If he sounded a bit wistful, it would have been because he had abstained from speculation in stocks directly involved in munitions lest they "might open me to criticism" that he had profiteered in his preparedness promotions. Yet by no means had he suffered financial hardship as a consequence of his scrupulousness. He could still boast of being worth "some eighteen or twenty million dollars."[59]

The administration began to take notice of his aggressive advocacy of defense preparations. With his friend Secretary of the Treasury McAdoo acting as an intermediary, Wilson invited Baruch to the White House for the first time in September 1915, to present a scheme for a "Businessman's Commission" to study industrial preparedness for war. A month later, Baruch sent Colonel House a formal outline of his preparedness ideas. It included a plan for college graduates to serve six to nine months in the military and five years in the reserves; a 150,000-man army would be created.[60] It did not matter that his proposals were neither profound nor original: his bringing them to the White House publicized the need to interest businessmen in industrial mobilization. And they promoted Baruch's reputation as a business leader of the preparedness movement.

The preparedness tempo accelerated in the spring of 1916, and talk of a Council of National Defense took legislative form. Anxious that the parade would march without him, Baruch reminded Colonel House that "although I am not looking for any work, I would be glad to open the way for such an organization, or even if it were found necessary, to help continue its work." He was by no means the only industrial mobilization enthusiast. Wilson could turn to someone like Howard Coffin, an automotive engineer then in the forefront of movements for war preparedness and for scientific management in a rationalized society. So we can imagine Baruch's pleasure when in May the president assured him, "I remember the stimulation I received from our conversation about [industrial mobilization] and it has ever since been at the front of my thoughts."[61]

Another presidential audience followed in June. For an hour and a half, Baruch and Wilson discussed preparedness and politics, for they were being ineluctably intertwined as the parties got ready for the November elections. Although still a political novice, Baruch did not hesitate to recommend to the president strategy for the coming campaign. He audaciously impugned the loyalty of some cabinet members and offered to spare Wilson the embarrassment of a confrontation by firing them in the president's name. (It was Baruch who carried the message to McCombs when Wilson removed him as chairman of the Democratic National Committee.) To protect the administration from being rent by factional squabbles, he urged Wilson to use a firm hand in patronage matters. He suggested that Secretary of the Navy Josephus Daniels, then embroiled in a fight with steel companies over the price of armor plate, be replaced by Baruch's Wall Street friend, copper magnate John D. Ryan. On the other hand, he lavishly praised Wilson's recent appointment of Newton D. Baker as secretary of war. For himself, Baruch claimed to seek nothing from the president: "he had plenty of money, his country place in the South and in Scotland and . . . he intended to enjoy life and . . . nothing but some great crisis would ever make him want to have an office of any kind."[62] If Baruch's cheekiness disturbed Wilson, then his loyalty and wealth were qualities that would compensate in the coming campaign.

Of course, the "great crisis" that would enlist Baruch's eager services was at hand. Incidents at sea and expanded U.S. investments and trade with Britain brought the nation closer to war in Europe. Wilson very deliberately orchestrated the politics of preparedness, which climaxed on 29 August 1916 in congressional approval of an army appropriation bill that created a Council of National Defense composed of relevant cabinet officers with an Advisory Commission of interested citizens appointed by the president. The twin bodies had little power except the power to educate Americans to the need for mobilization.

On 12 October, Baruch learned while reading his morning newspaper of his appointment to the Advisory Commission, along with Daniel Willard, president of the Baltimore and Ohio Railroad; Howard Coffin, vice-president of Hudson Motor Company; Dr. Hollis Godfrey, president of Drexel Institute in Philadelphia; Julius Rosenwald, president of Sears, Roebuck and Company; Dr. Franklin H. Martin, director general of the American College of Surgeons; and Samuel Gompers, president of the American Federation of Labor. Walter S. Gifford, a young statistician for the American Telephone and Telegraph Company, and Grosvenor B. Clarkson, a public relations man, were later appointed director and secretary of this commission, respectively. All had been active in the industrial preparedness movement.

That day, Baruch called Colonel House to say that he was "sorry" the president had included him on the Advisory Commission. House really was sorry. He regarded Baruch as a disingenuous poseur and expressed privately reservations that would be heard often throughout the war to come: "I doubt his sorrow as much as I doubt the wisdom of the President's making the appointment. He might have chosen a more representative business man."[63]

The press release announcing the Advisory Commission listed Baruch as a "banker," a euphemism rather than an accurate description. As House indicated, the administration wished that Baruch were "a more representative businessman." No sooner would he be appointed than he would be accused of profiteering from preparedness, an accusation leading to his congressional defense in January and a redefinition of his occupation as "investor-speculator." Had he not established his probity then, his career in government would have ended before it began. Yet the same charges and similar investigations would haunt him for the next two decades. As a Wall Street short seller, Baruch was a political liability. "Stockbroker" could not deflect the contempt many Americans held for his kind of moneymaking. More than most men in government, Baruch had to establish many times over his innocence of any conflict of interest or taint of illegality in his business life. Even among certain denizens of lower Manhattan the immorality of his accumulation was self-evident. Not until he grew old did he qualify for a legitimate political status in the eyes of most Americans. Until then, Baruch had to proclaim his own respectability as a businessman and benefactor of good causes.

One of the good causes that mattered to politicians was campaign contributions. To Wilson's campaign for reelection he gave at least $35,000, a great sum for those times. Given his freewheeling generosity and his eagerness to find acceptance among politicians, it is likely that he invested a good deal more in other Democratic campaigns. Baruch and New York lawyer Thomas L. Chadbourne served as the party's chief fundraisers in one of the closest presidential races in American history, which saw the incumbent running as an underdog and pulling ahead only on the strength of late returns from California. Baruch may not have been representative of businessmen, but that is why he deserved some reward for this risky speculation. Few businessmen had considered the president worth a contribution despite Wilsonian prosperity. They were backing Charles Evans Hughes, a safer Wall Street commodity.

Baruch's audacity and arrogance bothered some people, but not apparently the president. It would be simple to dismiss this tolerance of him as a reflection of his financial contributions, but that assessment ignores his inherent political gifts. Moreover, it overlooks the political inexperience of most of the president's men. The 1916 campaign was only Wilson's third try for public office. The Wilson Democrats, with some exceptions, were a gang of neophytes who had upset such established national political leaders as Champ Clark, William Jennings Bryan, William Howard Taft, and Theodore Roosevelt. The brash Baruch was in the right sort of company.

And, vanity aside, Baruch had a gift for dealing with people—one that any politician prized. For instance, he could flatter sincerely. In an awkwardly phrased handwritten note to House shortly after the election, he lavishly praised the colonel and the president, declared how much he valued their friendships, and stated: "I am supposed to be a successful man by the world but I have learned anew many things from my contact with you." He seconded the president's ideals and policies. Following the election, all sort of rumors and gossip concerning the speculator's notoriety surfaced; within the White House they were interpreted as indirect assaults upon the administration. Baruch treated the attacks as a cause for martyrdom: "If a man has an ideal he must at some time suffer for it." To some that sounded like pomposity; to others it was devotion. He would vindicate himself, vindicate the president, and thereby doubly prove his loyalty.[64]

Baruch's beginnings in government were uncertain because the Advisory Commission's role had yet to be defined. "The position of the Commission is rather a curious one," Baruch observed; "the only thing definite about the law is that we serve without compensation." Although the commission met several times during December and January, its members accomplished little except getting to know one another. The commission had no precedent, little knowledge of its responsibilities, and virtually no political base. From the start, Baruch displayed his ignorance of government's workings and his dependence on personal sources. He suggested to Walter Gifford that if he wanted all pertinent information on copper and steel manufacturing capacity, he ought to get in touch with his friends Daniel Guggenheim and John Ryan. After all, that is what Baruch did in Wall Street to gain particular knowledge. Gifford retorted that he already had inventories of twenty-seven thousand industrial plants and could find the necessary facts on metal resources in the U.S. Statistical Abstract and the Geological Survey of the Bureau of Mines.[65] It was not an auspicious start, but it foretold much about Baruch's way of operating.

In February the commission divided responsibilities according to seven economic groupings, and Baruch drew the raw materials assignment. The commission began to organize in anticipation of a real mobilization for war. It considered Germany's insistence upon unlimited submarine warfare as making U.S. involvement in the war inevitable unless, as McAdoo put it, "she recedes from the position she has taken." Yet, despite the imminence of war, the council was unable to act upon Baruch's call for total mobilization and McAdoo doubted that "it would be possible to induce Congress to take such drastic action unless we were actually engaged in hostilities."[66] Baruch had much to learn concerning political possibilities.

So Baruch bided his time by trying to assemble an informal mobilizaion apparatus. He was not very systematic in his approach, except for relying upon his personal connections in Wall Street to obtain pertinent industrial information. But, as it has been argued, that technique was as valid in 1917 as the standardization mania of an engineer like Coffin or the flow-chart passion of a corporate manager like Gifford. In New York, Eugene Meyer recalled, "he'd go out and do the selling job. He had a following and people he'd recommend."[67] He excelled in such personal contacts, and it had to be his style in Washington. He began with "no organization, no files, nothing." But he was an operator, not an organizer. He brought knowledgeable friends like Meyer to Washington and let them organize the office, do the paper work, and recruit an office staff. Meanwhile, Baruch recruited corporation executives to assume large responsibilities relating to the industries from which they came. Many of them had to be persuaded to give up lucrative jobs for dollar-a-year posts in government. Baruch spent much of his time in promotional work. Inevitably the engineers and statisticians in other sectors of the war bureaucracy cast aspersions on the untidiness of his operations. But within raw materials he built a devoted following; within big industry and big finance he developed a respectful constituency; and within the Democratic administration he earned gratitude for his harmonious, effective relations with industry.

On 2 April 1917, Woodrow Wilson informed Congress that Germany had left the United States with no choice but to make the world safe for democracy. Congress, notwithstanding fifty-six dissenters, made war on the German Empire. Bernard M. Baruch sent the president his personal thanks for the war message: "To those of us who had followed you like crusaders through the toil and trouble of the last few years, it is but the expression expected from our leader."[68]

CHAPTER TWO
THE WAR INDUSTRIES
BOARD

The congressional declaration of war concluded America's defense preparedness and ought to have inaugurated a full-scale war mobilization. But the mobilization of World War I, America's greatest public endeavor since the Civil War, never measured up to the anticipations of preparedness enthusiasts or to those of its allies. In the months following the call to arms the mobilization process was plagued by a lack of coordination, conflicts of authority, and a pervasive mismanagement that embarrassed efficiency devotees scattered throughout the emergency bureaucracy. Partly because of these problems, American troops and American supplies did not figure in the battles until early 1918 and not in any substantial degree until the middle of the year. And it took equally long for a total economic mobilization and stabilization scheme to be improvised. The German haste to seek victory in the early part of 1918 was motivated not by what Americans had produced but by their expected output in 1919.

Ignoring the fact that the Europeans had been at arms for more than two and a half years, the United States treated mobilization either as an original organizational problem or as an extension of its experience in the Spanish-American War. A genuine struggle over policy and power between civilians and generals ensued. Civilian planners in the Council of National Defense (CND) sought innovations to meet the technological and logistical requirements of modern warfare, the engineers and entrepreneurs suggesting that the U.S. Army knew more about chasing western Indians or Mexican bandits than supplying tanks for combat against one of the great industrial powers of the world. Additionally, businessmen wondered if the military appreciated or cared about the social consequences engendered by the fulfillment of its needs upon a modern corporate economy. The War Industries Board (WIB) was created in May 1917 at the behest of businessmen who saw that the War Department's orders would so drastically alter supply and demand as to destabilize the price system.

Yet, the WIB, like the Advisory Commission to the CND, was confined intitially to the status of official kibitzer. Essentially it was still the War Department's war, as only that cabinet agency could decide matters governing its own supply and procurement. Though the Council of National Defense reigned supreme in a civilian hierarchy, it had all the advisory power of a president's cabinet. Conflicts between military and civilian authority erupted with increasing frequency in the first year of the war as the WIB strove to centralize control of the economy in the hands of those who produced materials rather than those who expended them. After months of administrative uncertainties and outspoken public and congressional complaints, President Wilson finally conferred the WIB chairmanship upon Baruch on 4 March 1918, giving him broad authority to accomplish whatever was necessary to win the war without wrecking the society.

Baruch became the government's "general eye" upon industrial problems, the president's "Dr. Facts," the leader who provided that America would emerge from the crisis with its economic structure intact and its prosperity insured. Such a role came naturally enough to a man accustomed to soothing clients anxious for their portfolios. But, despite congressional passage of the Overman Act in May, separating the WIB from the CND and making Baruch directly responsible to the president, Baruch's jurisdiction remained ambiguous enough to require his own definition of the role. Improvisation was the order of the day. Although he often threatened to put all industry under his direction, and often boasted later that he had, the fact is that Baruch was too good a politician to control anything more than discussion. He instituted many industrial practices that terminated with the war and advanced others that endured because business support for them had been widespread since before the war. Yet he proved himself the ideal leader for industrial organization because of his penchants for self-promotion and opportunism, qualities found lacking in predecessors holding the WIB chairmanship.

With the war the government assumed economic functions hitherto unimagined by a private-enterprise system. Ironically, Washington promoted economic activities in wartime it had prosecuted in peacetime. Corporations that had surreptitiously attempted to exchange information on production and prices within an industry-wide organization before the war were given license by Baruch and the WIB in 1917–18 to form associations of dubious legality under government supervision. Baruch reassured industrialists that they could not be held in violation of antitrust laws if the government was a party to the conspiracy in restraint of trade for reasons of national security. The WIB set industrial production quotas, fixed prices, determined wages and hours, and established priorities governing the distribution of raw materials. Though not seeking a planned economy, Baruch and his comrades desired as much control and predictability as they could achieve within the ideology of a profit-making private-enterprise system. Supply and demand were immutable laws, Baruch and the Wilsonians believed, but the organically free market had to yield for the time being, and probably all time, to the managed market. Business as usual was incompatible with winning the war and social stability.

Although they had not intended it, the war managers knew that they could not avoid challenging America's basic articles of faith—liberty, property, and individualism. But without discipline, sacrifice, and patriotism, America could not make war and insure domestic tranquility. The nation had to organize a community. Washington solicited industry's agreement to defer personal pursuits until peace. The war managers projected the ideology of cooperation—cooperation between government and industrialists, cooperation among all producers—for the higher good of the nation and its components. Practical men had to espouse idealism without mawkishly compromising their realism. The war gave the illegal cooperation credo an underpinning of patriotism; there were those like Baruch who hoped that its precedent and experience would be remembered and practiced, with Washington's tolerance, after the war. These progressive entrepreneurs were not unmindful of the fact that today's expedience could become tomorrow's virtue.

Baruch considered himself one of those enlightened capitalists, and enlightenment for him meant acquiescence to temporary despotism. Beginning with the demand to centralize all mobilization and stabilization authority in the WIB, he graduated his rationalization of the marketplace to include nationalization of certain industries, conscription of uncooperative corporations, setting of civilian production quotas, controlled allocation of materials, standardization and simplification of output for civilian needs, conservation of resources, and management of prices. But he was too shrewd a politician to take enormous powers for himself, preferring always that industrial committees make the hard decisions for which he could take credit or elude blame. At the same time, Baruch earned the gratitude of the president, who could not understand why other businessmen feared his paternalistic interest in their welfare; he transformed himself from an almost notorious Wall Street short seller into a Washington statesman, won national and international fame as Wilson's confidant and advisor, and emerged as a mover and shaker in the Democratic party instead of a mere financial angel. The war gave Baruch a chance for prominence and a taste for celebrity status, feeding his insatiable vanity enough to bring him back time after time for public activity that increased his influence and power.

How was it possible for a Jewish Wall Street speculator to achieve command in a Christian nation that doubted the morality of his business?

War is the most expedient of all enterprises, a redeeming venture that allows even a crook to become a patriot—or a speculator to become a statesman. Somebody had to win the president's confidence by succeeding as his domestic general, winning victories on the all-important industrial mobilization front. The secretive and inaccessible Wilson, known personally and liked by so few men, needed a leader who could organize industry with the utmost loyalty and grace. Making this even more imperative was the fact that Wilson was a vulnerable president. He had been a minority president in his first term and had won a second term by the narrowest of margins. Lacking even the illusion of a mandate, Wilson could lead only if his domestic generals brokered well within a political and bureaucratic complex while exercising the highest skills of publicists. These talents, it developed, Baruch possessed.

Nothing about the circumstances of 1917–18 was familiar. Most governmental and industrial responses had to be innovations. The cliché that all armies fight the last war held true: in the Spanish-American War, U.S. soldiers in the tropics had been furnished with the heavy blankets suitable for winters in the high plains and mountains of the Indian campaigns; in Europe in 1918, supply officers wondered what to do with the mosquito nets given them by the War Department. Americans had not fought in Europe before, and had not fought as allies of Europeans. Weapons like tanks, planes, and chemicals required new generalship and new industrial plants. The American economy itself had undergone radical changes in the previous two decades. The modern corporation had evolved as a private industrial organization functioning in behalf of its stockholders; somehow it had to be put to work in behalf of an extraordinarily specialized public enterprise. Washington had no history to learn from; established departments proved to be incapable of a knowledgeable response. World War I was, in the words of two business historians,

a task new to all concerned. There were many unanswered questions in September of 1917. Who was to build these new industrial ventures? Private industry? If so, on what terms? And who in government was to negotiate the contracts? Or would the government itself build the required factories? If so, where would it get the manpower, organization, and managerial and technical talent? All of these were real questions, and there was no consensus either in or out of government as to how they should be answered. Adding to the confusion was the shortness of time. The war demanded rapid solutions. There was little opportunity to sit back and formulate an overall plan.[1]

To build the necessary war machine, you might as well have a speculator in charge.

Others could have won fame as head of the War Industries Board before Baruch did, and, in fact, others had the opportunity before he became Wilson's logical choice for the assignment. But only Baruch, among Wilson's choices, had the acumen, shrewdness, timing, and personality to become WIB "czar." Adversaries inevitably deprecated his achievement. Correctly, they pointed out that he inherited an organization that had begun to assume the characteristics manifested under his leadership. Correctly, they argued that he guilefully expropriated the ideas of others. Correctly, they observed that he possessed few managerial talents and depended upon lieutenants for the day-by-day administration of the WIB. Correctly, they accused him of using either his money or his friendships to inflate his status. All these charges, and more that portray Baruch as a slick, wily operator, assist us in understanding his success. His faults were his assets. He allowed an assembled organization (assembled partly by him) to function and recruited good strategies and good men to run it while unashamedly putting his personal wealth and contacts to work for him. He was not a "mere figurehead"; he was an impresario with a talent for upstaging the ensemble he zealously promoted. He needed all the deviousness his enemies saw in him.

As a Jew and a short seller, Baruch was accustomed to dealing with people who disliked him on reputation alone. Though blessed with a commanding and handsome appearance, he worked hard at ingratiating himself with people, deflecting their hostilities and displaying his charm, humor, graciousness, warmth, and good conversation. He impressed colleagues with his "sweet" disposition, his "calm, deliberate toleration" of difficult individuals and adverse events, his "friendly, affable" working relations, and "his quickness of understanding, his untiring energy and patience in conducting negotiations." He actually inspired certain subordinates to believe that working with him was a privilege—even if they initially did it only out of patriotism.[2]

Baruch's wealth was an extension of his personality; he used occasions and nonoccasions to bestow gifts upon people he wanted as friends. He did not bribe anyone; he simply displayed his thoughtfulness. His gift giving was a form of courtly flattery, a way of telling others that this esteemed man valued them. For example, personages like the attorney general, the secretaries of the Treasury and Commerce, and U.S. senators, mere acquaintances in some instances, received freshly killed ducks from South Carolina; or the wife of a WIB colleague received potted Scotch heather for Christmas. Just as his wealth was used to prove his consideration of others, so it could testify to his support of programs, as when he bought a million dollars' worth of Treasury bonds during the war. He looked for ways to flatter. He would tell a prominent government official "in confidence" how important that person was to Baruch, that he was performing yeoman service to the nation, or that "any line from you would have the required weight" with the president. That was heady stuff coming from a man himself widely believed to swing a lot of weight in the White House. And Baruch literally wined and dined his associates. Invitations for breakfast, lunch, and dinner were frequent, as were offers to share his cabs or his private railway drawing room.[3] Men of wealth abounded in wartime Washington, but few of them used or cared to use their money so skillfully as Baruch.

Artful flattery could be his means of gaining someone's loyal service. He could afford to share praise with subordinates the public rarely heard about; their achievements boosted his public image as head of the industrial effort. "I find very great success (although it takes time) in getting these men to suggest the changes I want them to make," he once bragged. "It is a great thing to always let a man think he has a new idea, show him how to do it, and pat him on the back and tell him how well he has done it." It was not an idle boast. According to a lawyer who witnessed Baruch's dealings, he handled bureaucratic underlings and rivals "very cleverly." Although Eugene Meyer resented Baruch's theft of credit for innovations Meyer claimed to have originated, even he conceded that Baruch was essentially loyal to colleagues.[4]

Outside the WIB, Baruch's vaunted successes drew the envy and anger of his adversaries in bureaucratic politics. Newton Baker, for instance, credited a predecessor as chairman of the WIB, Frank Scott, with originating the powers and processes that later brought Baruch fame. Neither Baker nor Scott liked the shadow Baruch cast upon their wartime contributions. Yet Baker was not wrong. The apparatus for governing industry, whatever its shortcomings, was there prior to Baruch's command. He had not, contrary to the claims of the WIB's publicist, "helped build the machine in every part from the earliest days," nor had "the general plan . . . originated with him."[5]

He was hardly the sort of person who could sit at a desk working on bureaucratic problems for hours at end. Day-to-day administration bored him. Visitors often found him woefully ignorant of organizational details, such as who was responsible for a particular WIB task. But why should he have known such matters? He had good lieutenants to worry about them. Baruch described his task, in the course of advising a mobilizer in the next world war: "Get your men and place them in charge[,] giving them full responsibility, at least just as much as you think you have." Baruch found competent executives who handled the details of administration in his name. As Baker and almost everyone who came into contact with Baruch recognized, one of his greatest talents was for surrounding himself with capable assistants and getting out of their way. A friendly journalist believed that "Baruch has an utterly disordered mind"; yet the same man considered Baruch "one of the distinct successes of war-time Washington."[6]

Aside, then, from picking good administrators, what was Baruch's contribution to the WIB? He excelled in policy making, industrial contacts, and political intrigue. All of this required the sort of personal touches his gregarious nature thrived upon. He could spend hours probing companions for useful information or indulging in nothing more important than gossip. He picked brains, always alert for a concept worthy of calling his own. He was an artful participant in policy sessions. At meetings, according to Herbert Hoover, he played the role of the synthesizer, thereby moving the participants to a satisfactory resolution.[7] But, most of all, Baruch was ubiquitous in Washington, the quintessence of what Eugene Meyer called "a very personal operator, good at getting men, backing them, trusting them and keeping his equanimity." Also, as Meyer recalled, "he played politics, I think, pretty well."[8] Because his very presence in wartime Washington was a cause for congressional suspicions, his continued survival and success depended upon his political savvy. He gathered about him enough Democrats to keep Wilson's party content and enough Republicans to claim nonpartisanship in war administration. He transferred his speculating from Wall Street to Washington. He liquidated all stockholdings except those in gold, sulfur, and tungsten mines and invested his cash in Liberty Bonds. The latter, he insisted, constituted the only means by which he could profit from the war.[9]

Baruch's emergence in Washington depended upon Wilson and the men closest to him. Baruch spent a great deal of time making certain that he was one of the men around Wilson and reminding others of the connection. In fact, this galled Robert S. Brookings, a nonadmiring WIB committee head: "Whenever Baruch was met by anyone he was always on his way to the White House or just coming from there. He was constantly parading his intimacy with the President."[10] If the claim is true, it is safe to say that Baruch's standing was worth parading. It made men envious and respectful. Few could doubt that he enjoyed close alliances with the men closest to Wilson, like McAdoo, House, and Admiral Cary T. Grayson, the president's personal physician and confidant. But being a friend of a president's friend never made anybody influential in the White House. Significantly, Wilson himself liked Baruch.

Upon elevating Baruch to WIB leadership and defining his executive authority, Wilson created the "war cabinet," an informal body of war agency heads that convened on Wednesdays, with Baruch sitting on a little black rocker at Wilson's left hand. Here were the men whom Wilson most relied upon to make war and peace in 1918–19: McAdoo, director of the Railroad Administration and secretary of the Treasury; Josephus Daniels, navy secretary; Baker, war secretary; Harry A. Garfield, fuel administrator; Herbert Hoover, food administrator; Edward N. Hurley, Shipping Board and Emergency Fleet Corporation chairman; Vance C. McCormick, War Trade Board chairman; and Baruch. "It is interesting to note," wrote one insightful observer, "that with the exception of Hoover every one of these men is an intimate personal friend of the President, and collectively they are exercising all the administrative power which the President is not exercising through the regular Government Departments." All of them had been businessmen of a kind; all of them were regarded by Wilson as, like himself, "practical idealists," men who sought to improve mankind without succumbing to the "sentimentalism" of perpetual reformers. While claiming to be nonideological, they saw themselves as foes of special privileges and pecuniary materialism that debilitated liberal democracy enough to lead to a hegemony of wealth or a dictatorship of the proletariat. They considered themselves humanists and humanitarians who would protect organic processes from arbitrary disruption. In the words of WIB historian Robert D. Cuff, the war cabinet is "best understood not as an administrative, technocratic, managerial or business elite, but as a patrimonial band of loyal followers, a partisan, political directorate, and a group of gentry-professionals. . . . Wilson, by his association, had not only raised these men, and others into History; he had also, they felt in some curious way, put them into deeper touch with themselves, something for which they would be eternally grateful."[11]

Devotion to Wilson and the higher goals he represented had given them access to the White House and the power it could bestow. That made them at once colleagues and rivals. It is doubtful that they shared the haughty Colonel House's complaint that Wilson had "a tendency to dampen both enthusiasm and initiative." They relished the excitement and tension of wartime responsibilities. Although often frustrated and disappointed in personal pursuits for power, they, like Baruch, found Wilson "an inspiration to us all."[12] They had been raised by their ambitions, zeal, and luck from mere commercial success to positions of idealistic command in America's greatest crusade.

About Baruch, however, what in particular had attracted the president to invite him to his side on those Wednesdays in 1918? Certainly the speculator shared the war cabinet's aforementioned beliefs and traits. Still, among those men, only McAdoo was more of a nonpareil than Baruch. Why did he become a Wilson favorite?

Simply put, few of the others had Baruch's political instincts or geniality. Time and again he spared Wilson from political embarrassment
while providing him with excellent company. On the other hand, Hoover
—the humanitarian, engineer, and organizational and promotional genius—created unnecessary public controversy and conflict while suffering
from a humorless presence. The others lacked the public relations apparatus of Baruch, Hoover, or McAdoo, which might have raised their
political visibility and value for Wilson. It might also be conjectured that
Baruch possessed qualities that Wilson admired and even wished he had;
for Baruch was acknowledged by his critics to be "masterful, dignified,
urbane, quick of decision, unflinching in purpose, above all skillful in
selecting men and unstinting in the support given to his lieutenants."[13]

Baruch's personality made his career in politics. In an administration
committed to a government of men above one of legal or organizational
technicians, the personal operator par excellence won prominence because he won the commander in chief's confidence. All this had little to
do with institutions or functions. What mattered more than the science
of government was the conviviality of men: Wilson and Baruch, practical
idealists, transplanted southerners, comrades. "Upon Baruch's entering
the room, the barometer of Wilson's spirit, if previously disturbed, would
subside a degree or so toward serenity," Mark Sullivan claimed. "Wilson
trusted Baruch absolutely, had perfect confidence in his wisdom, and
—what was important in the case of Wilson—was fond of Baruch
personally, liked to have Baruch near him."[14]

HOW BARUCH BECAME CHAIRMAN

Baruch's rise provided controversy for considerable gossip in wartime
Washington. Each successive appointment of Baruch to a mobilization
post—the Advisory Commission, the Allied Purchasing Commission, the
General Munitions Board, the War Industries Board, and, finally, the
WIB chairmanship—was marked by strong opposition. Moreover, a
principal detractor was the key man in military mobilization: Secretary
of War Newton D. Baker, a former progressive mayor of Cleveland.
Others in the cabinet shared Baker's antipathy to Baruch. Baruch himself later admitted he faced widespread opposition to his "ill-advised"
promotions: "I know of no men other than the President and Mr.
McAdoo, who, in the beginning, were favorably disposed toward me."
Reasons reflecting negatively upon Baruch's abilities were seldom given.
Pressed to articulate their hostility to his advancement, belittlers usually
complained that he personally offended them or that he was politically
the wrong "type" of man for a sensitive job. What did that mean? It
meant, as Colonel House directly said, "I do not believe the country will

take kindly to having a *Hebrew Wall Street speculator* given so much power."[15] Both his Jewish origins and his manner of making money were repugnant in Washington and deemed a liability to Democrats across the nation.

Baruch advanced to the pinnacle of war leadership in part because others either failed or felt the press of other business. His obligations and values allowed for a public career along with private pursuits. He did not manage a giant corporation, and his personal business would not suffer greatly if he simply deferred operations until peace returned. For that matter, he genuinely felt that the WIB represented a public enterprise more worthy than his private endeavors; he had a sense of community usually absent among businessmen. Like other children of immigrants, he probably meant every patriotic cliché he uttered. His perspective and background contrasted sharply with that of Baker, a midwestern, WASP lawyer. As a quasi pacifist and libertarian, Baker appeared out of place in a wartime War Department. Not Baruch: Baruch believed in war as an extension of policy, especially this one. As chaos and uncertainty slowed the mobilization effort through 1917, his was a confident voice amid uncertainties. By 1918 his leadership had become inevitable to all but those adamant against a Wall Street Jew operating the war machine.

Wilson quietly espoused one-man control for the war mobilization, and 1917 had been spent in search of a suitable dictator to resolve fundamental problems a liberal society faced in war. Could the private sector ignore the public commitment to war? Would the federal government have to direct the entire economy in order to fulfill its war needs? Would the federal government have to intervene in the economy to stabilize it and to prevent shortages of materials and rising prices? As early as 1916, on the advice of a British economist, Sir Walter Layton, Baruch had been persuaded that nothing short of an arbitrary designation of societal priorities would facilitate war mobilization. But Baruch was not about to regiment the nation without any recognition of its democratic ideals. Committed to a partial conscription of resources, Baruch emerged as a spokesman for an enlightened conviction that extraordinary circumstances required extraordinary responses. Like the progressives of recent years, he expressed the supremacy of public need to private greed. He would achieve that community goal through the liberal ideology of voluntary cooperation.

The immediate concern was a balky war machine. The War Department maintained an antiquated system of supply incompatible with the industrial system that furnished its needs. Military procurement created confusion and turmoil in both sectors. Industry produced with either ignorance or indifference toward warmaking, and the army bought with no concern for the civilian consequences of its purchases. Moreover, the army actually competed with its European allies in purchasing U.S. production, a circumstance that Baruch resolved by centralizing all purchases of war materials. Competitive buying was an anathema to an efficient war machine, because it spurred inflationary prices and war costs. Baruch's solution was to compel cooperation. Still, Baker and the army resisted demands for coordinating the waste of war with its production.

Nevertheless, the demand for centralization of government purchasing was endorsed by Secretary of the Treasury William G. McAdoo. When discussions concerning a purchasing commission were inaugurated in the late spring of 1917, Baker opposed both centralization and McAdoo's quest to install Baruch as the centralizer. Vance McCormick and Colonel House briefly sided with Baker; they could accept the commission, but they feared that Baruch's leadership of it constituted a political hazard. McAdoo prevailed and Baruch took on the added assignment of heading the Allied Purchasing Commission.[16]

In July the White House moved to alleviate the procurement dispute by converting the Advisory Commission (AC) into the War Industries Board. However, Baker made certain that the WIB remained subordinate to the CND and powerless to control the mobilization system. Though the WIB continued the AC's organization of industrial committees (a violation of antitrust statutes), their relationship to the war effort remained uncertain. "Concentrated control is absolutely essential," insisted McAdoo; he warned Wilson that the uncoordinated mobilization would fail, and "we shall have to pay a heavy price for the experience." Baruch seconded McAdoo by advising Wilson that the WIB setup was not an improvement upon the existing structure. It was a victory for Baker: the War Department continued to control purchasing and the WIB could not influence it if the army and navy refused to cooperate.[17]

The uncertainty of war mobilization continued. Its impact upon the marketplace increasingly disturbed businessmen. More complaints concerning the unpredictability of war requirements were heard in Congress. The army and navy, Baruch charged, continued their purchasing without WIB civilian consultation. Moreover, the WIB lacked assertive leadership. Chairman Frank Scott's health failed, and he left the WIB in the autumn of 1917. Railroad magnate Robert Lovett temporarily replaced him. Lovett, in turn, soon departed and was succeeded by another railroad executive, Daniel Willard. Because both Lovett and Willard were more concerned with their railroads' problems than with those of the WIB, the War Department was left comfortably in charge of mobilization. The board still needed both power and leadership.[18]

Baruch considered both centralized civilian authority and his personal leadership indispensable to mobilization. In a typical comment, concerning the problem of tin prices and tin's use in food conservation, Baruch told a Food Administration official: "The various departments who are handling this should be brought under one head, and if it met with the approval of all, I should be glad to take it under the War Industries Board, and be responsible." Only he seemed to comprehend adequately the price problems created by war demands and the need for market planning. Yet all he could do during 1917 was express his misgivings to Josephus Daniels and other sympathetic listeners. Within the board he was respected enough to serve as chairman in Scott's absence, but fellow member Julius Rosenwald opposed a permanent chairmanship for Baruch on the usual grounds—he was a Jew and a Wall Street speculator. Besides, for a variety of political and economic reasons, President Wilson was not yet prepared to grant the WIB the authority Baruch envisioned for it. As the speculator acknowledged, "No one wants to give the power to one man."[19] He might have added, "least of all to Baruch."

But the faltering mobilization favored Baruch's quest for the chairmanship of a centralized and supreme war agency. During the winter of 1917–18, newspapers voiced business and congressional concerns by clamoring for a minister of munitions to resolve the military-industrial muddle. If neither the War Department nor the impotent WIB could win the war without wrecking the economy, then Wilson had to improvise better institutions with new leaders. The Senate Military Affairs Committee, led by Senator George E. Chamberlain of Oregon, began hearings on the war mobilization. Businessmen pleaded with the senators for somebody to forestall economic chaos by assuming complete command. Baker and the military continued to resist alternatives to the current structure, but the political dangers of the controversy were more evident in the White House. The issue came to a head in January when Willard resigned, issued still another call for a strong WIB organization headed by a single mobilizer, and went home to care for his financially sick railroad. His departure left the WIB leaderless and its future in doubt.[20]

Washington was gripped by a sense of overwhelming despair during the winter of 1917–18. Work was slowed when the worst blizzard in forty-one years struck on 18 December. Even without a natural disaster, the work load was staggering. Dollar-a-year men found themselves laboring harder than most had when salaried by private corporations. Complaints of physical and mental strain were commonplace. One government official wrote in his diary: "Major Phil Sheridan dropped dead yesterday. The number of sudden deaths—young and old—scares me badly. It is due to overwork under pressure and to the great nervous strain and responsibility. Four Senators, several Congressmen, [British Ambassador] Spring-Rice and Sheridan—all in forty days is alarming." At the WIB, Baruch, in his quest for order, railed against the mounting confusion: "No one has a plan and all seem too tired to do anything except to criticize." He too had a taste for criticizing, but others confirmed his sense of the war effort's disorganization and low morale.

THE SPECULATOR

Although Baruch would not have done so, some people blamed the White House. All activity seemed to hinge upon presidential decisions that were not readily forthcoming. In the words of one State Department man: "Washington is distinctly depressed. Everyone complains against the lack of coordination in the Government. There is no War Council, no one body of men making war, no Secretary of Munitions. Everything great and small must be referred to the President, who receives no one, listens to no one, seems to take no one's advice; consequently, there are many delays and precious time is lost because of the necessity of referring everything to the White House."[21] Clearly, when Wilson eventually selected Willard's successor, he would have to delegate considerable power to that man.

In such an atmosphere of confusion, anxiety, and exhaustion, even a Hebrew Wall Street speculator could merit expedient consideration for command. However, Baruch could not afford to seem too eager. He knew that Wilson opposed the ministry of munitions concept, and he followed suit. At the same time he knew that McAdoo boosted him for the WIB chairmanship, that his value to Wilson was rising, that most of the cabinet had reappraised him favorably, and that the Congress considered him politically tolerable. And so he sat tight and tried not to seem overambitious. The issue no longer was whether a single authority ought to rule industrial mobilization; that seemed settled. As Felix Frankfurter put it to the recalcitrant Newton Baker, "I wonder if there is much doubt left in your mind by this time that the creation of a single-headed manager to direct the industrial energies of the war is inevitable."[22] So the issue had become, Should Baruch be that manager? Weeks would pass before Wilson would finally give an answer.

At the first hint of Willard's resignation, McAdoo begged Wilson to "consider Baruch for the vacancy if Mr. Willard leaves. He is by all odds the most capable man for the position." Days later, Baker sent for Baruch to sound him out on the WIB chairmanship. Of course, Baruch wanted it, but he insisted that the position must have expanded authority. When the CND met, Baruch's possible nomination headed its agenda. Significantly, the progressive Daniels argued for Baruch on the grounds that he was that rare businessman, a Wilson loyalist. Baker agreed that Baruch had demonstrated his devotion to Democrats, but secretaries William Redfield of the Commerce Department and David Houston of the Agriculture Department maintained that Baruch lacked necessary executive and organizational talents. Everyone conceded that the WIB's power had to be enhanced, but Baker preferred copper tycoon John D. Ryan as its new leader. It was fortunate for Baruch that McAdoo, House, and presidential secretary Joe Tumulty distrusted Ryan as a Republican without any Wilsonian attachments. House and Tumulty were hardly admirers of Baruch, but they firmly believed that at this critical time loyalty to Wilson ranked ahead of organizational wizardry. Through an assistant, House sent word to Baruch "to sit tight."[23] A newspaper reported that Baruch would be appointed WIB chairman, in an obvious effort to test the public opposition to him. Wilson ordered Baker to confer with Baruch on revamping the WIB's role in the mobilization structure. Still, on the verge of the big move, Wilson hesitated. Daniels defined the conundrum: "In capacity to do the work and in loyalty Baruch is the best man, but whether under all these conditions and prejudices it would be wise to name him now is debatable." Did Wilson dare to court more controversy by giving the Jewish speculator such great power? The president responded with the observation that Congress was "learning very fast to have a very great confidence in Baruch" and that he had achieved greater respect than his enemies appreciated.[24]

And yet the WIB chairmanship remained vacant as Washington awaited Wilson's next move. On 7 February the president conferred with Baruch on the mobilization reorganization but gave him no assurance that he would be the new WIB head. Baruch now feared that—with Ryan's loyalty in question—another Baker favorite, Edward R. Stettinius, would get the position. Meanwhile the president asked the CND to ratify a Baruch-Baker agreement that granted the WIB supreme mobilization power and independence of the CND. Baruch was in limbo. He was hopeful of the president's nod, but, failing that, also prepared to join McAdoo at the Railroad Administration or to aid McAdoo in the formation of the War Finance Corporation (WFC). On 25 February, apparently not aware that Wilson had informed Baker and Daniels the day before that Baruch would be the new WIB chairman, McAdoo wrote to Wilson requesting that Baruch be assigned to the new WFC. "My dear Mac," responded Wilson:

> I am mighty sorry but I can't let you have Baruch for the Finance Corporation. He has trained now in the War Industries Board until he is thoroughly conversant with the activities of it from top to bottom, and as soon as I can do so without risking new issues on the Hill I am going to appoint him chairman of that board.
> This is strictly confidential.[25]

In March the president made official Baruch's appointment as chairman of an enhanced WIB.

DOLLAR-A-YEAR PRIMA DONNAS

A major portion of Baruch's success in the WIB is attributable to his ability to select "men who knew their business" and to his giving these corporate managers a free hand to develop their own operations and then backing them up. Hardly a manager himself, Baruch depended upon the skills and loyalty of his executives. Their success would determine his.

Personality figured prominently in the way Baruch attracted technicians into the WIB. He always had to prove that he personally was "the kind of man people like to work with." Although their employer was officially the U.S. government, the person they were subordinate to mattered a great deal. After all, many of them were ambitious corporate executives who had laid their careers aside temporarily for a task that gave them no compensation other than any self-satisfaction to be derived from being in the midst of the bureaucratic action in a time of crisis. In principle they were "without-compensation (WOC)" men, volunteers whose service would be its own reward. The costs of America's first modern war were so extravagant that the administration believed it could ill afford to spend for salaries what should be spent for supplies. Moreover, as we shall see later, it reasoned that a man working for a salary was less valuable than one who served out of a spirit of patriotism. Thus, the WOC men, or "the dollar-a-year men," toiled for the nominal check that one day would be framed upon a wall to demonstrate their patriotism in the nation's hour of need. Baruch's task was to make their service as pleasant and professionally rewarding as nonprofitable enterprise could be.

Baruch's first approach to a potential recruit stressed the businessman's love of country and Baruch's lack of hubris. He dared others to follow his own self-proclaimed example of humility. Anyone who refused this affable, self-made millionaire's blandishments to do something for his country ought to be left with the nagging suspicion that he appeared both disloyal and materialistic. Additionally, at a time when younger men of their class joined the military's officer corps, Baruch convinced his recruits that civilian war service would be as meaningful and as elitist as any officer corps. How could a man resist the flattery Baruch employed on, for example, Chandler P. Anderson, a Republican lawyer needed as a special counsel on international affairs:

> In the course of our conversation he told me that his assistant Legge
> was responsible for my selection, and that as I had probably noticed
> the men around him formed a very efficient group which had
> organized itself into a close corporation, and it was really a great
> compliment to me that they were all so anxious to have me join the
> group. He said that I would be interested to know that after our first
> conference there, they each came to him separately and said that I was
> just the man they wanted, and he must make sure of getting me to join.

Any *gentleman* invited to join an exclusive society on the recommendation of an International Harvester Corporation vice-president, with the assurance that his position in the WIB was important, could hardly refuse. After consulting with his mentor, former Secretary of State Elihu Root, who assured him that the group appeared illustrious enough and the assignments worthy of his talents, Anderson accepted. Two weeks later came "another attractive invitation of Baruch's, which was to attend the regular meeting of his entire group of assistants to discuss and criticize the work of the office. This invitation was extended to me on the ground that I was now a member of the official family, and he wanted me to be on the inside of everything which was going on. I was sorry to miss the opportunity."[26]

Baruch had to make the WIB an appealing organization because he sought some of the most desirable second-line executives in American industry, men with reputations for being hard-driving and ambitious. Yet he had to persuade them to take leave from their corporations at critical moments in their careers. Baruch insisted that he wanted no "laurel-crowned, . . . acclaimed kings of industry"; rather, he desired tough "fighters and diplomats, good salesmen as well as good executives." Among them he developed an esprit de corps that relied greatly upon their affection for him. They respected him enough to call him "Chief." Between Baruch and his men there grew up a genuine affection and loyalty that would carry them along through the war and, for some of them, beyond.[27]

WIB camaraderie and cohesiveness, at least among the men closest to Baruch, was unusual in the Byzantine politics of wartime Washington. The war crisis, instead of being an occasion when ambitious men set aside personal goals, provided aspiring leaders with opportunities for power and fame. Well-connected hustlers like Franklin D. Roosevelt and Herbert Hoover, along with Bernard M. Baruch, made the most of their associations to perpetuate their sudden prominence. Wartime Washington provided a springboard for many a political career. Not only did the normal executive-congressional conflict prevail and even escalate,[28] but the proliferation of war agencies multiplied the possibilities of bureaucratic political combat. The established executive departments looked resentfully upon real and imagined encroachments by the emergency agencies. Indeed, the very presence of crisis agencies pointed up the inadequacies of cabinet departments in dealing with the war requirements, as well as Wilson's inability to define their overlapping roles. Clashes between cabinet and war cabinet abounded: between the State Department and the War Trade Board, the Agriculture Department and the Food Administration, the War Department and the War Industries Board, and so on.

Conflict, inevitably, was not limited to clashes between the established agencies and the upstarts. Although the members of the war cabinet shared a special devotion to Wilson in appreciation of his having recognized their genius and having raised them to leadership in a time of greatness, the war cabinet—"We Band of Brothers"—fought among themselves some of the most bruising bureaucratic battles ever witnessed in Washington. Most of them were, perhaps as Wilson intended, strong-willed and aggressive egotists. Each one of them believed that his personal relationship to the commander in chief gave him a license to prevail. While maintaining the amenities of fraternity, they did not disguise their rivalries. Like barons in the court of a king they gave Wilson their fealty, ever mindful that they too might someday be presidents or president makers. As Wilson once told reporters: "My troubles with the war are slight compared with the difficulties of satisfying my distinguished dollar-a-year associates. Each thinks he ought to have all attention and is unhappy if any is given to others of his group. The result is that I am like an opera impresario, every member of whose troupe wants to be recognized and applauded as the prima donna."[29]

Publicity and nearly arbitrary decision making did not appease their vanities; they desired power and the trappings of power. To gain these objectives they raided each other's staffs and coveted even the scarce office space of Washington; bright men and ample quarters were the accoutrements of importance. One of the losers in these bureaucratic struggles, Walter S. Gifford, who saw Baruch's WIB superimposed on his CND, later recalled: "Everyone was overflowing with pet ideas and new schemes for winning the war, . . . if they had the power. . . . As it was[,] these men butted into others who had other pet ideas and each picked flaws in the other's plans." Gifford noted their agility at appropriating their colleagues' schemes—especially his.[30] For relative newcomers to Washington, they proved remarkably adept in bureaucratic politics, perhaps proving that there were really no behavioral differences between corporation and governmental bureaucracies.

Part of Baruch's success in the war cabinet depended upon building and maintaining the WIB's hegemony over other bureaucratic empires. Lesser agency heads sought direct access to the president to further their designs, but only the men at cabinet and war cabinet levels enjoyed this prerogative. When Gifford wanted to get out from under Baruch's sway, the speculator and his entourage calmly "suggested to him that instead of the War Industries Board leaving the Council, the Council would have to leave the War Industries Board," a divorce that seemed advantageous to the up-and-coming WIB. Similarly, another bureaucrat in Baruch's shadow, Edwin F. Gay, enlarged his Division of Planning and Statistics from its creation in February 1918 to include over three hundred academic and corporate economists at the Armistice, only to find himself frustrated by a status that demanded accountability to the president without access to the White House except through Baruch's WIB. At the same time, Baruch piled special tasks upon the zealous Gay, who tried to console himself by believing that his importance grew in proportion to the number and size of his responsibilities. Yet the temperamental Gay ("a regular bull in a china shop," a WIB man said of him), without a direct line to Wilson, remained powerless as his assignments from Baruch mounted. No wonder he complained that dealing with the wily Baruch required "playing a typical game of Washington poker—a game which I thought I had won last week, but which I must now commence all over again from the beginning."[31]

Within the war cabinet, Baruch's most formidable competitors were Herbert Hoover and Vance McCormick. His ally within Wilson's inner circle was Secretary of the Treasury William G. McAdoo, who had pushed Baruch as sedulously as he had once promoted his transit enterprises. Baruch made his own ambitions subordinate to McAdoo's, whom he might serve someday as a Warwick. Others in the war cabinet were weaker politicians. Fuel administrator Harry Garfield, lawyer, businessman, president of Williams College, and son of a president of the United States, demonstrated considerable integrity when he issued directives that outraged manufacturers not tied directly to the war effort: he obviously lacked political acumen. Edwin N. Hurley of the Shipping Board, a retired manufacturer, seemed less intent upon empires for himself than upon acquiring overseas commercial empires for U.S. businessmen. Josephus Daniels, a North Carolina newspaper editor, unduly antagonized businessmen with his profit-cutting progressivism while administering Navy Department contracts. These three took their patriotism more seriously than most businessmen and incurred more corporate enemies than a blossoming political career allowed. Only Daniels would see government service following the war.

Hoover was emerging as one of the war cabinet's stars. Before Wilson invited him into the administration, the wealthy mining engineer had carved for himself an independent niche in public life as a war relief administrator in Europe. Public relations came naturally to him. In the list of war cabinet members, only Hoover's was a household name. But it remained to be seen if he could translate his talents and growing fame into bureaucratic and electoral political success.

His fame, even his slight infamy, made him the envy of Washington's bureaucratic politicians. Although they respected him for his organizational talents, many of the people who came in contact with Hoover found him unnecessarily brusque and intimidating. Congressmen resented his assertion of dictatorial powers in directing the production and distribution of foodstuffs. His first encounter with Edwin Gay, according to the latter's biographer, was "a pitched battle." Moreover, he sometimes lacked the decorum that kept these contretemps out of the public eye. A State Department official accused Hoover of seeking to protect himself by carefully making "a written record for future reference . . . [to] lay the blame for all failures . . . on other people."

As might be expected, Baruch's vanity and conniving were matched by Hoover's. The Baruch-Hoover battles were classics in the annals of bureaucratic warfare. Both men lusted for *lebensraum*, protesting their office space insufficient to carry out their important tasks. On one occasion, Hoover waspishly accused Baruch of "robbing" him of key Food Administration assistants; Baruch retorted that they had approached him, and furthermore, he had "troubles enough keeping people off my preserve and certainly do not wish to get on yours." Another time an irate Hoover complained that the WIB had usurped Food Administration responsibilities: "I would be glad indeed if the War Industries Board would take over the whole Food Administration!!" Baruch denied such overreaching designs and haughtily advised Hoover of his newly written bureaucratic rule: "to always believe that others are seeking at all times to act upon the best intent."[32] When it came to good intentions, Baruch believed that nobody surpassed Baruch.

Vance McCormick presented Baruch with a different sort of rivalry. The Pennsylvanian was both War Trade Board (WTB) chairman and chairman of the Democratic National Committee, thanks to his extensive contacts and political experience. Baruch respected the party credential more because it made McCormick more formidable than others in the war cabinet. Even so, Baruch proved his own political mettle. When McCormick attempted to block Baruch's accretion of power early in the war, he found himself "waved aside by the President." Baruch eagerly sought McCormick's friendship, but agency interests frequently brought them into conflict. The WIB and the WTB bumped heads over negotiations in Paris and London concerning the purchase of raw materials, an incident that led a Baruch partisan to complain loftily that the "very grumpy [McCormick] . . . does not accept gracefully any criticism from us." Fortunately for Baruch, however, McCormick did not imitate Hoover's reach for personal power. As a good party man, he made his paramount interest the political protection of the president, a concern mutually held by Baruch. Thus, because neither expected to head the parade, they were more likely to cooperate than quarrel needlessly.[33]

Bureaucratic imperialism being what it is, Baruch even had differences with his patron, McAdoo. Early in 1918 the Railroad Administration petitioned the president to transfer out of the WIB the authority to designate all transportation priorities. But Wilson rejected his pleas, leaving his anguished son-in-law with "an unfortunate condition with which I feel that I am unable to cope." McAdoo's failure to wrest power from Baruch did not rupture their alliance. A few months later, Baruch was able to intercede as peacemaker in another controversy, this time between

McAdoo and Garfield.[34] A McAdoo-for-president boom was germinating during the war, and the two transplanted southerners needed each other to fulfill their political goals.

Wilson attempted with little success to treat these bureaucratic battles with olympian disdain. He admonished his agency chiefs not to raid each other's staffs, urging them to set aside their own interests in favor of common goals that he defined. In January 1918, when Garfield ordered all industrial plants east of the Mississippi to shut down for nine consecutive Mondays, beginning 28 January, in order to conserve precious fuel, a great public outcry ensued; and Baruch, ever anxious to show himself loyally cooperative, rushed forward to assure the president of his support. Wilson thanked him, remarking, "It is extraordinary how some people wince and cry when they are a little bit hurt."[35]

Not Baruch: in what some people might describe as an obsequious manner, he made an ostentatious display of himself as selfless team player. Any unpopular administration decision brought a swift Baruch pledge of support in writing. To listen to Baruch, nobody in Washington was more selfless, loyal, or idealistic (realistically idealistic, of course). From time to time he sent Colonel House, who came closest to being the president's confidant, handwritten notes deprecating unnamed rivals for "passing the buck or getting an alibi ready" and suffering from "a bad case of rattles." "A lot of fellows," Baruch complained, ran to Wilson with problems they ought to have solved themselves. Not Baruch: "I try to keep everything I can from the President, having him believe that my problems are simple and that I am solving them all. . . . He is so kind and generous with his strength."[36]

The speculator worked hard to portray himself as a bureaucratic leader who uncomplainingly shouldered enormous obligations while other war agency heads engaged in fruitless backbiting. Possessing almost carte blanche authority over war production, Baruch shrewdly allowed other agency heads to wrest responsibility from his centralized domain. If they were foolish enough to take on more duties than they could successfully discharge, it would be further evidence of his magnanimity and their excessive ambition. And all the while he would retain his accountability to the president. It was a bureaucratic strategy that would confirm his loyalty and wisdom.

THE PRICE PROBLEM

Early in his Washington career, Baruch was both naive and disingenuous. He actually believed that his Wall Street contacts were all he needed to succeed in that overgrown village on the Potomac. He thought that he had much to teach the Wilsonians about politics and the national economy. That he lasted is a tribute to his capacity to learn, which prevented his arrogance and confidence from being misspent. One of his earliest tutors on Washington's role in the marketplace was Josephus Daniels, the Raleigh, North Carolina, newspaper editor who was then secretary of the navy.

On 14 May 1916, Colonel House introduced them, and Baruch expressed to Daniels interest in knowing him better and discussing the impending preparedness drive. (Thirty-seven years later he told Daniels's history-writing son, "I no sooner knew your father than he and I became very fast friends.") It was, at first, typical of Baruch's flattery and disingenuousness. Later he telephoned House and told him: "I believe Daniels is a good, honest, simpleminded jackass who is trying to do well." But Baruch, a self-styled political expert after a few short years of involvement, considered Daniels, a Bryanite and spokesman for southern progressivism, an administration liability. He recommended that Wilson remove Daniels "because the country did not believe in him" and replace him with copper magnate John D. Ryan. In other words, the job needed a business administrator rather than a misguided reformer. Even after Wilson's reelection, Baruch still campaigned to take away Daniels's portfolio because some of his friends believed that Daniels was bad for business. It would be Baruch's good fortune that he failed in this exercise of influence.[37]

American intervention in Europe's war changed Baruch's mind about Daniels. Neither man wanted "business as usual" when the national need called for mobilization of industry. Ironically, the issue that inspired the anti-Daniels effort was the issue that later earned for Baruch Daniels's friendship—the price of steel plate. Daniels had been battling with the steel industry over the cost of armor plate for the navy. Corporate collusion in bidding, he was convinced, prevented the navy from building ships at lower costs. The only way to get fair prices and prevent this monopolistic exploitation of a single buyer was for the government to build its own armor plate factory. Needless to say, the producers opposed this harbinger of government competition. The industry insisted that its stability and profits required a single price for a singularly large buyer. Daniels, however, charged that that practice led to unfair profits for industry, which justified a federally owned armor plate factory to serve as a yardstick for steel prices and for the quality of plate delivered by the industry. At the time of his introduction to Baruch, Daniels's proposal for the federal armor plate factory was incorporated in a bill en route to passage by Congress.[38]

The Daniels drive for fair steel prices proved instructive for Baruch. Hoping to head off government intervention in the marketplace, he personally endeavored to convince the metals industries that patriotism was not incompatible with profits. On 30 March 1917, Baruch appealed to

Judge Elbert H. Gary, whose influence at United States Steel and the American Iron and Steel Institute was decisive, for voluntary steel price reductions. A similar approach through his friends in the oligopolistic copper industry, the Guggenheims, already had brought about lower copper prices to the government, much to the delight of the cost-minded Daniels. Having already tasted fame for saving tax dollars on copper in the nation's hour of need, Baruch confidently told Daniels that he expected the steel industry to be "generously helpful." But the steel men were not as close to Baruch as the Guggenheims, and Baruch then had no power in his WIB post. Moreover, he became enmeshed in Gary's long-festering feud with the Wilson administration over steel prices. Gary rebuffed Baruch, leaving the speculator torn between Daniels's patriotism and Gary's right to command a price based upon Washington's need for steel.[39] When Daniels pressed him to turn his attention to other metal prices, Baruch accommodatingly agreed: "We must fix prices and we must fix a power to deliver on those prices." Enforcement was a sticky issue. Baruch believed in the need for a price policy governing all raw materials used in manufacturing munitions, but he hoped to negotiate it by appealing to the producers' patriotism. He wanted the steelmakers to fix their own reasonable prices. Although impressed by Baruch's success in copper, Daniels knew Gary well enough to doubt that Baruch could deliver in steel. Daniels insisted that the Munitions Board or Baruch's committee on raw materials determine what constituted reasonable prices; then the producers "would be compelled to furnish [the commodity] to the Government at the price thus fixed." Baruch demurred before resorting to such arbitrary action. Pointing to dwindling supplies and mounting prices, he urged Daniels to buy what his department needed at any price or face shortages later. But Daniels stubbornly refused to play steel's game.[40]

Washington had to consider drastic action: if it could not get a fair price for steel, then nationalization of the industry was its only alternative. Prices that summer were out of control and the government was not just another customer. The situation was intolerable to Daniels, who argued that "relief to all could be accomplished if the government fixed selling prices" of munitions and raw materials. Hoping to keep Congress out of the pricing muddle, steel agreed to talk with the administration. At a meeting with steel representatives, the WIB challenged their cost figures and demanded one fixed price for the government, its allies, and the public. If it were not forthcoming, Baruch warned, then Wilson would have to nationalize the mills. To this threat, one steelman, an old friend of Baruch's, shouted at him: "Bernie, the steel people thought you were friendly to them but they've found out you're their archenemy. They'll never forgive you as long as they live." Nevertheless, the threat to commandeer the mills brought the steelmen around in September. They agreed to restrain their prices in order to restrain public demands for a government takeover.

Actually, such threats were hollow. As long as the steelmen did not call the administration's bluff, "cooperation" prevailed. In a few instances, with the Fuel Administration's cooperation, the WIB later put teeth into its "gentlemen's agreement" by withholding fuel from obdurate steel companies; but usually threats of commandeering saved the WIB from resorting to really tough measures. Meanwhile, the steelmen were learning that Washington provided them with a convenient forum for achieving a stable price consensus.[41]

Indeed, Daniels fretted that the arrangement worked too well for big steel. With Baruch's support, a representative of the navy was installed upon the price-fixing committee. Yet Daniels still feared that the smaller steel companies were at the mercy of Judge Gary, who virtually controlled price-fixing strategies. The necessities of war were against the smaller producers, who could not manufacture steel as quickly and efficiently as the larger ones. The war, Baruch observed, obliged "a number of firms to consolidate, or take the work as a unit and distribute it among themselves [i.e., pool]." The small either grew big or had to pool contracts. Big steel commanded the markets in peace or war, and its cooperation proved viable because price-fixing proved beneficial. Significantly, when the war ended, Gary urgently appealed to Baruch to continue WIB price-fixing.[42]

Despite price-fixing's ultimate benefits to big steel, the hostility between Gary and Baruch was quite real. During a February dinner at Sherry's in New York, U.S. Steel's Henry Clay Frick engaged Baruch in a conversation that ended with Frick accusing the speculator of being "a leader of the socialistic movement" and threatening "to get even with him in some way for forcing down the Government's price for steel products." Baruch returned steel's distrust and dislike. At a price hearing, Gary offered the plate needed by the army, the navy, and the Shipping Board for three cents per pound; Baruch whispered to the Shipping Board representative, "Billy, if the old fox says three cents, about two and a half is right." In the 1920s, Gary and Baruch would clash again, and years later, Baruch bitterly remembered the judge as "a man who did not believe that we would need all the steel (because he could get such big prices for it), who did not believe in price fixing, who was willing after a battle to let the government have what it wanted but desired the allies and the civilian population . . . [to] pay what they had to[,] whose idea of defense was first of Company[,] then government." The experience with steel diminished Baruch's faith in business cooperation. In the later stages of the war he urged a government takeover of the steel plants; but the war cabinet viewed that as only compounding the administration's problems.[43]

Politically, however, Baruch benefited from big steel's enmity. It sharpened his loyalty to Wilson and his "courage to fight the privileged crowd." It gave him an image of progressivism otherwise unattainable by Wall Street speculators. But political advantage did not diminish his sincerity. Baruch, despite his earnest devotion to the marketplace as the sole force governing prices, was preeminently a nationalist. Profits had to yield to the national interest in price stabilization if the two were in conflict. To him, that was the practical idealism of war. Wars necessarily created abnormal markets because government competed with civilians for materials, and such competition inflated prices. In order to prevent the social disruption attendant on inflation caused by too many dollars chasing not enough materials, the government had to assert its paramount authority. It had to define priorities for the use of materials and set their prices. Of course capitalism would not be abandoned. Because reasonable profits were guaranteed by the government, Baruch saw priorities and price control as a maintenance of the system rather than its socialization.

Washington had to define the national interest. Baruch's speculative instinct told him that the competition for world markets would favor the nation that maintained the lowest price structure during the war and then quickly converted to civilian production for an invasion of the export market. But few businessmen possessed such a cosmopolitan perspective. The Wilsonians were convinced that they alone understood America's special place in world markets. Gary and his kind "typified the problem which WIB faced in educating American businessmen to the new facts of life," Baruch wrote in his memoirs. "They had not made the transition in their thinking from Main Street to Washington, and their values were still the values of the marketplace. Their pride in their achievements of industry and their mistrust of government made it difficult for them to put national interest above unenlightened self-interest."[44] Baruch could tolerate their taunts of "socialism" when he advocated priorities and price controls because he considered himself an enlightened businessman. Corporate parochialism and individualism had to be subordinated to the common interest. And he knew that, not only would the nation benefit, but the big businessmen themselves would gain the most from America's arrival at the acme of world economic power. In time, Baruch would become the foremost advocate of the idea that the national interest required a decision by Washington to control prices whenever it contemplated making war.

However, the WIB in 1918 really did not fix prices, even though a price-fixing committee was established within the WIB. Commissioned directly by the president, yet subordinate to the WIB, the committee relied upon WIB section chiefs for enforcement of its decisions. It was headed by Robert S. Brookings, a sixty-eight-year-old retired St. Louis businessman, former president of Washington University, and philanthropist. As chairman of the WIB, Baruch was an ex officio member of the committee; but the pompous Brookings was intent upon preventing his junior (by two decades) superior from upstaging him during its deliberations. Like Edwin Gay of Planning and Statistics, Brookings relished his presidential commission and chafed under Baruch's authority. Price-fixing was difficult enough without the intrusion of personality clashes and bureaucratic politics.

Moreover, the committee was initially handicapped because it conducted meetings with a great dearth of information basic to industry prices under consideration. Patriotism and intimidation were the committee's chief weapons for arriving at fair prices; but it remained to be proved that industry was patriotic or could be intimidated. Brookings often began sessions with recalcitrant industrialists by lecturing them on their civic responsibilities. In a sense he had no choice, because the meetings were really bargaining sessions in which only one of the two parties knew the facts of costs and inventories. Negotiating for the government required all the bluff and finesse of poker. If Brookings was dealing with a monopolistic or oligopolistic industry, he trimmed its proposed "fair" prices on the assumption that the public interest required something lower and that the monopoly could afford it. But Brookings preferred dealing with highly integrated and rationalized industries because they reacted more quickly to his blustering threats of nationalization. Highly competitive industries with smaller units rarely responded with any semblance of coordination and were too chaotic to be commandeered by the government anyway—and they knew it. So Brookings would order the competitive industries to form an industry-wide committee to coordinate their interests and represent the industry in bargaining with the government's committee. From one industry to another, "price-fixing" lacked procedure, formula, figures, and consistency.[45]

It did not help price control when the controllers, Brookings and Baruch, clashed repeatedly. They shared only a zest for holding profits and prices in check. Brookings believed that an excess profits tax would sop up undeserved earnings, whereas Baruch saw the tax as broadly inflationary. Moreover, Baruch regarded Brookings as ineffectual, inefficient, fussy, and tiresome: he could not command the respect of industrialists. As described by a partisan Baruch assistant, Brookings's "method of conducting the meeting was to make a long rambling speech largely autobiographical about the other things he had accomplished and to threaten everybody present with a heavy fine and imprisonment if they did not do something which he frankly admitted he could not formulate because he knew absolutely nothing about the business. The whole thing was futile and everybody was bored and the trade representatives were disgusted to find themselves in his hands instead of Baruch's." Also, Brookings may have distrusted a Jew who had traded well, "true to his

1. *The Price Fixing Committee of the War Industries Board, 1918. Baruch is seated second from left. On Baruch's left is the distinguished-looking Robert S. Brookings, chairman of the committee. Directly behind Baruch in uniform is John Hancock, who would be a frequent collaborator with Baruch in the 1940s. (Courtesy Seeley G. Mudd Manuscript Library, Princeton University)*

race." On the other hand, according to Brookings's biographer, Baruch was insensitive to the needs of manufacturers because he had not been one himself.[46]

Personalities aside, the fact is that the WIB principally raised the producers' consciousness that the society at large paid for their high profits. But the price-fixing committee could do little more. Through service committees, the WIB threatened, cajoled, and pleaded with industrialists to remember a higher cause than their profits. In the end, there was no price-fixing without the consent of the businessman whose price was fixed.

The government really curtailed prices through the judicious use of priorities. That was a real power Washington wielded to extract involuntary accord. Since 1916, Baruch had seen priorities as a way of bludgeoning corporations into cooperation with the government by withholding materials for civilian production. It would not be necessary to fix prices arbitrarily, Baruch and Daniel Willard pointed out, if the government simultaneously could prevent nonessential manufacturing and stimulate war production. Yet that proposal appeared to ignore the diminution of civilian supplies without a concomitant reduction of public demand. Consumers would still have too much money to spend. Benjamin Strong, governor of the New York Federal Reserve Bank, argued that consumption taxes were needed to discourage demand, along with credit controls that stifled production in civilian industries. Although the instances when the government acted arbitrarily against particular businesses were dramatic, and collective bargaining between management and labor was enforced in most industries, the war administrators went out of their way to reassure businessmen that such actions were only for the duration of the war. Threats of commandeering were implemented as a last resort when Washington was confronted by an intransigent monopoly like Western Union. Otherwise, the WIB *negotiated* prices. It never intended to fix them. As Brookings ambivalently explained, "We do try to agree with the industry, but failing in that, our instructions are to fix prices, and if we cannot fix it by agreement we have to fix it by order, although we do not like to do that."[47]

More than two decades later, another generation of potential price-fixers preparing for World War II judged the WIB's efforts a failure. Assistants in Franklin Roosevelt's Treasury Department believed that the key to conducting a war without serious domestic disruption would be to expand military production without shutting down the civilian production that absorbed demand dollars. The WIB had not done that. In a New Dealer's words, "*The Board never succeeded in expanding production*; it merely diverted production from civil to military purposes." Accordingly, "the Board never succeeded in stopping inflation."[48]

That was not quite fair. Though it is true that, according to statistics kept by the Price Section of the WIB under the direction of Wesley C. Mitchell, the index of all commodities rose from the March 1918 level of 188 to 201 at the Armistice (base, average prices July 1913 to June 1914 = 100), the index since the Declaration of War the previous April had risen from 170, a steeper jump. Thus, after the WIB received its presidential commission to stabilize industry in March 1918, the pace of rising prices was distinctly slowed. Furthermore, it might be inferred that the board had done its work well because the index showed no change in the closing three months of the war. After Baruch assumed command of the WIB, inflation slowed nearly to a halt. Indeed, the indexes suggest a personal triumph for Baruch's price controlling. The metals group index, under the speculator's own supervision, fell from its July 1917 high of 330 to 211 for the year 1918. Overall, the worst war inflation occurred during the sixteen months preceding the U.S. entry; then the index of all commodities rose from 115 to 170.[49]

Of course, it can be argued that the price rise slowdown in 1918 was a natural leveling off and would have occurred despite Baruch and the WIB. Some evidence suggests that this was the case. According to the

WIB's *History of Prices during the War* (compiled and written by the statistics division under the leadership of Edwin Gay, one of Baruch's bureaucratic competitors), Baruch "did not during the whole war formulate and advertise any general or dominating principles of industrial control." He resisted hard-and-fast rules for prices, relying at first upon his personal powers of persuasion to win industrial restraint, rather than upon government control of prices. In the case of copper, price-fixing worked because of Baruch's long association with the Guggenheims and because the government bought the industry's entire output and was really fixing a price for its own purchases.[50] But steel's intransigence demonstrated that not all monopolies were so cooperative. In industries where producers and buyers were numerous and competitive, such arrangements were unlikely and unfeasible. Nevertheless, Baruch's first goal always was to erect a government-trade association partnership on prices.

Many businessmen, however, enjoyed high profits too much to settle for anything less than price maintenance at high 1917 levels. Price rollbacks were out of the question; Wall Street friends cautioned Baruch, "No matter whether people applaud or not, do not ask for too low prices." Certainly he had to keep the lid on prices, but in 1917 he could not expect increased production without the incentives of high prices. Price control could not entail profit control. "Beyond a certain point," Baruch reasoned, "restriction of profits will restrict the production of these vital materials." Baruch suggested that his faith in markets required production incentives by asking, "How far can we reduce prices, yet keep wages up and keep production at full blast?" Therefore, it was in the government's interest not to employ price-fixing, just as it was in industry's interest to cooperate on price negotiations in order to avert fixed prices. But unorganized industries could not negotiate. So the commodity sections had to inspire trade association activity, if only so that the government might have a negotiating partner on prices.

For an industry like cotton textiles, trade association activity was "revolutionary." Little industrial cooperation had previously existed among the hundreds of mills, a condition that the war did not change. Cotton prices floated freely upward, and no industry figures on textile costs were available. Not until the summer of 1918 were cotton goods prices set, and these still gave maunfacturers prices 64 to 87 percent above the general price level while raw cotton advanced more than 61 percent. According to the head of the WIB's Knit Goods Section, corporate collusion on government contracts was widespread, and many manufacturers refused government contracts in favor of the more lucrative civilian trade. "We made it pretty smooth for the mills," he later recalled. The government not only found scarce materials for the mills, it also discharged workers from the army to fill their depleted labor supply.

Prior to the government's limited intervention, textile prices were "simply wicked." Even with government regulation of textile prices, profits remained strong and were bolstered by a flourishing black market.[51]

Ambivalent themes permeated Baruch's and America's experience with price control in 1917–18. Baruch and his fellow nationalists asserted that "business as usual" had been suspended in favor of a higher law of public interest and patriotism. Yet, despite the suspension of the free market, they also insisted that the ideology and folklore of capitalism had prevailed. Price controls and profits were not antithetical. In a crisis circumstance such as the war, a noncoercive price control mechanism was imperative for stabilizing the marketplace and preserving fair profits; and stabilization was imperative for preventing the social unrest that followed price extremities, lest the disorderly market give rise to socialism or communism. Acutely sensitive to the increasing popularity of socialism during the past decade, and keenly aware of charges that this was "a capitalist's war," the Wilson administration sought to cleanse its crusade by abolishing profiteering without abolishing profits. Price controls sought only to penalize the businessman's greed and opportunism. The profits system remained intact because nobody quarreled with the basic premise that America could not fight Germany without expanding war production, and war production would not expand without profit incentives. And profits inflated prices. So the administration opportunistically "fixed" prices in monopolistic industries where it wielded a priorities stick with the carrot of substantial, if not excessive, profits.

But the stick was mostly intended to serve the government's own needs. In industries primarily affecting the public's cost of living, the WIB tended to operate by exhortation rather than edict. The government argued justifiably that it could not plan its own budget when the costs of war were constantly escalating. Lest materials be lured by consumer dollars, it restrained civilian trade by deferring civilian needs. Thus, the war administrators exuded the mystique of Machiavellian authoritarianism while insisting that the voluntarism of a cooperative business community had worked. They had it both ways.[52] Ironically, as Baruch would learn later, few people really believed that price-fixing had worked without coercive management; suspicions of profiteering in World War I would not easily be allayed. And, for that matter, even Baruch was not convinced of voluntary cooperation's effectiveness.

But Baruch and others believed that price-fixing served America's interests in international markets. A restrained price structure dampened social unrest and helped defeat Germany during the war, and the warmakers anticipated that it would likewise defeat their allies in the markets of South America and elsewhere after the war. From its inception, the Wilson administration had encouraged businessmen to expand their Latin American commerce. In 1917–18, it viewed the war, with its attendant disruption of overseas trade and management of foreign properties, as a golden opportunity for U.S. competitors to supplant the British, French, and Germans in the commerce of the Americas.[53] Without stabilization of American production, U.S. commodities could not compete in the coming race for those overseas markets. Wartime price control served postwar commercial ambitions.

At any rate, the last word on price control remained to be written. Maintenance of a low cost of living was a difficult task. Not until mid-1918 did the war managers develop devices for restraining civilian prices. And then they showed a genius that a free society could not fully appreciate.

"THE INVOLUNTARY VOLUNTARY METHOD"

What, which, or who should come first?

Priority went to the marrow of industrial planning for war. It raised no less a question than "How free ought the marketplace to be?" For Baruch and the WIB the answer was based upon expedience: as free as the needs of war and stabilization of the economy would permit. Therein was the first definition of priority, one that asserted the supremacy of nationhood above individualism, of community stabilization above corporation profit, of public above private property, of soldiers above sellers. Priority possessed revolutionary potential. It bestowed upon the government the right to deprive a producer of market advantages in the name of the national market's postwar advantages. It directed materials where they did the most good for the war effort. To prevent inflation it conserved materials; standardized, rationed, and simplified consumer goods; and taxed income—by edict. In principle, priority would discipline the entrepreneur and regiment the investor to manufacture and capitalize according to society's needs rather than consumer demand. It defined and dictated a community interest hitherto unknown in U.S. society. Few men considered its feasibility beyond the current hostilities—unless they contemplated a transition to socialism or state capitalism. Baruch assuredly did not allow himself such thoughts.

The logic of patriotic voluntary cooperation called for private enterprise to defer to the paramount public venture; industry would produce and sell on command for a single buyer in Washington before it went to the marketplace. The free market, unorganized and unplanned, constituted an internal threat to a nation at war with an external enemy. Freedom diverted materials away from armies unless government could afford the prices that it unwittingly but ineluctably bid upward. Baruch reasoned that, having provoked the chaos that beset a wartime civilian market by its unwelcome intrusion, government had a moral obligation to real patriots to stabilize their commercial environment. That duty justified price management which, by itself, was an insufficient stabilizing force. At least priority asserted the supremacy of society above personal selfishness. It curbed superfluous growth. Priority planned industrial output to conform to the needs of war and the principle of a finite market.

In later years, the WIB leaders naturally liked to hear encomiums that testified to their success; and they were particularly fond of the German general von Hindenburg's florid celebration of U.S. industrial mobilization: "Her brilliant, if pitiless, war industry had entered the service of patriotism and had not failed it. Under the compulsion of military necessity, a ruthless autocracy was at work and rightly in this land at the portals of which the Statue of Liberty flashes its blinding light across the seas. *They understood war*."[54] Leave it to a vanquished German militarist to appreciate the paradox of a democracy at war.*

Flattery aside, the mobilizers of 1918 really "understood war"—and they acknowledged that priority had been their tool. There was no inconsistency with the patriotic theme of voluntary cooperation, maintained Alex Legge; "priority was the mechanism through which the voluntary agreements were carried out." The war managers were almost as adept as von Hindenburg at playing with the ambivalences of a liberal society at war. Anyhow, Baruch asserted, the priority board made only six rulings and none of them were appealed to the president; did that not prove that the inner compulsion of patriotism had prevailed? He conceded that the mere threat of a priority judgment usually sufficed in winning industry's cooperation in the form of an out-of-court settlement: "It was found that when the representatives of the various interests knew a decision would be reached for them by the chairman, they did it themselves by mutual understanding."[55] Industry came to understand war.

For that matter, the WIB found an even easier way to avert a priority decree; it simply avoided a confrontation with industry. In a sense, then, priority was much bluff and bluster. Its legality was moot and its administration was lodged in section committees staffed by business executives from industries they administered. Moreover, the WIB's priority

---

*And well might Hindenburg have envied American industrial discipline in war; it appeared to be greater than Germany's. Having planned on no more than two years' fighting, German industrial organization proved to have fallen far short of the mark by the time of American entry into the war. For its war economy, Berlin blended state and private sectors, but the latter's right to profits always remained supreme. As much as in the United States, industrial cooperation in war meant subsidization and incentive prices for producers. Priority controls and civilian conservation programs were innovated, but nothing proved so unpopular as profit curbs on heavy industry. As late as 1918, at a time when the WIB struggled to win the cooperation of American industrialists, the German War Bureau found that "whereas the workers were agreeable to military control of industry, the factory owners were not, and 'refused to submit to the military authorities.'" Gerd Hardach, *The First World War, 1914–1918* (1977), pp. 55–73.

power often depended upon its control of major levers of influence, fuel and transportation; but fuel and transportation were administered independently of the WIB. In some industrial situations, the WIB's casual procedures allowed manufacturers to attach their own priority ratings to government orders. Despite these vagaries, the war effort benefited by the creation of the priority board on 27 March under the chairmanship of Judge Edwin B. Parker, a man whose shrewd manipulation of industries led some observers to rate him as more important to the WIB's work than Baruch.

The priority board at least gave the WIB an illusion of power following the failure of voluntary cooperation. It represented a fulfillment of Baruch's campaign for centralization and control of mobilization. Other war managers reinforced Baruch's demands for real authority to compel industrial cooperation. Harry Garfield, beset by urgent claims upon the Fuel Administration's allocation function, had pressed Baruch for a commitment to priorities even before the Parker board's creation. But the board did not automatically improve war production. In May, Alex Legge admitted: "There has not been one week that we have been able to meet our obligations from a military standpoint." More than a year after the United States went to war, it still could not procure its war needs or those of its allies.[56]

The priority board approached an industry as a friend in need, appealing to its patriotism and solicitous of its well-being. "It is a large part of our responsibility," said one member, "to see that the industry is not unduly disturbed and is not unduly starved, during the [war] period. Just as much as it is part of our responsibility to see that materials are forthcoming for war purposes." To the priority board fell the diplomatic assignment of satisfying the materials requirements of war industries without depriving civilian industries of their life's blood. To the priority board fell the onerous task of organizing what Baruch candidly described as "the tremendously competitive system with which we had so much trouble in directing the use of our facilities." To the priority board fell the obloquy of twisting industrial arms, putting what Eugene Meyer called "a little bit of pressure in back of our advice"; it adopted, said the sardonic Meyer, "the involuntary voluntary method." The war managers had no choice but to replace the worn illusion of voluntary cooperation with a fresh illusion of priority power. In the words of a Shipping Board man: "Such a thing as voluntary cooperation for production as a matter of public service was almost unknown, and, yet, that was what the war had demanded."[57]

Dollars always had priority over patriotism. Baruch and other WIB leaders privately said so during the war. Members of the war cabinet knew who they were dealing with. Observing management-labor relations in the shipbuilding industry, businessman Edward Hurley commented, "I find no patriotism on either side when it comes to money." Nobody worked only for the flag. Manufacturers of acid threatened not to sell to the government unless it offered a "stimulating price" instead of a reasonable profit. Labor administrator Felix Frankfurter sniffed that businessmen in government were no more defenders of the public interest than their counterparts in industry: "Business men are trained to make money and that is their view point." (Frankfurter believed that lawyers had a patent on the public interest.) Still, there were many business executives in the WIB who sincerely put the government's interest in victory first. In difficult industrial negotiations, when all else had failed to elicit cooperation, a section chief would ask his opposite number, "Haven't you a son in the Army?"[58]

Baruch reinforced priority with threats to seize intransigent industries. The speculator righteously insisted that corporate property was no more sacred than the common good. However, he emphasized that a seizure would be used only when negotiations collapsed. As old friend George Peek recalled, "We were looking for production and it was a rare thing to discuss taking over somebody's plant. We felt that the men who had grown up in the business . . . were in a better position to operate it than some Government clerks." They would never trust production to people who had not met a payroll. Baruch concurred, but, facing a businessman's hostility, he would commandeer a plant or even an industry. He threatened Judge Elbert Gary with a takeover of U.S. Steel. "You haven't got anybody to run the Steel Company," Gary said, and Baruch retorted, "Oh, we'll get a second lieutenant or somebody to run it." He may have been serious.

Du Pont's profiteering on explosives so outraged Baruch that he nullified a contract with the company and sought federal production of nitrates. He became such an avid booster of commandeering production for war that in late August 1918 he requested centralization of the power in his office. Hoarded materials were a choice target for government seizure. Baruch put a detective on the WIB payroll, gave him the title "Chief, Stored Materials Section," and sent him into warehouses to impound hoarded materials kept from the government's watchful eyes; he then sold them to foreign governments at higher prices.[59]

The war managers had a penchant for a bit of state capitalism. But they were not consistent or of one mind. When Harry Garfield advocated government purchase and operation of coal mines, the war cabinet rebuffed him. Pennsylvania's Vance McCormick denounced it as "not good business" (or good politics, he might have added), and the assembled businessmen turned their attentions to financing public utilities, a project earning Baruch's warm support. McAdoo and Hurley demanded that private financiers match Washington's capital in any venture. To Hurley, federal financing of industry was another example of businessmen's desires "to help themselves to the Government money." Ideologically, he deplored any trend toward government ownership of production. President Wilson seemed more pragmatic. State capitalism was preferable to socialism. He was considering permanent public ownership of railroads, steamship lines, and utilities; it was said that he hoped nationalization would steal the thunder of "the radical element," a policy that could be "classed as one of expediency rather than conviction."[60] Even Baruch, as zealous as he was to expropriate property in the name of patriotism, as eager as he was to augment private capital with the Treasury's billions, as anxious as he was to second every presidential opinion, might not have tolerated this intrusion upon capitalist conviction.

Nevertheless, during the war, free enterprisers in the administration were willing to cast some business dogma aside in favor of the national interest, which, according to Wilsonian doctrine, served businessmen even if they were too myopic to appreciate that fact. Certainly some businessmen benefited by war orders more than others. A key word in the priority board's vocabulary was "essentiality," which meant that if a manufacturer's product did not have immediate utility to the war machine, then it should not be made. Many small manufacturers suddenly found their availability of materials curtailed; their wholesalers and retailers had nothing to sell. The priority board did not want anyone to manufacture refrigerators, stoves, baby buggies, and so on, because they consumed vital materials for products the war machine deemed "nonessential."

Ultimately, however, for the benefit of intractable automobile manufacturers, Judge Parker claimed that "we have eliminated the word ["nonessential"] from our vocabulary." That conformed with the president's wishes. After all, Wilson had warned his war cabinet against "an unnecessary curtailment and destruction of the less essential industries," thereby articulating a concern for the small manufacturer that may have been shared in the war cabinet only by Josephus Daniels. Who defined "unnecessary curtailment" or "less essential"? That was the job of the priority board, whose chairman, Judge Parker, once commented, "All essentiality is relative." The small manufacturer not only had to produce for war in order to stay alive, but he had to do it as efficiently as his big competitor. If this required an economy of scale, then small manufacturers had to join forces. Baruch, a longtime advocate of industrial consolidation, insisted that, if a small manufacturer had trouble "getting the [war] work done"—that is, bidding against bigger competitors —he should pool resources with another firm. Pooling, Baruch believed, "would not violate the Sherman [Antitrust] Law, provided the Government was a party to it." Baruch carried his mania for essentiality to the extreme of demanding "immediate stoppage, if possible, [of] all activities not necessary to the winning of the war." He once lectured Herbert

Hoover, "If our man power becomes further lessened, it seems to me that we must arrive at a time when we will have to stop the production of certain foods that are not essential for the preservation of life, and only produce those which are necessary to keep the civilian population in good condition." The food administrator sharply retorted that Baruch should stick to eliminating nonessential jobs. Neither man could afford to be outdone in the quest for "essentiality." Wilson's fear that his war cabinet was capable of destroying enterprises producing solely for the civilian market was well founded.[61]

But the game of essentiality would not have been necessary if businessmen cooperated. Baruch admitted that Wilsonian visions of enlightened selfishness played no part in most wartime business considerations: "It is curious that in a great situation like this when men should be thinking in terms of winning the war and of the great benefit that is going to come to countless generations coming after us, that these very men are thinking of what small profit or position is going to come to them." There was nothing enlightened about this selfishness, nor was it confined to a few small chiselers; it was widespread among the biggest entrepreneurs. Big industrialists would not produce for Uncle Sam unless assured a fair profit. As his biographers have written of Pierre S. Du Pont, "Others might rely on the surge of patriotic zeal for motivations, but for the president of the Du Pont Company, the one way to assure success was to pay for it." Baruch's tendency to wrap himself in the flag must have amused Du Pont, Ford, Gary, Frick, Durant, and other moguls. Some of them hoarded materials, flouted the blacklist's prohibition on filling orders from neutrals for delivery after the war, and otherwise played the competitive market as if they did not know a war was on. Only a threat to deny fuel to U.S. Steel prevented the corporation from giving preference to civilian customers. Only a tip from a French government official enabled Baruch to find some two hundred thousand tons of American ships withheld from government service in favor of bigger profits in civilian trade.[62]

The automobile industry deserves special notice in this connection. The WIB dragged most automakers screaming and kicking into the war. Civilian demand had risen considerably just prior to the U.S. entry, and the automakers, at that time the nation's third largest industry, consumed enormous quantities of skilled labor and materials without the slightest willingness to convert to a government market. They tested the WIB's ability to stabilize the economy while filling war needs. Other manufacturers pressed the WIB to explain why they were denied materials, fuel, labor, and transportation while the automakers still turned out pleasure cars. Finally, in March 1918, the industry magnanimously offered to reduce production of passenger cars by 30 percent in return for war orders. The offer was not as generous as the automakers intended it to appear: as Daniel Willard pointed out, they had contemplated an increase of 30 percent above the previous year's output anyway, instead of the 50 percent reduction of 1917's output sought by the WIB; they were merely offering no increase.

A steel shortage toughened the WIB's resolve to recruit the automakers for war. Amid rumors of steel hoarding in Detroit, the WIB began to consider priority restrictions against the automakers unless real voluntary curtailments were forthcoming. The industry blamed the steel crisis on the WIB for its failure to expand production while steel mills operated at 50 to 75 percent of capacity. John Dodge wanted the government to finance expanded steel production; clearly, some manufacturers did not share the war cabinet's ideological aversion to state capitalism. As Dodge put it, "The trouble seems to me that we are not getting sufficient government assistance." Nobody could accuse him of unrealistic, laissez-faire views. What he wanted was expansion, not industrial conversion, and that ran counter to Wilson's policy of restraining wartime construction of plants that could become surplus capacity following the war. Washington had no alternative to curtailment of auto production. "We have been going back, back, back," Alex Legge declared in May 1918, concerning the government's failure to fulfill its military commitments. Baruch pleaded with the automakers for a voluntary attempt to enlarge their war effort, a plea buttressed by the threat to shut them down if cooperation were not forthcoming. But, he insisted, "We don't want to be arbitrary." The automakers were prepared to call his bluff. One manufacturer reminded Baruch that if the WIB closed him down, "I'll be alright enough; it won't affect me at all, but . . . it does vitally affect at least 1,000,000 people,—it will absolutely paralyze them. . . . The credit of the working man who has bought his house on credit and is trying to pay for it, all this will go." The specter of a million unemployed voters in the midst of a war had political significance for Baruch.[63]

Baruch blustered in a crisis that called for action. In June, Fuel Administrator Harry Garfield, who had a reputation for making the tough decision regardless of political consequences, ordered an allocation for the automakers of only enough fuel to enable them to produce 25 percent of their passenger car capacity. Garfield, having taken the onus for an auto cutback from the WIB, stiffened Baruch's determination and strengthened his hand in negotiations. Meeting again with the industry association's representatives on 16 July, Judge Parker confronted them with evidence that General Motors and Dodge had been hoarding materials. One company president was not easily shamed: "Of course we have; we would be damn fools if we hadn't." But the industry representative conceded that cutting off the supply of materials would hurt the automakers because only 8 or 10 percent of their capacity was committed to any kind of war production. The WIB pressed its demand for a 75 percent conversion to war production. "If you put that act through," an auto man warned, "you will precipitate the worst panic the country had ever seen, and I am your friend in telling you so. . . . It is absolutely confiscation of the industry." But this time, Baruch would not retreat: "You won't get your steel; that is all." Parker even threatened to seize their hoarded steel if the automakers did not comply. The WIB would go to the country to see "whether we will give the boys in khaki their supplies or give the automobile industries theirs." Still, Washington's coercion of Detroit depended upon Pittsburgh's cooperation; the automakers were betting that steel would not turn its back on its best peacetime customer while the WIB gambled that it could intimidate both industries into cooperation.

In August the automakers offered the WIB a compromise of 50 percent. Their decision to enter the military market was based less upon patriotism or WIB pressure than upon economics—car sales were slumping. Again, Baruch, for all his tough talk, seemed eager to accept industry's terms, but Parker sent a stiff demand to Detroit: convert *everything* to war production by 1 January, "for in no other way can you be sure of the continuance of industry and the preservation of your organization." To prevent stockpiling, he ordered sworn inventories of materials for car production from the manufacturers. The 100 percent demand incited screams of outrage from auto dealers who would have no new cars to sell in 1919. The WIB retreated while accusing the producers of precipitating a crisis by not accepting even 25 percent. By then the automakers were willing to go along because civilian fuel limitations had reduced car demand and, to fill that gap, Detroit needed Washington's war orders. However, their minimal collaboration would never get a real test because the war would be over three months after cooperation began.[64]

People and institutions less powerful than the automakers could not afford the luxury of defying Washington's demands for cooperation. Baruch denied builders materials for private construction during the war, an edict that really depended upon the assent of the American Iron and Steel Institute. Civilian deprivation stemming from priority decisions abounded. New York City was told it could not build schools, and Yale had to suspend dormitory construction. Some priority schemes were not so sensible. Daniel Willard pushed for a public resolution to notify manufacturers and merchants that the government was "discouraging Christmas-giving as inconsistent with war-time economy." If Willard had had his way, Uncle Sam would have put Santa Claus out of business in 1918.[65]

Conservation was a central feature of civilian life during 1918. Hoover's Food Administration gave Americans victory gardens, meatless and wheatless days, and "Hooverized" meals based upon recipes using tasteless meat and wheat substitutes. Its objective was a moderate expansion of production coupled with a reallocation of anticipated stocks abroad. Fearing excessive social dislocation brought on by excessive economic expansion, Wilson preferred to divert as many resources as possible to war uses. For that he needed widespread civilian conservation. Critics of Wilson like Chandler Anderson ridiculed such conservation because "the nation was being drugged by Hooverism, by being told every day that food will win the war, and most people thought that they were doing all that was required of them if they ate chicken instead of beef, and rye bread instead of wheat, and contributed their spare cash to Y.M.C.A. and Red Cross work."[66] By fall 1918, Anderson could have added gasless Sundays, nighttime closings of gas stations, and Daylight Saving Time to his list of superficial voluntary measures. Anderson's point was that the situation was urgent enough to warrant greater regimentation, such as rationing, not mere pleas for patchwork cooperation.

Labor conflict added to the list of instances of noncooperation. On the one hand, workers in boiler factories and in coal mines would rather fight than build boilers or mine coal, as the lesser of the hazards. Miners and boiler workers were refusing military deferments and enlisting in the armed services, thereby depleting the labor supply in vital industries. That sort of patriotism the WIB could have done without.[67]

Inflation of prices and corporation profits justified war worker demands for higher wages. But industrialists resisted both their workers and the government, the latter's interest being in guaranteeing war production by mollifying labor. Government imposition of the eight-hour day in war production was a particular source of business resentment. Looking ahead to peace, Pittsburgh steelmakers wanted to remove the war precedent of an eight-hour day before their workers took it for granted. Southern cotton mills refused army contracts restricting the use of child labor. Business would concede nothing that labor had not enjoyed before. From his vantage point in war administration, conservative businessman Edward Hurley commented:

> My greatest disappointment in the labor question is from the fact that the employers take the position that [the war] must not cost them anything for increased wages. They do not want to co-operate with the Government. In fact, they desire the Government to pay all the bills and seem to have lost interest in what wages the men demand as long as the Government pays the toll. After my work in behalf of the employers of the country, to find this feeling prevailing in most quarters is most disheartening.[68]

Cooperation, Baruch hoped, would lead to a more generous attitude by capital toward labor. He liked to believe that industry converted to war production and stabilized prices without exploiting labor. Employers had voluntarily given their workers eight-hour days, time-and-a-half for overtime, and the right to organize and bargain collectively. Guided by the higher idealism of mutual interest, labor and capital had set aside all differences. Samuel Gompers sat upon the Advisory Commission and Hugh Frayne, an organizer for the American Federation of Labor, headed the WIB's Labor Division as symbols of the workingman's participation in industrial mobilization. Labor-capital cooperation was symbolized in the WIB seal, a mishmash of eagle, stars, shield, ships, and soldiers; prominent in the foreground were two hands clasped in a handshake, their sleeves representing the employee and the employer, under a pennant that fluttered from the beak of an eagle bearing the inscription "Together We Will Win." Significantly, perhaps, labor's hand appeared on the right. The WIB's motto was taken from the words of Woodrow Wilson: "The highest and best form of efficiency is the spontaneous cooperation of a free people."

The WIB, through the use of priority power and the ideology of voluntary cooperation, endeavored to erect a social-minded capitalism that subdued the exploitation of robber barons. Liberal capitalism "had found that [from service in war] came business profits, the development of new sources of raw materials, the wisdom of paying good wages, the new relationship between capital and labor, the new relationship of business and government," all of which enabled America's triumph as "the economic leader of the world." Forty years after World War I, Alvin S. Johnson, a former member of the board's Division of Planning and Statistics, affirmed that liberal capitalism had evolved from the war experience:

> The old capitalism of Morgan had no adequate answer to Lenin. The new capitalism of Bernard M. Baruch has a wholly adequate answer.
>
> Democracy under Morgan's capitalism was a dream. Under Bernard M. Baruch capitalism-democracy became a reality.

Beyond altruism or public service, the war managers considered voluntary cooperation a rebuttal to the specter of communism. The Russian Revolution had jolted the Wilsonians. In the urgent words of the CND's 1919 annual report, "the social responsibility of the business enterprise has become a much more serious matter than it used to be. In the light of world developments it is obvious that our business system must prove its resourcefulness."[69] Yet the experience of the war cast doubt upon the notion that most businessmen voluntarily demonstrated their social responsibility.

"A LIBERAL EDUCATION
IN MANY UNEXPECTED DIRECTIONS"

"One gets the impression," economist Edward S. Mason has written, "that during World War I the accomplishments of economic warfare were much greater than in World War II." Mason theorizes that the World War I effectiveness was due to Germany's reliance upon its navy to procure raw materials for its war production and to overcome its vulnerability to blockade. Germany's capacity for ersatz raw material production could not stand the test of a long war. The matter of raw materials was a special theater to U.S. economic warfare, and it was Baruch's theater in the CND. Among raw materials, nothing proved so intricate and vital a problem as securing nitrates for production of food and explosives. Germany had prepared itself to produce vast quantities of synthetic nitrates while effectively denying the Allies their chief source of nitrates in Chile by demanding that Chileans adhere to strict neutrality.

Nitrate of soda was an overriding concern for the WIB, for it was the key ingredient in manufacturing explosives and fertilizer cheaply enough to stabilize prices of munitions and consumer needs. Without an abundant supply of nitrates, the Allies could not effectively kill the enemy or clothe and feed themselves. Chile, a neutral nation with considerable British and German investments in its nitrates plants (oficinas), was the only known source of natural nitrates. Germany was cut off from Chile by submarine warfare but was able to depend upon its own potash sources or nitrogen fixation plants to extract from the air what it could not acquire from the earth. Although the U.S. government, at Baruch's insistence, began construction of three fixation plants during the war, U.S. industry depended upon its Chilean source until after the war. Thus, Baruch had to discover a way to obtain quantities of nitrates at prices that would not disturb domestic markets. As the WIB's official historian dramatically put it, "No part of the industrial-military grapple was more tense and breathless than that of the nitrate sector."[70]

The story of our quest for nitrates in 1917–18 is so arcane and complicated that few men then in the WIB or the State Department knew enough of its details to describe a portion of it. To a large extent, a coherent narration and understanding of this significant episode depends upon the diary of Chandler P. Anderson, international lawyer, protégé of Elihu Root, and experienced hand in negotiating with and for Latin American government officials. In November 1917, when the British proposed an Allied pool to buy Chile's nitrate of soda production, Baruch recruited the Republican lawyer to direct the WIB's international negotiations. It was typical of Baruch: find the right man, give him responsibility, and share in the glory.

The problem as defined by the British was simple enough: the Allies' war effort was jeopardized by high nitrate prices controlled by a Chilean cartel; they proposed to break the producers' cartel with a buyers' pool, thus reducing the market to one purchaser for one producer.

However, the nitrate issue was complicated by a host of international intrigues worthy of spy fiction or of amateurs in diplomacy with fertile imaginations. Involving novices like Baruch and his business cohorts in the WIB, plus a crafty and experienced hand like Anderson, in economic warfare was certain to lead to unpredictable developments. All of this wartime intrigue over nitrates contributed in small ways to America's improved investment position in South America in the next decade. "What was important," a historian has written, "was that by the end of World War I, U.S. direct investment was challenging European hegemony" in South American markets.[71] The nitrate cooperative venture accelerated U.S. penetration of foreign markets.

U.S. interest in Chilean nitrates had developed gradually in the early twentieth century and was influenced greatly by the cartel's manipulation of prices. Four American firms imported nitrates from Chile, but none sought to break the British-German-Chilean cartel until the Du Pont Company bought its first property in 1910, following a break in prices. War between Germany and Great Britain, South America's primary foreign investors, increased American interest in the southern continent. As the price of nitrate lands declined in 1914, their desirability rose. Chile emerged as the object of greater investment interest than any other South American country. With German properties available at bargain prices, DuPont considered investing its excess working capital in additional *oficinas*.[72]

Chilean nitrate lands also attracted the interest of Baruch's Wall Street friends and erstwhile investment partners Daniel Guggenheim and Eugene Meyer, Jr. Guggenheim, who along with his brothers already had explored Chilean copper properties, proposed that J. P. Morgan and Company join with him and his brothers in a confidential investment association that would discreetly send agents to investigate options on British and German properties in Chile, with the cooperation of the Chilean government. The war in Europe offered American investors such an "unusual opportunity" that Guggenheim was eager to capitalize on the misfortunes of belligerency.

On account of war, Guggenheim argued, "the opportunity is now presented of organizing this great nitrate field into a modern, up-to-date, American industry, capable of yielding a greatly increased profit upon a greatly increased capitalization." Indeed, the Morgan people sought Chilean nitrate properties. In association with a group headed by Meyer, they bought a large tract from a major British developer in Chile, Gibbs and Company. The combination of increasing demand and declining supply drove nitrate prices up, thereby assuring investors in *oficinas* of a good return if various marketing problems could be overcome. By February 1916 nitrate of soda sold for 56 percent higher than its prewar average, and by September 1917 the figure was more than 100 percent.[73]

The high price caused the British to worry that the cost of foodstuffs and explosives would reduce their capacity to pay for other vital war materials. London proposed a boycott of Chilean nitrates for the three months ending 1917 while plans were perfected for a single buyer and distributor for all the Allied governments. The U.S. agreed to end its competitive buying. The boycott worked so well in depressing prices that the *oficinas* retaliated by restricting output. However, the Allies' need for full production gave the Chileans the upper hand.[74] Furthermore, negotiations over the proposed nitrate-buying pool, dubbed the International Nitrate Executive, bogged down over conflicting U.S. and British needs and designs.

The War Industries Board negotiated the Nitrate Executive proposal with the British Ministry of Munitions through the State Department in London. At the outset the Americans agreed to locate the Nitrate Executive in London; the British conceded the American Congress's demand for a hundred thousand tons of nitrates for U.S. farmers. Baruch and his WIB assistants—former International Harvester executive Alexander Legge, one-time chemical engineer and J. P. Morgan aide Leland Summers, and Chandler Anderson—represented the United States. Their paramount objective was to secure enough nitrate to win the war and at a cost low enough to avert further disruption of the Allied economics. They gave lip service to cooperation with the British intention to corner the market on this valuable raw material. The WIB, however, wanted its own direct line to Santiago, in addition to negotiations on nitrates through London. The WIB's strategy, as conceived and directed by Anderson, called for cooperation with the British in knocking down producer prices; but as Anderson pointed out, it certainly did no harm to suggest to the British that the United States could afford to act alone in order to get its needed share of nitrates.

Then, too, there was the matter of German *oficinas*, which normally accounted for about 25 percent of the annual Chilean output, but now were idle for lack of fuel. The Americans generously offered to supply oil for the German plants, giving a boost to nitrate production that would benefit U.S. explosive and fertilizer makers and the Chilean treasury. Chile's ambassador to Washington was pleased, especially when the Americans suggested that his son, an employee of the National City Bank of New York, serve as lessee for the German plants, a position that would personally net him $40,000 or $50,000.[75]

Baruch wanted the output of German *oficinas*. Getting it, however, required the complicity of Chilean government officials in effecting a takeover of German properties, U.S. oil to fuel the German *oficinas*,

British jute bags from India to package the nitrates, and U.S. ships to transport the precious cargo from South America. Could a takeover be accomplished without violating Chilean neutrality? Would the U.S. oil companies deliver oil at lower contract prices? Would the British deliver the jute without charging exorbitant prices? Would other U.S. war agencies share their ships for carrying the nitrates? Would British and American authorities wink at the blacklists intended to prevent their nationals from trading with the enemy—in this case the German owners of nitrate fields who anticipated some compensation for Allied use of their properties? As Allied nitrate stocks dwindled through the winter of 1917–18, Elihu Root called it "perhaps the most important and delicate situation in the war."[76]

Having established its own Santiago connection, the WIB turned its attention back to London. It had to act quickly in concert with the British if the proposed buyers' pool was going to control the 1918 price for nitrates. Through the auspices of the State Department, Anderson sent instructions to the American embassy in London to proceed with the formation of the pool, with U.S. Consul General Robert P. Skinner as Washington's representative. Quickly the trans-Atlantic nitrates combination took shape. The British promised jute bags from India to package the German-owned nitrates produced with American fuel. To tighten the buyers' pool against destructive competition from Japanese purchases, both sides agreed to invite that Asian power into the pool. But what about Du Pont's independent purchases in Chile, the British asked? The WIB assured London that Du Pont acted solely as Washington's agent and would act as one of the pool's buyers. Du Pont, of course, relished an opportunity to supplant the Germans in the nitrate fields of Chile. By December 1917, Anderson believed that the Nitrate Executive's arrangements were "practically completed."[77]

As Anderson noted, the Americans "were practically going into partnership with the Chileans in the production of nitrate." Chile had to be assured of oil before it moved on the German *oficinas*. As the WIB discovered, Standard Oil was already under contract to supply all *oficinas* with their 1918 fuel requirements. The Americans then needed a Chilean intermediary as a local buyer of the German output. To Anderson's surprise, he found that the navy had anticipated his search for an intermediary. Louis McHenry Howe, assistant to Assistant Secretary of the Navy Franklin D. Roosevelt, already had retained Chile's assistant minister of war, Enrique Cuevas, at $10,000 annually. Unfortunately, however, Cuevas was later reassigned as Chilean minister to Uruguay, and the United States had to find another government official to act as its man in Santiago.[78]

Meanwhile, the British viewed the American initiative as a threat to their commercial interests in Chile. If wartime cooperation increased

Du Pont's business in a strong British market, then the British were correct in suspecting U.S. commercial ambitions. In fact, the WIB considered other executive organizations to buy raw materials essential for munitions. Anderson believed that other buying pools should "apply to many mineral products of which Great Britain has a monopoly, and it would be advantageous to this country not only during the war, but may lead to some general international agreements along the same lines in peace times." Baruch urged Colonel House to discuss more such executives with the British. Yet the only other executive established in 1918 concerned tin, a metal seldom found in the United States, which consumed more than half of the world's output. Much of the tin came from the Dutch East Indies; the British were accordingly more amenable to a buyers' pool.[79]

"This all goes to show that this war business is a liberal education in many unexpected directions," the urbane Anderson wryly commented, upon hearing a banker complain that the buying pools would diminish his foreign exchange role. Businessmen in and out of government were apprehensive about the WIB's overseas activities. On the positive side, its initiatives opened markets for Americans that had been dominated by the British and the Germans. But, as in other government economic ventures in World War I, some businessmen feared that Washington's leadership brought unwelcome interference in their trade. Nevertheless, the WIB men were committed to private enterprise as long as businessmen put patriotism ahead of profits. They took pains to assure corporations in the nitrate trade that they would profit by the large 1918 purchase, even to the point of asking the four dominant British and American firms to recommend a means of protecting themselves against losses if the war ended that year. Although the profit motive had failed to ensure the nation of an adequate supply of nitrates, Baruch and his fellow private enterprisers planned to lease or sell public nitrogen fixation plants following the war.[80]

Early in 1918 the boycott intended to cut nitrate's price had seriously depleted Allied stocks. The British minister of munitions, Winston Churchill, dourly forecast that French and Italian nitrate reserves would be exhausted by the end of January and British stocks would be down to one hundred thousand tons. Americans suspected that the Allies had withheld some nitrates from the pool; the British could not forgive U.S. insistence upon nitrates for its farmers. "The nitrate situation is getting worse and worse," Anderson observed in late March, "and the only possible relief at present is to shut off entirely the use of nitrate here for agricultural purposes."[81] Such use had political priority, however, as long as the Allied armies maintained any semblance of firepower.

But American farmers would not get their share unless those German *oficinas* could be put to work for them. Ironically, the Germans sought in

Chilean courts to block American oil shipments to German *oficinas* operated by the Chileans, and the courts agreed that oil deliveries violated Chilean neutrality laws. It was the sort of result that benefited only the Chilean secretary of the treasury, who doubled as German counsel in the oil litigation and organizer of a combination to drive the price of nitrates still higher.[82]

After Baruch and Anderson decided to turn the entire nitrate negotiation with Chile over to the International Nitrate Executive, Winston Churchill, as head of the executive, became a shield behind which the WIB operated. Baruch dispatched Anderson and Summers to London for firsthand supervision of American interests. At the same time, President Wilson granted the WIB sole U.S. control over the nitrate negotiations, officially charging it with responsibility for a vital phase of economic diplomacy.[83]

Baruch and the WIB virtually controlled U.S. economic foreign policy. Baruch had sent Anderson and Summers to London to conduct U.S. economic warfare, personally assuming the cost of the WIB's foreign mission. It would amount to $63,752.25, money well spent for his personal foreign policy. If it proved successful, he told Anderson, additional missions to South America would be arranged. The objective of the London mission called for "joint control . . . of practically all the raw materials in the world[,] . . . a plan of vital importance to Great Britain." The British sought additional buying pools that would control other raw material prices. Fearful that the United States would emerge from the war with a preponderance of capital and ships, London sought to involve Washington in arrangements that would limit competitive bidding for the world's raw materials by dividing the output among industrial buyers. In this way they hoped to stem the American unilateral advance into European colonial markets. Of course the Americans were keenly aware of their advantages in the impending rivalry with the British, and the WIB's foreign mission was not about to let London have its way on buying pools.

The topic of cooperation with the Allies always stirred internal U.S. debate. In such discussions, Baruch liked to take the high ground of Wilsonian practical idealism. According to Anderson, "Baruch expressed the view that the only way to win the war was to pool our interests with the Allied Powers, and until we had made sacrifices equal to those already made by the others, the question of making the others pay for our contributions to the war, was not only bad policy but inconsistent with the altruistic and unselfish purposes for which we entered the war." Yet the longer the war, the more prominent the U.S. role. The Allies had been depleted of manpower, materials, and money. Looking ahead in mid-1918, it was apparent that the United States would dominate the fighting, the supplying, and the financing of the Allied side of the war. In Anderson's view, such expectations seemed to make it necessary for the United States to have "a controlling voice in all these matters, and to reserve the right to determine how our power should be exercised for the benefit of the others." When the British suggested raw materials pools, Americans tended to reject such proposals as unnecessary to a nation wealthy in metals and minerals. The associates in war were rivals in peace. The British, some American businessmen complained, were already returning to South American markets while erecting trade barriers in the empire. Hurley caught this spirit of a trade war within a shooting war when he told Baruch: "While the bloodiest war in history is progressing, every nation is preparing not merely to get its share of foreign trade, but trying to find out how much it can take away from other nations. The question as to what nation will control the raw materials of the world is uppermost in Europe. Whatever nation does control them (unless it be America) will make other nations pay a heavy toll."[84]

Baruch, for all his sanctimonious lecturing on the need for economic cooperation with the Allies, appreciated the opportunity the war presented for American commercial ambitions. He believed that the WIB, with its extensive domestic and overseas responsibilities, was peculiarly suited to assert Washington's new power. Meeting with his WIB assistants on 11 June, Baruch agreed that the time had come for the United States to inform the British that they were no longer the senior partner in this cooperative venture. That would be the message the foreign mission, Anderson and Summers, would carry to London. The United States, "being the reservoir of strength, . . . should insist upon having the deciding voice in determining how our strength should be applied and utilized to the best advantage of all concerned." The WIB would demonstrate that it, unlike the War Trade Board, could not be "seduced by the British influences." No longer would the WIB rely upon the State Department to represent it in pool negotiations. Future executive arrangements "were apt to prove to be one sided" unless the WIB went abroad.[85]

On the day before Baruch's forty-eighth birthday, Summers sent him a triumphant message from London: "We have put the War Industries Board on the international map and you will have to come over and show yourself."[86] Summers headed a delegation of twelve businessmen intent upon displacement of British businessmen in Latin American markets and low prices for raw materials originating in the British Empire. Postwar cooperation called for American access to British markets.

The Americans arrogantly demanded that the British reform their business procedures. The British government, the WIB foreign mission asserted, had not organized its industries as efficiently as the WIB had organized American industry. Private industrial committees in Britain performed work equivalent to the WIB's without the governmental authority or the prestige enjoyed by the service committees in Washington.

The drawback of the British arrangement, as the WIB saw it, was that it allowed two sets of prices—one for government and one for business. It did not disturb Americans that His Majesty's government bought at a price lower than the market level; it did annoy them that Washington paid the higher market price. After all, Wilson had guaranteed a uniform price for all buyers, domestic and foreign, private and governmental. But the British businessmen kept two sets of prices, exploiting the U.S. government as if it were a British customer. Therefore, as a precondition to future buying pools, the foreign mission cockily demanded that British industrial committees control their prices the way the WIB controlled American prices. British businessmen rejected the demand. Then the Americans asked Whitehall to step in and represent its industries as the WIB represented American industries. Again, the British turned aside American intervention in their business system.

The next American step was an "ultimatum." The foreign mission demanded one price for jute, the Indian fiber woven into bags in Aberdeen and Manchester for the nitrates of Chile. Intent upon setting low prices for nitrates entering the American market, the WIB challenged prices commanded by British mills for their precious bags. To back up this demand, Summers threatened to withhold U.S. silver, the metal used to support the price of the India rupee, unless jute bags entering the U.S. market arrived at the same price paid by the British government. The intimidated British agreed to establish an Anglo-American committee that would set jute prices. The Americans were exultant. The moral of the story, according to Summers, was: "If you want to make unjust trade unpopular, you must make it unprofitable." By threatening the stability of colonial India, Summers extracted his price from the British jute weavers.[87]

The WIB men bragged a good deal about the jute arrangement, mostly because they had little else to show for their extraordinary foreign mission. They broke the price of Dutch East Indian tin, but failed to lower the price of rubber emanating from British and French colonies.[88] Although Summers continued to demand negotiations with Whitehall instead of the industrial committees representing British cartels, the British were intransigent. Summers fulminated but got nowhere.

Had the war not ended in November, an Allied-American steel combination might have been set up, to American satisfaction. The United States exported more steel than the British produced in entirety, and Summers demanded a steel committee chaired by an American. By this means, Americans could direct British and French distribution of low-priced U.S. steel and assure themselves that the Allies were not diverting it to civilian production for postwar commerce. Summers complained that he found among British businessmen "a spirit rampant of getting ready for trade after the war and no opportunity is neglected to improve industrial position." Anticipating peace and a diminished dependence upon U.S. output, the British sought to reduce their American orders for pig iron by half. The WIB responded by insisting that "the English take their full tonnage of steel ordered by them whether peace comes or not."[89] Clearly the United States would miss its captive buyers when the Armistice was signed.

Anglo-American economic cooperation neared a collapse as the war neared an end. The British hoped to check U.S. competition in postwar world markets. They were especially alarmed by the American construction of a great merchant ship fleet that would not be in use until 1919. The ships posed a direct challenge to British maritime supremacy, and competition would be costly to London. Would the Americans be interested in pooling their ships with British merchant vessels, Lord Reading inquired of Hurley in September? Wilson found that "an extraordinary proposition" and advised Hurley to tell Reading "that we are sure it will not be possible for us to make special arrangements with any one nation, inasmuch as it is our fixed policy and principle to deal upon the same terms with all." In a few months the United States would possess all that it needed to open the markets of the world to American businessmen. In late October, Wilson cautioned the members of his war cabinet to desist from publicly discussing foreign trade lest they undermine cooperation and further unnerve the already anxious British. Nevertheless, "a just and continuing peace," Baruch declared in October 1918, "must include a just and equal access to the raw materials and manufacturing facilities of the world." This theme was repeated elsewhere in the war administration. As McAdoo wrote Wilson in November, "It is obviously important that the United States should retain the utmost freedom of action in the disposal of its resources." American capital, ships, and steel were negotiable only on Washington's terms. If London wanted shipping pools or other forms of economic cooperation, McAdoo and Wilson agreed, the British would have to come to the United States, "thus concentrating all important negotiations and decisions in Washington." The center of the western economy had crossed the Atlantic. Cooperation would always be considered, in Wilson's words "whenever the advantages to be derived therefrom are demonstrated."[90]

American economic diplomacy in 1918 had gravitated into the hands of Baruch, Hoover, et al.—the ad hoc war cabinet. Individually they were aggressive and assertive men whom the State Department found "not altogether easy to handle." They had their minds set on trade expansion. Baruch foresaw great possibilities for the merchant marine in the postwar world: "Ships will help to make certain the great part we are to play in the days to come," he told Hurley, "for America has emerged from her isolation and her ships will project her friendship and commerce over all the world's waters." Indeed, Hurley could not wait for the war to end so that the U.S. merchant marine could enter the South American ports vacated by Allied and German freighters. He advised Wilson that the United States should

> send an important commission to Argentina, Peru, Chile and Barzil [*sic*], consisting of men representing finance, manufacturing, particularly the electrical industry, and railroads, with the thought in mind of developing the water power of the different countries visited. Commerce should be developed in these countries, not so much for the purpose of selling our goods to them but for the financing of local enterprises. My object is to assist these countries in extending their railroads, both steam and electric, and finance the municipalities on sound and conservative lines, and become interested in their mining properties, particularly the materials that we require for our needs. The financing of these local enterprises would be a safe investment and it would prove to the citizens of the respective countries mentioned that we are endeavoring to develop these countries and offset the charge so often made against America that our whole game is to sell our wares and take money and profits out of the countries we sell to.

With Wilsonian practical idealism, Hurley asserted that U.S. expansionism, unlike that of European imperial powers, was unselfish. Because "the world's money markets are in most cases depleted," the United States would also finance China's development. In China, U.S. investments would be helpful "to leave the door open to the rest of the world. Our associates in the war, England, France and Italy, may feel that we would be taking advantage of their present positions, but I am sure this can be explained to their satisfaction."[91]

Thus, the Nitrate Executive, begun in the spirit of wartime cooperation, faded into the economic nationalism of the Paris Peace Conference of 1919. As run by business expansionists, U.S. economic diplomacy shifted from expedient cooperation to natural competition.

READJUSTMENT

"The War Industries Board died with the war. It has no history worthy of mention after November 11, 1918," the first chronicler of the board has written. "The magnificent war formation of American industry was dissipated in a day; the mobilization that had taken many months was succeeded by an instantaneous demobilization." In November the WIB proclaimed its disbanding on the first day of the new year, a promise it kept. The act of self-destruction seemed deceptively simple: when the war ended, the war agency went out of business.

But not all war agencies concluded their affairs that abruptly and expeditiously. 1919 found the War Trade Board, the Food Administration, the Shipping Board, and the Railroad Administration gradually winding down their activities with speeds varying according to the needs of their principal constituencies or according to the strength of their statutory mandates. In fact, the War Finance Corporation not only met a slow demise, but, led by Baruch's Wall Street and Washington comrade, Eugene Meyer, was revived in the twenties to finance America's expanding foreign trade. Surely, Baruch and other war managers who had been so sensitive to the chaos engendered by the transition to war anticipated economic dislocation in the postwar reconstruction. Then why did the administration make "no more preparations to leave the war than it had to enter it"?[92]

As suggested by its negotiations surrounding the Nitrate Executive and schemes for other cartels, the WIB closed shop partly because much of the war cabinet's attention through 1918 was riveted upon the prospect of postwar foreign trade expansion. The war had provided American financiers and entrepreneurs with great opportunities to enlarge their shares of the world's business substantially. Having mobilized the nation for war, the war cabinet now mobilized it to take advantage of peace. Americans enjoyed a plethora of resources that competition for foreign markets demanded: hundreds of new ships for trade, a supply of most of the world's known raw materials, and abundant credit for foreign customers. With planning to protect its industrial system from the extremes of unchecked inflation and massive unemployment, the nation could look forward to a postwar boom in 1919 and the twenties.

During the war, Baruch professed that postwar world markets were concerns furthest from his mind. Even in his memoirs he asserted that in late October 1918 he had responded to discussion concerning overtures for an armistice by saying, "I've been thinking so much about war, I haven't given much thought to peace." If that were true, Baruch was undeserving of his reputation for forecasting.

However, he was being less than candid. Knowing that Wilson appreciated nonmaterialistic devotion to America's crusade, Baruch exaggerated his own idealism. Yet almost a year before, Baruch had evidenced considerations that were not confined to a mobilization for victory alone. "If one must think in terms of business," he apologetically observed, *"after the war the country which can demobilize the quickest will have a decided advantage over the others."* Put another way, to be first in the race for world leadership, a nation had to be first in the race for reconversion to peacetime production. (Nor was he unmindful of the fact that the British had created a Ministry of Reconstruction in 1917.) Eleven months later, the young journalist Walter Lippmann expanded upon this design, albeit with more elegant phrasing: "We can take it as an axiom that the stability, the prestige, and the effectiveness of the governments which make the [peace] settlement depend above all on their skill in demobilizing. That applies to us without question. If the American Expeditionary Force is not gotten home promptly when it is time to come home, and if when it gets there it is set adrift, our whole body of ideas will tend towards being discredited. Reconstruction at home will be the rod by which our international program is judged." To paraphrase one of Baruch's favorite aphorisms, the nation needed productive work. It was not hyperbolic to declare that the very survival of America's social system depended upon a quick revival of peaceful output for available markets. "It seems that the civilization and Government are rocked to the very bottom," Baruch told industrialists. "Unless [civilians] get the materials to get them to work, they will have idle hands and idle minds and you know what the result of that is."[93] Already the red devil's workshop had come to Russia and now it menaced all Europe. That nothing less than capitalism itself was at stake during reconstruction had crossed many minds during the hostilities.

The administration quietly encouraged entrepreneurial prospecting for overseas markets, not only in the interests of U.S. ambitions and prosperity, but with consideration for the stability of its capitalist allies. From the White House's perspective, no discrepancy existed between American competition with its associates and its concern for their welfare. The Wilsonians equated U.S. economic expansion with capitalist durability. America had both the opportunity to produce the necessities of a devastated western civilization and the responsibility of doing so. All industrial nations required their output, Baruch told a meeting of steel producers: "There is really one country today that is able to supply those [materials] and that is the United States." He urged them to keep their prices as low as possible in anticipation of overseas orders. Throughout the WIB, commodity section heads alerted businessmen to the opening of foreign markets. In August 1918 they had agreed that they should prepare industries "for greater export business when the War is over." Nor had the WIB been alone in the anticipation. For months the War Trade Board, the Shipping Board, and the War Finance Corporation had been advising their business clients to expect a postwar boom in overseas trade. Little wonder, then, that when the war was over a large delegation of businessmen descended like "a hungry pack" upon the Shipping Board to demand immediate annulment of government controls on foreign trade and shipping.[94]

Businessmen were not of one mind on the matter, but many of them desired a sharp reduction of government planning in meeting the challenges of postwar economic expansion. Demands for a speedy end to blacklists, shipping orders, WIB priorities, price management, and wage stabilization inundated the war agencies. Small Nevada copper producers chafed under the price ceilings Baruch had arranged with the Guggenheims; their costs had risen and the year-old fixed price benefited only volume producers. Reluctant to submit to the guiding hands of government agencies during the war emergency, most businessmen were even less willing to allow their prosperity to be orchestrated from Washington in peacetime. They would accept unsolicited Wilsonian advice concerning business expansion at home or abroad only if it came without strings or restraints.

An exception to this passion for government withdrawal from the economy was big steel. Two days after the Armistice, Judge Gary and his cohorts arrived in Washington to beseech Baruch to stabilize steel prices through large government purchases. Baruch, never greatly sympathetic with big steel or high prices, suggested that Gary would have to learn to live again without the federal government as a heavy buyer. Similarly, big finance resented the end of restrictions on capital announced by Baruch.

Political considerations worked against continued controls. Baruch was mindful that steel users were more numerous than steel manufacturers and did not appreciate administration policies that supported high steel prices. Demand in the marketplace was substantial enough without Washington's competitive buying. "Don't forget, gentlemen," Baruch warned the steel producers, "we have all got politics in front of us." The marketplace seemed to call for a lowered government profile. The construction industries eagerly awaited a building boom once Washington withdrew priority and price regulations that had deferred civilian projects. The National Association of Manufacturers observed that "the factories and stores of the United States are at present almost depleted of their usual stock and that our country is on the threshold of a most unprecedented business expansion owing to this domestic condition." Dark hints were dropped that if the Wilsonians did not act quickly to restore the prewar business-government equilibrium, the administration could expect the newly elected Republican Congress to act for decontrol. Soon after Armistice Day, the politically sagacious Daniel C. Roper, then commissioner of Internal Revenue, advised the White House:

> You have doubtless observed within the last day or two, as I have, that the Republican leaders purpose to seize upon the issues of economy and retrenchment in Government activities now that the war had ended. To permit this would be extremely unfortunate, and to prevent it effectually, the President must take immediate and strikingly effective action. . . .
>
> The wisdom of adopting and pursuing aggressively from now on a definite policy of economy and retrenchment in Government expenditures not only rests upon the soundest possible economic basis but is vitally necessary for political reasons which will be obvious to you. . . . It would be inadvisable . . . to rely upon heads of depart-

ments and independent establishments to curtail their activities and expenses. . . . Their failure to do so will simply result in having the Appropriations committees of Congress lop off the appropriations and the Republicans will endeavor to take the lead and keep it in this desirable course.

The White House considered this "confidential" message significant enough to pass it along to Baruch.[95]

Wilson did not need Roper's reminder. He had been a reluctant mobilizer; only the unexpected prolongation of hostilities could compel him to empower the emergency organizations with stringent authority for intervention in the nation's normal affairs. He preferred a minimum of economic dislocation with a minimum of emergency bureaucracy. Expansion in both industry and government would be limited unless absolutely justified by war exigencies. He preferred to convert existing industries to war production and to employ conservation, price management, and priority regulations to stabilize domestic markets. He eschewed war plants built with public capital that had doubtful postwar utility. "The war demands must, of course, be met, but it has become necessary that they should not be anticipated," he told the war cabinet in July 1918. He feared that the priority apparatus would create "an unnecessary curtailment and destruction" of domestic industries. War production, he believed, should never enlarge the nation's productive capacity beyond what its domestic and foreign markets could absorb in peacetime:

> I am solicitous that our war programme should be carried out with as little disturbance of our usual industries and our normal economic fabric as possible, and with this in mind suggest that it is of paramount importance that existing plants which have been rendered idle or are likely to be rendered idle by the curtailment of non-essential production should be converted to war uses as far as possible. The present tendency in many cases is to create new plants or enlarge old ones. . . .
> . . . No new facilities should be provided without consultation with the War Industries Board. If these suggestions are acted upon, many of the hardships that would fall upon business may be lessened or avoided altogether. The War Industries Board is in a position to know the business that will have to be curtained [sic], because of the withdrawal of materials and their adaptation to other uses.[96]

Wilson proposed that a war fought with a minimum of disruption to the civilian economy would insure minimum reconversion upon the outbreak of peace. For that matter, reconversion of the economy was hardly necessary when there had not been any substantial conversion. Business would resume in peace almost as if there had not been a war. The government would simply cease whatever it was doing and transfer its enterprises to the private sector. Its wartime recruits and tasks would be automatically discharged. Wilson encouraged discussion of reconversion in November, but shied away from any planning that suggested a need for considerable reorganization. Chandler Anderson, ever ready to denigrate Wilson, believed that "although he is making a very public appearance of encouraging and organizing the government activities for reconstruction work, behind the scenes he evidently is paralyzing all effort in this direction." To those who pleaded for a more gradual demobilization of the armed forces and industry, Wilson appeared to turn a deaf ear. By his lights a quick demobilization was feasible because there had been no full-scale mobilization. Accordingly, on 8 November, the WIB issued a public statement reaffirming government contracts but promising to release raw materials for civilian and export purchases; restrictions would cease with the war's end.[97]

Wilson's perspective on economic organization was unrealistic. It ignored the genius of his managers. Through the use of priorities, conservation, standardization, and simplification, the WIB had streamlined the civilian marketplace. Had the war continued, it had plans to reduce the civilian market further. The need for price stabilization justified these extraordinary schemes. The American family would be reduced almost to wearing uniforms, so standardized would the selection in clothes have been. This would restrain the price of clothing by reducing its costs of production and limiting demand for unattractive items. Yet the basic idea had been the massive conversion of existing plants to war production without the building of additional factories to cater to expanded demand. The wartime civilian market had been dislocated for its own postwar benefit. Prices from mid-1918 until the end of the war had been checked. But the plans that accomplished that feat required plans to disestablish them in an orderly manner.

Two weeks of peace passed amid public discussion of a comprehensive demobilization policy deemed superfluous by Wilson. But he could not prevent business and congressional discussion of it. Rumors of imminent reconversion announcements often got the better of reality. Although it should have been apparent that Baruch was moving toward abandonment of controls, Secretary of War Baker and Secretary of Agriculture Houston went scurrying to Wilson to complain that reconstruction would be discussed publicly at a forthcoming WIB-CND dinner. Such talk without any presidential guidelines could only incite unwanted congressional and business speculation regarding the status of the government's contracts. Policy dictated that Wilson, then preparing for a December departure for Europe, keep silent on the nation's economy. Meanwhile, the British, advised by Baruch that he would disband the WIB, wondered whom they would deal with in Washington concerning economic agreements.[98]

Reconversion after World War I was primarily negative—mostly a matter of governmental withdrawal from the economy. Public planning was not needed to restore the supremacy of a private sector. At a war cabinet meeting on 20 November, Baruch and McAdoo expressed satisfaction that "reconstruction would take care of itself." When Washington canceled its munitions orders, they predicted, private enterprise would find other work for war laborers. Public works jobs for former war workers were deemed unnecessary. However, Baruch's disposition "for cutting loose everything at once and allowing everybody to bring about his own readjustment as quickly as possible" worried some Democrats. Robert W. Woolley called it tantamount to hanging out a sign reading "Welcome Bolshevism."

Still, there was limited, improvised planning. The war managers considered unemployment compensation desirable because it was "better to pay labor till [business] adjusted than use it in what is not needed." The vast quantities of raw materials purchased for war making ought to be stockpiled, Baruch argued, because "in the present circumstances the Government should not compete with producers." Stockpiling would prevent oversupply and give producers incentives to meet civilian demands, thereby buttressing prices and jobs. By hoarding its raw materials the government would encourage orders "and start anew the wheels of industry." Later, if demand drove up prices, Washington could release its stocks. Did Baruch appreciate the irony of his advocating a government practice in peace that he considered unpatriotic in industry during war? But it was not a time for reflection. Agreeing with Baruch, Wilson ordered the navy to maintain its stocks of raw materials. In December the WIB could report with satisfaction that "the Departments will hold certain raw materials, until a sufficient market develops."[99] This was hardly laissez-faire; it was government restraint designed to create enough of a raw materials shortage to foster production at higher prices. Just as Baruch told Gary that Washington would not buy, so he told others that Washington would not sell. The Wilsonians would employ public inertia to stimulate private expansion.

On 27 November, Baruch officially implemented a policy of decontrol. "The work of the War Industries Board is actually over," he told the president. "The American people would resent, I believe, the continuance of apparent war powers; and further continuance of the War Industries Board, shorn as it is of its powers, would create a lack of respect for the government which sought to maintain its unenforceable regulations. Therefore, I think the sooner it closes up its work and leaves, the better it will be for all concerned." The war had been the WIB's sole raison d'être. Once it was bereft of that expediency for legality, Baruch and

Wilson concluded that peace compelled its dismantling. In no way, they hoped, did this invalidate the WIB's activities in the areas of business regularization, standardization, and cooperative organization. Those efforts at industrial efficiency ought to be continued; to that end, the WIB promised to will its files and projects to the Departments of Interior, Commerce, and State. The board itself was politically expendable, but many businessmen and Wilsonians regarded its principles and goals as indispensable to economic stabilization.

Two days after Baruch sent his letter to the White House, the war cabinet, minus Hurley, who was abroad, met without Wilson to discuss "the general question of a return to normal conditions." The need to clarify reconversion policy was deemed urgent; the president was due to sail for Europe in less than a week and public uncertainty was great. Baker then acted as spokesman for the war managers, who conveyed to the president their concern about the lack of a perceived policy. What kind of a policy did they seek? Nomenclature became important here. The term most often used to characterize the period of transition was "reconstruction," but an administration containing several southerners and dependent upon the support of southern-led Democrats in Congress eschewed any "reconstruction." Moreover, the idea of reconstruction contradicted the Wilsonian concept of war without mobilization and demobilization. Thus, carefully measuring their terms, the war managers assured the president, "Reconstruction, as applied to this country's problems is a misnomer; *we did not so convert the industries of the country to war purposes as to require governmental action to reconvert them. The present problem is not one of reconstruction but of readjustment.*" Baruch was among those who would replace "reconstruction" with the less offensive "readjustment." Perhaps he never appreciated the irony that the British government, which he had once accused of not disciplining its industries enough for the war effort, had a Ministry of Reconstruction. Still, the turn to peace called for expediencies not too unlike those justified by war. In the collective words of the war cabinet:

> The resumption of American industry and commerce is a matter of removing from the enterprise of America those restrictions, temporary in character, which it was found necessary to impose during the period of the war. The absorption of material and labor of the country into the production of war supplies necessarily created shortages so far as domestic consumption was concerned. In order not to allow such shortages to bear unequally or to create unnecessary hardship, restrictions were imposed by the several emergency administrations created under the authority of Congress. Now that the war conditions have abated, all that is necessary for the industries of America to resume is that these restrictions should be relaxed and removed, and

this is being done rapidly, with the expected result that American enterprise is taking advantage of its opportunity to reestablish the business of the country.

The war managers called upon the president to signal Americans that the crisis had passed and once more it was business as usual. For the time being, at least, that was the extent of the administration's "chart to business." Industry and trade should be urged to look abroad for business because "the United States is freeing ocean commerce to profitable opportunity." A year of anxiety had passed and businessmen could again be "certain as to their obligations and their resources for the resumption of former or other production." Wilson conveyed this message to Congress on 2 December. The American "readjustment," he proclaimed, called for the people to "go their own way."[100]

The WIB went its way. Its sections expressed their appreciation to their respective industries for wartime cooperation and perfunctorily asked for suggestions on the WIB's role in assisting their readjustment. Baruch sent his personal thanks to every government and business official with whom he had had contact. Later he mailed each of the more than thirteen hundred members of the WIB a gold pin showing a flag-bearing eagle above the inscribed words "United States War Industries Board," with a printed note that read: "This is a reminder of my appreciation of your part of the work we did together. Bernard M. Baruch."[101] As the war agency died, Baruch kept its spirit alive with his private national fraternity, complete with pin, motto, and even the reunions that would be held later.

The WIB had to die. "It's a dead cock in the pit," he told Hugh Johnson. "Let's turn industry absolutely free. Everything that made us possible is gone—the war spirit of cooperation and sacrifice—the vast purchasing power of the government—the scant legal authority we have had—and the support of public opinion." Politically the WIB was not worth fighting for; the anticipation of normal market demands denied it popular support for its regulations. A few businessmen in and out of government argued that a WIB presence during the readjustment period made enough economic sense to overshadow its political liabilities. In his memoirs, Baruch ruefully conceded that subsequent inflation, labor strikes, and then depression in 1920–21 had proved a need for the WIB's continuance: "Had the WIB been empowered to carry on its direction of the economy, much of the waste and disorder accompanying reconversion might have been avoided. But we had no authority to do so."[102]

In the context of 1918, the dismantling of the WIB had a logic of its own, no matter what economic dislocation it might have prevented. Peace had terminated its mandate. It was an expediency that had been deprived of its motivating circumstances. Perhaps more importantly, it was a harbinger of state capitalism that threatened the existing private system. Moreover, because it symbolized the corporate state more than any other agency, the WIB contradicted Wilson's assertion that war mobilization had been a liberal adjustment to ephemeral circumstances. Finally, Baruch had personal reasons for wanting to terminate its operations: his own nascent political career called for a change in his theater of operations.

Baruch knew that, with the Armistice, Washington ceased to be the object of public attention it had been during the war. The president would be going to Paris to negotiate the treaty of peace; the eyes of the world would follow him and his entourage. Baruch longed to be part of the delegation at Wilson's side instead of presiding over a superfluous bureaucracy. He justified a possible shift to diplomacy on the grounds that his participation on the Allied Purchasing Commission and his direction of the American end of economic warfare had given him sufficient credentials. Unmentioned was the fact that the Nitrate Executive had whetted his appetite for international activity and fame. If he had not been known to the Allied governments before, the foreign mission of 1918 had made him a familiar name in the government corridors of London and Paris. British ministers like Arthur Balfour and Winston Churchill knew him as the powerful individual guiding Summers's overseas activities. To maintain his reputation as a man of considerable influence in Washington, he had to go to Paris.

The day after the war ended, a report circulated through Washington that Baruch would soon be going abroad. It was premature. No, he insisted, he could not gracefully abandon the WIB in November. Besides, "without being unduly conceited," Baruch believed that the president needed his advice on business and on averting political difficulties. He could not leave for Paris before mopping up in Washington. He agreed with WIB counsel Albert C. Ritchie, who wrote him: "You must be on the peace commission. You are not only needed there because of your knowledge of conditions here, but this would be a wonderful way to end and end now, while the going is at its very best, and when the work is really over, your work here." Thus, the WIB's need for a quick conclusion and Baruch's need for a new start coincided. All that remained was to find a dignified opportunity for accomplishing both.

Washington's rumor mills favored Baruch. Because he was seen as one of the president's most trusted advisors, it was supposed that a new role for him was in the offing when changes and appointments were made in response to peace. The resignation of his friend McAdoo from his twin posts heading the Treasury and the Railroad Administration presented him with a dilemma of sorts. Baruch believed that the Treasury was his if he desired it, but he did not. He later claimed that he turned down the Treasury post because his wife wanted him home more, hardly a good reason for a man ambitious for a Paris assignment. Although he enjoyed some degree of congressional support, Baruch still feared that his appointment to the Treasury would be an embarrassment to a progressive administration that deplored Wall Street's influence upon the economy.[103] Though there was much reason for that consideration, Wilson had run such risks before. However, Baruch was intent upon accompanying Wilson to Paris and finding a place in world politics as he had in Washington's. Neither the WIB nor the Treasury department posts could prevent him from attending that gathering of the world's notables.

CHAPTER THREE
PARIS, 1919

Throughout his public career, Baruch made it his policy not to take an assignment that called for an indefinite commitment. He liked short-term positions. The WIB chairmanship had suited his eclecticism and restlessness by involving him in a variety of tasks of short duration. Also, it gave him high public visibility and proximity to powerful policy makers; he attained recognition as a statesman. During the waning weeks of 1918 he helped shape economic policy, found himself the object of rumors of pending cabinet appointments, and sought another outlet for his energies and ambitions.

Fortunately for Baruch, his quest for further service was matched by Wilson's desire to find a place for him. The president did not let Baruch suggest a farewell any more than Baruch really intended a departure from public life. "I do not mean to let you go yet if I can help it, because there is much remaining to be done, and I do not like to feel that I am going away and leaving it to be done by inexperienced hands," Wilson told him in late November. Baruch recorded Wilson's letter in his memoirs with the comment, "When the President said he did not mean to let me go, I had no idea that he was thinking of having me serve as one of his advisors in the making of the peace."[1] True enough; there is nothing in the letter to suggest that Wilson wanted Baruch in Paris. It was Baruch who was thinking of himself as one of the president's peace advisors.

Wilson had tapped Baruch to succeed McAdoo as secretary of the Treasury. Baruch could have taken the appointment in December or again in the summer of 1919, but he declined it. The nature of the position conflicted with the nature of Baruch's business, opening him to charges that he manipulated market conditions to his own benefit. A Wall Street gambler in the Treasury would embarrass Wilson, Baruch told a friend. That and the fact that he was a Jew were the reasons he later gave an Englishman, adding for proper effect, "I want nothing and prefer to get back to civil life."² Had Baruch been as much of a political liability as he portrayed himself, he should have retired from the Wilson administration. Instead he sought the role of economic advisor to the president at the upcoming peace conference.

Baruch always had a good speculator's instinct for shifts in the public spotlight. He had been in on the ground floor of the preparedness drive, and it had led to his WIB chairmanship. Now he was eager to demonstrate that he was an international statesman. The Allied Purchasing Commission had given him an initial taste for foreign negotiations, and he knew that the war had focused American attentions upon international affairs. A year before the war's end, a colleague observed, "He seems to be fascinated by the international game, and is evidently going to transfer his activities from the financial field to international politics."³ No matter what excuse Baruch gave for turning down the Treasury offer, it was very apparent that he preferred to go to Paris. After the WIB's machinations with and against the British concerning the world's raw materials, one could hardly expect him to turn to something less exciting. After all, he had practically been secretary of state for economic affairs during the war. His ambassadors, Summers and Legge, were still in Europe. And when he heard that the president himself would go to Paris, that must have removed any doubts concerning his next move.

The logic of Baruch's inclusion in the American delegation had been apparent to others as well. In October, Colonel House had urged Wilson to include members of the war cabinet as economic advisors. When Wilson did not respond, House continued his efforts through members of the State Department, such as Gordon Auchincloss and Frank L. Polk. They especially wanted Vance McCormick, but, in the words of one historian, Baruch was "Wilson's personal choice" for inclusion in the economic group. Considering House's distaste for Baruch and the State Department's unhappiness with his intrusion into its field, it does indeed seem probable that Wilson wanted Baruch in Paris more than they did.⁴

We can only conjecture why Wilson wanted Baruch in Paris, but certain factors are more obvious than others. Considering the importance of economic matters, it would seem likely that the chairman of the War Industries Board should be at hand. Also, there could be little doubt concerning Wilson's personal regard for Baruch both as an advisor and as a loyal friend. Baruch had demonstrated his support many times over as a financial contributor. Evidence suggests that Wilson used Baruch to defray $150,000 in costs for his Paris trip, pending recompense by Congress.* It would have been ignoble of Wilson to solicit funds from Baruch

* "Senator Lodge told us that in the estimates for the additional $850,000 which the President has asked for the peace conference expenses, an item of $150,000 was included to

and then not grant his wish to go to Paris, where the president could use his experience, loyalty, judgment—and purse.

Throughout November rumors circulated through Washington that Baruch would join Wilson in Paris. Wilson had confirmed them on 3 December in discussion with Harry Garfield, who had urged him to take Baruch. On 7 December, Wilson sent word to Baruch that he was "sure we shall need you within a very short time." Baruch's bags were packed. The only question in his mind was which WIB personnel would accompany him. In Washington he feared that he would be an embarrassment to Wilson, but not in Paris. On 18 December, word was received that Baruch and McCormick were to leave as soon as possible for Paris without any entourage other than their personal secretaries.[5] Having helped to make war, Baruch was eager to share in the making of peace.

PRIMA DONNAS ABROAD

Of course, Baruch was not unique in his bid for the prospective power, fame, or influence that might result from rubbing elbows with all the great men of his time congregated in Paris. Thousands of men from America and Europe viewed the conference as a main chance for making contacts that could lead to greatness, fortunes, or the fulfillment of idealistic dreams. In the reawakening that followed the carnage of World War I, Paris was the place where great decisions would be made by the Atlantic powers. After Wilson's decision to go to Paris, almost every national leader or would-be national leader considered his own presence there a must. There would congregate, not only the leaders of the Allies, but among others, a future prime minister of Britain (Winston Churchill), a future U.S. president (Herbert Hoover), a future U.S. secretary of state (John Foster Dulles), a formative economic philosopher (John Maynard Keynes of the British Treasury), and a Vietnamese baker in quest of an impossible nationhood who would later take the name of Ho Chi Minh.

Many in Paris sought lesser goals than greatness or a place in history books. The conference was an event—perhaps the grandest or even the last grand event of that epoch. Any New York or Washington correspondent aspiring for more than a routine beat had to cover Paris. But Paris was also a party where poseurs and parvenues played hard; for them, the conference was not the main chance; it could be the last chance. With revolution coming out of the east, having already overtaken Moscow and apparently about to sweep through Berlin or Budapest, scions of an

---

be paid to B. M. Baruch to reimburse him for money advanced for presents and contributions made by the President to the crowned heads of Europe and charitable institutions during his visits abroad." Anderson Diary, 21 September 1919.

ancien régime from all the capitals of old Europe descended upon Paris, perhaps in quest of a final good time, perhaps to be with their own kind when the deluge hit, perhaps, if they were optimistic, to scheme for a restoration of times when titles automatically elevated them above the crowd. For them the real tragedy of the war was that it had involved the masses in matters of power; they conceded that democracy was on the march, either to leave them in its wake or to trample them in its path.

Either way, Europe had not seen a gathering like this since the Congress of Vienna in 1814–15, and the only similarities between the two would have to be in the dancing rather than the diplomacy. The ministers in Vienna restored, but the ministers in Paris would refashion. Leaders in 1919 had to speak to the peoples of all nations. Any politician who could not adapt to the rhetoric of democracy could not expect to be taken seriously. With the masses and prices both on the rise, it was no time to expect the superiority of one's lineage and breeding to find a place in a postwar world that one had not worked for. Politicians understood the case, but there were on hand a great many human relics of the nineteenth century who flaunted their titles as if they still mattered. As a Democrat from Pennsylvania told his diary: "Lunched at Mrs. Hyde's with French and Italian titles. There are so many of them about that they seem cheap and common but some people choose them. If I saw much more of this kind I believe I would become a real out and out Socialist." Democracy was on the march, Woodrow Wilson was its champion, and liberal America its savior! Alas, as Vance McCormick discovered more than once, even some Americans did not recognize these truths: "Dined with Mrs. Whitelaw Reid to meet Bishop Brent. These reactionaries are delightful socially, but have no vision and everything done by the administration during the war was wrong, and Mrs. Reid is so taxed that she can only give Jean Ward an income of $150,000 per year. Poor child!" The elites of all nations were there to complain and play and the Americans were no different from the Europeans. "So many Americans with axes to grind were allowed to come," grumbled a U.S. official. Certainly no operator or partygoer would pass up this affair. "Nearly everyone," a technician assigned to the American delegation observed, "wants to be in Paris. The result is a flood of parasites and grafters besieging the Crillon and seeking through influence of some sort or other to attach themselves to the Peace staff. A young Boston aristocrat and loafer, whom I saw at his ease in the Ritz the other day, has secured, I am told, the job of carrying letters between Paris and Rome. Others of equally ineffective type have been assigned to more important positions."[6]

And onto this scene of grasping charlatans, enthusiastic nationalists, and fearful aristocrats arrived Bernard Baruch on 11 January. He seemed to belong to all those categories. His capacity for reaching beyond his grasp was never more evident than when he donned the mask of international statesman. One of his problems was that he could not decide which role suited him best. On the one hand he chose to affect the manners of aristocracy. Not content with the American delegation's comfortable but confining quarters at the Ritz where it lived or at the Crillon where it worked, Baruch rented a villa near St. Cloud where he could entertain a dozen men for a weekend economic conference. In the words of his compatriot, McCormick, it was "an ugly, modern, French house, attractive grounds but small. Paris for me."[7] It was obviously a matter of taste. Unlike most others in the American delegation, Baruch had the money with which to wine and dine and impress. Paris was expensive; food was scarce enough for a dinner for four at Larue's to cost 230 francs, or about $40. His guests had to be grateful when the generous Baruch either picked up Larue's tab or invited them to St. Cloud. Away from the conference table there was gaiety, fun, and entertainment. The American delegates and advisors worked hard, to be sure, sometimes almost exhaustingly hard; but when they sought to escape the ennui of negotiating, they played hard. They attended the opera, the Folies-Bergère, the races, and the wrestling matches. They entertained themselves with dinners and dances, festivities that Baruch excelled in giving because so many were invited and so much was spent. The luncheons and dinners, at least, were not solely frivolity, for that was where the politicking, negotiating, and strategy planning continued. And they carried their quest for simultaneous negotiation and relaxation onto the golf courses and tennis courts of the City of Lights.

Sundays were ostensibly days of rest and recreation before the torrid pace was renewed, but the nature of Baruch's activity and that of other Americans often depended upon the weather. With the onset of spring, they took to the countryside to see for themselves how war had brought them abroad and made them Europe's creditor. Even a motor tour of rural areas or remote towns was really an extension of their Paris business, rather than an escape from it. Beyond Paris they found the waste and devastation of the war. It was all, as the French and Belgians intended these tours to be, instructive. Baruch was affected by what he saw:

> The destruction in some places is beyond description; and when one sees it, one has to rub his eyes to realize that it is not an illusion. In Belgium I visited what appeared to have been one of the finest little steel mills I had ever seen. It produced about 200,000 tons of finished product a year; starting with their own coal and their own iron ore, and carrying it through to such finished products as rails, joints, rods and ship-plates. The Germans had removed from the plant all the engines, and every machine and machine tool. They had taken down the stacks plate by plate; and the day before the armistice was signed

they wantonly dynamited the buildings and the remaining structures. This was a typical case.

In the invaded and destroyed areas of France not alone have towns been wiped out; but there is no evidence of the existence of some of them, excepting a sign saying that such and such a town was there. Acres upon acres are pitted with deep shell holes, and all kinds of hand grenades and explosives are still in the ground, rendering it dangerous to till; and the tilling cannot take place until the holes have been filled up. This is going to take a long time.

On a snowy, cold day in the early spring, Vance McCormick visited an American cemetery on the edge of the Argonne Forest.

> We returned via Rheims and Chateau Thierry. I never saw anything like the miles and miles of desolation, old trenches, barbed wire, shell holes, ammunition lying about tanks, aeroplanes, every conceivable war implement lying in the field; most desolate and depressing and nothing apparently done yet to clean up.
>
> We lunched in Rheims in a partly destroyed hotel, with temporary roof and a temporary wall. About four thousand people had returned to their homes and the Boche prisoners had cleaned up the streets but no buildings repaired as yet.

On another weekend tour, McCormick saw flooded mines and destruction similar to that of Rheims, leading him to comment, "Each destroyed town and surrounding country exactly alike, a desolate waste, churches, houses, everything gone."[8]

Always the Americans noted the dilatory manner with which the French repaired their lives. Of course the French were in no hurry to rebuild, because they wanted the world to see what they had suffered so that the bill for German reparations might be suitably high. In a sense, then, the horrors of the war-torn areas were an extension of the spectacle in Paris. Tourists and newsmen were welcome everywhere to ensure that the Americans got the message.

The Americans were hardly novices at public relations, but nothing prepared them for the propaganda barrage they encountered under the tight orchestration of the French government. The French papers were vitriolic at the least suggestion that their government's demands were excessive. The American delegation warily cast about for support and, according to McCormick, found the Paris edition of the *New York Herald* "a rotten anti-Wilson sheet" intent upon embarrassing the president. Toward their own journalists the Americans became suspicious and somewhat distrustful, Gordon Auchincloss going so far as to compose lists of U.S. and European newsmen whom he considered reliable or hostile.[9] In Paris the press did not merely write and report; increasingly it was a participant in the making of history. Like everyone else, the members of the fourth estate were eager to run errands for powerful men and perform other favors for which they wanted to be remembered. They too knew that Paris, 1919, could be a springboard for their careers.

A meticulous historian of the Paris Peace Conference has observed that the American delegation "comprised a number of different groups, whose only real link was the President, who had the final word."[10] This suggests some of the problems that beset the Americans in Paris. First, except for the selection of the peace commissioners, the delegation had not been planned with any forethought concerning the harmonization of personalities or political ambitions. Secluded from much of the turmoil about him, Wilson seldom confronted issues or personalities until he could no longer ignore them. The State Department and Colonel House sent him constant reminders and suggestions, but Wilson chose to delay personnel selections in a vain hope that he could keep the numbers of Americans at a minimum.[11] The result was a delegation beset by egotism, confusion, and intrigue, with the president inaccessible to all but the strongest intriguers and averting decisions until the drift of events demanded his command.

The peace commissioners—House, Secretary of State Robert Lansing, General Tasker H. Bliss, and Henry White—played little role in the conference except as public symbols of experience and integrity. Bliss had been a member of the Interallied Council and thereby served a military function outmoded by the Armistice. Lansing was a weak secretary, but his office deserved representation. White was an elderly diplomat chosen mostly for his Republican affiliation, although he was scorned by at least one GOP international lawyer as "distinctly unsuitable." Loyalty to the president mattered in most selections. When Gordon Auchincloss later asked Undersecretary of State Frank Polk why Wilson appointed White, Polk recalled that he had disagreed with the president's choice, but "the President said that he could not trust other prominent Republicans, and therefore, he put Mr. White on."[12]

The principal figure in the American delegation, besides Wilson, was Colonel House. House had had more contact with the Allies than any other American during the war and was seen by them as the president's personal voice. House enjoyed that prestige and used it to cultivate special contacts in England and on the Continent. In Europe, said Walter Lippmann, House was "the Human Intercessor, the Comforter, the Virgin Mary." As early as 2 September 1917, Wilson had given House authority to create a special organization known as "The Inquiry" for the purpose of planning America's postwar diplomatic negotiations. House installed his brother-in-law Sidney E. Mezes as its director. However, before very long, Mezes and House had lost control of its composition and direction to others. Yet the Inquiry went to Paris with a group of scholarly and journalistic "experts" whose advice figured only nominally in the conference; House was left an influential but isolated figure in the American delegation.[13] Measuring his own power by the fact that his office had twice as many rooms in the Crillon as those of the other commissioners put together, House abandoned "his anonymous, background position; his personal power was now clear to all, and dissatisfaction began to spread in the Delegation. However, his position was safe as long as he continued to enjoy the confidence of the President."[14] As it turned out, one of the more dramatic stories of the conference would be the disintegration of that confidence.

Prior to the conference, House urged Wilson to include in the delegation economic advisors from his war cabinet. House and his son-in-law, Auchincloss, especially sought the services of McCormick and Hoover, but could find no way of excluding Baruch and Hurley from the group.[15] Thomas W. Lamont and Norman H. Davis were designated by Secretary of the Treasury Carter Glass as special financial advisors.

The American delegation functioned on at least three different levels in the earliest stage of the conference: at the lowest were the comparatively anonymous members of the Inquiry or the State Department whose task it was to share their learnedness or diplomatic experience with the higher levels; at the middle level were the economic advisors who negotiated the reconstruction of Europe; and at the leadership level were the president and his surrogate, Colonel House. A superficial glance at the delegation's organizational chart suggested no problems; yet the Americans were beset by poor internal communication, mushrooming rivalries, and a dearth of command. The knowledge and skills of the lower levels were usually bypassed in favor of the political needs of individual Americans in more prominent assignments. The economic advisors, in particular, were constant sources of mischief; all the rivalries within the war cabinet were grafted upon the delegation. At the outset their assignments were undetermined, leaving it for each of them to carve out a small domain— something they had been doing throughout the war anyway—although it remained to be seen if such competitiveness would work in Paris as well as it had in Washington. Thus, a common complaint among observers and anonymous functionaries was that "no one had thought out any systematic plan of work. The President was not interested in the problem. There was no man in charge of the [economic] group; each was left to work out his own salvation."[16] At that they were indeed experts.

McCormick and Baruch posed the largest organizational problems; they had no logical reason for being in Paris other than that House wanted McCormick and Wilson wanted Baruch. For reasons that are not apparent, the colonel's group considered McCormick an able ally in its intrigues with the war cabinet; it would soon discover that McCormick's only loyalty was to Wilson. Obviously the president had counted upon their loyalties as well as their carefully tuned political sensibilities when he asked for McCormick and Baruch. They arrived together and conspired together, and when they left Paris together with the president, House's star was in descent while theirs glowed brightly.

As McCormick wrote, "This entire history of the inside conference will make interesting reading someday." It is the story of war cabinet jealousies and maneuverings by men keenly aware of their places in history and determined to augment their roles. It brought to Paris what British official Robert Brand referred to as "the Byzantine system of the government of the United States." The British took a very lofty view of the American disorganization, even though by May it would be very apparent that both delegations were divided internally over the issue of reparations. By London standards the Americans were diplomatic amateurs. Witness senior British official Lord Robert Cecil's description of a meeting of the Supreme Economic Council: "More wrangling over the German exports. Very hopeless because the Americans were quite divided amongst themselves as to what they wanted. That is one of the difficulties of dealing with them: they have no organisation particularly. Five different Americans attend the Economic Council, all apparently of equal authority, and rather jealous of one another. . . . one or two of them apologised afterwards to me for their behavior." Another time, Cecil, who was chairman of the Supreme Economic Council, asked House to name an American to a special committee, and "the moment I suggested there should be one American representative, he asked me whether the plan was to make a big fight in the Crillon, for they were all jealous of one another as prima donnas, and it would be quite impossible to send any one of them to represent any of the others. Truly their ideas of organisation are extraordinarily primitive." House was a source of much of their contentiousness, but even without him they would have had each other to create acrimony and friction, and absence of collegiality or leadership.[17]

Hoover, for example, was a source of enormous irritation to his fellow economic advisors. Hurley believed that Hoover sought to wrest control of shipping from him; McCormick accused Hoover of attempting to dominate blockade policy. Baruch was told by Leland Summers when he reached Paris that Hoover was "trying to make personal capital out of his work over here." "Hoover gets into a good many fights unnecessarily," the admiring Auchincloss conceded. To Auchincloss's chagrin, another favorite of his, McCormick, bitterly resented Hoover's infringement on his efforts to coordinate economic policy. McCormick-Hoover clashes occurred frequently, and the Pennsylvanian tied Hoover to House's machinations. Although McCormick respected Hoover's talents and intellect, as did almost everyone else who came in contact with him, Hoover offended McCormick in other ways; McCormick noted, for example: "Hoover's manners very brusque. I don't see how he holds his popularity."[18]

Baruch's role in the delegation was ambiguous from the beginning to the end. In his memoirs he related how, when he arrived at the conference,

> for some days I sat around wondering why I had been called to Paris. I had the clear impression that my arrival had not occasioned unalloyed enthusiasm in the Colonel's personal entourage. Then the President learned of my presence, and I received my assignments.
>
> I was hardly at a loss for jobs and titles. I found myself a member of the drafting committee of the Economic Section; a member of the Supreme Economic Council, and Chairman of its Raw Materials Divison; a Representative on the Economics and Reparation Commission; and an Economic Adviser to the American Peace Commission.

This is deceptively clear. Baruch knew that he had been called to Paris because he had been wangling an invitation since early November and that he got it only because the president wanted him. He leaves us to assume that his jobs and titles were conferred upon him by the president, yet Wilson merely made Baruch an economic advisor and left him to find those other niches for himself.

In his own memoir, financier Thomas Lamont renders his version of Baruch's role in the delegation:

> Bernard Baruch was a roving ambassador. He had not come to the Conference with any one duty. But he made himself useful in almost every direction and showed the same capacity for handling problems and persons he has always displayed. At times he was active like the rest of us on the reparations problem. He was a great favorite of the President and commanded his complete confidence. The intimate acquaintances that he cultivated among members of the British delegation from top to bottom were no doubt of great value to the President. We all worked together as an harmonious group, with all questions of precedence eliminated.

This is a superior job of gentlemanly insight, filled with the sort of inference, innuendo, and indirection that compels us to read between the lines. Forgotten is Lamont's 1919 opinion that Baruch "knew nothing but had the faculty of gathering about him able men who guided him."[19]

Lamont's observations of Baruch were not wide of the mark. In December 1918, following Wilson's assurance that he would soon be summoned to the conference, Baruch's first thoughts were of surrounding himself with "good men" who would tend to the detail work while he concerned himself with policy and politics. However, Wilson wanted his advisors to travel light and send for their technical experts later as they were needed. Moreover, Chandler Anderson, drawing from his extensive experience in overseas negotiations, counseled Baruch that he misplaced priorities in preparing for the conference. Baruch first had to assure himself of a significant role in the conference, lest his personal organization become the conference's excess baggage. Baruch was hardly one to be satisfied with being "on the fringe of things," so he had to attain "definitely recognized status" at the conference. That began in Washington, where he threw a sumptuous farewell party for himself, entertaining correspondents with roast duck, champagne, and tales of his WIB exploits.[20]

Baruch shrewdly sought out McCormick and attached himself. McCormick, also in search of status, seemed to appreciate that the old war cabinet could serve as a vehicle for establishing it. They had dinner together the first day and tea the next, joined Hoover and Hurley for dinner with the president and Mrs. Wilson the third, and lunched together with members of the French delegation and dined together with members of the British delegation the fourth. By that time it was evident that most of the conference's real work was being done at informal conferences among the various Allied representatives. So Baruch went out of his way to impress Lord Robert Cecil with his importance. According to Cecil Baruch "spent the whole evening in explaining what a great man he was, and how he had had the complete dictatorship of American industry throughout the war. A man of great power but not attractive."[21] The Baruch manner attracted some Englishmen, like Churchill, while offending others, like Cecil.

Although much could be accomplished informally at the conference, it could be done only by men with formal authority. The conference officially opened on 18 January. McCormick and Baruch let House know that they wanted assignments on the Economic Council, which Hoover sought to monopolize for himself. To minimize friction, Baruch got the Reparations Committee position, and his place at the conference and in diplomatic history was assured.[22] He then went after the chairmanship of both the American delegation to the Reparations Committee (McCormick, Baruch, and Norman Davis, with Lamont as Davis's alternate) and the committee itself. But the United States had less interest in reparations than the Allies, and it soon became evident that what they could get from the Germans would be "bound to disappoint everyone." Thus, an American chairman would be a political mistake. Baruch quickly drew back from that quest.[23]

When it came to organizing the Supreme Economic Council, where U.S. interests required strenuous vigilance and defense, once more the war cabinet rivalry was renewed. All five economic advisors—Baruch, McCormick, Davis, Hoover, and Henry M. Robinson, a California banker who had served on the Shipping Board and replaced Hurley in Paris—represented the United States in the Supreme Economic Council, thus giving Washington five ambitious delegates. Baruch and Hoover sought the council's chairmanship (McCormick taking instead the quiet and diffident route to power), which went to the Frenchman, Etienne Clémentel, and rotated to Lord Robert Cecil, where it remained out of respect for a very dignified peacemaker and out of fear that further rotation would ignite an inferno in the American delegation.[24]

That did not quiet the Baruch-Hoover rivalry. As the conference confronted complex economic problems, new committees had to be formed, and again the two egotists vied to be the American representative. In May the rivalry took a slight turn. When it came to forming the European Economic Committee, Baruch magnanimously deferred to Hoover as the American representative. Hoover briefly accepted, then thought about it, and then deferred to Baruch, insisting that the speculator was "better qualified." Baruch was not about to argue with what he considered to be obvious and so he went.[25]

Baruch also had strained relations with the finance specialists, Davis and Lamont. He had played a role in the financing of American railroads before and during the war, might have become chairman of the War Finance Corporation, and incessantly told Europeans that he had declined the Treasury portfolio. He considered his claim to a place on the Reparations Committee justified by his financial experience. But Davis and Lamont, Morgan men, were contemptuous of Baruch's banking knowledge. Baruch sensed, correctly, that they were deliberately excluding him, with the tacit consent of the House group, from a stronger role in negotiating reparations. Undoubtedly, as Auchincloss believed, to some extent "it was Baruch's own fault that he was not called in." Lamont intensely disliked Baruch and considered him a vague thinker who "talked disconnectedly" and was full of "fruitless" or "silly" ideas. Lamont was hardly the only person in Paris to consider Baruch shallow or an expropriator of other's schemes. However, Lamont's judgment of Baruch should not be the last word. The Morgan company had an animus against Baruch that went back to his Wall Street days and was aggravated by the war. Also, we cannot discount the possibility that Lamont's own ego competed with Baruch's. At an April meeting of the Big Three, Lamont noted, "I sat at left of Pres. and he paid me more attention than B.M.B."[26]

In a sense all the economic advisors wanted to sit at Wilson's left and monopolize the president's attention. Baruch once confided to Cecil that he was, in Cecil's words, "intriguing to get the control of the financial policy, and to do so glosses over the fact that the main question is financial, laying stress on the commercial aspects of the problem, so that the President shall not call in the financial experts." If that were the case,

2. *American delegates and advisors to the Paris Peace Conference of 1919. Seated from left to right are Hoover, Tasker Bliss, W. S. Benson, Baruch, Henry M. Robinson; standing are Thomas W. Lamont, Whitney Shepardson, Norman Davis, Edward M. House, Gordon Auchincloss, and Vance McCormick. (Courtesy Seeley G. Mudd Manuscript Library, Princeton University)*

then Baruch should not have been quite as resentful later when he noticed that "Davis is very secretive about what he is doing, and . . . does not keep me conversant." He also observed that a Morgan publicity man had arrived in Paris; his arrival accounted for "the appearance in the press of the two articles regarding Lamont's speech" and inspired a vigorous protest to McCormick that Lamont threatened the delegation's harmony and success.[27]

Auchincloss's somewhat enigmatic remark that it was Baruch's fault if the president consulted Lamont and omitted Baruch on matters of international finance suggests that Baruch often did not tend to business. In Paris he had earned a reputation of missing meetings. In his peripatetic manner, he tended other irons in the fire or buried himself with gossip or conniving, thereby avoiding the tedious negotiating and paperwork involved in the conference. His style was better suited for Washington than for Paris. His presence was demanded at meetings that endlessly debated turgid international quarrels. His contributions at conferences were usually limited to a few undistinguished sentences while McCormick, Davis,

and Lamont carried the brunt of the American side of the debate. He still
thought that others could do his work for him. Some of his confusion is
suggested in comments made to a friend: "The situation over here is a
little different from what I thought it would be. On the economic side we
are trying to establish broad principles, and leaving it to the various
departments involved to carry out the details, which will have to be taken
care of by the technical men who understand these matters." He was
wrong. He had to be more of his own technical man than he appreciated.
He had established his status in the conference, but in late February he
sought WIB comrades who could be his surrogates at those tendentious
sessions.[28]

The European political atmosphere differed markedly from Washington's, and some of Baruch's stratagems did not go over as well with the
French and British as they did with U.S. congressmen or bureaucrats. To
begin with, his background disturbed the French, if we can take the word
of Charles Seymour (of the House camp): "He is a mystery to the French;
they cannot understand how a Jewish speculator can be in the position
he holds." Yet Baruch struck up good friendships with French officials
like André Tardieu, Louis Loucheur, and Count René de Rougemont,
who seemed taken with this man of great wealth, influence, and ideals.
At his initial meeting with foreigners, Baruch usually attempted to impress upon them that he was a statesman of power and vision. That was
the approach he used with both Lord Riddell, a British publisher, and
Cecil. Cecil was more taken with Baruch's power than with his vision.
The day Cecil became chairman of the Supreme Economic Council, Baruch requested that they dine together so that they might discuss economic matters. Cecil found their conversation pointless and nebulous;
Baruch proceeded to outline problems, leaving Cecil curious as to what
he was driving at. Cecil often found himself embarrassed by Baruch's
"asseverations of his own honesty by equally vehement assertions of
mine." But Baruch had moments when he could engage Cecil in "a rather
interesting talk" concerning European finances over dinner. Gradually,
Cecil learned that Baruch had cultivated the art of indirection—throwing
his listener off guard with assorted trivialities that tangentially drove
home his point. It was his way of charming and engaging his adversaries
so that they felt courted rather than cornered. Cecil described one encounter thus:

> At 10:30 on Tuesday I went to see Baruch who wanted to explain to
> me exactly the attitude he took up about economic assistance to
> Europe. I was there for nearly three-quarters of an hour, and on the
> whole very much amused. Baruch wandered about over the subject,
> interspersing a number of personal appreciations of himself, and many
> protestations of his complete honesty and high-mindedness. I really

believe he is an honest man, and should have no doubt about it if he did not so constantly assert it. There was a long passage about his methods of doing business, which at the time I thought merely one of his usual irrelevancies, but from what I have heard subsequently I think he intended it to be a kind of indication of the way in which he thought the economic problems of Europe should be dealt with.[29]

Never certain whether his reputation as an unscrupulous speculator had preceded him, Baruch worked overtime in those years to prove that his motivations were pure, that he merited his place in Wilson's coterie of unromantic idealists, and that his national interests surpassed his personal interests.

No matter what House, Hoover, Davis, or Lamont thought of him, Baruch's value to the president appreciated during the conference. He gave Wilson the utmost loyalty, even seconding the president's position when it contradicted his own. At the same time, there can be little doubt that Baruch conspired, but with whom and for what is not clear. Two years later, Lansing was told by a former Democratic senator that Baruch had plotted with Henry Morgenthau and unnamed others to undermine and get rid of House. Although the report surprised him, Lansing did not doubt its authenticity. Morgenthau reached Paris in March at about the time when House's standing with Wilson began its gradual but certain decline. We can be sure of three things: (1) the president lost confidence in House; (2) House had antagonists in the American delegation, including Baruch, Morgenthau, McCormick, Lansing, and others who distrusted and resented his influence with Wilson, although it is not clear that they schemed together to undermine him; (3) Baruch and others were the beneficiaries of Wilson's loss of confidence in House. In Baruch's quest for enhancing his influence with Wilson there is nothing unusual or sinister. According to one historian, there is evidence of "direct and seemingly unprovoked intervention by Baruch" in early April, and "thereafter he chose the road to the President directly." If others could not likewise skirt House in an effort to reach Wilson directly, then they must have envied Baruch for his access to the aloof president. House believed and Herbert Hoover repeated the conventional wisdom: "Now that Colonel House had faded into the background, McCormick and Baruch had more personal influence with the President at this time than any other Americans in Paris." It was the highest status Baruch could attain at the conference, but considering the outcome and consequences of the conference, Hoover may have intended to be damning with faint praise.[30]

"TO SET THE WORLD AT WORK AGAIN"

Despite the spectacle of American delegates to the conference jockeying for position or for acclaim, disagreements among them were usually differences between personalities or dissents in degree. At the highest levels of the American delegation, misgivings concerning U.S. stands were set aside in favor of unity on all the major issues. It is the judgment of Arno Mayer that "none of the more prominent members of the American delegation ever considered resigning" as a protest against the announced terms, although five young experts at the lowest echelon did.[31] But none of them compared in stature to John Maynard Keynes, economist for the British Exchequer, a draftsman of key British proposals, whose resignation denounced two British representatives on the Reparations Committee. And no American wrote such a vitriolic dissent as Keynes's *The Economic Consequences of the Peace*. Though high-ranking Americans like Hoover and others had misgivings concerning the treaty's terms, none of them went on record as did the South African general, Jan Christian Smuts. The Americans believed that, given the confines of national politics, they had achieved as much as could be expected.

The American delegation began its conference work with a policy consensus, and further developments only sharpened it. Wilson was the undisputed leader of the delegation, a point that may seem too obvious to be worthy of mention except for its contrast with the British delegation: there the nationalists dominated reparations, to the dismay of the liberals and Prime Minister Lloyd George. Wilson often temporized, but when he gave a signal he could be certain that it would not incite any major defections from his delegation or scandals at home. In part, the American solidarity can be explained by the obvious fact that the issues were much less crucial to Washington than to the Europeans. In the parliaments of Europe, governments with great majorities could be toppled if the wrong decisions were made at the conference table; the prosperity of Europe appeared to hinge upon the terms written into the treaty. The United States had emerged from the war as undisputedly the richest nation in the world, a condition nothing at the conference could disturb.

The Wilsonians came to Paris confident of achieving their primary objective—a League of Nations—and the tumultuous welcome for their president seemed to prove that Wilsonianism had taken hold in Europe. They assumed, and their personal examinations of the war-devastated zones confirmed their bias and hardened it into a platitudinous conviction, that Europe simply had to be made productive again. Davis and Lamont perhaps said it more elegantly than Baruch and Hoover, but they agreed that Europe had to find a way of going to work again. Briefly elaborated, what they meant was that, following the waste of war, Europeans had to learn again the importance of productive capital, productive industry, and productive labor. Failing this, the future boded ill with instability, more war, and the spread of Bolshevism.

But the Europeans did not want such amorphous prescriptions. They demanded that the Americans find the capital for the renewal of enterprise. If it was not forthcoming from New York, then the Allied nations were left with little choice other than to extract it from the defeated culprits in the form of reparations and indemnities. Thus, a central issue of the conference concerned the extent of reparations and when that sum should be fixed.

Baruch went to Paris believing that the reparations issue was an international price problem affecting the economics of all nations. What Germany would pay the Allies would have a direct impact upon U.S. trade and prices simply because Germany was the most populous market of western Europe, the most productive, and a major trading partner for all industrial nations. Although the American strategy called for allowing the British and French partners to set the tone for the reparations, Baruch and his colleagues knew that no settlement could be reached without the direct involvement and tacit approval of the United States. The Americans never doubted the moral wisdom of Germany's compensating France for the devastation of its industry and agriculture, Belgium for a small portion of its industry and the violation of its neutrality, and Britain for the destruction of its merchant ships and overseas commerce. However, they doubted the practical wisdom of weakening Germany through reparations so as to assure French security from renewed German militarism supported by its revived industrialism. The Americans counted upon a more calculating British self-interest that looked toward the need for restoring Britain's former trading partner in central Europe. Yet such economic logic seemed evanescent in December when the British went to the polls in the wake of Lloyd George's campaign promise to "squeeze the pips until they squeak." Now the word "indemnity" found its way into the diplomatic vocabulary in spite of American protests that it contravened pre-Armistice assurances to the Germans and threatened to delay European progress toward stability. In January, the Americans, who had earlier looked to the British for reasonableness on settling with Germany, confronted a British delegation divided between the moderate attitudes reflected in its Treasury advisers and the nationalistic hardness found among some of its politicians, and led by a politician whose own mind was uncertain. Vance McCormick succinctly stated the American case against punitive damages: "'If you ask the indemnities you want from Germany you will kill her and get nothing but Bolshevism.' . . . [The] Allies cannot get indemnity paid unless Germany can produce." John Foster Dulles, counsel to the American representatives on the Reparations Committee at Baruch's request, also voiced the economic advisors' fears when he wrote: "We here are very much impressed by the urgency of settling the indemnity question, which is operating to arrest the renewal of trade and industry. In France there is considerable idleness directly traceable to this."[32]

The Americans were concerned that the French allowed their industry to lie dormant pending the announcement of terms for their expected indemnity. And, to assure that there would be an indemnity for them, the French had formed a coalition of small nations who could anticipate nothing in the way of reparations but hoped to extract something from the Germans in war costs. To the Americans, it suggested a conspiracy by the British and French to extract from the Germans enough money to repay the Americans for wartime loans. Or the Allies would demand a deal from Washington—no indemnities for cancellation of their war debts.

The Americans argued that war costs could not be lumped with reparations without increasing Germany's indemnity to $100–120 billion, well beyond Germany's capacity to pay within a reasonable period of time. That would retard European economic recovery. The American dilemma was portrayed by one U.S. commissioner:

> Mr. [Thomas] Hughes of Australia [third British member of the Reparations Committee] is claiming that Australia is a house with a mortgage on it, which mortgage can reasonable [sic] be assumed to be due to the war, is as much an injured house requiring reparation as a house in Northern France or in Belgium with a shell-hole in it. In short, as they represented it, the universal demand was that under the head of reparation the Germans should be made to pay for all the expenses of the war, including the maintenance of armies by the governments and all direct and indirect losses. This, of course, would mean a staggering claim against Germany. . . . Privately certain other members of the Committee, such as the Belgians and French, were opposed to the claims set up by Mr. Hughes and others for the reason that they foresaw a greatly diminished chance of their getting out of Germany for themselves that they had expected. Nevertheless, they were not disposed to actively oppose Mr. Hughes but apparently hoped that the United States would make the fight for them and they would then apparently consent. This would put the United States in the attitude of opposing the wishes of the other members of the Committee and might lead to the claim by them that if the United States prevented them from getting what they claimed, the United States should assume itself the financial burden of satisfying their claims.[33]

The Allies were isolating the Americans on the reparations issue. It appeared that the British were "getting the little fellows lined up with her to include war costs, with the idea of taking over any shares that these countries might receive in payment for debts owing to England." Thus, Lloyd George's strategy seemed geared toward either obtaining Britain's funds for reconstruction from the Germans or at least fulfilling his election promise of making a supreme effort toward that end while blaming the Americans for obstructing it. "The result," Cecil acknowledged, "is considerable friction between us and the Americans."[34]

The Americans countered with a two-pronged strategy: first, to put the reparations matter into the Supreme Economic Council, "on the theory that most of these economic problems are of temporary character only," and then to build an alliance with the Belgians, who had the best case for reparations among the smaller nations. Hoover suggested "tying up with Belgium" on reparations with an inducement not readily available to others—"giving them priority" on a loan from the United States. At a dinner on 16 February with the Belgian delegation, the American economic advisers gave assurances that if Belgium "decided to come out boldly" for the American position, it would be entitled to a separate class of reparations that would include "costs of war" denied other nations. It was, after all, the idealistic as well as the practical thing to do. The United States broke out of its isolation at the conference by befriending poor, defenseless Belgium. As Lamont neatly put it, "We thought we had on the whole done quite a strike."[35]

Not quite so: the American position against huge indemnities had already begun to slide toward compromise in its quest for Allied political and economic stability. The delegations were not free merely to negotiate with one another; as politicians, they had to satisfy their constituencies, most of whom looked forward to, and had been led by their political leaders to expect, nothing less than punitive damages imposed upon the Germans. Economic logic aside, the American delegation had to satisfy European political conditions:

> We personally are disposed to adopt as liberal a construction of this agreement as to reparation as is possible as our opponents make a strong popular argument and one difficult to answer without appearing to be bound by legal technicalities. We have refused, however, to accept the principle of inclusion of war costs. . . . You will understand, however, that the political situation in almost all countries will make it most difficult for their delegates to take any attitude other than insistence upon complete reparation which they have promised their people and which all our inquiries show the people of the Allied countries feel to be just and due them. While the representatives of the Allied countries generally recognize, and privately admit that it will be impracticable to secure actual repayment of war costs on account of limited ability of the enemy to pay, they seemed determined upon recognition in principle of complete reparation.[36]

Ever attuned to democratic politics, McCormick took the lead in modify-ing the American demands. In return for an Allied concession on war costs, the Americans would acquiesce in European insistence upon not fixing total reparations until all the damage in the Allied countries could be assessed, a compromise made necessary by the fear that "otherwise governments will fall." Besides the danger to the leaderships of France and Great Britain, there loomed a chance of Germany's succumbing to Bolshevism. This put McCormick in a mood to "make peace and discuss details afterwards."[37] That, however, was late February, and for all the American willingness to accommodate the political needs of its Allies, the conference still had a long way to go to reach a formula minimally satisfying to a maximum number of countries.

But McCormick seems to have been more tractable on the issue of reparations details than were his American colleagues. Baruch, Hoover, and Davis argued the necessity of fixing the amount of Germany's repa-rations as soon as possible in order to restore a flow of capital that would revive industry throughout the west. French, British, and German economies would stagnate while their politicians haggled over Germany's obligations, with the consequence that investors would not invest and legislators would not tax until everyone knew what the German bill amounted to. Delay could lead to widespread disorder. The Americans had a sense that, with Germany possibly verging on revolution, they were "living on top of a volcano." But Lloyd George, explained one British delegate, was "trying to ride 2 horses on Reparation," attempting to keep his parliamentary coalition happy while berating the French for their "unwarranted, ridiculous and grossly exaggerated" claims on the Ger-mans. At the same time he mediated a bitter split in his delegation. The conference marked time through most of March.[38]

Baruch sympathized with Franco-British demands for reparations "jus-tice," but he believed that they had to measure Germany's capacity to pay without pauperizing her or, consequently, Europe. As he succinctly summarized the American dilemma: "We should give the German people an opportunity to work but we must make them pay to the fullest extent possible for the terrific damage done to the devastated countries." The French, he confided to an American visitor, "want to kill Germany and then collect." He could see that if Germany were to "be made to pay to the utmost penny," then it would have to "be helped to pay and live." Doubting that Germany had enough wealth to pay and prosper made Baruch, like other Americans with such thoughts, susceptible to French accusations of German sympathies: "I do not wish in any way to express any sympathy for Germany, nor to lessen her burdens; for she should be made to pay everything she can pay, and brought to a full realization of the crime she has committed against civilization; but it would be a great mistake to be a party to promising the already over-burdened tax-payer of the Associated Governments with the hope of a payment which will never be collected." If the Allies took from Germany territories rich with raw materials, then "the Germany that will have to meet the payment will be vastly different from the one that entered the war." Instead of subtracting from Germany's wealth, Baruch urged that ways be found to augment the credit of war-ravaged Europe in order "to set the world at work again."[39]

The British would have welcomed an American contribution to the Old World's recovery even in the negative form of cancelling inter-Allied debts. However, the Americans were every bit as ready to defend the interests of their taxpayers as were the British and French. The British especially sought ways to increase their portion of the damages bill. In actual physical damage, except for shipping, the British claim was slight when placed against that of France. The United States endorsed a larger British claim, but the British refused to bow to American pleas for fixing Germany's bill; and in late March the British added a new category of German liability—pensions. All Lloyd George intended by the pensions gambit was to improve, in Lamont's appropriately inelegant jargon, Britain's "division of the swag with the French."

To the dismay of his economic advisors, Wilson acceded to Lloyd George's ploy. Meeting with Baruch, Davis, Dulles, Lamont, and Mc-Cormick at 2:00 P.M. on 1 April in the Crillon, Wilson made it clear that he would accept the inclusion of pensions. Despite Lamont's argument that pensions were *"most unwise"* and could only revive claims to other war costs, Wilson bought the Allied argument that without them, the "consequences would be grave." The advisors persisted in pointing out that pensions were consistent with war costs and that war costs were inconsistent with the Fourteen Points; if they gave way on one type of costs, they logically had to include all others. To that, according to Lamont's account, Wilson retorted: "I don't give a damn for logic." Or, as McCormick told his diary; Wilson "was very clear in his mind that there was no intention of including pensions when the peace and armistice terms were discussed and that particular categories of that character were not considered by themselves and that he felt that as pensions were such a just and equitable basis of claim, he would support them upon the French basis of valuations and it was particularly important to do this, *otherwise England would not get what she was entitled to in proportions to the other countries*." Wilson had altered the American position. Even on the issue of when the reparations would be fixed, he gave in to the British quest, known by the delegates as "postponing the evil day." Again, McCormick: "We all agreed to the Lloyd George proposal which established a commission to determine the amount Germany can pay and the amount of the claims before 1921 *which will relieve Great Britain and France from making public the small amount they are to get from reparations because both Prime Ministers believe their governments will be overthrown if the facts are known.* I am afraid this camouflage will not work but it may, as the people forget so easily." It is clear that Wilson had bowed to European politics as a means of securing quicker writing of a treaty that included his League of Nations. As Auchincloss wrote, Wilson "could not well contemplate starting Peace negotiations all over again with new governments." Yet it remained to be shown that his compromise would indeed facilitate agreement, either with the Allies or with the Germans.[40]

Wilson's advisors anticipated additional Allied demands for concessions. They persisted in their quest for a stated sum, as opposed to Clemenceau's "roofless proposition," on the grounds that capital could not be kept waiting to know when or how to go to work and that the Germans would not sign something that left them vulnerable to the whims of Allied politics two years hence. Davis reminded the French, "In conceding pensions we did so on the theory that this would not increase materially the actual amount that Germany would have to pay." But the French were unwilling to set an amount or allow a commission to do it. Davis feared "in working on this new basis we tend to abandon our principle that Germany should pay measured by her capacity."

Having made important concessions, Wilson too was decidedly disappointed by Allied intransigence. Irritation between the Americans and the Allies increased sharply in April. Wilson ordered his ship, the *George Washington*, to prepare for departure, an undisguised threat to leave unless the Allies showed some amenability to American insistence on a fixed sum and other moderate terms. McCormick reflected his chief's and colleagues' impatience on 5 April: "I am thoroughly disgusted with Allies' selfishness and constant effort to use the United States for their own selfish purposes and throw the blame on us when we have been ready for some time and they are temporizing and playing politics; afraid to tell their people they cannot get them what they promised them at election time. I feel more discouraged today than at any time since I came over." Still the talking dragged on. British moderates asserted their helplessness to influence the hard-liners or their prime minister.[41] But now they began to realize that the Paris muddle had weakened American idealism.

UNILATERALISM

The reparations tangle encouraged latent economic nationalism among the American delegates in Paris. For all the exigencies calling for cooperation with the Allies during the war, national self-interest had never been far from the minds of the war cabinet chiefs who now served as economic advisers. Cooperation had been a fragile branch, easily snapped by the prospect of peace. The WIB's foreign mission had been a harbinger of revived competition, and Baruch kept it in Paris through early 1919. The squabble over reparations further suggested to him and other Americans that the French and British were less interested in a cooperative postwar effort to put capital and people to work throughout the world than they were in depleting their German foe.

Ever a keen nationalist himself, Baruch distrusted European imperialism. And, as Hoover noted, Baruch had the ability to synthesize the ideas of others. Because he undoubtedly borrowed concepts from his colleagues (something we can be certain that they all did), when it came to defining the interests of the United States and representing them, Baruch usually spoke for the consensus. Because Baruch was often forthright and told the British what they did not really want to hear, they sought to confirm that his ideas were truly American policy. In at least two instances, Britons confirmed that Baruch accurately portrayed American positions.[42]

The policies pursued in Paris were enunciated in Washington during the waning months of 1918. Baruch put them in terms at once aggressive and altruistic, thus conforming with Wilson's practical idealism. Heeding the advice of the president, Baruch approached cooperation with the big powers with caution.

The United States adopted the role of protector of small nations' commercial and manufacturing interests. It presented itself as the advocate of opportunity in the new and less-developed nations of the world; as Anderson noted, "Baruch's interest in this matter is growing rapidly as he goes into it more fully, and appreciates its importance." He was intent upon the dismantling of special conditions that had made imperialism. All nations should be treated equally and accorded the rights of commerce hitherto reserved for one or a few favored nations. Investment capital should not have its opportunity obstructed by political barriers any more than raw materials should be reserved for the speculations of a privileged few. Coming from the nation with the greatest capital reserves, with a merchant marine that verged on meeting the British in every port of the world, with raw materials that gave its manufacturing capacity unmatched self-sufficiency, and with an appetite for more raw materials to satisfy its needs for investment and manufacturing, the idealism of Wilson and Baruch appeared to the Europeans as an exercise of economic supremacy.

Yet Baruch presented it as a blueprint for an enlightened international political economy that assured a restored or an enhanced prosperity for all nations who subscribed to its liberalism in principle and in practice. Baruch outlined this prescription for Wilson on the eve of the president's departure for Europe:

A just and continuing peace should include a just and equal access to the raw materials and manufacturing facilities of the world, thus eliminating preferential tariffs. No nation, including neutrals, should be allowed to enter into [an] economic alliance, to the detriment of any other nation. . . . Without the determination of some such basic policy, geographical lines or spheres of influence may predetermine economic and industrial conditions affecting a whole nation or the whole world.

. . . The passing of new spheres of influence to anyone of a number of nations without this policy of equal opportunity, might seriously affect or entirely hamper each and every other nation. I am not suggesting that this will be done, but knowing the ideal task to which you have set yourself, I am bringing it to your attention. Industrial inequalities have caused dis-satisfaction and revolution within countries or forced wars to relieve intolerable conditions. Therefore, each nation must be given equal opportunity.

Inherent in the manifesto was a call for the supremacy of international competition and private enterprise, as opposed to multinational cartels promoted by governments hoping to foster enterprise in their capital-hungry nations.[43]

The Wilsonians considered the British Empire an international cartel that violated liberal principles. In dealing with the British at the peace table, Baruch assured Josephus Daniels, he would be cold and firm; "I intend to carry as many weapons to the peace table as I can conceal on my person." He disagreed with Newton Baker's restrained liberalism and advocated aggressive economic expansion and a global open door that would benefit the world community:

I am rather of the opinion that we should do all we could in this country to increase the production of new lines of commercial industrial activity, and an impetus should be given to any policy which would either increase raw materials or give additional access to them. In reference to "the seeking of the world's markets," we should say very frankly that citizens of the United States should have an equal opportunity to enjoy the world's trade, not with any advantage over anyone, but certainly not to the disadvantage of its citizens, and we should stand for equal opportunity for others as well as ourselves.

At another time he wrote: "It is not too much to say that the very life of the nation depends upon her unrestricted access to remote points; it might be even better to say the very life of the world, since the fate of the world is so indissolubly bound with that of America and her associates.[44]

Obviously, however, it would take time to persuade the British to accede to America's leadership. In the meantime the Americans had to anticipate a dogged British defense of her erstwhile naval supremacy and protected markets. Wilson hoped to keep up the appearances of cooperation, lest the Americans alarm London and "give England an opportunity to say that, well, America is not only in this to make this world a place worth while to live in, she is also anxious to get all the business she possibly can." Until Wilson negotiated a League of Nations that established rules governing the freedom of the seas and equal access to all markets, the economic might of the United States had to be restrained in order not to offend and antagonize Old World reactionaries. As Edward Hurley put it, "Without a League of Nations England and America are liable to become bitter rivals for commercial supremacy." From London in December 1918, Hurley confirmed European trepidations concerning U.S. wealth and intentions:

> In all the conferences I have had on this side, I have been impressed with the fact that it is not the league of Nations, nor an International Court, or even the Freedom of the seas that is feared by Lloyd George, Clemenceau, Orlando or their associates. What they are thinking about, as you are probably aware, is the increased power of our shipping commerce and finance. In every conversation the commercial question has come to the front. France fears that she will not be able to get the raw materials she needs at the same price as other nations; Great Britain fears that we will have a bigger merchant marine than she will be able to build, and that our government will operate it, regardless of cost, so that we can capture the best markets of the world.

The Europeans had to be persuaded that American private enterprise could thrive without governmental support overseas except to enforce rules of fair competition. The United States did not seek to wage economic warfare against Europeans. It merely sought a worldwide new freedom. As Hurley told Wilson:

> I am convinced that the principles you have applied to American business are adaptable to the international situation. The European nations are really suffering from an attack of "nerves." . . . The British are fearful that under a League of Nations the United States, with its present wealth and commercial power, may get the jump on the markets of the world.
>
> If it can be made clear to them that the essence of the League of Nations is international fair-play, that membership in the League is dependent upon square-dealing and that a member of it would not be able to put into effect retroactive and confiscatory legislation against foreign interest, as Mexico did to England's disadvantage and our own, I am convinced that whatever opposition there may be will be swept aside.[45]

However, the Hurley-Hoover relief mission in Europe turned into an exercise of raw economic muscle that left the Allies expecting the worst. While the two men squabbled over whether their respective control over ships and food entitled either man to dominate European relief, the Europeans were left without doubt that it would be an American project no matter who ran it. Neither Hurley nor Hoover was about to deliver all the supplies, ships, and finances for the relief of Europe into the hands of a multinational commission dominated by British, French, and Italian government officials. The Americans wanted to control the flow of their materials and money into Europe because their distribution influenced prices in American markets.[46] But Europeans would wonder if the Americans were less intent upon relief than upon dumping surplus commodities in Europe. Europe would have to learn that Wilsonians blended their economic self-interest with their humanitarianism.

In Paris, Baruch lectured Europeans on the need for free enterprise. Get rid of government restrictions at the earliest possible convenience, he advised Lord Riddell, so that the world can get to work again. Also, a quick settlement of economic terms with Germany would release raw materials and other manufacturing necessities and reestablish trade. A month later he told Cecil much the same thing, with the difference that, in the intervening time, circumstances such as the Allied unwillingness to lift the blockade of Germany had converted the blend of American humanitarianism and self-interest into an assertion of power. Baruch bluntly told Cecil that European manufacturers desperately needed raw materials and credits, of which the United States had plenty. Cecil noted that "his panacea is to sweep away all government control and direction, and to encourage private individuals to work out their own salvation; for which there may be a great deal to be said, but I doubt any continental government accepting it." Despite Baruch's insistent idealism, Cecil perceived that the "result undoubtedly would be, as he indeed plainly stated, to give America the commercial predominance of the world."[47] As the Europeans saw it, the Americans were anxious to dump their raw materials and manufactures in Europe as soon as London and Paris opened their markets and Germany's, too. Trade barriers would remain in place until the Americans offered something in return for those markets (like cancellation of inter-Allied debts, or cheap credits) or until European businessmen had sufficiently recovered from the war, with the aid of their governments, and were ready to resume the race for markets.

The cooperation of the Allies depended upon their respect for America's principles and sovereign economic strength. When Wilson heard from reliable sources that the Allies were conspiring to pool the total cost of the war and extract a proportionate share from the Americans, he became "considerably exercised" and ordered his economic advisors to discuss no financial matters that did not relate directly to Germany. The

Americans demanded an end to the Allied blockade of Germany. They maintained that recovery would not be forthcoming "if governmental restrictions of all kind are not removed and business permitted to become normal." But a month after the Americans arrived in Paris the blockade remained in place despite agreements in principle to the contrary. That served to harden U.S. unilateralism.[48]

On 11 February, Baruch huddled with Davis, Hoover, McCormick, and Henry M. Robinson to map out a strategy for opening European markets to American products and investments. Part of the problem involved public opinion. The French had marshaled their people behind stringent demands upon Germany and a continuation of the blockade. Although the Americans could do little about the government-controlled French press, it became apparent to them that they were neglecting their own public. Cooperation, they had to tell their public, had become a conspiracy by Allied governments to weaken U.S. economic strength through artificial trade barriers. The Europeans were playing dangerous nationalistic games that delayed the economic recovery of all countries. As Baruch wrote to Wilson, "There are not enough people in the world working in order to produce the things the world needs and to create enough wealth on which credit can be founded to start the new governments and keep the world going. *This can be accomplished only if the governments will remove restrictions, as we have done in the United States.*" Thus, the Allies could best serve themselves and their potential trading partners in central and eastern Europe by abolishing embargoes and following the U.S. example in normalizing trade through the removal of government restrictions. Moreover, and perhaps uppermost in Baruch's mind, the emancipation of European trade would open up the Continent to American surpluses, *"the large over-production in the United States of food and materials*, with which we undertook to help win the war." Maintenance of the high American standard of living called for finding outlets for the enormous wartime production in Europe.

Therefore, Baruch wrote, "To break down the blockade and set things going again, we suggest the following remedies": First, the American businessman should be encouraged "to find a market for his materials in the markets that Europe formerly occupied, and that Germany formerly occupied," a reference probably to areas like Latin America. A U.S. commercial invasion of old colonial markets would cause the Allies to reconsider their trade obstacles. Secondly, the United States ought to erect retaliatory trade barriers on nonessentials from France and Britain. The limited application of the Allies' own medicine against them would not detract from the U.S. argument. Thirdly, because of U.S. inflation, Washington should extend credits to the new nations of Europe "to buy only the things that they require . . . only on condition that all import and export licenses and restrictions should be removed, except those with enemy countries." Hopefully, these credits would originate with private sources, but the economic advisors would endorse pending legislation in Congress to authorize European loans up to $1.5 billion. Baruch saw this as an incentive for Europe to do things the U.S. way: "We shall then be able to say to the world that we stand ready to help those who are willing to help themselves, but we can not and will not finance those who are not willing to help themselves." Finally, to stabilize domestic U.S. prices, the War Trade Board would police large purchases by foreign governments of U.S. raw materials.[49]

The American delegation embraced unilateralism. When the Allies demanded that all sequestered German property, including ships commandeered in ports, be placed into a pool until all claims against Germany were decided, the American commissioners refused because "the United States should not allow the disposition of such property to be decided by anyone but itself." The Allies' insistence upon cooperation on their terms encountered American counter-demands for cooperation that respected U.S. economic supremacy. Wilson endorsed Baruch's principle that the United States should offer to share its wealth only upon terms favorable to its political goals. "I think it is perfectly legitimate," Wilson advised Davis at a later date, "that we should ask ourselves before each of these credits is extended, whether our colleagues are cooperating with us in a way that is satisfactory."[50]

Clearly they were not. McCormick grumbled that the Allies were "holding us up on every hand for money whenever we asked for [a] relaxation of [the] blockade or anything else." French propaganda accused the Americans of wanting to end the blockade in order to dump pork and other food commodities upon Germany and soak up the assets Paris considered its rightful indemnity. The French would sooner starve Germans than agree to peace terms. That worried the Americans and the British. The French were unwisely debilitating Germany with the blockade, leaving it susceptible to Bolshevism and retarding recovery. Cecil scolded the French representatives for their obstructionism at a meeting of the Supreme Economic Council. It was time, he believed, to dictate food terms to the French and "make these Latins behave properly."[51]

The French were right on one thing: the Americans wanted German raw materials as payment for food. Also, Baruch brusquely demanded an American "open door" in Rumania, fearing a British and French grab for its oil. The United States would withhold credits from any nation where its businessmen did not enjoy "equal opportunity with all other nationals." In the Raw Material Committee of the conference, Baruch was a lion in defending and promoting American interests. "I made a fight . . . for an equal opportunity for American goods—no matter what they were," he later boasted for the benefit of the chairman of the board of Standard Oil. Baruch demanded parity for U.S. cotton and copper in

European markets. "I am very anxious to get the cotton markets opened up," the South Carolina-born speculator admitted. The textile mills of Lodz, Poland, needed the South's cotton and Baruch wanted to accommodate them.[52]

The best hope to protect the peace of the world, Baruch believed, was a strong American navy. This belligerent opinion was a harbinger of, as Lamont saw it, "a big fight between us and England." It involved nothing less than a challenge to Britain's naval supremacy. Although the war had ended with the U.S. navy numerically inferior to the British, U.S. ambitions threatened to close the gap by 1925. This suited Wilson's diplomatic strategy. Knowing that the British were not about to countenance a freedom-of-the-seas provision in the League of Nations Covenant, Wilson used naval construction as a bargaining device in Paris. Lloyd George played right into his hands. According to Cecil, the prime minister was "anxious to use his assent to the League of Nations as a lever to compel Wilson to give up increased naval construction." Moreover, as a sop to the big navy enthusiasts in Washington, the prime minister had to affirm the validity of the Monroe Doctrine in the League Covenant.[53]

Britain desperately pressed for an Allied pool of U.S.-seized German ships, lest the Americans use them to augment their burgeoning merchant marine. On 23 April, Lloyd George came to Wilson's house to appeal for the German ship pool. Wilson claimed that he could not accommodate the prime minister because Congress already had refitted many ships and put them at the service of the Allied cause; besides, he added, "the United States' claims for reparations would be very minor" and it did not intend to assert a claim to pensions, as the British did. Therefore, Wilson considered the ships to be America's just reparations. Lloyd George countered by reminding Wilson of Britain's staggering shipping losses, its dependence upon ships for its very economic life, and the action of its navy in driving German ships into U.S. ports during the American neutrality period. Wilson agreed that neutrals should not benefit by British naval success; but the U.S. would keep those ships, although he at least gave assurance that Britain would get a share of their dollar value.[54]

The British wanted a return of a great deal of their money that had crossed the Atlantic during 1914–17. European recovery, Cecil thought, called for the United States "to undertake large additional financial obligations," but his afterthought was correct: "I doubt if she is ready to do so." Cecil did what he could to change that, dropping broad hints with Americans "that they must be ready to shoulder their fair share of the burden of the war." He urged Frenchmen "to persuade the Americans to help [with French finances], for there was no solution of the European economic question without the assistance of America."

But, as Cecil recognized, American financiers were awaiting some sign that the Allies would help themselves, in addition to taking what they could get from the Germans or the Americans. Americans suspected that the Europeans were interested in nothing other than their dollars. As Baruch put it: "I find on every side the tendency to force the United States into a position in which it will be assuming a larger part of the indebtedness incurred in the war. They are approaching this . . . by obtaining loans from us on a plea of inability to finance themselves in any other way, until we shall be in a position where we shall have practically assumed a larger share of the war debt." Baruch was deeply suspicious of any cooperation with the Allies. He saw the reparations controversy as a ploy that really sought to grab dollars, of which there were so many in 1919. He wondered, if the United States became a party to a reparation settlement, what would be "our obligation, moral or otherwise to see that it is paid?" Though America was willing to provide the credits Europe needed for reconstruction, Baruch believed that the recipients had better be ready to contribute large quantities of their own.[55]

Until western Europe decided how it would return to business, the Americans were intent upon taking their dollars and materials to eastern Europe. By assuring Belgium of American credits, they made it an example of what great America could do for the new governments of eastern Europe, who, McCormick felt, were "looking to the United States to protect their interests." Tell the Belgians, Wilson instructed Lamont, that they would be remembered by the United States to the extent of $500 million. The next day, Lamont asked Wilson if he were convinced that the United States "*must* help the small nations . . . and he said *yes*." Lamont added, without elaboration, "To me this is very significant."[56] It signaled an American financial interest in the small nations of eastern Europe, then coveted by the British and the French.

In a conference with Wilson and House on 21 April, Baruch developed the themes of Wilsonian liberalism. He argued that the United States had a humanitarian mission to perform, "that we could not very well depart from Europe and leave the people here in their present condition." In particular, the small new nations would fall prey to the predatory established powers. America should help, "but only to the extent that they would help themselves; . . . we should not lend money with a free and open hand but with a stinted hand." Eastern Europe would have to open its markets; upon these terms the United States would give aid. What might be called the "Marshall Plan of 1919" was not munificence given freely:

> A prime condition of our granting aid should be the establishment of
> equality of trade conditions and removal of economic barriers. Any
> credits we give should be contingent upon the cancellation of
> preferential treaties and trade agreements now existing, and upon an
> understanding that the monies advanced by any of the governments

should not be held as a special charge against the customs or duties or public utilities of any country. All advances should be made with the understanding that the nationals of all countries should receive equal opportunity to do business in the country to which the money has been advanced, and that no preference or special consideration should be given to the country making the advance, *except that where commercial credits are granted the material should be bought in the country making the advance.*

To achieve "the restoration of economic life in Europe, particularly in the new states," Baruch in May proposed that European buyers of American products become eligible for War Finance Corporation (WFC) credit arrangements. To keep new European governments alive until their revived commerce brought in revenues, the Treasury would make direct advances to them. In these ways, the richest nation in the world would fulfill its obligations to the newest, and the United States would benefit handsomely by its idealism.[57]

Baruch's recommendations came close to representing a consensus among Americans. Congress had put the WFC in the business of financing foreign trade in March 1919. The concept of credits for the Europeans had been kicking around the Treasury and banking circles since the Armistice. Later in May, Lamont and Davis also prescribed credits to the eastern Europeans, U.S. raw materials for the factories of western Europe, and capital infusions for tottering non-Allied governments, basing their proposals "on the grounds of almost immediate self interest rather than on grounds of generosity and humanity."

In June, Eugene Meyer, chairman of the WFC and a man whom Baruch had suggested earlier as an economic advisor, arrived in Paris to act as America's overseas banker. Hoover gave a luncheon for Meyer and invited a group of British, French, and American delegates to meet him. Afterwards, the Britons and the French left the Americans alone with Meyer. His colleagues asked for his impressions of the financial negotiations. Scanning the round table where they ate, Meyer informed them, "I think the shape of the table here is wrong. You ought to have a long, narrow table with all the Americans on this side and all the foreigners on the other side. That's the economics of it. You sit around and let them tell us what to do. Why don't you take the lead and tell them what they should do and what we can do for them if they cooperate along lines that are practical?" Like his fellow Americans, Meyer wanted to "make our credits and bank loans contingent upon [European] production." He conceded that "this is treating our potential creditors in a highly paternalistic way," but it gave the United States "our greatest leverage" after the treaty was signed and was justified by "altruistic" goals.[58]

By the time Meyer gave the conference the benefit of his conventional wisdom, most of its anguish was behind it. The future of Allied-American cooperation was in doubt. Aside from some last-minute discussion of the workability of reparations without a fixed sum or a fixed time limit, all that remained to be decided was the future of international economic cooperation with the Supreme Economic Council as its vehicle.

The Americans unanimously favored scrapping it. For almost four months, the Supreme Economic Council had been a theater for discord between delegations. It seemed to sharpen national differences instead of softening them. Worse yet for the Americans, it bound them like Gulliver among the Lilliputians. McCormick wrote in his diary: "Hoover, Baruch and I discussed future of Supreme Economic Council and all are unanimous we should not continue its *control* after peace. Our Allies want us tied up to them; Italy through fear of her other Allies; France for somewhat same reason and hope to use us and Great Britain to hold us down to her level in trade until she gets on her feet as she fears our competition." Cooperation with the Europeans was impossible without allowing them to stifle American initiative, production, and trade. "What Europe needs," McCormick maintained, "is freedom of action and to learn to stand on its own bottom, cut out paternalism and let the economic laws assert themselves." The Continent would not be safe for American capital until equal opportunities reigned and private investors were unfettered by government restraints. The conviction was at once ideological and national. The United States owed it both to itself and to the well-being of Europe to make its own decisions.[59]

The conference headed for a conclusion. Wilson conferred with his economic advisors on 13 June at 10:00 A.M., an hour before he met with the Allied leaders. Lloyd George wanted Allied control of food purchases whose costs, he claimed, would ruin Europe. Wilson opposed this on principle, but he wanted to know what Baruch, Davis, Hoover, Lamont, and McCormick thought. Their arguments were firm: no price control and no inter-Allied buyers' pool. Baruch and McCormick doubted that a combination of the Allies would be cohesive enough to prevent the Americans from commanding a free market price. Hoover was confident that an Allied combine to get a lower price would instigate lowered production and higher prices than the Europeans bargained for. Lamont, the Morgan man, wondered how the Allies could hope for American credits if they waged economic warfare against American prices. Davis depicted the situation as a struggle between state-run economic systems and private enterprise; after too many years of war, "they are trying to wean us into their way of doing things, and we decline to go along." Wilson agreed; Europe would have to take high American prices immediately, free its markets, and await the day when prices would find a lower organic level. However, for appearance' sake, the United States would allow a special commission to study food purchases as long

3. Posing outside of King's Palace, Brussels, Belgium, 18 June 1919, are advisors to the American delegation at the Paris Peace Conference—Baruch, Norman Davis, Vance McCormick, and Herbert Hoover. (Courtesy Seeley G. Mudd Manuscript Library, Princeton University)

as Hoover headed the group. But Americans would no longer suffer Europe's complaints. America's wealth and power, her representatives believed, deserved more respect than they had been accorded at the Paris Peace Conference.[60]

The Supreme Economic Council continued to meet, but its discussions had less meaning than ever. On 22 June the economic advisors decided without a dissent to abolish the council, although they thought it prudent to postpone announcing their unilateral action until after the signing of the treaty. The next day, Wilson approved the decision.[61] The Americans were going home, but a part of their business would always be abroad. This would not be isolationism; it would be unilateralism.

A "JUST PUNISHMENT"

The American delegation believed that the United States had interests in Europe that would have to be protected long after the conference ended. It never considered a political withdrawal into isolation: American enterprise then would be disadvantaged in European markets. For his part, Baruch was convinced that politics and economics were inseparable, that governments had roles to play in developing the political economies of their societies. He admired President Wilson as a political leader who carefully defined where free enterprise ended and state responsibilities began. Yet the experience of the conference suggested that Europe did not comprehend Wilson's distinctions and pursued a statist course. If American businessmen were ever to have a chance to buy and sell freely in Europe, the Wilsonians had to reassert a balance between state encouragement and private enterprise's freedom. Reparation was an issue of crucial importance in the quest for free enterprise in Europe.

In January reparations had been primarily a European problem. The United States had no war claim against the Germans; and it had no reason to expropriate German wealth that, when Germany was productive again, could benefit the United States and everyone else in trade. But the extreme claims of France and Italy, and of Britain to a lesser degree, presented challenges in principle. The Allies wanted nothing less than to develop spheres of influence throughout central and eastern Europe that would exclude American businessmen. The Allied governments threatened to put Germany to work for them for an indefinite period, expropriate territory and property, impose concessions for their own merchants, and erect barriers against outside traders. Shocked by Allied vindictiveness, frightened by the potential consequences posed by Germany's and eastern Europe's captive trade, and determined not to finance Europe's tragic mistake, the Americans reluctantly jumped into the reparations debate. The American economic advisors sensed a disaster in the making, although they were nearly powerless to prevent it. Compelling Germany to pay an unlimited reparation would boomerang against the extortionists, argued Davis and Baruch. The day would come, they reasoned, when the actual burden of reparation would be thrown upon Britain and France. A Germany that shipped capital abroad could not be a customer for the world's producers. Desperate for foreign currency, the Germans would dump their surplus output on world markets for whatever it could bring, "thereby causing severe competition with the Allies." They warned that the outcome could be "greater economic damage to the Allies than the benefits they will derive from the reparation."[62]

Baruch's political antennae indicated more trouble than the fight was worth. In April he confided to his diary, "I am fearful in having the United States Government tied up even in an indirect way in the reparation that is to be paid by Germany, because of the disappointment that some day may come to the people of the world in not receiving as much money as had been indicated by the Reparations Commission's report." He continued to stress that the Allies would not and could not collect as much from Germany as people were led to believe, "particularly for the first few years, as she would be very much handicapped by the economic and industrial structures put upon her."[63]

In May it became evident that these doubts were not peculiarly Baruch's or American. British liberals hoped that the conference would set lenient terms for Germany. However, at this point Baruch became ambivalent. Almost echoing the French, he maintained that Germany had to "feel the weight of her misdeeds" and endure a "just punishment." Over lunch in late May with Winston Churchill, "who envisioned a prostrate Germany seized by Bolshevist hordes," Baruch argued for setting a reparations figure higher than that advocated by the Englishman! Baruch quite sincerely considered Germany a hoodlum nation who had to be penalized severely enough so that she would not do it again, but not so severely that she would be of little use to world society. Although he did not want Germany to pay lightly, he believed that stabilized international finance and commerce required immediate knowledge of Germany's terms. On 31 May he wrote concerning a German counterproposal: "I thought there was something in what they had said; and that what moved me more than anything else was the necessity for fixing a sum for reparation." "On that," McCormick observed, "we all agree."[64]

Breakfasting with Lloyd George on 2 June, Baruch pressed the case for fixing the sum right away. The prime minister offered two alternative propositions, including one for fixing the amount in three to four months. Baruch countered that they would probably know little more then about European economic conditions and ought to settle the matter while they had the Germans at Versailles. Lloyd George asked to discuss it with the U.S. president, and Baruch agreed to arrange a meeting immediately. With Wilson the prime minister made it clear that what troubled him was a potential occupation of Germany if the enemy refused to sign the treaty. Now he was amenable to softening the terms cosmetically in order to get the German signatures on the document. That suggestion exasperated Wilson, who saw Lloyd George taking an American position that Wilson had compromised for the sake of harmony with Britain; now Britain would delay the treaty by having it rewritten in accordance with the original U.S. position. By this time, Wilson just wanted a treaty.

Wilson's economic advisors still wanted the amount fixed, if they could get the French to agree. McCormick would set it at $25 billion ("Baruch, I think agrees"), which Davis thought was too much. Some in the American delegation argued that the sum itself mattered less than the fact of an agreement, which German business needed to know. Thus, the French could get a high figure, as long as everyone else knew what it was in 1919 rather than waiting for 1921. But the French would not give way, Tardieu even urging the United States to stand with the French and arguing that "Lloyd George would change his mind again." Meetings with the French went back and forth on 3 June. Britain had anticipated that the United States, rather than approve punitive terms against Germany, would finance the British and French themselves. But the Americans barely opened their purses, took the hard terms, and surprised the British, who were more dependent upon a German trade that could be crippled by the treaty.[65]

The outcome satisfied nobody. Some delegates were more outspokenly unhappy than others. Wilson and Lloyd George agreed to allow Germany four months in which to present its version of a reasonable fixed sum, to which the Allies would reply in two months. Although Hoover argued that the treaty would crush Germany and was unworkable, Baruch and McCormick hewed to the Wilson line that it was just and would be made to function. With the example of John Maynard Keynes's resignation from the British delegation, Hoover threatened to resign if the Allies reimposed the blockade in order to intimidate Germany into signing; McCormick dismissed Hoover as a "very exaggerated talker."[66] It was late in the game for cautious men to resort to antics: sometimes one had to make the best of what nobody wanted, if only to move ahead to confront awaiting dangers.

THE THREAT OF BOLSHEVISM

In any examination of the Paris Peace Conference, the subject of Bolshevism is never far from the center of attention. That is as it should be. The conferees were there to establish a new international order and, though they may have disagreed on its character, they formed a consensus on the exclusion of Russia from the conference and on quarantining its infectious Bolshevism from Europe. Russia distracted the conference by its absence. As early as January, an Englishman noted: "In the discussion everything inevitably leads up to Russia. Then there is a discursive discussion; it is agreed that the point at issue cannot be determined until the general policy towards Russia has been settled; having agreed on this, instead of settling it, they pass on to some other subject."[67] On Bolshevism, however, no disagreement could be found among the delegates: if Russia chose a Bolshevist course, its neighbors must not be allowed to follow. And, although it is indisputable that "Wilson spear-headed various Allied efforts to tame the Russian Revolution," it is not true, from the perspective of the economic advisors, that "in fact, these efforts came to be central to Wilson's overall peacemaking strategy."[68]

Baruch and his colleagues were anti-Bolshevik but did not allow the Red threat to monopolize their considerations. Baruch worried less about eradicating Bolshevism in Russia or preventing its spread through middle Europe than about advancing Wilson's vision of a world free from the old diplomacy of alliances, power balances, and traditional imperialism and free for the new diplomacy of popular influence, open markets, and nonmilitarist competition. The Wilsonians intended to practice humanitarianism toward the Russian people and hostility toward any Moscow government that espoused antiliberal principles. That went not only for the Bolsheviks, but for the anti-Bolsheviks in Russia led by Admiral Alexander Kolchak as well. Baruch explained to Winston Churchill "that the recognition of Koltchak would depend upon whether or not he represented the reactionary forces in Russia; that if he really had at heart the aiding of the masses of Russia, that I would do all that I could to help him; but that the American people would never stand for putting back in power the reactionary element."[69] Churchill, in Cecil's words, was "mad to intervene in Russia and destroy Bolshevism." Intervention was not what the Wilsonians desired. Baruch advised Churchill "that I had the greatest sympathy for Russia, that humanity was going through its greatest struggle there; and that if he had a concrete plan, I should be glad to assist him in carrying it out."[70] But making war against Red Russia had low priority for liberal Wilsonians.

Certainly, Baruch wanted to throttle Bolshevism, but not by going to Moscow. Rather, he and the Wilsonians hoped to contain it. Upheavals rent eastern Europe in 1919; in March, Bela Kun came into power, proclaiming a Soviet Hungary. Even before then, Europe had buzzed with talk of the chaos that permeated revolutionary Germany, McCormick noting a widespread belief that Germany had entered its "Kerensky period" and that Bolshevism was bound to strike it. But McCormick coolly noted that Germany was unlike Russia in that "too many people own their own property" there. By March reports from Germany left McCormick considerably less confident that German economic institutions were impervious to revolution. Germany was being starved by the Allied blockade, on which the French would not relent. On 8 March, Lloyd George pleaded for an end to the blockade to save Germany and Europe from Bolshevism, telling the revanchist French minister of finance, Louis-Lucien Klotz, that when Bolshevism succeeded in Germany, three statues would be erected—one to Lenin, one to Trotsky, and the third to Klotz. The Americans too were persuaded that food and supplies could save Germany and the Baltic states from revolution. Toward that end, McCormick thought that the creation of the Hungarian Soviet could prove salutary: it would temper hard demands for reparations and hasten a liberal peace.[71] Significantly, that hope proved illusory.

Did the Wilsonians seek a moderate peace with Germany to prevent

4. *In Paris, 1919, Louis Loucheur, Winston Churchill, David Lloyd George, and Baruch. (Courtesy Seeley G. Mudd Manuscript Library, Princeton University)*

Berlin from going the way of Moscow? Certainly it was always a consideration, even when it did not have priority. At a war cabinet meeting back in October, Wilson had told the story of a senator who called him to insist that "the Kaiser must go." Wilson said that he responded by inquiring who the senator preferred to have ruling Germany, the kaiser or the Bolsheviki. The senator responded in favor of the kaiser and then recommended that the American army drive on Berlin to impose upon Germany a government acceptable to Washington. With the observation that such military action would require two years of fighting for success, Wilson stated that he hoped to achieve the same goal through diplomacy.[72]

Wilson sought for Germany what historian N. Gordon Levin, Jr., calls "reintegration." In quest of "a peaceful and open order of world liberal-capitalism free from military and economic alliances and from socialist revolution," the Wilsonians believed that American interests were the world's best hope for prosperity and stability. The Wilsonians sincerely believed that a Pax Americana would benefit everybody; "as was normal in Wilsonian thought, the needs of America's expanding capitalism were joined ideologically with a more universal vision of American service to suffering humanity and to world stability." American material and moral interests were twins. Thus, the United States had a duty, "as the leader of liberal opinion of the world, as the selfless and trusted arbiter of international problems, and as the disinterested defender of a new world order against both traditional imperialism and revolutionary socialism," to employ its power and influence in Germany or in eastern Europe in behalf of its liberal values.[73]

The American delegation did not go to Paris bent upon the destruction of Russian Bolshevism, and that goal never became ascendant on the American list of priorities. But anti-Bolshevism complemented other American objectives. Typically, McCormick complained in April that the blockade was "choking trade and commerce, causing idleness and making Bolshevists." Put positively, what the economic advisers wanted was productive work for their money and materials and strengthened liberalism throughout the world. That naturally made them anti-Bolshevists.

Germany had to be punished, but the Wilsonians believed that a punitive settlement worked only to aid France, which furtively did business in Germany while the blockade excluded American materials. The Bolshevist menace enabled the Americans to intimidate European capitalism with the threat that if the Allies did not give the Germans a quick and merciful peace, the Germans would give the Allies another Bolshevist state to contemplate. British diplomat Harold Nicolson saw Bolshevism as the German "trump card." The Germans would "go Bolshevist the moment they feel it is hopeless to get good terms." Some pessimists envisioned a debacle in which the Germans would "join up with the Russians and Magyars, and present us with a Red Mittel Europe."[74]

Gradually the Wilsonians came to believe that peace, even at less than desirable terms, and prosperity were the best antidotes for any Bolshevik poisoning. Except for brief moments of doubt and for the Cassandra-like Hoover, they were optimists. Being good promoters, they believed they had something to sell the world that would be bought in any free market. Their liberalism had to triumph if they practiced it for the benefit of all. It struck a balance between the reactionaries and the Bolsheviks, offering justice and abundance beyond the capacity of either extreme.

But by 9 June it had become difficult for Wilsonians to remain confident. That evening, at a dinner given by Cecil, the speeches were morbid with anticipation of a "revolutionary tendency in the world." Only Hoover spoke for the Americans and, though he was certain not to enliven the occasion, he did give an excellent ideological exposition of American liberalism grounded in his own philosophy of history. Lamont gives us this description of the polemic:

> The problem was a very grave and complex one; the population of the world was such that we must maintain our productivity. Can we maintain that productivity and still make proper division of it, for the moment that we divide up the yield of it too much, at that moment we delay (or dull) individuality and initiative. *We must be both conservatives and radicals at the same time*. We must give labor a larger share in the management of industry and a larger fruit from its product. But we must not go to the other extreme. Russia was giving an example of that extreme of altruism. How has it resulted? Russia was formerly the greatest exporter of food in the world. Now, because of the loss of initiative, of individuality, she is unable to raise enough food to feed herself.[75]

The Wilsonians believed that America would give the world a demonstration of the way free markets could benefit mankind with food and a fair distribution of productivity. Bolshevism anguished them. The dictatorship of the proletariat was a loathsome prospect. They abhorred the notion of a society without rewards for the speculator who ventured his capital. They believed that all men should aspire beyond their immediate grasp; Bolshevism only promised to reduce everyone, especially the few who excelled, to the lowest common denominator.

But they did not consider themselves merely anti-Bolsheviks. They considered themselves progressives concerning the maintenance of order, sharing power with the humble as befitting a land of opportunity, expanding the marketplace to abundance lest any man go hungry. They resented the way Bolshevism cast them as reactionaries, confident as they were in their own minds that they were the enemies of the true reaction-

aries—the inefficient imperialists who distorted parliamentary governments and markets with special privileges that denied *the people* liberty
and freedom.

Possibly the richest of the Wilsonians, Baruch tried to sound the most
progressive. He went out of his way to inform reporters and delegates
from other countries that the aspirations of the working class had profoundly moved him. The haves of the world had to come to terms with
the have-nots, he declared. Men concerned with the public purse needed
"greater vision, and not the cold calculating point of the lead pencil." As
for his own purse, he told an Englishman, " 'So far as I am concerned, I
am prepared to give up voluntarily, through the medium of taxation, a
very large part of my income. I am convinced that, unless the wealthier
classes take that course, they may have everything taken from them.' "
It was Wilsonian practical idealism at its most enlightened and opportunistic best.

In order to be both radical and conservative at the same time, as
Hoover put it, Baruch endorsed the concept of welfare capitalism. A kind
of participatory capitalism should evolve: "Labor should be granted representation on the boards of directors of corporations, in order that they
[*sic*] might have a voice in the making of regulations, and see how the
property was run, and what the profits really were." He probably felt
outrageously radical as he sprung that notion on Morgan man Tom
Lamont, "who I was surprised to find, agreed with me."

But Wilsonian liberalism also had meaning for the world. Late in
embracing welfare capitalism and progressive taxation, the United States,
Baruch realized, ought to stand for political independence and free markets in the new states. Because the new states were "the children of the
Great Powers," they had to be afforded special treatment or else they
would be the victims of the great powers. At home or abroad, America
had to redress the balance between the rich and the poor; about that,
Baruch wrote, "I feel very strongly. . . . It sometimes looks as though the
rich and powerful always get the best of it. We have been pushing very
hard the claims of the farmers and of the smaller peoples, but the ship-
owners, and that class of people, seem to be getting the best of the
bargain."[76] He would have to fight harder for Wilsonian liberalism at
home. He would work to show the world that the United States was a
progressive society furthering the cause of an orderly world.

THE TREATY FIGHT

Politically, the Wilsonians could not win. If the French or the British or
the Germans did not make the treaty a liability, then the Senate, with its
Republican majority, could inflict the ultimate setback. Too many national

and domestic political interests were involved in the treaty to satisfy all parties. The Wilsonians' first quest had been to secure an agreement that upheld American interests; then they had to ensure its congruence with Wilsonian ideals. Having satisfied themselves to the extent that compromise would allow, they had to assure the political protection of their Allied negotiators, lest their zealousness in behalf of self-interest destabilize Europe. Finally, they had to demonstrate the triumph of all these principles to the American people and their antagonists in the United States Senate. This was the most difficult task of all: how could the complexity of enlightened self-interest be explained to the satisfaction of an uncomprehending public whose definition of interests did not allow for appreciation of other interests? Thus, as the Wilsonians prepared to depart from Paris with their arduously negotiated treaty, it was evident that Frenchmen and Britons were not the only obtuse adversaries with whom they had to deal; the politicians of the Senate defined their political needs as narrowly as did those in Whitehall. Moreover, they resented Wilson's exclusion of them from the Paris deliberations and were intent upon exercising the one power that the Constitution conferred upon them: the last word.

The Wilsonians usually patronized others. Throughout the war they had been the sole interpreters of an enlightened self-interest. While claiming to act only in concert with the voluntary cooperation of all sectors of the economy and the body politic, they had employed coercive wartime powers to impose their conceptions of the national interest upon a host of interests whose dissent from Wilsonian leadership had been defined by the war managers as selfish or seditious. The "readjustment" to peace inaugurated an era in which the Wilsonians were no longer the arbiters of enlightened self-interest. Their behavior no longer carried the authority of national emergency. Not only would they have to persuade a brooding multitude of antagonists, they would have to assuage the unpersuadable— those adversaries who defined national interest differently and scorned convoluted Wilsonism.

The Wilsonians were attacked from all sides. Senatorial debate in the spring had already suggested that opposition to the treaty would be "very formidable" and debate would be "bitter." The Wilsonians looked to their friends in business for encouragement, believing that they were entitled to support in return for their strong advancement of American credit and commercial interests overseas; but businessmen came away from Europe discouraged by its nationalism and disorder, feeling that "in such a mess . . . cooperation at the present is impracticable, and that therefore it might be better for us to go it alone until things straighten out."[77] That made the League of Nations, the political vehicle for equal opportunities, dispensable for the time being. Moreover, articulate progressives were dismayed by the discrepancy between the Fourteen Points in theory and the treaty in practice; the *New Republic* and other voices of enlightenment were raised against the political crassness that prevailed in Paris. Wilsonians were practical idealists, but now they were being abandoned both by practical men and by idealists; the result was a suggestion that the two were incompatible.

With his usual self-confidence, Baruch endeavored to demonstrate the practical idealism of the treaty. Called to begin testimony on the economic sections of the treaty before the Senate Foreign Relations Committee on 31 July, he floundered through two hours of Republican questions which suggested that American interests were badly represented in the document. Later that day, Baruch by chance met Chandler Anderson, the attorney who had served him so well in the WIB's foreign activities. Anderson was just the counsel he needed, Baruch was convinced. A prominent Republican international lawyer, an associate of the GOP's chief opinion maker on foreign policy, Elihu Root, Anderson could serve Baruch as a technical expert and serve the cause of ratification by dividing the GOP opposition. Anderson obligingly accompanied Baruch to his second day of testimony and came away with the opinion that Baruch made "a poor witness" because he appeared ill informed. Nevertheless, Anderson thought that Baruch probably disarmed the senators by giving the impression of being "very obliging and good natured about trying to answer questions." A third day of testimony passed without serious consequence and Baruch was excused.[78] He retired to behind-the-scenes bargaining with treaty opponents and to promoting a public education campaign.

Led by Senator Henry Cabot Lodge, a group of Republicans put forward reservations and amendments to the treaty designed to put a GOP stamp upon it. Isolationist opposition from a handful of irreconcilables could not be negotiated, but Lodge's Reservationists sought a quid pro quo in return for their votes. The Reservationists centered their attack upon the League of Nations, insisting that it subordinated U.S. sovereignty and abridged the Monroe Doctrine. Their amendments and reservations, they claimed, would protect American interests. Thus, the price the Wilsonians would have to pay would be a concession that they had not been as practical in guarding American interests as they believed. That would be tantamount to a confession to a sin of omission, but most felt that it would be worth paying the political extortion to ransom the treaty's freedom from the Reservationists.

When Senator Philander C. Knox of Pennsylvania, who had been President Taft's secretary of state, sought indirect contact with the Wilsonians in the Senate and in the White House to facilitate some understandings concerning the reservations, Baruch served as a "reliable channel of communication" between the Wilsonians and the Reservationists. Baruch, along with lawyer Bradley Palmer for the Wilsonians and Anderson, now representing the Reservationists, sought to bring about some agreement "between the two more reasonable groups in the opposing camps." President Wilson briefly raised hopes that some form of mild reservation would bring about speedy ratification, but Lodge and other Republicans were not thinking of compromise. When Anderson informed Lodge that Baruch hoped to find an area of compromise with the Mild Reservationists, Lodge "said that no compromise was possible; that the Republicans had the power to make reservations . . . and if the Democrats did not agree with them promptly they ran the risk of having the entire Covenant thrown out of the treaty, because the opposition to the Covenant was growing very rapidly throughout the country, and would soon be so strong that mere reservations would not be satisfactory." The message was clear; either Wilson accepted Lodge's reservations or he ran the risk of no treaty at all. To Wilson the reservations constituted an abridgment of his word. He correctly concluded that further efforts to compromise would be fruitless.[79]

Wilson believed that legislators in all countries were behind in their thinking and that his conception of national interests would find responsive chords among the people. Thus, he abandoned his Washington negotiators to build public opinion against the Reservationists, certain in his heart that Lodge had misgauged sentiment on the treaty. Traveling across the country for weeks, Wilson suffered a physical breakdown in late September; he returned to Washington, where he was struck by cerebral thrombosis that paralyzed the left side of his face and body. Never one who easily delegated his power, he would thereafter guard it all the more jealously. Compromise needed his personal touch, but the president became nearly incommunicado.

Still, Baruch carried on his personal crusade to bring Lodge and the Senate Democratic leader, Gilbert M. Hitchcock, to their own treaty compromise. In mid-October, Baruch happened to meet Anderson at the Shoreham Hotel, and as they strolled toward the Pan American Building, they discussed possible compromise arrangements. Baruch by then approved reservations, provided they were not in effect amendments to the treaty. He was anxious to avoid any more delay. Anderson agreed that he would take the matter up with Lodge while Baruch called upon Hitchcock. Whatever good intentions they might have had, Baruch and Anderson were not controlling personalities in this fight, while Wilson and Lodge clearly were. Wilson would not accept even the Hitchcock reservations, let alone Lodge's. Moreover, the Republicans read the Hitchcock reservations as a signal that Democratic senators might subscribe to Lodge's reservations rather than lose the treaty altogether.[80] That proved to be a miscalculation: loyal Democrats stood with the president, and the treaty failed of ratification in November.

The scene between the frail president intractably upholding his honor and the equally determined Republican leader was replayed in March

1920. Baruch urged compromise upon the president and was rebuffed. Despite Wilson's accusations of apostasy, Baruch remained close to him for the rest of the president's days, closer to him than anybody else except for Mrs. Wilson; Secretary of State Bainbridge Colby; Wilson's secretary, Joe Tumulty; and his doctor, Admiral Cary Grayson. But the maintenance of that relationship required that Baruch publicly eschew reservations.[81] In the end, it mattered not what compromises Baruch and his friends wanted as long as others remained fixed in their autumn 1919 positions.

ENCOUNTER WITH *The Economic Consequences of the Peace*

On 19 March 1920, the day the Senate refused to approve the treaty with Lodge's reservations, John Maynard Keynes was on the minds of Baruch and his fellow Wilsonians. For about a month, Washington had buzzed with gossip concerning Keynes's recently published book, *The Economic Consequences of the Peace.* The English economist, a technical representative for his government in high-level financial negotiations at the Paris Peace Conference, had sharply assailed the treaty as inconsistent with the Fourteen Points' liberality and as the product of tawdry backroom political compromises that would bleed vanquished Germany and eventually disrupt the victor's peace. That argument reinforced Reservationist accusations that Wilson's wiles and wisdom had deserted him in Paris; American interests demanded better protection than could be found in a treaty that essentially catered to French and British political and economic requirements. Whatever hope had remained that the Senate would ratify the treaty, *sans* reservations, seemed to have been obliterated by Keynes's charges.

Baruch firmly believed that Keynes's malicious dagger was the one that ultimately killed the treaty. A month before the vote, a Wilsonian senator had told Baruch that he found Keynes's book more compelling than any other interpretation of the treaty. No doubt others whom Baruch sought to convince used Keynes to suggest that they were otherwise persuaded. He was incensed that people did not see Keynes as dishonest and duplicitous: "He may be a good economist; but the impression he left upon all of us in Paris was that of an able man of liberal views, yet who was always jealous of the position of the British Exchequer. We never felt certain after discussing a matter with him that his understanding was ours if it suited him otherwise."

Toward Keynes, Baruch bore a resentment the rest of his life. Baruch had other enemies, rivals, and adversaries, all of whom he treated with civility and equanimity, even with a touch of geniality. Life was too short to bear grudges—except against John Maynard Keynes, one of the few persons to qualify as a Baruch bête noire. In 1950 he would tell Winston Churchill that Keynes, then dead for more than four years, "was the man who did more to destroy America's steps toward international cooperation after World War I, than all the others put together. It was his devastating, unfair criticism of Woodrow Wilson that caused America to turn its back upon Europe." He repeated the charge in his memoirs, adding the irony that his "pernicious book, *The Economic Consequences of the Peace* did so much to bring about the very consequences he claimed to fear."[82]

What crime had Keynes committed? He had demeaned and deprecated the practical idealism of Wilsonian liberalism for American liberals. But was Keynes or his book responsible for the defeat of the treaty and the reemergence of isolationism? Keynes's biographer, Sir Roy Harrod, argues that the book's appearance in the United States came too late to influence the treaty vote: for all the furor it engendered, the book probably only reinforced a few hostile opinions; it hardly ordained the treaty's defeat.[83] Of course the book contributed to postwar disappointment. But Baruch and the Wilsonians themselves contributed to the incipient isolationism with their constant depiction of the British as cunningly pursuing their own national designs at the expense of American taxpayers and business interests—even if the characterization was essentially accurate! As we have seen, divergent Anglo-U.S. interests inhibited postwar economic and political cooperation; Keynes merely confirmed the fact that mutual assistance had given way to national competition.

What embittered Baruch enough to exaggerate Keynes's importance was the English economist's savage attack on Wilson. Baruch was correct in his appraisal of it; it was devastating and unfair. "*The Economic Consequences of the Peace* takes its place as one of the finest pieces of polemic in the English language," asserts Harrod, and it is unlikely that his biased claim is errant. Its language has an elegance, wit, and sting often imitated by Keynes's disciples but never duplicated. Baruch was ruefully in awe of Keynes's "literary barrage," as well he might be. Looking at the book as a work of history or economics or as a contemporary tract, it is difficult to disagree with Harrod that it is "a great masterpiece, . . . a work of art." Paradoxically, Baruch could concur with Keynes's arguments concerning the issues of peace; at best, their policy differences were subtle, concerned with national interests and the levels of reparations and their timing. Yet their economic prescriptions agreed in principle. They both wanted to limit the sum of reparations and to fix the figure soon enough to restore Germany to her place in the west's economy; they both dreaded inflation, albeit less than state price controls that would limit free enterprise. What enraged Baruch was that Keynes appeared to have affixed blame for the conference's failures upon the

Americans' incompetence and intransigence; and he hurled his accusations with "ruthless and terrible character sketches [and] . . . invective."[84]

Wilson disappointed Keynes: "We had indeed quite a wrong idea of the President." He had seemed very different to Keynes during the war. From afar, Keynes saw in Wilson the intellectual qualities that Baruch perceived up close. But in Paris, Keynes saw another Wilson: "The President was not a hero or a prophet; he was not even a philosopher; but a generously intentioned man, with many of the weaknesses of other human beings, and lacking that dominating intellectual equipment which would have been necessary to cope with the subtle and dangerous spellbinders whom a tremendous clash of forces and personalities had brought to the top as triumphant masters in the swift game of give and take, face to face in Council,—a game of which he had no experience at all." Keynes had anticipated an intellectually worthy adversary, but Wilson turned out to be "a blind and deaf Don Quixote" dealing with shrewder, more cultivated politicians. Celebration in 1918 turned to condescension and contempt in 1919. Europe waited upon the most powerful nation in the world to lead, but its leader "had thought out nothing; when it came to practice his ideas were nebulous and incomplete. He had no plan, no scheme, no constructive ideas whatever for clothing with the flesh of life the commandments which he had thundered from the White House. . . . he could not frame their concrete application to the actual state of Europe." Moreover, Wilson arrived in Paris "ill-informed," which Keynes considered understandable. Less forgivable for him was Wilson's apparently "unadaptable . . . unresourceful . . . slow-minded and bewildered" response to the "swiftness, apprehension and agility of a Lloyd George." Keynes's portrait of Wilson reinforced American misgivings that Yankee virtues were no match for European artifice.

The president's economic advisers were of little help, according to Keynes. Without mentioning Baruch, Keynes appraised them as "a very able group of businessmen; but they were inexperienced in public affairs, and knew (with one or two exceptions) as little of Europe as [Wilson] did." Yet Keynes suggested that Wilson might have done better had he followed the lead of his economic advisers.[85]

The corrosive cynicism of *The Economic Consequences of the Peace* challenged Wilsonian idealism. "The main difficulty with brother Keynes," wrote Baruch, "is that he has no faith in human nature. He thinks everybody is a knave and fool, and will do nothing that is just and wise, but only things which are destructive, selfish and without wisdom." Baruch did not quarrel with the view that Keynes was a brilliant analyst. In human relations, however, Baruch considered him sophomoric, "a petulant and spoiled child."[86] To him, Keynes was temperamentally incapable of adjusting economic logic to political complexities.

Keynes had crossed swords with the Wilsonians in Paris; in the words of a countryman, he was one who had "thrown up the sponge and gone away." He had pressed the Americans to employ their enormous wealth in behalf of European recovery by the simple step of cancelling inter-Allied debts. The Americans had steeled themselves against such blandishments. In April, Keynes advanced a broad scheme for financing European prosperity with what "amounted to a sort of Marshall Plan, albeit on a small scale." Vance McCormick's initial response was cautiously favorable, if only because it was right that the richest nation should aid its bankrupt associates. But, he quickly noted, "the more the plan is studied the less enthusiastic our people become. It is the same old game, . . . to get the United States to underwrite their debts." The Wilsonians were fearful of a British raid upon the American Treasury. When Wilson asked Thomas Lamont for an opinion of Keynes's plan, the banker was quick to label it "impracticable."[87] By early May the Wilsonians had firmly rejected Keynes's scheme.

The affair left Keynes badly wounded. Lord Robert Cecil noted that he was "very depressed about it." Keynes himself privately conceded "most bitter disappointment [over] the collapse of my grand scheme for putting everyone on their legs." The Americans turned it down, he said, "as a most immoral proposal which might cost them something and which senators from Illinois would not look at. They had a chance of taking a large, or at least a humane view of the world, but unhesitatingly refused it. *Wilson . . . is the greatest fraud on earth*." Keynes's illusions had been shattered; his idealism had turned sour. Worse, he took it as a personal defeat. Cecil's perspective on Keynes attests to that:

> The difficulties of the position are a little complicated by the peculiarities of Keynes' character. He has a mind of very exceptional ability, slightly academic in its character and very intolerant of fools. Recently he produced an extremely ingenious scheme for providing large sums of money for everybody by a kind of joint guarantee of German indemnity bonds. The Americans rejected it, and for various reasons I think they were right; but Keynes is bitterly grieved, and rather inclined to say, "If you won't have my scheme, no other is good."[88]

That was mid-May, a time when Keynes admitted to being "utterly worn out, partly by work[,] partly by depression at the evil round me. . . . I am quite at the end of my tether and must have a holiday." Still he worked on another financial plan, which Baruch found generally acceptable. But by then nothing could alleviate his fatigue or detract from the impending tragedy of an unjust treaty. Keynes had to flee Paris. On 5 June he sent Lloyd George a letter of resignation and told Norman Davis, "I am slipping away on Saturday from this scene of nightmare. I can do no more good here. You Americans are broken reeds, and I have no anticipation of any real improvement in the state of affairs."[89] Within a few weeks he began to write *The Economic Consequences of the Peace*.

"My mind has crossed a Rubicon. I have struck my tents and am on the march," he boasted to Davis months later amidst public uproar surrounding the book. He found it "comical" that the bitterest denunciations of his book and most vehement defenses of the treaty came from the United States. He was indifferent to the howls of outrage that emanated from the Wilsonians. Even so, he exchanged ideas with Norman Davis in an effort to show his American adversaries that though "we agree so much, . . . I can only regret we don't agree more."

They agreed on what the treaty should have said, but disagreed on the one that existed. Davis argued the Wilsonian view that expedience in the name of achieving political stability justified a disappointing treaty; adjustments of reparations would follow in a world at peace and rational again: "With a quickened public conscience and even a more enlightened selfishness, the defects of the Treaty should take care of themselves." But Keynes retorted with a forecast that two years hence at the most the treaty would be a dead letter, done in "by the mere march of events." Keynes professed to be amused but otherwise unconcerned by the political division engendered in the United States over his book. That it encouraged greater American isolationism caused no regret in his mind, nor did he perceive it having any impact upon Europe. He declared prophetically: "There is very little you can do for us at this moment. But a time will come again, not too long hence, when it will be for America to decide very great issues." Besides, Keynes had intended to undermine the political standing of the treaty's signers. His book was designed to achieve "a far-reaching revulsion of opinion on the part of the *general public*" against the politicians. As for his characterization of Wilson, Keynes denied that he had intended malevolence toward a man whom he considered "a pitiful and tragic figure, for whom I feel a genuine sympathy and who in spite of everything was the one member of the Four who was *trying* to do right." Keynes gave Wilson the moral benefit of his doubt by portraying him as an inept victim of Europe's sinister diplomats. Considering the "perfidious Peace," Keynes believed that he had done Wilson a service by treating him as "a fallen hero," although he could appreciate that the Wilsonians might not see it that way.[90]

But the Wilsonians needed to show Americans that in the world of European realpolitik they had succeeded as well as Americans could. Therefore, they had little choice but to defend the treaty and their president against the accusations by Keynes and their political opponents that they had been made dupes of by the wily Europeans. That need to justify himself, Wilson, and his colleagues in the eyes of American public opinion would be the occasion of Baruch's initial foray into the world of books, *The Making of the Reparation and Economic Sections of the Treaty*.

Baruch had no facility whatever for writing books, but he felt deeply that some response to Keynes and Wilson's domestic enemies was called for. Moreover, it was not merely a matter of affirming the American delegation's superior morality, but also one of answering, in the words of his book's dust jacket, "the all-important question for this country: Were America's interests protected at the Peace Conference?" Baruch assuredly answered in the affirmative, but *The Making of the Reparation and Economic Sections of the Treaty* was his book only in that he was its impressario. Some of the economic and technical advisors in Paris did the actual writing and editing of the book, the foremost contribution coming from the U.S. counsel on the conference's Reparations Committee, John Foster Dulles.

About two months after the appearance of Keynes's book in Washington, Baruch sent word to Dulles that it was worth $10,000 to Baruch for about two weeks of Dulles's time to prepare a book on the writing of the economic sections of the treaty. Dulles responded with a draft on the history of the reparation sections, the work he was most familiar with; others would write on various economic sections.[91] A few weeks after he accepted Baruch's commission, Dulles began to circulate drafts of the book to Norman Davis, Vance McCormick, Bainbridge Colby, Thomas Lamont, and others, urging them to give it a careful reading because Baruch was "very anxious that the final work represent the story of what happened in a way which all of us who worked on this part of the Treaty will agree with." Thus, Baruch wanted a definitive Wilsonian response to Keynes. Even senior officials in the Department of State read galleys of the book, at least a couple of them commenting regretfully that it was such an obviously biased interpretation as possibly to diminish its ultimate impact.[92] Despite the department's desire for a more judicious view of the treaty, Baruch saw the book as a necessary weapon in a polemical war.

Written in the first person, Baruch's book asserted that all virtue in the treaty was directly attributable to the best efforts of Wilson and the American delegation. For example, the "minimizing of the vengeful elements of the treaty were due in largest measure to Woodrow Wilson." Only the American delegation presented "any definite scheme of reparation"; other nations persisted in offering vague declarations of the wrongs done them by Germany. The Americans argued heroically against extravagant Allied demands that Germany pay war costs, but finally yielded to pleas by British liberals for understanding of their domestic political needs. British leaders would not fix moderate reparation sums. At the same time, the Americans had to protect their claims to Allied debts. They were practicing the fine compromising art of the possible. In a passage that seems written in direct reply to Keynes, Baruch argued: "To expect that these problems could receive any wise final solution at the Peace Conference itself discloses a visionary confidence that ignores the complexity of the questions and the difficulty of the conditions under which the peace negotiators had to labor." So the Americans made concessions postponing resolution of the issue of reparations in order to secure a treaty.

Baruch's book fared better with Keynes than it did with the State Department. Keynes was less bothered that Baruch's book was an apologia than that Baruch's publication of confidential documents enabled him to relate "a fuller tale than any Englishman could, and on the whole a faithful one." Baruch, Keynes said in a *Manchester Guardian* review, was "one who (to my way of thinking, at least) held during the conference broad and enlightened views, and did his best to uphold them (though not to the death), and now explains without temper, with much candour (that is to say, if we sometimes substitute for the printed words what one can discern between them), and a singular freedom from personalities, why he acquiesced in something so very far from what he himself thought wisdom." Baruch's version of the conference elicited Keynes's sympathy. The Americans had compromised their ideal peace in favor of stabilizing European governments. Thus, Baruch's central theme, as interpreted by Keynes, was that "it is not fair to criticise the American delegation for what they yielded without making allowance for what they withstood." And in that, Keynes declared, "I agree with him." Baruch celebrated American compromises that Keynes considered "unsound solutions"; "but one sees what he means," the reviewer said. Indeed, Keynes conceded "that the President being what he was, and the Allied leaders being what they were, then in the situation that Mr. Baruch describes the result could not have been otherwise." Nevertheless, Keynes was dismayed that Baruch and his fellow Americans were so sincere and so sound, and yet put their signatures to a document they knew to be "empty and [full] of professions which are disingenuous."

Though Baruch best remembered the Keynes review for its characterization of his "colorless" style, he did note that Keynes applauded the book's "significance as a human and historical document." He commented in his memoirs, "I suppose I should have been grateful to have escaped so lightly, and not to have been subjected to a full Keynesian literary barrage." Actually, Keynes was more complimentary than Baruch cared to recall. Keynes applauded the book's "enlightening method, . . . simplicity [and] candour." Although it was ponderously written, Keynes believed that

> if it were written with more art, it would tell less. It powerfully
> illumines history, and reveals the secret springs of human nature.
> It takes the private citizen of discerning mind behind the scenes of
> the modern world of diplomacy and tells him how "able and high-

minded persons" justify their presence there. I wonder if Mr. Baruch is always aware how much he here discloses.

. . . Mr. Baruch's book is sincere, and he has done truth a service.[93]

But Baruch never forgave Keynes for his cavalier treatment of Wilson in *The Economic Consequences of the Peace.*

Some of Baruch's friends in the early 1920s worried that the fading Wilson wielded too much influence upon the speculator. In the opinion of a journalistic crony, Baruch possessed an intellect that recognized Wilson's mistakes and a heart that adhered completely to any cause of the fallen president. That was simplistic nonsense. Wilson's political errors aside, the foreign events of the early postwar era demonstrated to Baruch that the Wilsonian analysis was being confirmed. Wilson's blunders were not nearly as great as America's. Without America in the League of Nations, Baruch told Louis Loucheur, Europe would witness a German resurgence and domination of the western half of Eurasia while Japan held sway over its eastern half. Stabilization was improbable, he warned: "Most anything can happen in Europe when there is an absence of a balancing wheel such as America was during the Peace Conference." If Germany established its hegemony over Europe, then America would have to share responsibility for the consequences, "because we did not live up to our promises to our allies or to the written promise given to Germany in the terms of the Armistice." Intellectually, he insisted, the treaty had been a triumph. Baruch was convinced that "the American businessmen at Paris held their own with the trained diplomats of Europe." Then what went wrong? His diagnosis was terse and inelegant: "America welched." No matter, like Wilson, like his fellow Wilsonians, and like the liberals in the United States and Great Britain, including Keynes, Baruch saw the outlines of the future with enough confidence to predict, "America will have to take her place in the world sooner or later."[94] And when that day came, Baruch would be there playing his role as a torchbearer of the Wilsonian faith in an American role in world stabilization.

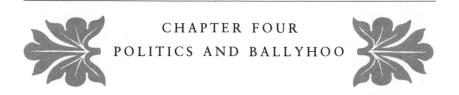

CHAPTER FOUR
POLITICS AND BALLYHOO

Baruch was at a crossroads in 1920. The eclipse of Wilson from public life was coincident with the failing health of both his parents. He often pointed to the president and his father as the men who had the greatest influence upon his public life. Both had imparted to him a sense of the spiritual quality of public service in behalf of good causes. It was only natural then that, at a time when both declined in vigor, Baruch should pick up their fallen flags. The influence of Wilson upon Baruch came well into his maturity, but it actually reinforced the example of public involvement set by his father, Dr. Simon Baruch.

Dr. Baruch was a prosperous and socially prominent physician who sought to influence New York's thinking on issues of public health during the progressive era. A considerably more verbal man than his eldest son, distinguished in his seventies by white hair and a white goatee, Dr. Baruch was in demand as a public speaker and not at all bashful about using the editorial pages of the *New York Times* to propagate his opinions on health and social controversies. Dr. Baruch's activities and his life's experiences made good press copy. He was a Victorian gentleman who could speak extensively about the chivalrous men he had seen on both sides during the Civil War. By this time he was an elder statesman of American medicine who constantly reminded his audience of his half century of experience. His image as a venerable sage, presented to the public during the first two decades of the century, would be projected over the next three decades by his son, albeit on other issues.

Foremost among the causes dear to Dr. Baruch's heart, and perhaps the least controversial, was hydrotherapy. Long a crusader for free public baths for the poor, he had cajoled the city of New York into building a bath on the lower East Side in the late nineteenth century. In 1911 he battled for free public baths in Coney Island, expressing misgivings about a location "not convenient to the dwellings of the working people," but determined that if it were built it should be free to them.

Any lecture by Dr. Baruch on the "health-giving" effects of baths was newsworthy, and he could not resist commenting upon matters beyond hydrotherapy. In one letter to the editor of the *New York Times*, he warned that the city was foolishly filling its rivers with sewage and that "when the schoolboy of the future shall be asked to describe Manhattan Island he will answer—a body of land surrounded by sewage." Because the river currents could not be depended upon to flush the waste into the sea, "rapid transit for the health-menacing sewage is at least as urgent as rapid transit of rent-menacing population." Likewise, he warned that pasteurization of milk for babies was a social imperative. But one of his greatest health crusades had less to do with the mass of Americans than with its elites: he wanted a spa at Saratoga to equal any in Europe.[1]

Dr. Baruch also joined the debates that resulted in the Eighteenth and Nineteenth Amendments to the Constitution, those decreeing prohibition and women's suffrage. His opposition to alcoholic beverages was moderate and based principally upon fears that society was being fed nonsense concerning the health benefits of alcoholic beverages, which encouraged immoderate consumption. He derided arguments that alcoholic beverages had "a certain food value" or were an agreeable stimulant. His opposition was confined to distilled liquors, rather than beer or wine: he endorsed beer on the grounds that its refreshment kept workingmen away from hard liquor.[2]

The most controversial of Dr. Baruch's crusades was against feminism, and in this matter he was joined heartily by Mrs. Baruch. Belle S. Baruch chaired the antisuffrage committee of the City Federation, a responsibility which led her to celebrate that men "have always guided and protected us" while denouncing "the unholy alliance of suffrage, feminism, and socialism."[3] Dr. Baruch likewise assailed feminists for thinking that they could contribute to medical research. Women were intelligent, he affirmed, but they were biologically incapable of any originality leading to the expansion of knowledge; he did allow, however, that they could be suited for a practice of medicine. When Professor Charles A. Beard of Columbia University accused him of spouting antidemocratic theology, Dr. Baruch responded by leaning on his half century of observation and charging the historian with demagoguery.[4]

Significantly, Dr. Baruch's manner and use of the press to establish himself as a public sage on health and social issues would be duplicated later by his son on matters of political economy. Baruch *fils* was a chip off the block. What he learned from his father was to use the newspaper columns and his own prominence to advance public causes dear to his heart and field of special interest. He later remembered his debt to his father by contributing handsomely to causes and institutions Dr. Baruch had espoused.

Likewise, in Baruch's mind, Wilson assumed a Christlike significance; Baruch assumed the role of a disciple who would carry the word long after the passing of the martyred president. In a sense that was what Wilson himself intended. In the waning years of his life he had drawn about him the most faithful of his followers and had exhorted them to collect others who would preach the gospel of liberalism and the League of Nations. The teachings of Woodrow Wilson would have to be carried on by the likes of a reformed Wall Street gambler named Baruch, and for that task he indeed considered himself blessed.

Wilson himself had encouraged Baruch to gather about him all the publicists he needed for the propagation of Wilsonian policies and to buy newspapers that would teach the American people what Wilson had taught Baruch. He personally implored Baruch and other Wilsonians to involve themselves ever more intimately in politics and policy making. He encouraged them in believing that they had been morally correct and that, if they were true to his precepts, they would witness one day the fulfillment of his preachings, although he would not be there to enjoy it. This was a spiritual crusade, he advised them, and such undertakings transcended material endeavors. The day following Wilson's death, Baruch, though personally agnostic, indicated that he took his apostolate seriously by articulating the religious metaphor:

> The greatest figure of the century has passed, but no man of any age has left a richer, truer heritage for mankind. As the Ten Commandments and the Sermon on the Mount have for thousands of years survived sneers and disobedience to remain the true outline of the relationships that should prevail among men, so Woodrow Wilson's concept of the League of Nations will survive disparagement, blindness and attack as the true outline of the relationship that must prevail among peoples. The human race, oppressed by greed, ambition and war, will trace its evolution into world peace to the thought and labor of this eminent American.[5]

Wilson would have relished Baruch's sentiment on that occasion, for his final years had been preoccupied with the American entrance into the League of Nations, in order to implement a lasting peace. Although the Wilsonians knew that the League's day in America was past, their leader had prepared them throughout his presidency for influence upon a great range of issues confronting policy makers in the twentieth century.

Baruch's use of the word "peoples" was in itself consciously Wilsonian. When talking about the League he might have used "countries," but Wilsonian ideology always aimed at peoples rather than the governments.

Thus, his war message had been intended for the Germans who would rebel against the kaiser's "imperialistic rule and military autocracy." When Wilson discoursed upon the problems confronting Europe and America following the war, he could be a spellbinding instructor. "I have never witnessed in any one individual a more complete and masterly understanding of such wideflung interests and such complicated problems," wrote one acolyte following a presidential analysis of the state of the world.[6]

Wilson sought to convince his followers that his ideas were indispensable in building world stability in the twentieth century. Yet, he warned, they should not equate stability with social inertia or the reestablishment of reactionary ideas and power. For this reason, in conversations concerning possible candidates for the Democratic nomination in 1920, Wilson rejected the name of John W. Davis, his solicitor general, because he was "a formalist. If you want a standstill, he is just the man to nominate." But, continued Wilson, "it is dangerous to stand still. The government must move, and be responsive to the needs and wishes of the people. Revolution is everywhere in the world and any body of men who think they could drive down stakes and pull the world up are the most dangerous enemies that our country has." Later he would warn his friends that the election of Harding would mean the sort of reactionary government that might inspire revolutionary discontent in the United States or war with Mexico as a diversion from brutal industrial conditions north of the border. Labor had to be mollified at once or capital would suffer horrendous consequences later: "The President spoke of the labor conditions and the impossibility of forcing labor back into the position it occupied prior to the war. He said that forces of this kind were like great rivers and that they could be dammed, but that ultimately these restraints would be broken and that there would be a great flood and then he added, rather quizzically, and there isn't apt to be any Noah to rescue us."[7]

His fear was that the United States would lack the leader it required to deal with such problems, a Noah that would enable society to endure. He proudly claimed that, despite some mistakes, he, like Theodore Roosevelt, "had accustomed the people to the idea of leadership and that it was better for a President to make mistakes than it was to do nothing and permit things to drift." A president had to have a program in domestic and foreign affairs and a determination to implement it. The White House was still a "bully pulpit." Stability called for the president to be enlightened and willing to enlighten others:

> He went on to say that the world had been safe for democracy, that that was an accomplished fact, that there was no sort of possibility that military government or autocratic power or hereditary dynasties would ever again control the destinies of the human race. But he said

Democracy itself had not yet been made an instrument of justice and the difficulty with the present situation is that it contains the elements of popular upheaval sweeping and even revolutionary in character, and that the need of the present moment was men in public life who sensed this situation and who had the character and the vision to apply the proper remedies.[8]

From the utterances and writings of Baruch and other Democrats, it is plain that Wilson hammered at these points with them, cajoling them to be true counterrevolutionaries by eschewing class interests in favor of progressivism that defused conditions ripe for disorder and radicalism. Although never greatly sympathetic to proletarian causes, Baruch was receptive to enlightened strategies in the nation's interest.

Seeking to broaden his contacts with intellectuals who wrote for the *New Republic* and others who called themselves social progressives, Baruch proclaimed his deepest devotion to Wilsonian idealism. "My heroes," he told William Allen White, "have always been those who have fought for an ideal or for a principle. Among these heroes whom I worship there are more who have failed than those who have succeeded during their lifetime." He would follow his martyred leader's failing principles regardless of the low degree of public acceptance. He assured Wilson that he would be eternally grateful "for your having pointed to me the finer and better things that men should be happy to live for, and if necessary, to suffer for. . . . victory for your ideals is merely deferred." Like Wilson, he recognized that labor was on the march; its direction required flexible responses by capital, lest the consequences include chaos or revolution. Fresh from Paris in 1919 he had told the press:

> We have all got to wake up to the fact that we are never going to have back the world that existed in 1914.
>
> First, and foremost, we have got to wake up to the new terms on which labor must be treated. Labor never again will be satisfied with the old conditions. A proprietary share in what he produces must be given to the working man, and he has to be taken into the management of the corporations by which he is employed. The working man must sit on the Boards of Directors. These conditions are here, and must be promptly recognized. Capital, instead of hanging back and passively resisting, should run to meet the advancing conditions, or else labor may not be satisfied with what it is entitled to and may demand more than its share.

Fairness required a rational response by the haves in order to forestall irrationality by the have-nots. More than anything else, everyone ought to have equality of *opportunity*. If, Baruch lectured a fellow Wilsonian, in the opening of this door of opportunity, human rights come in contact with property rights, property rights will have to give way enough to let human rights move on.

Equal opportunity, and the asserting of human rights above property rights does not in any sense mean Socialism, or the destruction of personal initiative. Every man and every woman with equal opportunity should be paid fully for his brain or brawn, and for his application. This does not mean there should be a levelling, or advancement, except by *one's own* effort.[9]

But how were "entrenched interests" to be persuaded that to yield a bit to the worker was not only morally correct but in the reactionaries' best interest? Here is where Baruch hoped that the "spirituality" of Wilsonism would take hold of the businessman and convince him that the struggle between capital and labor was not one to divide spoils but one of decency and destiny—"to make this country and the world what it should be!" If capitalists listened to the moral arguments of the worker, they would not be blinded by their fears. In Baruch's enlightened capitalism, those "who are endeavoring to improve their condition" and "give expression to higher motives and aspirations . . . have always been the great moving force in the world."[10]

However, Baruch was not about to change society overly much at once. "We must move slowly," he told one progressive, "then pause to consolidate our position, and move on again." He feared that "there is a mental Bolshevism confusing the minds of all the people of the world and none more so than ourselves." Lest some of his sympathies for the working man be misconstrued, Baruch declared, "I am not a Socialist, and I think their propaganda a mistake." Wilsonian liberalism sought to humanize an otherwise harsh system, to create a society amenable to orderly change, to stabilize the world, and to deter communism. The choices were quite simple: "The world must decide between the constructive radicalism of Woodrow Wilson or the destructive radicalism of Lenine."[11]

Baruch considered the prosperity of the twenties illusory and ephemeral. Republican policies ran counter to Wilsonian idealism. He tried to influence Mark Sullivan's history *Our Times* to portray the "spiritualism" of Wilson in sharp contrast to the Republican administrations that succeeded his. He also attempted to convince the political writer Frank Kent that basic differences between the two parties illuminated the innate progressivism of the Democrats. Democrats stood for equality of opportunity regardless of birth: "That is what has attracted the foreign population so much to the party." With Wilson's "Golden Age of Noble Purpose," as Baruch dubbed it, the true character of the Democratic party had been made plain. Here Baruch's "idealism" reached absurdity: "Our party has more of inspirational or, if I may say so, religious fervor back of it. If Christ had been mortal, he would have been a Democrat—certainly not a Republican. So all the great figures of history which [sic] have tended to liberate the thoughts and the corporal existence of man would have been Democrats."[12]

At any rate, he had cheerfully accepted the responsibility of furthering the careers of Democrats who reflected Wilsonian idealism, publicizing policies he construed as consistent with this philosophy, and molding himself into a vehicle for the triumph of Wilsonian stabilization. Essentially then, his life's work called for the propagation of stabilization concepts for the United States and the world.

THE PRIVATE SIDE OF A PUBLIC MAN

Baruch was determined to achieve a unique kind of fame, status, and power in American public life. That goal called for careful cultivation of a popular reputation for high-minded public activities suggesting sagacious statesmanship. People had to be led to believe that Baruch the speculator had been a casualty of the war; now his money labored mightily in behalf of public service, rather than redundant wealth.

The decision to find a different postwar career was made shortly before his appointment as head of the WIB. Not only did the WIB service have political value in mitigating his onerous reputation, but it was also consistent with the progressive ethos of the lawyers, publicists, and former businessmen who infested the Wilson administration. The Wilsonians sensed that, in the words of historian Christopher Lasch, "Private pursuits came to seem sterile and unproductive unless invested with political meaning." So Baruch took measures designed to signal onlookers that he would no longer pursue a speculator's career. He instructed his secretary and business manager, Mary Boyle, to advise his Wall Street landlord that he would not sign a lease for two years beyond 1918 because he did not anticipate remaining in business that long. Following his return from Paris in 1919, reporters outside the White House asked him if, because he denied political aspirations, he would be returning to Wall Street. "Never again," he replied. "I was a gambler once, and for many years was a member of the New York Stock Exchange, but I am through." The sale of his seat on the exchange was meant to have both real and symbolic significance. He was above all else a Wilsonian dedicated "to the cause in which we are all enlisted." A servant to that cause had to be chaste, believing in "service without reward" of political office or financial gain.[13]

Cynics and Republicans doubted that the gambler could reform or refrain from pursuing personal privileges. At a Senate committee hearing on campaign funding in May 1920, he was asked about his business activities. "I haven't had time to get back into business. . . . I'm just a private citizen. I'm spending most of my time writing some books on economic subjects," he replied. At the time, Washington buzzed with rumors that Mrs. Wilson, Tumulty, and Baruch virtually ran the administration for the partially paralyzed president; thus, the senator must have felt safe in inquiring of Baruch, "You are assisting in some governmental activities, are you not?" Baruch's response was a crisp and swift "That is not correct. I am not." He told friends that as a consequence of wartime service his fortune had dwindled to about 60 percent of what it had been in 1916 and that he had had to sell off some of his bonds to pay his bills. Of course, he was hardly a pauper, but his diminished wealth and continued abstinence from business activity testified to his Wilsonian idealism. "This has not only been avoiding evil, but even the appearance of evil," he declared. To a senator from Iowa, who must have been doubtful that old speculators could learn new habits, Baruch averred:

> I saw clearly what the future was going to bring forth. In March, 1920 I publicly predicted that we had reached the zenith of scarcity and, therefore, of high prices. You know what followed. In December of the same year I publicly stated that we had reached the bottom of our troubles. Between . . . these two events it would have been possible for me to have made millions of dollars had I cared to speculate. But, again I repeat *that I have neither bought nor sold, nor entered into any gainful pursuit of any description.*[14]

However, Wilson's departure from the White House and Harding's normalcy made him feel less virtuous. Late in 1921 he confided to friends that he was about ready to make initial moves to return to business. For a long while he had entertained opportunities to buy a newspaper, a business venture that carried with it the redeeming virtue that Wilsonians desperately needed a press organ for their ideas on public policy. But by the last quarter of 1921 he had come to the conclusion that it would be a bad investment that even idealism could not improve. By the mid-1920s, Baruch was back in Wall Street, albeit without a seat on the exchange. He conceded that again he "made some money," but without any great personal satisfaction. He still wanted to run a railroad, in particular the New York Central. It was an unsettled mid-period in his life. Fresh from his public triumph, uncertain of his next move, he probed for new public and private endeavors without gaining any immediate gratification. His plans were uncertain: "I am 55 years of age, and I should like to get something to do for twenty more years." Yet on Wall Street he had to proceed cautiously, for every sudden rise in security prices revived rumors that he had resumed heavy speculative operations. The *New York Times* checked out these rumors and described him as an "investor" or "banker." He was no longer a Wall Street "operator." When Baruch leased new offices in the financial district so that he would be better located to oversee his business interests in the late 1920s, the *Times* reported: "Mr. Baruch has large security investments, but he has not been 'in the market' in the sense that Wall Street understands that term."[15]

Baruch professed no longer to understand Wall Street. During most of his speculative career he had been a bear. Prices that rose sharply alarmed him. One stock that paid handsomely for him was Texas Gulf Sulphur, yet the speculative fever that caught up with the stock in 1927 unnerved him. Advising his friend General John J. Pershing that he did not agree with tips that it should be purchased, Baruch argued that it already sold at almost twice what it was worth. So he gradually began to sell off his 121,000 shares, leaving others to take big risk gains in the next two years. As he reminded Pershing: "I told you some time ago that I was out of step with the market, and I have not gotten in step since."[16] But the prices would fall in line with Baruch by late 1929.

In a peripheral way, Baruch went back into railroading when Daniel Willard asked him to be a director of the Baltimore and Ohio in 1927. His longtime contacts in industry proved helpful to the railroad's declining traffic. During the next few years, Baruch interceded with American Smelting and Refining, Texas Gulf Sulphur, National Dairy Products, and International Harvester in an effort to send more business the railroad's way. The price to be paid for such favors was revealed when he began giving Willard advice on how to run his railroad. He urged B&O to increase profits by paying greater attention to freight than to passenger traffic, a point with which Willard was in hearty agreement. Later, in the depths of the Great Depression, he admonished Willard against overloading his payroll with unnecessary workers, lest the road find itself in greater debt to the banks and the Reconstruction Finance Corporation. Willard fretted that the Pennsylvania and New York Central holding companies might attempt a consolidation reminiscent of Morgan's Northern Securities Company, thereby bringing a revival of antitrust activity or at least foreclosing justified consolidation for years to come; could Baruch say something to his friends at Central? In 1935, Willard would acknowledge Baruch's services, writing, "I feel that you have a large uncollected bill against the company because of services rendered while you were on our Board of Directors."[17]

That Baruch could be of service to the B&O was possible because of a decades-old network of business contacts. His fortune had been made by knowing the people who dispensed significant inside information. As chairman of the WIB he broadened that network to include businessmen whose businesses seldom brought them in contact with a Wall Street speculator, many of whom were second- or third-level executives with great promise. In the 1920s he nourished those contacts through WIB reunions staged, when practical, every 11 November. He needed these contacts especially because he distrusted the usual published advisory services, and the speculative economy of the twenties baffled him. Moreover, he had less time than formerly to devote to purely business affairs; political activities increasingly claimed his attention.

And every summer he sailed for Europe, where he would renew his great friendships in England and France with Churchill, Clemenceau, and Tardieu, among other notables, and entertain the leisure class, or those who aspired to that status, at a rented estate—the ten-thousand-acre Fettersee in County Kincardine, Scotland—hunting grouse, pheasant, and snipe, with aristocratic retinues of servants to wait upon the hunters when they returned from the fields. He had to renew his fortune in order to enjoy this grand style, which included his fabulous South Carolina estate, Hobcaw Barony; there he showed hospitality to businessmen, politicians, and opinion leaders in the press, who came every winter at his invitation (one not easily declined) to enjoy the masculine recreation of hunting quail in the marshes and exchanging gossip with one of the most personable raconteurs one could ever hope to call a friend. Baruch spent profusely, and money always seemed to be a secondary consideration. He lavished it upon his causes—especially those that enhanced his reputation as a benefactor. People counted upon him for money, either for themselves or for their causes. He could not let them down, he could not continue to deplete his principal, he could not be a successful public man without being a successful businessman. With less time for business, with more obligations in public affairs, with more causes that required his financial interests, Baruch had need to replenish his fortune. He would never retire from speculation.

He was especially generous with Wilsonian friends and causes. Admiral Cary Grayson got $10,000 to invest in Continental Can; William G. McAdoo earned a retainer of $15,000 while he made the transition from public service to private practice in 1919; Hugh Johnson and George Peek were carried through their business crisis; the cost of publishing Samuel Gompers's autobiography was partially underwritten; and so on. Those were his unpublicized uses of his money. Other ventures in public service got press treatment: he helped subsidize Harry Garfield's Institute of Politics at Williams College; he contributed $250,000 for a study of war profiteering to be conducted by the Walter Hines Page School of International Relations of Johns Hopkins University.[18] Agricultural cooperatives were preferred social investments: he helped wheat farmers in the middle border states, tobacco farmers in Kentucky, and boll weevil-stricken cotton farmers in South Carolina.

Baruch subordinated his family to his public ventures. His wife and three children did not figure prominently in his life and are barely mentioned in the two volumes of his memoirs. In a rare mention of his wife after 1917, he wrote: "My wife had never enjoyed public life. She was happiest in the privacy of her family, pursuing her interest in music and in antique furniture, quietly helping good causes." One of his biographers called it "a relationship carefully screened from the public."[19] She seldom traveled with him or served as his hostess when he entertained outside New York; it was believed that she detested Washington and would not go to Hobcaw. Perhaps this arrangement satisfied Baruch because he considered her something of an alcoholic and frowned on any woman who took more than two drinks on any social occasion (even though some of his best political friends were seldom sober). His children disappointed him. At age twenty-one each received a legacy providing wealth and independence—another source of his later regret. His son and namesake married showgirls more than once and otherwise preferred obscurity to his father's fame. One daughter, Belle, never married; another, Renee, married but never had children. In his old age, Baruch would mourn the absence of grandchildren to carry on his name.

Baruch was very much of a womanizer; in the words of one woman friend, he was "a philanderer." Baruch admitted only to his reputation. "Sure, there're lots of lurid stories about me and women," he conceded. "I haven't denied them. Why should I bother?" He professed his love for his wife and expected that affirmation to be sufficient answer to any questions concerning his relations with women. But it was not always so. When Baruch was under consideration to head the WIB, Elihu Root was "very much disturbed" by stories that he was "taking up" with another man's wife who had previously been someone else's mistress. Chandler Anderson went straight to Baruch to learn that she was merely an old friend and "certainly is not his mistress at present."[20]

He was a very attractive man. Whether young or elderly, dark or white-haired, he was tall, distinguished, loquacious, courtly, masculine, a bon vivant. He enjoyed the company and attention of women and never seemed to be at a loss for them. "Women were forever finagling introductions to him," Helen Lawrenson remembered. While Annie Griffen Baruch stayed home minding antiques and social causes, Baruch availed himself of the adoration of women he encountered in Europe, Washington, or Saratoga. He might have had affairs, but he remained an ostensibly happily married man. His parents were greater objects of love than any living woman could have been. He confided to a friend, "Much unhappiness has come to me different times because I have never forgotten the woman I idealized as a young southern boy. It is very seldom they can come up to it." Baruch was a momma's boy, a fact that may account for Lawrenson's surprise upon discovering that her Don Juan was naive about sex.[21]

Still, reputation counts, however undeserved it may be, and Clare Boothe Luce enhanced Baruch's Lothario status. She met him while she was between marriages, when she was known as one of New York's most beautiful actresses. Fashion publisher Condé Nast, a friend and fellow womanizer, introduced them, and it soon became evident that Baruch did not consider her a passing fancy. He was sixty-one and she was twenty-nine when he took her to the Democratic convention in Chicago. It is probable that Baruch wanted exclusive rights to the much-sought-after Clare Boothe Brokaw, but marriage was out of the question for him, whose code did not include divorce for himself. (Mrs. Baruch lived until 1938; Baruch never remarried, although he outlived her by more than a quarter century.) Clare married Time-Life publisher Henry Luce, but she and Baruch remained friends. A decade after Baruch had taken her to the Chicago convention, Franklin Roosevelt recalled their affair: "You know she was Barney Baruch's girl. . . . Yes, he educated her, gave her a yacht, sent her to finishing school, she was his girl."[22]

It cannot, however, do any good to speculate further about Baruch as a family man. Suffice it to say that his correspondence is full of loving references to his children, and the file on his namesake son is evidence of a concerned father who hoped his son would follow in his footsteps. Undoubtedly he can be accused of patronizing "Mr. Junior," but even a purchase of a seat on the stock exchange can be an act of love. A public man, he set his own standards as a husband and a father.

THE "AMERICAN DISRAELI"

Baruch never considered standing for elective office. In fact, he considered himself a potential liability to others in politics because of his enormous speculative wealth and Jewish birth. Both made him hesitant to accept appointive office. He may have been paranoid on this matter, but regular and frequent assaults upon his heritage and business justified such paranoia.

Washington had many Jew-haters, many of whom were Baruch's friends or acquaintances. He was either the exception to or the confirmation of their prejudice. Respectable Jew-haters preferred their Jews poor and quiet; their stereotype was that Jews were rich, egotistical, and ostentatious. It was bad enough that Jews frequently made their money in disreputable ways without their conspicuously flaunting that wealth. When President Wilson had discussed a position for Baruch with Josephus Daniels, the North Carolina editor reminded him that Baruch was "somewhat vain," to which Wilson responded, "Did you ever see a Jew who was not?" The young Eleanor Roosevelt liked the lawyerly, crusading Louis Brandeis and the genteel Morgenthau family, but they were exceptions to her distaste for Jews. Invited in 1918 to a party for Baruch, she swore she would "rather be hung than be seen" there; she went and later reported, "The Jew party [was] appalling. I never wish to hear money, jewels and . . . sables mentioned again." Lincoln Colcord was another progressive with greater regard for the uses of Baruch's money than for wealthy Jews; he courted Baruch's friendship in 1917 even as he confided to his sister that "Mrs. Baruch is a typical rich bounder of a Jew woman, who is trying her damnedest to marry her daughter" to the Colcords' brother.[23] (Of course, Mrs. Baruch and her daughter were Episcopalians.) It is difficult to say who among Baruch's political friends was not a Jew-hater.

In late 1919, in the waning years of the Wilson administration, he could have had any of several cabinet openings. The president's secretary, Joe Tumulty, favored Baruch for the Department of the Interior; the resignation of William C. Redfield as secretary of commerce set off a spate of rumors that Baruch would be his successor; and it was said that McAdoo wanted Baruch as his successor in the Treasury and that Baruch "had hypnotized the President." But even to consider Baruch seemed "incomprehensible" to some Democrats. Complaining that stock speculation was at its highest point in fifty years, one governor of the Federal Reserve Board opined that "to choose the star stock gambler of the country would be disastrous to the Democratic Party." Apparently Wilson concurred, as did Baruch, that politically Baruch was unavailable.[24] He was odious either as a gambler or as a Jew.

He was a Wall Street Jew. He never denied either part of that combination; he felt no reason to be ashamed of the way he had made money and he had no reason to be ashamed of his ancestry. Besides, he believed that he had earned his money without depriving anyone else of an honest dollar, and his Jewishness was a matter of his family's history. As a nationalist and a firm believer in the public interest, he was hurt by accusations of putting pecuniary interests and the circumstances of his birth ahead of his Americanism.

Yet there were politicians, journalists, and other public figures who exploited the notoriety attached to his prominence. In the spring of 1920 an Illinois congressman accused him of making windfall profits in copper speculations early in the war; after nine months the Republican repeated his accusations. Then Baruch hit back calling him "an ordinary damn liar" and daring him to prove the accusations. The next day three senators rose to Baruch's defense, and by the middle of 1921 Baruch was proclaiming his victimization by unprovable slurs.[25] During the 1920 campaign, William Randolph Hearst accused Baruch of leaking to Wall Street secret provisions of the treaty pertaining to the League of Nations. Earlier in the election year much was made of the fact that Baruch was a prime contributor to Democratic coffers. Nothing illegal was proved, but the mere suggestion that a Wall Street Jew gave money to elect Democrats suggested something sinister. Baruch complained that newspaper cartoonists "depict me as a man with hat in hand . . . as the most ugly and disagreeable Jew that they possibly can. . . . It is deliberately meant to arouse prejudice." Then, through his *Dearborn Independent*, Henry Ford stirred some anti-Semitism by charging Baruch with political ambitions, with wanting to become "America's Disraeli." At least, a friend puckishly wrote Baruch, "it assures to America a better looking Disraeli than England had."[26]

But Baruch was not amused by bigots, xenophobes, and anti-Semites in the early twenties. It was the heyday of the Ku Klux Klan, the aftermath of the Red Scare, a time of resurgent nativism; immigration restriction brought an end to the flow of fugitive peoples from the more remote parts of Europe. Some German Jews in Wall Street and their "unprejudiced" friends welcomed an end to the migration of Jews from eastern Europe to the United States, believing that Slavic Jews confirmed Jewish stereotypes. As Baruch complained of Ford's caricature of him, "he tries to make me out a boastful character, uncouth and uncultured."[27]

Baruch's friend, respected columnist Mark Sullivan, was among those who deplored the prejudice of the time, particularly because it "fails to discriminate—between the old Jews who have been with us and who are Americans like the rest of us; and, on the other hand, this new immigration of Jews which is different in many ways." Sullivan very carefully assured Baruch that nobody meant ill will toward German Jews, "whom everybody regards as the salt of the earth." They only became a problem because German Jews supported unrestricted immigration: "In short, I think these older Jews ought to be Americans first and Jews afterward." Baruch heartily agreed with this. He always claimed to be an American before being a Jew. He told Sullivan, "There is no room for argument on the point you raise. . . . I am never denying, but always stating the fact that I am a full blooded Jew . . . and I take second place to no one in being a pure American and in my pure Americanism."

Baruch believed that bigotry was the product partly of benighted lower-class minds, best exemplified by the Ku Klux Klan, and partly of the peculiarities of the victims themselves. He was ambivalent on the subject of discrimination. He could inquire about the difference between anti-Semitism in the Harvard Club and in the Ku Klux Klan and, in the same paragraph, approve the club's discrimination: "Mind you, I don't deny the right of any man to exclude from the club anybody he wishes. I do not quarrel with that whether they exclude the person for race, creed, color, fact, or fancy."[28]

Yet he represented himself as a victim of bigotry. When Mark Sullivan goaded him to take a leadership role in the Democratic party, Baruch declared that he could consider it "if it were not for anti-Semitism." Telling McAdoo that he would make a great president, he commented as the 1924 campaign approached, "It is too bad that you have to bear an additional burden of having me as a friend." Rather than exempting him from Jew-baiting, Baruch's wealth and fame seemed to beckon slander. He took his martyrdom in stride. He cautioned associates in public endeavors to anticipate vilification "because of my previous Wall Street connection and my race," urging that, "when I become a liability, please say so, and I shall become as quiescent as I have been active."[29]

But Baruch was less a victim of anti-Semitism than he would have us believe. Indeed, bigotry served his purposes. His prominence as the most publicized Jew in American public life in his time* automatically assured him of crank attacks from Henry Ford and Adolf Hitler. Yet he freely associated with biased Americans who discriminated against every Jew but Baruch. He allowed them to use his association with them to demonstrate their absence of the ordinary prejudice that characterized the lower-class bigots who joined the Klan. In turn, anti-Semitism served him with an excuse for operating in politics behind the scenes rather than seeking office. It was a crutch upon which he leaned to explain his extraordinary political function. This is not to say that he exaggerated anti-Semitism; its abundance in his time and in his milieu could not be inflated beyond belief. But it would have been overcome by Baruch if it could have been overcome by any Jew.

MCADOO'S WARWICK

In 1919, with the decline of Colonel House, many people in Washington suspected that Baruch had become what House had been, the president's chief advisor and confidant. Some power watchers called Baruch "Wilson's Warwick." Baruch considered such gossip "100 percent nonsense,"[30] and he was not usually given to false modesty. Besides, he could eschew such a role in the declining Wilson administration because it would be his in a succeeding McAdoo administration.

McAdoo and Baruch were natural allies within the Wilson administration. Both had been members of the New York Southern Society and promoters who had failed in their efforts to control railroads but had succeeded in Wall Street as mavericks (although McAdoo's wealth could not compare to Baruch's and McAdoo had not been the plunger Baruch was), and both looked to Woodrow Wilson for spiritual enrichment in public life. Son-in-law to the president, McAdoo was referred to, both in private conversation and in the press, as the "heir apparent" or the

---

*From the diary of Colonel House, 25 March 1920, comes the report that a Democratic official, Harry Marsh, "said that he has kept the dictograph record in which Baruch figures. Among other things, Baruch tells his companions that he expects to rank in history as the greatest of all Jews. In Baruch's opinion, Disraeli was the greatest, but times were so different then and opportunities were no [sic] so much wider to do big things that he felt certain that he could eclipse him."

"crown prince." McAdoo's was one of the success stories of the administration. Among its many southerners he was a charismatic leader. In
obtaining the WIB chairmanship, Baruch personally owed much to Mc-
Adoo's energetic and influential support. Assuming that Wilson would
adhere to the two-term tradition, both men looked forward to a McAdoo
run for the presidency in 1920.

Of all their promotions, making McAdoo president would be their
most challenging. Only days after Wilson's reelection in 1916 Baruch
discussed it with his WIB comrades. He planned to turn the WIB state
organizations into political vehicles for McAdoo—unless Wilson wanted
a third term. On that last point, Baruch seemed uncertain. Thus, Mc-
Adoo's decision to run for the White House hinged at the onset on a
future decision by the incumbent to step aside. But no such decision had
been made. While Baruch and others in 1919 moved the scene of their
operations to Paris, McAdoo sought a return to a law practice. In resigning his dual posts at the Treasury and at the Railroad Administration, he
professed interest only in replenishing his depleted personal fortune. Baruch did not think that McAdoo's private pursuits would interfere with
his presidential quest.[31]

McAdoo's departure from the administration came at an awkward
moment. Democratic setbacks in 1918 congressional races stunned both
Wilson and the party, and at a dinner of party leaders shortly after the
election, McAdoo was the object of some blame for the losses. He had
many enemies as well as friends. Some resented his occasionally high-
handed manner of administration. He had had numerous bureaucratic
conflicts, the railroad problems having given him an unwelcome visibility
in dealing with the nation's torturous transportation situation. And he
often served as a convenient surrogate for Wilson antagonists. His departure, an unexpected "thunderclap to Washington," together with recent
Democratic defeats, suggested reasons for resignation other than those
given by McAdoo. It was said that he was "financially embarrassed" by
living in wartime Washington while employed solely by the government.
Some gossip centered upon a possible policy dispute between McAdoo
and Wilson concerning government ownership of the railroads and ships
Washington had consolidated and built for the war exigency. Ever the
railroad entrepreneur, McAdoo objected to a governmental monopoly.
Also, and perhaps more importantly, it was rumored that McAdoo disagreed with another developing decision of the president: to seek a third
term. Contrary to earlier expectations, McAdoo would not enjoy the
president's support in 1920 because Wilson withheld it in favor of his
own candidacy.[32]

Nevertheless, Wilson insisted that he was not a candidate, although he
did not close the door on that eventuality. Early in 1919 he asked Vance
McCormick, then chairman of the Democratic National Committee,

whom he considered prospective candidates for president. McCormick replied that there were none announced, but McAdoo was the most active of the unannounced candidates. Colonel House then volunteered Hoover's name as a Democratic possibility and Pershing for the Republicans. Wilson said nothing about these names, launching instead into a discussion of his own political status. Circumstances might arise in which, he said, "he might be compelled to run." Significantly, Wilson's old fund raiser, Morgenthau, let it be known that McAdoo did not have his endorsement. Some Democrats, like Frank Polk, concluded that the early front-runner was losing ground. When Wilson took to the stump in pursuit of popular approval for his treaty, it did not require much imagination to liken the tour to that of an active candidate for reelection. But then Wilson was stricken, and his political availability faded with his health.[33]

During this time, Baruch remained certain of McAdoo's candidacy. Not only did he put McAdoo on a retainer, but among those with whom he talked politics he made it clear that there was only one candidate for him—McAdoo—and only one issue—the League. Yet Baruch knew that Wilson could put an end to the McAdoo campaign any time he chose. He was still the party's leader, whom it dared not repudiate, besides being the most visible personality in the Democratic party. Wilson, Baruch wrote, "is such a great Colossus that he has dwarfed us all."[34]

McAdoo's protean candidacy could not have its own life until Wilson withdrew. As Democrats prepared for the primaries and conventions that would select delegates to the 1920 national convention, Wilson let it be known that he wanted an open convention with delegates uninstructed for any candidate. Baruch quickly fell in line with that ploy, denying published reports that he was financing McAdoo's undeclared campaign and insisting that uninstructed delegates to the San Francisco convention best served the interests of representative democracy. Thus, McAdoo was a noncandidate, Wilson was a noncandidate, and Baruch was a nonsupporter. Baruch even went to the extent of denying knowledge of a McAdoo campaign organization because "Mr. McAdoo is not a candidate, as I understand it. . . . He doesn't want the nomination." Yet there existed what one senator called "this invisible McAdoo campaign," rounding up delegates without the tacit direction of McAdoo or of those closest to the noncandidate himself.[35] The stage was set for a clash between supporters of a McAdoo draft and those supporting the declared candidacies of A. Mitchell Palmer and Ohio Governor James M. Cox.

With almost three-quarters of the delegates to the convention uncommitted ten days before the convention, McAdoo seemed the nearly unbeatable favorite. Then in late June the picture changed radically. Wilson gave a *New York World* reporter an interview calculated to demonstrate that he was still physically and mentally fit for his job. That same day,

McAdoo announced the "unequivocal" withdrawal of his noncandidacy. The next day the *New York Tribune* headlined, "McAdoo Refuses to Enter Race, Wilson May Seek Third Term." Dining that night with Chandler Anderson, Baruch "seemed very much put out about" McAdoo's pullout. "Disgruntled," Baruch guessed that Cox or John W. Davis would be the most likely convention choices; he did not anticipate a last-minute boom for either Wilson or McAdoo.[36]

But the McAdoo candidacy was far from moribund, even if McAdoo had officially terminated it. Though his most obvious supporters, like Baruch, stayed away from San Francisco, delegates there waged a leaderless fight to give him the party's nomination. The alternatives to McAdoo made this necessary. Cox was the choice of anti-Wilson Democrats, but his antiprohibition stance made him an anathema to Bryanites. Davis was too much of an unknown quantity. The McAdoo candidacy continued to excite delegates enough for him to lead in the early balloting before Cox won the necessary two-thirds of the delegates on the forty-fourth vote. The Democrats were devastated.

The nomination fight caught Baruch between loyalties. Wilson evidently wanted a third-term draft, but staunch followers like Carter Glass and Baruch could not bring themselves to tear the party apart over the League and kill the president himself by pushing him beyond what his health could endure. At the same time, Baruch had been committed to McAdoo, whose sudden withdrawal had to leave his backers chagrined at the least. Baruch did not attend the convention because he no longer had a real candidate. He was still a Wilson man, endorsing the president's choice, Homer Cummings, for chairman of the Democratic National Committee, because to do otherwise would be "false to the old man."[37]

When Cox declared himself for the League following a visit with Wilson, Baruch lent the campaign his purse and hopes, for he could do no less. But he expected Cox's defeat, although the magnitude of it stunned and angered Baruch. "There was no referendum upon the League of Nations," he told Wilson. It was "a reflection of people's temperament rather than their judgment"; the "hyphenates" had voted for their former homelands.[38] In the wake of the debacle of 1920, the Democratic party needed Baruch. It was disorganized and heavily in debt. The Cox-appointed chairman of the Democratic National Committee, George White, and Treasurer Wilbur Marsh were incompetent and managed to alienate Wilsonian financial angels such as Baruch. Baruch prudently refused to join the ranks of Democrats calling for White's removal early in 1921. However, White proved unwilling to leave his party post of his own volition after six months of Baruch's patient anticipation. On 10 August 1921, Baruch suggested to Cox that the time had come to find another chairman. Asked by Senate Democrats to raise $40,000 for the party's candidate in a special New Mexico race, Baruch angrily told them that the party would not receive his further assistance while White retained the chairmanship. Joe Tumulty urged Baruch not to attach conditions to his money, but Baruch made it clear that he expected his wealth to give him influence in party affairs. On 21 September, White bowed to the pressure from Baruch and others and resigned. Congressman Cordell Hull of Tennessee replaced White, but Baruch insisted that a changeover did not give the party a lien on his fund raising.[39]

Labeled constantly as a McAdoo man and a barometer of McAdoo strategies, Baruch attempted to put himself above party factions without losing the McAdoo tie. He did not want to be taken for granted. While others gossiped that his money would buy the 1924 nomination for McAdoo, Baruch was telling McAdoo not to count on it. In 1922, Baruch informed McAdoo: "We do not know what the issues will be and it is wrong to tie the great Democratic party to the coat-tails of any individual." At the same time he told opinion makers like Mark Sullivan that "thoughtful men" such as his friend Otto Kahn rated McAdoo highly as a leader. Baruch wanted it both ways: to promote McAdoo without losing his independence of action. For, as another McAdoo backer noted, "McAdoo still has the advantage over any other one man, but he is losing ground—and has been for at least six months past." Baruch rebuffed McAdoo's request for a private railroad car for campaign trips, insisting that such a convenience would detract from his common man's image. He even suggested that both he and McAdoo would benefit if they scaled down the extent to which they were identified with each other by the public.[40]

Following Democratic gains in the congressional elections of 1922, Baruch edged closer again to McAdoo. Although he still had an open mind on a candidate as late as December 1923, he hailed McAdoo as "the logical man . . . the most available man . . . head and shoulders above every [other] man," and urged friends to "do whatever you can to spread a good opinion regarding McAdoo." But McAdoo ignored Baruch's advice against launching his candidacy early and against entering the Illinois primary.[41] He was determined to avoid any suggestion that his 1924 candidacy would be as hesitant as that of 1920. Baruch's words of restraint were ignored.

Early in 1924 disaster befell the McAdoo candidacy. On 1 February, oilman Edward L. Doheny, having already admitted to a Senate committee that Interior Secretary Albert Fall had been given money in return for oil leases at Teapot Dome, Wyoming, named McAdoo as another recipient of a retainer. McAdoo had done nothing wrong. He had served as special counsel to Doheny, who now openly conceded that he had been in the practice of bestowing money upon politicians where it might do him the most good. However, this raised the question in the public's mind whether McAdoo's retainers carried unsavory connections. McAdoo could deny any impropriety and insist that they constituted nothing more than the usual attorney-client relationship, but could he dispel suspicions that he was tainted with scandal?

The news broke just as McAdoo headed east to be at Wilson's side for what would be the former president's final illness. The sad occasion brought Wilson adherents together, including Baruch; and it was on 7–9 February that McAdoo learned how seriously Doheny's retainer had damaged his candidacy. Baruch reminded McAdoo that he had ignored earlier admonitions against accepting retainers from the rich. Along with his fund-raising crony, Tom Chadbourne, Baruch now counseled McAdoo to withdraw and announce that he sought to spare the Democratic party any harm, and subsequently denounce those who slandered his good name. Then a wave of sympathy would revive his candidacy. Others agreed on the strategic withdrawal. But campaign manager David Ladd Rockwell held firm to the charted course. Baruch and Chadbourne agreed that the accused McAdoo would have to prove himself in the court of public opinion.[42]

But Baruch brooded over his rejected counsel. He was "very much irritated" that political managers did not heed political financiers, but he responded to a plea for $10,000 because he "did not want to be in a position of not having helped at a very critical time." He told McAdoo, "I feel satisfied that if you had been left to your ideas, you would have done as I suggested, and I think you would have been a very great deal better off in every way." With the McAdoo campaign eroding and beset by dissension, the unhappiness of Baruch and Chadbourne stood out. As Breckinridge Long asked, "Who is going to put up the money if they don't?" In late March, Baruch bluntly told Long that McAdoo could not be nominated and that he would not make further contributions or encourage others to give. "We must not fool ourselves," Baruch admonished McAdoo, "in thinking that there is not considerable seepage going on amongst your people."[43]

McAdoo showed surprising success in spring primaries and state conventions. By mid-April, Baruch realized that he could not abandon McAdoo. In politics loyalty to a loser can sometimes be forgiven by winners; desertion of a winner is never forgotten by anybody. "I, of course, am going to stay along with McAdoo as long as he wants me to and as long as he desires to run out his string," Baruch told a mutual friend of theirs. McAdoo had been in telephone contact with Baruch, full of stories of successes yet unknown to the press and other politicians. By the end of May 1924, Baruch instructed his political client, Governor Albert Ritchie of Maryland, to be sure that two tickets were allotted Baruch for the July convention in New York's Madison Square Garden.[44]

It was the most embattled convention in American political history. McAdoo and Governor Alfred E. Smith of New York fought for days until John W. Davis, Wilson's solicitor general, took the nomination on the 103rd ballot. Baruch wearily paid Davis the perfunctory compliments owed the winner and left for a vacation in Europe. In time, Baruch would also put some distance between himself and McAdoo. He had been consulted by McAdoo throughout the convention and, after the seventieth ballot, had gone with Chadbourne to Smith looking for an arrangement whereby the New Yorker would withdraw in favor of their candidate. What they offered Smith is unknown, for Smith was on record against taking a vice-presidential nomination as a consolation prize.[45] It was Baruch's last effort in behalf of McAdoo's quest for the Democratic nomination.

When Baruch boarded the *Aquitania* on 10 July, he sailed away from Davis and McAdoo. In fact, he later claimed to have left *all* preconvention struggles behind him. He would ever after claim neutrality between Democratic contenders, explaining, as he did in his memoirs, "I learned a lesson from the frustrating events of 1924. I made up my mind never again to take part in the internecine fighting for the Presidential nomination. I would support the Party's candidates if I could. I would take my stand on issues. But I was determined that, from this point forward, I would have nothing to do with divisive and destructive political warfare between personalities. I have clung to that resolve to this day."[46] That was prudent of him. It enhanced the value of his money to the nominee. More importantly, if one discounts the significance of a preconvention commitment, Baruch would never be persona non grata in the winner's camp where his presence and words carried as much weight as his money—a concern that figured more prominently in the mind of a man who yearned to be appreciated for his advice as much as for his purse.

Baruch had concluded that it was in McAdoo's best interest and his own that he keep McAdoo from future presidential quests. But he did this as a good friend should, redirecting McAdoo's interests with loans of at least $55,000 for speculative ventures in real estate. Eventually, McAdoo would concede that he was out of politics, in search of more lucrative activities than his law practice, and grateful that Baruch had been "willing to carry me on those loans."[47] But he had come away from the 1924 convention determined to capture the next Democratic nomination or at least block Smith in the effort. Early in 1927, Baruch told McAdoo that he would not participate in another McAdoo campaign. Though he admired McAdoo's "sterling personal qualities," as a matter of principle he would abstain from any fight for a presidential nomination. To this, McAdoo responded that sometimes a fight is preferable to party harmony; besides, how could the differences of Smith's and his positions on prohibition be reconciled? Baruch ignored his question. Disclaiming support for any contender, he told the financially troubled

McAdoo that he should fulfill his business ambitions. He soothingly urged McAdoo to concentrate on his own best interests, politically "saw wood and make a living for yourself." After all, McAdoo was in his mid-sixties, Baruch was a decade younger, and "we have not much more than fifteen active years before us."

(More than two months before he gave this discouraging advice to McAdoo, Baruch had promised commitment to Governor Albert Ritchie of Maryland, agreeing to arrange "to give you a great send-off" in pursuit of a presidential nomination. His tone with the almost diffident Ritchie contrasted sharply to that taken with the enthusiastic McAdoo: "If a man wants to be President of the United States," he admonished Ritchie, "he can't get there by waiting for the office to come to him." McAdoo did not need to be given that pithy wisdom. But neither was McAdoo offered the use of Baruch's ample political resources.)[48]

We can only imagine Baruch's relief when it was announced in September 1927 that McAdoo had sent George Fort Milton, editor of the *Chattanooga News* and staunch McAdoo booster, a letter declaring that he would not be a candidate for the Democratic presidential nomination. For a decade a McAdoo candidacy had been synonymous with Baruch money. While the news from Tennessee took one man's name from the running, it made Baruch's war chest accessible to all available men deserving of his influence. Now he could be any Democratic president's Warwick.

"BARUCH'S CONSTITUENCY"

Although Baruch would never be as committed to another presidential candidate as he had been to McAdoo prior to 1924, Governor Albert Cabell Ritchie of Maryland came as close as anyone to becoming the man for whom Baruch would be kingmaker. Of course, for the record, Baruch denied that Ritchie was his man. But by 1927, Baruch's praise of Ritchie had the timbre of an endorsement.

Meeting Ritchie in person, one could say of him what had been said of Harding, that he looked as if he had been cast in Hollywood as president. His striking appearance prompted Gordon Auchincloss to note in his diary that Ritchie was "one of the best-looking men I have ever seen." But being handsome and a delightful companion never qualified anyone for the presidency. Ritchie had been Maryland's attorney general when Baruch asked him to take on an additional assignment as War Industry Board counsel. The next year, 1919, Ritchie ran for governor with a $5,000 contribution from Baruch. Thus began a fifteen-year tenure as governor, the longest in the state's history. He was an ultra-conservative in politics, interpreting Jefferson as literally as Bryan interpreted the

Scriptures. A strict states' rights man, Ritchie opposed prohibition only because it was an infringement of federal government upon individual rights. Ritchie also was a balanced-budget enthusiast who could tell a Chamber of Commerce meeting that America needed "more business in government and less government in business."[49]

The Ritchie boomlet for president was launched in 1924 at a Jefferson Day Dinner in Annapolis that featured Baruch; his crony and editor of the *New York World*, Herbert Bayard Swope; and Senator Oscar Underwood of Alabama. Despite an occasional sojourn outside Maryland, Ritchie in 1924 was little more than a favorite-son candidate with scattered backing elsewhere. Behind McAdoo, Smith, and Davis, he was the darkest of dark horses. His biggest financial backer, Baruch, remained nominally committed to McAdoo. His best publicists in the national press were *Baltimore Sun* editor Frank R. Kent and David Lawrence, the former a keen admirer of Baruch, the latter a borrower from Baruch. Ritchie was valued for his servility to Baruch: he did as Baruch told him.[50]

Baruch in 1924 complained bitterly that politicians valued him only for his money, not his advice. Democratic leaders, Baruch told Senator Pat Harrison of Mississippi, "look upon me more as a thing with some money than anything else. . . . They are going to be very much astonished, as they are getting to be, when they find I am not going to let them spend my money." He urged the party to undertake a $100,000 publicity campaign prior to the convention, a proposal Norman Davis considered excellent for its own merit and because "it would increase Baruch's enthusiasm very much to have his suggestion adopted, since he often complains that none of his suggestions are followed." Baruch demanded to be taken seriously as a political strategist, not merely because he possessed "a sugar barrel here." If the 1924 Democratic candidate proved unacceptable to Wilsonians like himself, Baruch threatened to spend his summer in Scotland.[51]

And that is what he did, sugar barrel and all. He spent a fine summer entertaining prominent politicians and businessmen from Europe and America who gave him greater respect than Democrats who took his money without his advice. He insisted that he held nothing against John W. Davis, but when the new Democratic finance director, Jesse Jones, had asked Baruch for a contribution, Baruch gave "some contribution but not a conspicuous one." In late September he asserted that he had "no interest in the political campaign except the making of a small contribution (all of which has annoyed my old associates very much)."[52]

How much it annoyed them Baruch learned a few days later. "I . . . wonder how you expect us to really wage a vigorous fight when you refuse the kind and extent of support that you are so well able to give," Jesse Jones wrote in a scorching letter. Conceding that the Democratic party owed a great deal to Baruch for past support, Jones reminded him that without it, "B. M. Baruch the stockbroker or Wall Street speculator would have no standing in the councils of the world. He would have no influence in the affairs of our own Country." Not only did Jones accuse Baruch of ingratitude, but he confirmed the speculator's suspicions of the national committee's interest only in his bank account. In strident tones that suggested the desperation of the floundering Davis campaign, Jones demanded a contribution from Baruch of $120,000 instead of a "miserably small check" and lectured him "to thank your God every night" for his fortune and ask for humility. It was not the sort of letter that would elicit either humility or $120,000 from Baruch.

Professing to be "amazed and hurt" by Jones's "intemperateness of tone and recklessness," Baruch retorted that he did not believe in "a system of barter and sale, of contributions and resulting recognition, which seems to be your conception of politics." However, Baruch wanted any contribution to be "spent wisely and not foolishly," these terms to be defined by the donor. Though Baruch honestly claimed to seek no "favors" for his contributions, control over the uses of his money was a favor that Jones had refused to accord him.[53]

Following the party's 1924 debacle, Baruch emerged as the indispensable Democrat. Debts reaching back to 1918 threatened to strangle the party unless Baruch removed the lid from his sugar barrel. Campaigns in 1926 for congressional seats and in 1928 for the presidency were lost before they were begun unless either good fortune or Baruch's fortune blessed the party. Moreover, as Baruch increasingly made his point that Democrats must take his advice with his largesse, Democrats could either find other financial angels or give Baruch the larger role in party affairs he demanded. His suggestions would be given more respectful attention thereafter. Baruch was a bear market man and the Democrats of the 1920s presented a woefully underinvested market.

In the mid-1920s, Baruch found House and Senate races political investments that were safer, less noticeable or notorious, and more likely to provide a return in terms of influence—having his "suggestions" adhered to. Ten or twenty thousand dollars spent in a nonindustrial state primary or election could mean the difference between victory or defeat and at least the temporary gratitude, pending the next election, of a Democratic congressman or senator. Urged to persuade the New York Democratic party to nominate Frank Polk for senator in 1920, Baruch had declined on the grounds that he really could not influence the situation.[54] New York was a high-risk state for political contributions. It had alternative financial sources; it could be won by Republicans. But Baruch could finance a Senate primary fight in the South or West that would guarantee victory without a contest in November; and the winner would have a vote equal to a New Yorker's and probably more impact upon legislating.

Democratic candidates were eager to become part of what Senator C. S. Thomas of Colorado referred to as "Baruch's constituency." The year 1926 ought to have been a rebound one for the Democrats, given the normal expectation that the party without control of the White House gains seats in Congress during the off-year election. But the extent of the off-year effect could not be forecast. As reporters noted, Democratic officials in Washington were apprehensive that 1926 would be "a lean year so far as contributions are concerned." That certainly did not diminish Baruch's enthusiasm. Charged by congressional Democrats with the responsibility of electing candidates in Kentucky and Maryland, between February and mid-October Baruch contributed $46,500 and exhorted friends like Thomas Fortune Ryan and Thomas L. Chadbourne to give another $45,000. Baruch specified four beneficiaries, two of whom lost. Still, Elmer Thomas of Oklahoma and Alben Barkley of Kentucky won their seats knowing that they had received a big assist from Baruch. For that matter, Barkley had won the Senate nomination largely because Kentucky friends of Baruch had urged his intervention when the party divided during a fiercely fought primary. Following his success, Barkley acknowledged his obligation to the speculator with "deep gratitude" and assured him, "I shall be glad at any time to have the benefit of your council and judgment."[55]

Baruch claimed that his contributions carried no ulterior motive. In fact, "I have supported very heavily the Democrats for what I think is the most important thing—good government," he told Mark Sullivan in 1926. Such declarations, he knew, were not apt to be believed. Three decades later, Baruch would characterize the expectations of political contributors: "Those who contributed had a friend at court. I really don't think anybody got anything more than a right to present a visiting card and be heard." Baruch claimed to be innocent of anything sinister: neither the giving of a contribution nor its acceptance implied a deal then or sometime in the future. In his old age he would assert, "It is a shocking thing that anyone can believe that any member of Congress was venal. I have been in contact with them for over forty years. I have yet to know one."[56]

A big contribution was a way of gaining an entry to a politician's office for the purpose of being heard. Both the giver and the recipient needed each other for reasons having nothing to do with a tainted arrangement—unless the act of giving is itself implicitly sordid. Baruch wanted access to men who made policy and laws for reasons that some people would have considered selfish, but Baruch sincerely believed his purposes to be in the public interest: the national welfare dovetailed with his own. Believing that he had significant ideas on national economic policy, he yearned to be heard by people who made that policy. And he had the money with which he could buy an audience. Yet the intrusion of a multimillionaire who professed to speak only in the name of a general interest seemed paradoxical. Only his earnest manner and overwhelming generosity convinced people that the speculator's motives were as noble as he claimed.

His wealth and his persistence in distributing it to politicians who could share his ideals or learn from his ideas opened doors in Washington. He could write a lengthy letter on taxation to the senate Democratic leader, insist that he was motivated to advocate tax policy that affected him only to the extent that he would "have a little more or less to spend" (a hint that he would have more or less for political campaigns?), and conclude by stating a broad principle underlying his recommendations with which few capitalists could disagree: "Personal initiative is what we want to keep going."[57] Here was a man as generous with ideas as with political contributions, Washingtonians ought to have believed.

Baruch built friendships with most of the Senate Democratic leaders of the 1920s and 1930s. Such a relationship might begin with a chance introduction and be followed with a letter that advised the senator on impending legislation. Lawmakers constantly hear from constituents, but Baruch was no ordinary constituent. They gave him their very respectful attention, and in time there would come an invitation for a vacation at his South Carolina estate, where "Mr. Baruch" became "Bernie." There might be benefits for senators other than contributions and advice. Three years after Arkansas's Joe Robinson began to take Baruch's policy wisdom, he began to receive Baruch's investment wisdom. In 1926, Baruch invested $60,000 in the Southwest Joint Stock Land Bank of Little Rock, a venture in which Robinson had a considerable stake. Their relationship grew; a Baruch trip to Washington would be certain to include a meeting with Robinson. If Baruch was en route to Hobcaw he might urge Robinson to come along and bring a friend or two from the Senate. He flattered Robinson, telling him that a man of his experience and intelligence needed time for contemplation, which a few days in South Carolina would afford him. At Hobcaw, the affairs of state could be discussed among gentlemen in a rustic setting while they were attended by all the appurtenances of the leisure class. On the eve of the convening of the Seventieth Congress in 1927, Robinson, then the minority leader, would tell Baruch that the organization of the party's Senate structure awaited his arrival in Washington. Baruch would plump for a prestigious committee assignment for the freshman New Yorker, Robert F. Wagner. (Baruch had wagered on Wagner's opponent, the aristocratic Republican James Wadsworth, an act for which he was quick to atone.)[58] All the while, Robinson would urge Baruch to invest more in their Arkansas banking enterprise and likewise encourage his Wall Street friends. Baruch's closest Washington friends grew to include Senators Key Pittman of Nevada and Byron "Pat" Harrison of Mississippi. By the early 1930s, Robinson would be the

5. Baruch, Vice-President Charles Curtis, Churchill, and Senate Democratic Leader Joe T. Robinson on a visit to the Capitol building in 1929. (Courtesy Seeley G. Mudd Manuscript Library, Princeton University)

Democratic leader in the Senate, Pittman would be the ranking Democrat in the Foreign Relations Committee, and Harrison would be the ranking Democrat in the Finance Committee; and Baruch would be a frequent expert witness at congressional committee hearings that made the front pages of America's newspapers.

Baruch had come a long way in politics. He had begun as a hanger-on, helping finance local candidates and then Wilson's presidential campaigns of 1912 and 1916. But only Woodrow Wilson seemed to understand Baruch's desires to be known as something more in politics than a Democratic party financial angel. In the WIB and in Paris, Wilson allowed Baruch to fulfill some of those ambitions. That satisfaction, however, only instilled greater expectations in Baruch, expectations that politicians other than Wilson refused to consider. In part that was Baruch's fault. Had he been intent on being more than the Democrats' financial resource, he would have accepted Wilson's proffer of the Treasury secretaryship and played a role in guiding the postwar political economy; by rejecting it he appeared to admit that he was not equal to the task. His later regret that he had refused the post has the tinge of recognition that at a crucial moment in the making of the Baruch legend for sagacity, he had suggested that he was too lightweight for policy making. And Baruch made another mistake. Freely doling out his money to a debt-ridden Democratic party only impressed the politicians that he was an easy mark, the sort of person who would cover campaign costs in 1918 by writing a check on WIB stationery. Even McAdoo had failed to heed his political wisdom. Baruch would never again allow himself the luxury of public ardor for an undeserving presidential contender.

Notwithstanding Jesse Jones's wrath, 1924 confirmed Baruch's place in the Democratic party. Since 1920 congressional Republicans had been spotlighting illicit political contributions to the Democrats. Allegations that big contributors earned special favors in the Wilson years deterred big givers who shunned publicity. But Baruch throve on publicity and, so it seemed to Democrats, had the courage to face down unfounded charges of misconduct. Democratic hard times amid Republican prosperity endeared the party to the devoted Baruch. His wisdom gained in currency. In 1925 party chairman and congressman Cordell Hull wrote him: "In view of the approaching session of Congress and the early consideration of revenue and possibly other economic measures, I shall be delighted to have the benefit of such comment and suggestions as may occur to you. I know of no person possessing a wider range of economic information, or more constructive ideas relative thereto, than yourself. I shall be much interested in hearing from you."[59] Baruch had become an advisor to policy makers.

He had discovered that he had no need to play Warwick to the man in the White House when he might assume the role for the Senate.[60] He knew well the Senate's place in making economic policy. He had tasted victory in the election of men like Barkley, and among ninety-six senators, a few, a veritable fraternal group in politics, could determine the course of economic policy. Moreover, he had tested senators and found them uncertain in their comprehension of the business system, insecure in their own status, and extremely deferential to a man who, by virtue of his capacity to fund their careers freely and entertain them on a level of extravagance they could only dream of, empirically had demonstrated that his insight into the economic system brought wealth without venality. Like Joe Robinson, many in the Senate wanted his investment in their careers, maybe his investment in their investments. And even if they could not attain the latter, in the course of a couple of days at Hobcaw they would have the pleasure of being told by this great and famous man that he savored their company and might even be told what corporations the speculator currently invested in. His attention to them could sustain their careers and increase their financial worth. He effectively bought for himself a powerful audience for his monologues on the American political economy. He articulated their "convictions," daring them to take the "demagogic" route in favor of their constituents. More of them voted with their constituents than with Baruch when the urgings of the two did not coincide, but this man of sweet temperament seldom begrudged a politican the expedient of eschewing good principles in favor of votes.

The purpose of his influence in the Senate, which caused others to wonder about it, was more influence. His influence with the Senate increased his influence with the public. He demonstrated that politicians gave him their attention. His access to the White House, his public role as "advisor to presidents," depended heavily upon his capacity to talk reason with the Senate club. And, to complete a circle, his public image as an advisor to presidents gave him the ability to call down upon the Congress an outpouring of mail demanding that legislators pay heed to this sage. Washington did not have to follow his wisdom, but it could not afford to ignore him. Baruch would become an institution by himself in Washington.

BIGOTRY AND DEMOCRATIC PRINCIPLES

"I think the money I spent in the last election bore some fruit," Baruch observed in 1927. "I can't say that generally of the money spent at other times." He was now a confirmed neutral in any presidential sweepstakes. "I shall not be a party to destroying our organization, such little of it as does exist, by fighting over candidates," he insisted. "I am trying to get the Democrats together on some principles."[61]

Baruch and other Wilsonians sought a device for institutionalizing a party apparatus and party accountability. Norman Davis and Cordell Hull had discussed conferences that might "steer the Party away from issues that will merely bring internal dissension," like prohibition and religion, and that might bind Democrats to the party's 1928 nominee. Davis suggested that about a half dozen party angels ("those who might help supply the sinews of war" was the delicate way he phrased it) should confer early in 1927 to plan for a larger conference; his list consisted of John W. Davis, Tom Chadbourne, Owen D. Young, Baruch, and a few others, like Franklin Roosevelt and Frank Polk. The group met on 21 January, and it became apparent soon after that Washington Democrats feared a rump New York group intent upon issuing a manifesto that claimed to speak for the party. That fear killed the larger conference before it was born. To Baruch's disgust, the Democrats continued to flounder through debates over liquor rather than economic policy. Party government in America seemed to Baruch to be incapable of producing a program or the organization by which to implement it. "The only difference between the two parties," he told a friend in 1927, "is that the Republicans have not done anything and could do something if they wanted to, whilst the Democrats have not and could not do anything if they wanted to."[62]

The Democrats were concerned over the probable nomination of Governor Alfred E. Smith of New York, a Roman Catholic, for president in 1928. Indeed, no sooner did he know the results of the 1926 elections than Baruch was drawing invidious comparisons between the front-running Smith and his client, Albert Ritchie. Portraying Ritchie as a candidate acceptable to both sides of the prohibition issue ("Ritchie carried wet Baltimore and the dry Eastern Shore"), he maintained that the Maryland governor had great support in the vital border states. Yet Baruch carefully left a door open to later endorsement of Smith: "He is an excellent man, and I have supported him ever since he ran for Sheriff, and I have unlimited faith in his integrity and ability." Smith's problem, as Baruch saw it, was his close identification with Tammany Hall and its historic record of corruption, although he conceded that Smith's tenure as New York's governor had been free from scandal. Disclaiming any backing of Ritchie, Baruch merely recommended a news story for an alert journalist: "I would suggest that you write a little piece about Ritchie some time. . . . I am not advocating this man as candidate, because I have no candidate, but it is well to put before the country the fact that there are other white hopes so that the Smith people cannot preempt the whole thing and so that the Republicans themselves cannot drive this religious issue in." In effect, Baruch had joined a "stop-Smith" drive.[63]

Baruch spent most of 1927 cautiously suggesting Ritchie as an alternative to Smith's volatile candidacy. He privately accused Democrats in New York, New Jersey, and Massachusetts, states strong for Smith, of never supporting "any interest at all in the whole party unless they have some special candidate," now obviously the man in the brown derby. He assured his senatorial friends that they would not have to share a ticket with Smith because "a Moses will come out of the bullrushes" to snatch the nomination from Smith's grasp. He wishfully depicted a press assault upon the New Yorker as "the kibosh on Al Smith's campaign." Late in the year, when it should have been apparent to a shrewd observer of politics that Smith had the nomination all but locked up, Baruch expressed his "hope that we may be able to get a candidate whom we can all get enthusiastically behind and elect."[64] Smith was not that man.

But 1927 also proved that Ritchie was not Baruch's Moses. However striking Ritchie was in the convivial company of men on the hunt for quail at Hobcaw, he was a vapid politician on the hunt for national backing. Baruch cajoled him with comments like "I think if I had any candidate for President, I would not let him sit back. . . . He must get out and attack the other party." Go west, he urged Ritchie; talk about the iniquities of the Republican tariff or the plight of agriculture. So what if Ritchie knew little of agricultural policy or problems; Baruch knew enough for the two of them and would find the right positions on agriculture for the governor of Maryland: "You could say you are . . . " In May, Ritchie toured the Midwest, speaking in Chicago, Omaha, Lincoln, and

Kansas City. Ritchie also found summer audiences in Atlantic City, Indiana, and Michigan for didactic talks on the need for reviving states' rights. By the spring of 1928 the Ritchie boom entered an unseasonal hibernation from which it never emerged; the governor himself took to denying that he was a candidate.[65]

In March 1928, Baruch extended himself in behalf of the favorite-son candidacy of another client politician, Joe Robinson. At a dinner in Baruch's New York home in Robinson's honor, the host was asked by reporters where he stood on the candidates. Baruch described himself as friendly to Smith, leaning to Ritchie, ready to work for Robinson. "I certainly am not going . . . to oppose anybody whom the Democrats may nominate," he told a die-hard McAdoo backer. "Whoever we nominate let us elect. . . . If Smith gets a majority of the Convention, I think we ought to nominate him right away and go home and do the best we can."[66] But few of his southern friends shared Baruch's sangfroid concerning the impending wet, Catholic, Tammany nominee of the Democracy. So he mostly talked about the dark horses. He assured the governor of South Carolina that Owen Young would make a very great president, the editor of the *Chattanooga News* that he shared his high opinion of Cordell Hull, and Claude Bowers that Alben Barkley should be considered a contender. Then Smith scored a smashing victory in the California primary over Senator James Reed of Missouri and Senator Thomas J. Walsh of Montana; Baruch foreswore any association with the stop-Smith campaign. "There evidently is stronger sentiment for Smith than anyone has yet realized," he told George Fort Milton.[67]

The Smith success changed Baruch's tune on prohibition. In 1920 he had told Bryan that he could "neither support nor vote" for a wet. In 1925 he had been certain that no wet candidate could be nominated for president because prohibition had contributed to prosperity by the "purchase of necessaries and luxuries with money which in former days was spent in the saloon." In 1927 he reassured McAdoo that the Democratic candidate would have to declare for enforcement of the law and the Eighteenth Amendment. However, in 1928, Baruch lauded Smith for his consistency in opposition to prohibition and proclaimed his disgust with "the hypocrisy of our elders on prohibition."[68]

Baruch was welcomed into the Smith fold like a long-lost brother. In Houston his friend Robinson got the vice-presidential nod following Smith's first-ballot victory. Smith asked Baruch to be the party's finance committee chairman, but Baruch declined, saying that he preferred an unofficial fund-raising role; he recommended Herbert Lehman in his stead. Reasoning that Smith might attract wet Republicans, Baruch contended that Smith had a reasonably good chance of defeating the GOP nominee, Herbert Hoover. Yet no campaign could prevent Baruch from taking a summer vacation in Europe. To reporters who saw him at dockside as he departed on the *Leviathan* on 4 July, he gave Smith his unqualified blessing.[69]

Besides fund raising, Baruch performed a quartet of self-appointed functions in the campaign. First, he reassured businessmen that the election of a Democrat would not impair the apparent prosperity of the times. Second, with Hugh Johnson and George Peek in tow, he prepared agricultural position papers for Smith and utilized his very extensive farm organization contacts to argue that Smith was safe for farmers.[70] Then he sought to assuage southern fears concerning Smith's Catholicism and antiprohibition stance. Finally, he vainly endeavored to bring McAdoo and his admirers into the Smith camp.

The latter two assignments proved the most disheartening. "Really, there is only one issue—and that is religion," Baruch confided to Winston Churchill in September. Because most of the Smith antagonists were his friends or political allies in better times, he should have known that he could not treat their prejudice with rationality. "I cannot see what the South is going to gain by a bolt or secession from the Democratic party," he told Carter Glass of Virginia. "When you get down to the bottom of it, the opposition to Smith is based upon religion. When people say he is going to Tammanyize the government, the people of the state of New York are amused because that is the kind of stuff ghost stories are made of upon which they feed children and ignorant people."[71]

To his consternation, Baruch discovered that some former McAdoo backers were engaged in a holy war. Foremost among the crusaders was Chattanooga editor George Fort Milton. In his paper, Milton editorialized that Smith appealed "to the aliens who feel that the older America, the America of the Anglo-Saxon stock is a hateful thing which must be overturned and humiliated; to the northern Negroes, who lust for social equality and racial dominance; to the Catholics who have been made to believe that they are entitled to the White House; and to the Jews who likewise are to be instilled with the feeling that this is the time for God's chosen people to chastise America." Baruch assailed this as "nauseating." Later he would label Milton one of the few people in politics for whom he had contempt.[72]

To counter the likes of Milton, Baruch and the Smith people had need of an endorsement from McAdoo. But McAdoo wanted a modification of Smith's prohibition stance. McAdoo appeared to desire rapprochement with Smith to save himself politically from "self-stultification," but, according to McAdoo, Smith was unwilling to meet him partway on prohibition. In the end both men saved face by suspending the negotiations, McAdoo choosing silence on the campaign.[73]

Again a losing Democratic campaign enhanced Baruch's stature in the party. Baruch had given the hopeless Smith candidacy his unflagging loyalty—and his money.[74] He had made good his boast of preconvention neutrality among candidates and postconvention loyalty to the nominee. Aside from members of Congress, he would be the most powerful Democrat in Washington, and he was determined to direct the party along the path of sound economic principles.

THE FOURTH ESTATE AND BARUCH

Baruch and politicians had a symbiotic relationship: he had the wherewithal for victory; they had the public mandates with which to implement his ideas. Baruch and journalists also were symbiotic: he impressed them with his munificence and a good sense of what was newsworthy; they publicized him and gave articulation to his ideas. Baruch recognized the press's peculiar role in American society and exploited it better than almost any public figure in his time; he knew that the line between journalist and publicist was thin enough for an easy obliteration.

Predominantly middle class in background and perspective, journalists in Baruch's time were ill-paid parvenues who had embarked upon a career in their craft out of a romantic "love of the game." Convinced that they tested "the pulse of the world," journalists, in order to fulfill their role as the scribes of their times, hungered to rub elbows with the rich, powerful, famous, and infamous. The more ambitious the journalist the more likely he was to be a historian of the elites. Unfortunately for even the most brilliant of them, the complexity of elitist activities often confused them, and the significance of their observations escaped them. In the words of two rare scholars of the early twentieth-century profession, "Most of them admit that their knowledge is superficial, but they make nothing of this." Confident that intellectual curiosity could overcome the handicap of insufficient knowledge or experience, they read widely and watched carefully. But nothing seemed adequate to prepare them for reporting from Washington.

Reporters tended to be insecure, and with good reason. "Don't go into journalism if you do it just to make a living," went the wise old editor's advice to the young cub. More than ever that was true in the 1920s. The number of jobs available to reporters was shrinking. The heyday of journalism had passed, the zenith of low-cost competition being 1892–1914. Inflation during and after World War I contributed to the downfall of many big-city dailies whose costs of production outstripped any return on advertising and circulation. Investors forced mergers, built chains, and liquidated losers.[75]

There was a time when Baruch depicted himself as a potential newspaper owner, and for about a decade following the Great War he was rumored as the buyer of every major city newspaper known to be for sale. The press was an extension of Baruch's ambitions in politics. Democrats constantly mourned the comparative dearth of their funds for propaganda. They bemoaned the preponderance of Republican-owned newspapers and the difficulties of getting an adequate hearing for Wilsonism; as they looked for funds that would pay for that voice, they looked to Baruch. Having flaunted the availability of his money for candidates, Baruch let it be known that his money could buy Democratic daily newspapers. "I am more convinced than ever that we must get some newspapers in order to get our views before the public," Baruch told Colonel House in mid-1918; and to a New York newspaperman he declared, "I would like very much to become the owner of some good paper." Moreover, he was encouraged in this by Wilson himself, who pronounced his plans to buy a newspaper and make it a Democratic voice "Bully!"[76]

He wanted to please Wilson by giving him a major ideological organ and to impress his fellow Democrats with this undertaking, but he could not do this at the cost of violating his own business sensibilities. And the economic problems inherent in newspaper publishing at the time made it a very questionable venture. Moreover, he prided himself on being a person who rarely acted without substantial information to support his decisions, and the newspaper business was more mysterious to Baruch than railroads or raw materials.*

Part of his hesitation also stemmed from the fact that he would be something of an absentee owner, dependent upon the good judgment of a veteran journalist. Baruch probably never trusted a journalist to do anything but write what he was ordered to write or suggest public relations. Newspapermen were either technicians or publicists for Baruch, but he would not entrust a balance sheet to their management. He wanted a newspaper that would perform a service for the Democratic party and Wilson, not create a financial embarrassment for Baruch. Inevitably, most available papers already embarrassed someone else. Nevertheless, the mere prospect of that purchase added to the importance of Baruch's name within the Democratic party. Progressive-minded journalists, eager to run their own newspapers, likewise sought his money for the purchase of a metropolitan daily. This is not to say that Baruch was the only Wilsonian to articulate interest in molding public opinion through a newspaper. During 1918–20, Herbert Hoover toyed with the idea of buying the *Baltimore Sun* or the *New York Herald* or the *San Francisco Chronicle* for the purpose of "exerting a greater influence on the situation from outside than from in." Although he bought shares in newspapers in 1919, little more developed. Also, Thomas W. Lamont bought the *New York Evening Post* in 1918 in order to make it "the leading organ of

---

*A Baruch confidant once told me this story. A friend asked Baruch if he knew why the *New York Daily News* had the world's largest circulation. Baruch, who avidly read opinion, responded that it had the best editorial page. No, the friend explained, it had Dick Tracy. Baruch did not know whom his friend was talking about.

opinion in the United States."[77] Eugene Meyer, Jr., would buy the *Washington Post* in 1933. But what made Baruch a favorite among Democrats was his loyalty to the party, something not shared by Republicans Hoover, Lamont, or Meyer, or by most other men of wealth who sought to educate the American public to the new realities of world and national politics.

During the war, Colonel House tried enticing Baruch into the newspaper game. Ever eager to find outlets for Baruch's money and to serve his own purposes, House introduced Baruch to Lincoln Colcord of the *Philadelphia Public Ledger*, a reporter who dreamed of his own newspaper as a vehicle for making the world safe for progressivism. Along with H. B. Brougham, editor of the *Public Ledger*, and reporters Raymond Swing and William C. Bullitt, Colcord campaigned to persuade Baruch to buy a New York newspaper that would serve as a major voice for Wilsonian liberalism. According to Swing, their first target was the *New York Tribune*, which they believed could be bought by their "angel" so that it could, as Colcord put it, "save the country from social and industrial chaos." Baruch met with them several times, demanding to know the *Tribune*'s real and potential earnings. Just when Swing had amassed the necessary data, Baruch was appointed chairman of the WIB and declined to go further in the *Tribune* negotiation, lest it be a conflict of interest with his administration position.[78]

Still the Colcord-Brougham efforts to get Baruch to buy them a newspaper continued, with assists from House and his son-in-law, Gordon Auchincloss. The object of their interests shifted to the *New York Evening Post*, then owned by Oswald Garrison Villard, whose pro-German sympathies had diminished its readership. Baruch showed interest in picking up an option on it and on the *New York Herald*. But Morgan partner Tom Lamont bought the *Evening Post* in mid-1918 to satisfy his own journalistic hankerings and his passion for educating Americans on the need for a League of Nations. Still, Baruch encouraged the House circle to believe that he seriously wanted a paper for propagandizing Wilsonian philosophy. As he told Colonel House, "Every day I see the necessity for us to have some organ through which we can express the views for which we have fought and the ideals for which we stand. These ideals are in the ascendancy, and we should have some method of nailing them down so they never can be changed." He asserted in early 1919 that he was prepared to spend ten million dollars on a string of newspapers with the *New York Herald* as the flagship property (House's son-in-law, Auchincloss, had the British news agency Reuter's in mind as another Baruch purchase). Baruch professed to be willing to sustain heavy losses to fulfill his ambitions and ideals.[79] But he and the House circle were growing apart in 1919, just as the Colcord-Brougham partnership was drifting away from the House orbit.

Other journalist friends sounded him on buying newspapers. In late 1919, Herbert Bayard Swope hoped Baruch would buy the *New York Mail* and fulfill their mutual yearnings. The following year, Arthur Krock laid out a scheme for Baruch to invest his money in a syndicate that would operate a chain of Democratic newspapers from New York to California. Bruce Bliven went shopping in behalf of Baruch for the *New York Globe* in early 1921. But by March 1921, Baruch began to express fears about tying up too much capital in a losing venture, even if it was "a public service." He had little faith in the likes of Swope, Krock, Colcord, and others who wanted to run his property; as he asked Mark Sullivan, "What is the use of having a vehicle or any organization unless you have a man to run it?" With 40 percent of his wealth eroded since 1917, Baruch had no desire to invest in a poorly managed, capital-starved, cost-intensive enterprise that paid a small profit, if any at all.[80] He still believed in publicity for advancing his causes, but the medium could no longer be a newspaper.

Baruch alone could publicize his causes with greater economy than could any newspaper. His friends in journalism would assist. Why should he buy a publicist's organ when he could create one—the legendary Bernard M. Baruch! He accomplished with selective investments of $50,000 or less what other crusading moguls accomplished with investments of a million dollars or more, because he understood journalistic economic problems and the art of publicity better than most journalists. Opportunities in journalism abounded; many magazines and newspapers sought heroic investors willing to propagandize in red ink. Did he want to buy *McClure's? Everybody's?* the *Independent?* These were leads that came in the mails; we can only imagine the verbal offers to sell that came almost daily. Purchasing one organ would have made him a competitor of others, perhaps shutting him out of their columns; investing in many organs, however, made them beholden to him: they opened their columns to a man who had something to say and who was, not incidentally, a benefactor. He gave a $12,500 loan to *Our World* magazine, an unknown amount to M. Lincoln Schuster to begin his publishing house, $25,000 to Josephus Daniels to save the *Raleigh News and Observer,* and unknown amounts to save *Vogue* and *Vanity Fair* for his good friend Condé Nast.[81] Some of these loans would be repaid and some would not. Probably there were many others as well. All of them were good investments in terms of the small amounts of capital required, the freedom from responsibility, the nonassociation with disaster, and the good friendships that advanced his name and ideas.

Cultivating contacts after Baruch's fashion was the mark of a successful Washington correspondent. "Gossip in the capital has become institutionalized," observed one student of the capital scene. Everyone in Washington, from the president down to the lowliest bureaucrat, thrived on gossip. The Washington correspondent listened rather than read. "It is an atmosphere which is not conducive to a sober analytic perspective," Leo Rosten wrote. "It fosters a dominantly impressionistic political orientation. In Washington, news becomes a disjointed combination of event, conjecture, and inference." As newspapers took on more features that duplicated magazines via the op-ed page, the political publicist found a regular niche as a columnist. News, gossip, and publicity melded into an indistinguishable mélange of print.[82]

Lest gossip lead naturally to fabrication, editors demanded that their correspondents furnish unimpeachable sources as authorities for their news. This dependence made the reporter, in the words of a veteran newspaperman, "a servitor, a satellite," to his well-placed sources, whom he flattered and befriended in the manner of an acolyte.[83] Baruch ruthlessly exploited the Washington correspondents. He constantly favored certain friends with choice tidbits of gossip that hardened into fact because their source was the authoritative Baruch. The alternative to believing Baruch as a source might be a story without an "angle," and Baruch was a source who radiated charm, shrewdness, and all the arresting traits of a statesman. Playing the role of a visible tipster whose demeanor suggested integrity and insight, Baruch made them his willing publicists, and they thanked him for the opportunity that enhanced their work. Most of them venerated his economic judgments as the most practical and scholarly wisdom—because his means gave ample testimony to that wisdom, because politicians likewise deferred to it, and because their own knowledge of the workings of economics was so meager. For many of them, Baruch was the only textbook on an increasingly complex political economy. Ever impressionists, most Washington correspondents freely confessed that they were woefully unprepared to explain and interpret Washington economics to an economically illiterate public.[84]

Either as an identified source for background information or as a witness before a congressional committee, Baruch became a public authority on economic behavior for a great part of the American public that read newspapers. The more freely he talked to correspondents, the more they wrote about him; the more they wrote about him, the more they heeded him; the more they heeded him, the more of an authority he became; the more of an authority he became, the more freely he would talk. It was reassuring that someone could loquaciously and lucidly and reassuringly explain the system.

Baruch's experience in the war had taught him that newspapermen were "a pretty useful lot of citizens" who could have a "potent effect on the public." In the 1920s, he and his fellow Wilsonian Herbert Hoover became skilled Washington practitioners in the art of publicizing policy as it ought to be, that is, lobbying the issues of government with the public. He had the instincts of a journalist—the capacity to engage people easily in conversation and elicit significant information that aided his analysis of events.[85] He had a better nose for news than some reporters. In certain instances he could make a mundane scene newsworthy because he had dramatized it as such for reporters. Correspondents who witnessed his capacity to highlight the "real significance" of an event fondly saluted him as "our old fellow reporter."[86]

In the press the most powerful vehicles for Baruch were certain Washington columnists. His longtime friend Herbert Bayard Swope invented the op-ed page at the *New York World* in the early 1920s, creating expanded space in newspapers for columnists who purveyed either Washington gossip or insightful political analysis. The craving for fresh information or understanding made Baruch a particularly helpful friend of the columnists. He would interpret for the interpreters, a role that was made to order for him. Writers found that editorializing and prognosticating could be dangerous business unless they buttressed their insights with information from an authority like Baruch. Craving the company of powerful men, they basked in the reflected glow of his power as represented by his easy access to congressional Democratic leaders and to the White House. And the more they wrote of that accessibility, the easier it became for him to maintain it. Moreover, their value to him was increased by the fact that most of them wrote for the aristocracy of the American press between the wars, the eastern papers like the *New York Times*, the *Baltimore Sun*, the *New York Herald-Tribune*, the *Washington Post*, the *Washington Star*, and (prior to its demise in 1931) the *New York World*. These were the newspapers most widely read in Washington by both the members of government and the press itself.[87]

Baruch cultivated the editorial and social friendships of columnists. Among those who regularly drew wisdom and camaraderie from Baruch were the three men most often hailed as the originators of their genre— Mark Sullivan of the *New York Herald-Tribune*, Frank R. Kent of the *Baltimore Sun*, and independently syndicated columnist David Lawrence—and *New York Times* columnist Arthur Krock. They became his pals, with Sullivan a frequent guest at Hobcaw and Kent often accompanying Baruch on a summer tour of Europe. While they relaxed as his guests he would ply them with gossip and insight worth many columns to them. His correspondence with them regularly recommended topics or perspectives for columns. And, as they had aided Baruch in his public ambitions, so he assisted them in their journalistic aspirations. When David Lawrence founded the *United States Daily* in 1926, Baruch invested $50,000 intended to lure other speculative capital needed for the extraordinary venture of a national daily. Seven years later it folded as a daily, liquidated (Baruch wrote, "It was my loss which I willingly take, so do not give that part another thought"), and became *United States News* and, following World War II, *U.S. News and World Report*.[88]

Krock was the quintessential recipient of Baruch's journalistic advice. For more than thirty years, Krock was a powerful journalistic voice in Washington, the first opinion many officials read in the morning throughout the Roosevelt and Truman years. Yet most of his writings on economic matters were mere echoes of Baruch's words.

Krock was editor of the *Louisville Courier-Journal* when he went to the Paris Peace Conference and became a sidekick of Herbert Bayard Swope, who introduced him to Baruch. Back in Louisville, Krock sent an anxious appeal to Swope to inquire of Baruch if he was "enough interested in me, or attracted to me, to attach me to his staff [of writers] in any way that I would desire? . . . I hope if you discuss this matter with him you will explain it's confidential and give him my word that I am decidedly— *persona grata*." Krock did publicity work for the Democrats in 1920, but it would be nearly three years before he permanently left Louisville for New York to serve as an assistant to Will H. Hayes, president of the Motion Pictures Producers' Association. Krock seems to have spent most of his months there firming up his connections with Swope and *World* editor Frank Cobb before he received a coveted invitation to join the *World*'s editorial staff. Again he was restless, and in 1927, Baruch, who had attempted as early as January 1923 to move Krock from Louisville to the *New York Times*, convinced Adolph Ochs to hire him. Five years later, Krock was sent to Washington to reorganize the *Times*'s Washington bureau.[89] His column, "In the Nation," either paraphrased Baruch or quoted him directly on almost any economic topic. The two men were known to be close: even Baruch later acknowledged that Krock "knows about what I think in most any given circumstance." Indeed, Krock wrote some of Baruch's speeches, just as Baruch gave Krock his perspectives on economics. Their relationship was not greatly different from that of Russell Leffingwell and Walter Lippmann, respectively advisor in financial policy and publicist of the former's perspectives.*

Baruch had need of publicists like Krock. In the early twenties he openly took several on his payroll, a practice begun during the war. Publicity became a major preoccupation of his life. "I am gathering around me a group of young men of spirit, high faith, education," he had wanted Wilson to know, and they would keep Wilsonian ideals before the American public. In addition to Lawrence, Kent, and Krock, many

---

*In researching a biography of Walter Lippmann, Richard Rovere "found instance after instance in which Lippmann had written Leffingwell asking him to explain and give his opinion on some current dispute. Leffingwell would oblige, giving him a lengthy analysis . . . and in a few days, that response, shortened and paraphrased, would turn up in Lippmann's column." Rovere, *Arrivals and Departures* (1976), p. 136. However, the Baruch-Krock relationship was different to this extent: although there were probably many times when Krock solicited Baruch for his judgment concerning the issues of the day, there were more times when Baruch did not wait for Krock to ask.

less familiar names in American journalism performed numerous publicity tasks for which Baruch paid them well. First came the necessary publicity for his exploits in the WIB and in Paris, leading to the widely distributed WIB report and *The Making of the Economic and Reparation Sections of the Treaty*. Then came the long-planned effort to memorialize the WIB and Baruch, Grosvenor B. Clarkson's *Industrial America in the World War*. As Clarkson said of his well-advanced history, "Baruch seems to be happy over the book and I hope he will continue to be. I sincerely tried to please him, to get his point of view, and to give him the place in the sun he so richly deserves." Few seekers of fame have been blessed with so dedicated a publicist as Clarkson. Hearst press reporter John E. Nevin often did publicity favors for Baruch, including telling the story of how Baruch personally and philanthropically paid the passage home for female war workers from Washington following the Armistice; for his services, Nevin received several gifts and loans from Baruch, each totaling between $500 to $1,500. *Baltimore Sun* reporter S. M. Reynolds wrote a piece at Baruch's behest on the WIB, for which he received $250. Several articles on industrial preparedness for war, international debts, the farm problem, and the state of the economy in general appeared in magazines and newspapers early in the 1920s under Baruch's name but written by journalists like Theodore M. Knappen and Samuel Crowther. Some of them also wrote his public addresses. All of them had the ability to turn his "colloquial and idiomatic English into readable prose."[90]

These publicists merely served Baruch as technicians; the speculator was himself the supreme strategist on publicity. Baruch took special care to see that everything he did caught the attention of people whom he believed ought to know about it. He drew up extensive mailing lists of prominent people in business and government whom he wanted to influence and saw to it that they received copies of everything with his name as author. He was conscious of his news value and subscribed to clipping services that regularly sent him every news story containing his name. A careful reader of "All the News That's Fit to Print" in the 1920s might have learned that Baruch, abroad for the summer, had lunch in Prague with Czech Prime Minister Beneš and spent a week with Clemenceau at Vendee; that Baruch had rented for the summer the second largest estate in Scotland; that Baruch had dinner with Calvin Coolidge in the White House, during which they presumably discussed farm relief; that Baruch entertained Clemenceau in New York and gave him a departing gift of twenty-five live terrapin from his South Carolina estate; that Baruch and John W. Davis attended a 1925 performance by Will Rogers at the Ziegfeld Follies and Rogers singled them out for attention that called for the audience's applause; and, least but still found worthy of being printed on page 2, Baruch had played jokes on Admiral Cary Grayson while they were turkey hunting at Hobcaw—nothing earth-shattering here, but newsworthy enough for the *Times*.[91]

One did not have to peruse gossip columns to find out that Baruch was a celebrity. Where he went reporters were sure to follow, confident that the man they stalked was newsworthy. He very consciously generated publicity: his mind automatically turned to promotion in most of his endeavors. His proposal for organization of Al Smith's campaign focused upon the imperative of "unifying propaganda," a central feature in his own activities. A formal dinner at the Baruch home in New York was news because the guest of honor often was a prominent international personage on the level of Clemenceau, Winston Churchill, or Jan Christian Smuts, and those who attended were the most prominent names in finance, politics, or publishing; Baruch made these dinners all the more memorable by supplying his guests with souvenir guest lists they might show to their friends or use as references for their diaries or memoirs.[92]

His exploitation of the fourth estate was predicated upon his quest to become the fifth estate. His orchestration of his own promotion as a newsworthy person of trust was calculated to make him a public sage and soothsayer in whom the American people might have confidence. Although he ballyhooed himself, most of the time he focused public attention upon issues and policies. He was a propagandist for causes dear to his heart and fame: the integrity of Baruch would bestow integrity upon his ideas.

The manipulative technique was by no means peculiar to Baruch. If anything, it paralleled Herbert Hoover's techniques in the Food Administration and in the Department of Commerce. The Great Engineer held the conviction that public relations had become in the 1920s "an exact science" and indispensable to governing people. Desiring to make himself a man "of large affairs," he hired publicists and disseminated thousands of his reports and writings to newspapers and libraries throughout America. He zealously cultivated some of the same journalists who attended Baruch—William Hard, Mark Sullivan, and David Lawrence. For Hoover, of course, the task of being a celebrity was made easier by his position as secretary of commerce. Baruch envied the public attention given Hoover. When Hoover became president, Baruch commented, "The present incumbent of the White House is the greatest propagandist the world ever saw."[93] But Baruch was a worthy challenger for that title.

THE FIFTH ESTATE AND HERBERT BAYARD SWOPE

Preeminent among Baruch's retinue "of young men of spirit" dedicated to advancing the twin causes of Wilsonian policy and the image of Baruch was the most ingenious and intrepid journalist-publicist of the 1920s and perhaps of all time (even if one is at a loss to measure such things)—Herbert Bayard Swope. It is not hyperbole to call Swope the most celebrated newspaperman of a decade celebrated by contemporary journalists and their successors as a golden age of the craft. For, between 3 November 1920 and 1 January 1929, the period in which Swope ran Joseph Pulitzer's *New York World*, that journal "was a newspaperman's newspaper, brilliantly written, tautly edited, politically and commercially independent, effervescent, irreverent, combative, liberal."[94] All these characterizations of the *World*, save "commercially independent," could apply to its prime force, Swope. Swope's talents and personality invite ornate adjectives because of what he did and the manner in which he performed; besides, ornate adjectives were part of his vocabulary. Swope had chutzpah, or, in the words of Westbrook Pegler, he was "all gall, divided into three parts—Herbert, Bayard, and Swope." It would have been impossible to envision the *World* without Swope during the twenties:

> The *World* was an extension of Swope's personality as newspapers have not often been since the heyday of personal journalism. He moved with utmost ease among the eminences who conducted or appeared in the Page Opposite Editorial columns. He was equally at home among politicians, high-echelon professional and amateur gamblers, and in the Wall Street, Broadway, racetrack and prizefight communities. He talked incessantly, played croquet as if it were a joust to the death, was slow to forgive a slight, met deadlines but was seldom on time for an appointment, wrote letters of advice to anyone (including Presidents of the United States) about anything at all, became a millionaire through shrewd speculation in the market, was a lavish host to guests who came to his Long Island home and sometimes stayed for years, amiably overlooked alcoholic proclivities in good reporters, and in general viewed life generously.[95]

Swope had genius. Almost nothing intimidated him, he spoke and wrote incessantly and glibly, and he befriended the great men of his time with an ease that constantly suggested their need for him. Two of Swope's ambitions drew him to Baruch's side and kept him there for the rest of his life, in a friendship—a companionship—that lasted forty years: he wanted money to live in the grand style and he nurtured Baruch as a means toward publishing his own newspaper. But he never achieved that latter goal and, despite the millions that he made, he never had enough money to replace the millions that he spent. In his last decade he knowingly admitted, "My whole capital is my knowledge of things and acquaintances with people."[96] That should have been sufficient for anyone but Swope, for his retention of facts was breathtaking and he certainly seemed to know anybody worth knowing in New York or Washington at any time between 1918 and his death in 1958. Most of all, he knew Baruch; for four decades their names were nearly inseparable—as they were themselves.

Their first meeting probably occurred during Wilson's 1916 campaign for reelection. Swope loved politics, admired Wilson, and considered himself a good liberal Democrat. In late 1917 he embarked for Washington on a *World* assignment that called for a scrupulous investigation of the mobilization program; but he went to Washington looking to be co-opted by the administration he already believed in. By early 1918 he began performing unofficial duties for Baruch while still reporting for the *World* on mobilization. Swope drafted speeches and letters for Baruch. A natural publicist, his dispatches to the *World* celebrated Baruch in glowing terms. When Baruch became WIB chairman, Swope wrote: "That he possesses the President's confidence to a marked degree has been known for some time; that he deserves it is now generally admitted even by those who opposed him." Swope had wanted to get into government work ever since the United States entered the war. On 19 August, Baruch's birthday, Wilson approved Swope's membership on the WIB, a welcome present to Baruch. For the remaining months of the war, Swope put Baruch's ideas into serviceable English and performed as a WIB propagandist—not too different a function from his efforts at the *World*.[97]

Swope believed that going with Baruch was a momentous step in his life. The decision had "future possibilities" that made it worth "putting my eggs in his basket." Theirs, Swope felt sure, would be an extraordinary relationship. "When two men understand each other as I know we do," Swope wrote Baruch upon the conclusion of the war and the WIB, "expression in words becomes superfluous." Swope frequently dealt in the superfluous and obsequious: "By nothing have I been helped so much as by the influence you have exerted upon me. It has stood for all that is fine and kind and decent. I do not believe that an impure thought could find lodgment in your mind. I feel myself a better and a sounder man from my all too brief association with you." Back on assignment with the *World*, Swope followed Baruch to Paris, where he churned out more dispatches promotional of that "tall, distinguished figure, Bernard M. Baruch, who will handle all questions of the world's raw materials, so vital at this period of reconstruction." A correspondent friend urged Swope on: "Use your relationship to Baruch. He has aspirations through which you may realize your own. That main chance must be seized, sooner or later."[98] It is doubtful that Swope needed to be reminded of the opportunities Baruch afforded him.

Swope's services did not come cheaply. Wherever he went he was sure to run up a sizable bill. Of that, Baruch did not need to be informed. Rumor had it that Swope's job at the WIB carried with it "a very comfortable salary," rather than the usual dollar a year. At the WIB, Swope charged an enormous number of personal long-distance phone calls to official business.[99] But Baruch believed that the best things cost a great deal, and he recognized that Swope was one of the great publicists of his time.

Not all of Swope's schemes for using Baruch's money suited Baruch, however. Swope wanted his own newspaper. In November 1919 he cajoled Baruch to buy the *New York Mail*, arguing, "You will find a deeper satisfaction in it than in anything you have ever done before, for nothing equals the opportunity a newspaper offers for true service, for altruism, for courage and for initiative, and for each of which I know you to hold a passionate purpose."[100] But even Baruch's close alliance with Swope could not get him to buy a daily of his own, much to Swope's enduring consternation.

So Swope remained at the *World* during the twenties, working full time in building fame for himself and the newspaper and part time in maintaining fame for Baruch. When it would become apparent that, past his prime, Swope would never achieve the goals he had set for himself with Baruch's money, a certain bitterness would poison his attitude toward his senior partner. Much of his publicist's work required an anonymity that went against his personality. His public association with government work came from his association with Baruch; he was laboring, Swope's wife once said privately, for "the glory of God and Bernie." It was Mrs. Swope who first called Swope Pygmalion, acidly suggesting that people saw only what her husband had created. Swope also believed that he had molded Baruch to be a fifth estate for service to mankind. Still, as a biographer has remarked, "The appraisal was probably unfair to Baruch, a man who, after all, had striking natural endowments."[101]

It is indisputable that Baruch owed much to his alter ego. Intellectually, Swope was the more brilliant of the two, Baruch the more clever. In his life, Swope publicized two major institutions, the *World* and Baruch: the *World* recorded history, Baruch made history. Yet Swope rued the fact that history would record only Baruch, not Swope. Considering what they attempted, however, one personality had to be subsumed to the other. Baruch had fame before they met; Swope augmented that fame. He introduced Baruch to other publicists, like Arthur Krock, and performed the introductions with a style calculated to impress the others with Baruch's greatness. Some of the fastidiousness with which Swope would later promote Baruch's name is suggested in a *World* memo written in 1926: "Please tell the Sports Department in referring to Mr. Baruch never to call him 'Barney.' His name is Bernard M. Baruch, and he is to be referred to in that way, or as B. M. Baruch."[102] But he was much more than just the best publicity agent a celebrity could have. Swope claimed (and Krock agreed with him) that he had invented Baruch's postwar public career, "devised a pattern for him to live by and be known for; . . . kept him from being presented and recognized . . . merely as a rich man[,] . . .

staged him as a Pro bono publico—as a servant of the people—as one
with a passion for service." Baruch's written prose was, by his own
admission, "incoherent and inarticulate," but Swope polished it into
acceptable reading. Baruch lived in a world of ideas, but he confessed,
"When I try to be intellectual which means talking a lot of hooey I just
flop."[103]

Even so, Swope was not Professor Higgins, and Baruch most definitely
was not Eliza Doolittle. Swope's service to Baruch involved less promotion and polishing than Swope admitted. He performed as an intermediary between Baruch and his public, sorting entreaties for the use of his
name or money. Would Baruch serve on a public service committee?
Would he contribute to a public service cause? By 1930 it was known
widely that Baruch wanted special pleaders to go first to Swope, who
would decide whether the cause was worthy of the great Baruch name. In
this way, Swope acted as a filter. Organizations wishing to tender Baruch
honors first sounded out his impresario. A charity seeking a large contribution had to ask Swope whether its was the sort of philanthropy worthy
of the Baruch name. But always the final decision was Baruch's. Swope
could not commit Baruch to a cause; Baruch had his own notions of
what constituted a Baruch cause. The impresario was only as good as his
cooperative performer.

Swope usually played backstage to Baruch and sometimes performed
merely as court jester. Always garrulous, Swope kept up a running patter
for Baruch's benefit and that of his guests. Alone together, Swope was the
genial companion, full of humor and good ideas. "You know, it's a great
thing just to have somebody to talk to," Baruch said of his buddy. In his
notes for his memoirs, Baruch called Swope his "Right hand." How
much Swope subordinated his career and his real worth to Baruch is
pointed up in an exchange between Dwight Eisenhower and Arthur Krock
many years later, following the passing of both Swope and Baruch. As
Eisenhower recalled, "I met Bernard Baruch and Herbert Swope back in
1930. Strangely enough, at that time, I did not realize that Mr. Swope
had been such an important figure in the newspaper field. I regarded him
primarily as a satellite and merely a close companion of Mr. Baruch."
Krock responded that Ike's untrained eye may have erred on Swope's
own fame, but that he had captured the essence of their relationship.[104]

As his biographer notes, Swope consciously fused his career with Baruch's, seeking to share the acclaim that the great man would reap. Such
is the way of the publicist. "I'm willing to sink myself into him for the
rest of my life," Swope wrote in a 1939 memo:

> I must do something and I want to do it with him. And he, too, has
> need of sort of companionship I can supply with love and admiration.
> I can help him express himself and in so doing express myself. There

is much that he has to do, all of which can be done better together.
. . . The relationship would give me an outlet for my energy and
imagination. And, for him, it would coordinate his efforts and help
give them direction. And it would bring two people together who
are—at least, one of them is—happiest in each other's company.[105]

Baruch found it easy to keep Swope happy by funding his debts. In 1921
and in 1931, Baruch advanced Swope $76,500 and $487,575 in return
for stock certificates as collateral; Swope would have the right to repur-
chase the stocks at agreed-upon prices.[106]

But loans could not relieve Swope of his keen desire to command a
metropolitan daily. When the *Washington Post* went on the block in
1933, Swope vainly pleaded with Baruch to buy the property for him to
operate. Baruch had no intention of buying the *Post*, whatever Swope's
ambitions. It passed to Eugene Meyer, and Swope switched to promoting
the *New York Herald* and the *Philadelphia Public Ledger* as potential
Baruch properties. In all likelihood, Baruch led Swope on, never discouraging his ambitions and never committing himself to buy.[107]

Baruch catered to Swope's enthusiasms because he valued the publicist's
talents. (Maybe that is why Baruch never bought him a newspaper: why
should he share Swope's talents with the public?) Also, Baruch enjoyed
the company of rambunctious individuals with talents useful to him but
clearly subordinate to or even dependent upon him in financial affairs.
Although Swope had a good business as a publicist following his *World*
career, and enjoyed associations independent of Baruch, he never escaped
Baruch's orbit. And helping to build the great image of the legendary
Baruch, the advisor of presidents, the park-bench statesman, "pro bono
publico," as Swope put it, would be his major task. But the advice, the
ideas on America's political economy, the influence with policy makers—
these would be Baruch's own creations.

CHAPTER FIVE
THE SEARCH FOR
ECONOMIC ORDER IN
THE 1920s

PRICE TURMOIL IN 1919

Bad times follow good. In the capitalist folklore of the times, the business cycle taught producers that inordinately high prices must be followed by declines. The war economy's orgy of production would reap the misery of reduced demand. The Wilsonians had anticipated that war demands would inspire an overproduction that, unless checked during the war, must create postwar havoc. Through priority management they sought to displace normal civilian industrial production, so that only a comparatively minor readjustment to peacetimes would be required. Of course they knew that they had not necessarily succeeded; in particular, the agricultural sector had been lured into an expansion that could have disastrous consequences in peace unless the United States maintained its foreign markets through extraordinary means. But producers could not expect continued demand once the government withdrew from the marketplace. Thus, Baruch's announcement that he was dismantling the War Industries Board immediately following the war could be seen as a harbinger of lower industrial prices—welcome relief in some quarters, a calamity in others. Hoover would stay with agriculture a while longer and go to Europe intent upon forcing America's expensive agricultural surplus down Europe's throat. At best, all the American marketplace could hope for was a postponement of lower prices.

Baruch professed to be undismayed by that prospect because wartime prices were artificially high. Any speculator knew that lower prices were salutary following a high-demand period; the economy would go through a brief wringer and new money would enter the market to take advantage of lower prices. If the government retained its stockpiles of raw materials and encouraged producer cooperation, that boom would come sooner than expected.

While Baruch embarked upon his diplomatic career at the beginning of 1919, fears that he had folded the WIB precipitously gained strength in certain quarters of Washington and big industry. A skeleton staff of the WIB had been transferred into the Commerce Department, where it came under the vigorous leadership of Commerce Secretary William Redfield. Consistently with his fellow Wilsonians, Redfield stressed the importance of continued industrial cooperation and trade expansion overseas. To accomplish the former he established within his department an advisory board of former WIB officials—industrial executives themselves, whose mission it would be to spread the gospel of cooperation among their kinsmen. Of those advisors, George N. Peek had been closest to Baruch. Peek was a former Deere and Company vice-president for whom producers' cooperation was the gospel. In January he was among those businessmen who lamented the WIB's hasty departure from the marketplace. As he told a former WIB comrade, "There is going to be a lot of unemployment, I feel sure, and I think it is extremely unfortunate that the demobilization could not have taken place in a more orderly way."[1]

The Commerce Department made itself a new hub of government activism in the postwar period. From WIB alumnus William M. Ritter came a plan for an industrial board within the department that would carry on the WIB's proselytizing for cooperation, preferably employing the government's purchasing obligations as an incentive. In early February the Industrial Board's role remained undefined, and as events would confirm, its purposes created confusion. The basic issue was, Would the board coordinate an orderly retreat in prices to a lower level or would it organize cooperation to prevent an immediate decline? A consensus existed on the inevitability of a price decline and the need for Washington to brake the slide, but disagreement arose as to what constituted a reasonable price at which the government should hold the line. The conflict was between the advocates of "stabilization" and those of "modification" of prices: the stabilizers would lay a strong floor under prices to arrest their decline; the modifiers would catch prices with a net and gently ease them to lower acceptable levels. The stabilizers most wanted the Industrial Board to fix minimum prices, but the modifiers represented strong business interests that welcomed lower prices to stimulate consumer purchasing.

Despite political misgivings that the Industrial Board violated the antitrust laws, it had enough support to be recommended by the cabinet to the president. Baruch appraised the plan with the eye of a man who had seen it before in war. Then the antitrust laws were not enforced, but one of his motives for abandoning the WIB so hastily was that what succeeded in war was not necessarily acceptable in peace. National security no longer justified restraint of trade. "Of course you realize," he told Wilson, "that although this may be called a stabilization of prices, it is a fixing of minimum prices."² Indeed, stabilization was a euphemism for price-fixing at high levels. Nevertheless, Baruch endorsed the scheme and Wilson gave it his approval.

With the board under the Commerce Department's jurisdiction, it fell to Redfield to recommend a chairman. He wanted either of two Baruch cronies for the job: Peek or Alexander Legge, a former International Harvester vice-president. Legge deferred to Peek in part because he believed his own industrial position made him more vulnerable to congressional accusations of conflict of interest. Peek, then employed by Baruch, was released to accept Redfield's offer on 18 February. He was determined to check any "critical" slide in prices—any that might approach catastrophic levels. Baruch advised him that it was a "most difficult undertaking, . . . even a more difficult task than that with the War Industries Board, but I am sure that your courage and patience, knowledge and experience, good judgment, and that never failing fine disposition of yours will pull you through."³

But Peek's commitment to stabilization did not always permit an exercise of patience and good judgment. Assuming that an obscure mandate for his leadership existed, he ignored real controversy over the board's mission. He mistakenly believed that the board had powers of arbitration and that the board's price-fixing powers were sanctioned by the Sherman Act because the government was the fixer. The WIB had floated that notion once before, but had never pressed it. Peek seemed to swallow it whole. Throughout March the board met with several industries, the most important being steel. Steel's prices were firm, its orders holding firmer than Peek had anticipated. Peek saw the board as a catalyst to increase buying, but steel still operated almost at capacity. Nevertheless, the board won cooperation because big steel saw the board as a useful tool to hold prices when demand declined. Magnanimously the steelmakers agreed to a reduction in the cost of steel, anticipating orders for steel rails from the Railroad Administration. "It was the unanimous opinion of the Board," Peek cabled Baruch, " . . . that these were the lowest prices obtainable without threat of wage reductions."⁴

Peek's satisfaction over the steel agreement was short-lived. The day after it was reached, the Railroad Administration rejected the price, asserting that it was too high by $2 per ton. Furthermore, the Railroad Administration hinted that it would not accept the coal industry's and the Fuel Administration's prices for coal. Peek mobilized Redfield and Fuel Administrator Harry Garfield to plead his case with the uncooperative Railroad Administration. Also, he urged Baruch to intercede with Wilson: "The President must back us up without delay." The prices, he insisted, were fair to buyers; and labor would benefit by prices that protected wages. Now it was up to the Railroad Administration to buy rails and coal at prices lower than it could have obtained three weeks previously. If the railroads depressed the price still further, Redfield noted, then other big purchasers would demand comparable prices that were destructive of steel's profits. Without a presidential directive to the railroads to buy rails at the negotiated price, Redfield feared that the board and its cooperative spirit were finished and that a "calamity" would follow in their wake.[5]

But those orders were not forthcoming. "The position of the Railway [sic] Administration seems to me entirely reasonable," Wilson told Baruch, "and yet I do not want to do anything which will make this attempt to start business on a new basis a failure." Of course this equivocal statement, coming on 1 April as crucial Paris negotiations reached a climax, was made by a distracted man. Wilson preferred to temporize and hope that the antagonists might resolve the matter themselves. At the same time, he gave others an opportunity to express themselves and build pressure for a decision. Attorney General Palmer adjudged the board an effort "to fix prices in all the basic industries by agreement instead of by competition"; Redfield vehemently denied the charge, preferring instead to call the board an attempt "to inform the commercial world of the precise situation in respect of production costs of each basic commodity, in order that buyers may know the level of deflation which justifies a vigorous invasion of the market." To the attorney general it was collusion; to the commerce secretary it was a buyers' guide. Secretary of the Treasury Carter Glass, never known for his fondness for high prices, joined sides with the Railroad Administration.[6]

Peek undoubtedly expected Baruch to sway Wilson. The Industrial Board, after all, was an offshoot in policy and personnel from Baruch's WIB. However, circumstances now were different. It was rumored in Washington that Baruch was among those who preferred private stabilization agreements and lower prices to government-imposed prices in peacetime. Try as Peek did to lobby with Baruch, his effort proved futile. On 7 April, Baruch suggested that the steelmakers should offer lower prices. Legge buttressed the advice, hinting that old conflicts might have made railroad leaders intractable in the struggle.[7]

In principle, Baruch could support the Industrial Board's stabilization efforts. But it was the wrong institution, benefiting the wrong industry, building cooperation at the wrong time. Baruch preferred an agency that operated with the expressed approval of Congress, endorsed lower railroad costs, and allowed lower prices to prevail, except when and where prices were already too low.

The board had to go. In May, Wilson ordered Redfield to dismiss it. Peek was bitter, and the WIB men were certain that history would vindicate their postwar organization as the only rational alternative to chaos. But the gradual deflation reversed itself that summer and a sharp inflation ensued. Amid soaring prices, Baruch and the Wilsonians condemned business price-fixing and hoarding of materials as contributors to the inflation. Markets, Baruch was confident, would return to normal when production returned to full peacetime pursuits. Late in 1919, Peek reflectively asserted that "the controversy over steel was merely incidental," although he was unclear about what was central to the dispute.[8] Yet the Industrial Board of 1919 served as an interesting precedent for federal antideflationary activity prior to the New Deal.[9]

In the confusion of early 1919, the administration had no antiinflationary policy. Baruch and the Wilsonians had anticipated falling prices that would not come until mid-1920. Rising prices in 1919 took them by surprise. Production of civilian goods had not revived swiftly enough; Hoover's dumping of agricultural surpluses overseas kept domestic prices high; completion of government orders for ships and raw materials to be stockpiled induced inflation; and businessmen freed from government controls charged all they could get from the buying public. Wilsonians, determined to demonstrate their sympathies for the workingman, now confronted workers resorting to strikes in efforts to keep their wages from falling further behind rising prices. The industrial turmoil Baruch had witnessed in Europe had arrived in America.

In August, Wilson discussed with Baruch a proposal that he call a conference of leaders in industry and labor for the purpose of establishing cooperation with the government "in lending such aid and guidance as may be possible and wise, to our foreign commerce in these critical days of dislocation." Afraid that industry would not produce for overseas markets, Wilson dispatched Baruch to Judge Gary. Could the foreign trade conference serve to keep labor peace? Gary insisted that no threat of disruption was real, that his workers were content except for a small minority of malcontents, and that there would be no strike because 85 percent of his employees opposed one. Less than two weeks later, Baruch repeated Wilson's suggestion and Gary again refused to make his workers' discontent a topic for the foreign trade conference. Wilson desperately sought to head off the capital-labor confrontation and had Admiral Grayson telegraph Baruch, his emissary to Gary, "The President begs that you will urge his advice upon Judge Gary as strongly as possible." Baruch responded that Gary expressed his regrets; but Baruch recommended that Gary be invited anyway to the industrial conference. Thus, Wilson's conference for expanding foreign trade also became one for resisting a strike-induced reduction of steelmaking.[10]

But by the time the conference met on 6 October the steel workers were on strike. The conference organized itself into an employers' group, a labor group, and a "public" group, the latter under the chairmanship of Baruch and including Gary and other industrialists. The proceedings of the public group were anxiously watched for signs of a strike settlement. But two weeks passed and the two sides were at loggerheads. The conference disintegrated. Baruch later claimed that the failure of the conference made him more aware of industry's "obtuseness and stubbornness" in resisting collective bargaining, the eight-hour day, and government mediation of strikes. At the same time, Baruch discovered that labor was an interest group as indifferent to Baruch's paternalistic "public interest" as was management. Incredibly, an industrialist later accused Baruch of a labor bias, saying that Baruch wrecked the conference in order to preserve the administration's standing with the labor vote.[11] That is unlikely: Baruch was more at ease in the company of management than in that of labor. Moreover, he believed that the resolution of price problems lay with producers, such as industrialists or agrarians. And it was to producers that he turned for a reasonable discussion of the price problems of the 1920s.

A "PROPERLY CONSTITUTED ARBITRAL AUTHORITY"

The Industrial Board of 1919 died shortly after birth and would be forgotten quickly by all but those who were parties to its brief life. But its model, the War Industries Board, would not be soon forgotten. Baruch and his comrades would see to that. Clarkson's *Industrial America in the World War*, subsidized by Baruch and distributed to libraries and individuals throughout the nation, carried the message that America's industry had won the war. The final report of the War Industries Board would likewise emphasize the theme of a cooperative industrial democracy organized for war; it too would have the advantage of Baruch's money in carrying its celebration of industrial patriotism throughout the land. Then there would be annual reunions of the War Industries Board members, drawing hundreds of businessmen from across the nation to New York, in a gathering of luminaries that publicized the ideas and people favored by their "chief." One theme, repeated often and widely by WIB orators, emphasized the postwar significance of the war experience and drew a moral for the public. Sometimes that moral called attention to the need for industrial mobilization plans for any future war; sometimes it stressed the peacetime application of wartime industrial organization. To many who had served in a war agency the experience of economic planning was akin to a revelation that left its witnesses wondering when they would perceive it again.

It is probable that some postwar mechanism such as the Industrial Board of 1919 had been discussed during the WIB's life. Even before the war some businessmen believed that government assistance in the rationalization of their enterprises was imperative. They needed more information, freely exchanged among themselves, which would improve their cost-accounting systems and minimize losses through competition. They hoped the Federal Trade Commission would allow the growth of trade associations that would encourage standardization of products, uniform cost-accounting procedures, and other regularizing of businesses in behalf of stabilization that would attract investors. Price-fixing in some industries during the war whetted their appetites for continued price-fixing in 1919: it could prevent a precipitate decline of prices that brought about depressions to plague every generation.[12]

Price-fixing, trade association organization, consolidation of competitors, and government supervision of commerce seemed to Baruch and his contemporaries to be the waves of an orderly future. Efficient planning of markets within industries and the eliciting of cooperation from government were preferable to chaos or ignorance. But Baruch could not ignore the fact that planning suggested the antithesis of liberal democracy and private-enterprise initiative. In war an abridgment of private enterprise had been justified by the need for conscription of resources to serve society. Even then an artificial voluntary cooperation masked the coercion by government that suggested the absence of patriotism and the imperative of fabricating it. Such state activity without the moral justification of war amounted to either statism or socialism—a negation of private enterprise by any name. Price-fixing, even to achieve domestic tranquility and economic order, went against the grain of the system. As Baruch told the American Society of Mechanical Engineers in 1924:

> The thought naturally arises, why if regulation of prices and distribution of production can be done in war time, they cannot be done in peace time. The answer is that this cannot be done. In war there is the urge of common danger and common sacrifice and a spirit of service which, in my opinion, cannot be brought about in peace time. Nor have we found a substitute for personal initiative. Even during the war, when regulations were put into effect, the endeavor was always made to leave as untrammeled as possible personal initiative and opportunity to gain from it so far as it did not affect the general interest.[13]

However, Baruch was already committed to increased governmental supervision and regulation of the economy in ways that could not possibly avoid tampering with markets. He saw this as a response to economic realities, to a drift of events toward what he once characterized as "a sort of medievalism of industry" into guild organization under government's watchful eyes. Edwin B. Parker, who guided the WIB's priority operations during the war, argued that the trade associations encouraged by the war would continue to require the government's cautious observation in behalf of a public threatened by inflation: "Now that the supervision is removed, some of these organizations become a real public menace and are, in a measure at least, responsible for some of the post-war profiteering. Under existing conditions, which are essentially different from what they were at the time the Sherman Act was originally passed, I do not think the remedy lies in dissolving the associations, but rather in regulating and supervising them."[14] Therein was the consensus among former WIB men and members of the war cabinet: the government had to work with businessmen to stabilize the economy. It might be done possibly through a supervisory agency like the Commerce Department and possibly through a regulatory agency like the Federal Trade Commission, preferably by establishing lines of cooperation that allowed for industry's self-regulation, and most definitely by eschewing the antitrust laws. "I have been thinking along the lines of cooperative markets ever since I have been on the War Industries Board," declared Baruch. "We did so well with regulation during the war that the thought naturally occurs to one—Why couldn't it be done in peace times?" It was hardly the first time the thought had occurred to him, but after brief consideration he added: "I am inclined to believe that you can have cooperation but not [government] regulation."[15]

Baruch had a penchant for consolidation of economic power in the marketplace. During the war his voice had been the loudest calling for a single authoritarian figure to run the WIB. In the war cabinet he was usually the quickest to demand nationalization of a recalcitrant corporation or industry. He appeared to relish his bouts with Elbert Gary and the threats of a government takeover he so frequently hurled at the steel baron. In war his zeal for fixing prices arbitrarily carried a patriotic flavor, something even some businessmen could respect. That passion did not abate after the war; although he distrusted legislative intervention in the marketplace, he still desired a decisive power to stabilize prices. On the matter of strikes and collective bargaining at the industrial conference of October 1919, he declared that "it would be possible for a properly constituted arbitral authority to adjust such difficulties with justice and fairness to all."

Baruch's "properly constituted arbitral authority," in effect, would settle price disputes. In some quarters of American business, such rational price making outside the marketplace would have earned Baruch opprobrium as a socialist. He was prepared for such charges. "I am not a man who is set on precedents," he insisted in 1927.

> This gray-bearded grandfather stuff does not "get over" altogether with me.
>   In discussing with various friends of mine the subject of price-fixing, I often ask them, "What makes the price of money?" They all say, "The law of supply and demand." You and I know that a man could wander the streets of New York until he wore his legs off and not find any difference in the rate that any bank or trust company would pay as

interest on deposits. The clearing-house system fixes that. And when he wants to borrow money, you know very well that is governed by the Federal Reserve System. When people talk about price-fixing, I am not afraid of it; it is a question of how it is used. . . . Price-fixing is like power—it is all right if it is well used; if it is not well used, it is bad.[16]

Believing in a well-used power, Baruch began a career of proselytizing for the "properly constituted arbitral authority" that would resolve price disputes—between seller and buyer, labor and management—independent of the marketplace. Who would fix prices, and under what circumstances? Would Congress allow for a circumvention of the antitrust laws? Would the authority be consistent with a free market?

Baruch's prescription took different names at various times: "supreme court of commerce," for example, or "high court of commerce." The authority of his court had numerous definitions, all of them vague. The concept had been discussed during the WIB days, when the dollar-a-year men dreamed of perpetuating their disinterested economic planning after the Armistice. Usually the favored notion amounted to a supervisory Department of Commerce combined with a regulatory Federal Trade Commission, with perhaps another federal agency thrown in, "centering up in higher authority." The prospect of a stabilization mechanism excited men who dreamed of a great American community and its destiny. An editor of the *Washington Post* wrote Baruch, "Your 'Commerce Court' idea opens up a big field. It is a step toward the wonderful British system, which puts the government behind industry, where it belongs; or rather consolidates government and industry, making them one. How can individual Americans go up against that?"[17]

Few people opposed the high court of commerce proposal; most just ignored it. Baruch tried to get it written into the Democratic party platform of 1920. His cabled proposal read:

> The Democratic Party never has and never will tolerate unfair methods of competition and unreasonable restraints in trade and commerce and will continue to demand the vigorous enforcement of all proper measures for their suppression. But this essentially negative policy of curbing vicious practices should in the general public interest be supplemented by a positive program and to that end we advocate transforming the Federal Trade Commission into an *enlarged tribunal* with broad constructive in addition to inquisitorial powers under strict governmental supervision [encouraging] such cooperation and coordination in industry as shall tend to eliminate waste[,] conserve natural resources[,] increase production both in quantity and quality[,] promote efficiency in operation and reduce costs to the ultimate consumer.

It was a hodgepodge of progressive principles and catchwords that usually drew nodding agreement.

Following the convention, Baruch took the idea for an economic tribunal to Democratic nominee James M. Cox. Baruch conceded that WIB table talk could not be made an issue in the coming campaign, particularly as it called for "modification" of the Sherman law: "You can see that this subject, in the present state of the public mind, would not receive proper consideration. Further, it would be taken up by the opposition and would be used . . . to our disadvantage." Nevertheless, he wanted the party's candidate for president to know the sum of the WIB's thinking. Invoking the concept of his judicial-administrative fourth branch of government, he described it for Cox as an institution "before which business men could go in times of severe underproduction . . . , and in times of over production, when there would be serious competition and economic losses involved." He was unclear on what the institution would do for businessmen in the latter instance, but he hinted that his court would issue edicts limiting competition and reducing output, actions that amounted to price manipulation. Even if such an institution were not feasible, Baruch hoped that a Cox presidency would establish a bureau making economic statistics available to businessmen who urgently needed to know more about the markets in which they operated. Also, government should be more responsive to businessmen: "The business men should have a closer affiliation with the Department of State, the Department of Commerce, the Treasury Department, the Department of the Interior, the Department of Labor and the Shipping Board." He envisioned advisory committees of businessmen for all these agencies. Workers and farmers would be represented on those advisory committees, too. Then informed American diplomats would, "in so far as is legitimate, carry our industrial interests to the corners of the world." He concluded with the assurance that a great corporate authority in Washington would eliminate the worst waste besetting business—regulatory laws. "We have enough laws upon our statute books if a *strong but wise hand* uses them."[18]

Cox's defeat and the Republican ascendancy did not inhibit Baruch from carrying his scheme to Washington. A month after the inauguration he took the commerce court plan to the new commerce secretary, Herbert Hoover. We can be certain that it was not the first time that Hoover had heard anything like this proposal; and Baruch knew that; taking it to Hoover was merely his way of establishing authorship with a former bureaucratic rival he suspected of adopting other people's concepts. Also, Commerce was the executive department most likely to push it.

Even if Hoover had not heard Baruch's concept before 1921, it is likely that he had heard of Harry Garfield's "industrial cabinet." The fuel administrator in early 1919 had proposed that Wilson create by executive order seven commissions representing the basic industries of the nation to serve as advisory bodies on essential economic questions. Needless to say, this scheme recalled the Advisory Commission of the Council of National Defense. It was a nebulous proposition that conferred unlimited discretionary powers upon the president and coincided with the creation of Peek's Industrial Board in the Commerce Department.[19]

"It looks as though we were all working along the same line," Baruch remarked when Peek sent him a draft for a bill to create a "federal board of trade," a statutory version of the Industrial Board and the high court of commerce. Indeed, in the 1920s and 1930s there would be a multitude of people working along the same lines toward rationalizing a chaotic business system with a corporatist solution. Baruch might have become silent if he had believed that the commerce court was an isolated bit of quackery. Instead, with the return of more prosperous times by the middle of the decade, with the return of old fears of overproduction and ruinous competition, he was emboldened to make his proposal public. At the 1924 WIB reunion dinner, attended by the press, Baruch renewed his call for the commerce court. His emphasis was upon remedying overproduction and competitive prices, which were abetted by the "inquisitorial" FTC and an intimidating Sherman law. Arguing that the regulatory agencies and the federal courts ought to follow the election returns, he interpreted the results of 1924 as a solid mandate for corporate consolidation and cooperation. Americans needed larger economic units: "These combinations, by their production, increase the standard of living by placing in the hands of the greatest number of people many of the things which they need for comfort and luxury." An omniscient commerce court would discipline great industrial aggregations in the public interest. Six years later, Baruch would again invoke the commerce court dream of stabilization; then, however, it would be presented as a solution to the business slowdown that followed the 1929 Wall Street panic.[20]

Baruch believed that the commerce court would be serviceable in all phases of the business cycle and to all groups in the economic system. To him its quasi-judicial quality would obviate partiality. It would be as skeptical toward bankers, as resistant to exorbitantly high prices ("profiteering"), as sympathetic to labor's quest for collective bargaining (although the court could negate undesirable results of free bargaining), as encouraging of producer combination and consolidation, and as antagonistic to legislative intervention as he was. In fact, the commerce court might almost eliminate the need for Congress. It would permit industrial self-government, private self-supervision and self-regulation, in the "many things that could best be done by the people [that] are being done by Government institutions which are not exactly fitted to do [them]." It would take politics out of the marketplace. In 1929 he enthusiastically backed President Hoover's request for a tariff bill that would allow rate adjustments by the chief executive, reasoning that tariff changes "should no more be undertaken by politicians than should a mastoid operation on one's dearest child by the neighborhood butcher. . . . Congress is political purely." However, because Americans could not always be certain of having a president as free from political expediency as Hoover, Baruch could not resist asking, "Why not take this question out of politics forever?" Answering himself, he declared: "The whole question should be removed from politics and placed in the hands of an Economic Commission not inferior in its own proper circumstance of dignity and equipment to the Supreme Court in its peculiar field."[21] It was an undisguised plea for his commerce court.

Of course there would be something of the commerce court in the New Deal's National Recovery Administration (NRA) led by Baruch's protégé, Hugh Johnson. But it would not be as free from politics as his commerce court. The NRA's life would belong to a politically minded Congress and president who could snuff it out at renewal time; or, as would be the case, a conservative Supreme Court doubtful of its constitutionality. Baruch's court was more supreme than the Supreme Court. Still, the NRA would owe its life to the high court of commerce idea and all the other industrial self-government concepts. And, in Baruch's mind, the NRA's demise would strengthen the need for a commerce court. He would witness decades of continued industrial strife and instability, ever quietly publicizing his "properly constituted arbitral authority" as a panacea for America's economic ills. Following World War II he would press it upon Truman administration officials as a means of combating inflation, strikes, and other economic turmoil of 1946. A half dozen years later he wondered if stabilization during the Korean War might be enhanced by it (by then the publicist believed that "perhaps it should be called a high court of equity," in deference to an age conscious of such matters).[22]

Baruch celebrated a decade of peace in 1928 by publishing an article that nostalgically summarized what he depicted as the war's beneficial consequences to industry. Americans were more self-sufficient in their use of raw materials, the production of which had been immensely increased the world over. In part this was in response to expanded manufacturing capacity. Much of this growth, he maintained, would have taken place without the war, but certainly the war accelerated that growth. Moreover, Americans had learned to organize their enterprise more along the lines of "a collective scheme" that made corporate planning possible. Industries were integrated through pooling and standardization. Baruch could be almost maudlin in recalling how, so he believed, the war had brought out the better angels of man's nature by appealing to America's sense of community. In that sense, his quest for a commerce court based upon the war experience was a bid to recapture forcibly a nonexistent moment in U.S. history when workers received wages commensurate with the importance of their labor, when farmers found markets and prices to their liking, when bankers followed credit practices that were socially acceptable, when the profiteering businessman had been condemned by Baruch in Teddy Roosevelt fashion as a malefactor, and love of country favored the corporate balance sheet. Men were "inspired" by a vision of growth and community: "It was a spiritual development that made possible this great material development."[23]

HOOVER, BARUCH, AND VOLUNTARY COOPERATION

Despite the apparent eccentricity of the supreme court of commerce idea, Baruch was only a synthesizer of business concepts of stabilization in the twenties. All he did was put his brand upon strategies for stabilization that had been discussed in private and in public for more than a decade. Similarly, he publicized the organization lessons of the Great War that had been evident to the Wilsonians and numerous business spokesmen. A multitude of business observers engaged in a cross-fertilization of stabilization concepts that were voguish between 1918 and 1922. Despite the failure of the Industrial Board in 1919, Wilsonians and other business philosophers still looked to the Commerce Department for the most practical implementation of orderly price changes. Individualism and anachronistic economic attitudes among politicians made Congress a potential barrier against cooperation, but education had to begin in the executive branch—and the Commerce Department seemed the choice of business philosophers for the initiative. Under the leadership of Wilson's secretary of commerce, William Redfield, a start had been made. It seemed probable that no matter which party won in 1920, that portfolio would continue to grow in importance. Some Wilsonians may have believed, both for partisan and for philosophical reasons, that the Republicans were not as likely as the Democrats to strengthen the business leadership role of the Commerce Department. Republicans tended to support either the grossest monopolies or anarchistic economic philosophies. But to the relief of the Wilsonians, one of their own took the Commerce Department post—Herbert Hoover.

"Hoover has the biggest job in Washington," Baruch commented a few days after the inauguration with not a little bit of envy. He stood ready to give Hoover unsolicited suggestions, "but I fear they would not be taken graciously." The old antagonism of the war years remained. It flattered Baruch that Hoover asked Alex Legge for assistance and appeared likely to seek out other WIB men, thus confirming the wisdom of Baruch's own talent searches and of WIB organizational concepts. He conceded admiration for Hoover's executive ability and his brilliant mind. However, "I wouldn't put my finger in his mouth; but that's another story." He had considered Hoover an idea and personnel thief during their war days. In

Baruch's strongest terms, Hoover "was a white livered yellow dog who was forever damning every body else and taking all the credit for everything that was successful, and shifting all the blame on the President or any one he could find for his failures."[24] He blamed Hoover for the high agricultural prices that contributed to the inflation of 1919. Nevertheless, relations between the two remained correct and cordial, and Hoover and Secretary of Agriculture Henry C. Wallace invited Baruch to their conference on agricultural marketing in June 1921. Yet even then, Baruch was irate over the similarity between Hoover's proposed marketing and credit plan for grain farmers and one he himself had made public seven months previously. Side by side in parallel columns, Baruch arranged his items next to Hoover's to show their similarity; he wrote in the margin, "Has Hoover borrowed another's plumes . . . ?" Sending Hoover a copy of his own propositions, Baruch called his attention to the closeness of their recommendations. "I have not always agreed with you," Baruch reminded his rival, as if it were necessary, but added that he was pleased to "advise on any subject" with his creative colleague. Privately, Baruch wrote: "Hoover is either a very ignorant man or a very ungenerous man, for he gives credit to no others for those wonderful ideas that have suddenly come down from the sky to him."[25]

Hoover would emerge as the Warwick of the Harding administration and the foremost spokesman in America for the industrial self-government concept. It was what Baruch expected of Hoover because, whether he recognized it or not, the two men were alike. If opposites attract and likes repel, Baruch and Hoover could never have been real friends. Differences between them abounded, but, just as Baruch's parallel columns of his proposals matched Hoover's alleged plagiarism, so their personalities, techniques, concepts, and ambitions unavoidably duplicated each other. Baruch had been a speculator in mining operations and had worked many years with the Guggenheims; Hoover had been a mining engineer previous to his government career and had rejected an offer from the Guggenheims to accept the Commerce Department post. Both men had a galaxy of able followers, and now some of Baruch's were spinning off to join Hoover. Both men were persuasive in small groups and enjoyed inundating less-informed adversaries with an avalanche of facts that appeared to support their arguments. Both men were shrewd publicists for their causes and themselves. Neither was shy about telling others how to improve the nation and the world, but both were uncertain of their oral and written abilities to express themselves. Yet their dissimilarities should not be neglected. Hoover was the superior intellect, more widely read, a more systematic thinker, more capable of a philosophy of history than Baruch. Baruch was the more likable personality, more ingratiating and gregarious, more tolerant of the nuances of politics, and more willing to call himself a party man than Hoover.

In war, Baruch and Hoover had coveted autocratic powers they believed necessary to overcome chaotic individualism and organize industry and agriculture to serve community interests. In peace, both men pursued stabilization without the coercion required by an ephemeral administration. Both men disdained the irrational policy making of parliamentary government and the costly bureaucracy of executive government. How could they achieve national stabilization without Washington? They shared enough of a paternalistic attitude toward businessmen to know that the desired organization could not come through "spontaneous cooperation" in peace any more than it could in war. That left the job of education, coordination, and supervision up to agencies in the federal government and to their business organization satellites. Even then, incoherence might dominate a program without centralized leadership. Hoover intended to give American business that leadership in the Department of Commerce. Had he been given the opportunity, and taken it, Baruch would have done the same. Yet the results would have been different.

Baruch lacked Hoover's organizational zeal, executive drive, and strong faith in the ultimate efficacy of voluntary activity. To the fundamental question whether a liberal capitalistic society could stabilize itself without institutionalizing monopoly or could act as an ultimate arbiter without regard to the marketplace, Hoover had answered in the affirmative; Baruch was ambivalent. Whereas Baruch argued that organic market forces of supply and demand would set their own just prices, from experience and observation he knew that men organized markets and rationally fixed their own prices. Moreover, because the whole trend of recent economic history was toward consolidation of corporations into larger units and organization of industries into trade associations (with the inducement of his own WIB practices) and workingmen into labor unions, it made sense to him for some neutral body to involve itself in the economic arena to umpire between hostile interests. Although Hoover did not steer clear of Baruch's commerce court, he seems to have preferred private corporatist stabilization arrangements to those involving government in any form.

Craig Lloyd has neatly capsuled the paradox of Hoover's behavior and personality in the title of his book *Aggressive Introvert*. Similarly, Ellis Hawley, who probably understands and has synthesized the conflict of Hoover's ideas and practices better than Hoover himself or any Hoover acolyte, has described him as "The Anti-Bureaucrat as Bureaucratic Empire-Builder." That Hoover overcame his own shy nature and philosophical underpinnings suggests a hard determination. Richard Hofstadter reminds us that "there is evidence that he had developed a vein of arrogance beneath his matter-of-fact exterior."[26] He did not suffer fools or wrongheaded adversaries with equanimity; he intimidated them with an avalanche of information and undercut them with unexpected initiatives. It took him and his hagiographers volumes to catalogue the successes of those initiatives and to attribute his failures to his opponents. Hoover seldom committed sins of omission. And, like Baruch, he made prophecy part of his stock-in-trade; he knew the shape of the future. Unlike Baruch, he sought accountable power to influence history; for this he was prepared to document the wisdom of every action meticulously. Before Franklin Roosevelt initiated the practice of presidential libraries filled with documents of self-justification, Hoover's colleagues had published volumes of state papers in support of their side; eventually a Herbert Hoover Presidential Library would supplement the monumental Hoover Institution at Stanford. Hoover might lose a battle, but he never lost an argument.

Hoover appealed to the better angels of man's liberal nature. His new order would be humane, solicitous of individual liberties, and rationally executed. Never the rugged individualist or laissez-faire champion depicted by the New Dealers who succeeded him, Hoover sought to preserve individual freedom within an enlightened community led by men who rejected monopoly, statism, and collectivism. Having used direct and indirect coercion during the war era, he now preached voluntary cooperation to enable Americans to avert the polar evils of chaos or collectivism. Through conferences and a myriad of commissions and other cooperative organizations, he would teach the people the superior attributes of voluntary action. Many historians have attributed this strategy to Hoover's Quaker background or his rural origins, as if to say that it was peculiar to him. It was not. Hoover was as much an interpreter of the Wilsonian synthesis as Baruch—or Norman Davis, or Harry Garfield, or Franklin Roosevelt, or Cordell Hull, and so on—all men who subscribed to the efficacy of "enlightened selfishness," private profits subsumed to public welfare. To Hoover's credit—or condemnation—he placed a greater premium upon the means toward his goal of stabilization than did Baruch and defined that strategy with less flexibility. He did not envision Baruch's "properly constituted arbitral authority" to stabilize American society when voluntary action failed.

Hoover's ideal was corporatist even if it was not statist. In an infrequent admission of uncertainty, relating in this instance to the farm problems of 1926, he wrote: "I confess I do not know how to go about it at the moment, but if we could get 25 sensible men in a room together without the pressure of either publicity or politics I believe the agricultural industry of the United States could be put on a basis more stable than any other industry."[27] One wonders how different would have been the composition and deliberations of this group of twenty-five "sensible" men from those of Baruch's supreme court of commerce. Both notions betoken an impatience with parliamentary democracy and a preference for rule by an economic and intellectual elite. To Hoover's credit, however, the remark was only whimsical; Baruch might have implemented the scheme if given the chance. As secretary of commerce, Hoover would organize "a type of private government" for which "the commerce department was to become a department of economic development and management; other agencies would still be responsible for special sectors of the economy, but commerce would serve as a general policy coordinator. In effect, as S. Parker Gilbert once put it, Hoover would be 'Under-Secretary of all other departments.'" Under Hoover's aggressive leadership, Washington "would act only as a clearing house, inspirational force, and protector of international rights, not as trader, investor, or detailed regulator."[28] It would develop and supervise the practice of industrial self-government.

Hoover created bureaus and boards and agencies in response to advances in technology and deficiencies in organization. All were designed to render information or service to the business community so that it would function more efficiently, more rationally, and more predictably. He expediently expanded the purview of his sector of the federal government, confident that it was evanescent pending the day when a multitude of trade associations, whose existence he had fostered, would provide their own enlightened leadership for stabilization. He justified *his* big government because, "like the war to end all wars, it was the bureaucratic empire to end all bureaucratic empires; and in theory at least it was supposed to wither away once the new order was built."[29] For those who celebrate constructive activism by government, this Hoover comes as a refreshing surprise. Yet as someone once said in defense of master road builder and city destroyer Robert Moses, if he had not built those highways, someone else would have built them sooner or later; it should be cautioned that if Hoover had not accelerated industrial organization and rationalization, there were other like-minded corporatists ready and willing to perform. Their performance might have been less aggressive, less encompassing, less thoughtful, and even less successful. But Hoover was not the indispensable man of the 1920s that his publicists portrayed.

In a selfish economic system, Hoover hoped to elicit cooperation. Baruch, as accustomed to the pits of Wall Street in his youth as Hoover had been to distant mining pits, was cynical concerning such expectations. However, Baruch was not less of an idealist, for what is a cynic if not an idealist soured by experience? Hoover had had much the same wartime experience as Baruch (the first government service for both came in wartime), and he was a man of the world; yet he seems to have clutched the utopia idealized by Baruch more firmly than the speculator. Baruch was less consistent; and it was in his cynical moments that he would have rammed his corporatism down the profiteering throats of businessmen whom Hoover still believed were persuadable. Which man would have benefited the community more—the one who put the means to stabilization above the goal itself? In the end, Hoover failed. As Ellis Hawley reminds us:

> Viewed from the altered perspective that took shape after 1929, his emerging private government seemed increasingly undemocratic, oppressive, and unresponsive. . . . And the leaders of his new order, revealed now to be far less altruistic and far less prescient than Hoover had hoped they would be, seemed unable either to sustain expansion, solve festering social problems, or check the greatest economic contraction in the nation's history. . . . Ironically, by demonstrating that they could not achieve the sustained expansion, rising living standards, and decentralized, non-coercive planning that they were supposed to achieve, he helped open the way for "big government" and state-enforced market controls in the 1930's.[30]

In a sense, Hoover's defeat was political, stemming from an inability to translate his philosophy from his personal vehicle to an institutional one. The concept of industrial self-government did not necessitate a party affiliation in an age of increasing voter estrangement from party loyalty. Besides, the two parties are nonideological. But the politicians themselves were still party loyalists and were not about to embrace a corporate concept that could deprive them of real power. Hoover was correctly Republican if he recognized the GOP as historically the proper place for such a nationalistic commercial scheme to root. However, he had chosen the wrong party as a vehicle, both for himself and for his philosophy. Industrial self-government, no matter how strongly it recalled the centralizing tendency inherent in the New Nationalism of Theodore Roosevelt, was essentially Wilsonian and Jeffersonian in its antigovernment bias and quest for decentralized order. And, because the concept was so Wilsonian, the Democratic party was where it belonged, where its publicists could inveigh against both bigness and chaos even as they sought more consolidations along decentralized lines. The rhetoric of voluntary cooperation usually sounded more natural coming from a Democrat than from a Republican. It paid homage to the party's nineteenth-century Jefferson-Jackson tradition even as it ruthlessly disavowed passive government. No wonder industrial self-government would find fruition in the early New Deal, whereas it passed from the Republican party with Herbert Hoover's decline. (It would reemerge as "Modern Republicanism" with Ike, whom Baruch would endorse!) Baruch had chosen wisely in becoming a Democrat, whereas Hoover endeavored to apotheosize himself and his utopia above party.

Hoover usually was a loner in government. While Baruch built a large reservoir of political IOUs throughout the war years, Hoover played a loner's game that kept even his governmental associates ignorant of his party affections. That was possible during a bipartisan war administration, and it might have been to his advantage had Hoover chosen to translate his personal popular following into a Democratic attachment. Certainly, Hoover was at home with the Wilsonian philosophy of government. The Democrats' interest in Hoover's political future was intense during 1919, and historians are fond of recalling the irony that among the most interested in Hoover's potential as a Democratic contender for the presidency was Franklin D. Roosevelt. Why not—considering that he was the most visible of the Wilsonians? In February 1920, Democrats, aware that Hoover verged on a declaration of party affiliation, anxiously sought to assure themselves that it would be for the party whose administration he had served. Breckenridge Long initiated an interview with Hoover, and Hoover responded by complaining of the similarities of the parties, their "political degeneracy" and "platitudinous platforms." Long answered that Hoover the great organizer ought to understand that political organization was imperative and that the party was "an agency to an end and to carry out real ideas." Hoover then launched into a discussion of current issues, denouncing nationalization of the railroads and other industries. Long did not disagree with Hoover; he merely urged him to formulate these ideas more positively. About the presidency, Hoover professed an indifference that Long thought "becoming." But Hoover's distaste for parties, Long believed, would be "likely to lead him to trouble."

Three days later, Democratic National Committee chairman Homer Cummings also sounded out Hoover on party affiliation and availability for the presidential nomination. Democrats wanted Hoover's luster at a time when their own fortunes were on the wane, and Cummings made no bones about it. Cummings interpreted Hoover's willingness to talk with him as a signal of his receptivity to the party's organization. Apparently, Hoover had absorbed Long's lecture on the need for parties, for Cummings was impressed with Hoover's belief that "a person who was elected President would regard the party organization as entitled to consideration and respect" and with his statement that "he favored party regularity and discipline." On current issues, Hoover found nothing in Democratic positions to quarrel with, and he went out of his way to invoke frequently the Wilsonian phrase "equality of opportunity." Cummings told Hoover that "it seemed to me that he was a Jeffersonian Democrat, that I could not gather from anything he said that he would be at all uncomfortable in the Democratic household." Hoover agreed. Unlike Long, Cummings found Hoover "engaging" and "amiable," and he was led to suspect that Hoover was shrewdly shopping for a party. But, several days later, Hoover let it be known through intermediaries that he identified himself as a Republican. Cummings was especially disappointed because Hoover's "method of expression reminds you of Wilson" and Hoover "seems to understand W.W." However, Cummings noted that Wilson was stronger for party government and personally doubtful of Hoover.[31] The Wilsonians lost a viable leader for the 1920s. Ironically, that loss may have been a blessing, for it left them alive and ready for a resurgence in the 1930s. Hoover would fail, but not the concept of "voluntary cooperation."

Hoover seems to have suffered from an excess of principle that went against the American political tradition of expediency, as witness Hofstadter's comment that "Hoover can always be acquitted of the charge of revising his ideas to cater to mass sentiment." Baruch railed against that public image in the 1920s, and others corroborated a Hoover flexibility on principle. But Hoover was merely inconsistent in his attachment to principle. As a publicist he stressed his adherence to principle, another of his political postures that the public would find "becoming." In private, regarding his Wilsonian devotion to the League of Nations, Hoover was crafty, somewhat devious—and a good politician on the make. Proselytizing for the League of Nations in 1923, Lord Robert Cecil naturally sought out Hoover, whom the Englishman had known as a believer in Paris four years before. The secretary of commerce went on at length about national and international economics before Cecil steered the conversation to the purpose for his visit. Then he found Hoover "evidently apologetic for his attitude about the League[,] explaining that you cannot do more than you can do." He strongly encouraged Cecil to continue his quest for U.S. support for the League and to persuade its opponents, who were strongest in Hoover's Republican party, "that their enterprise is impractical." Then, Cecil wrote, "as I went away he begged me to tell any newspaper men who asked after our interview that we had discussed the world position of commerce and say nothing about the League."[32] Hoover was proposing a half-truth that Americans would come to appreciate from expedient politicians like Franklin Roosevelt. Of course, it was a clumsy one because it belied the well-known reason for Cecil's mission; but historians seldom fault Hoover for attempting to play politics, just for failing to do so.

Baruch's constant complaint of Hoover's deviousness was more than sour grapes. The speculator angrily admired Hoover's skillful self-promotion with the public even as he privately sought to undermine it with policy makers. He resented newspaper editorials that attributed many of Hoover's commerce programs to 1921 beginnings; Baruch was certain that campaigns for standardization and waste elimination in industry had their origins in Wilson's administration—even before the War Industries Board. Nevertheless, in 1928, Baruch would tell Hoover that "we seem to have different views regarding the philosophy of government." Of course they had some differences, but it was mostly Baruch's attachment to party and loathing of Hoover that inspired disagreement. Hoover's popularity intensely annoyed Baruch:

Hoover has delusions of grandeur now. He really believes all the wonderful things he has written about himself are true. As a mining engineer he never had a success in his life. I know of no business that he has ever directed successfully, except for himself. Nor do I know of any great question on which he has not taken one position and then shifted it at least once. One must take off his hat to him on the way he has publicized himself so thoroughly. All the things that Mr. Wilson told him to do he took unto himself. Now he is a great prophet of prosperity which is the economic consequence of the war due to the genius and hard work of our business leaders.[33]

Let us not forget that Baruch's tirade came in the heat of the campaign as a reaction to Hoover's campaign rhetoric and deserves some discounting. Even so, there is more than a little truth in Baruch's emphasis upon the continuity of Wilsonian policies and the impact of wartime innovations.

THE FARMER'S FRIEND IN WALL STREET

Addressing in 1921 a conference of twenty-five leaders in business, labor, and agriculture—in Hoover's mind the proper-sized group to resolve the problems of America—the secretary of commerce asserted that "an infinite amount of misery could be saved if we had the same spirit of *spontaneous cooperation* in every community for reconstruction that we had in the war."[34] Like Baruch, Hoover missed the motivating force of patriotism for organization. Nevertheless, he recognized that cooperation had to be mobilized through Washington or the political economy would be chaotic. And in certain sectors of the marketplace the chaos was more pronounced than in others. During the war, Hoover had dealt with the most fragmented area, agriculture, whereas Baruch had begun with the most noncompetitive, raw materials. Though Hoover centered his organizing attentions in the 1920s upon the bituminous coal and textile industries, which were plagued by excesses of competition and resultant low prices, both Hoover and Baruch dabbled extensively in movements for agricultural relief and farm cooperatives.

Of all America's producers, her farmers were the most competitive and overproductive. Hoover's Food Administration had fixed high incentive prices that could not be maintained when global markets were restored in 1920. Yet the farmers could not adjust their productive abundance to conform with emerging competitive realities. Their surpluses had been aggressively marketed by Hoover and by Eugene Meyer's War Finance Corporation in the year following the Armistice, but then the administration abandoned its overseas brokering for farmers in favor of defeating domestic inflation. The ensuing deflation spelled disaster for the farmer.

For the ideologists of cooperation, Baruch and Hoover, the farmer's plight became a stern test of the efficacy of voluntarism. If agriculture could be cooperatively organized to achieve good incomes for producers without the hand of government operating the price controls, then industrial self-government would be feasible in any sector of the economy. And the antitrust-minded farmers could hardly deny other producers the legal and political right to stabilize their markets through cooperation once they had done it themselves.

Baruch savored the irony of his entry into the farmer's movement of the 1920s. Late nineteenth-century social attitudes had suggested that organized farmers were automatically radical and dangerous to the market advantages of all other groups. Baruch himself seems to have held such a perspective, but he mostly attributed it to his comrades in the financial district. Upon his return from Europe in 1919, Baruch made a fetish of his proclaimed democratic ideals. He enjoyed shocking acquaintances in his milieu with his advocacy of recognizing the Soviets in Russia; domestically, he cast about for a cause upon which to lavish his contrived egalitarianism. The Industrial Conference of 1919 marked a brief fling for him on the side of the organized workingman, but Baruch did not communicate well with men he saw as essentially cost factors in production. On the other hand, farmers were true producers—for that matter, capitalists not unlike copper operators and other raw material producers whose supply and demand concerns called for stabilization planning. Farmers were businessmen like his friends in the extractive industries, desiring only a fair price for their output, and no more radical than any entrepreneur who took the corporate form of organization over the proprietary.

His chance came early in 1920 when he received an invitation from J. C. Mohler, secretary of the Kansas State Board of Agriculture, to contribute his judgments on the agricultural depression. Knowing that he was one of many prominent persons whose advice for farm recovery had been solicited as a device for alerting opinion makers to hard times on the farm, Baruch seized the opportunity to broaden his alliances. He went to Kansas to investigate the problem firsthand, which meant establishing contacts with farm organization leaders, newspaper editors, and political leaders like Senator Arthur Capper. To become an instant agricultural expert, he sought a sample of insights from those who best understood the problem. He employed economist W. Jett Lauck to gather data on agricultural finance, the role of middlemen, and basic costs. He personally inquired of Secretary of Agriculture E. T. Meredith what services his department provided farmers in the marketing of crops abroad ("relatively little compared to Commerce's aid to manufacturers," came the reply). He discussed marketing with corn belt spokesman Henry A. Wallace.[35] But Baruch was not a novice in farm affairs.

He had been dabbling behind the scenes in government agricultural policies during 1918–19. Good bureaucratic imperialist that he was, he was not about to leave Hoover alone with agriculture during the war, particularly where southern cotton was concerned. Baruch seemed to believe that his South Carolina manners entitled him to a voice in the matter of fixing cotton's price. With some assistance from brokers, including Will Clayton of Houston, Baruch argued strenuously that cotton ought to have a market price except when there were signs of an impending scarcity. Even without high price incentives, cotton production never suffered from the glut induced by Hoover's artificial price on wheat and other commodities. Baruch later pointed to this particular difference between himself and Hoover as evidence that, of the two of them, Hoover was more of a price-fixer with less insight into agriculture.[36] Baruch had been telling Farm Bureau leaders that agrarians should market their commodities in conformity to real costs and should lobby for legislative assistance to farm cooperatives in the export trade. Because his own lobbying brought him in touch with Senator Capper, he was not unfamiliar in Kansas at all.[37]

On 3 December 1920, Baruch sent his reply to Mohler in a lengthy letter simultaneously released to newspapers. Professing a modest insight into agriculture, Baruch attributed marketing problems to war-stimulated overproduction combined with financing of U.S. agricultural exports. Describing it as essentially a problem of finance qualified him to speak with acumen. Under the rules of Wilsonian equality of opportunity, the American farmer had to compete in world markets, a circumstance made treacherous because of commodity overproduction and money-starved foreign markets. American producers found it advantageous to finance overseas buyers. In particular, the farmer needed capital to finance storage of commodities in warehouses or grain elevators until buyers could be found at prices higher than cost. Baruch preferred private stockpiling (he had advised Wilson to stockpile raw materials in order to stimulate production at higher prices), but he believed that the government should provide facilities if they were not forthcoming at reasonable rates from private sources. With warehouses the farmers could launch cooperative marketing systems. Cooperative marketing, in turn, would enable the farmer to sell at a propitious time and command more reasonable credit than he could obtain as an individual producer.

Credit was the key to businesslike farming. Cooperatives "should be large enough and so officered that they would gain the confidence of the investing public." Baruch wanted big farm corporations and conservative management. "Bearer certificates based upon carefully guarded advances on farm products" would attract investor interest. Because the Agriculture Department was of little use to farmers who sought to regulate their output to domestic and foreign consumption, Baruch argued for regular government-supplied information to marketing corporations that would enable them to time their sales to meet demand conditions. Cooperative marketing, even on a local or regional basis (although Baruch preferred national organizations to avoid geographic competition), was desirable; however, Baruch inveighed against cooperative buying that might disrupt a potential harmony of interests in the rural community.[38]

For all Baruch's posturing as a Wall Street radical, his letter was a profoundly conservative document filled with prescriptions designed to consolidate farming to make it attractive to big finance. His hints that he would use government facilities to store commodities and would sell them overseas in tune with government data on markets were consistent with proposals that antedated the war and had been debated for years. And his injunction against cooperative buying smacked of cronyism when we recall that some of his closest associates in the WIB were in the farm implement and fertilizer industries!

The Baruch manifesto caught the attention of Aaron Sapiro, an articulate California lawyer who had become a major publicist for agricultural cooperatives. Praising Baruch's analysis of foreign trade conditions as "unusually interesting" and his recommendations for warehousing and financing as "keen," Sapiro nevertheless complained that Baruch was ignorant of existing cooperative associations and their operations. "Mr. Baruch would be an enormous factor in American agricultural life if he would try to understand the real co-operative movement in its fundamental aspects," Sapiro wrote. Others likewise criticized Baruch's financing plan and questioned his understanding of agricultural marketing.[39] Even so, the Kansas letter accomplished the purpose of injecting Baruch into the farm debates of the 1920s.

The year 1921 was a busy one for Baruch. Not only did he play a role in Democratic National Committee maneuverings, he became heavily involved in the farmer's movement. He put his letter to Mohler into pamphlet form, and its circulation brought it attention as one of the first programs to meet the postwar agricultural crisis. It attracted the interest of the Grain Marketing Committee of Seventeen of the American Farm Bureau Federation, a collection of agricultural leaders charged by the parent organization with developing a plan for nationwide marketing. The Committee of Seventeen had been traveling and studying cooperatives in California and in Europe. A scheme was developed for cooperative grain elevators and an export corporation. Asked to help the farmers develop a finance corporation, Baruch met with the Committee of Seventeen at a public gathering in Kansas City and then left for the South to persuade cotton farmers to a similar scheme for marketing and warehousing. When a larger conference of the Farm Bureau met at Chicago in April, it was apparent that grain growers were divided over the question of compulsory pooling of a percentage of each farmer's crop. In a sharply divided vote it was decided to form the United States Grain Growers,

Inc., a marketing and warehousing corporation for farmers.[40] Then the farmers turned to Baruch and offered him the job of running their financing operation.

Baruch turned them down. Fissures in the Grain Growers organization had begun to develop, and Baruch had come under attack by the Hearst press, which accused him of representing a Wall Street conspiracy to control grain marketing. Alex Legge, on behalf of farm equipment manufacturers who sought to stabilize farm prices and farmer buying habits, implored his WIB chief to take the finance post. Baruch was flattered by this plea but urged them to find some bankers instead.[41] Baruch wanted to advise farmers and not involve himself in their internecine fights or in their battles with the Grain Dealers Association. As the movement for grain grower cooperation floundered, Baruch would say only, "Their organization is sound in principle and I believe it ought to be saved. But the people to do it are the farmers themselves."[42]

Generous with his advice and his money, Baruch was chary about involving himself further with farmers. Besides the grain growers, he was exhorting tobacco and cotton farmers to form cooperatives along the lines he prescribed. With Robert W. Bingham, publisher of the *Louisville Courier-Journal*, Baruch assisted large tobacco growers in Kentucky to form a cooperative association that elected Bingham its president.[43]

Significantly, when Baruch turned his hand to cotton cooperatives, he no longer was satisfied with stockpiling and marketing a commodity; he sought crop reduction, a more direct influence upon price and income. Without foreign buyers or diminished costs, cotton farmers had to reduce their output. As Baruch told the governor of South Carolina, "If you will notice, the copper producers have undertaken something along the lines of my suggestion to you." Obviously, Baruch believed that cotton and copper were somewhat analogous, but that belief ignored the fact that copper production was oligopolistic, whereas cotton production was competitive despite loosely organized cooperatives. Besides, what inducement would a farmer have for reducing his cotton acreage when doing so correspondingly reduced his income? For the time being, Baruch wanted cotton farmers to warehouse their cotton and take bank loans, using their cotton as collateral. If banks were unwilling to gamble with cotton markets, then Baruch proposed a finance corporation that would raise at least a million dollars selling notes on the warehoused cotton. But bankers were unwilling to speculate that withholding cotton could drive its price up to acceptable levels. Baruch still went ahead with a plan worked out between himself and the governor of South Carolina: he subscribed $500,000 to a finance corporation and the State of South Carolina matched that amount. He was betting that his money and the state's would lure other investors to assist in the cooperative manipulation of market prices.[44]

The caution of bankers disgusted him, and he stood ready to help farmers' finances any time he believed that their enterprise was soundly based. For instance, when Northwestern Wheat Growers wanted a $6–8 million loan on their wheat stored in elevators, Baruch offered to buy 10 percent of the certificates issued for the wheat. The alleged radicalism of the Nonpartisan League did not frighten Baruch, who thought enough of its cooperative efforts to subscribe to its bonds and contribute to the career of its political spokesman, Congressman William Lemke of North Dakota. Baruch preferred to speculate on warehoused commodities, but he also contributed to such causes as a conference on cooperatives.[45]

By the spring of 1921 he had earned a reputation among agrarians as a businessman enlightened enough to assist their organizational efforts. Hence, Baruch was angered by Hoover's call for a Washington conference to discuss his own marketing plan, given the similarity of the commerce secretary's scheme to Baruch's Kansas proposals. Neither man had an especially original idea, because both embroidered upon the apparently successful efforts of California cooperatives, but Baruch resented Hoover's poaching on his territory as a business sympathizer for agriculture. Still, they agreed on the general outlines of dealing with the agricultural depression and the necessity of promoting voluntarism and heading off political solutions. In the end, Hoover's conference accomplished nothing other than demonstrating Washington's interest in the growers' plight.[46]

But the conference's underlying motive had been to mobilize opposition against the Norris Farm Export Bill, which called for a government corporation to buy farm surpluses for sale abroad. Hoover, Secretary of Agriculture Henry C. Wallace, and War Finance Corporation Chairman Eugene Meyer, Jr., united behind a substitute measure that became part of the omnibus Agricultural Credits Act of 1921. Yet Hoover complained that parts of the law called for too much government involvement with disproportionate benefits going to middlemen rather than to farmers. Baruch concurred with that assessment: "I don't think it is going to be of much help to the individual farmer, but will be of very great help to the man that buys and moves his products." However, he doubted that Hoover had more to offer farmers; "I hear a whole lot of committees being appointed [by Hoover]; but I don't hear of them doing anything at all." Also, it seemed to Baruch that the whole tenor of the Harding administration was more solicitous of bankers than of farmers.[47]

For Hoover the federal government served as a coordinator of cooperatives and the last resort for financing and marketing his commodities; for Baruch the first choice lay with cooperatives, but he suspected that the last resort was close at hand. When he first became involved with the grain growers' cooperatives, Baruch eschewed government involvement in marketing, a position that aligned him with Hoover. Following some involvement in the cooperative movement, Baruch edged closer to the concept of government assuming a greater role in farm markets.

Fundamental to the Baruch approach in agriculture was a frontal assault upon the antitrust laws. "Modernization" of agriculture called for large farm corporations that would regulate their output in order to set commodity prices, action that would have brought swift antitrust action if those corporations had been manufacturers. "So the farmers affirm the necessity of amending those laws," asserted Baruch, blithely ignoring the fact that the Clayton Act usually was interpreted as exempting cooperatives from antitrust prosecution. Still, Baruch insisted that the antitrust statutes carried "many intimidating suggestions of violations" by cooperatives. The farmers needed an "affirmative law" that would approve consolidation and integration in manufacturing corporations as well. Then the farm corporations could integrate their producing and marketing functions. Baruch hoped to create a community of interests between agrarians and industrialists, both of whom would be better situated to control market forces than before. Industrialists ought to welcome farm cooperatives because their structure would imitate that of steel manufacturers, and the farmers' improved market position would assure industry of customers with enhanced buying power. Baruch envisioned a common front of farmers and entrepreneurs for bigness, marketing control, and the corporate structure. Moreover, farmers and industrialists both had need of overseas markets. In fact, when Baruch was asked by an interviewer to identify "'the most important thing to be done immediately in aiding the farmer,'"

"Fully restore his foreign markets," was the laconic answer.
"I mean in the United States," I explained.
"I mean in the United States, too," was the emphatic reply, "for the foreign markets are to be opened up primarily by action taken right here at home. We've got to abandon this isolation policy and get into the world circle initiatively, if we expect to do business with other countries and get our share of international commerce."[48]

In summary, Baruch encouraged organization of farm cooperatives that would become big agricultural corporations emulating industrial confrontations with the antitrust laws and lust for foreign markets. It was hardly a new prescription for the farmers' ills. But in the context of changes that had developed in American industry over the previous quarter century, it amounted to a large dose of corporatism for individualistic, proprietary agriculture:

Why should not the farmers be permitted to accomplish by cooperative methods what other businesses are already doing by cooperation in the form of incorporation? If it be proper for men to form, by fusion of existing corporations or otherwise, a corporation that controls the entire production of a commodity, or a larger part of it, why is it not

proper for a group of farmers to unite for the marketing of their common products, either in one or several selling agencies? Why should it
be right for a hundred thousand corporate shareholders to direct 25 or
30 or 40 per cent of an industry, and wrong for a hundred thousand
cooperative farmers to control a no larger proportion of the wheat
crop, or cotton, or any other product?

Implicit in Baruch's reasoning was a strong defense of large concentrations of productive power in any industry. In consonance with his advocacy of the commerce court concept, Baruch urged bringing laws and
government in line with the new realities of contemporary corporate
structure. At heart a voluntarist, he argued that realities dictated larger
government involvements:

> I am opposed to the injection of government into business, but I
> do believe that it is an essential function of democratic government to
> equalize opportunity so far as it is within its power to do so, whether
> by repeal of archaic statutes or the enactment of modern ones. If the
> anti-trust laws keep the farmers from endeavoring scientifically to
> integrate their industry, while other industries find a way to meet
> modern conditions without violating such statutes, then it would seem
> reasonable to find a way for the farmers to meet them under the same
> conditions. . . .
> We have traveled a long way from the old conception of government
> as merely a defensive and policing agency.

This had the ring of progressivism. All he wanted for farmers was parity
with industry—equality of opportunity. Farmers would achieve real market power with the cooperative-corporation structure. Farmers who subscribed to cooperatives might learn to appreciate corporate organization:
"The one is a lumbering democracy and the other an agile autocracy,"
Baruch declared. But he knew that it would be a long time before farmers
were united enough to manipulate their prices as readily as steel companies controlled theirs.[49]

While Baruch courted farmer acceptance of modern corporate levia-
thans, he also proselytized among businessmen for approval of farm
cooperatives. He derided industrial fears that agricultural organizations
would disrupt their businesses. When a friend from WIB days moaned
that the market for his fertilizer-manufacturing firm was "absolutely
gone," Baruch was unsympathetic; businessmen, he declared, had invited
bad markets by their hostility to organized farmers. He endorsed, over
resistance by bankers, the appointment of a "dirt farmer" to the Federal
Reserve Board, where he could protect agricultural credit interests: "There
is too much mystery about finance on the part of the bankers anyway.
Banking is the simplest business in the world. The farmers are quite right

in trying to get somebody more favorable to their interests than those heretofore have been." He was happy in his irony-laden role as the enlightened Wall Street advocate of farmer causes. In January 1922 he told an Iowa senator: "It may interest you to know that I am lunching today with the New York *Times* people to discuss with them the wickedness of your agricultural bloc. You and I are going to get into a bad way, because you are going to be tainted with me, and I am going to be tainted with you."[50] Yet Baruch was not the only business supporter of the farm movement, if only because his old cronies from the WIB—Alex Legge, George Peek, and Eugene Meyer—also promoted the concept of a community of interests among farmers, manufacturers, and bankers.

But cooperation among farmers did not take hold as its publicists wanted. By 1922 the Grain Growers had tired of cooperation and ousted their old leadership in favor of advocates of political action. The Farmers' Finance Corporation was dying for lack of investor attention. Whereas Baruch and Hoover had endorsed farmer voluntarism, the farmers insisted that they needed Washington's intervention to manage their markets.[51] In this new phase of the 1920s farm movement, George Peek emerged as an agricultural agitator and the focus shifted from cooperatives to Congress. Baruch already operated on Capitol Hill with ease, and because his agricultural synthesis included a role for the federal government, he had no problem making the changeover.

"OBLIGATORY" COOPERATION IN AGRICULTURE

The administration had called a National Agricultural Conference for January 1922 at Washington, where the most articulate voices for the farmer would be heard debating agricultural issues. For George Peek it was an opportunity to seize farm leadership. Since leaving the Industrial Board fiasco he had returned to the farm equipment-manufacturing business, this time working for himself as head of Moline Plow Company. However, in an industry that depended upon the farmer as a customer, Peek found nothing but trouble in 1920–21. Along with his associate at Moline Plow and friend from WIB days, Hugh S. Johnson, Peek intently studied the agricultural problem; by December 1921 they had written a forty-eight-page pamphlet entitled *Equality for Agriculture*. In it they argued that manufactures and wheat existed on two different price levels, the former protected in a domestic market, the latter vainly pursuing foreign customers for its surplus. Simply put, wheat prices would rise in a domestic market if those surpluses could be marketed overseas by cooperatives assisted by the federal government. The pamphlet earned Peek and Johnson an invitation to the conference, and on its second day, Peek took advantage of an offer to speak for ten minutes and launched an hour-and-a-half discourse on his solution to the price gap. How many converts he made is impossible to say, but the conference adjourned only after passing a resolution that Washington ought to act to "re-establish a fair exchange value for all farm products with that of all other commodities." For Peek it was the beginning of a crusade.

By the mid-twenties he became a publicist, organizer, and lobbyist for legislation that would have put his ideas into practice—the controversial McNary-Haugen bills. The bills were unassailable in their intent to equalize agricultural commodity prices with other commodity prices, but their intended machinery and practice opened them to controversy. Establishing a federally capitalized agricultural export corporation, the bills would have put a floor under commodity prices at home by selling surpluses abroad. This inspired a myriad of objections: the government would have to go into business in behalf of farmers and thereby erect an interest-group bureaucracy; dumping surpluses would bring retaliation by other countries and trade wars; farmers organized by the export corporation potentially threatened the profits of processors; and finally, the concept inadvertently encouraged overproduction by assuring farmers that the corporation would find buyers. However, from the start the bills had considerable appeal to farmers, and in time, Congress passed them; in 1927 and 1928 only vetoes by President Coolidge prevented varying versions of the McNary-Haugen bills from becoming law.[52]

Baruch's role in the McNary-Haugen campaigns is ambiguous at the least. He was known as a supporter and he was one. But, as in the case of his support of McAdoo's presidential candidacy, it may be that both Baruch and some contemporaries—and we might add historians to the list—exaggerated his prominence in the McNary-Haugen movement. Merely lending it his name gave it some respectability in certain conservative circles. Still, Chester C. Davis, Peek's lieutenant in the fight for the legislation, later recalled that Baruch's main contribution to McNary-Haugenism consisted of "money and moral support" given entirely through Peek; otherwise his connection "was a very tenuous one." Baruch withheld direct support for the movement, but proved loyal to his friend Peek. "There is no doubt in my mind that Baruch could have accomplished something if he had really wanted," Davis said. "Baruch could have been a powerful aid here."[53]

Baruch's role in the farmers' movement was mostly one of "money and moral support" for cooperatives; otherwise, he was unlikely to involve himself organizationally. To do so seemed to him an unnecessary risk of his political capital, both with policy makers and with the public. Besides, his statements suggest that he was still uncomfortable with the farmers' "radical" image, which he defensively explained as a quest for equal opportunity. Even so, Baruch was one of the few men identified with big capital who dared to attach himself in any capacity to the farmers' movements of the 1920s.

Baruch attended the Washington conference of 1922, but he did not embrace the Peek plan. He spoke positively of it because it was promoted by a man he admired. A firm believer in the overproduction thesis, Baruch was torn between supporting cooperatives that limited yields through acreage reductions and endorsing Peek's proposal to exploit foreign markets. He watched farm legislating carefully and freely gave to Senators Capper and Kenyon and other mainstays of the farm bloc his unsolicited advice. He wanted farm bloc senators to know that he was their friend regardless of party affiliation. The election of 1922 excited him, not only because it augured well for Democrats, but because it gave the farm bloc the prospect of holding the Senate's balance of power. He hoped it would use its power to help the cooperative movement, but would refrain from legislating parity. The corporate organization of farmers was fundamental to his thinking. "The farmer must be taught to be loyal to the cooperative" and to learn that individualism brought overproduction. He would have to organize to plan his markets in order to achieve parity with industry.[54]

Mostly out of respect for George Peek, Baruch worked for the McNary-Haugen bill of 1924. In March he gave a grand dinner at his home, to which a wide assortment of notables in New York journalistic circles were invited to hear Peek and Hugh Johnson discourse on farm parity. Also, he extolled the bill to friends in business and finance in an effort to elicit their support for it. He preferred to have it limited to wheat, a restriction that he knew was unlikely because it would reduce the bill's appeal to farm legislators and guarantee its defeat. He assured financier Otto Kahn, "I favor the *principle* involved in the McNary-Haugen Bill only because it meets a crisis." Because it was presented as a short-term palliative, not as a panacea, he told Senator Thomas J. Walsh, "the mistake would not be so great."[55] But the Congress was not yet ready for Peek's plan and the McNary-Haugen bill.

The Coolidge landslide of 1924 jolted the farm movement. Opponents of McNary-Haugenism launched a propaganda campaign that emphasized the improvement in farm incomes under the Republicans while ignoring the disparity with industrial prices. George Peek counterattacked, moving to Washington, where, as president of the newly formed American Council of Agriculture, a coalition of cooperatives, he directed his own publicity and lobbying effort for farm equality. During 1925 local midwestern banking and merchant interests began to coalesce behind their agricultural clients. And a movement that had been confined to the West and Midwest began to get tentative expressions of support from southern lawmakers. Another effort to pass the McNary-Haugen bill, by then a compromise measure designed to combine a broad variety of farm concerns, failed in 1926. It was evident, however, that there would be a more forceful push for the equity legislation in 1927.

Through 1924 and 1925, Baruch had been a mainstay in the financing of Peek's organization. Also, he lobbied with southern Democrats in the Senate for an alliance of "corn and cotton." Still he remained a tepid McNary-Haugenite, a position in part dictated by his need to negotiate between free-trade-minded southern brethren and Peek's unyielding high tariff views. Besides, he shared "a common ground" with Hoover on agriculture (by which Baruch meant that he had not abandoned the cooperative formula for attacking the farm problem). Unlike Hoover, Baruch liked tough persuasion in his "cooperation." He explained his contradictory support of cooperatives and Peek's plan this way: "The McNary-Haugen Bill is really cooperative marketing carried to the Nth degree; it makes it *obligatory* and not promissory. I believe almost any of the ideas would work if we could all get behind one of them. However, *obligatory* cooperative marketing would be better than the other form because everybody would share in the profits and no one could stay out and be used by the dealers to snipe at the rest of the farmers."[56] In principle, he favored cooperation; in practice, he favored intimidation. In principle, he opposed the Peek scheme—but he hoped that it would organize farmers.

Would his southern friends in Congress join with Baruch in favor of a plan that went against free trade? A glut of cotton was on his side. "For the life of me I can't understand why Pat Harrison is opposing this legislation," he responded when Peek complained that he was "unable to understand the apathy of some of your friends." By the end of 1926 southern farm leaders agreed that under the Peek plan, much of the surplus cotton would have been sold abroad. While some parts of the South attempted cooperative acreage reductions, and Texas passed a law prohibiting the planting of cotton two years in succession, Baruch exhorted his fellow South Carolinians to withhold their crops from the market. But by early 1927 many southerners despaired of local or cooperative efforts to control their surplus production. Aaron Sapiro, the high priest of farm cooperation, reported that he found growing support for the McNary-Haugen bill among southern cooperative associations. When the bill passed Congress that year, it was with the aid of southern votes that had gone against it in previous years.[57] President Coolidge vetoed it, but hopes among the McNary-Haugenites rose in anticipation of another passage in 1928 and an override of another veto.

No longer important to the cause for his contributions or his influence with southern legislators, Baruch in 1928 stressed the need to persuade western farmers to vote Democratic. The Republican Peek agreed in 1928 to throw in with Al Smith—a move that surprised nobody who knew that Peek detested Hoover on a philosophical and personal level. Following Hoover's election with a sizable Republican majority in Congress, Baruch began to act as a brake upon Peek in any intentions of reviving his quest for a McNary-Haugen law. He now opposed a McNary-Haugen bill that would dump surpluses without dealing with the fundamental problem: the production of excess supply for insufficient demand. In lieu of his contributions to Peek's farm relief schemes, he invested in a Peek enterprise for manufacturing building materials from cornstalks. It was not the sort of enterprise Baruch expected to yield a good return on his $25,000, but he hoped that it would give his friend something else to do. Peek attracted more investors who hoped to raise farm incomes by finding a use for the waste part of corn, but in five years the National Cornstalk Process Company went bankrupt.[58] In less time than that, George Peek would again be a name on the lips of American farmers.

Baruch was an anomaly in the farm movement; what was a Jewish Wall Street speculator who kept a home in South Carolina doing among those predominantly Protestant farmers from the wheat belt?

Baruch not only *contributed* money to the farm movement; he *invested* considerably in agriculture-related enterprises. For instance, he bought shares in cotton warehouses and counseled his investor friends to follow suit. Following the creation by Congress of Intermediate Credit Banks for farmers in 1923, Baruch purchased $250,000 of tax-exempt debentures paying 4.5 percent interest. Baruch's investment portfolio included shares not only in Peek's faltering Moline Plow, but also in other farm implement corporations whose profits by 1928 were so good that their managers feared farmer resentment. He also speculated in farmland. These agricultural investments were consistent with his political activities and his direct farm investments.* Agriculture did not add much, if anything, to a man's riches in the 1920s. However, Baruch had personal motives: the publicity he won as the farmers' Wall Street friend fed his massive ego and increased his influence in the Senate, where more men owed their careers to Baruch. (We can only wonder how many farm leaders like George Jewett heard these head-turning words from Baruch: "If you ever want to run for the Senate in your country, let me know; I should like to help you.")[59] His farm activity was a touch of romantic altruism that blended well into his conception of a community that practiced enlightened selfishness.

---

*Contrary to what Rexford Tugwell has written, and Tugwell believed that Baruch was evil incarnate, Baruch was not in league with food processors in the 1920s. In fact, Baruch's support of cooperative marketing and the agricultural export corporation put him and Peek in direct conflict with processors. One of the Peek-plan's primary attractions to farmers was that it went against the interests of middlemen. Tugwell, *The Brains Trust* (1968), p. 456; James Gray, *Business without Boundary: The Story of General Mills* (1954), pp. 87–89, 193.

Agricultural cooperatives were necessary ingredients in Baruch's "practical idealism." The least organized and the most competitive of economic sectors had to organize cooperation before it would tolerate the legalization of industrial consolidations and cartels. Farmer organization was in the interest of other businessmen; as Baruch put it, "The better satisfied the farmer is, the less he will object to what other people do legitimately."[60] What he meant was the inverse of this: the more dissatisfied the farmer was, the more he would object to legalizing industrial cartel activity or railroad consolidations.

Beyond what the adoption of his scheme brought him in ego gratification and stabilization of his investments, Baruch had other stakes. Railroad consolidation would bring him substantial profits on his rail securities, but he probably would have believed in the stabilization virtues of mergers even if he had owned no transportation stocks. *The nation's well-being was always identical with his own.* It was a part of his enlightened selfishness. Baruch's vision was not parochial. As an investor he sought a harmonization of business interests in all sectors. He sought universal organization of the market to prevent any single group's exploitation.

As he saw it, all businessmen—whether manufacturers or farmers—suffered from success. A persistent theme in his economic pronouncements was overproduction: "I am wondering whether the producers of other things may not be facing the same things that the farmers are facing—overproduction. . . . The greatest problem of agriculture is caused by [the] inability to get rid of the surplus in a proper way. That is also a real problem before every industry, raw and finished. For instance, the copper and oil people are over-producing. Practically every manufacturing industry in the country is over-producing."[61]

Stabilization began on the farm. In 1927, Baruch wrote in a business journal that if farming ceased to be profitable, then farmers would leave the land and the reduction in their numbers would precipitate a "painful and disorderly" decline in production. (It would be a form of reducing acreages by natural selection: Baruch vehemently opposed acreage reductions unless planned by cooperatives, and even then he preferred storage of the surplus to its nonproduction.) Agricultural overproduction, he warned, would haunt other industries: lower incomes for farmers meant diminished sales for other producers. "The big question before us now is whether we can solve the problem of overproduction. We have learned how to create wealth, but we have not learned how to keep wealth from choking us and from bringing on widespread poverty to producers in the midst of their abundance. *We have to learn to keep from glutting the market without curtailing such market as there is.* It is a matter of relating production to consumption in such a way that production will surely pay."[62] Significantly, this observation encompasses the economy as a whole, rather than agriculture alone. Baruch did not prescribe a solution, but he favored association activity instead of legislation to plan curtailments.

Farming was no different from any other raw material industry. All raw material producers dreaded overproduction and gluts that depressed prices. In the latter part of the decade oil companies would preach "conservation" and withhold some of their output from the market by mutual agreement. Technically, Baruch argued, such behavior was not price-fixing. So long as it stimulated a better market price for producers, that was the type of legitimate action that Baruch hoped a supreme court of commerce would uphold, whether it was indulged in by copper producers or by an agricultural cooperative. Although the United States was the principal customer, he admired the way in which the British protected their rubber producers by regulating output to prevent ruinous prices; if the price dropped too drastically, London would withhold rubber from world markets. And, of course, other producers—like those of copper, zinc, tungsten, and so on—could cooperate in international markets to adjust their prices to profitable levels. All producers would prosper, to the benefit of their consumers, who could count upon sustained production at fair prices.

What Gilbert Fite has written of Peck might be said of Baruch: "Thus by indoctrinating farmers with the idea of *compulsory* cooperation and group action, Peek helped to usher in an era of collective action among farmers. It is not too much to say that this was a major turning point in twentieth-century agricultural policy. The idea of *forced* cooperation set a precedent for the Agricultural Adjustment Administration Act four years later." Yet that opens Baruch to the same charge Hoover leveled at Wallace, and indirectly at Peek, in his memoirs: that he "was in truth a fascist, but did not know it, when he proposed his price- and distribution-fixing legislation in the McNary-Haugen bill."[63] Actually, Baruch vacillated between Peek's state corporatism and Hoover's private corporatism, but his agricultural involvement of the 1920s is one more instance in which Baruch looked to Washington for inducing national community planning. Despairing of any real voluntary cooperation, Baruch, as was his custom, embraced "obligatory" cooperation. In that sense, his definition of a national education for voluntary cooperation was somewhat different from the more patient Hoover's.

THE REJECTION OF GOVERNMENT OWNERSHIP

Baruch believed in free enterprise, but he seldom allowed ideology to obscure the goal of stabilization. If stabilization of agriculture called for the creation of a state corporation to direct the marketing of exports, then the ends justified the means. However, he believed that the marketing of commodities on a domestic level called for collective action in the form of cooperatives and then consolidation of cooperatives into national associations—all privately owned and controlled. In other words, Baruch saw nothing wrong in socializing the export market for the benefit of private corporations.

His approaches were consistent with business thought and congressional action during 1919–23. The Webb-Pomerene Act of 1918 had exempted corporations in the export trade from the antitrust prohibitions, thereby replacing competition with cooperation for the pursuit of overseas markets. The Edge Act of the following year allowed banks to consolidate for the purpose of facilitating America's export trade with large reservoirs of credit. In the spring of 1919, Baruch had been, in the words of an acquaintance, "very decided on developing foreign trade; [he] thinks it should be done by the government, that if the government starts the next step would be for the Government and the exporters to extend credit jointly."[64] Baruch unhesitatingly would use public capital in order to guarantee the flow of private capital into export markets. At the same time, domestic markets would be made safe for private enterprise.

Foreign trade was the only area where government enterprise had a Baruch-approved role. Otherwise, Baruch was downright platitudinous on the subject of the government's role in the economy. He deplored "dependence" upon the government to deal with problems that individuals could solve: "We must teach more of the doctrine of self-help and self-reliance and less of the idea of help by a reliance upon the Government," he wrote in 1925. It seemed to him that governments throughout Europe threatened to assume functions of private capital and to retain enterprises nationalized as a wartime expedient.[65] Baruch had been one of the strongest advocates of temporary nationalization of essential industries during the war. But he opposed retention of nationalized properties such as the railroads and the power plant at Muscle Shoals.

For Baruch the wartime success of the Railroad Administration had been a triumph—not for the principle of government control, but for the concept of consolidation of smaller units into more efficient giant aggregations. As a longtime stockholder in railroads he had welcomed the government's take-over because it promised stabilized rates, increased investment, and modernization of rolling stock and tracks. A half billion federal dollars were pumped into the rails during the war to bring about the most effective American rail organization seen in a generation. But, like most rail investors, Baruch wanted control restored to private hands, the higher wartime rates retained, the wartime public investment left intact, and the wartime consolidations also kept. With the Transportation Act of 1920 he got all but the latter.

The issues of government ownership of transportation, communication, and energy sources remained alive during the twenties. Baruch consistently advocated consolidation into larger units under private ownership. In response to agitation by the railroad brotherhoods and some farm groups for government ownership of the rails, Baruch insisted that the issue had already been decided in the negative. Each successive election he interpreted as a mandate for consolidation and against government ownership of the railroads. Despite the wartime experience, despite his own postwar dissatisfaction with railroad management ("the men who operate the roads now, even at the big salaries, are nothing to brag about"), Baruch lobbied strenuously for private control. He believed that nationalization of one would be followed by others: "If we take over the railroads, we must take over coal, oil, and power." Government ownership of the rails would lead to government ownership of the rails' energy sources as well, and possibly other raw materials too. Therefore, he rallied Democrats against the proposal: "I really feel that any party that takes over the railroads will destroy itself politically for many years." He lectured farm cooperative leaders on the necessity of railroad consolidation to achieve more stable shipping rates. He asserted that the creation of a federal department of transportation would bring shippers in closer touch with government regulators. Even municipal take-overs of transportation, like New York City's purchase of its subways (in which Baruch had investments), he opposed as harbingers of nationalization of all railroads, a step toward greater inefficiency and the transfer of the investment burden to taxpayers. He drew from Washington's wartime control the moral that the rail barons and their Morgan allies in finance had been correct in their earlier endeavors to consolidate the rails in private hands. Baruch's solution to railroad inefficiency was a government-approved monopoly.[66]

Muscle Shoals presented a slightly different problem, but Baruch's reaction was essentially the same. During the war he had been largely responsible for the government's decision to build the Alabama power plant on the Tennessee River for the production of nitrates that could make explosives in war and fertilizer in peace. And he remained thereafter what one historian called the "loudest voice in the defense of the practicability" of the Muscle Shoals project. But Baruch pointedly maintained that it had been merely a wartime expedience and that its peacetime operation ought to be as a private enterprise. He chose to overlook the fact that American capital had ignored hydroelectric power development in the South because, as his good friend L. L. Summers observed, "that region cannot consume this power" in quantities sufficient to yield a great return on the investment. Yet "the fundamental motive underlying the selection of Muscle Shoals" as the site of the nitrates project, Summers hinted, was that the Wilson administration sought to boost southern economic development. Accordingly, southerners during the 1920s approved efforts to put that inactive plant to work for development.

In 1921, Henry Ford offered to buy Muscle Shoals from the government and produce nitrates on terms highly favorable to his own interests. For about three years controversy raged in Washington over acceptance of Ford's offer; but the Senate, led by the public-power-minded George Norris, blocked the sale. Baruch's position was that the government ought to accept Ford's offer if it in any way aided agricultural development. Baruch opposed Norris's counterproposal for government development on the vague grounds "of its inherent disadvantages." In favoring the Ford offer, Baruch made a display of disinterestedness, which was enhanced by the fact that the anti-Semitic car manufacturer had assailed him as a Jew and for his farm activities. Baruch linked the Ford proposal to his campaign for peacetime industrial preparedness for war, thereby making it more estimable in the national interest. But farm groups charged that Ford would unnecessarily raise fertilizer costs. When the issue of Ford's offer came to a head in 1924, Baruch disregarded the Norris alternative and argued, "I think he [Ford] would make more out of it for the common interest than anybody else."[67]

Baruch and America had moved far from the nationalization policies he advocated in 1918. He no longer was so intent upon impressing progressives with his own enlightenment concerning public interest when it alienated businessmen from the Democratic party. Nationalization had been merely a wartime expedience. The elections of 1920, 1922, and 1924 had demonstrated to Wilsonians that government ownership did not appeal to the electorate. As in Europe, where socialism's attractions to voters dwindled and corporatist solutions to festering problems assumed more prominence in the bourgeois quest for stability,[68] in the United States private enterprise enjoyed an ideological resurgence. The alternative to government ownership, Baruch and other American corporatists argued, was for Washington to encourage private enterprise to achieve economies of scale through consolidation and cooperation.

INTERNATIONAL COOPERATION AND COMPETITION

Baruch was an internationalist without illusions. He believed that if the United States joined the League of Nations it would advance American commercial interests. He did not want Americans to miss out on opportunities: as creditors to the world, he believed that it behooved Americans to act the part, developing ties to erstwhile colonial areas of the world and using U.S. financial resources to broaden U.S. trade. Moreover, America ought to assume the role of arbiter of Europe's festering reparations questions, thereby hastening its economic recovery and helping it to function as a vital U.S. trading partner. The lingering reparations issue not only retarded the resumption of business as usual in Europe; it also postponed the payment of the debts Europe owed the United States from the war, a sensitive political issue both in Washington and in European capitals.

Baruch believed that American policies, or sometimes the lack of foreign policies, exacerbated our own economic problems. A proponent of international cooperation, he nevertheless believed in exacting concessions from competitor nations through the exercise of economic strength. America's abundance of raw materials made it a Samson among nations; unfortunately the tariff was a debilitating scissor that Americans wielded on themselves. Were American producers freed of the tariff and its retaliatory consequences, they could capture enormous overseas markets for their surplus commodities. Artificial political barriers made sense only to economically underdeveloped nations or insecure empires. Without hospitable foreign markets, choking surpluses could only depress prices in the United States and inhibit producer confidence. The removal of American tariffs would bring welcomes to Americans in ports where Yankee traders seldom visited. At the same time, increased imports would improve the purchasing power of American consumers. As a nationalist and as an internationalist, Baruch found tariff and trade incompatible.

American prosperity was tied to world markets, and the tariff hindered U.S. accessibility to them. "A just and continuing peace should include a just and equal access to the raw materials and manufacturing facilities of the world, thus eliminating preferential tariffs," Baruch wrote to Wilson on the eve of the president's departure for the Paris Peace Conference. American businessmen could hardly invade British colonial areas protected by imperial preference, or break France's monopoly of eastern Europe's trade, if they insisted upon barriers to their own markets. Why should farmers pay exorbitant prices for manufactured products and sell fewer commodities because they were confined to domestic markets in both buying and selling? The agricultural crisis of the early 1920s confirmed his point. He lobbied against the protective tariff in Democratic hearings on the 1924 platform. He worked hard to wean George Peek from the traditional manufacturers' high tariff to the logic of receptive foreign markets for farmers' surpluses through a low tariff. Of all farm relief proposals, Baruch considered tariff revision "more important than anything else."[69]

Like the path to industrial consolidation and cooperation, the path to internationalism began with the farmer. Baruch saw isolationism as politically real where the farmer and other American commercial interests were concerned. The tariff contributed to this isolationism because it deterred trade with the outside world. "Unofficial" relations through banks resolved nothing: "We must enter into some kind of association with [Europeans]; we must get away from our policy of isolation." Not only did the tariff contribute to an inequitable price structure at home, it also reinforced the chauvinism that resisted the rationality of "enlightened selfishness." As Baruch told Senator Harrison of Mississippi, "The farmers' ills are very much mixed up with our foreign policy, which you and I cannot discuss without losing our tempers."[70]

As good promoters, the Wilsonians at the conclusion of the war had been eager to assist American businessmen in developing their foreign markets. The president himself encouraged government officials to demonstrate "their readiness to help and their knowledge of how intelligent assistance can be rendered" to businessmen interested in overseas trade. That set the tone for government involvement. Although Eugene Meyer and his War Finance Corporation preferred private capital to do the job, they were prepared with statutory authority to assist Americans in the export trade. The failure of the Versailles treaty in the United States signaled another instance when political developments failed to advance with economic developments and threatened to retard American prosperity. The interdependence of nations called for American international participation, Wilsonians insisted. The United States, Norman Davis argued, "must render service to the world by cooperating . . . from a purely enlightened selfish standpoint." That meant, said Baruch and Meyer, that Washington should subsidize, if necessary, a viable American merchant marine capable of competition with Great Britain's.[71] American prosperity and international participation would simultaneously benefit the United States and the world. Personal interests were fused with altruism.

A British observer, Lord Robert Cecil, confirmed the American paradox of economic internationalism and political isolationism during a tour in 1923 intended to convince Washington that it belonged in the League of Nations. Although Secretary of State Charles Evans Hughes "indulged in a long dissertation explaining the total powerlessness of the Government in foreign affairs," by no means did Cecil find that Americans were isolationists. To the contrary, he found among businessmen a "great amount of interest . . . in international affairs." Believing that New York financial magnates were very influential in determining foreign policy, he approached Wall Street with caution, especially because the prominent Otto Kahn, a good friend of Baruch, had opposed the League in 1919, fearing that it "makes it incumbent upon us to act henceforth as policeman for Europe and Asia," an imperial role the United States should avoid. To his relief, Cecil found that the majority of financiers he spoke with were "against isolation and in favor of England and a considerable majority in favor of the League." New York businessmen still distrusted British motives in urging the League upon them, but "every one here agrees really that a policy of isolation is impossible, and that it is to the interest of the United States to maintain the peace of the world."[72]

But that was an internationalism of resignation; Baruch demanded an enthusiastic internationalism. With Wilsonian fervor and idealism, he called upon the United States to be Europe's moral leader, not just its moneylender. America was important to Europe; not only did it fill a vacuum for financial leadership, it was the Continent's "balancing wheel"—if it chose to assume that role. Only an America involved in European affairs could restore Germany as a viable trading partner for the west and restrain French ambitions to make Poland "a military appendage of France." For Baruch it became a point of American honor, responsibility, and greatness. "America must not stand aloof," he pleaded. His tone was reminiscent of that of the advocates of America's imperialism at the turn of the century; the nation had a "manifest opportunity and destiny to lead the world." As he advised Mark Sullivan: "Financially and commercially America is now distinctly at the parting of the ways. She must go ahead and be the leader." The nation had defaulted on its assurances to Germany and to its allies; Americans had "shirked our responsibilities." As he told Senator Kenyon during the financial crises that beset the Continent in 1923: "There will be no peace in the world until America takes the position to which her power and wealth obligate her—yes, I should say, give her the privilege to take. The question of whether we are our brother's keeper was answered in the affirmative long before history was written." America should not go into Europe merely out of altruism, but because U.S. prosperity was inextricably linked to it. In the midst of the 1921 depression, Baruch reasoned: "Business is not going to be good, and never will be good again until we get into the game and take our share in straightening out the world's problems." That meant resolving the reparations tangle from the war, for without that settlement on terms fair to Germany, businessmen could not make plans for future enterprises. Then, when Europe had recovered sufficiently to become a valued trading partner, "we must learn to mobilize our finances if we want to occupy the first place in the world of finance and trade."[73]

Until then, World War I remained with the world in the form of the reparations issue. Baruch's position was clear, as clear as he could make it in attempting to mold indifferent public opinion. Though he could influence public perceptions of this arcane international problem, in truth, Baruch had little impact upon its policy making following Wilson's move from Pennsylvania Avenue to S Street.

Yet no issue, except perhaps agricultural relief, served Baruch as well in keeping his name before the public as did that of debts and reparations. Throughout the twenties he maintained a steady stream of pronouncements and interviews with reporters that tended to simplify the debts and reparations question for the public while assuring it that Baruch was a statesman whose opinions were trustworthy. In an age of democracy, Baruch believed that people were educable and that finance and foreign policy were not topics for discussion solely by bankers and diplomats. As was customary when he adopted a cause, Baruch propagandized and lobbied vigorously for his point of view. As was his habit with issues about which he never really was comfortable, he took a position representing the consensus view of informed leaders.

The debts-reparations issue had been fixed in Baruch's mind since Paris. He rejected the British effort to link Britain's debts to German reparations. What the Allies owed America had no relationship to the cost of damages Germany inflicted upon the Allies; those debts had been incurred prior to the American entry into the war and therefore could not be considered costs sustained while fighting "in common cause" with the United States. As to the contention that Americans could not expect the Allies to exact reasonably low reparations charges from the Germans while they faced monumental debts to the United States, Baruch took the position that would best be articulated by the taciturn Calvin Coolidge: "They hired the money, didn't they?" Cancellation was out of the question, and debt reduction was unlikely.

A nationalist and a politician could not afford to take any other position than the one Baruch took. Concomitantly, he strenuously maintained that the British and the French ought to reduce the burden reparations placed upon the Germans. Germany had to be stabilized quickly so that its industrious people might resume their prominent place in the western economic community, resist the radicals among them, and serve as a capitalist counterweight to the Soviet Union in eastern Europe. However, he would never permit Germany to rearm; he endorsed all French security demands. But France had no unilateral right to seize German economic resources while demanding high reparations payments. Moreover, France had to put its own financial house in order by taxing its people enough to balance the government's budget and service its debts. As for Britain, Baruch took the British at their own word that they were still a great imperial power. Imperial preference in the British colonies rankled among Americans every time the British preached international cooperation. Baruch always extended the British his sympathy and affection, but he credited them with more economic resources than they acknowledged. He never resolved the inherent conflict between his desire for international cooperation and his hostility to competitors.

Internationalists in the 1920s forecast a new war caused by economic problems outstanding from 1919 because the United States had not asserted its corporate right, derived from its prestige and its economic might, to act as Europe's arbiter. However, in those instances when the

United States entered the international arena as an agent of cooperation, its efforts frequently met rebuff by the Europeans. Internationalists then prescribed that the United States actively pursue enlightened selfishness in world markets until its economic prowess enabled it to prevail in liberal, nonstatist competition. Politicians would govern best if they would simply allow national problems to find a private-enterprise solution. [74]

"We have all got to wake up to the fact that we are never going to have back the world that existed in 1914," declared Baruch upon his return from the peace conference. Normalcy was an illusion. The Wilsonians believed that America could not return to prewar aloofness from Europe, even if politics dictated the stance that reparation was a matter essentially between the Allies and Germany. In fact, Baruch and his Wilsonian comrades wanted an American presence in the League of Nations, on the Reparation Commission, and on the Rhineland occupation commission. American interest in German reparations, Baruch told the Senate Foreign Relations Committee in 1919, is not impersonal because "our markets are there." At a public dinner more than a year later he repeated the contention that America needed Germany as a customer for her manufactures and raw materials but would be denied that market as long as the Germans labored to pay reparations still awaiting determination. [75]

The Making of the Reparation and Economic Sections of the Treaty contributed nothing to American debate or to the establishment of Baruch as an influential policy maker. The reparations sections of the book were widely known to have been written by John Foster Dulles, and additionally, State Department previewers criticized his treatment of the economic sections of the treaty as narrowly nationalistic. [76] If Baruch knew of their adverse remarks he did not let them dissuade him from becoming a foreign policy spokesman. His credentials entitled him to a public hearing, and his connections with the *New York Times* and other journalistic organs assured him that he would have an audience as long as an interviewer or ghostwriter was available.

Prior to the Allies' first reparations claims against Germany, Baruch endorsed a punitive settlement against the former enemy. Advising French industrialist-politician Louis Loucheur that "the only way to make the Germans come through is to do it by force," Baruch nevertheless urged that German markets be left prosperous enough to buy American agricultural commodities. He launched his own campaign against American indifference toward the settlement, forecasting expanded trade following a reparations agreement that allowed the revival of German industry. But where precisely was the point at which France punished the Germans for their transgressions against civilization without making central Europe an enslaved region for French industry? [77]

British liberals rejoined that, if Americans supported French claims for a pound of German flesh, then the United States ought to be willing to relinquish debt claims against the Allies—claims that would be more difficult to pay without Germany as a substantial trading partner. Again, Baruch denied any relationship between the Allied debts and the German reparations. In 1922 he launched a propaganda campaign against the British, accusing them of duplicity at Paris and in their current demands. Cancellation of debts was bad business and France's claims were justified by security needs. Although Baruch summered in Scotland, cultivated friendships with Winston Churchill and other tories, each day he sounded more and more like an Anglophobe. At one point he even sent a public letter to a leading Senate Republican isolationist, William E. Borah of Idaho, ridiculing British claims to forgiveness for their debts; it made page 1 of the *New York Times*. He even recommended that Americans answer British cries for debt cancellation by withholding purchases of United Kingdom bonds.[78]

The French occupation of the Ruhr in 1923 diverted Baruch's attention from the debt question. More than ever the speculator favored an American hand in renegotiating the reparations questions. But though he wanted the reparations figure decided upon in 1921 scaled down, he assured the French ambassador that he believed France had every right to action to protect itself, and he even went so far as to suggest a regional defense arrangement that would include an American presence in Europe. The Ruhr occupation reopened the whole reparations question and provided a wedge for American participation, not only in the settlement but in European markets. As Baruch told Senator Harrison, "All we want is a place where we can sell our production, and the opportunity is open in the settlement of the reparations question." The United States should finance German payment of its reparations, Baruch recommended.[79] Of course that is what was already being recommended during talks among American government officials and bankers and European government officials: the reparations burden for Germany would be reduced and American loans would help build its economy to pay the war costs.

In the latter part of the decade the focus shifted to the debts question. Baruch railed against the debt settlements of 1926, but urged Senate Democratic leaders to support the administration's agreement because the commission that negotiated them was bipartisan and "we [Democrats] must remember how we felt when the Senate refused to act on the Versailles Treaty." When the newspapers called him for comments on the settlements he deplored lowering interest rates, but on the other hand recognized that if Americans were not more lenient creditors, they would cause excessive hardship. Thus, the right settlement was one that was "morally right and economically sound"—an unarguable position. In foreign policy, Baruch served as a public interpreter, much like a journalistic analyst who enjoyed easy access to those who actually were involved. It would be unfair to Baruch to leave the impression that he simultaneously took two positions, an inoffensive political science. On issues that he really cared about he assumed very strong stances certain to alienate powerful people. But he desired to create correct impressions, to say "something very intelligently, but with usual good taste, as a gentleman would and should say it."[80] Thus, his pronouncements appeared designed to attract commendations of his perceptions and sagacity, perhaps even consideration of him as the next Democratic secretary of state.

Baruch's experiences of 1918–19 might have been pointless if he had been unable to broaden his background in foreign economic policy. As early as 1917 he had indicated to Chandler Anderson that he intended to make international politics a specialty. Through his ability to travel widely and his ingratiating personality that developed associations, Baruch projected the imprint that he moved with men of power on the international scene. And he did. As one reporter observed, Baruch was "on terms of intimacy with the elite of the *deux cents familles*, with military men, with high politicians, the small group that governed France." When he traveled to France every summer in the 1920s it would be reported in the influential *New York Times* that he had visited Clemenceau; the former leader's protégé, Tardieu; and Loucheur, a powerful figure in his own right. Indeed, Baruch's correspondence is full of letters to these men and to French aristocrats; he really was close to them. A side trip to Czechoslovakia brought him an interview with Prime Minister Beneš. When he arrived in Berlin he had to deny rumors of an impending American loan for the stricken German economy. New York and Washington read about his meetings with Smuts of South Africa, Hughes of Australia, and Lloyd George of England, all acquaintances from 1919 who took time to confer with this private citizen about matters of state. When he debarked in New York, waiting reporters were treated to a discussion of what concerned the great European financiers with whom he had recently consulted. Every major development in international economic diplomacy found reporters ensconced on Baruch's doorstep waiting for his analysis. When Clemenceau or Churchill visited New York, it was noted that they were his guests.[81] A friend of important international figures had to be one himself.

Notwithstanding, Baruch was still an outsider. He had no impact on the Dawes Plan or on the reparations settlement of 1929. Democrats and financiers participated and were consulted, but Baruch was not among them. Any influence he had upon the major international economic debates of the 1920s came indirectly through the press or through his contacts with senators. He did not shape events, but he never seemed to be far from them or ignorant of their significance. He was a strong voice against isolationism. Eventually his sustained prominence would translate itself into international participation again.

LOWER PRICES

One of the legends concerning Baruch is that he anticipated the crash of 1929. Perhaps nothing contributed more to his later fame as an economic soothsayer than the fact that he came through the crash and depression with his fortune apparently intact. There is something admirable about a man who at a time of great depression is able to loan or give hundreds of thousands of dollars—perhaps millions—to charities, political campaigns, and friends. Many millionaires continued their habits of conspicuous consumption until the money ran out, but Baruch's conspicuous spending never exhausted his money. How he achieved this is less important here than the fact itself. For it is likely that if he had had to retrench as a consequence of the depression, his power and his influence could not have flourished in the early 1930s as they did. But he remained a winner in an age of losers.

The wild speculation in stocks of the 1920s had not deceived Baruch. He abhorred the easy money the Federal Reserve had made possible in 1927, which generated the boom that preceded the bust. Preferring to buy rather than sell, he was deterred and frightened by rising prices in 1927–29. Safety usually dictated that he sell when others were buying. He did not consider this formula a personal secret: he shared his doubts about the boom with his friends and the public. If they were foolish enough, they could discount his counsel as that of a man out of touch with his times—which he freely professed to be—and some of his friends did turn a deaf ear to him. It is hard to say which discomforted him most—his doubts about the economy or not being heeded by the public.

Baruch did not like the role of a prophet of gloom. For a time in 1929 he went along with the price euphoria and forecast even greater prosperity. He wanted to be the bearer of good news—in fact, the *first* to bring the word. Of course, in 1929 he was hardly original with a prediction of continuing prosperity. All he accomplished by it was an exhibition of vulnerability. He had yielded to uncertainty concerning his pessimism. For posterity's sake, that was a mistake. His contemporaries soon forgot it and focused only upon his reminders that he had left the market before most of them; but historians of the liberal persuasion would take delight in unearthing Baruch's 1929 article of optimism and ritualistically holding it aloft as an example of the era's distorted perspective. Yet his own magnificent affluence testified that he had indeed anticipated the worst and taken measures to protect himself against it.

As the 1920s came to an unforgettable end, Baruch was financially and politically well situated. His connections in the national Democratic party were strong and growing stronger. For the minority party, the 1920s had been a political depression during which Baruch had been its major benefactor. An economic depression would not alter that relationship. Furthermore, his image of influence considerably enhanced his position in the nation's press. It had begun to recognize that Baruch carried considerable weight with Democratic senators and not a little with House Democrats. It was the sort of prestige that not even a Republican president could ignore if he hoped for a compliant opposition. And Herbert Hoover would need Democratic cooperation to achieve legislative approval of his program.

Though personally distrustful of Hoover, Baruch agreed with the Great Engineer's principles of economic strategy and organization. In certain ways, both men espoused concepts that diverged from the mainstream of American business thought. Such concepts as cooperative organization and stabilization planning had had a progressive tone in the 1920s; Republican mossbacks had branded Hoover a socialist during the preconvention fight of 1928. What made Baruch and Hoover "progressive" was their quest to achieve economic stabilization by altering the terms of business competition. They preached the gospel of cooperation—the self-regulation of business through quasi-cartelistic associations. Both men would involve the federal government in business to a greater degree by enhancing its role as a coordinator of economic decisions. Baruch called for a theoretical tribunal of community elders, akin to a blue-ribbon grand jury, that would adjudicate market conflicts with a mythical public interest as its guide. Hoover, as secretary of commerce, had to operate on a more practical basis; that meant the creation of regulatory commissions for technologically innovative commerce—like radio and aviation—which increased the power of the federal government and allowed the regulated industries to avoid the debilitating effects of over-competition. Also, he initiated conferences in industries beset by price-depressing competition in the hope that they would organize cooperation and stabilize themselves. Essentially that was the tactic both men used in their agricultural incursions. The route to prosperity in most economic sectors lay through organizing self-regulating, cooperative associations and public studies that monitored economic data to allow a flexible private response.

It was a corporate panacea whose time might have arrived. Baruch and Hoover rejected legislative solutions to economic problems that only compounded the turmoil by transferring economic conflict to the political arena. Although they encouraged increased activity for Washington, they considered Congress meddlesome. Except on pet issues such as planning for industrial mobilization for war, Baruch's influence upon Congress was negative, intended to act as a restraint upon law making that hindered a corporate solution to economic concerns. Indeed, if Baruch had any personal political ambition, it was to become secretary of state, a policy-making post less likely to collide with Capitol Hill than was the

Treasury or any other secretaryship. Perhaps in no other area was the Congress as permissive of corporate solutions that diluted its own authority as in foreign affairs.

Understandably, Baruch welcomed the passing of the 1920s. The depression confirmed his own economic sagacity. As a speculator and a deflationist, he welcomed the return of low prices; they warranted real optimism. As a Democrat, he saw bad times as a harbinger of party victories in 1930 and 1932, maybe even the presidency. As a would-be policy maker, he found that his prominence in the press and in politics gave his advice greater authority. The depression promised for Baruch, then entering the seventh decade of his life, the realization of his ambitions for power *pro bono publico*.

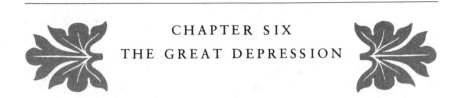

CHAPTER SIX
THE GREAT DEPRESSION

THE MOST POWERFUL DEMOCRAT IN HOOVER'S WASHINGTON

At a time when the collective wisdom of Wall Street was called into question with each new panic that depressed stock prices, shriveled credit, and lengthened lines of unemployed people, Baruch nimbly avoided the increasing public hostility toward America's financial leadership. He availed himself of a multitude of forums from newspaper interviews to committee hearings to speaking engagements (preceded by press releases of the text) that both reassured the nation and vaguely prescribed for the depression malady. Without official or professional title, Baruch relied greatly upon his past credentials as Wilson's advisor, his continued prominence as a personage who traveled in the international circles of great men, and his own very evident wealth to mark him as an authority.

As Hugh Johnson once said of his chief, "His effectiveness as a practical economist is suggested by his own magnificent solvency." Implicit in the designation "practical economist" was disdain for academic economists. Indeed, Baruch and Johnson jestingly had organized their own "society to shoot all statisticians and economists." Anyone who believed that economics could be studied quantitatively and isolated from normal human behavior or political developments would be fair game for their verbal fire. Theoretical study gave a man insufficient credentials as an economic genius. In the words of Felix Frankfurter, John Maynard Keynes was "a professor and a maker of money, which apparently validates ideas." As in previous panics and depressions of the twentieth century, Baruch increased his wealth. In one of his favorite soliloquies, he told a radical friend, Helen Lawrenson, "I have a talent for making money, the way Fritz Kreisler has a talent for playing the violin and Jesse Owens has a talent for running. I buy when stocks go down, I sell when they go up.

When prices go up, production increases, consumption decreases, and prices then fall. When prices go down it's vice versa. I got rich, Madame Fathead, by remembering those words."[1]

In Washington, Democrats listened carefully. For many in the Senate it had become a habit that the depression reinforced. Hoover was cognizant of this when he consulted Baruch. Moreover, the frequency of those consultations increased following the election of 1930, which saw the depression erode strong Republican majorities and create the most dead-locked Congress in history; the deaths of some representatives gave the Democrats a majority of five by the time the House convened in December 1931, and a Republican majority of one in the Senate. Given the propen-sity of anti-Hoover Republican progressives for opposing the president, the cooperation of Democrats became more crucial to head off public works measures proposed by dissatisfied Democrats and Republicans. With his Senate "constituents" properly in tow, Baruch fashioned the congressional consensus that dominated legislating during the winter of 1931–32. He did not hide the fact—he advertised it. His power was suggested by his attendance at congressional debates, whereas formerly his public appearances had tended to be limited to prize fights, Broadway shows, and the Saratoga racetrack. He gloried in his role, bragging to Agnes Meyer in February 1932 that he was "passing Hoover's legislation now," and she, no fan of his, conceded the likelihood of his claim, "as he is supposed to have more control over the Democratic side of the Senate than anyone else."[2]

How had he achieved that control? As noted earlier, he had been a big contributor to Democratic campaigns for the Senate in the 1920s, and this factor remained no small part of his power. In the 1930 campaign fourteen candidates for the Senate divided $38,800 that Baruch funneled to them via the Senate Democratic Campaign Committee. He could be counted upon for this generosity. When the committee ran a deficit of $2,281, he made up $2,000 of it. "You jump a lot of fences between campaigns," teased columnist Frank Kent, "but when the bell rings for the horses to go to the post, you are in front, check book in one big paw and fountain pen in the other."[3] But it would have been unwise for Democratic senators to take him for granted or to take only his money.

He was their crony and he was their economic advisor and he was their political strategist. Baruch always entertained in style, and many in poli-tics, savoring the company of great wealth, looked forward to being his guest at Hobcaw, at the fights, or just at dinner in the grand style. It was the sort of wealth a senator did not attain at an annual salary of $10,000, even if it was augmented by nepotism—putting a relation on the payroll, as so many of them did. At the least, Baruch might reveal a sound invest-ment for that few thousand dollars a politician had stashed away; or he might allow himself to be persuaded by a political friend to put a small part of his own substantial capital—say, $50,000 or more—into a favorite venture of the friend's.

He gave political advice with the anticipation that it would be listened to. Whenever he visited Washington in the early 1930s, telegrams to Joe Robinson, Key Pittman, and Pat Harrison preceded him, with the request that they come to his Carlton Hotel suite. They responded to those messages,[4] thus giving Baruch Capitol informants consisting of the Senate Democratic leader and ranking Democrats on the Foreign Relations and Finance committees. As their friend he often urged that they relax at his South Carolina plantation retreat, hunting quail; there, without a phone for miles, only Baruch could raise reminders of the momentous issues they helped shape. In 1932, Pennsylvania's David Reed might join them at Hobcaw or at the fights or at the Carlton; it did not disturb these Democrats that Reed was a Republican, one of the few senators liked by Hoover, and the opposition in an election year. After all, Reed's presence firmed up the bipartisan consensus on economic issues that dominated the legislating of that year, and Baruch had been one of its principal architects.

He believed that economics was too important to be left to politicians. A few wise leaders should resolve issues before they went to the marketplace. In 1928–29 he had restrained the combative George Peek from rallying his Senate allies around another farm program that invited conflict with Hoover, telling Peek "to wait with an open mind and a kindly spirit for what Mr. Hoover has to propose. . . . Indeed, we should go further and aid him wherever we can." During the special session of 1929 that dealt with the tricky farm and tariff issues, he urged Robinson to proclaim bipartisanship on farm relief, following Hoover "so far as you can consistently, supporting him in getting his measure and in endeavoring to make it effective. I think this is good morals and good politics, rather than to offer a substitute." Steer clear of alignments with dissenters, Baruch counseled. Democrats would better impress the electorate with bipartisanship than with legislative victories at the expense of the president.[5] Besides, Baruch basically agreed with Hoover's proposed farm board and the flexible provision of the tariff bill that allowed rate adjustments up to 50 percent by the president without congressional approval. Anything that made for diminished law making would be welcome to old Wilsonians like Hoover and Baruch.

But Democratic electoral successes in 1930 had threatened to sharpen policy differences in Congress. Baruch did his best to blunt party conflict during the depression crisis. Joe Robinson assured him that his Senate leadership would exhibit caution, but Democratic organization of the lower House, which was less amenable to Baruch's persuasions, would likely disrupt a Hoover consensus. The last thing Baruch wanted was to suggest obstructionism to a Hoover program. "Let us be careful not to get in a position where the Republicans will be able to unload this onus upon us," he advised his Senate friends. "The country is in a highly excited condition. What it needs is rest, not any more changes. . . . Let us not try to rectify too many things now." At the acme of his influence with a minority party, Baruch feared its premature emergence as a majority. For he truly believed that Hoover would enjoy an improved economic situation by the next election because his policies were fundamentally correct. In the spring of 1930, Baruch had forecast that Hoover would be "fortunate enough, before the next election, to have a rising tide and then he will be pictured as the great master mind who led the country out of its economic misery."[6] Shortly after the market broke he advised a business friend that it appeared "all technical and forced liquidation [was] about completed." If businessmen could restrain themselves from bearishness and show confidence in recovery, then an upturn would shortly follow; after all, "business cannot remain very bad in this country long." By nature, Baruch was sanguine when the economic trend was bad, dour when it was good. In October 1930, Baruch declared that raw material prices had bottomed out and that "natural curative forces have set themselves in motion." In April 1931 he told McAdoo: "The process of readjustment is going on day by day. It is very unpleasant but I do not believe government can do anything to help it. Every time government steps in they [sic] make it worse."[7]

These were mean times, but Baruch thought smart men had to hold their ground against the herd instinct to run in the wrong direction. Barbarism knocked at the door. "Go out to the Baltimore and Ohio station," he wryly suggested to Frank Kent, "and see if it is still there and if the tracks are still in the roadbed. . . . Do the people in Baltimore still eat and wear clothes? Or are we all going back to savagery?" Civilized people knew that economic adversity brought out the worst in men. Chatting with some younger, unworldly college professors attached to the Roosevelt campaign in 1932, he calculatingly shocked them by declaring, "Business must go through the wringer and start over again." But, exclaimed one of the academics, there would be riots in the streets. "There is always tear gas to take care of that," Baruch replied. He was not heartless, but he had little feeling for the unemployed. When B&O Railroad president Daniel Willard attempted to pay a dividend to stockholders and provide jobs for men "who because of conditions beyond their own control find themselves without money and without work, and in many cases with others more helpless dependent upon them," he turned to one of the prominent directors of the company, Baruch. "Of course I am sympathetic with giving these men some work," Baruch responded, "but I think we have to be careful about borrowing money for anything that is not absolutely necessary now, until we know more about how we will be able to meet our March maturity."⁸ The investor always had priority over the laborer.

Baruch was not ignorant of real conditions. His favorite industrial observers, Hugh Johnson and George Peek, had been candidly and consistently reporting the worst. In mid-1930, Johnson traveled through the industrial Midwest and privately reported that he could not find "one fundamental sign of improvement." Despite presidential pleas to the contrary, "wage and salary cuts—some under cover, some boldly—are general." With every index heading downward, Johnson predicted, "The last half of 1930 will be worse than the first in nearly all lines." He forecast "further recession" in 1931 and provided the unwelcome opinion that "this government is going to have to provide between five and six billion dollars this winter for the relief of unemployed in nearly every industry." However, not even the warning from George Peek in 1932, "One need not be very smart to see that the proletariat is on his [sic] way and will get [the rich] if constructive action is not taken shortly," could dissuade Baruch from his opposition to government spending for public works jobs. He continued to insist that job inflation was wrong and credit inflation was justified, even after Peek commented that "it is hard to keep a barrel full of water by pouring it in at the top when there is a hole at the bottom."⁹

Amidst such stern realities, Baruch sounded a note of confidence. On 12 November 1931 a front page headline in the *New York Times* proclaimed, "Baruch Sees Nation Rising from Slump." Such forecasts of new eras of prosperity could be expected at War Industries Board reunions involving 150 prominent industrialists and financiers. Yet there is something ludicrous about that story, appearing next to news about 65,700 people registering for emergency federal employment in New York and only 7,000 actually being placed.

In public observations and prescriptions, Baruch tended toward bland exhortations for courage and confidence, not greatly unlike those of Hoover. But then, on the eve of the convening of the Seventy-second Congress, he preferred to allow the president to propose and Democrats to dispose. This strategy combined Baruch's senses of caution and patriotism with his belief that the president's course was fundamentally correct. In private, however, Baruch revealed a growing desire for federal leadership. Like his fellow Democrats, he began to part company with the Hoover program.

First, he cast doubt upon the efficacy of Hoover's international strategy. Allowing that prosperity could not be restored without the solution of America's foreign economic problems, Baruch maintained that those overseas matters should not obscure the fact that the depression's "vortex" was internal: "Regardless of the feeling of interested bankers, only a relatively small proportion of domestic depression can properly be traced to [foreign sources]." Like the Senate isolationists, whom he usually differed with, he believed that disarmament of all nations would be more effective than the ephemeral moratorium on debts. The practical course of action lay in domestic efforts to contain the depression.

Ever a master publicist, Baruch faulted Hoover as a propagandist. Obviously the president's campaign for confidence had not stemmed the tide of pessimism. Rhetoric was no longer a sufficient weapon against the pervasive despair. The nation needed action. What did Baruch propose? He would have the president promote the consolidation of railroads and allow rate increases as a means of stimulating profits in America's principal transportation network. Then, recognizing that unemployment, as Hugh Johnson reported, "has been woefully underestimated—that acute and very wide suffering is in prospect—that the possibilities are explosive—that provision is wholly inadequate," Baruch urged that the president boldly declare that the jobless were Washington's responsibility. Relief of the unemployed would cease to be solely a local or voluntary mission. Such an announcement by itself would be "heartening." It would come to grips with the reality that the "millions of innocent and helpless sufferers from a national economic misfortune . . . [,] practically one-fourth of our population," could not survive without relief. Baruch would not give the jobless charity or put them on a federal dole, but would offer "closely supervised and administered small loans . . . to tide them over the winter months." Implicit in this was an understanding that the federal government could not balance its budget and perhaps would turn millions of wage earners into debtors to it and, ultimately, perhaps, defaulters. Had he gone public with this proposal, we can imagine how his standing might have suffered among conservatives. His only recommendation for federal work relief called for a "vigorous decentralized organization" under War Department leadership performing unspecified projects; although tersely ambiguous, it suggested what would become the New Deal's Civilian Conservation Corps. Significantly, Baruch believed that "responsible federal administration [of work relief for the unemployed was] preferable to non-responsible voluntary organization."

For business, Baruch wanted to broaden credit. Sensitive to "a fantastic paradox" that America enjoyed an abundance of most necessities of life while many of its people could not afford them, he urged finding "some vehicle for carrying frozen collateral," so that banks would not exacerbate the financial panic that already existed. Though this would bring about an undetermined inflation of credit, Baruch otherwise recommended an "equalization of deflation" by vigorous federal pressure upon industries and economic sectors whose prices had hitherto resisted commensurate declines—"e.g., electrical rates." But Baruch never went public with this program, for, whatever his personal ruminations, his own political strategy called for seconding the president in the hopes that Hoover would hang himself or really bring recovery.

Never at home with the cultural politics of the 1920s, Baruch looked forward to the economic debates of 1932. With no remorse whatsoever, he abandoned prohibition and swung behind repeal so that government could tax the bottle. In fact, he would tax everything that was not a clear necessity of life. The White House indicated that its strategy for Hoover's reelection would be based upon blaming Congress for an unbalanced federal budget that hurt business confidence. Therefore, Democrats had to out-tax and out-economize Hoover. That may have been dubious logic to some politicians who equated electoral success with responsiveness to public pleas for federal spending, but Baruch felt that the Democratic leadership had to fight Hoover on his ground.

Besides, once again politics complemented principle. Democrats did not want public activity to detract from the potential revival of private enterprise. Moreover, public spending would inflate the dollar. At a time when the British boldly devalued the pound to bring about a more competitive position in international markets, Baruch reassured an aristocratic French friend that America's dollar would hold as firmly as the franc. "We will tax our people to the uttermost limit to keep our dollar good," he promised, "and we have plenty upon which to base our taxation. The dollar will remain sound." Declining revenues had to be made up by consumer taxes. If the Republicans hoped to portray Democrats as antibusiness, then it became imperative for the Democratic tax proposals to show, as Pat Harrison put it, that they would "not disturb business any more than Mr. Mellon's plan will."

Because the Democratic majority on the House Ways and Means Committee had the nominal responsibility of initiating the revenue bill of 1932, Baruch took it upon himself to make sure that it conformed with administration demands for a sales tax that would balance the budget. He sent an emissary to House Majority Leader Henry T. Rainey and personally told the Illinois Democrat, "A balanced budget is the first and greatest requisite of reconstruction. This is your policy and I think it well to announce it now." In March, Baruch still played consensus politics. Hugh Johnson visited Undersecretary of the Treasury Ogden L. Mills (a Baruch partner in Alaska Juneau gold mines) to assure him that House Democrats would not be an obstacle to balancing the budget and that Baruch "would in no event be placed in the role of an adversary of the Treasury." Although the House Ways and Means Committee handily passed a revenue bill containing the sales tax, Baruch proved unable to deliver the lower chamber's Democratic membership. On 24 March 1932 it rebelled against its leadership and killed the levy. The Democrats would not balance the budget as Baruch had wanted.[10]

Baruch and the Senate Democratic leadership then waged a two-pronged attack against Hoover. On the one hand they goaded him into reaffirming the administration's support of the sales tax and the balanced budget principle while they moved ahead with plans to use federal loans to revive state and local public works activity. In the first instance the Democrats maneuvered Hoover into a position where he remained the lone public proponent of the rejected sales tax. At the same time, Baruch personally dared Hoover to reduce government expenses. Hoover denied that further retrenchment would be practicable without additional revenues, but Baruch retorted that the Treasury could save a few billion dollars if it really wanted a balanced budget. Hoover could not win politically. He was either profligate or parsimonious.

To assure that Hoover would appear heartless, Baruch and Hugh Johnson gave Joe Robinson a plan for instituting "self-liquidating" public works. Robinson publicized the Baruch scheme, thereby beating Hoover's announcement of an administration public works bill by one day. Perhaps not coincidentally, the Robinson and the Hoover plans were so similar that the press referred to them in the singular, "the Robinson-Hoover plan." The lawmakers who had defeated the sales tax were certain to be dissatisfied with the coalition's cautious public works spending, but Baruch promised "to hold the Democrats to this limited program." He could not. The House Democratic leadership did not follow Baruch as closely as Senator Robinson did. As a result, it took a Hoover veto of another public works bill before the Congress virtually confirmed the Robinson-Hoover plan as the Emergency Relief and Construction Act of 1932.[11]

The congressional fights of 1932 diminished Hoover's political power, but not apparently Baruch's, although they did mark him as an unreconstructed deflationist at a time when Democrats were increasingly leaning toward measured inflation. Still, Baruch had the ear of Senate Democrats in a way that Hoover could only envy as he found himself increasingly isolated from his own party's congressional leadership after 1932. Not only would Baruch retain the attention of Robinson, Harrison, and Pittman in 1933, at a time when the first was majority leader and the others were committee chairmen of Finance and Foreign Relations, he could look foward to the rise of South Carolina's James F. Byrnes, a comer first elected in 1930 and very much a Baruch man. However, what had made Baruch and the Senate Democratic leadership so important in 1932 was the balance of political power in Washington and the absence of an alternative opposition leader of national reputation. The nomination and election of Franklin D. Roosevelt would change that. Even so, 1932 had confirmed Baruch as a powerful Democrat with whom even a Democratic president would have to deal.

COMMISSIONS AND COMMITTEES

Baruch's center of power lay in the Congress, but he consistently favored a reduction of its role in the economic life of the nation. The depression confirmed his preference for executive or private organizations for dealing with economic problems. Liberal democracy seemed a poor forum for economic reconstruction. That is why he remained a staunch defender of the Federal Reserve System in principle, even as he had castigated its 1927 liberalization of credit for inducing speculation. He constantly reminded Carter Glass that the theory of the system remained valid and that any reform of it should not make it an agency beholden to pluralistic politicians. He sometimes thought that arbitrary bodies like a supreme court of commerce best mitigated marketplace anarchy, particularly in times of crisis. But the court notion was too arbitrary to be acceptable to free enterprise or organized labor. If Baruch hoped to diminish the evils of competition in the business and political marketplaces, he would have to do it piecemeal, one sector at a time. That is what Hoover had been doing in the 1920s; that is what seemed practicable, without surrendering the broader commerce court idea, in the early 1930s.

Aware of corporatism in Europe during the 1920s, Baruch sought similar arrangements in the United States that would divorce politics from business. Like Hoover, he would confront a market problem with a body of experts, men with broad vision and acute insight who would form a commission to resolve conflicts of competing interests. The tariff appeared to be the outstanding instance of pluralism's ineffectiveness during 1929–30. Baruch disliked Hoover's flexible provision for presidential tariff revising only because it conferred inadequate tariff-making power upon the wrong institution. He privately espoused an "economic commission" to divest politicians of this age-old source of demagogy. As he reasoned: "Congress is political purely. Presidents are somewhat and sometimes but never sufficiently less so. If we could always have as President a man of Mr. Hoover's antecedents, and if we could be sure that, in the face of political pressure, such a man would remain sound in economic outlook and not become soggy-minded between political expediency and economic necessity, then, while approving of neither, I would prefer him to Congress as an operator on tariffs, but I would hesitate the risk of a statute preferring a President to the Congress in every case."

Why not take this question out of politics forever?[12] However, it would have taken a political decision to eradicate politics from the tariff issue, and the history of the Hawley-Smoot Tariff, the highest in American rate making, tells us that logrolling prevailed as usual. Baruch blamed both strong manufacturers and weak politicians for succumbing to greed and expedience. The macroeconomic general interest again had been betrayed by special interest law making. Now, amid the developing crisis, he questioned whether the political economy could function as it had: "Representative government in every part of the world is permitting strong, strident and noisy minorities to interfere with . . . the law of supply and demand which . . . will only prolong the present agony." Alternative institutions were more imperative than ever. Industrial self-government was to be preferred to interest-group politics in any form.

Although he had been attracted to the idea of "obligatory" cooperation for farmers, he desired free cooperation for industry. "I believe in industrial cooperation but only in free conference," he insisted. "Enforced cooperation is an absurd contradiction in terms."[13] The vehicle for legitimate cooperation by industry was the commission. Formally and informally, Hoover had been its prime proponent. Commissions neatly eliminated public debate. Moreover, relying upon prestigious persons to advance a cause was just good public relations. Hoover organized other commissions and committees for unemployment relief and most other depression concerns that could be dealt with outside the legislative framework. Once in 1931 a reporter asked Baruch to account for American difficulties in combating the depression. "Commissions, commissions, nothing but commissions," he expostulated. Yet less than three weeks later he recommended to the governor of South Carolina that he and other southern governors attack the problem of cotton surpluses by each appointing "a commissioner or a commission of not more than three members, vested with full powers, and that a conference be called to discuss the whole problem and settle upon a common policy." It would be an effective device to circumvent parochial politicians who dealt only with their constituents' concerns. That was the story of the inception of the Reconstruction Finance Corporation (RFC). First came conferences with bankers, then conferences with Baruch and Andrew Mellon on the need to bail out banks approaching insolvency. Baruch's unique influence with the Senate Democratic leadership made him exceptionally important to Hoover's efforts to effect a financial-political collaboration. Eugene Meyer, Jr., former head of the War Finance Corporation under both Democratic and Republican presidents, similarly figured in selling the concept to New York and Washington. Both Meyer and Baruch were slated for the RFC board until it was deemed politically unwise to appoint two Wall Street men. Baruch graciously deferred to Meyer. Significantly, banking friends of Joe Robinson and John Nance Garner filled other vacancies on the board. Thus, an informal commission arrangement created the formal body that dispensed Treasury funds for debt-burdened banks.[14]

The railroads, hard pressed to prosper ever since the government had given them back to the shareholders after the Great War, also could borrow from the RFC. That kept the railroads alive for another year of "staggering deficits." Certainly their creditors were anguished. In the fall of 1932, seventy-two investing institutions, representing insurance companies, banks, and four major universities, asked Baruch, Calvin Coolidge, Alexander Legge, Alfred E. Smith, and Clark Howell to form the National Transportation Committee (NTC) to study and make recommendations for the restoration of the rails' profitability. But even this distinguished panel could not agree upon a course, an inability that suggests how unlikely industrial self-government was without government's arbitrary authority.

Of course, any commission examining the railroad problem had to be somewhat biased with Baruch as a member. His speculative involvements with the rails were extensive and spanned three decades. Throughout the twenties he had criticized rail management resistance to consolidation and its refusal to effect economies of scale. In his role as a director of the B&O he had urged the company to acquire trucking and distributing corporations and jettison some of its passenger lines. Baruch brought Hugh Johnson to the NTC as his personal economist and hired A. A. Berle from the Roosevelt campaign as his personal counsel on the committee. There could be little doubt that Baruch would push for rail consolidation, a recommendation he explored in correspondence with B&O president Daniel Willard. Sure enough, the report argued for regional consolidations that eliminated wasteful lines and duplicated equipment, while "looking eventually to a single National system."

True to the spirit of voluntary cooperation, the report called for the railroads to effect their own consolidations without government intervention. But the Johnson-written report took no chances on rail recalcitrance: "Consolidation is so vital to the public welfare that, unless it is voluntarily accomplished within a reasonable time, the Government should *compel* it." Baruch and Johnson did not want to take any chances that cooperation and consolidation would be rejected by the rails. But there would be no shotgun marriage of rails, and later Baruch would blame the major eastern systems, the New York Central and the Pennsylvania, for being the chief "objectors" to consolidation.[15]

Another obstacle to rail cooperation lay in the competition with motor vehicles for freight hauling. In the committee, Baruch and Johnson clashed with Al Smith, a business-political partner of John J. Raskob and the Du Ponts, major stockholders in General Motors, and Smith's second, Robert Moses, who would become New York's master highway builder. Johnson and Moses, equally pugnacious and proud of their verbal abilities, argued their cases so strenuously that they nearly came to blows. The Baruch side contended that automotive transportation had an inherent financial advantage over the rails because the public subsidized and maintained the roads through taxes on automobiles and fuels. Also, the comparative lack of regulation of interstate trucks and buses and the undertaxation of vehicles in some states gave motor transportation a competitive advantage over the rails. Smith answered these claims in a separate Moses-written report. Agreeing that "the fundamental problem" for the railroads lay in the method of consolidation, "compulsory or voluntary," Smith inclined to the former if the railroads resisted the latter, particularly because the rail stockholders insisted upon behaving as "a preferred class of investors." But the battle lines were really drawn when Smith assailed the committee's report for exaggerating highway competition with the rails. He vehemently denied that additional taxation of trucks and buses would be equitable in the public interest. If highway transportation prospered, its growth was attributable to superior economy and efficiency, not public subsidization of roads.[16]

No commission or committee could resolve the transportation conflict, any more than it could lead the United States out of the depression by itself. The National Transportation Committee had no mediation authority. But it was another important experience for Baruch in dealing with the conflict of compulsory and voluntary schemes for economic planning. Also, his sidekick Hugh Johnson was about to play a significant role in the Roosevelt "Brain Trust" and the New Deal's National Recovery Administration, and the NTC may have confirmed the wisdom of compulsion in Johnson's mind.

A STRANGE BEDFELLOW IN THE BRAIN TRUST

During the presidential campaign of 1932, the wife of a member of Franklin Roosevelt's advisory "Brain Trust" observed that it had become "increasingly evident that the Democrats have many strange bedfellows in their party."[17] Considering his recent legislative alliance with Hoover, Baruch may have been the strangest Democrat in the Roosevelt entourage. He was a late arrival on the Roosevelt bandwagon, having joined it after the New York governor had won his party's nomination. Moreover, Baruch's deflationist determination conflicted sharply with the inflationist thinking among many of the Roosevelt backers and Roosevelt himself. But the candidate was flexible and receptive to all influences—and Baruch was eager to exercise his influence.

Baruch and Roosevelt were not strangers to each other. It is difficult to say when they first met or how well they knew each other in 1932. It is conceivable that Roosevelt knew Baruch as a political contributor in New York as early as 1912. During the war the assistant secretary of the navy certainly knew of Daniels's extensive dealings on raw materials with the War Industries Board. In 1920, Roosevelt, the Democratic candidate for the vice-presidency, mindful of Baruch's influence in the New York Democratic party via his campaign benefactions, had sought to align the speculator behind Frank Polk's senatorial candidacy, only to have Baruch deny that he either could or would "put it over." Their contacts in the 1920s must have been mostly through the Smith organization in New York. Roosevelt was respectful of the venerable Democratic money man; aspiring politicians could not afford to alienate him. Baruch, however, privately appraised politicians much as he judged racehorses. Early in the governor of New York's first term, Baruch patronizingly opined, "I am afraid that Franklin Roosevelt will not be a great governor. He has enthusiasm, but I don't know whether he has balance and, unfortunately, the poor fellow is not as strong as he should be." Translated, this meant that Baruch had misgivings about Roosevelt's sudden independence of the Smith people and about his paralysis from polio. Following Roosevelt's reelection in 1930 and his emergence as a prominent contender for the 1932 presidential nomination, Baruch retained his doubts but sought to extend his policy influence with Roosevelt. He urged Roosevelt to follow a strategy of allowing the Republicans to take the initiative against the depression.[18]

In the campaign for the 1932 nomination, the Roosevelt people suspected Baruch of aiding and abetting a block-Roosevelt effort. Baruch's coolness toward Roosevelt was evident. When one party financial angel told Baruch in early 1931 that Roosevelt was his candidate, Baruch supposedly declared that he would not give one cent to the party if FDR were nominated; Roosevelt had been a good governor, "but he's so wishy washy." The Roosevelt camp watched warily to see which way Baruch would fall. At the War Industries Board dinner in November 1931, Baruch put in a plug for Ritchie, and the next day the *New York Times* reported on the front page that Baruch "sees Ritchie in the White House." Was Ritchie the man to stop Roosevelt's drive? Roosevelt probably knew that while Baruch was publicizing Ritchie, Smith adherents John J. Raskob and Pierre S. Du Pont were encouraging the Maryland governor to become a candidate.[19] But Ritchie could not mount a campaign because he uttered states' rights platitudes that had increasing irrelevance to the times. The Ritchie candidacy was hopeless. Baruch must have realized this, for he denied that he had given Ritchie an endorsement. "I am very friendly with Ritchie and think he is a wonderful man, but I have in no way made up my mind," he told Carter Glass. Baruch sent Roosevelt a personal avowal of neutrality; certainly, Roosevelt responded, he understood that Baruch would not work surreptitiously against his candidacy. Yet the governor knew that "some people who profess friendship" nevertheless spread false innuendos "with the blissful assumption that they will never be repeated." Roosevelt probably was aware that Baruch had been telling friends that the Roosevelt candidacy was puffery, that he "did not know anybody who is really interested or doing anything in regard to it," and that Owen Young and Newton

Baker were the men to watch. Nevertheless, Roosevelt let Baruch know that the door was open to his influence.[20]

Baruch went to the 1932 convention in Chicago with an entourage that included the very attractive actress Clare Boothe Brokaw, but he had no candidate. As soon as the nomination was Roosevelt's, Baruch and Hugh Johnson went to his convention headquarters and demanded to see a copy of the acceptance speech. It did not matter that several drafts had been floating about Chicago hotel rooms and that the final version was en route from Albany. Louis Howe, Roosevelt's campaign manager, appreciating that Baruch had signaled his eagerness to join the Roosevelt camp, gave him a couple of drafts to study. An entente was sealed. Hugh Johnson was welcomed as Baruch's ambassador to the Brain Trust, a group then consisting primarily of Adolph Berle, Raymond Moley, Rexford Tugwell, and Sam Rosenman. Baruch was given input for every campaign address. For his part, Baruch publicized his role as a business conservative for Roosevelt, enabling newspapers to report that Democratic divisions were being mended. Baruch went to Hyde Park in September to assure the nation that business had nothing to fear from Roosevelt, who stood "for the preservation of the fundamental institutions of the nation."[21]

Significantly, politicians in the Roosevelt campaign greeted this late-comer more warmly than did the Brain Trust. Moley and Tugwell were suspicious of Baruch's power. When Baruch had requested to see the acceptance speech drafts, Moley had feared Baruch's deviousness and Tugwell was "aghast." The Columbia University professors had traveled in different New York City circles than Baruch and knew only his reputation, and that they considered sinister. Tugwell later wrote that in 1932 "Baruch's was a history few people were familiar with."[22] But there were also policy differences between Baruch and the Brain Trust.

Baruch wanted the Democrats to assail Hoover for his failure to practice "genuine and effective economy" and to accuse the Republicans of "reckless squandering" of taxpayer dollars. He wanted Roosevelt to vow to reduce government spending by $1 billion. Baruch's antidepression program called for a balanced budget to encourage private investment, "equity" for farmers, and repeal of prohibition and taxation of liquor. Like the Roosevelt people, he endorsed public works expedients for emergency employment and insisted that the crisis had a domestic solution. This did not mean that international action would not be useful: he endorsed bilateral trade agreements like those being recommended by Roosevelt's strongest supporter in the Senate, Cordell Hull of Tennessee.[23]

Roosevelt himself accepted the principle of government economies. Baruch was consulted on every major campaign address, from the Commonwealth Club speech that heralded a Wilsonian merger of the interests of big business and government, in order to seek markets abroad for

American production, to the Pittsburgh address that promised more effective government retrenchment than the Republicans could provide. Wilsonian ambivalence on government's role in economic planning could not be resolved in a presidential campaign. And both Baruch and Roosevelt were Wilsonians.

Baruch was encouraged to foster a dialogue within the Roosevelt campaign on proposed economic policy, as is shown by this Berle memorandum of July:

> The program proposed by B. M. B. was discussed by Moley, Tugwell and myself. Most of the practical proposals seem like common sense; we have not discussed the tax program.
>
> When he gets under principle, B. M. B. poses the essential issue between the two wings of the party. Like most eastern businessmen, B. M. B. wants to permit free play to business, which in practice means freedom to six or eight hundred large corporations and banks to fight among themselves [for] the ultimate mastery of the situation. He believes that individuals must suffer for and rectify their own mistakes. Unfortunately, the result reached is that the "forgotten men" suffer for the mistakes of the individual leaders, who come off relatively unhurt.
>
> The obvious line is to agree on definite measures without committing on questions of philosophy or principle.[24]

Baruch was more at ease with the Brain Trust than it initially was with him. He considered Roosevelt no more a threat to economic institutions than he himself. His tranquility of purpose unsettled Roosevelt advisors who depicted themselves as progressives and Baruch as a tory. They doubted his fidelity to Roosevelt. Yet Baruch assured them of his loyalty to Roosevelt by confiding that the Hoover Treasury Department had sought his silence on fiscal policy while it carried out various inflationary devices designed to boost confidence and stock market prices. Instead, Baruch hammered away at Hoover's government-induced inflation and hoped that Roosevelt would as well. During September, Roosevelt saw more of Hugh Johnson, whom Tugwell considered representative of the "sinister influence" of Baruch. In October it was feared that Hoover enjoyed a resurgence, and Roosevelt reacted by vowing to cut the federal budget by 25 percent. Tugwell later called this "a piece of unforgivable folly," but Tugwell was singular in his antipathy to Baruch. By then, Berle was under retainer to Baruch for the National Transportation Committee and Moley was "softening" on Baruch.[25]

Baruch's other obvious contribution to the campaign was money. He was intent upon surpassing all other givers. In the 1920s he had lectured Democrats on the need to broaden the party's financial base, insisting that it must not appear to be "a plaything of a few rich men." Nonetheless, in 1932, Baruch gave from the heart. On election night he whispered to Moley, "I gave 200,000 dollars." Frank Freidel has tabulated $53,000 of Baruch's money in the campaign, but that figure seems too low: it cost Baruch $50,000 just to get Johnson attached to the Brain Trust. Years later, Senator Claude Swanson, who had worked in the 1932 presidential campaign, recalled that he had requested $25,000 from Baruch to cover certain expenses and received $35,000. Moreover, it appears that some of John J. Raskob's contributions were made possible by Baruch's willingness to cover some of that businessman's money difficulties. Whatever the records show, it is likely that the figure Baruch gave Moley is what the entire campaign cost him, whether or not it was attributed to him.[26]

Following Roosevelt's triumph over Hoover many Democrats wondered what Baruch's notorious money had bought for him. What did he expect in return for his contributions? Office? Influence? How obligated to Baruch did Roosevelt feel? Were their views on economic policy compatible enough to allow Baruch to find a place in policy making? Baruch did not need to be told that contributors held no lien upon a successful candidate. The least he could expect was the sort of civility in which the officeholder kept an open door to his benefactors. Beyond that, it depended upon what role Roosevelt bestowed upon Baruch. It was a concern for many Democrats in the months to come.

TO BE KEPT IN LINE

Roosevelt kept the nation guessing about what the election had determined. His signals on antidepression policy seemed contradictory, although they leaned decidedly toward more intervention in the economy from Washington. But what kind of intervention? Indications of the new president's remedial policies would come with the announcements of his cabinet. The political company kept by Roosevelt would be seen as a reflection of his economic thinking. The lines were drawn on fiscal policy with Baruch on the side of deflation. Having pragmatically conceded that productive and self-liquidating public works spending by the RFC had a legitimate place in 1932, Baruch now stood adamantly against additional spending. Carter Glass, the arch-deflationist of the Senate, liked to say of him, "Bernie is dogmatic as hell about two and two making four," and this was true about Baruch's hostility to inflation. He seldom missed an opportunity to preach against the slightest inflationary action (except where investment was concerned); in early 1933 this attitude could only be seen as the grossest obtuseness. How could prices go lower? Something had to be done to increase the value of productivity. Baruch countered that that could be achieved only by a restoration of business confidence in *real* values, with investment incentives enhanced by low prices. He seemed to ignore the nagging suspicion that private investment capacity had been mostly paper, which the depression had diminished to a true value, so that supplementary public investment was justified even at the risk of public indebtedness. Besides, where would producers find customers when perhaps fifteen million workers and their families were without any income and millions more lived on reduced wages? Baruch's arguments for government economy seemed to ignore this desperation, but he carried the attack against inflation in defiance of burgeoning sentiment for it. Roosevelt leaned toward inflation. Berle, the most cautious of the Brain Trust, had argued that planned inflation could only be considered as a last resort; Baruch retorted that it could not be considered at all. The inflationists girded for the postelection struggle.

Baruch was ready for them. Two weeks after election day he lunched with twelve senators and twelve representatives and warned that high taxes might wreck the government. Every chance he had to talk with Roosevelt was spent didactically discussing the need for drastic budget cutting. Quoting portions of the Pittsburgh address, Baruch gave Pat Harrison an idea of what Roosevelt probably heard: "Now it may have been good politics last year to accede to and accept all the Republican budget unrealities, but is it so now? . . . Isn't our first move in bringing back the confidence so necessary to recovery a little truth to restore public faith in the pronouncements of government to the people?" To those who answered that *controlled* inflation should not be confused with unchecked inflation, he retorted that any allowance for inflation was promiscuous. He did not oppose government spending for relief of the unemployed; he insisted only that it be paid for through borrowing rather than deficit spending. The bonds sold by government would later be financed by broad-based taxes.[27]

There was nothing furtive about Baruch's campaign. What he said in private he repeated before the Senate Finance Committee on 13 February. For most of the morning and the afternoon, Baruch gave an exposition of the sound money case. The depression, he explained, had been caused by the extraordinarily high prices induced by the war and its impact, which continued for a decade after; by the taxes and debts incurred by governmental "nonproducers"; and by overproduction (not to be confused with "underconsumption," he insisted) manifested by "excess productive capacity" wrought by the war, especially in farm and mineral output. Whether he intended it or not, it amounted to an admission of guilt that the Wilsonians had not been successful in restraining the wartime expansion. But that was a lesson to be learned by those who would artificially expand the national economy to meet the current crisis. What could the legislators do to repair the damage of 1933? "Reject all plans which oppose or postpone the workings of natural processes." This did not mean that the Congress ought to do nothing, rather that it ought to discriminate between measures of an ephemerally remedial nature and those likely to sustain recovery for years to come. Relief of human suffering came first, but repair of federal credit and the liquidation of private debt followed closely behind. The *New York Times* found this "good advice." Most of his statement to the committee inveighed against monetary inflation; as Senator Tom Connally of Texas would observe during the questioning that followed, it was the eastern creditor's argument against the debtor's desire to pay off his debt with cheaper dollars. Even Baruch's friends in the Senate were no longer sympathetic to a long-term solution that extended short-term misery.[28]

In discussions of possible cabinet appointments, fellow deflationist Carter Glass received serious attention for secretary of the Treasury and Baruch was considered for secretary of state. Baruch's appointment as the chief foreign policy spokesman might have been seen as a vindication of Wilson. Baruch had been an advocate of American participation in the League, although flexible enough on the treaty to seek compromise with the reservationists. His credentials as a Wilsonian remained impeccable; he articulated positions closely identified with other Wilsonians. On trade matters he was an internationalist without illusions about the probability of cooperation. On debts questions he enjoyed a common ground with the isolationist William E. Borah, ranking Republican on the Senate Foreign Relations Committee. On international monetary questions he predictably disagreed with advocates of abandoning gold, and this position was a serious obstacle to his appointment in 1933. Except for that, Roosevelt seemed to agree with Baruch's foreign policy positions.

But did Baruch want to be secretary of state? Gossip had it that his frequent foreign policy pronouncements of the 1920s and early 1930s were part of a campaign to get the State Department portfolio in the next Democratic administration. Later he would assert that he had decided against any position in Roosevelt's cabinet, preferring "to act in the capacity of pinch-hitter or trouble-shooter." We will never know if he would have accepted an offer of the secretaryship of state from FDR because it was never tendered. Jimmy Byrnes thought he "might like" it. Baruch met with Roosevelt at Warm Springs in February, expecting Roosevelt to discuss cabinet appointments: "That includes any possible relationship that I might bear to the new Administration."[29] Roosevelt made Baruch his coordinator of preparations for the World Economic Conference to be held later in London, a task that suggested policy-making influence without administrative authority.

The State Department was not offered Baruch because Roosevelt obviously did not want him there. Of the party's elder statesmen, which included Newton Baker, John W. Davis, and Norman Davis, Roosevelt considered Owen D. Young "the only one with an adventurous mind." However, Roosevelt did not want anyone connected with big finance, which eliminated Young and most of the names that appeared in the press. Joe Davies and Senator Byrnes had pushed Baruch's name in conversations with Roosevelt's political circle, as did William Randolph Hearst, a strong campaign contributor and, like Baruch, an opponent of foreign debt cancellation.[30] But Roosevelt did not want Glass in the Treasury or Baruch in the State Department because he desired a flexible financial policy instead of the orthodoxy they espoused. RCA's David Sarnoff disapproved of Baruch's deflation stand. If some businessmen could not subscribe to it, the politicians would be even less willing to undertake such an agenda. Political advisor Homer Cummings believed that Roosevelt needed a "well-ordered inflation program." Finally, there was Roosevelt himself, who declared: "We are not going to throw ideas out of the window simply because they are labeled inflationary."[31]

"Politically, I am very far off on the side-lines," Baruch conceded in January, "but economically I am very close to the center of things." It was a fair appraisal then, but even his influence on economic policy was eroding. Some insiders considered Baruch a better contender for the Treasury than the State Department portfolio on the grounds that his sound money views would reassure business. Others argued that he remained a manipulator of the markets who should not be trusted with any position of power. Roosevelt himself privately repeated rumors that inspired distrust of the speculator. That still left Roosevelt with the problem of finding some safe personality who would reassure business that his New Deal did not mean a radical departure in fiscal and monetary policy. Roosevelt half-heartedly sounded Glass out for secretary of the Treasury, but the crusty old Virginia senator wanted guarantees that there would not be the slightest touch of inflation in the New Deal. Roosevelt refused, and by 8 February, Glass had removed himself from consideration. However, as Moley observed, the Glass situation was still unsettled. Baruch, believing that "the first announcement of the Cabinet will have a very big effect one way or the other," intervened to try to persuade Glass to reconsider; but the president-elect, having talked with Glass three times, now wanted William Woodin.[32]

Even so, Roosevelt could not afford to offend Baruch. Baruch was too adroit a publicist to be left to speak against him. Also, Roosevelt had to have the cooperation of Congress: he appreciated Baruch's sway over Robinson, Pittman, Harrison, Byrnes, and other Democrats. Robert W. Bingham, chosen to be ambassador to Great Britain, entreated Secretary of State-designate Cordell Hull to give Baruch some attention: "I felt it was highly important that the administration should have his support; that he was disgruntled and disappointed and likely to become antagonistic. . . . Senator Hull agreed with me entirely on the course to be pursued with Baruch and also stated that he thought his general position on financial matters was perfectly sound." Roosevelt himself served notice upon Tugwell, his principle advocate of governmental economic planning, that they had to respect Baruch's power: "He leaned over the desk to tell me that Baruch owned—he used the word—sixty congressmen. That, he said, was power around Washington. He said he didn't know himself why this effort was made and this control established. That could be speculated about. But those sixty congressmen had to be kept in line."[33]

And so Baruch had to be kept in line. Roosevelt's task would be to make him an occasional consultant and an indirect participant. Roosevelt loved such political sport and Baruch relished the attention. Each had something to gain from amicability rather than antagonism. Baruch would be given a place in policy making without a role in policy implementation.

"UNOFFICIAL PRESIDENT"

Roosevelt wanted the endorsement of Democratic conservatives like Baruch without necessarily having to take them into the administration. Baruch was the most useful and safest of the party elders because he wielded real influence with Congress, never envisioned himself as president, and genuinely expressed a willingness to be helpful. Roosevelt, although he had promised a New Deal, needed continuity to maneuver through the crisis of 1933. His own banking bill was drafted in the previous administration's Treasury Department; he thereby managed a Hoover settlement of the banking crisis without Hoover. Then Roosevelt asked Congress to slash the federal budget by a half billion dollars; it did so within two days. "Under the leadership of Franklin Roosevelt," William E. Leuchtenburg writes, "the budget balancers had won a victory for orthodox finance that had not been possible under Hoover."[34] And he moved to end prohibition, thereby offering a myriad of governmental authorities an opportunity to tax consumers and ease the strain on their budgets. Roosevelt's first steps understandably satisfied deflationists like Baruch.

Roosevelt had been mindful to give Baruch a sense of participation without prominence or power. An international conference on monetary stabilization and the festering debts problem, scheduled for London in mid-1933, provided Roosevelt with that opportunity. During a discussion of cabinet prospects in January, Homer Cummings had suggested using Baruch in preparations for the World Economic Conference. Roosevelt then had recoiled from the idea, but William Randolph Hearst let it be known that he would be reassured by Baruch's presence in the conference planning. Hearst had invested his money in the Roosevelt campaign as insurance against cancellation of Europe's debts, a position with which Baruch heartily concurred. In addition, Ray Moley recognized that important senators like Pittman and Byrnes were close to Baruch. In early February, Baruch was made chairman of the ten-man preconference planning group. It was, Roosevelt reasoned for Tugwell's benefit, "a way of keeping him out of the cabinet."[35]

Although it included the Brain Trust and advisors in Hoover's State Department, the ad hoc committee had no legitimate influence. Following the inauguration, Baruch conferred with Cordell Hull, informing the new secretary of state of the group's activities. He received no indication that the committee's deliberations or he himself would be a part of the London conference. He had been tantalized by the prospect of an assignment in foreign affairs, and he was hurt that it seemed to come to nothing more.[36]

The planning for the ill-fated conference in London proceeded without Baruch through the spring.[37] Investment banker James P. Warburg, a recent addition to the White House's circle of economic advisers, assumed a key role in the planning for the conference and the composition of the U.S. delegation. Warburg was hostile to Roosevelt's predilection for including big contributors, the "Patronesses of the Democratic Campaign." Exercising a Wall Streeter's bias, he especially deplored inclusion of short sellers like Baruch and Joseph P. Kennedy. Moreover, if Baruch were appointed to a delegation that already listed Warburg and Henry Morgenthau, Sr., Warburg feared that it would look like "an International Jewish Congress." And Roosevelt's 19 April announcement that the United States had left the gold standard was a foreign economic move that Baruch could not approve of. At that moment it seemed unlikely that the veteran of Paris in 1919 would advise again at London in 1933.[38]

Also, suspicions of Baruch as an "inside investor" who used privileged information for personal speculative purposes flourished among New Dealers—and Roosevelt was a chief subscriber to them. It was a believable if not verifiable charge, reminiscent of tales concerning Baruch's wartime speculations. When Cummings had proposed Baruch for the conference back in January, Roosevelt had responded that something about Baruch troubled him and he wondered what to do about it. Cummings gasped, "Oh Gosh," and Roosevelt went on, "That is it exactly, oh gosh." He proceeded to tell Cummings that he had heard Baruch had bought about $3 million of Missouri Pacific bonds at 15 "evidently" because he knew of an impending Reconstruction Finance Corporation loan and had sold them when the RFC loan sent their price to 50. Furthermore, Roosevelt said, Baruch had an option on a silver mine's production and the London conference would be dealing with matters influencing the price of silver. Roosevelt, Cummings noted, "looked at me whimsically. 'Now what can one do with a situation like that?' There the matter rested."[39] Baruch's investments were so extensive that it would have been impossible for him to avoid a hint of conflict of interest unless he divested himself of them. That he had done in World War I, but he usually insisted that an investor's patriotism ought to be assumed unless a failure of it was proved. Baruch never denied that he speculated in gold and silver, a fact that was broadly known because he considered that it confirmed his economic wisdom. He saw no conflict of interest between his investments and the national interest.

Whatever the truth of Roosevelt's allegations, Baruch in the spring remained a New Deal pariah who eagerly sought entry. But Roosevelt could not ignore the logic of including Baruch in the conference delegation, especially if he sent a nondescript Texas banker to London. Besides, Raymond Moley had become a fan of Baruch, and Secretary of State Hull, a former senator, knew Baruch's value to the administration. Finally, on 26 May, much to Warburg's consternation, Roosevelt agreed that Baruch would act as a Washington-based advisor to Undersecretary of State Moley during the London conference. Because Baruch never embarked upon any task without a second, he brought Herbert Swope into the picture. That suited Moley and State Department economic advisor Herbert Feis, whose friend Felix Frankfurter already had urged Swope upon them.[40]

The delegation headed by Secretary of State Hull arrived in London on 8 June while its backup group headed by Moley awaited events in Washington. From the beginning the administration had given domestic recovery a higher priority than reconciling international monetary differences. The British were off the gold standard, hoped to undersell the United States in world markets, and only wanted cancellation of their war debts. The French remained tied to the gold standard and haughtily considered those who floated their currency in the markets as less holy than they. The Americans wondered whether stabilizing international prices before domestic levels had been established made any sense. Therefore, it was not surprising that the conference quickly hit an impasse. It was then that Moley decided to join the delegation in London.

Moley's ambition may have gotten the best of him. The former Columbia University professor had originally chosen not to accompany Hull to London because he preferred staying close to Roosevelt; besides, the likelihood that the conference might be discredited and take the reputations of its participants down with it was high. He calculated that if he ought to go, a late arrival as special representative of the president would be more prestigious than traveling as assistant to Hull. When his moment came, Moley took Herbert Swope with him for speechwriting and publicity purposes.

Now it appeared that Baruch was in control of the U.S. delegation on both sides of the Atlantic. Warburg jealously wondered if Baruch were "in the saddle" in Washington and the man responsible for Roosevelt's decision to reject a stabilization scheme that Warburg had developed. Just prior to departure, Moley had told the press that Roosevelt had made Baruch coordinator of economic counsel in Washington. To emphasize his importance, Moley told reporters that Baruch would occupy his office. While Moley and Swope were en route to London, Baruch, the "mystery man" of the administration, as one reporter called him, was being heralded on the front page of the *New York Times* as "Unofficial President." Subsequent stories discussed Baruch's misgivings on stabilization agreements before domestic programs had been tried, and headlines noted that "Senators Approve Baruch's Program."[41] Meanwhile, Roosevelt was on a vacation cruise and let Moley and Baruch bask in their brief glory.

By his insistence upon bringing Baruch and Swope into the picture, Moley invited more political intrigue than he could handle. Considering the recent drift of Roosevelt toward inflation, Baruch's emergence posed a contradiction. How could Roosevelt float the dollar when Baruch defended the gold standard as good policy for a creditor nation? As Herbert Feis commented years later, "In short Moley had selected a *locun tenens* whose views were quite the opposite of those which the President was soon to adopt." But the injection of Baruch into the London muddle meant more than a confusion of goals; it suggested to the press a struggle for power in the three-month-old administration. Swope in Europe fed dissension in the delegation; to Warburg, he was Baruch's "sycophant," to Bingham, a source for inside speculative information for Baruch. It did not help matters that Baruch and Swope were known to be in constant contact via trans-Atlantic telephone.[42]

Baruch believed that international cooperation satisfactory to the United States would not be possible. The British sought to modify their debts out of existence, the French to stabilize currency at a price favorable to themselves. America's course emphasized "national self-containment" that required "a chance to work" before it was tested in international markets. How could values be stabilized internationally when they were unknown domestically? Any international agreement would bring uncertainty of recovery, whereas "it is a restatement of the obvious that our improvement, now so definitely underway, will be the greatest contribution we can make to the good of the world." As George Foster Peabody had told Roosevelt in February, "Confidence here at home [is] absolutely vital before we can expect to revive it among other people." The Americans wanted time to work out their own recovery. "Until we make up our minds at what price the dollar is to be stabilized in reference to gold nothing can be done except temporizing with the situation," Baruch telegraphed Swope when he was en route to London.[43] However, to great fanfare, Moley had landed in England with a compromise proposal for multilateral stabilization.

Now Moley was the star and Hull, the chief American delegate, had been upstaged. Considering that it was already a fragmented delegation in which egos outranked policy, experienced observers might have been reminded of the worst aspect of Paris in 1919. Bingham became the "horizontal" ambassador because illness put him on his back through most of the proceedings; the arrival of Swope added to his discomfort. Key Pittman was alternately drunk or devious, or both; and when he was not playing with Lady Nancy Astor he was working out silver agreements beneficial to his personal Nevada interests, which were the only substantive developments originating from the London meetings. James M. Cox sulked and Hull's temper flared. Somebody's career was certain to be in eclipse following the London conference.

After negotiations with the French and British concerning his proposals for a compromise, Moley on 30 June was certain he had made progress. Baruch was disbelieving. By telephone he suspiciously inquired of Moley three times whether all terms had been understood in their translations and were indeed acceptable. Both Swope and Moley assured Baruch that there was nothing temporary or tentative about the stabilization program that had been agreed to by all parties. Baruch finally, after consulting with William Woodin, Dean Acheson, and George Harrison at his end, assured the London tandem that they had the support of New York (where Baruch had transferred his operations following Moley's spotlighting of him in Washington). As the Moley diary described it, "The conversation ended with Baruch expressing for himself and the others heartiest congratulations upon what they regarded as our victory, and suggested that we come home at once, since the step we had taken had advanced the President's program."[44]

But did the president view developments their way? Did Roosevelt want his secretary of state to endure Moley's insubordination, especially when the diplomatic results were of such dubious consequence? The answer swiftly came in the negative.

The following evening, Baruch knew what a euphoric mistake he had made in attaching himself to Moley's apparently rising prominence; Roosevelt refused to endorse Moley's declaration. Speaking to Swope, Baruch wondered if someone in London had wired the president information that deflected him from their chosen course. In any event, "Baruch's attitude was that nothing more should be done—the President had spoken." Baruch had no stomach for being caught in opposition to the president, especially because he shared so many doubts concerning Moley's compromise. Then came Roosevelt's "Bombshell Message" to the conference, which seemed almost to denounce the conference for endeavoring an ephemeral arrangement in currencies that would placate international bankers at the expense of national interests. It effectively ended the conference;[45] it effectively abbreviated Moley's career in government; it effectively put Baruch back on the periphery of New Deal developments.

To Moley's chagrin, Baruch swiftly moved to patch up relations with Roosevelt by eschewing Moley's rejected scheme and congratulating

Roosevelt for his courageous stand. Moley could pout that Baruch went to "absurd" lengths to protect himself, but the speculator never stayed long with a loser. Moley was on the way out and Baruch had other irons in the fire; he liked Moley, but the emotional professor had allowed his ambitions to get the best of him. Besides, Baruch, ever suspicious of British and French designs, could subscribe to Roosevelt's trepidations. Also, Baruch had little use for fanfare that could not be viewed benignly by the president: in London, Swope had trumpeted that Moley made foreign policy while Baruch ran the government in Roosevelt's stead. Baruch did not want to be portrayed as an "acting president" or an "unofficial president" or just an "assistant president." Swope could not understand why Baruch suddenly was aloof and objective concerning their declining fortunes. It was one more hurt Swope endured for his benefactor. In September, Moley would leave the State Department to begin a writing career.

Baruch, of whom it had once been said that he was too important to the New Deal to take his customary summer sojourn in Europe, departed for France via the liner *Majestic* on 21 July, sardonically telling reporters that he would avoid London because someone might call him "a delegate, a prophet or something." The trip was strictly personal, he assured the press, and even if he visited London it would be to see his old friend Winston Churchill, "but remember he is out of the government now." When asked what he thought of the press characterization of him as "assistant president" during the recent conference episode, Baruch responded with an epithet and laughingly dared reporters to repeat it in their dispatches. He emphasized that the trip was merely his annual summer excursion to take the baths at Vichy and "boil some of the wickedness out of me." Six days later he told reporters in Cherbourg, "I am just a private citizen. I am a good soldier, or I hope so. I certainly do not intend to say anything about anything." He gave the press an itinerary that called for celebrating his sixty-third birthday in Vichy three weeks hence and then hunting in Czechoslovakia with Cary Grayson. He obviously hoped that Roosevelt would forgive and forget all those press tales concerning his alleged power and that following a month abroad he could return to the president's good graces.[46]

"THE LOGICAL CHOICE" FOR AGRICULTURAL PLANNING

Between the inauguration in March and the London economic conference in July, Baruch's reputation inflated to an extent that made him uneasy. He had enjoyed fairly discreet influence with the Seventy-second Congress, but the press buildup of 1933 focused public attention upon him as a backroom operator with only quasi authority and no administrative responsibility. His influence with Congress was intangible; now his power in the administration was defined by the emergence of his cronies, George Peek and Hugh Johnson, as the New Deal's administrators of agricultural and industrial recovery. Baruch himself was depicted in the press as a policy maker without portfolio: "And here is Mr. Baruch, advertised far and wide not only as Acting President, Acting Secretary of State and Acting Secretary of the Treasury, but as the great man who thinks this morning what will be thought this afternoon by General Johnson, our Czar of Industry; by Mr. Peek, Prime Minister of our Czar of Agriculture, and by Mr. Swope, Personal Conductor of the Professor on his Thrilling World-Saving Tour of the World." Roosevelt had conferred the *illusion* of influence upon Baruch. He encouraged journalistic puffery that could only embarrass Baruch. Popular political analysis claimed that, little as it seemed to be generally appreciated, the president appeared to have made Baruch the most powerful person in his administration, in both foreign and domestic affairs—and, moreover, without giving him a title, official recognition, or credentials of any sort; both Roosevelt and Baruch, however, knew that this claim amounted to hollow hyperbole.[47]

Baruch's indirect power in the early New Deal gave him treacherous prominence. He appreciated this because he was quite familiar with the weaknesses of Peek and Johnson, his alleged surrogates in power. Both men were adept at mounting effective publicity campaigns that promoted their causes or their own visibility. But neither had had administrative success. Johnson was completely untested, and Peek had failed in his only governmental effort, the Industrial Board of 1919. Both were volatile personalities. Both were self-righteous. Both lacked introspection about their abilities or their knowledge. They did not work effectively in large organizations.

In Peek's case, his 1919 experience should have been a clue that he could not suffer opposition gladly, that in bureaucratic battles he could not compromise enough to fight another day. But his remarkable management of the McNary-Haugen movement suggested that here was a publicist and lobbyist of extraordinary talents. His broad following and respect among farmers and congressmen caused Roosevelt and the New Dealers to overlook the Industrial Board episode. Although they did not agree with his agricultural doctrine, they valued his abilities in promoting their own, if he chose to do so. Peek sought an external resolution to the agricultural crisis while they emphasized internal adjustments. However, flattered by their attentions, he agreed to administer *their* program in the hope that he could simultaneously put across his own. Anyone familiar with his history could have foreseen a tumultuous collaboration.

The primary interpreter of New Deal farm policy was Secretary of

Agriculture Henry A. Wallace. The son of Harding's secretary of agriculture had more in common with Peek than his historical reputation as a liberal visionary might suggest. Both men had been active in the 1920s movement for putting farm prices at a parity with industrial prices. It was a practical goal, for both men had made their livings by selling to farmers with low incomes—Wallace selling hybrid seed corn and a farm journal, Peek his machinery. They were corn belt businessmen who needed prosperous customers. Like many men involved in the agricultural market, they disagreed on the most effective method of achieving their common goal. This disagreement could obliterate the common base and trust they shared.

Although reserved and ill at ease in New York, Wallace had been bold enough to seek an introduction to Baruch in 1931 for the purpose of financing his enterprises. He would have dealings with Baruch for the next fifteen years without ever understanding him. He tended to stereotype Baruch's associations and interests. Baruch and his southern political friends were "very skilled in meeting human beings"; Baruch's corporation friends were "hard-headed, efficient" types, and Wallace apparently saw himself as quite the opposite of them. Wallace considered Baruch a Wall Streeter in business and a southern conservative in politics, but he was dumbfounded upon learning that Baruch also had contributed to "radical" North Dakota congressman William Lemke's campaigns: "I can't figure it," Wallace confessed. In time, Wallace came to appreciate that Baruch was more eclectic and perceptive than he earlier had given him credit for, admitting, "He has seen deeper than many people in the United States, because he's had wider European contacts." That observation of Baruch may again tell us more of Wallace's estimate of himself.[48]

Because Peek considered Wallace "one of the best economists in the farm field and . . . exceptionally well informed on agricultural conditions" in the 1930s, Baruch made it his business to probe Wallace's mind, even if he would not trust his money with Wallace. Wallace responded, making certain that a trip to New York in 1932 was not without a visit to the farmer's friend in Wall Street. They pursued a dialogue on agricultural policy, and although their correspondence clarified differences, it also sharpened broad areas of agreement. Assuring Baruch that he was not a "convert to any one idea," Wallace nevertheless promoted the domestic allotment plan for restraining agricultural output to increase farm income through higher consumer prices. Baruch cautiously advised that such an experiment be limited to one commodity at a time, preferably wheat.[49] For cotton, Baruch liked cooperative crop reductions to limit surpluses and boost prices when the controls were invoked by organized farmers and state statutes. But it remained to be seen whether he would endorse "voluntary cooperation" at the federal level for all or most commodities.

It might generate broader inflation if it evoked a responsive rise in industrial prices.

While policy differences between Baruch and Wallace were being sharpened, both men were intent upon achieving a consensus. Peek, whose ideas on farm recovery had not progressed beyond the McNary-Haugen plan for dumping surpluses abroad, had to be a part of that consensus. However, in the early 1930s the domestic allotment scheme had gained significant adherents, Roosevelt and Wallace tentatively counted among them. Shortly after banking and economy measures were overwhelmingly passed by the special session of Congress in March, the president and his secretary of agriculture decided to strike for an omnibus agricultural recovery bill. First, they hastily convened a conference of farm leaders and skillfully sold them on a package plan. But, recognizing that the farm bloc in Congress was conservative and that acute policy differences could not long be suffused with the ethos of emergency, they sought passage of the administration's agricultural adjustment bill through an alliance with Peek and Baruch.

Baruch had been expecting overtures from the New Dealers. "They really have no representation in Congress," he observed shortly after the election. Wallace had nominated Peek for secretary of agriculture in mid-November, but Peek never even received a Roosevelt inquiry as to his availability. Still, Wallace ingratiated himself with Peek and Baruch by the mere thought and act of recommending Peek. Later, through a mutual friend, Wallace advised Peek that the cabinet post would have been his had it not been for his friendship with Baruch, whom Roosevelt "did not entirely trust"; at the same time, Wallace was anxious that this gossip not be repeated to Baruch.[50] Any farm program would have to reckon with Baruch's sway over Congress.

Baruch in later years persisted in repeating the story that *he*, not Peek, had first refusal on heading the Agricultural Adjustment Administration (AAA) because the processors and farmers wanted him. Wallace denied ever offering the job to Baruch and maintained that if he had figured in considerations for it, it had been out of "politeness." But there is no denying that Baruch was asked to nominate a candidate. Baruch gave Wallace two names, Charles C. Teague of the California Fruit Growers Exchange, the model for cooperatives of the early 1920s, and Peek. Peek probably was the only one seriously considered for the job. Besides being well known in the farm belt and in the Congress, he had the endorsement of most farm organization leaders and of former governor Frank Lowden of Illinois, himself a spokesman for agricultural equity. On 20 March, Baruch sealed Peek's appointment by sending Wallace a terse telegram, "I think George Peek is the best of the list of men mentioned." Wallace hoped to win the Senate Democratic leadership's support for domestic allotment with Baruch's aid. But a snag in the wooing of Baruch and Peek developed when Peek declined the first offer to head AAA.[51]

The New Dealers needed Baruch and Peek to reassure not only Senate Democrats, but agricultural middlemen as well. Rexford Tugwell, Wallace's assistant secretary of agriculture, made the case in his diary:

> We have puzzled a good deal—H. A. and I—about the adminis-
> tration of the farm act, the Agricultural Adjustment Administration.
> I think we have pretty well settled on George Peek. There are reasons
> for and against. But he carries much weight and will enlist with himself
> the whole Baruch faction. We do not like this crowd particularly and
> would rather have a hard-boiled progressive. But this is a new thing
> and much depends upon cooperation amongst the processors who are
> affected. If we do this we shall advance in our chosen direction
> more slowly, no doubt, but perhaps more surely.

Looking back upon these observations from the vantage point of many years hence, Tugwell, without being clear why, believed that he had been "both perceptive and naive" in his judgment of Peek.[52]

The former Brain Truster believed that Peek never mistrusted the processors as much as he—a judgment verified by the subsequent history of AAA—but Tugwell stands history on its head when he calls Peek the processors' "agent." (Tugwell had made his first effort at becoming a presidential advisor in 1928 and had failed to become Smith's agricultural consultant because "Peek was more practical than a Columbia professor"; his pique endured.) Peek no doubt felt more comfortable with businessmen, even processors, than with academics or Harvard-trained lawyers. But Peek's was another history Tugwell knew little of. Ever since they launched their crusade for agricultural parity, Peek and Baruch had clashed repeatedly with the processors. For over a decade, Baruch and General Mills' James F. Bell had not even spoken to one another because of Bell's 1922 attack on a Peek parity scheme. In 1924, Baruch had complained about middlemen: "It always happens that whenever we try to do anything for the benefit of the farmer, we have the opposition of the Chicago Board of Trade, the millers, and the grain dealers."

In March 1933 the Baruch-Peek combine, along with Hugh Johnson, began negotiating for the "voluntary cooperation" of the processors. They must have enjoyed the exchange immensely because it was so reminiscent of the informal arrangements that characterized the WIB. From the first, Peek noted, they were confronted by "all kinds of dire mutterings" from the businessmen. Jim Bell came to Peek, "whined" about how AAA would destroy his thirty years of work in milling, and vowed to fight it on constitutional grounds. When Bell attempted to strike a bargain by voluntarily reducing his export trade, Peek reminded him that General Mills already operated extensively in Canada. Baruch met with a similar response from a packers' representative, whom he advised to cooperate. One session between the packers and Baruch wound up with Baruch declaring that he was out of patience with their failure to cooperate and that they deserved all they were about to get from the government. Another time, Peek ambiguously recommended "the Big Stick to force cooperation of [the] processors." In the writing of the agricultural adjustment bill, Baruch, Johnson, and Peek brokered among the administration, the processors, and Congress, effectively neutralizing corporate resistance to the bill.[53]

Of course, Peek and Baruch were solicitous of the processors' profits. Clearly the administration's scheme would make business more cumbersome, but not threaten it. Yet the Baruch group retained mixed feelings toward domestic allotment. At first, Peek considered it a modified McNary-Haugen plan, but Johnson was "fierce" in his denunciation on the grounds that it rewarded nonproduction, augured a planned economy, and would tax either businessmen or consumers, neither of whom could afford it when investment and purchasing power were sharply curtailed. However, its cooperative principle appealed to Baruch. He wanted a trial for statutorily reduced production of a commodity or two, but he shied away from any broad experiment. He ambivalently conceded that domestic allotment was a vehicle worth trying in order to attain voluntary crop reduction in the style of 1918.[54]

Peek wanted the farmers to reduce their acreages and market their production cooperatively (abroad, it was hoped) while the processors worked through their own trade associations to fix their costs and prices, "just as the W.I.B. administered industry during the war." Domestic allotment offered that opportunity. The agricultural adjustment bill, Baruch and Peek believed, could be administered well in their hands, but not in the hands of its original drafters: Tugwell, agricultural economist Mordecai Ezekiel, and New York lawyer Jerome Frank. Baruch wanted to redraft the administration's bill, with the wheat millers, packers, and cotton millers represented by Bell, Thomas Wilson, and Robert Stevens respectively.[55] It was typically Baruch: secure industry arrangements and cooperation from the strongest producers and the rest would follow on the assurance that their interests were protected. Small wonder that Tugwell saw Baruch and Peek as the advance agents of a processor takeover!

Although they wanted "sympathetic" administration of the bill, neither Baruch nor Peek desired to head the new agency. They recommended instead an "advisory council" for AAA where processors, producers, and Baruch or another industrial self-government proponent could manipulate policy. Wallace endorsed the proposal and immediately offered Baruch a place on the suggested council; Peek noted that "Tugwell obviously was not pleased with the trend of affairs." Intent upon making sure that AAA would "follow the War Industries Board precedent," Peek assured Wallace that he would work to win congressional approval of the administration bill. But Peek wanted Baruch to head AAA. If the administration accepted the principle of industrial self-government, why should it settle for an acolyte when it could have the prophet himself?[56]

On April 2 the fragile alliance of different planning philosophies verged upon disruption. For days, Peek had been complaining that nobody could take the leadership of AAA with "such men as Tugwell and Ezekiel in a position to run circles around him and perhaps around the Secretary, and appealing to the President." Two days later, Roosevelt called Baruch to arrange a meeting with Peek. Baruch urged Peek to take the AAA job if Roosevelt offered it, provided that Peek could "come directly to [the president] with the Secretary," which would assure AAA of equality with the Department of Agriculture in the hierarchy. Meanwhile, Wallace and Tugwell put misgivings about Peek aside and began to consider him indispensable to AAA's approval in Congress. On 5 April, Peek conferred with Roosevelt and demanded a direct line to the president with the job. Two days later, Peek returned to the White House with Baruch and Lowden and outlined several objections to the bill. Roosevelt agreed to all Peek's demands. A month later, Peek became agricultural adjustment administrator.[57]

Baruch still wondered if AAA were unconstitutional or if the inflation it would generate would defeat the deflationary effects of the Economy Act and a balanced budget. But he resisted an urge to take his trepidations directly to the president. Perhaps he felt that it was too soon to sound a negative note; perhaps he did not want to jeopardize Peek's performance in AAA. He need not have worried about the latter. Peek's differences with Wallace's "internationalist" resistance to dumping surpluses and Tugwell's "idealist" efforts to prevent the processors from passing the taxes along to consumers made for a very unhappy tenure in office. AAA became a battleground between Peek's men and Tugwell's. As Peek began to lose control of AAA in late 1933, Baruch complained to Joe Robinson about those "underlings in the Department of Agriculture who desire to change our philosophy of government without much idea of what the farmer gets out of it."[58] By then the quarrelsome Peek had to go. It was an easy decision for Roosevelt: Peek could move over to the post of special advisor on foreign trade, and his assistant, Chester Davis, would take over AAA, sacrificing nothing in AAA philosophy or administration. Just seven months after taking the job, Peek resigned. The outcome could have been predicted in April by those familiar with Peek's history or personality. Yet it is likely that he would have been offered the job anyway. Peek and Baruch had become the sine qua non for launching a program of agricultural planning that would endure for generations to come.[59]

THE GENERAL FOR INDUSTRIAL RECOVERY

Peek had been a very useful person, the president commented during a discussion with political advisors in December, but a good deal of a prima donna, and in that respect he was very much like General Johnson.[60] The comparison was unavoidable. Peek and Johnson were former business partners, veterans of the WIB, publicists of the industrial self-government ideology, and mainstays of the "Baruch faction." They were emotional, headstrong, and dogmatic in their pursuits. As advocates they could be intimidating; as organizers they could be inspiring; and as adversaries they could be uncompromising. As subordinates in an organization they were invaluable for their fecund minds and indefatigable energies; as leaders they became zealous megalomaniacs who brooked no opposition. Yet Roosevelt conferred power upon them in the New Deal's two most vital planning agencies.

Like Peek and Baruch, Johnson had a history the New Dealers had little familiarity with. Although a talented man, Johnson had advanced mostly because of two patrons who had been attracted by his personality and ability—General Enoch Crowder and Baruch. Raised in a small town in Kansas, Johnson had gone to West Point, where he demonstrated "a greater predilection for hazing than for his studies." ("He's a well-developed bully," Baruch once told Frances Perkins.)[61] Thus began an army career noteworthy only for what Johnson did on his own time before he attracted Crowder's interest. Johnson, an omnivorous reader since boyhood, spent his army days between the Spanish-American War and World War I on remote posts from the Mexican border to the Philippines writing western stories for pulp magazines—"potboilers," he called them. But they demonstrated a great flair for language. The effects of that phase of his army career undoubtedly remained with him and later contributed to the oft-used adjective for his salty volubility—"colorful." (As head of the National Recovery Administration, he once denied to reporters that he harbored political ambitions, insisting that all he wanted was "to be down between Brownsville and Matamoros where the owls fucked the chickens.") Impressed by Johnson's industriousness, Crowder picked him in 1914 for training as a lawyer for the judge advocate corps. Promotion then came swiftly, climaxing in a wartime appointment to the WIB as the army's representative that brought him to the attention of Baruch.

Following the war, Johnson resigned his commission and went into business with Peek, a disastrous mix of personalities and profits. But

Baruch, who esteemed Johnson's candor and writing and organizational skills, hired him as a personal investigator of businesses and macroeconomic conditions. Baruch supplied the capital for Johnson's investment recommendations and Johnson took 10 percent of the gains or losses. The Johnson-Baruch relationship could never deteriorate as Johnson's partnership with Peek had: Baruch was always called "chief" by both men.[62]

Johnson's descriptions of business conditions in the early 1930s are some of the most insightful to be found anywhere, perhaps because he knew more about business than did journalists and wrote with less self-deceit than most businessmen or politicians. Honesty was one of his most endearing qualities—and sometimes his most offensive. In addition, he was a missionary for industrial self-government. As one of the authors of the War Industries Board final report, he believed that a similar peacetime institution was imperative in order to rationalize the business system. The Great Depression only confirmed that judgment and lent urgency to his advocacy. Johnson's schemes for recovery went beyond Baruch's orthodoxy. He obliged Baruch to consider expansion of federal public works for the reemployment of the jobless. He wanted parity payments for farmers. In 1933, Johnson was the lone industrial self-government proponent in the Brain Trust.

It was later written that Baruch had "loaned" Johnson to Roosevelt, but Johnson's status in the New Deal owed something to his aggressiveness and expressiveness. He had dashed off biting assaults upon Hoover for the Roosevelt campaign and had battled the professors and lawyers on the proper relationship between business and government. His intellect was as sharp as his vocabulary. He seemed inexhaustible, juggling his obligations to Baruch in 1932–33 with the Brain Trust activities, the railroad commission, and other matters. Part of his energy seemed to be derived from liquor, an old army problem. He always appeared belligerent and excited during those excitable days. Roosevelt was quite entertained by him. Had Johnson not been a Baruch man, he might have received an assignment at the very outset of the new administration. Instead, he was left in limbo during March as the White House focused its efforts upon business reassurance and agricultural recovery.

Johnson could not resist injecting himself into the struggle for an agricultural adjustment bill. His involvement with agricultural relief went back as far as Baruch's and he had extensive contacts among processors. He disliked—which may be too mild a word to use for Johnson—the domestic allotment plan and vehemently defended the processors' interests. When Peek urged Johnson to write a memorandum detailing his objections for Roosevelt, Baruch interceded to insist that only Peek should speak for cooperation during the writing of the agricultural bill. So Johnson forwarded his memorandum through Peek and waited. He expected

Baruch to lead AAA and take him along as a lieutenant. When it became evident that Baruch would not be AAA head, Johnson was agitated and blamed it all on Tugwell. He told Peek that Tugwell was "a damned Communist, and that the whole idea of benefit payments was communistic": Baruch had to be protected from those people. Johnson considered himself indispensable to agricultural planning. Only he could bring about processor cooperation. Baruch relented and gave him a green light to go to the White House. But Johnson's intervention seemed to confuse both the White House and the processors: had Baruch and Peek had a falling out over differences on the agricultural bill? Baruch then moved in to assure all parties that Peek's role suited him perfectly. That put Johnson back chafing on the sidelines. In mid-April, Baruch commented to Peek that he worried about Johnson. Later in the month, Raymond Moley, beleaguered by his varied roles for the White House and the State Department, happened upon Johnson at the Carlton Hotel and begged him to help in the drafting of the administration's industrial recovery bill. Johnson surely did not require much encouragement.[63]

Then Johnson was on his own. Even Tugwell, who was "used to thinking of him as Baruch's man rather than an independent personality, not doubting, of course, the strength of [his] character and real brilliance," was impressed with Johnson. But, as all parties later emphasized, nobody asked Baruch if Johnson should lead the National Recovery Administration (NRA). Baruch approved of Johnson's participation in designing an industrial recovery bill, knowing that he would be a good advocate for industrial self-government. An alternative scheme for industrial planning came from a congressional-Commerce Department group, and by mid-May a compromise draft of the industrial recovery bill was introduced in Congress. In June, Congress approved the National Industrial Recovery Act (NIRA), a vague charter that awaited definition from its administrator—Hugh Johnson.

As Johnson later told the story, one day while he and Roosevelt discussed the proposed organization, the president said: "Hugh, you've got to *do* this job." Johnson grabbed the offer without any of Peek's sort of temporizing. He was eager for the battle that would accompany NRA's creation. "It will be red fire at first and dead cats afterward," he told friends. "This is just like mounting the guillotine on the infinitesimal gamble that the ax won't work." Apparently he did not confer with Baruch, although they had business plans and Johnson had financial troubles that made him dependent upon Baruch's help; but he "knew exactly what Bernie would tell me to do."[64]

Soon after news of Johnson's appointment hit the newspapers, Baruch went to Secretary of Labor Frances Perkins. He wanted to know if the newspapers had it correctly and Perkins affirmed that they did. "He isn't fit to be head of any of these things," the troubled Baruch declared.

Startled by this deprecation, Perkins exclaimed, "Why, Mr. Baruch, I thought you thought a lot of him and that he was one of the people who worked with you." "Sure," he said,

> he's worked with me for years, but Hugh's got lots of weaknesses. He's not fit to be the head of anything where he has to carry heavy responsibility. He just can't do it. Hugh's always got to have somebody to keep him in order. He's got lots of ability, but you have to handle it. Hugh isn't one of the men I trust. Hugh's my number three man. I don't give him anything to do that is responsible and independent. He's fine when he works right with me, or right with Hancock, or right with somebody else, working under them, with them telling him what to do. He's got lots of drive, but you've got to lead him, to show him how. He isn't fit for this. You must intervene with the President. You must go tell the President this.

Perkins did not want to be the bearer of Baruch's bad tidings. "You should be the one to tell him," she admonished him. "Well, I can't," Baruch declared, and he pressed her again to carry his message to Roosevelt. Reluctantly she agreed.

When Roosevelt heard about Perkins's visitor, he professed to be astonished. "Have you seen anything wrong with Hugh?" he asked her. "No, I've only known him these few weeks," she said. "I've seen nothing wrong with him. The man is touched with genius. He's slightly unstable at times. That I can see. But he is a driver and able." Roosevelt was still more intrigued about why Baruch did not deliver the message himself, a matter he seemed to find of greater significance than the message's content.[65]

Johnson considered Baruch the intellectual father of NRA. All that Johnson did in NRA, he claimed, was guided by principles enunciated by Baruch earlier in the depression. The foundations of NRA lay in Baruch's War Industries Board report, his 1930 speech before the Boston Chamber of Commerce calling for a supreme court of commerce, his calls for suspension of the antitrust laws, his pleas for cooperation among producers to achieve stabilization of their markets. Johnson even attributed NRA's emblem, the Blue Eagle, to Baruch's address to the Brookings Institution on 20 May 1933, in which Baruch suggested mobilizing public opinion through an insignia to be displayed by those who cooperated "voluntarily." These speeches probably were written by Johnson himself, but Baruch gave the words importance and the ideas were as much his as Johnson's.

If Baruch was the father of NRA, Johnson was, by his own reckoning, the dutiful son. He hurled himself into the task, working eighteen hours a day to effect industrial self-government through codes agreed to by the industries following hearings often presided over by Johnson himself.

Disappointed by Roosevelt's administrative separation of the recovery statute's two titles, giving the Public Works Administration to Interior Secretary Harold Ickes and thus depriving NRA of an incentive with which it could command industrial cooperation and set national production priorities, Johnson determinedly proceeded to energize his program. He made no bones about suspending the antitrust laws through trade association collusion to fix minimum prices. Johnson shocked manufacturers by insisting that this meant that even labor's price would be fixed with minimum wages and maximum hours. Subscribers to their industry's codes would display the Blue Eagle and its motto, "We Do Our Part," on labels, store windows, and newspaper mastheads. He employed warlike patriotism, complete with a massive parade down New York's Fifth Avenue and a propaganda campaign that beseeched consumers not to practice thrift but to "Buy Now." He even toured the country, exhorting cooperation from ordinary Americans who should "Buy! Buy now! Buy within prudence everything you need and have so long denied yourselves. It is the key to the whole situation." Was all this not what Baruch had intended?[66]

It was not. In May and June, Baruch bombarded Johnson with names of "right" people to staff the new agency, undoubtedly hoping that they would surround Johnson and make him perform as he ought to. And, when Johnson terminated his salary from Baruch in order to avoid an appearance of any conflict of interest with his governmental obligations, Baruch extended the financially pressed Johnson loans to sustain him.[67] But Baruch knew that what mattered was NRA's policies: he did not like what he saw and heard of them. NRA under Johnson was not compatible with Baruch's preference for deflation or noncoercive cooperation.

"I think there is much to be said about promoting the industries and getting together with the idea of forming something like the War Industries Board," he told economist Harold Moulton in March, "but I am not in favor of giving any guarantee against losses." He could not support a floor under prices because he believed that prices had to find their own organic depths. Also, he knew the difficulties of winning industrial cooperation without the moral equivalent of war. Thus, Baruch emphasized the mobilization of public opinion as a key to any WIB revival. As he told his Brookings Institution audience: "While we agree fully that Industry must voluntarily accept and ask for coordination, and that any appearance of dictation must be avoided, the power of discipline must exist. At least we found it so in the war experiment." When was voluntary cooperation voluntary? Where was the line drawn between it and governmental coercion? Was the real issue *competition versus cooperation*, or *chaos versus discipline*? Baruch publicly insisted that it was through *self*-discipline that the nation would be converted into a congregation of believers in their own cooperative faith. The Blue Eagle propaganda was imperative to spread that faith. "With all earnestness let me say that if this policy of *enlightened cooperation* is not the actual method of the new industrial coordination it must fail." Industry must restrain its own prices or "bring us face to face with the necessity for governmental supervision."[68]

Baruch had urged that two provisions be made a part of the NRA: "one to prevent the sweating of labor and the other the exploitation of the public."[69] Thus, industry had to pass the benefits of stabilized prices along to its workers in the form of minimum wages and maximum hours and put a ceiling on the prices it charged consumers. The WIB had accomplished that goal by first negotiating prices with the most concentrated industries at levels that assured handsome profits, and by providing assurances that these quasi cartels would be free from antitrust prosecution. These were quiet arrangements free from any threats or intimidation. They had set the tone for collusion within an industry and with government. NRA did not imitate the early WIB. To Baruch's consternation, he found upon his return from Europe in the late summer of 1933 that General Johnson had threatened regimentation for slackers in this war. From St. Louis, Johnson had spoken to the nation via two radio networks and had branded noncooperative businessmen Judases among the apostles. Mixing his metaphors, he promised to deprive any Danny Deever of his Blue Eagle epaulets, causing him to suffer "a sentence of economic death." Johnson had employed his last resort first. He had used threats instead of Baruch's honeyed tones intended to enlist industrialists in a great cause that netted sweetly reasonable profits. "Chief," Johnson had said to Baruch when he took on NRA, "I wish I had your faculty for getting things done through charm and astuteness and polish and your genius for saying things positively but so gently that nobody ever takes offense." Baruch replied that Johnson ought to be himself, and in time the slugger would learn to be a crafty pugilist (a favorite Baruch metaphor). After the St. Louis speech, Baruch was not so sure. Johnson's intemperate ballyhoo and frenetic pace worried him.

In the late afternoon of 2 November, Johnson flew to New York to confer with Baruch. That evening, Baruch gave the general a memorandum outlining his grievances: NRA lacked the voluntaristic principle; Johnson's speeches failed as clear expositions of NRA's reason for being and its intentions or failed to emphasize the importance of real cooperation and the ephemeral character of NRA. Also, Johnson attempted too much. Price-fixing had to begin where it was welcome—in raw materials like copper—and proceed only where industries were noncompetitive and eager for government sanction. He warned Johnson that "if you arrive at the point of demanding fair code practices for all industries, it will result in a revolt . . . even greater than that against prohibition." Essentially, Baruch believed that the government should supervise monopolies and cartels, giving them exemption from the antitrust laws. Labor, to be sure, ought to have its eight-hour day and a minimum wage, as well as abolition of child labor and the sweat shop. Beyond that, government ought not to go. He also urged Johnson to ignore Gerard Swope's proposal that the U.S. Chamber of Commerce assume NRA's functions; only the government could do the job.[70]

Baruch returned to his favorite solution to price chaos: the supreme court of commerce. He regarded NRA as a flight from political reality. It was unlikely that NRA could succeed with all the hostility it engendered from businessmen, antimonopolists, and government planners. It had fragile legislative underpinnings and would have to be renewed in 1935. Baruch continued to conjure up a supragovernmental institution that by its blue-ribbon nature would command the respect of all parties to an economic conflict; its findings would be saluted by all of capital and labor simply because of its impartiality and prestige. "This is the concept we are working for," he lectured the errant Johnson, "not a bureaucracy but Government with its guiding hands upon business and a determining body which shall sit like a great court of justice." He envisioned a five-member "court" responding to industrial appeals for codes or initiating codes where the members decided one was needed. Because it was likely that its docket could very easily become crowded with cases that overwhelmed the five members, he would relieve the congestion either with mediation panels for industries or with regional lower courts, with his five-man supreme body sitting as an olympian court of last appeal. It would be above Congress, the executive branch, and the federal courts. For the sake of industrial peace, it would be above politics.[71]

Baruch's criticism of NRA was quite similar to Tugwell's, although their solutions had nothing in common. Both condemned the "blanketing" effect of codes in industries where resistance was likely; but where Baruch would have left them under voluntary cooperative supervision, Tugwell would have put some of them under public ownership. Both men agreed, however, that the public should not be promiscuously exploited by corporations or unions that used their NRA licenses to inflate prices needlessly. Price control was imperative. "We think these codes are going through with a very serious lack of attention to the problem of price control," Tugwell commented. Baruch advised Johnson that "every rise [in prices] must be examined most carefully to see if it is justified by the facts," and if higher wages or materials costs were not evident, the higher prices "had to be fought on the ground of improper and unwise profits."[72]

Meanwhile, NRA foundered. A review board headed by Clarence Darrow criticized it for encouraging monopoly while simultaneously recommending regulation by government and trust-busting. Organized labor bitterly condemned the company unions that flourished under section 7(a) in the absence of real collective bargaining. Internecine warfare between Johnson and his general counsel, labor lawyer Donald Richberg, had erupted. Under assault from all sides, NRA was torn by factionalism. Johnson did not possess the equanimity to withstand such pressures. His gruff army manners and passion for the striking metaphor in his speech invited controversy. Self-publicizing came naturally, and early in NRA he handled his own publicity, which meant reading press handouts and checking every word. His immediate subordinates were under orders to report the names of every person with whom they conferred. Stories circulated that all this hard work and old army habits made him drink excessively. The excess seemed to lie with his workaholic tendencies rather than with any alcoholic problems; he was either bleary-eyed from lack of sleep or under medication for his fatigue; and both factors contributed to an appearance of drunkenness.

NRA often was depicted by opponents as American fascism and the general as its Mussolini. Johnson himself got carried away with his new-found power. In September, George Peek visited him at Walter Reed Hospital, where he was being treated for exhaustion. Johnson was keyed up and said that the Blue Eagle campaign gave him "the greatest following of any man in the country; that he could have anything in the country he wanted; that of course he could not cash in during the present administration." Peek attributed his ramblings to medication. Yet Johnson already had told reporters privately that because he got more publicity than Roosevelt, "naturally some folks were jealous and trying to knife him." Although he denied having any political ambitions, few people doubted that he was an arbitrary man who deserved their fear if not their respect. As Henry Wallace told a reporter, "Johnson is a determined man and usually gets what he wants."[73]

In early 1934 it appeared that Johnson's days in NRA were numbered. He still worked incredibly long hours, although at least once he took a vacation with Baruch at Hobcaw in order, he quipped, to "formulate a code on ducks and quail." Roosevelt still liked him and apparently thought more highly of his organizational and administrative talents than did Baruch. As for the general's outbursts, Roosevelt professed to be amused and firm in the belief that every administration needed to have a Peck's Bad Boy. But the general's skin seemed to be stretched thin and increasingly weak to attacks from outside and within the administration. In February he supposedly called Baruch and sobbed that he wanted out of NRA. That tantrum passed, but the annoyances continued. For Roosevelt, what had seemed a colorful intellect a year before appeared to be the actions of a man unhinged. In June, Roosevelt sought Baruch's assistance in ridding himself of Johnson for a while: could Baruch take Johnson to Europe for a month's vacation? Baruch tried, but Johnson refused to go. In August, Johnson offered to resign and Roosevelt graciously refused. A few days later, Roosevelt asked Johnson to tour Europe and study recovery programs on the Continent. That night, Johnson wrote the president a lengthy, emotional letter of resignation that spoke of humiliation before his "enemies" and sent a copy of it to Baruch. Then he wired Baruch: "Boss said today under no condition will he willingly consent for me to leave him as long as he is on job. Wants me to take more important station as soon as can be spared from present job and said no kicking upstairs. Says he can never spare me. What shall I do? This may be dead cock in pit. Expense heavy with wife seriously ill requiring two nurses. Broke. Cactus."[74]

Roosevelt wanted Baruch to take back his former industrial investigator and sent Frances Perkins on that mission. To Perkins's astonishment, Baruch declared that that was impossible: the general's head was swollen, as witnessed by his refusal to take Baruch's advice on two or three NRA disasters. "Sometimes he won't even talk to me," Baruch confided. "When he does talk to me, he doesn't say anything, or he isn't coherent." Johnson was "a born dictator" and following NRA he would be "just utterly useless" to Baruch. Baruch would not take him back, and he remained with Roosevelt. A month later, Johnson set off another public furor with a speech on the textile strike. Rumors circulated that Johnson would resign and Baruch would replace him, which Baruch promptly denied. However, it was true that another Johnson resignation had been accepted by the president. Johnson's tenure at NRA had finally ended. Donald Richberg replaced him and the NRA embarked upon a phase that stressed the virtues of competition without eliminating the cartelism of industrial self-government launched by Johnson.

In May 1935 the Supreme Court unanimously ruled NRA unconstitutional; only some New Dealers, some businessmen, and Roosevelt himself mourned its passing. It is doubtful that Baruch joined them. "You know I wouldn't have done some of the things he did because I don't believe in them," he told Peek.[75] Baruch did not elaborate with Peek because he did not have to.

A week after Johnson left NRA, Baruch phoned the White House to assure Roosevelt that the "Johnson situation is all right." He spoke too soon. A month later, Baruch began to pass the word along that Johnson was at work on a book dealing with his NRA experience. "I have been using whatever influence I have to bear upon him to say whatever he has to say as a detached scholar, not as for or against anything, and I have had a great deal of difficulty," Baruch reported. He had no control over the "bullheaded" general. Johnson saw the world in terms of friends and foes. His enemies would be named and indicted in that book, he had sworn to Baruch. "I am trying to get him so that he won't be in the position of talking about things he should not," Baruch said. "I don't want him to ruin himself." Johnson became a Scripps-Howard columnist, a natural outlet for a man with a fluent pen and definite opinions. The latter were not complimentary to the New Deal. In 1935, Johnson's columns and the serialization of his book, *The Blue Eagle From Egg to Earth*, in the *Saturday Evening Post* put the administration under assault from an apostate New Dealer. Baruch advised Louis Howe to avoid a public response that would stir more controversy. He had been trying to restrain Johnson, but to no avail. He had asked Johnson to confide in him before publication of his attacks and the general had replied, "You would only bawl me out." So Baruch disassociated himself from Johnson's vituperations, obviously hoping to remain welcome at the White House.[76]

Nevertheless, in Johnson's small pantheon of heroes, Baruch always stood out because he returned the general's loyalty. In fact, Baruch asked Roosevelt to take Johnson back into the administration in 1936 as head of the Maritime Commission, a post he merited politically, Baruch argued, because his columns devastated Republicans, as well as New Dealers, during the 1936 campaign. Roosevelt conceded that Johnson had only kind things to say of the president, but he suspected that Johnson had become a "confirmed toper" and was untrustworthy. So Johnson stuck to his writings, occasionally performing for Baruch such personal services as speech writing or business research. Baruch never disavowed the cantankerous Johnson. When Johnson became seriously ill in 1941, Baruch paid his nursing bills for the rest of his days.[77] It was a last act of respect for a fallen comrade in the war for industrial self-government.

GOLD IN THE VAULTS

By the autumn of 1934 both "Baruch men" had lost their positions of leadership in the New Deal. Nevertheless, recovery by cooperation remained a motif in the administration's agricultural and industrial programs, although Peek and Johnson were no longer its principal voices. Actually, Roosevelt was the strongest advocate of cooperation planning; he would be the leading mourner for NRA and AAA when the Supreme Court struck them down in 1935 and 1936. Baruch could tolerate some inflation, but not a general scheme for higher prices. Stabilization demanded a more cautious approach. Whereas Roosevelt was innovative in creating machinery for higher prices, Baruch was innovative in erecting institutions for price restraint. Roosevelt, committed to higher prices, considered Baruch's deflationary preferences discredited by the depression experience. Both Roosevelt and Baruch wanted planning, but they disagreed upon the incentive: the producer's higher price or the investor's lower price.

The philosophical conflict between Roosevelt and Baruch was part of an evolving relationship between them. Neither man desired a struggle that ended in alienation. Roosevelt perceived Baruch's influence in the Senate as both a threat and potentially useful, depending upon whether the speculator accepted a subordinate status in Washington circles of power. Baruch, eager for access to the White House, consistently deferred to the president. New Dealers who forecast an open confrontation between Roosevelt and Baruch would be disappointed by the latter's quiet submission. Baruch kept his policy dissents from the public. He would be useful to Roosevelt, partly because of what the president knew of his speculations in gold.

It was not that Baruch had done anything illegal in buying gold. But his activity would have suggested to the public that he was hoarding the precious metal at a time when its flow was away from the United States, and Wall Street bankers were again earning the opprobrium of the nation for their greed and selfishness. Any publicity that Baruch had speculated in gold to the detriment of national recovery would have cast serious doubt upon his self-generated image as a patriot who unselfishly put his nation's needs ahead of his own profit. Moreover, it would have seriously impaired the efficacy of "voluntary cooperation" articulated by the industrial self-government advocates. Clearly, Roosevelt wished no harm either to Baruch or to the cause of industrial self-government, but the allegations of financial impropriety gave the president a lever with Baruch. He could convert a policy dispute into a breach of ethics.

Baruch had initiated his personal gold-buying campaign in March 1932. He bought gold bars from European sources and from Alaska Juneau Gold Mining Company, a firm in which he and Eugene Meyer had had interests for at least two decades. That went on until February 1933, Baruch by then having bought sixty-six gold bars that he stored in a New York bank vault. He ceased buying gold before Roosevelt's inauguration, but not without first discussing the new administration's gold policy with the Brain Trust.

On April 5, Roosevelt issued a proclamation calling for the return of hoarded gold.[78] Did Roosevelt know then that Baruch held gold? Probably, because the knowledge seemed widespread among Baruch's friends in Washington.

It was even discussed in the cabinet. When Baruch refused to take his low opinion of Hugh Johnson's leadership qualities to Roosevelt and took his qualms to Francis Perkins instead, she had wondered why Baruch steadfastly declined to go to the White House. Roosevelt understood why. Baruch realized that Roosevelt knew that he had opposed abandonment of the gold standard and government sequestering of gold at a time when "the greatest single [individual] holder of gold bricks was Bernard Baruch." Now he supposedly was afraid to face Roosevelt. Members of the cabinet who had been in Congress—Hull, Swanson, and Vice-President Garner—warmly endorsed the president's gold policy when he announced it at a cabinet meeting. Garner chuckled, "Well, of course, it'll put a lot of people in a very embarrassing position, Mr. President." Roosevelt said that it ought not to; but, Garner, a Texas banker who had never been close to Baruch, persisted: "Well, you know, one of our great friends has got a great hoard of gold." "Who's that?" someone in the cabinet innocently inquired. "Baruch," Garner gleefully disclosed. "I understand Baruch's got a whole bankful of gold bricks."[79]

How Garner learned of Baruch's cache is anybody's guess, but it is likely that Garner was not alone in his knowledge. A couple of months before this cabinet conversation, Baruch, testifying before the Senate Finance Committee on economic recovery, found his deflationist views under careful scrutiny by inflationist advocate Senator Tom Connally of Texas. Connally deftly steered the questioning to the subject of gold, asking, "Do you know anybody that has got any actual gold now?" "Somebody must have it," Baruch parried. "But you do not know where it is?" Connally persisted. "No." The Texan then changed the subject, but several minutes later he returned to it. Remarking that Baruch had expressed fears that any threat to the gold standard would encourage gold buyers to hoard, Connally inquired, "As far as that is concerned they are hoarding gold to-day, aren't they?" Baruch tersely replied: "Hoarding money and credit."[80]

Widespread knowledge of Baruch's gold seriously handicapped his influence on monetary policy. Following Roosevelt's casual statement on 19 April that the country was effectively off the gold standard, Baruch drafted a letter to South Carolina's Senator Jimmy Byrnes, insisting, "This country cannot go off the gold basis." However, he thought better about sending it and kept his silence. Later that first year of the New Deal, Roosevelt, going along with the recommendation of Professor George Warren of Cornell that the government buy gold, announced that all newly mined gold would be purchased at a price fixed well above the market price. It was inflationary, but the owners of Alaska Juneau ought not to have opposed a policy that temporarily raised the value of their securities. Still, the inflationary intent annoyed Baruch, as did Roosevelt's cavalier fixing of the price. "I think they should have paid the market price for it," Baruch privately complained. "I do not like the idea of having the Government declare an emergency and seize a thing without due compensation." Roosevelt had reasoned that any individual or government with $50 million could drive up the price of newly mined gold unless the government put a ceiling price on it. The program proved ineffectual, and by January, Roosevelt had abandoned it. Alaska Juneau's price slid back to its old low.[81] Roosevelt's failure in monetary policy freed Baruch to give his advice not to fix gold prices in 1934. Also, he began to urge that the administration buy up silver in order to compel an international stabilization agreement.[82]

With his partners, Meyer and Ogden Mills, Jr., Baruch invested considerable capital in Alaska Juneau during 1935; in late 1936, following passage of the undistributed profits tax, they pressed the engineer in charge of the mine to extract a higher grade of ore from it, in spite of the engineer's warnings that such efforts would jeopardize the future of the mines. Using his influence with Joe Robinson, Baruch campaigned to reduce the capital gains tax on profits from investments in mines after 1 January 1935.[83]

Many people believed that Baruch's activities in government were at least partially motivated by the desire to gain information or exercise influence for personal gain. Baruch always insisted that his public role was that of an interested citizen whose sole concern was for the nation. Certainly the personal interest and the national interest coincided, both consciously and unconsciously, in Baruch's mind. Yet there is evidence that he was not above pursuing policy or legislation that benefited him in clear conflict of interest. He benefited from the New Deal's policies of buying gold and silver. To his credit—or perhaps he could not hide it—he freely disclosed the "fortuitous circumstances" that made him in the mid-1930s a richer man among poorer people.[84]

AT PEACE WITH THE NEW DEAL

During the 1930s, Baruch assumed new relationships in Washington. He liked to be invited to the White House and he liked his status as a Democratic elder statesman; so he learned to keep his peace, or to oppose by indirection the inflationary policies of a Democratic administration. Moreover, even Baruch's constituency in the Senate missed his presence during the New Deal's first year. "I have kept away from men like you and Pat [Harrison]," he informed Joe Robinson early in 1934, "because you are in a somewhat different position under a President who is the leader of the party."[85]

Always a New Deal outsider, he had to avoid becoming a Democratic exile. It was evident that participation in the New Deal would have required political credentials indicating that he had been for Roosevelt before Chicago; he could not buy his way in afterwards. But could he influence policy from the periphery? The appointments of Peek and Johnson gave the illusion that he could be a policy molder in 1933. Yet at the peak of his supposed power during the London economic conference, he privately described himself as "just a messenger boy running around the country." For a time he spoke kindly in public of everything Roosevelt did, as a loyal Democrat should during the new president's response to a crisis. He warmly cheered Roosevelt's initial actions, all of which were as deflationary as Baruch's prescriptions: no problem there. When businessmen spoke guardedly of the business outlook under the Democrats, Baruch was bullish. He told Roosevelt personally that he had acted during the first month as "an inspired man of very great courage" who had reawakened the American people's confidence in themselves. At a 1933 university commencement, he lashed out at the Republican policies of the twenties and assured the graduates that America's new leadership would give individuals "reasonable protection against any recurrence of seasons like this."[86]

Inflation was politically unavoidable. During his 1933 summer tour, Baruch told friends abroad that Roosevelt would be compelled to raise prices by monetary means if he failed to do so through AAA, NRA, and the Public Works Administration. Tinkering with currency, though abhorrent to him, would be inevitable. The inclusion of the Thomas Amendment to the agricultural law, giving the president monetary inflation powers at his discretion, had demonstrated the political appeal of higher prices at any cost. In November the *Saturday Evening Post* published a Baruch article describing the dangers of *inflation*—complete with photographs of Germans in 1923 buying coal by the pound and throwing millions of worthless marks away—a clear warning that it could happen in the United States. It suggested adverse criticism of the New Deal. Baruch claimed that he had written it back in March, innocent of the administration's intentions to inflate or the *Post*'s intentions to publish the article at a time when it placed Baruch so diametrically against Roosevelt. Almost frantically he sought to assure the White House that he did "not want to be in a position of being publicly opposed" to an administration that he truly supported. He told political friends that his silence was necessary if he were not to "bring down upon my head a terrific amount of personal abuse." Key Pittman reassured Roosevelt that "Bernie . . . had rather injured the effect of his argument by admitting that there had been no inflation as yet."[87]

Even so, Baruch spoke privately of the New Deal's inflationary manipulations of 1933–34 as if they heralded the decline of western civilization. "I think we are going to level everybody down," he darkly wrote to Winston Churchill. The great skyscrapers of Manhattan would be "as useful as the pyramids." Capitalism had not failed: "the madness of wars and speculations are bound to upset any system." Mistakes had been made, but they could not be rectified by the nostrums emanating from Washington:

> We are now in the clutches of the professors of another class
> than that of 1927 and 1929 who told us that we were on [sic] an era
> of removal of all poverty. Now we are going to remove poverty
> by edict.
> I still have old-fashioned ideas (you know they make fun of

everybody old-fashioned and orthodox) that the world can progress only by privations and hard work.

To Baruch, the New Deal set class against class, siding with debtors in a manner certain to reduce all people to poverty instead of elevating them to prosperity. Increasingly he found himself in the social company of the Du Ponts and other wealthy Democratic antagonists of the New Deal. He filed among his papers this parody of the Twenty-third Psalm:

Mr. Roosevelt is my Shepherd
I am in want
He maketh me to lie down on park benches
He leadeth me beside the still factories
He disturbeth my soul
He leadeth me in the paths of destruction for the party's sake
Yea, though I walk through the valley of depression
I anticipate no recovery, for he is with me.
His policies and his diplomacies, they frighten me.
He prepareth a reduction in my salary, and in the presence of mine
    enemies
He annointeth my small income with taxes, and my expenses runneth
    over
Surely, unemployment and poverty shall follow me all the days of
    my life.
And I shall dwell in a mortgaged home forever.

Did he know that only a short time before bonus army veterans had a similar parody, the most significant variation being that it began with the name Hoover?[88]

But he never joined Democratic tories in the Liberty League or allowed a public impression of alienation from the New Deal. By early 1934, as Roosevelt began to reconsider gold-buying and other currency inflation gambits, Baruch began to insist, "As a matter of fact, there is little that I object to in what is being done." He composed a balance sheet for the New Deal policies; and he found many assets in them. He was a good Democrat, and after twelve years of opposition, it was good to enjoy the fruits of majority status and executive power. He reasoned that "the tinseled structure" of the 1920s economy, with its illusions and speculations, had made the New Deal necessary. He liked Harold Ickes's caution in his management of the public works program. He brushed aside charges of financial waste in the Civil Works Administration and approved the way it had "taken people off the streets." Indeed, the New Deal's relief policies made more sense than its recovery stratagems. Inflation made the workingman "much worse off" because of the artificially higher prices produced by NRA's and AAA's planned scarcities. Even that was not solely the New Deal's fault: "If the truth is told, it must be admitted that the manufacturer added too much to his price." The New Deal had acted hastily, but it had had to do so. Although Baruch would have done things differently, he recognized that "we have drawn away from financial collapse. Our people are better employed and life is much easier. Great efforts are being made to level out conflicts, injustices and impracticalities, and above all, the graft, venality and incompetence." Roosevelt's good intentions mattered more than his mistakes: "I think there has been an unwarranted but inevitable invasion of certain privileges but the pendulum will swing back." A believer in cooperative planning, Baruch certainly did "not weep at the bier of rugged individualism." The only issue was *who* should determine the uses of government and their "spiritual values." He was satisfied that the recovery and relief programs provided a "high purpose" missing in America's leadership since Wilson left the White House.[89]

In good conscience he could be a friend of Franklin D. Roosevelt and the New Deal. He wrote: "I do not sympathize with those who have lost their property because they abused it, nor will I shed any tears for those who have been deprived of their power because they have misused it." Given the diversity of the New Deal's programs and administrators, he could find a rightful place and policy within it. He was a believer in a consensus that depended upon dissent. He preferred affirmation to cynicism; he offered alternatives, rather than merely hostility. He was, above all else, a patriot; he deplored fellow businessmen who paid first allegiance to their earnings. In 1934, as the New Deal began a struggle over taxation, Baruch proposed that the government not deprive men and corporations of wealth upon which the system depended for the creation of jobs and materials. But he did not want to be on the side of personal selfishness. He understood the imperatives of public planning in a crisis. "You see, Mr. du Pont, I have occupied both positions—that of the man making the article and that of the man getting it for the Government," he reminded a founder of the Liberty League. "In case of war, if I had anything to say about it, I would have you in the front line in your shirt sleeves and I don't think you would be talking much about profits."[90]

That was the Baruch who had sounded so progressive in 1918. He offended others of his class with such talk, but he truly believed that in war or peace the system would be saved by men of public conscience. The poor were no more virtuous than were the rich—perhaps less so. The elite had a duty to the disadvantaged and deprived. Men of principle had to practice goodness and not uphold injustice. Thus, as the New Deal moved into its social security phase of 1935, Baruch addressed his "fellow" southerners:

There is no more ardent advocate of state rights than I and no greater defender of the Constitution—so much that I am opposed to any change in it. I am considerably of a stand-patter in this respect. . . . I have never seen an amendment since the Bill of Rights that was worth a damn. Even slavery would have disappeared by itself.

But to come to the point. I sometimes wonder whether we in South Carolina are not so engrossed with our states rights . . . that we do not close our eyes to some of the things we ought to be doing for ourselves. What I have in mind for instance is child labor. What are we doing about it? . . . Another thing I think we ought to be studying for ourselves is the question of what we can do for the tenant farmer. We know more about the question than does Washington. . . .

That applies also to the question of aiding the unemployed. South Carolina should be able to take care of a lot more people than they have. We certainly could increase the standards of living of our own people.[91]

It was simply an appeal for enlightened selfishness.

Some of his fellow conservatives sneeringly referred to New Deal reforms as "idealism," and Baruch agreed with them. However, he believed that if reforms were administered by the right people, they were "practical idealism." He believed, as he told South Carolinians, that stabilized working conditions would attract more industry to their state. As for farm tenants, Baruch envisioned them joining the ranks of minor capitalists with a line of credit and a stake in the system; every farmer ought to own the land he worked: "The spread of ownership of the land is something that will be good for the country and good for our people."[92]

Aside from their need to avail themselves of Baruch's influence and power with the Senate, New Dealers discovered through personal contact with the odious speculator, usually to their astonishment, a compatibility of goals they had not imagined previously. The personal contact was important, but it is significant that their policy differences were those of devices and degrees. In 1937, following his reading of a collection of position papers, Baruch wrote Henry Wallace: "I doubt the wisdom of some of the conclusions. But you and I start with one common basis, that is that 'the unfortunate one-third' must be taken care of by those who are more fortunate. And to my mind it doesn't make any difference whether they are so because they can't help themselves or because they won't help themselves. But the amount of help that is given them should depend upon their willingness to try to fend for themselves."[93] The haves had a responsibility to the have-nots. New Dealers interested more in results than in methods discovered in Baruch an unexpected collaborator.

Savoring his reputation as an enlightened capitalist whose career had been marked by support for higher farm prices and collective bargaining for labor, Baruch often sought to impress businessmen with his broader perspective and their need to emulate it. In 1938, Alfred P. Sloan, Jr., chairman of General Motors Corporation, solicited Baruch's interest in improving what he considered industry's number one problem—public relations. Baruch responded that he believed industry had a greater problem in its hostility to laws concerning collective bargaining, minimum wages, maximum hours, and child labor. Why, he demanded to know, has there "never been a law written in Washington to meet changing social conditions that has not been fought tooth and nail, instead of our people trying to work it out?" Industry ought to stop "fighting a losing, rear-guard action" and achieve a better understanding with labor and the general public.

"Frankly, Mr. Baruch, I am rather surprised to receive a letter like this from you," came Sloan's response. General Motors had favored collective bargaining under NRA, but industry ought to fight, "if it has any 'guts,'" the one-sided Wagner Act. As for the minimum wage, "Frankly, I do not believe that your viewpoint is based upon sound economics," Sloan wrote; it would "dislocate industrial balances" by eliminating smaller employers and creating more unemployment. Baruch was not looking for an argument with Sloan, but he pointed out that the U.S. Chamber of Commerce still demanded repeal of the Wagner Act: "Could anything be less realistic, less sensible, more calculated to challenge the political and labor community (now in sort of working agreement) than this proposal?" Would it not make more sense to have the law "modified" in a manner fairer to business without sustaining the impression that big business was reactionary? "We cannot dam the tide of such reform, and it should not be dammed," Baruch admonished Sloan. "True prosperity cannot be legislated, as you say. But wise legislation can aid in permitting the operation of those economic laws which, as you also say, are the sources of stable prosperity." Therefore, he urged, declare that General Motors favored collective bargaining and work for the law's modification. Now it dawned upon Sloan that what Baruch had been advising was directed to the subject of his initial letter—public relations! Industry had to *advertise* its acceptance of the changes in labor relations even as it worked to ameliorate them. As Sloan conceded, "I see, from what you say, that you and I agree just 100%." Sloan had sought support for a proindustry publicity campaign and unexpectedly got more: a substitute promotional idea and consensus legislative strategy from one of the nation's outstanding political publicists. Decades later a historian would write: "The enemies of the New Deal were wrong. They should have been friends."[94] In effect, that was what Baruch told Sloan.

ELEANOR AND FRANKLIN AND BERNIE

The year 1934 had been another watershed in Baruch's life. He had only two choices: he could retire from Washington, join increasingly alienated conservative Democrats in their plans for the American Liberty League, assail the New Deal, and then fade away to be marked by triumphant liberals as a reactionary out of touch with his time; or he could join the fray, maintain his contributions and his influence with Democrats in the Senate, sustain his public image as an elder statesman through appearances before congressional committees, speaking engagements, and myriad contacts with the press, and engage New Dealers in a dialogue that both enlightened them and penetrated the bureaucracy. His decision was obvious to himself. After all, if businessmen could be wrong about the New Deal, New Dealers could be wrong about businessmen. Baruch needed a forum where he could be a spokesman for stabilization. A kibitzer, he was on his way to setting new standards in the art.

First he conducted a strategic retreat from odious Wall Street in order to become the ubiquitous and omniscient elder statesman venerated by even New Dealers. He announced his "retirement" from business; he was closing his Wall Street office and opening one in uptown Manhattan. "I don't want anyone to think I'm getting rusty and am going to retire [altogether]. I'm not, positively," he pledged to reporters. "I'm going to be as active as I've always been. But it will be a different kind of activity." He could not yet define that activity. Once he had styled himself a "speculator," but now that would no longer serve him. Appearing before the House Foreign Affairs Committee, and confronted with the familiar first question asking him to state his name, address, and business, Baruch responded to the last stammering, "Uh-uh-I hardly know how to say what my business is." Then he quipped, "Off the record, though, I'm not on the dole."

For the record, when he first announced his withdrawal from Wall Street, he claimed to be beginning a new career as a writer, his first project being his memoirs. "And there'll be no ghost-writing," he asserted. "I'm going to do it myself. It may not be good as literature. But at least it'll be my own." John Foster Dulles, Hugh Johnson, Herbert Bayard Swope, Arthur Krock, and the numerous journalists who wrote his books, articles, speeches, and sometimes even letters for him during the previous twenty years must have been amused by that bit of disingenuousness— especially when he volunteered that he now employed Marquis James, prize-winning biographer of Andrew Jackson, to "help collate and arrange" his papers![95]

His arrangement with James, dating from February 1934, put the writer on a salary of $750 per month for over two years until he delivered a two-volume manuscript. But it was never published. Baruch kept it, but in 1936 it must have seemed to him either inappropriate to his purposes or just incomplete for a man engaged in a new career in his sixties. His life was in flux. Good public relations man that he was, he was willing to amend the symbols of his life that offended the public. Just as he moved his office uptown, so he surrendered that remnant of leisure-class living upon which he thrived—Hobcaw Barony, his huge estate in South Carolina. Donating it to his native state, he replaced it with a more modest retreat for vacations and entertaining, "Little Hobcaw," in Kingstree, South Carolina. "It has become difficult to maintain the place," he said, explaining his decision to Churchill, "both because of the expense and the fact that the people are being taught that it is anti-social to enjoy such things." He suggested a keenly felt need to bow to the egalitarian feelings of the masses on the march.[96]

His interests centered on Washington. He did not give up his speculative habits, not only because they were ingrained, but also because so many people looked to him for investment advice. But he spent more time in Washington's Hotel Carlton, tending to his political contacts. "You see," he confided to an old acquaintance in 1937, "I do not know so many people in industry any more because I have not kept in touch with them."[97] Most of his prewar or wartime business associates had long since either retired or died, and Baruch knew few of the younger generation of executives.

He was not happy with the New Deal's social legislation and tax proposals of 1935. Moreover, he felt keenly the antipathy of administration figures such as Tugwell, Harry Hopkins, Harold Ickes, and a wide assortment of second- and third-echelon administrators. A few New Deal congressmen considered him persona non grata, but they were insignificant in number: most Democrats, unless they could count upon other sources, learned to value his campaign contributions. Baruch tried to keep his criticisms of the New Deal out of print; even in private conversations he tried to focus his comments upon issues rather than personalities. Not only did he exempt Roosevelt from adverse comment, but he frequently went out of his way to commend the president publicly.

It was the world's worst-kept secret that Baruch yearned for invitations to the White House no matter who was its occupant. Those visits brought him public attention. Even the loyal Herb Swope deplored what he called "B. M.'s desire occasionally to run with the hare and hunt with the hounds." But power flowed from the presidency and Baruch could not influence events unless he had access. So he bided his time during Roosevelt's first term, maintaining his contacts in the Senate, accepting occasional invitations to the White House, performing a favor or two for the president, and keeping a sharp eye open for a chance to be of some service for the administration in any arena. As Henry Wallace once remarked, "Baruch always gravitated to where the power was and the power seemed to gravitate to where Baruch was. It was a magnetic relationship."[98]

The Roosevelt-Baruch relationship alternated between warmth and frigidity. The president often told people that Baruch could be brought over to his side any time he allowed him to put his feet under his dining room table. Roosevelt probably said it because it was both true and demeaning to Baruch. Roosevelt missed few opportunities to gossip about Baruch. In 1937 he revealed an ancient grudge, involving the time in 1917 when the assistant secretary of the navy had been compelled by the Raw Materials Section head of the War Industries Board to give up some options on copper at prices lower than what the WIB had negotiated. Baruch, who prided himself on getting the lowest possible prices from industry for the government during the war, challenged FDR to verify the truth of the 1917 incident. The president had the navy research the issue; the navy concluded that "both the President and Mr. Baruch were right in their recollections, but each had in mind different transactions." The matter seemed to be resolved with each expressing a sense of camaraderie with the other. But it did not prevent Roosevelt from telling other stories that encouraged distrust of Baruch. Baruch knew what Roosevelt was doing, but was willing to ignore it as long as, in the words of a reporter, his back was "stroked the right way by an occasional audience with F. D. R."[99]

Why did the president even bother to stroke him? Sam Rosenman explained that Roosevelt genuinely valued Baruch's judgment on economic issues and found "Old Bernie" useful as an intermediary with prominent Europeans whom Baruch visited during his summer jaunts. The evidence of his utility as a problem solver is abundant. Although Baruch's opinions on the economy were somewhat predictable, Roosevelt had learned to appreciate his insights on monetary policy. But most of all there was Baruch's political clout. It was both intimidating and useful. As Roosevelt told Perkins late in the 1930s: "Baruch can raise rumpeses [sic]. He can put things in our paths. He's got lots of influence on the Congress still. We kind of need him to keep [congressmen] in line. . . . He helps out tremendously in keeping the more wild members of Congress, the Southern members of Congress, kind of down and reconciled. . . . Barney's a great help to us in keeping them in line, keeping them pacified, keeping them from doing reckless things."[100]

It was an extraordinary relationship, one filled with respect and conviviality, distrust and deceit. Had Roosevelt not been president and had Baruch not been as influential as he was with key senators, it is inconceivable that they could have been friends. In fact, they had not been cordial before 1932, although these two New York Democrats and veterans of the Wilson administration had many mutual friends. Yet Baruch usually saw or reached the president at whim. His letters and messages to Roosevelt were given special attention. Baruch often channeled his messages through press secretary Steve Early or Missy LeHand, whom, along with Louis Howe, "Pa" Watson, and Mrs. Roosevelt, he later credited with bringing him into the White House's "inner councils" when others, such as Hopkins and Rosenman, sought to keep him out. He volunteered insights into business conditions, recommendations for executive reorganization, and suggestions for foreign economic policy to Roosevelt. He hunted with Watson and lavished on him gifts for himself and his wife. In 1940, Watson and Early were among the recipients of the ten life memberships Baruch bought in the Jefferson Islands Club for Washington Democrats. Baruch claimed that his influence had won the appointment of Joseph P. Kennedy as chairman of the Securities and Exchange Commission. However, Roosevelt knew that giving Baruch easy entry to the White House carried certain hazards. Baruch slyly leaked White House gossip to favored reporters, thereby reminding his public that he was privy to presidential power.[101]

In the New Deal bureaucracy, Baruch was disdained as a Wall Streeter, a deflationist, and an antagonist in earlier party battles. But he had persistence and personality on his side. "How Baruch gets into anything always has the same answer—he wants to get in," James Warburg once declared. "He was scratching all the time." As Baruch himself told Hopkins's biographer, "Harry didn't want much to listen to me, but I kept at him." Contact with New Dealers usually favored Baruch in the long run, for they found that he was not the ogre they were told to dread. He was genial and intelligent, and he usually made bright conversation even when others could not agree with him. Even a radical journalist like Matthew Josephson found him "approachable, garrulous, and also disingenuous." Baruch savored a good argument with "idealists" and a chance to heap scorn upon what he considered their ignorance and illogic. But he was not a quarrelsome man. Immovable in his convictions, he came prepared to disarm adversaries and to negotiate differences. A first encounter with Baruch took many people by surprise. "We met at 10 in Baruch's study," State Department economist Herbert Feis reported to a friend. "Baruch was cordial and contrary to all the pictures I had built up of the man. He is of a rather smiling and understanding nature."[102]

Of course, in those days of ideological infighting, no matter how pleasant Baruch was, most New Dealers knew that he was poles away from their convictions concerning the political economy. Only a year after Roosevelt's inauguration, the concept of industrial self-government was in retreat, in part because of the administrative ineptitude of Baruch's friends Peek and Johnson. The economic planners were bidding for the soul of AAA while the antimonopolists struggled to control NRA. With social security then in its protean stage, Baruch served as an old-order reference point. In some quarters, association with him was anathema; it could be interpreted as "going right." Raymond Moley, for instance, was depicted in 1934 by Brandeisians as abandoning the cause of reform in part because he had "been possibly a little too close to Barney."[103]

A New Dealer who dared to engage Baruch's friendship was Eleanor Roosevelt. The president's wife was both above ideology and unmistakably liberal. To many observers she was a soft-headed humanitarian who formed an anomalous alliance with Baruch, a hardhearted conservative. Such characterizations did each of them a disservice. They were close and dear to each other. To an extent theirs was an affair of the heart (they signed their letters, "Affectionately"), but it owed too much to their intellects to be considered as anything more than an attachment that sprang from admiration, trust, and support for each other. Sharing an appreciation of Victorian social graces, during frequent lunches or dinners they were properly no more than "Mrs. Roosevelt" and "Mr. Baruch." Each needed, used, enjoyed the other. Her biographer, Joseph P. Lash, is correct: "There was, no doubt, an element of calculation on both sides, but also there was genuine affection."[104]

How did Mrs. Roosevelt explain their misalliance? "I have always found that while it took a little tact and some flattery to get on with the old gentleman I got enough information with valuable experience back of it to make it worth while," she advised Adlai Stevenson in 1952. "He is not always a liberal and you will not always agree with him but fundamentally he is sound and I think it is valuable to have contacts with him, particularly unofficial ones." She shrewdly courted him with sincere encomiums that spoke well of her and fed his insatiable vanity. When Louis Howe was dying she brought in Baruch to promise to be helpful to Howe's son and to promise to underwrite a special political concern in the coming 1936 campaign; later she wrote Baruch, "You were wiser than the rest of us. You knew that it was medicine, food and drink to Louis to know that he was still in there fighting, doing something for Franklin." Many of her projects, like the Arthurdale settlement, were expensive, depending upon government funds that might not be forthcoming without Baruch's friends in the Senate, or upon private funds that he could contribute himself and convince other wealthy friends, who would never have given if he had not asked them, to contribute. Without experience in business herself, she needed practical advice that was not forthcoming from most businessmen because of the idealistic nature of her projects. His public approval of Arthurdale gave it the political and financial boost required to sustain it. But she seldom asked him to get up front with her, knowing that he preferred to be her "silent partner." Once she went against his advice, an act that prompted her to write him: "I hope you will feel I have acted wisely and have done what you would have done, for I value your good opinion and cooperation more than I can tell you."[105]

Baruch, as a female friend in the 1930s recalled, "liked women of spunk and talent, provided they were pretty, and he fancied himself in the role of mentor to their careers. Housewifely virtues did not appeal to him. He preferred a woman who could make a keynote speech at a political convention to one who could bake an apple pie." Clare Boothe Luce, to be sure, or the opera singer with whom he had furtive meetings at Saratoga, were women more to his liking. With Mrs. Roosevelt he could play impresario to a great political career. Besides, she probably caught the essence of his attraction to her when she commented, "Mr. Baruch looks on me as a mind, not as a woman." Perhaps this was said a little tongue in cheek, but if she could flatter him without losing any credibility, he could do likewise; his praise sustained her against the ridicule she often encountered, as when he paid tribute to her "rare combination of intelligence and great heart." He publicly defended her West Virginia project because of his desire "to see you carry out your ideas . . . [though] your critics were unfair and because I like you too." He deluged her with thoughtful gifts and at Christmastime every year sent her $500, not because she personally needed the money, but because he appreciated that she had many causes that did.[106]

Their mutual admiration and support was undoubtedly a cause for wonder among their friends and admirers. The New Dealers' attitude toward it is perhaps best represented by Aubrey Williams, executive director of the National Youth Administration, who once felt intense anger upon observing Baruch giving Mrs. Roosevelt a platonic kiss, "because he believed him to be 'a scoundrel, and unworthy of her affection.'" Her sons also deplored their affinity, although neither was a saint in their eyes. Their father, James and Elliott Roosevelt later claimed in books distinguished more by personal invective than by insight, shrewdly ignored Baruch's advice and blandishments, whereas their mother foolishly grasped Baruch's flattery and gifts. Indeed, the Roosevelt sons attribute Baruch's "infiltrating the White House" to the notion that the speculator "got to father through mother."[107]

Baruch used the Arthurdale project not only to ingratiate himself with Mrs. Roosevelt and to embellish his public image, but significantly to further his conceptions of political economy. Set in the poverty-ridden hills of West Virginia at Reedsville, Arthurdale represented America restoring itself through hard work and cooperation. It was a subsistence homestead where families would work the poor soil and create an indigenous industry. Mrs. Roosevelt had involved herself in it in the fall of 1933. Congress appropriated funds for homes, the first of which were completed in June 1934. She invited Baruch to the opening ceremonies,

6. *Mrs. Roosevelt and Mr. Baruch. (Courtesy Seeley G. Mudd Manuscript Library, Princeton University)*

and he quickly enlisted as a publicist for her. On the train back to Washington he told reporters who had been inspecting homes that they had missed "the most remarkable part of the whole trip." He exclaimed that he had never witnessed "a more dramatic scene" than the homesteaders gathered before embarking on their new lives: "you should have seen their joyous faces." He described one of the homesteaders turning to Mrs. Roosevelt and saying, "'I think we ought to offer up a prayer for the blessing the Great Jehovah has given us for sending this lady to see us.' And that is what they did." And that was what the reporters wrote. But Reedsville was in a depressed coal-mining area without capital for developing a profitable industry. Congress refused to finance a factory of doubtful productivity. Complaints about Reedsville's expensive experiment were heard in the House. Baruch sent Mrs. Roosevelt a handwritten letter of support, which he suggested she use as an endorsement for the project. In it he labeled criticism of Arthurdale "neither convincing, just nor quite fair." But no more public money was forthcoming. At Baruch's suggestion, Gerard Swope of General Electric was prevailed upon to operate a vacuum cleaner assembly plant in Reedsville for a brief period until a dearth of orders closed it.[108]

If Arthurdale were to survive as a homestead model of self-help and voluntary action, it needed private capital. The government contributed about a million dollars, mostly for housing, but there were necessities that could not be covered by that amount. For instance, an experimental school, dear to Mrs. Roosevelt's heart, operated on private contributions. Baruch kicked off her fund raising with a $22,000 check. "Win or lose it is really worthwhile," he assured her. It was right to experiment in "salvaging and redeeming old and young people." He believed that for Arthurdale to succeed, it had to break its umbilical cord to Washington and make basic decisions affecting its own welfare. It should decide how many houses the community needed, control its own school, and find industry profitable enough to enable every homesteader eventually to buy his own home from the government at a reasonable price.

Tugwell and others envisioned Arthurdale and the other homestead communities as experiments in state planning, but Baruch saw them as experiments in cooperative capitalism. In his mind, the rationale for them was no different from that for the cooperative farm credit institutions, with their principles of local control and private financing. They were speculative ventures that ought to be undertaken by Washington for both humanitarian and practical reasons. But, as with every speculation, it was important for the investor to recognize when a profit was no longer possible and to cut his losses. As a heavy contributor to the community's school, he before long urged that it become a part of the county and state systems. It was not just the school that he was writing off, but the community itself. Without a viable industry that provided jobs, it could not survive. He did not regret the experiment, for it served as an object lesson: "If we will learn not to put people where they cannot earn enough to care for themselves, whatever the cost, it will be cheap." But Mrs. Roosevelt and the Resettlement Administration persisted; in World War II, with a political assist from Baruch, the government built factories for an aircraft company at Reedsville.[109] State capitalism had returned to an Arthurdale that survived through the incongruous friendship of Eleanor and Franklin Roosevelt and the notorious Bernard Baruch.

"BARUCH APPARENTLY REFUSED TO VOTE"

The 1936 election was a touchstone for a Democrat's loyalty. Al Smith took a walk out of the party to join his Liberty League cohorts in cabalistic opposition to Roosevelt's "socialism." However, Roosevelt had given Baruch more cause for satisfaction than he had given Smith; after all, how many senators did Smith control? For Baruch, a delicate relationship was at stake. His reputation as an "advisor to presidents" depended upon his sway with Congress; but his authority with the lawmakers had been built in part upon his accessibility to the White House since 1917. He complained of much in the New Deal. But to join the opposition to Roosevelt was an invitation to be led into the wilderness. Old senatorial friends then would have to choose between Baruch and their party's leader in the White House, and the result would be unnecessary pain for all and banishment for Baruch. He could denounce the New Deal courtiers but he could never be so foolish as to strike at the king. He could disagree with policy as long as he quadrennially closed ranks with his party behind its leader. He could consider opposition to Roosevelt in 1936, but he dared not take the step.

On 3 March 1936, the day FDR sent a tax bill to Congress that enraged Wall Street, Baruch dined at Washington's Metropolitan Club with eight friends and acquaintances: Gerard and Herbert Swope, Jack Neyland, Arthur Ballantine, Averell Harriman, Condé Nast, Bruce Barton, and Raymond Moley. Their discussion naturally turned to the 1936 presidential election, and they polled each other on three questions. Who would the Republicans nominate? Five of them anticipated Governor Alf Landon of Kansas, two predicted Senator Arthur Vandenberg of Michigan, two could or would not say. Who would win the election? Seven were confident that Roosevelt would be reelected. Who would *they* vote for? Six of them declared they would vote *against* Roosevelt, two of them said they would vote for Roosevelt; Moley noted that "Baruch apparently refused to vote."[110]

Baruch must have believed that Roosevelt had ways of knowing what was discussed there, and he protected himself accordingly. (Harriman had been chairman of the Business Advisory Council created by Roosevelt in 1933 and was Harry Hopkins's link to industry.) But, in more private contacts, Baruch said things that encouraged anti-New Dealers to think that he would join them in opposition. He once lamented to an anti-New Deal columnist that "they" wanted to change the Constitution to suit their economic predilections. A glance at Republican Ogden Mills's anti-New Deal polemic, *Liberalism Fights On*, was enough to make him "believe I can subscribe to it all." But he continued to distinguish carefully between Roosevelt and "them." "I am decidedly persona non gratis [*sic*] with many of those surrounding the President," he conceded, but as long as invitations for visits and requests for favors came from the White House, he could not count himself as against Roosevelt.[111]

He kept his lines to both sides open and his finger wet in the wind. In May he visited the White House with fellow Democratic businessmen Owen D. Young and James M. Cox; two weeks later he wrote flattering words about Landon to Eugene Meyer, publisher of the *Washington Post* and an editorial supporter of the Kansas governor, adding, "I have been informed that the Standard Oil interests are opposed to Landon. Why do you fellows keep that secret? That wouldn't do him any harm." Two days following that letter to Meyer he called Steve Early at the White House with a message for the president that he anticipated improved business conditions and was "keeping an eye on" the activities of an oil company and an auto company's chief officers. He wanted the president to know he was still very much of a Roosevelt man.[112]

He believed Roosevelt was unbeatable. He did not go along with old Republican friends like Meyer and Smith Democrats in New York who looked for a revolt against the New Deal. Not even in Palm Beach, where rumor had it that a great deal of money was being bet against Roosevelt, could he find any takers. The odds, he assured Roosevelt, were running two to one in his favor. On leaving for his 1936 summer holiday in Europe, Baruch was asked by reporters to comment on rumors that Wall Street bets had begun to swing to Landon. "Take it from one who knows," he responded; "don't take stock in anything that comes out of Wall Street." He was asked if he knew about Al Smith's decision to leave the Democratic party before it was announced. No, he had not known before newsmen had told him, although he admitted that Smith personally had advised him that a statement would be forthcoming. His excursion to Europe conveniently prevented him from attending the Democratic convention that renominated Roosevelt.[113]

What else could a conservative Democrat do? Discussing the problem earlier with Frank Kent, he wondered what course Millard Tydings and Carter Glass and other anti-New Deal Democratic senators would take. "I do not know what I would do if I were in their places," he said. "Harakiri is not a pleasant thing to perform." He reasoned that he did not have to make such a choice because he was not a politician, but a test of his affections would come after the Democratic convention when he was tapped to contribute. To refuse to contribute would be to break with Roosevelt. With his anti-Roosevelt friends he kept silent on the matter of financing Roosevelt's reelection, but there could be no doubt that he had helped. In October, Moley thought Baruch "clung rather fervently to the idea that Landon has a chance." Baruch had managed to be ill during registration week; so he did not vote that year. When Roosevelt's victory was certain, Kent sent Baruch a telegram: "do you think we can get a recount if we holler fraud?"[114]

By the end of November, Baruch had gone to the White House and had involved himself in a number of agricultural, trade, and tax policy discussions. The election had not altered the status of either Baruch or Roosevelt—or their relationship. That is a tribute to the political dexterity of both men.

TAXES AND ''HUNTING IN THE TALL GRASS''

Taxation became Baruch's central point of contention with the New Deal. It ominously suggested to Baruch that the New Deal intended, not humanitarian adjustments, but basic alterations in the capitalist system. Through the devices of the capital gains and undistributed profits taxes the government threatened to deprive business of its venture capital. Nothing else went so directly and substantively to the heart of the system itself as the question of whose capital it was.

The issue had its origins in 1934. Antimonopoly Brandeisians had been waiting for an opportunity to swing the New Deal from cartelistic arrangements toward antibigness reforms. Believing that the power to tax carried the power to destroy corporate giants that inhibited competition and recovery, the Brandeisians passed the word to disciples of Harvard Law School professor Felix Frankfurter, scattered throughout the federal bureaucracy, that "Isaiah [Brandeis] wants to ride ahead hard with his full program, completely contemptuous of political obstacles." Roosevelt was less contemptuous of those obstacles that year, but by early 1935, Huey Long's share-the-wealth movement suggested that reform through taxation could give the president a political advantage. It is not necessary here to enumerate the offending tax proposals, for what mattered most was what they collectively suggested—conscription of wealth. In New Deal histories, Roosevelt is widely quoted as chortling when he sent Congress his tax message, "Pat Harrison's going to be so surprised he'll have kittens on the spot." Yet Harrison and his Senate Finance Committee cohorts delayed or defeated most of the administration's tax proposals while raising a few levies it had not requested. In the end businessmen nursed grievances against the administration for its intentions rather than its accomplishments. "If the President had said that the government needed the money, the conservatives would have understood and might have accepted the tax increases better," Herbert Stein has written. "But he refused to say that. He would only say that the society needed more equality."[115]

In January 1936 the Supreme Court provided Roosevelt with a good reason for what businessmen considered a bad tax. It ruled that AAA's processing tax was unconstitutional, leaving the government with a program it could not finance. The idea of an undistributed profits tax, a tax on surplus corporate profits not distributed to stockholders, had been discussed in the Treasury since late 1934. Now the administration put it forward as a measure designed to save parity payments for farmers and bring the budget into balance, reasons that appealed to the most liberal and conservative of hearts. Democrats in Congress, facing reelection with the president, put aside doubts and approved the undistributed profits tax. Perhaps nothing the New Deal did caused more collective fright among businessmen than this law.[116]

And nothing was more likely to involve Baruch in the legislative process than taxation. Usually he did not impose himself upon his senatorial clients; the favors they owed him for his contributions were to be husbanded until circumstances arose in which restraint had to yield to intervention. Also, he dared not antagonize Roosevelt over less consequential aspects of his program. His posture always had to be "constructive," which mostly meant supportive or at least silent. In 1932 he had exercised his power in the Senate in behalf of the Hoover tax program and met defeat when the House Democrats proved less amenable to his influence and more opportunistic. Having failed to secure passage of the sales tax that spring, Baruch mounted another effort during the lame-duck session of 1932–33 and found himself confronting the reluctance of the president-elect to have Washington adopt a fiscal device sorely needed by state governments. Roosevelt considered regressive taxes on consumers justifiable on state or local levels, but the federal budget had to be balanced by progressive levies. During the New Deal's initial two years, Baruch kept his counsel on taxes to himself. As long as Roosevelt himself sought balanced budgets by reduced expenditures or a processing tax, which the processors passed along to the consumer, Baruch had no real quarrel with the administration.

However, he anticipated that the New Dealers would be pressed by radicals to undertake "the exploitation of those who have by those who have not." He suspected that the failure of New Deal monetary experiments would turn Roosevelt to taxing the "successful." Baruch was all for social programs for the masses, provided that the masses paid for them:

If I were arranging a tax system, it would be on the basis of the highest tax that I could place upon the workers, to get everything I wanted for those who could not do for themselves, and for general governmental purposes, but I would limit that tax to the point at which I could get everybody going full tilt creating wealth and comforts in the greatest possible amount so that it could be distributed to the greatest number. That requires experience and wisdom. That policy like other government policies should not be touched by the feeling[s] of revenge, envy or jealousy.[117]

Social programs for the poor were economically correct as long as their financing did not inhibit investors from taking risks in new enterprises or reinvestment in expansion.

The lessons of Wilsonian policies had been that practical idealism could accommodate the masses' propensity for equity while preserving the inequity of wealth required for growth. Ever the Wilsonian, Baruch in 1935 reasoned that "during this period of strife it does seem to me as if the makers and doers can give up a little bit more than they are giving up now." If the "makers and doers" took that initiative, it would forestall the need for politicians to accede to demands by the electorate for taxes that soaked the rich. A pessimist on human nature, Baruch resisted the government's leveling tendency: "I do not believe that the world is educated up to the point where brother loves brother to the extent of working like the devil and dividing with him." He feared that the New Deal in its zeal to foster parity would reverse the process of recovery from the depression. "Business could not be controlled under N.R.A., but it can be destroyed by taxation," he lectured Joe Robinson in June 1935. He claimed to be avoiding his Senate friends at that time because the administration's tax program made him feel bewildered and helpless. Yet no less than freedom of enterprise itself might be trampled either by the masses or by a "man on horseback in the White House" they would someday elect:

The wisdom and forebearance with which this tax program
is handled will mark for many, many years, and perhaps for longer
than any of us realize, the future of the country and the world. If they
place too great a burden upon the doer, the maker and the saver, the
standards of living in the world will go down to a kind of Middle Ages
civilization. We rightly fight against the spoliation of the many by the
few but we should also see that there is not a spoliation of the few by
the many. The aristocracy of the proletariat wielding the knout is no
more beneficial to the masses than was the aristocracy of the Czars and
their nobles.

Baruch had overreacted to the administration's tax intentions. By that autumn he had the tax act of 1935 in perspective. (Also, his "man on horseback," Huey Long, who verbally flailed Baruch as an insidious Wall Street influence within the New Deal, had been assassinated, and one of the political pressures upon the tax act had been removed.) The prospects for business seemed "a little brighter."[118]

In December, Baruch took his case against the capital gains tax directly to Roosevelt and Morgenthau, arguing that it hindered new enterprises. In particular he had in mind new mining ventures such as expansion of Alaska Juneau, but he broadened his objections to the entire economy. Why was it that unemployment remained so high, he asked rhetorically. Assuring Roosevelt that he was cognizant of what was politically possible, Baruch offered reduced capital gains taxes as a means of creating jobs and winning reelection.[119] Roosevelt did not take Baruch's fiscal advice. In fact, to Baruch's astonishment, Roosevelt on 3 March recommended sweeping reforms in the tax system that removed a couple of corporate burdens but emplaced others—including the infamous undistributed profits tax.

Describing himself as "overwhelmed" by the proposed 1936 tax bill, Baruch again turned philosophical:

> The other day, being rather depressed, I went to Central Park to think things out. I said to myself, "what is the matter with me? I am a great deal better off than I was in the number of dollars I can get for my securities. As a matter of fact, most of my friends are." Then I looked into the question of taxes and said, "Of course I am very heavily taxed but still I have more than I need."
> So I kept asking myself what was the matter. Of course what is really the trouble is that we are fearful of the future. . . .
> There is demand by the incompetent, unwise and those unable to take care of themselves that they be given an opportunity.

The sixty-five-year-old Hamlet rendered a soliloquy to the effect that, through taxation, the poor had "gained on us." Confidentially denouncing Roosevelt's advisors to Frank Kent, Baruch complained that they waged a propaganda campaign in which individuals of "industrial and financial accomplishments . . . have been made to feel that success in their lines is unsocial."[120] Certainly, Baruch did not believe that his desire to exempt from taxation his earnings from mine operations begun after 1 January 1935 was unsocial. Yet that was his paramount interest in the tax bill. He wanted a tax bill permitting the investors who had accelerated extraction of gold ore from Alaska Juneau to reap the benefits of government purchases of gold.

Baruch's behavior during 1936 was erratic. He was frightened by the prospect of alienating himself from the White House or even from congressional Democrats. Hostile to Roosevelt's tax program, he seems to have been torn between loyalty to president and party and loyalty to class—or to self-interest. As we have seen, in March he had refused to disclose his true opinions on the forthcoming elections, and he feared that his longtime friends in the Senate, particularly Tydings and Glass, who had already spoken out against New Deal taxes, could not maintain their seats. He hesitated to speak even confidentially against proposed taxes, and when he did voice disapproval of the bill, he averted specific mention of the undistributed profits levy. By late April he cautiously added his voice to those denouncing the bill. In a manner totally out of character, he apologetically advised Joe Robinson, "There is nothing I dislike so much as to discuss financial matters in which the government is involved. But, it seems to me we have done so little toward creating employment." Baruch worried that he subjected himself to familiar accusations of tax avoidance by a very wealthy man. Yet he took his case directly to Roosevelt.

"The new tax bill is . . . open to the criticism that it penalizes the payment of corporate debts incurred for capital goods and prevents industrial reemployment in the heavy goods industry where it is needed most," he told the president. "*It is very clear to me that we are not only doing nothing to decrease unemployment but we are doing a lot to increase it.*" This constituted a tough indictment of the New Deal. It was not original with Baruch; in the words of Herbert Stein, "There was common recognition that to get up to high employment, or at least to get there without continued emergency expenditure by government, would require a revival of private investment." The administration asserted that it taxed only that money which did not find its way back into investment, a judgment businessmen could quarrel with. At any rate, in June 1936, Baruch hazarded the forecast that the tax bill, if passed with most of what the Treasury wanted, would create "more unemployment a year from now than you have today." As it turned out, the Roosevelt depression of 1937–38 began in August 1937. But it is uncertain whether the speculator was correct for the wrong reasons or truly perspicacious.[121]

In any event businessmen in 1937 were distracted somewhat from their preoccupation with taxes by the president's surprise bill to reform the federal judiciary, the "court-packing" scheme sent to Congress in February. Following Roosevelt's Second Inaugural Address, in which he declared, "I see one-third of a nation ill-housed, ill-clad, ill-nourished," the nation had anticipated an expanded social welfare program. Obviously, Roosevelt considered additional social legislation futile if the Supreme Court and lower federal courts invalidated such laws as the Wagner Act and Social Security. Therefore, he decided to reform the courts with additional judges more sympathetic to the New Deal.

The nation divided sharply over the proposal. The Senate reflected the alignments, and the search for compromises consumed much of its legislative time. Baruch had been an adversary of various "New Deal efforts to change the constitution" and could not have found this one to his liking. Yet he reacted with cautious noncommitment. The recent sit-down strikes in the automobile industry, which further antagonized the middle-class property owner, made the president's proposed reorganization of the judiciary untimely, Baruch advised Eleanor Roosevelt. For himself, he did not know what to think of it after having read the proposal three times. All he would say was that it seemed "a very ingenious and practical way of handling the situation. . . . I do not find myself shocked as others do." But he preferred to read it a few more times and talk with Roosevelt before taking a stand. About a month later he felt obliged to warn Roosevelt of "restlessness" in Congress. The fight over the Court bill dragged on through the spring as the Court itself went through a series of decisions approving New Deal legislation. There seemed to be less justification for the reorganization bill, but Roosevelt persisted into a hot, steamy Washington summer. "My heart goes out to you when you must be overwhelmed with the burden of always having the impossible thrust upon you," Baruch had commiserated with Joe Robinson, the reluctant leader of the administration forces. In July, Robinson assured Baruch that he felt physically "unusually strong" and mentally able "to stand the pressure very well." A compromise reform was in the works; the newspapers exaggerated the conflict in the Senate while the bitterness actually was less than anticipated, Robinson reported to his old friend.[122] Two days later, Robinson was dead from a heart attack.

Ten or fifteen minutes after he heard the news of Robinson's death, Roosevelt received a call from Baruch in New York, where he had been about to board for his summer's sail to Europe. He hoped that the president would now drop the Court bill and not kill any more senators! Roosevelt retorted that the stalled bill had not killed anyone; only its opponents were responsible. Obviously, Baruch was overcome with grief for a close friend with whom he had exercised considerable political influence, whose business ventures he had supported, and with whom he had socialized extensively. But it did not help Roosevelt's denial of killing senators when the *New York Times* the next day ran a story in conjunction with Robinson's death under the headline "Robinson is 23d Official Lost to Roosevelt; Ten of Senate Have Died in New Deal Regime."[123]

Robinson's demise did not diminish Baruch's influence in the Senate. Through Harrison, Pittman, and the increasingly powerful Jimmy Byrnes, among others, Baruch still exercised his voice in its legislating. Moreover, Colonel Edward A. Halsey, secretary of the Senate, remained a vital conduit for both solicited and unsolicited Baruch advice and funds. The prestigious *Times* columnist Arthur Krock, who got his job through

Bernard M. Baruch, often passed along unidentified Baruch economic opinions and exclusive tips to the public. More importantly, however, he sometimes celebrated Baruch in print, as when he wrote in April: "Mr. Baruch has long been one of the outstanding citizens of the world, and people have been heard to ask what qualities—in addition to his wealth and distinguished presence—have made him so. The answer would seem to be brains and the ability to use them, patience, industry and character." Because Krock was as widely read in Washington as in New York, Baruch could not have had a better publicist. How influential was he in 1937? Daniel Willard believed that Baruch could pull enough strings to alter the administration's posture toward sit-down strikers. Even antagonists in the administration and in the liberal press professed to see the hand of Baruch moving quietly and deftly against them. Almost paranoid, Brandeisians depicted Baruch as "mixing into affairs down here" in ways inimical to their best interests. Younger New Deal senators gossiped of how Baruch meddled in legislating. Liberal correspondent "Jay Franklin" echoed charges that Baruch sought to wreck administration relief efforts or block amendments to the Securities Act. Whether Baruch really did all he was accused of is moot; less arguable is the fact that his Senate "string" opposed the administration, a sign to New Dealers of Baruch's sorcery. He remained, in the New Deal's second term, a symbol of reactionary resistance among old Democrats, despite his best efforts to ingratiate himself with the younger liberals.[124]

Baruch, as he sometimes said, liked to think that he indeed did his "best hunting in the tall grass," meaning that he lobbied effectively with the president, administration officials, and senators through personal unpublicized contact. But the cultivated reputation of "presidential advisor" and public sage on economic matters required that he show himself enough to give his publicists—Swope, Krock, Kent, et al.—a chance to proclaim his wisdom. He did best, as we shall see in Chapter Seven, on issues involving foreign policy and national security, where he could operate as a patriot seeking only the national interest in honest difference with those who defined it otherwise. Issues of social or economic policy in the Great Depression were apt to suggest a selfish personal involvement he tried to avoid in public. But he was drawn ineluctably into the tax fight of 1938, the supreme concern of that year.

What made it so crucial was the economic reversal of 1937. The downturn gave heart to Roosevelt's corporate opponents—the "economic royalists" he had flailed in 1936—who pointed to his epithets and taxes as proof that the administration had killed business confidence; and business confidence, conservatives asserted, had more positive impact upon the economy than any of Washington's recovery and reform schemes. Nothing cast more doubt upon New Deal strategy than the very evident fact that after more than four years of assorted acronyms there were still at least ten million unemployed Americans. Baruch fairly gloated with satisfaction as the news of September 1937 appeared to confirm his warnings of 1936.

"If your economic advisers do not agree with me, I wish you would send them to me and let them convince me I am wrong," he challenged Harry Hopkins. "Punitive" and "stifling" taxation had broken business confidence, he asserted, and had resulted in conditions that offset previous relief efforts. A balanced budget, he lectured Henry Wallace, was always important, albeit not at the risk of reducing expenditures and creating unemployment. His support of federal spending in 1937 contrasted sharply with his devotion to economy in 1933 and demonstrated a capacity to learn through experience and to adapt to a new economic consensus. The new Baruch would reduce government expenditures only when there were clear signs of increasing employment and government receipts; an unbalanced budget was not a mortal sin after all! Thus, Washington should sustain its public works obligations and concomitantly reduce its taxes upon business in an effort to stimulate investment expansion. (Ironically, Roosevelt sought to cut spending!) It was the new economics of the 1930s *sans* Keynes; Baruch welcomed the recession as an excuse to relieve business of its tax burdens in the holy cause of generating jobs. "As much as a year ago, it was apparent to many that this would happen," he ungraciously reminded a Works Progress Administration economist. "It is too bad we must be burned to find out that fire does burn." The day after he wrote those words the stock market suffered a severe decline, which prompted him to call Jimmy Byrnes to assure him and others the selling was inexcusable, but understandable among frightened businessmen who dared not plan for an uncertain future.[125]

The clamor for lower corporation taxes proved overwhelming in 1938. Businessmen within the administration—that is, Joe Kennedy, Jesse Jones, and Marriner Eccles—broke ranks with the Treasury to urge publicly a repeal of the undistributed profits tax. Even Hopkins joined in the attack. Senate conservatives like Carter Glass could be expected to align themselves against it as they had before. Pat Harrison used a national radio broadcast to assail that tax and repeat the Baruch argument that the capital gains tax discouraged investment and development of new enterprises; business craved incentives for expansion, not "excessive or punitive taxes." However, Roosevelt remained a determined defender of progressive taxation. The administration's tax policies had been nothing less than "good morals and sound economics," he insisted; to change the existing laws would be to shift the burden of taxation to those who were least able to bear it. He would exempt smaller businesses from the stiff corporate taxes, a small modification. A fight was promised, but a Gallup Poll showed that only 31 percent of those Americans polled favored complete retention of the tax on corporate surpluses.[126]

Baruch finally left the tall grass and went public. Neither he nor the Treasury had wanted an open confrontation. Morgenthau was wary of his influence in the Senate. During an earlier Baruch lobbying effort for lower capital gains levies, the secretary had angered him, and Morgenthau's only consolation was that it was better to "have him annoyed at me than at the President." On 28 February, at the peak of the tax battle, Baruch appeared before the Senate Special Committee to Investigate Unemployment and Relief, chaired by Jimmy Byrnes—a presidential favorite who had turned against the taxes. Much of what Baruch said cagily applauded administration spending for recovery and relief, but the dramatized portions, which the newspapers eagerly picked up with big headlines, denigrated Roosevelt's tax policies. The ultimate indictment came in his words, "Unemployment is now traceable more directly to government policy than to anything that business could or should do." He would lower capital gains taxes (he noted that England had none) and "modify" the undistributed profits tax. Most of his testimony followed arguments he had used in Washington before; now he had pitted his personal prestige publicly against the president's, a confrontation Baruch seldom sought.[127]

Immediately after giving his testimony, Baruch sent a letter to Steve Early with a message for the president: the headlines, proclaiming Baruch's accusation that New Deal taxes put people out of work, had distorted the thrust of his views and he certainly intended nothing personal against Roosevelt. But Roosevelt found Baruch's behavior both "amusing" and "sordid." He asserted that he would have read Baruch out of the party, but he hoped "that a practical idealist like Baruch will help to finance Alben Barkley's campaign in Kentucky." When reporters inquired of Roosevelt if he had any comment on Baruch's testimony, the president looked surprised, moved his head from left to right, then up and down, feigning difficulty in recollection, and finally remarked with telling effect, "I'm sorry. I have only read the headlines."[128]

Baruch was afraid of what Roosevelt might do in retaliation. Not only did Baruch send him a message via Early, and circulate it to his friends in the Senate to assure them that he remained a Democrat in good standing, but he appealed to Roosevelt indirectly through a Krock column. Reminding the White House that Baruch had "remarkably refrained from controversial utterance, considering that hard won eminence in affairs leads the public to expect from those who have attained it candid expression when weighty matters arise," Krock pleaded with Roosevelt not to rely upon those damaging headlines but to consider the speculator's words "constructive criticism he should read." Baruch nervously asked Halsey and Byrnes to tell him what New Dealers in the Senate had to say concerning his testimony; he did not want them to think he had separated himself from the president. Byrnes soothed Baruch with the news that those who read his testimony did not regard it as "unfriendly" and that he should not fret over the headlines. Roosevelt then declared himself forcefully in defense of the taxes as instruments of equity. Once more, Krock wrote a column beseeching Roosevelt to read beyond the headlines and to remember that Baruch was "a lifelong supporter of the Democratic party, who on *no* previous occasion had publicly ranged himself against any of the president's taxation theories." In two late April columns, Krock repeated Baruch's arguments as reasoned truth rather than any political assault.

When the House-Senate conference deadlocked on taxes, Byrnes released his committee's report, which predictably seconded Baruch's prescription for lower taxes to stimulate industry and jobs. Columnist Joseph Alsop was inspired to write a piece depicting Byrnes and Baruch as in cahoots to embarrass Roosevelt; Baruch was not amused. And well should Baruch have been nettled by the effect of Byrnes's effort to pressure the conferees into accepting the probusiness Senate version; for it was interpreted by many Washington columnists as a decisive victory by Baruch over Roosevelt. Conservatives dubbed the 1938 tax bill "the Baruch bill." The Senate version prevailed: the undistributed profits tax was reduced and sentenced to die after 1939; capital gains taxes, much to Baruch's satisfaction, were substantially reduced on properties held more than eighteen months. Despite a Treasury recommendation for a veto because the bill was flawed with Baruch's insidious influence, Roosevelt allowed it to become law without his signature. No president had resorted to that tactic on a revenue bill since Grover Cleveland in 1894.[129]

Perhaps nothing else so evidently sounded the death knell of the New Deal. For himself, Baruch was anxious to remind Roosevelt and the New Dealers of his own commitment to measures of social justice such as maximum hours and minimum wages.[130] For he was a practical idealist, an enlightened capitalist.

THOSE MEN WHO WILL APPRECIATE BARUCH'S HELP

In an effort to generate more accountability in the Democratic party, the administration in 1938 employed its prestige against foes of the tax bill. By June, Roosevelt launched campaigns for opponents of anti-New Deal senators in state primaries. It was dubbed a "purge." Seldom, however, were the instances of White House intervention in primary campaigns clear-cut clashes between pro- and anti-New Dealers. In Iowa, for instance, Roosevelt sought Guy Gillette's defeat. His secretary of agriculture, Iowan Henry Wallace, maintained a strict neutrality between his boss and his state's Democratic senator. Not Baruch, however: Baruch went to Iowa's other Democratic senator, who was in Gillette's camp,

7. Baruch is depicted as a critic of Franklin Roosevelt and the New Deal in 1938 by Berryman in the Washington Evening Star. *(Courtesy Seeley G. Mudd Manuscript Library, Princeton University)*

plunked down a thousand dollar bill, and ordered, "I want you to see that this is used for Gillette." Gillette won the primary; but the president denounced "copperheads" in the Democracy, vowing to intervene in state fights where an issue of principle was at stake.[131]

Kentucky had a race where principle ranked well behind personalities. Governor A. B. "Happy" Chandler challenged Alben Barkley for his Senate seat from the Blue Grass state, but this time both Roosevelt and Baruch wanted to retain the incumbent. Barkley, chosen by a one-vote margin over Pat Harrison to succeed Robinson as majority leader, was a friend of both the New Deal and Baruch. The speculator long had had ties to Kentucky politics; he had bankrolled Barkley's first campaign and had counted upon him to answer the late Huey Long's personal attacks. Barkley in 1938 was in trouble because most of the tobacco elite who invited Baruch's intervention in the 1926 race had since either gone broke or died. Earlier in 1938, Roosevelt had claimed that he could not read Baruch out of the party because he needed money for Barkley's campaign. On the other hand, Baruch in later years asserted that Roosevelt had marked Barkley for defeat until, he said, "I went to bat and got him straightened out." It is possible that Roosevelt had feigned indifference to Barkley's fate in order to stir Baruch's concern that the populist Chandler would win. Certainly, Roosevelt wanted Barkley to win as much as Baruch did.[132]

But there were other Democratic contests that pitted Roosevelt's prestige against Baruch's money. In Maryland the president sought to oust Millard Tydings, who had opposed almost every significant New Deal measure since 1933. In Georgia, Roosevelt went after Walter George, a determined antagonist on social and fiscal issues. Neither man was especially close to Baruch personally, but Baruch had mixed in Maryland politics for nearly twenty years, and George was an integral part of the Senate club in which Baruch was an ex officio member. Jimmy Byrnes spent a lot of Baruch's money while directing the conservatives' defense.

The matter of principle was muddled in South Carolina, however, where both Roosevelt and Baruch held "Cotton Ed" Smith in contempt and both sought opponents to his reelection. The governor of South Carolina, Olin Johnston, desired Smith's seat; Baruch preferred Charleston mayor Burnett Maybank, who ironically had been close enough to the New Deal to be offered a position on the Federal Power Commission. Baruch's motivations were personal: in 1937, Maybank had given him assistance in a court case involving Baruch's liability for a failed bank in which he owned stock. But Maybank had his eye on the governorship, and Baruch, at Jimmy Byrnes's behest, eventually put his money on the anti-New Deal Smith, who won.[133]

Baruch lay low during the 1938 general election. For the most part he followed the advice of Jimmy Byrnes on which races deserved his money. Byrnes's sole recommendation was for the Wisconsin race, where Democrat Ryan Duffy faced "the LaFollette candidate," who may have been congenial to Roosevelt in spite of a GOP label. Byrnes counseled that Baruch assist Duffy and ignore requests for aid to Democratic senators running in New Hampshire and Kansas. Byrnes reminded Baruch that not every Democrat deserved his contributions: "You have done your part to help those men you know who, I am sure, will appreciate your help." Clearly, New Dealers did not qualify. It is unclear what Baruch did when Halsey begged him to "forget personalities" and remember all Democrats in need of his help, but it is likely that, following Byrnes's advice, he gave nominally and not particularly generously.[134]

The New Deal was an emotional issue in 1938 and after, but hardly one of great substance. Foreign affairs—the march of Fascism across Europe and Asia—distracted the nation from the old domestic battles of the 1930s. Recovery had not been achieved by the New Deal, as the economic crisis of 1937–38 so amply demonstrated. With foreign affairs as a backdrop, both Baruch and Roosevelt dusted off their favorite solutions for a stagnant economy—those prototypes for a modern national economic organization, the War Industries Board and the National Recovery Administration. Independently of each other they discussed what amounted to the same thing: corporate machines fueled by liberal hortatory rhetoric.

Essentially they were still preoccupied with the problems of competition and concentration, laissez-faire and collectivism, smallness and bigness. As Baruch observed, among those sets of alternatives, the first in each case no longer was viable; a dialogue was therefore academic at best. "Never in history has there been such a centripetal phenomenon as our modern concentration of business in a few institutions of overwhelming power, or such slaughter of small independents," he declared. Certainly nobody could mistake this as the plaint of a Brandeisian, for in almost the same breath, Baruch noted that "we are still in the era of destructive competition." Despite the "corporate collectivism" of industry, Americans had not developed policies and organizations for business stabilization. Americans were too individualistic and, as a consequence, "the peaks of prosperity became higher and steeper, but the valleys of depression grew deeper and more wide. . . . The trick is to scale down the peaks, to shore up the valleys, and thus to maintain equity and balance through the whole structure with due regard to the human equations involved." Until the nation took command over its business cycles, America could only anticipate "demoralizing booms or disastrous slumps. Both are failures of our economic system." Circumstances in 1933 had required action without ample weighing of alternatives for stabilization; in 1937, Baruch had urged that "measures reorienting our economic universe should now be given something more than hasty consideration." His planning was remote from Fabian or Marxist socialism. Man was eternally an acquisitive animal, and whatever system he devised would have to be respectful of individual initiative. Though philosophically nebulous, Baruch's warnings against excesses of regulation and competition amounted to a call for an organizing and arbitral peacetime WIB—an NRA with enough political savvy to cultivate industrial "voluntary cooperation."

Roosevelt seemed to concur. He had never quite given up on NRA. It had been too arbitrary, but he seemed to feel that it could work if Washington provided guidelines for business initiative. The antitrust statutes needed revision. He wanted the trade associations "to sit down around a table with the Government" and, calculating the output and demand of the country, "make a more intelligent group estimate" for the future, "*so that they won't overproduce.*" He denied that this solution would lead to price-fixing or a cessation of competition, but he conceded that "a lot of people are afraid of it." Roosevelt espoused a giant cartel: "I would very much favor making it a completely legal thing to do: to meet around a table to find out, with the help of the Government, what the demands are, what the purchasing power of the country is, what the inventories are."

Except for his protestations that he would "keep competition," Roosevelt's words could have come from Baruch. In April 1938 he sent Congress a message on monopoly that noted a "concentration of private power without equal in history," while price competition gave way to a "concealed cartel system." He recommended that Congress appropriate money to study economic concentration in America, a reasonable request that hardly anyone could quarrel with. As Ellis Hawley has remarked, "Reaction to the President's proposals reflected the general belief that they were relatively innocuous."

Baruch also saw these proposals as a bow in the direction of the Brandeisians. Referring to recent antimonopoly speeches by Harold Ickes and Robert Jackson, Baruch said of the president, "I knew Messrs. Ickes and Jackson had gotten him in Dutch, and now it looks as if the only way in which he can get out is to have a 'this study' made by his agencies." Despite the concession to antitrusters, which led to the creation of the Temporary National Economic Committee, Baruch did not doubt that wherever Roosevelt's heart was, his mind was with Baruch, even to the point of borrowing Baruch's phraseology.[135]

No matter, it was an inappropriate time either to inaugurate a reincarnation of a transmogrified NRA or to imitate cousin Teddy's trustbusting. Besides, neither Roosevelt nor Baruch knew precisely what the business-government relationship ought to be or where destructive competition left off and cartelistic collusion began. Resignedly, both men overcame their old passions for balanced budgets and economy and surrendered to the growing consensus in favor of government spending.

Spending was in the Washington air during the spring of 1938. "Your heroic Chief," Frank Kent scolded Joe Kennedy at his station in London, "has done what you (and me too) damned well knew he would—to wit, plunged into the old spending pool." Kent, whose heart belonged to the Liberty Leaguers and their economics, would have expected an opportunist like Roosevelt to resort to such expedience, but alas, he moaned, "even the estimable Bernie no longer sees the dim light." So true: advising Byrnes not to believe rumors that he would speak out against additional government expenditures, Baruch argued that he favored "certain expenditures as will be necessary in the future" and would give employment at low wages. He volunteered to give Byrnes a list of these needed projects, an offer Byrnes accepted. The "list" turned out to be a Baruchian generalization: "You know, a lot of money could be spent for rehabilitation of the Army and Marine Barracks, for airports and generally modernizing the Army."[136] His thoughts, like Roosevelt's and those of many Americans, were upon the need for military preparedness, increasingly justified by the conflicts in Europe and Asia during the last few years. But Baruch had had a longtime preoccupation with military preparedness and industrial mobilization for war. His time was coming and he was ready, even if nobody else was.

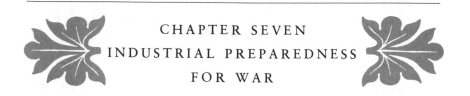

CHAPTER SEVEN
INDUSTRIAL PREPAREDNESS
FOR WAR

It was the summer of 1938. As was his custom, Baruch prepared to spend it traveling in Europe, a fact made noteworthy only by his comments to reporters at dockside and at the White House, upon his return from his previous year's holiday, that "the people in Europe have no hope any more; fear predominates," and that the Continent was "a tinderbox." He would not predict war, but then he did not have to. Civil war already raged in Spain and it was evident that the conflict was not isolated from other countries. Italy had already subjugated Ethiopia in Mussolini's effort to build a modern Roman Empire. And Germany was militarily resurgent, having invaded and occupied the Rhineland in a display of force that shook France's pretensions to military power. Then, in March, Hitler announced *Anschluss*, Germany's union with Austria, and the Nazis marched into Vienna. Czechoslovakia would be next. Great Britain earnestly debated its own military preparedness. In Washington a reluctant Roosevelt had turned to public works in a preelection effort to prime the pump, his action ostensibly carrying no military significance. Yet, prior to his departure, the watchful Baruch congratulated the president for "slipping in here and there" expenditures on airports, antiaircraft installations, "and other army necessities."[1]

But Baruch sought more than a few covert appropriations under the rubric of public works. Nothing less than the launching of full-scale mobilization, starting with the revival of a War Industries Board to guide the nation's industrial preparedness for war, would satisfy him. He pressed Roosevelt for a commitment and went away from the White House believing that he had one. Roosevelt even jotted a memo before Baruch's eyes, reading:

Defense Coordination Board
   To start Sept 1. and study & report to Pres. by Dec. 1st
Chairman—B. M. Baruch

Then Roosevelt put four lines underneath "Chairman" and ordered Baruch to spend his holiday abroad studying Europe's military preparations prior to assuming command of the "Defense Coordination Board" in September. Baruch left the White House confident that he would reenact his greatest triumph.

Baruch went to Europe exhilarated and filled with grandiose expectations. He savored missions for the president; and this one gave him authority to contact the defense heads of France and Britain with the private assurance that they would be talking to their soon-to-be-appointed American counterpart. He asked tough questions of them and came away disturbed. The French army did not appear as powerful as vaunted by Paris; the British seemed bereft of adequate armaments and dependent upon the French to supply what the French barely had for themselves. In August he placed a transatlantic call to Roosevelt and urged him to convene the Defense Coordination Board immediately; but the president was noncommittal. So Baruch extended his Scotland vacation into early September. On the third he sent Roosevelt two cables, the first beginning, "If still desirous appointing Board for coordinating defence." He could no longer be certain of Roosevelt's intentions, but, following another transatlantic phone call, he was confident that Roosevelt perceived the desperate need for the nation to rearm.

Even so, Baruch tarried in Britain another twelve days, departing amid a report in the *Evening Standard* of London that he "hastened" back to the United States "at the urgent request of President Roosevelt," who would confer upon him the task of coordinating national defense. The night before he embarked upon his return voyage he had been discussing events in Czechoslovakia with his old friend Winston Churchill, a stern critic of appeasement of Hitler. Both men anticipated war with Germany. Baruch would recall for the rest of his life Churchill's ironic forecast: "Well, the big show will be on very soon. You will be running it in America and I will be on the sidelines here." It looked that way then. Baruch's arrival in New York on the *Queen Mary* brought reporters to the dockside in droves. He denied that he had been officially commissioned by the president to undertake a defense assignment, but did not deny that he might be given the mobilization task soon. He would go to Washington within a few days and confer with Roosevelt, "if he asks me to."[2]

By then, Europe's war jitters had penetrated the consciousness of the U.S. administration. Roosevelt clearly saw the need for defense mobilization of a kind. But he was not about to give the job to Baruch. To some extent he must have been disturbed by Baruch's apparent self-advertising in Britain, but what seems to have outraged him even more were Baruch's proposals for filling the rest of the "Defense Coordination Board." Baruch wanted nothing less than a WIB reunion. In addition to Charles Foster, who had been vice-chairman of the WIB's priorities committee twenty years before, and J. Leonard Replogle, his old director of supply, his key men would include Hugh Johnson and George Peek! Baruch seemed totally oblivious of the political realities of 1938. After all, Johnson daily lambasted the New Deal in his newspaper column, and Peek had endorsed Landon in 1936.

When Baruch arrived at the White House on 23 September, Roosevelt was in a bad humor from a cold he had been battling for a week. His disposition was not helped by his anticipation of Baruch's proposals. In his cables from Scotland, Baruch had already broached the names of Peek and Johnson, evoking Roosevelt's laughter and a biting comment that Baruch had not progressed beyond 1917. Hearing the same names from Baruch in person, Roosevelt was testy, observing that he believed in the army tradition that a man ought to be an officer and a gentleman; Johnson was no longer an officer and he had never been a gentleman. Moreover, Peek was persona non grata in the White House. If Baruch recommended these renegades from the New Deal, why, inquired Roosevelt, didn't he suggest Raymond Moley as well? When Baruch departed he told waiting reporters that he and the president had discussed "world economics."[3]

The big show, World War II, was about to commence. When mobilization moved ahead full tilt in Britain and in the United States, Churchill would be prime minister, whereas Baruch would be mostly an informal power broker in the tall grass of Washington.

CONCEPTS OF TOTAL MOBILIZATION

Roosevelt was undeniably correct: Baruch had learned nothing new about industrial mobilization for war in twenty years. In fact, he had been repeating himself with monotonous regularity to audiences that ranged from congressional committees to the Army Industrial College to businessmen's groups to a friend engaged in casual conversation. Always the message had been the same, spoken with the authority of experience, the only experience America had known: modern warfare involved total populations and required a nation's total mobilization of its resources and total stabilization of its economy. He spoke with the insight of one who had directed much of America's mobilization in the World War and therefore was conversant with its successes and its failures. The latter he considered to be harbingers of a future disaster unless the United States could plan intelligently for the next conflict.

He anticipated war, but did not relish it. It was simply that he believed that the outcome of the Great War had resolved nothing. Modern wars, he argued, were not motivated by lust for territory. He was an economic determinist. (Not until the late thirties did he attempt to read Marx, and then he found what he read incomprehensible.) Baruch considered mankind to be naturally acquisitive and nations to be reflective of that behavior. Moreover, modern industry required resources beyond the grasp of most nations. Development of resources required more capital than individual enterprise possessed. Just as individual enterprise had evolved into corporate enterprise, so the corporate unit seemed to be evolving into the collectivist cartel. Competition in the twentieth century was a disappearing way of life, and concentration of economic power seemed inevitable. To forestall plutocratic tyranny or economic chaos, the government of any industrial nation had to devise collective strategies to protect the living standards of its people. This had been the case of Germany prior to the Great War and of Britain during the war. Having assumed the responsibility for the prosperity of their peoples, governments found themselves promoting competition for the resources of the world. The ineluctable consequence of this international corporate competition would be war.

The victor on the battlefield would be the nation that organized its economic resources swiftly and comprehensively. By itself war dislocated a society. Mobilization for war automatically disrupted commerce. All a country could do before a war, unless it intended to be the aggressor, was to plan for mobilization. Such planning required a government, through representatives of its military and its industries, to inventory continuously its industrial capabilities for conflict.

Again and again, Baruch rehearsed the liturgy of the five "Ms" of modern warfare. First came the mobilization of *manpower*, the drafting of young men to serve in the army. Once a nation resorted to that conscription, Baruch argued that it was morally bound to conscript everything that did not submit to the higher call of patriotism. However, a people educated to the righteousness of their struggle ought to respond to the call to arms voluntarily; propaganda, the mobilization of *minds*, would ever be essential to the conduct of war in these democratic times when the masses claimed a right to control their own destinies. He knew well that war was incompatible with the individual liberty articulated by capitalism. War called for public enterprise that superimposed itself upon private rights. Capitalists would rightly resist it if they did not benefit directly by it or perceive a greater community interest. Then it became the duty of government to regiment individual enterprise through conscription. That meant mobilization of *money*, the taxation of capital needed to pay for the war. Baruch preferred that capital be voluntarily subscribed through the purchase of government securities by individuals and credit institutions during the war and the payment of that debt through broad-based taxes following the war. Morally, and because the masses would not fight if they knew that a few were enriching themselves while many died in combat, it was imperative that government supplement its debt funding with taxes on profits in excess of normal peacetime profits. Baruch's other two "Ms" were *materials* and *manufacturing* for war. Government had to establish war priorities and direct these resources in a way that denied "business as usual," taking materials intended for civilians for warfare manufacture.

But triumph on the battlefield did not assure victory for the nation. For if nations fought for markets that bolstered their living standards, what good would it be for them to emerge from hostilities with distended and distorted home markets unprepared for peace? As a believer in the immutable law of supply and demand, Baruch appreciated that military expansion in war led inevitably to inflation of civilian prices. Mobilization without stabilization was an invitation to national tragedy no matter who prevailed in battle. The national economy had to emerge from the war with its price structure as low as possible, as near its level at the initiation of war as it could achieve. Otherwise, high prices would discourage postwar investment and consumer buying; extremely high prices would be followed by extremely low prices. Through taxation a government could reduce inflationary demand; it might exhort or require citizens to buy bonds with their consumer dollars, but neither of these methods would be effective without government controls of prices. Simply put, a free market had no place in a nation at war.

Even then, America had to plan for reconversion from war to peace before it was attacked! Here Baruch reasoned with the sorrow and familiarity of failure. Demobilization from the Great War had proceeded with little forethought. The Armistice had caught the Wilsonians unprepared, and they succumbed to pressures to decommission everything in the regimented marketplace. Postwar inflation, depression, chaotic speculation, and finally the Great Depression had been products of that oversight. The mistake could not be repeated again without inviting a cataclysm surpassing that of the thirties. Capitalism itself would be at stake. Preservation of private enterprise would demand a rational scheme for public enterprise.

In essence this was Baruch's message. Generalized as it was, it could provide only guideposts for planners. Conditions of warfare were changing, as were the economies that supplied the requirements of war. All he could hope to achieve was to bring the military and the industrialists together to institutionalize cooperation between them. Yet he knew that would be difficult to attain, because it had been one of the major problems of the Great War. Moreover, any planning institution for war would be rightfully suspect as a harbinger of fascism unless civilians led the mobilization, as had been the case when the WIB superseded the War Department in wartime procurement. Once again, the maxim that "war is too important to be left to generals" would come home to haunt the military. From the experience of 1917, Baruch knew that preparedness would be delayed unless Americans instituted wartime planning during the peace that remained.

However, most free enterprisers were apathetic, if not hostile to a public enterprise that submerged their interests and regimented them. Few among them wished to be reminded of the war in which Washington conscripted their labor, then supervised collective bargaining with industrial workers, conscripted their profits with excess profits taxes, allocated materials to suit the needs of war production, and even nationalized some corporations that dared to assert the freedom of their enterprise. Only the nostalgia-ridden mobilizers like Baruch freely discussed the subject of another industrial mobilization for war. Only a few business generalists would join the military and foreign policy bureaucrats in considering the apocalypse of war.

In another sense then, Roosevelt was wrong in his judgment that Baruch's thinking had not moved beyond 1917. As he stressed incessantly, Baruch offered Washington in those years, when the clouds of another war gathered in Europe, the experience of success and failure, so that it might again realize the former and avert the latter. Only Baruch, Baruch believed, possessed the familiarity with industrial mobilization for war requisite for attaining it with the alacrity and equity that planning and organization afforded.

WIB alumni believed that the War Department, as evidenced by the experience of 1917–18, knew little of modern economic organizations that were needed in war. Moreover, the military and its civilian leadership were more concerned with protecting their political flanks than with restructuring their systems. The War Department had failed to fulfill army essentials because it was infested with personal jealousies and selfish interests. Baruch attributed the War Department's supply problems to the fact that its wartime leadership, Secretary Newton Baker and Army Chief of Staff Peyton March, "were not working with us, but against us." Inevitably some of this contempt for the War Department found its way into Clarkson's history of the WIB and the board's own report, both of which naturally exalted the emergency agency at the expense of the regular department and resurrected the old charge that the department could not "state its requirements." The battles of the war administration were refought in peace. Baruch's Republican counsel on international law, Chandler Anderson, informed Secretary of State Charles Evans Hughes at the Washington Conference of 1921 that America's own "military and naval experts did not fully appreciate the importance of the industrial organization of a nation back of its fighting force." Sometimes the sniping became exceedingly petty, as when Baruch complained that "my boys" on the WIB did not get the military awards conferred upon other war board members (when the War Department decided upon a campaign to educate the public on civilian preparedness for war in 1923, it reversed an earlier decision and conferred Distinguished Service Medals upon WIB leaders).[4]

A broad area of agreement on two points prevailed: that there had been confusion in war mobilization and that an industrial mobilization plan was necessary to avoid a similar crisis in any future war. The National Defense Act of 1920, under the influence of the War Department, provided that the assistant secretary of war should have broad discretion in planning for mobilization of the nation's economy in time of war. The War Department seriously discussed plans and institutions for mobilization in 1921. Having made mobilization one of his pet postwar issues, Baruch then complained that the War Department "stole some of my thunder." The Army-Navy Munitions Board was founded in 1922 but proved ineffectual for most of its history, partly because the navy ignored it. In 1924 the War Department founded the Army Industrial College, an officers' school for studying mobilization problems. Former WIB leaders and other industrial statesmen were regularly invited there to discourse on the relationship between the army and business. For Baruch it provided an annual forum for lecturing officers on the lessons of his war experience.[5]

Mobilization planning for war was considered an unnecessary expense by the parsimonious administrations from Wilson through Coolidge. They were endeavoring to reduce federal expenditures incurred by the bloated wartime military establishment. Determined to protect its budget, the War Department drummed up a celebration of Defense Day on 12 September 1924. Despite the parades and demonstrations witnessed by millions of Americans in cities across the land, President Coolidge cut the military budget. Obviously the military had need of all the allies it could find, even critics like Baruch.[6]

Baruch considered Defense Day a "red herring." The War Department, he patronizingly observed, had not "grasped the big idea." Asserting that "no Assistant Secretary of War has done anything" since the 1920 law bestowed on the office the responsibility for preparedness plans, Baruch charged that it was "due to the fact that the Army is endeavoring to dictate the policy and keep control in its own hands, whereas it should be placed in the hands of a civilian." He was careful to keep these accusations out of the public arena, lest he embarrass the War Department to the point where it ceased providing him with forums for educating the "always reactionary" army. Personally he was most cordial to leaders in the War Department, like General John J. Pershing and Assistant Secretary of War Dwight Davis; but, in his judgment, "neither knows the industrial side" of the mobilization problem.[7]

Baruch took his case for business planning for war mobilization directly to Secretary of War John W. Weeks. Both Weeks and Army Chief of Staff Pershing were eager to give Baruch more of their attention. Baruch wanted a mobilization plan that envisioned a future War Industries Board, nothing less than a peacetime "board of industrial strategy or War Industries Board," staffed by the commodity heads of the war period.[8] But all he won was the Industrial College. By itself, that could never satisfy him.

Baruch's proposal for a permanent advisory WIB was considered "inadvisable" because it threatened the authority of the cabinet, which had been undercut during the war. Also, the plan relied upon businessmen who could only prescribe for an imagined contingency, and "consequently their interest would soon lag." Admittedly the army knew little of the impact that its demands might have upon an economy in war, but for that understanding it had created the Industrial College and would also seek the assistance of the Harvard Graduate School of Business Administration. Thus, whether Baruch liked it or not, that was as far as the army could practically and politically go in the 1920s.[9]

In consolation the army offered Baruch several sounding boards for his views on stabilization. At the Army War College he warned of greater confusion to be incurred in the next war if the War Department continued planning for its own needs without considering business's capacity to provide what was needed without destabilizing the civilian economy. At a Reserve Officers Association meeting he denied that his designs would impose "communist" authority upon business; rather, he insisted, they would encourage voluntary cooperation, a halfway station between chaotic laissez-faire and totalitarian socialism: "Our industry must be *led*—not driven." Industry would never submit to army regimentation. Baruch opposed conscription of labor; it might lead to conscription of capital. He adamantly rejected even the hint of a national service law, which would not be necessary if the government planned for priorities, controls, and taxes that stabilized without regimenting, thereby averting a "grotesque distortion of the price structure." The military willingly submitted to his scoldings for being remiss in its planning for the superagency of the next war. At times officers might have wondered if Baruch were merely a maudlin man who longed for a revival of the days when he had been of service to the nation. Indeed, by 1930 he was imploring the military to hasten in erecting an advisory board of WIB veterans, because in another decade or so they "will have passed off the scene or have become too old to be of any use." No doubt such trepidations pertained to the nearly sixty-year-old Baruch himself.[10]

In 1930, Baruch realistically had to settle for an army commitment to planning rather than an industrial strategy board itself. Fortuitously, a general receptive to planning was appointed chief of staff—Douglas MacArthur. Another officer sympathetic to planning became an assistant to the army deputy to the assistant secretary of war—Dwight D. Eisenhower. The position brought Eisenhower into Baruch's orbit, and as Eisenhower later recalled, it "gave me an early look at the military-industrial complex of whose pressures I would later warn. Except at that point, the pressures were exactly reversed." MacArthur, Eisenhower, and Baruch were instrumental in drawing up the army's first industrial mobilization plan, the "M-Day" plan, in 1930.[11]

But the M-Day plan could not be interpreted as an army embrace of Baruch. Baruch did not think the army program was comprehensive enough. Although he maneuvered the army into a discussion of the merits of his plan, his old antagonist Newton Baker disapproved of its rigidity and its price-fixing characteristics. Clearly the army preferred a more flexible plan; MacArthur would never be as much Baruch's fan as were other officers, such as Eisenhower.[12]

But Baruch always had many friends in the military. That they disagreed with his insistence upon civilian domination of mobilization did not bother either him or his military cohorts. A proselytizer by habit, Baruch always looked to educate and convert adversaries. Also, he shrewdly exploited their awe of the "big man." They were public servants who earned little; the wealth they did not possess impressed them profoundly. In those days officers could not count upon retiring to jobs in private industry. They needed friends like Baruch, who might supplement their meager government pensions. It is noteworthy that the military hero of World War I, "Black Jack" Pershing, borrowed $41,190.05 from Baruch in the depression. Baruch also had befriended a young officer he met on a Louisiana hunting trip in 1922—George C. Marshall. As an admiral reminisced later, Baruch "never lost touch with the military"; either they sought out his advice, or, as may have been more likely, he sought to confer his unsolicited advice upon them.[13]

Charged by Congress with reviewing its industrial mobilization plans every two years, the War Department would find Baruch and his string of senators handy, if somewhat hard to satisfy, allies. A small irony enters here: like businessmen, the War Department believed that Baruch's concepts did not rely enough upon voluntary cooperation. It insisted that the government could not regiment the marketplace as much as Baruch demanded. To some extent that was an excuse to avert civilian intervention in the process of procurement. The same conflict that had created bottlenecks in the Great War continued unabated into the 1930s. The services feared an abridgment of their prerogatives. Eisenhower neatly summarized the opposition to Baruch: "High officials believed that a war should be conducted through normal, peacetime agencies of government.

They did not favor price controls. They saw no reason for special organization. Those of us who believed in Baruch's policies argued that competition between departments of government would interfere with maximum industrial production. They would answer that co-operation between the Army and Navy departments would be enough to take care of the problem." Baruch was not amenable to compromising with the army's plan for a partial mobilization, because "we shall drift back into the old system." If America should ever go to war again, it would need a total stabilization plan "worked out from our past experience."[14] Thus, both Baruch and Eisenhower lobbied through the 1930s for the total mobilization of 1918 in preference to the chaos of 1917.

PROFITS AND NEUTRALITY

Meeting reporters for a press conference on 12 December 1934, President Roosevelt announced that later in the day he would be conferring with Secretary of State Hull, Secretary of the Treasury Morgenthau, Secretary of War Dern, Secretary of Agriculture Wallace, Secretary of the Navy Swanson, Assistant Secretary of the Navy Henry Roosevelt, Secretary of Labor Perkins, Federal Coordinator of Transportation Eastman, George Peek, Hugh Johnson, and Bernard Baruch. Having listed his conferees, he looked about the room at the puzzled press corps and puckishly observed, "Now I have got you all intrigued. Isn't that a funny combination?" A voice called out, "Is it for tea?" and the room broke into laughter. Then the president got down to business. Many mistakes had been made during 1917's mobilization because of haste, he said; however, he emphasized that no peacetime preparedness for war was contemplated. He was commissioning these men to prepare a plan whereby the government might be better prepared not to repeat the errors of 1917 through ignorance and, if war should come, not to cause hardship and inequity of burdens. "We have decided that the time has come when legislation to take the profit out of war should be enacted. . . . I regard it as one of the very important things that will be laid before Congress this winter." As chairman of the group he was appointing Baruch, "one of the principal students of that particular problem."

The next day, Arthur Krock, noting that certain senators considered Roosevelt's announcement a red herring across the trail of the Senate's committee studying the munitions industry in war, the Nye committee, assured his readers that a diversion from the goal of ending war profiteering could not happen with Baruch in charge. For Baruch had long been an advocate of a scheme to end such profiteering. Reciting Baruch's history in the matter, Krock noted that "this was the first time Mr.

Baruch's favorite brain-child has appeared in such magnificence" as a White House press conference. Krock believed that Roosevelt, having put Baruch in control of this old ignored problem, meant business: "Congress will know—and hear—of this commission."

Krock was a better publicist than prophet. While Baruch and Johnson went off to Hobcaw to prepare plans for the commission, *Business Week* rejoiced that the White House had stolen the thunder of the troublesome Nye committee. It is not evident that the Baruch committee ever met again, but Baruch and Johnson soon issued a report incorporating Baruch's oft-repeated notions on mobilization and stabilization. They were put into legislative form in January by the chairman of the House Military Affairs Committee, J. J. McSwain of South Carolina. Meanwhile, Roosevelt bowed to public pressure and, following a meeting with the North Dakota senator, agreed to endorse the Nye committee investigation. The Baruch commission was not heard of again.[15]

The Nye committee intended to "take the profits out of war," a slogan Baruch had been using for so long that he thought he might have invented it.[16] Early in 1935 the committee began to develop an alternative scheme for disentangling capitalism from war, the Flynn plan. Writer-economist John T. Flynn seemed to disagree with Baruch on several points. For one, he eschewed price controls, which he argued would be useless in curtailing profits based upon volume business in wartime. Instead he would tax the profits of munitions makers and assure through taxation that no individual had an income of more than ten thousand dollars a year during a war. The heavy taxation would also be justified on the grounds that it did not burden future generations with the debts of ancient wars. No socialist, Flynn proposed the conscription of management without actual conscription of its private property. His suggested national service legislation would erect an ephemeral system of state capitalism.[17]

On the issue of an equitable mobilization and stabilization, Baruch had staked out a politically enviable position: anything to the right of him endorsed unconscionable profiteering in wartime; anything to the left of him unpatriotically endeavored to change the economic system while the nation fought an external enemy. Baruch, by his system of priorities and controls, would socially discipline business without abridging its basic right to profits. Flynn's scheme, on the other hand, smacked of an undefinable radicalism. Nevertheless, the Nye committee invited Baruch in March to respond to the Flynn plan.

Not content merely to ask him to testify on taking the profit out of war, Senator Nye requested that Baruch furnish the committee with his tax returns for 1916–19, as well as information concerning his securities holdings for those years, explaining that the committee was studying "the industrial connections and income of various officials connected with the Government" during the war period. Ever since 1917, Baruch had been answering questions that sought a conflict of interest between his private speculations and his government responsibilities. As he would demonstrate to the Nye committee's satisfaction, he had been scrupulous in his interests during the war. Only his tungsten holdings suggested a conflict of interest. To Baruch's credit, he had tried to unload that potential embarrassment but had not been able to find a buyer. Still, he had arranged to stay out of all negotiations involving the metal, had indirectly sought to assure that its price would remain as low as possible in spite of its increased demand, and had arranged that his tungsten profits would be paid to the Red Cross during the war. He had anticipated Nye's questions eighteen years beforehand. Now Nye marked him again and roused him to fury. Taking care to alert his friends in the Senate to the need for a public defense of his integrity at a time when he was simultaneously under attack by Huey Long and Father Coughlin, Baruch mustered a publicity apparatus to match that of Senator Nye. In the end, Baruch made more of the issue of his supposed financial conflict of interest than did Nye. When it became evident that nothing but gossip existed as evidence, the committee remembered its primary intent and quickly turned to the matter of future profits in war.[18]

The publicity conflict shifted to the compatibility of the Flynn and Baruch plans. The Nye committee sought a comprehensive design for profit limitation, and the Flynn scheme for conscripting all corporate profits above 3 percent captured its attention. How would Baruch limit profits? The Flynn nostrum suggested a principle of equity with which Baruch could not argue without appearing to be intellectually fuzzy or to compromise with profiteers. For years, Baruch had tried to find a metaphor suitable for explaining his moderate approach to profit limitation. Whereas once he had advocated "freezing" prices, he now considered this "an unfortunate expression" because it suggested inflexibility. He flirted with the expression "building a wall around prices," but that had a clumsily vague ring to it. Finally, he settled upon a "ceiling" above prices, a concept that to him implied a maximum for all prices that could be adjusted from industry to industry. His proposal for price ceilings sharpened his differences with Flynn's plan for taxation and allowed Baruch to preempt the political center on the profits issue. Insisting that they shared "cordially and completely" a purpose of limiting profits, Baruch attacked Flynn (and indirectly the committee that had adopted the essence of his plan) for proposals that unintentionally were inflationary and intentionally endeavored "to abolish the present system in war." Flynn's plan, he argued, was counterproductive because industry had to pass the taxes along to the public or else absorb them in prices that would rob production of its monetary incentive. Flynn's 3 percent maximum profit would be suitable in certain instances, but not where high investment risks were involved. Commenting to a friend, "There are plenty of nuts around," Baruch maintained that he had been "willing to go down the road" with the Nye committee, "but not to the point where we would stop the flow of munitions and put people on the bread line[,] leaving them to the care of a bureaucratic government."[19]

The rhetorical clash between the Flynn and Baruch schemes continued beyond the committee hearings. Moreover, it was evident that Baruch had scored points in his suggestion that Flynn's scheme was inherently anticapitalist. In a radio speech, Nye lashed out at Baruch for characterizing business as unpatriotic. A right-wing Republican, Senator Arthur Vandenberg of Michigan, decried Baruch's "low estimate of the national patriotism," hinting that Baruch really sought "the collective state." Vandenberg privately confided to Baruch that his attack on the committee had been "exceedingly unfortunate" because of the way it intimated "that our plan to take the profit out of war might precipitate the end of capitalism. You have a large influence in this country. I felt your statement left me no alternative except sharply to challenge it." Thus, the dispute boiled down to which side more truly limited war profits while preserving capitalism.

Baruch wanted a truce in his fight with the Nye committee. "I would like to get into the position of being behind the Nye committee rather than in any sense against it," he told his public relations advisor, Swope. Both sides knew that no substantive disagreement existed. Rather, Baruch had been resentful of the committee's poaching on his specialty and its approval of Flynn as the author of a plan. It was a matter of public credit. As Baruch boasted to one of his press acolytes, "They have veered towards the adoption of practically all of my suggestions." He accused "Sly Nye" of employing "a rewrite man to . . . make it appear as if it was a new idea by changing some parts of it."[20]

In March, Roosevelt officially abandoned the Baruch commission and lent his moral support to the committee's bill. The following month, the House's McSwain bill went to the Senate, where Nye's provisions were tacked on. Then it was promptly lost in the shuffle of Senate Finance Committee business. "The bill is not bad but it should be modified," Baruch advised the committee's chairman, his friend Pat Harrison. The bill was guilty of the sin of being too detailed in a matter that required the widest discretion for the executive, Baruch pointed out. He clearly feared that Nye and Flynn would immobilize big business in war through taxation, destroying incentives for economies of scale in production for the military. "I am sure you concur with me," he wrote Vandenberg later that year, "that it would be most unfortunate to pass legislation that would injure our defenses instead of the legislation we all want—to increase our powers of defense."[21] To a large degree then, what Baruch sought was to increase the respectability and assure the profitability of industrial production for the military. The Nye committee incident threatened to have the opposite effect. But it proved to be a small victory for Baruch in that he emerged clearly on the side of the reformers while blocking any legislation that might have discouraged military production.

Although they could not restrain industrial profit in war, the Nye people hoped to diminish the likelihood of American involvement. European rearmament and the Italian invasion of Ethiopia spurred their demands for U.S. neutrality. It was the next issue on which they would confront Baruch.

On 2 October 1935, Baruch was at the Aberdeen Proving Grounds to receive, along with Newton Baker, the Army Ordnance Association's medal for outstanding service and to address 250 association members. The audience and the speaker were quite familiar with each other, but the times were strange to them. "Today," Baruch observed, "twenty-one years after the outburst of the volcano that shook the world, we see humanity in arms and embattled." Briefly appraising the international crises that beset the mid-thirties, he said: "Hitler and peace! The very terms are antithetical. He is today the greatest menace to world safety."

A little more than a month before, Congress had passed a neutrality bill while Italy readied to attack Ethiopia. Approved by Roosevelt, the law would prohibit all arms shipments to belligerents for six months upon notice given by the president that a state of war existed; Americans could travel on belligerent ships only at their own risk. Roosevelt reluctantly signed the measure, observing that it probably would "drag us into war instead of keeping us out." Now Baruch picked up that warning and rhetorically inquired, "What is neutrality?" It was an elusive goal and he was not "so completely a dreamer" as to recommend it. Modern war and international economic relations made true neutrality unlikely. "Wars are no longer dynastic," he noted pithily. "They are entirely economic in their origin." The scale of modern warfare made the enterprise prohibitive to any rational nation. "Wars are never won. Wars are only and always lost both by the victor and vanquished alike."

However, averting war was unlikely unless a nation was prepared for hostilities. Even then, the totality of war no longer allowed for a definition of contraband:

> I am sufficiently crass to say that if cotton is to be sold to a country from which it may find its way into the hands of a belligerent, then America should have the right to sell that cotton unless and until every other country agrees to withhold its supply. And so, too, with every other staple.

> Look at Germany. She is today, according to the press, selling
> munitions and other supplies to both Italy and Ethiopia. Why should
> we continue to be the great international Fat Boy at whose stick
> of candy other nations take an unwelcome bite.

The image of a powerful nation immobilized by timidity and victimized
by its foreign competitors was often employed by Baruch to make the
point that America's stakes in overseas markets and in world peace could
best be protected by planned mobilization for war. Neutrality laws could
not prevent involvement in overseas hostilities. Echoing Roosevelt, Baruch reminded his listeners of "the ever-present danger that strict neutrality, carried to its ultimate end, is almost certain to result in war
because, in itself, *it becomes an act of war*."[22]

The United States, he asserted, reserved the right to trade with any
country in protection of its economic rights. However, it could not embargo any materials without violating principles of free enterprise and
committing an act of economic warfare deserving of belligerency itself.
Insistence upon its neutrality invited an unrealistic curtailment of its
economic prerogatives. The need for trade made war itself inevitable,
particularly if the nation proved unwilling to protect itself from aggressors. Therefore, the government had to *plan* for war. Unless it planned
wisely at once, social chaos would result later when it was compelled to
mobilize. The process of mobilization, requiring discipline and regimentation of markets, was antithetical to the system. But without a design for
stabilization, without a planned and orderly marketplace, the totality of
modern warfare would bring havoc to both vanquished and victor. Only
the absence of a mobilization-stabilization design made Baruch an "isolationist." But he was very much of an internationalist. America's prosperity and its dependence upon foreign markets for growth and the maintenance of its standard of living required that it compete with other
world powers for markets on the basis of equality of opportunity. Baruch
was a patriot and an economic determinist in politics; isolation or neutrality was unthinkable.

Baruch saw the world in terms of spheres of influence. Immediately
following the Great War he envisioned a world system in which Japan
would dominate the Far East while a resurgent Germany would dominate
eastern Europe. Baruch once defined the economic relationships that
made disarmament unlikely:

> The Pacific question is a very serious one. Japan with 66 millions
> of inhabitants on an island smaller, I believe, than the State of Wyo-
> ming, is faced with either expansion or strangulation. We will not
> permit her to come here; nor will Canada or Australia permit her to

come there. On the other hand, we say we will not permit her to expand in China. That is the real gist of the Pacific question. . . .

Germany is the only power which can organize Russia and the Balkans, and start anew the languishing trade of the world.

The United States was on a collision course with Japan over its Far Eastern interests. Meanwhile, Germany would "rise to be a great power—even greater than ever. This will come about through economic penetration and German reorganization of [eastern Europe]." There it would confront British and French interests. In the 1920s, Baruch could afford to be somewhat clinical in his anticipation of these developments.[23] But the Great Depression inflicted a deeper wound upon the United States than upon any other nation, taking from it some of its magnanimity as the world's premier power. The economic threat to the United States posed by competitors less seriously hurt by the depression revived much of its nationalism. Baruch, for all his concern with military preparedness, was not a jingoist; but he was a chauvinist. He keenly felt rivalries.

He loathed Germany. In 1934, when George Peek argued for expanded trade with Nazi Germany in which the United States would benefit Baruch's beloved South Carolina by bartering cotton, Baruch responded to the proposition by blurting out: "I have my idea about the Germans—I think they are thieves. [However,] I would not want my judgment to enter into what was best for the United States Government. I wouldn't let them get a market for the maunfactured goods because we can make the stuff here. . . . You know there is no trade with them but what you are going to be finally cheated. The Germans will finally cheat you out of any trade they will make with you." Baruch detested Germany but he distrusted Britain. Whereas he considered the Germans unscrupulous traders, he thought the British were wily and shrewd. The former were antagonists, the latter adversaries. Wary in dealing with both, he preferred allowing the British an upper hand to conceding it to the Germans. A Europe in which the Germans held the balance of power, with the potential of displacing the British in overseas markets, would be treacherous for American interests. Throughout the thirties he fearfully attempted to monitor the revival of German trade in South America, discussing it often in the White House and in the State Department. On the other hand, the British were worthy competitors for markets, a stabilizing force in the world. The heart of his feelings would be expressed later, during the Battle of Britain, when he would tell an old friend, "I cannot visualize a world in which I would want to live without the continuance of the British Empire."[24]

Whatever his personal feelings, Baruch believed that the United States, without military preparedness, needed the time afforded by the tactic of neutrality. At the same time, as an astute publicist he sought to educate the American public to the improbability of genuine neutrality. In that spirit he first offered Americans the concept of "cash-and-carry" through an article published in the November 1935 issue of *Today*. He argued that whether they liked it or not, Americans confronted "the danger of involvement" in either the Italian-Ethiopian war or the Sino-Japanese conflict. Genuine neutrality required that the United States embargo *all* materials to the belligerents, not just those capriciously defined as contraband. Realistically considered, an embargo gave aid by indifference to the nation best prepared for war and most self-sufficient. For the plain truth was that "whatever we do, or do not do, we cannot avoid helping one belligerent or another. Which is to say that it is impossible to be neutral." Still, popular opinion demanded avoidance of war. How could America have both its commerce and its peace? He noted that three schools of thought existed on neutrality. The first insisted upon the doctrine of freedom of the seas, the national right to trade with anyone, including belligerents; this was "more likely to get a nation into war than keep it out of war." The second urged cooperation with the League of Nations, which old Wilsonian Baruch endorsed; but in 1935 such cooperation was not politically feasible because "public opinion in the United States is definitely committed against it." The third perspective was the congressional position on neutrality: that Americans traded and traveled with belligerents at their own risk and that all weapons of war were embargoed; sooner or later this policy would make the United States a combatant. Insisting that "we are not engaged in the hopeless effort to attain an ideal of neutrality; we are above all trying to stay out of the war," Baruch offered the "wholly practical" course of "come and get it." Any nation wishing to buy from the United States could do so, provided it sent its own ships or chartered an American vessel. "Now, this is not neutrality—not by twenty sea miles," he admonished. It frankly favored the nation that controlled the seas, most probably Britain. He denied being pro-British: "I am pro-American, and pro-peace."[25] It was a scheme by which Americans could keep their foreign trade with belligerents who could afford the merchandise and could afford to take the risks that would bring the United States, he hoped, peace and prosperity.

Baruch was intent upon making cash-and-carry the essence of a neutrality law to replace the one about to expire. Copies of his article went to every senator via the secretary of the Senate. He drew nationwide attention to cash-and-carry with a speech to the South Carolina Press Association. As Congress hurried to replace the neutrality bill due to expire on 29 February, Baruch lobbied with Joe Robinson and his Senate friends, ridiculing the Nye bill that attempted to define war materials. His point was that peace could not be preserved so long as certain powers were intent upon aggression. The craving of the populace to avoid war had to be respected, but, he asked, "Is there any price that this country can pay that will keep us out of war, short of permitting ourselves to be denuded of our property, having our standards of living lowered, and losing our self-respect?" Having already implicitly surrendered the principle of freedom of the seas, how could Americans do business and stay out of war?[26]

The neutrality law of 1936 neither adopted the cash-and-carry formula nor pushed the United States any closer to preparedness. It had a mandated life of one year, time enough for Baruch to publicize his cash-and-carry compromise. His 1936 *Current History* article elaborated upon the illusion of the current neutrality law and urged that, instead of breaking off all trade with belligerents, "for whatever we sell, we should have only one formula: 'Cash on the barrel-head.'" Like most of Baruch's articles and speeches to which he attached great importance, this one was reported widely as a news story. Also, he saw to it that all congressmen received reprints. In London that summer he declared that European governments were "arming more fiercely and quickly than ever before." Returning from a visit to Prime Minister Stanley Baldwin, Baruch told the press that Europe was beset by economic and armed warfare: "The astronomical sums spent upon armaments could give to the 'under-housed' living conditions approaching those which in our time and age they should enjoy. Not only hurriedly preparing with guns, gases, airplanes, bombers and all the lethal weapons, every country is like a bristling industrial fortress, endeavoring to surround itself by [sic] commercial Verduns and Gibraltars—all economic instrumentalities aimed at the life of other nations."[27]

"Cash on the barrel-head and take it away" caught on in 1936–37 as an expression of America's controlled commercial involvement in world hostilities. It offered Americans an opportunity to trade with the world on what appeared to be the most favorable terms under conditions of war abroad. Peace groups considered it vastly preferable to the existing neutrality law. However, a State Department memorandum depicted it for what it had been intended, a biased neutrality that drove home the ineluctable fact of involvement: "It would amount, in fact, to a benevolent neutrality in favor of wealthy nations and against poor ones. Its possible outcome would be to make us eventually the Allies of the former." Baruch's friends George Peek and Raymond Moley, though desiring both cash-and-carry and expanded trade with Nazi Germany and Fascist Italy, recognized that this device would, in Moley's words, "put us into the next war with a vengeance." Both distrusted Roosevelt and wanted Congress to define the embargo of materials. Likewise, a group of isolationists led by Senator Nye insisted upon a mandatory embargo of all trade with belligerents. Cash-and-carry loomed as a compromise between this effort to remove foreign policy from the hands of the president and the administration's insistence upon presidential discretion.[28]

In January, Key Pittman, chairman of the Senate Foreign Relations

Committee, incorporated cash-and-carry as a basic feature of the administration's new neutrality bill. Its enactment, Pittman asserted, would "keep us out of the next great foreign war." Pittman understood that Baruch did not subscribe to such euphoria. As the senator assured his interested friend, "In any and all statements that I feel called upon to make I couple our efforts to keep out of war with the necessity to be prepared to defend our Government and its citizens when it becomes necessary." Although Baruch continued to espouse his neutrality formula, it troubled him that the public saw it as a panacea, rather than a temporary expedient. It perpetuated the illusion of neutrality. For that reason, Baruch turned against it.

Using a national monthly as his forum, Baruch in March 1937 ridiculed the notion of neutrality, which itself constituted "taking a hostile position." He would not lend money to a belligerent, but he would demand the old right of freedom of the seas. Although not declaring, as he had once before, that such a demand could only bring involvement in war, he now disingenuously couched his argument for freedom of the seas as a point of national honor. Baruch had abandoned the sophisticated realism of his earlier advocacy. Now he lambasted cash-and-carry neutrality as a blanket embargo that amounted to "*scuttling and running* from our ancient doctrines" and raised the question "how far we are willing to go for *peace at any price*." International law and U.S. history bestowed on Americans rights upon the seas that they could not surrender. He used little subtlety in defining what their defense entailed: "For be certain of this: whatever rights we intend to assert we must be willing to defend by force of arms." The publicist of a mercantile cash-and-carry had abruptly become the publicist of militant neutrality.[29]

Following the enactment of the Pittman bill, the embodiment of his own prescription, Baruch stepped up his assault upon it. Before a receptive audience of the Foreign Affairs Council in Cleveland on 21 May, he inquired how Americans would respond under attack if other nations cut them off from materials they normally bought. Reiterating that the Pittman Act could be interpreted as an abnegation of freedom of the seas, he lashed out at cash-and-carry as "based upon the idea that we are no longer willing to fight" for our right to trade. Praising the administration's willingness to build the navy to its greatest strength while "withdrawing from the terribly dangerous salient of the Philippine Islands," he characterized the latest neutrality law as "a 'speak gently' policy. But the 'Big Stick' is just as evident."[30]

The Spanish Civil War beginning in July 1936 further contributed to the confusion of the neutrality legislation's meaning. Did it apply to a conflict in which the Spanish Republic defended itself against fascist rebels in its army? Germany and Italy aided the insurgents, whereas only the Soviet Union lent assistance to the Loyalists. The State Department interpreted the neutrality law as applicable to both sides, even if it was a civil struggle. Baruch disagreed; he favored aid to the Republic, reasoning: "It's a democratically elected government, the only constitutionally elected government in Spain's history." He saw the war as one of "individualism as against totalitarianism." Also, he feared that a triumphant Fascist rebellion could be repeated in Latin America. But in January 1937, Pittman introduced a resolution for embargoing all materials to Spain, a proposal that effectively worked against the Republic. Although Baruch quietly tried to persuade friends in the Senate to oppose the resolution, sentiment for it was so strong that it passed with but a single negative vote. Many Americans called upon Roosevelt to support repeal of the embargo, but the president allowed Secretary of State Hull to reaffirm it. "He's afraid of the Catholic vote," Baruch explained to a friend who supported the Loyalists. So was Baruch, who would not make his opinions public. The Loyalist cause was not important enough to Baruch for him to risk his position as a molder of public opinion on questions of economic or foreign affairs. Even his correspondence during the war betrays barely any interest in it. However, during the summer of 1938 he contributed $11,060 to the Abraham Lincoln Brigade—Americans fighting in behalf of the Spanish Republic. When a list of contributors became public, it brought Baruch an editorial rebuke from the Brooklyn diocese newspaper the *Tablet*. Baruch pusillanimously responded that he had donated $10,000 to bring wounded Americans home from Spain, and it "was in no way an expression of sympathy for the cause for which these young men volunteered. . . . I would have done it had they been helpless Americans, wounded while fighting for Franco."[31]

The administration moved in the direction of armed neutrality late in 1938. A month before the Nazis marched into Czechoslovakia in violation of assurances given British Prime Minister Neville Chamberlain at Munich, Senator Elbert Thomas of Utah introduced a resolution that would permit the president to distinguish between aggressors and victims, enforcing the embargo against the first and lifting it against the second. It amounted to a step toward collective security. Former Secretary of State Henry Stimson endorsed it and called for assistance to nations that had been attacked in spite of treaty assurances.

Cash-and-carry was all but dead by 6 April 1939, when Baruch testified on neutrality bills before the Senate Foreign Relations Committee. Much of his opening statement reiterated previous arguments, including an assertion that America could not trade and simultaneously claim its neutrality. Wars were not fought for "immediate results," but for "new markets, new trade, and new intercourse—always at the expense of the defeated and frequently of the neutrals. Therefore, it is accurate to say that in every great war the neutrals have a stake in the future almost as great as any of the belligerents." He was not yet prepared for involvement in a European war, preferring that the United States give its old allies all aid short of its own soldiers. The isolationists seized upon his candid admission that this was not neutrality and asked if logic did not compel an embargo of everything. No, responded Baruch, for that invited an "utter collapse of our economy," a price too great to pay for keeping out of a war. Still, he satisfied isolationists by observing that Americans "do not want to go in and fight in what they think is somebody else's war. That is what I think is back of all this neutrality legislation."

As Baruch stressed, the Thomas-Stimson collective security position was tantamount to a declaration of war by threatening a belligerent's capacity to fight it. Aggression was not a moral issue, Baruch contended: "Japan has about 70,000,000 people on some islands about the size of California. She wants to expand—she says she has to. I am not in the least condoning what Japan is doing to China." The United States simply had to protect its own accessibility to markets without going to war for them. But, suggested Senator Theodore Green, did a rejection of the Thomas-Stimson plan amount to a denial of the Monroe Doctrine? Baruch defended the principle of American freedom of action in the western hemisphere, but he denied Green's analogy in an answer that pithily summed up the case for nonintervention based upon economic advantage: "I perhaps am so imbued with the idea of keeping out of war that I would probably . . . prefer to keep the status quo unless we are prepared to take an action that could be construed as a declaration of war. We did not gain any commercial advantage by the Monroe Doctrine."[32]

Baruch had his testimony printed in pamphlet form and sent where it would "do the most good," but it did not command the State Department's support as had cash-and-carry. After four months of indecision, Hull and Roosevelt decided to push for repeal of the arms embargo and substitute proposals allowing for presidential discretion. But the congressional isolationists balked this bid for concentrating foreign policy in the hands of the White House. In September, Europe would go to war and Roosevelt would proclaim American neutrality.[33]

Throughout the neutrality debate, Baruch had rejected the economic strangulation of a full-scale isolationist embargo; nonetheless, he bowed to the popularity of the peace position. Scorning the pacifism of the isolationists, he sought time to erect an American arsenal that could command the respect of belligerents. Significantly, he denied that the morality of France and Britain's democracy mattered more than the self-interests of American enterprise. Much as he loathed Germany, he still believed that a semblance of impartiality best served American trade until the Nazis were a clearer danger to it.

WAR WITHOUT GUNS

Politically, Baruch walked a fine line between the isolationists' call for a total embargo and the internationalists' plea for collective security assistance to the democracies. In foreign economic policy, mostly at the behind-the-scenes policy-making level, Baruch used his influence to counteract the Fascists' advances. Although he publicly argued that economic warfare ineluctably led to armed conflict, he privately waged economic warfare, knowing its consequences. Throughout the New Deal years, Baruch had advocated foreign economic policies that treated the British as benign competitors, while encouraging the State Department to bring economic pressures upon the Nazis that would, he hoped, cause their downfall. He anticipated one of two consequences: either the toppling of an intolerable regime in Germany or the goading of it into a war for which the United States would be prepared. Also, he sought to align Britain's economic strategy with America's, carefully making certain that Washington's interests prevailed over those of the cagy people in Whitehall. In his mind the scheme for alignment was clear. As he had told a radio audience when sanctions against Italy for its invasion of Ethiopia were discussed in 1935, "If Italy can be brought to terms by economic pressure, so also can Germany, so also can Japan." Then "the world will have found a new way to keep peace without bloodshed."[34] On the other hand, if economic pressure brought war, then so be it—provided America was totally prepared with advance planning.

Baruch fancied himself an experienced and cunning strategist in economic warfare. In his preparedness speeches to the army he usually reminded the future generals of America how indispensable the government's operations in economic warfare had been to the battlefields of France in 1918. He boasted of how the WIB had plotted to confine Germany's ability to wage war through such schemes as buying up Swedish steel destined for Germany, while enhancing the Allies' war production through stratagems like the nitrate cartel in London that broke the price charged by Chilean suppliers.[35] If economic machinations could undermine an adversary's ability to wage war, they clearly might prevent a war. Or, failing that, if they produced a *casus belli*, at least a well-designed program of economic warfare would advantage the United States.

Only a free-trade purist or a special pleader could have eschewed economic warfare in the 1930s, and Baruch was neither. In fact, the Nazi search for markets in Latin America, while Germany was undertaking rearmaments, he considered a poaching menace in America's backyard. The Germans were after raw materials and U.S. customers. Like his old friend George Peek, Baruch anxiously desired overseas markets for cotton farmers and other producers, which would enable them to produce and produce and sell and sell. He could concur with Peek that "we must either sell it or quit making it." But whereas Peek would sell to the devil, even Germany, Baruch would first demand favorable terms. Despite American economic power, Baruch did not want Washington to allow Berlin trade advantages and credit that supported its militarism.[36]

Baruch's ideas on foreign economic policy meshed with those of Secretary of State Cordell Hull. They were old acquaintances from the days when the former Wilsonian congressman chaired the Democratic National Committee in the 1920s and learned to rely upon the speculator's generosity. In the 1930s, Hull resided in the Carlton Hotel, Baruch's regular Washington headquarters, where they occasionally took dinners together.

In 1934, a German request to buy eight hundred thousand bales of American cotton was received with consternation in the State Department. At the time, Baruch knew little of the circumstances of American-German trade; but George Peek, then special trade advisor for Roosevelt, turned to his old friend for consultation. Baruch thought that Americans bought more from Germans than they sold to them, when the truth was that Americans enjoyed a favorable trade balance with Germany by about two to one. However, given exchange problems and Germany's quest for additional credit, Secretary Hull feared American dependence upon Germany as a customer: "If we instruct our nationals to hold back purchasing from Germany, and Germany instructs hers to do the same thing, they would hold back two dollars to our one." Looking ahead, and considering that Germany was endeavoring to negotiate trade agreements that brought her exclusive trading rights with certain nations, Hull did not want extensive reliance upon German purchases. But Peek wanted— and Baruch agreed with him—to sell agricultural commodities wherever he could find a customer, "whether it was with the Nazi, Soviet, or the English Government." He did not contradict Peek's assertion that U.S. demand for most-favored-nation status with Germany was incompatible with the quest for reciprocal tariff arrangements. Nevertheless, for Baruch, "business as usual" had its limits where Germans were concerned. When Hull refused to allow the deal on terms sought by Berlin, the Germans persisted; so did Peek. Roosevelt went along with Hull, much to the consternation of his foreign trade advisor. It did not help matters when the Germans threatened to buy their raw materials elsewhere. To Hull, the Germans' insistence upon buying on their terms amounted to blackmail; to Peek, U.S. refusal to trade with Berlin amounted to allying the United States with Britain and France against its best economic interests. In 1940 the isolationist Peek, observing the Nazi *Blitzkrieg*, would say, "It begins to look as though probably the President had paid our money on the wrong horse."[37]

As the industrial nations of the world struggled for wedges of an economic pie diminished by depression, economic war heightened. Baruch's friend Joseph P. Kennedy commented on the desperation provoked by hard times: "A few more months of depression of values will have us and the rest of the world so deeply in the doghouse that war might seem to be an attractive out. That is the danger in world-wide depressions such as we have nowadays. Everybody gets to feeling poor and put upon at the same time. International tempers flare up. Pressure is brought to bear on those in authority to do something drastic to better the economic lot of their subjects." Kennedy had put his finger on the problem. Economic hostilities could lead to armed conflict. But the tide had been going out since at least 1934. After a six-week tour of Europe in 1936, Baruch told the *Evening Standard* of London that the Continent was building toward armed conflict:

> Not only is every country hurriedly preparing with guns, gases, airplanes, bombers, but it is like a bristling industrial fortress endeavoring to surround itself by commercial Verduns and Gibraltars—tariffs, quotas, depreciated currencies, trade barriers—all economic instrumentalities aimed at the life of other nations.
>
> In the guise of national preservation or greed, or to meet the competition of others, hours are lengthened and wages reduced to a point that results in almost inhuman conditions. It is easy to see how currencies that have been stabilized, or economic relations that have been agreed upon, can be entirely nullified by a reduction of wages or by a lengthening of the hours of labor.
>
> This barbaric sweating of labor can jump any tariff wall or undermine any currency stabilization.[38]

He had pointed a finger at Berlin. It had been an American fear since the early 1900s that German products, made by workers kept at a lower standard of living than the American, would inundate the American marketplace. A trade war was in the offing.

In a battle of plowshares, Baruch reached for a weapon with one hand and for an ally with the other. He coupled his warnings of conflict with a plea for international cooperation. He boldly bid for international agreements that fixed wages and hours according to formulas agreed to by collaborating nations. (He knew that they would have violated U.S. antitrust laws.) He seldom approached a problem any way but comprehensively. However, in this case he sought not multilateral cooperation but a bilateral economic alliance with Britain.[39]

Like most of Baruch's grand schemes that seemed to defy political feasibility, existing statutes, or institutional arrangements, the proposed economic alliance required some hard lobbying on both sides of the Atlantic. Less powerful men would have taken the proposal to journals of opinion, where it would have received a hearing from the intellectual, business, and political elite—and then probably have been forgotten. As with many of his forays into foreign affairs, Baruch sought to mold both elite and mass opinion. While cash-and-carry had been a ploy whose time had come, an economic alliance with Britain suggested a risky trade war against Berlin. So for the time being, Baruch floated the balloon with Roosevelt, Hull, and his Senate friends in Washington, as well as with Churchill and other British acquaintances. Even Prime Minister Stanley Baldwin heard a rough outline of it during Baruch's visit in the summer of 1936.

Baruch knew that he could not claim originality, because the State Department's thinking had been moving along a parallel course. In late February 1937, Hull invited Baruch to be the American delegate at an International Sugar Conference to be held in London for the purpose of discussing multilateral stabilization of sugar prices. Baruch responded by suggesting other individuals of lesser prominence, but opportunistically took advantage of Hull's attention to propose a broader agreement with England. He conceded that politically any economic treaty with the British would be suspect because of their war debt defaults. Nevertheless, he argued that Congress would buy an arrangement that brought currency stabilization while breaching the empire's preference system and opening new markets. Valuing Baruch as a useful congressional lobbyist for the State Department, Hull encouraged him. Six weeks later, Baruch urged that Hull "really put the heat on" the British, whose economy was in for more trouble than earlier anticipated. In fact, Baruch urged that negotiations with England ought to be held in Washington, where "it would show less anxiety on our part." He conveyed the same recommendations personally to Roosevelt. As in those happy days of 1918, Baruch waged economic warfare against Germany on one front and against British cartels on the other.[40]

Baruch's friendship with Churchill, his old British partner in the nitrate executive of 1918, helped facilitate his operations on the other side of the Atlantic, even if Churchill was then waiting in the wings for events to give him center stage. Providing his own interpretation of why Anglo-American economic cooperation collapsed in 1919, Baruch blamed "those great [London] trade interests which reach out into the colonies." Again, in 1937, they threatened to block Anglo-American collaboration by defending the imperial preference system for the British Commonwealth. "They think they have and doubtless they have, an advantage under the so-called Ottawa agreement," Baruch observed. But that was shortsighted; if imperial markets were opened to American merchants, it would "increase the trade and commerce of the world so tremendously, everyone would benefit." Statesmen had to assert the interests that ought to prevail over parochial commercialism. Other nations had erected trade barriers against America, believing that "the international fat boy" could be kicked around. Those nations hoped that America would raise the world's standard of living, but Baruch suspected that their tactics would inadvertently knock America's "down to the level of the rest. . . . For a better ordered world," he exhorted Churchill to work with him to develop "an understanding between England and America."[41]

The depression of 1937–38 and the increasing aggressiveness of Hitler in central Europe inspired that improved understanding. The connection between trade and defense assumed sharper definition. Baruch had been campaigning for a barter agreement with Britain: U.S. wheat and cotton for British rubber and tin. However, Commonwealth producers of wheat and cotton resisted. By the spring of 1938 the Chamberlain government faced the hard choice of whom to appease first: the nation's own merchants, its potential ally in Washington, or its potential enemy in Berlin. Political logic dictated appeasement of all. In the words of novice diplomat Joe Kennedy, then U.S. ambassador in London, "They are shooting the works in the hope that they can work out a general appeasement, once they are strong enough to stand up to the bargaining table with a few aces in the hole, and from that situation general prosperity may be revived." Rearmament, an Anglo-Italian agreement designed to wean Mussolini away from Hitler, and an economic alliance with the United States were among those desperately needed aces in the hole. But the British economy continued to decline pending the impact of expanded government spending for defense. Kennedy reported that more Britons were coming to believe that their economy needed to be in better harmony with America's.[42]

The depression and European crises were not the only concerns calling for Anglo-American collaboration. Nazi penetration of Latin American markets incited additional anxiety in London and Washington. Baruch noted that the increasing Nazi trade in the western hemisphere was part of Germany's effort to stockpile strategic materials; he campaigned for a similar American policy. Mexico's seizure of American oil properties in 1938 troubled him only because he believed in just compensation; without it, American capital would be less adventurous, and a contraction would be induced at home. However, he welcomed Mexico's economic nationalism (in 1919 he would have backed up the oil companies with intervention) insofar as it applied to Britain and Germany as well, and advised the White House, "We should take advantage of any trouble abroad, or even the possibility of trouble abroad, to cement our relationship[s] with Mexico, Central and South America, and show them the inadvisability of contacts with nations that might momentarily become embroiled in war." In other words, Europe would go mad with war and the Yankees would pick up the pieces wherever others were foolish enough to drop them. Indeed, Whitehall got the point. In late 1938 the two governments consummated the Anglo-American trade agreement calling for an exchange of British rubber for American cotton. For many reasons, the treaty delighted Baruch.[43]

Control of Latin American markets was central to Baruch's strategy of containing Hitler without resorting to war. This he articulated publicly. To him the Nazi reach for Latin America was evidence of Germany's imminent internal collapse. Only days before World War II began, when it should have been apparent that no Nazi crack-up would come in time to prevent the Panzers from rolling across more frontiers, Baruch still professed confidence in the ultimate efficacy of economic warfare. He beseeched Hull to promote blockades that would disrupt the flow of materials from Germany's partners in its international barter system. In Berlin the *National Socialistische Partei Korrespondenz*, in an editorial entitled "B. Mannes Baruch," branded him the American ruling class's "secret president" who now functioned as a Rothschild representative: "Mr. Baruch, already in control in the United States, wishes to safeguard his South American interests by having the United States control South America." At Senate Foreign Relations Committee hearings, Key Pittman gave Baruch an opportunity to deny that he held "a penny of interest in any country or anything south of the Rio Grande to the tip of Patagonia." That undoubtedly was so. But it was also true that Baruch exhorted the State Department to disrupt German trade relations and urged American businessmen like Eugene G. Grace, president of Bethlehem Steel, to "press very hard for business in Mexico, Central and South America," even if it meant selling at prices that competed without realizing profits.[44]

In the same vein, Baruch advocated that the United States buy gold "only from those nations with whom we have fair, cooperative relations." Washington had been purchasing gold from Japan, Italy, and Germany. For an ostensibly neutral nation, such an embargo "may be looked upon as a step towards war, but what have we now but war[,] with every nation, even our own, feverishly preparing for defense or offense and raising all kinds of economic barriers?" Baruch put this argument for economic warfare into a memorandum to Roosevelt. It struck a responsive chord with the president, who had waged economic warfare in behalf of naval interests during 1917–18. Obviously he had given the matter considerable thought in developing foreign economic policy in recent years, for he responded by telling Baruch, "Your memorandum sounds like a 100% endorsement of my Chicago 'quarantine speech' of two years ago!"[45] It would be more than another two years before Japan attacked Pearl Harbor, but the economic war with the Fascist nations had begun.

THE SIGNIFICANCE OF THE 1939 STRUGGLE
OVER THE WRB

While the United States waged economic warfare against Germany and Japan, Baruch did his best to see that the nation was industrially mobilized for the armed fight certain to come. Nevertheless, comparatively few Americans shared his preoccupation with preparedness for war. The War Department concerned itself with such contingencies, but it received little support from Congress; support came only from businessmen representing a minor sector of the economy—ordnance. The administration behaved in a perfunctory manner. Anxious not to alarm those harboring strong antiwar feelings in Congress, in the business community, on college campuses, and among pacifists and progressives of many stripes, Roosevelt at first mostly concerned himself with a "defensive" navy. But then the lingering depression of early 1938 provided military preparedness with an unanticipated rationale as public works.

Of course, even before then, Baruch and the military had given a great deal of thought to the unthinkable; both believed it to be their duty. For its part the War Department regularly reviewed and revised its 1931 industrial mobilization plan, producing new ones in 1933 and 1936. Each was essentially a variation upon the first. In the 1936 version, the Army-Navy Munitions Board would perform as a caretaker of plans until a transition to war was determined, then a civilian War Resources Administration would take over and act as the WIB had in 1918. All this remained an abstraction until Louis Johnson became assistant secretary of war on 28 June 1937.[46]

An ambitious man, Johnson, encouraged by Baruch and aided by headlines proclaiming aggression in Europe and Asia, pressed for rearmament. In 1937 he decided upon the creation of an advisory board on industrial mobilization to be composed of Baruch and "a disinterested group of citizens . . . whose review [of plans] will carry sufficient prestige to be convincing to the country at large." Inviting Baruch to submit names for the board, Johnson urged him to recommend "younger men whose services and interest may be available . . . should a future emergency arise." The shrewd Johnson must have anticipated Baruch's thinking on the matter, for Baruch predictably nominated nine men who had been associated with the WIB, including Hugh Johnson and George Peek. The only concession to youth was to have the WIB veterans nominate younger men as their alternates. Baruch trusted only experienced hands at such a task; besides, he probably knew very few younger business executives like those he had brought to Washington twenty years before. Louis Johnson, ever courteous and deferential to a man who figured prominently in the army's public relations arsenal, again tried to focus Baruch's thoughts on a board of predominantly younger men. But Baruch had no more names to suggest. When Johnson went to the president with a list of twenty names representing "elder statesmen," economists, industrialists, labor leaders, and clergymen for the proposed board, his list included only one name from Baruch's suggestions, the Peek-Hugh Johnson duo being conspicuously absent. Baruch's name headed the list. Roosevelt responded obliquely to the proposed board by requesting Johnson to investigate whether the Council of National Defense created in 1916 still had legal entity and might "perform the same function as your suggested 'Advisory Board.'"[47]

Already Roosevelt indicated a distaste for WIB-style planning for war. Baruch and Roosevelt each approached the matter of mobilization from the perspective of 1917, and each drew a different historical lesson from his experience. For Baruch it meant that without knowledgeable men drawn from key positions in the nation's industrial organization, mobilization would be chaotic, confused, and cumbersome. For Roosevelt it meant that responsible and honorable public servants could be temporarily displaced in an emergency by freewheeling promoters and executive types who usurped the regular channels of government and even the constituted authority of the president. Having begun the New Deal with emergency agencies headed by Johnson and Peek, neither of whom worked well with the cabinet departments, Roosevelt had returned to reliance upon the departments to carry the bulk of the New Deal's work. Interior Secretary Ickes had been a reliable organizer of the Public Works Administration; in time, Works Progress Administrator Hopkins would be commerce secretary. For what purpose did the president need a war cabinet if his regular cabinet functioned so well?

Shortly following his reelection in 1936, Roosevelt had met with the chairman of the President's Committee on Administrative Management, Louis Brownlow, who had been a commissioner of the District of Columbia during the war. For a while they reminisced about 1917–18 and the talk came around to the WIB, about which both had strong adverse opinions. Returning to the problems of the times, Roosevelt asked Brownlow to ascertain what authority still lay with the White House for economic mobilization for war. Brownlow reported that the Council of National Defense legally existed, although it could perform only advisory, not executive, functions. Roosevelt did nothing with this information until Louis Johnson brought forth his recommendation for a War Department advisory board. But it was evident that the president would not permit anything that might lead to another WIB.[48]

Baruch continued to agitate for preparedness through the winter and spring of 1938, the Czechoslovakian crisis giving his concerns added importance. Roosevelt's willingness to increase defense spending heartened him. In April he warned the White House that the United States possessed an insufficient reserve of strategic materials like manganese, chrome, tin, and tungsten, imploring Roosevelt to begin stockpiling immediately. Two weeks later a bill for the expenditure upon strategic materials of $25 million per year for four years was introduced in the Senate at the behest of five executive departments. Remembering Baruch many years later as both an ally and an antagonist, Henry Wallace could declare, "I found him more aware of the necessity for stockpiling back in the late 'thirties than any other individual except Herbert Feis in the State Department."[49]

History seemed to be heading Baruch's way. Confident that some mobilization was imminent, he went directly to the president with his concept of a defense coordination board, as noted at the beginning of this chapter. He no longer bothered to take his suggestions to the assistant secretary of war. But when he told the president that he wanted Hugh Johnson and George Peek to serve with him, Roosevelt was not nearly as understanding or polite as Louis Johnson had been. There would be no defense coordination board; mobilization would not proceed at the pace Baruch envisioned; and Roosevelt would be increasingly guarded in protecting his prerogatives as commander in chief from assaults by his speculator friend.

Shunned by the White House, Baruch retreated to exercising his influence upon Louis Johnson. The War Department developed a new industrial mobilization plan in May 1939, but it differed little from its predecessors except in conferring upon a war resources administrator more consolidated powers for coordination of mobilization under the direct authority of the president. Virtually every other administrator within the mobilization process reported to the War Resources Administration, thereby making it a super-agency whose hypothetical power was limited only by the president. It amounted to what Baruch had been preaching to the army for nearly twenty years. As Europe verged upon war in 1939, Roosevelt encouraged both Baruch and Johnson in their efforts to educate the public for preparedness. Johnson believed the time for action had arrived.[50]

Although charged by Congress under the Defense Act of 1920 with planning industrial mobilization, Johnson was blocked by his superior, Secretary of War Harry H. Woodring, an outspoken pacifist. When Woodring took two weeks of vacation in Panama beginning on 3 August 1939, Acting Secretary of War Johnson opportunistically proposed creation of a war resources board. By 8 August he had the president's approval to form a civilian review board for studying the latest industrial mobilization plan and recommending improvements. But Roosevelt did not want Baruch on it. Conferring with Johnson on the board's makeup, the president advised him, "Don't overlook Ed Stettinius" for chairman of the board. Stettinius, a Wall Streeter for Roosevelt, had been on Johnson's 1937 list of names for the proposed advisory board on industrial mobilization, as had "elder statesman" Walter S. Gifford and economist Harold G. Moulton, president of the Brookings Institution. Along with Karl T. Comptom, president of Massachusetts Institute of Technology; John Lee Pratt, a director of General Motors; and Robert E. Wood, chairman of Sears, Roebuck, these men composed the War Resources Board (WRB) created by Johnson on 9 August, with Stettinius as chairman.

Only the absence of Baruch initially stirred controversy. Unable to appoint him chairman of the WRB, Johnson could not have Baruch on the committee in any capacity without diminishing his importance. So he excluded the old warrior. His solution to this ticklish political problem was to stipulate that the board's first task would be to consult with Baruch. But that hardly resolved the matter. Army friends like Pershing expressed their surprise, and Hugh Johnson used his syndicated column to voice outrage over the absence of Baruch from the WRB. Having anticipated the outcry from the Baruch faction, Louis Johnson had promised that "other members will be appointed at a later date." In September the administration announced that John Hancock, a partner in Wall Street's Lehman Brothers and a Baruch friend since Hancock's days as the navy counterpart to Hugh Johnson on the WIB, also would serve.[51]

If the exclusion of Baruch upset his admirers, the inclusion of his surrogate, Hancock, frightened some New Dealers. They branded Hancock an enemy of the forces of reform in Wall Street. Thus, the fight over the WRB shaped up as not merely an issue of industrial mobilization and Baruch's role in it, but a struggle for the very soul of the administration. Behind the conflict were two basic premises: first, that the enemies of the New Deal ("economic royalists" who opposed social welfare legislation, tax reform, and antitrust prosecution) were behind the War Department's drive for preparedness; and second, that organization for war would undermine progressivism (as Harold Ickes believed that World War I had set reform back) unless it was run by New Dealers. Frances Perkins questioned why organized labor was not represented on the WRB, and Henry Wallace demanded that agriculture be considered in its deliberations; their respective constituencies vehemently concurred. Presidential economic adviser Lauchlin Currie challenged the use of the Brookings Institution as the WRB's source of economic sagacity. Midwestern businessman Cyrus Eaton attacked the excessive influence of the Morgan financial group, a reference to Stettinius, Pratt, and Gifford. Ironically, Hugh Johnson had foreseen the New Dealers' indictment of the WRB: "Do you suppose," he had asked Stettinius, "the present pack of semi-Communist wolves intend to let Morgan and Dupont men run a war?" Indeed, it was widely believed that Louis Johnson had "put one over on the President's New Deal supporters."[52]

Much speculation centered upon how Baruch felt toward the WRB. In theory the board represented a triumph for him. Not since he had walked into Roosevelt headquarters seven years before had liberals felt such a sense of impending betrayal. Compared to the WRB the old WIB had been a model of liberalism, for at least it represented a greater cross section of businessmen and it included nominal labor leadership. Hugh Johnson had hit the mark in pointing to the Morgan-related industrialists on the WRB; Dillon Read's James Forrestal considered it "discouraging" to anti-Morgan forces in Wall Street. Moreover, the announcement of the board's founding had stated that in the event of a threat of war, the board "would become an executive agency of the government with broad powers in many ways similar to those of the old War Industries Board."[53] The New Dealers were not unreasonable in their trepidations that this board would administer their downfall. Baruch should have been flattered by the WRB's formation.

But it wounded him. Although he said nothing for the record, he was hurt. The administration knew that Baruch was "sore as hell." Ben Cohen, who only recently had dined with Baruch and Tom Corcoran in New York, sought to assure Baruch that he and Corcoran had had no hand in deciding on the board's personnel. To rumors that he had turned down a proffered appointment to the board because he feared anti-Semitism, Baruch tersely declared, "That is not true." To Jimmy Byrnes he insisted: "I am not disappointed but I do not think it was a nice thing to do without saying something to me about it first . . . I do not think either Louis Johnson or [Secretary of the Navy] Charles Edison wanted me because of my activity in 1937 and 1938 in demanding that the Navy and the Army hurry up." A decade later he would confide to Arthur Krock, "Roosevelt dropped me and took up with the Stettinius Board." The WRB represented a personal setback for Baruch. After all his years of leadership in behalf of industrial mobilization for war, with Europe on the verge of hostilities in August 1939, the parade was about to commence without him at its head. It should have been a vindication of his mobilization doctrine, but instead Baruch mourned the WRB as a tragic loss. As Herbert Swope commented a year after the WRB episode, Baruch believed in his own indispensability, and "everytime another man's name is mentioned he spews upon it." In Byzantine Washington, power mattered more than principle even for Bernard Baruch.[54]

Roosevelt had power and could afford greater attention to principle. In this instance he operated on two principles: never share power with Baruch and/or his surrogates; and never allow even the emergency of war mobilization to become the occasion for erecting power bases that might rival the White House. Putting Baruch in charge of the WRB would have given it visibility and raised public anticipations beyond what Roosevelt intended. With Baruch's support in Congress and his hold on public opinion, he would have been almost impossible to dislodge once he had been appointed; on the other hand, Stettinius, accommodating and colorless, posed no such problem. As it turned out, when the WRB adopted the industrial mobilization plan of 1939, which Baruch characterized as "practically what I have been preaching for twenty years,"[55] Roosevelt dismissed the board and pigeonholed the report; it was not publicly accessible until after World War II. It would not have been so easy for Roosevelt to get rid of the WRB with Baruch running the show.

At issue too was nothing less than the fundamental question how the American government operated in an emergency such as war. The cabinet and the various New Deal agencies of relief and reform would not allow themselves to be reduced to caretakers of a civilian government while military and business executives directed mobilization—where the action by then was. Moreover, the New Dealers could not even expect military resistance to civilian encroachment upon the prerogative of procurement, as had been the case in 1917. As Baruch had told Stettinius when he thought that the WRB had graduated to WIB status, "Due to the education of the Army and the Navy as to their industrial needs, you have a much easier problem to deal with than we had to face in the last war." His unctuous self-congratulation aside, Baruch rightfully claimed to be the father of what others, including Dwight Eisenhower, would characterize as a "military-industrial complex." However, the New Dealers had not been as well educated in industrial preparedness for war as the military. The signs foretold their relegation to the sidelines. The potential elevation of Baruch to power and the acceptance of his ideas were unmistakable warnings. His trademark in mobilization was the emergency "war cabinet": "As a rule I have been opposed in war to anything but the usual activities in the departments. I like, in war, to see all operations in emergency organizations."[56] Here was a fundamental difference with Roosevelt.

Roosevelt interpreted the army's plan for industrial mobilization in the Baruch style as an "effort to cut the President out of any direct and continuing control of the industrial mobilization of the country." It would amount to a virtual "abdication" by the chief executive should he consent to it. The Baruch scheme called for conferring power upon another individual to direct the economy, the basic war effort, "even the public relations of the White House." As the WRB picked up the army plan and seemed intent upon perpetuating itself, Roosevelt slashed its requested allocation of $125,000 to $50,000 and, glancing at the board's comprehensive mobilization scheme, asked, "What do they think they are doing, setting up a second Government?" Recalling how the faltering organization of 1917 had impelled Wilson to go to Congress for each additional administrative innovation, Roosevelt wished to keep war management free of legislative interventions. If he conferred mobilization authority upon an individual or a committee, he would be delegating powers of the presidency to administrators not chosen by the American people. "I am inclined to think," he told Louis Brownlow as the WRB began its deliberations, "that the thing to do is to revive the old Council of National Defense and pull it straight into my own office." At the same time he discussed the feasibility of strengthening the military departments politically by appointing prominent Republicans as secretaries of war and navy. Hearing rumors of such a ploy, Baruch argued that it would be "a mistake" because the president ought first to "solidify" his own party.[57] Both Roosevelt and Baruch were inconsistent, each being primarily intent upon preserving power or grasping it. Still, Roosevelt was the president and he had intimated the outlines of his future mobilization plans.

The abrupt termination of the WRB in late September created a public uproar. In the first month of World War II the WRB issue had defined lines of a conflict that would persist throughout the war itself. Headlines in the *Wall Street Journal* sharpened the issue:

Left-Wingers on Top

Preparedness Plans
Will Be Handled
On New Deal Lines

War Industries Board [*sic*] Will
    Complete Report Soon and
    Then Disband

It Was Opposed by Liberals

Roosevelt's sacking of the WRB inspired jubilation among New Dealers. For them his decision to scrap the proposed super-agency concept signified nothing less than the preservation of the New Deal itself: when mobilization began, it would be a New Dealer's mobilization. Events would prove their joy premature: the WRB as material reality was moribund, but its theory lived. Historians are divided as to its legacy. "Though officially rejected in 1939," argues one scholar, "the principal proposals concurred in by WRB and the military were adopted during World War II." Another historian concedes that the agency development of 1942–45 was "reminiscent" of the Baruch-inspired WRB, but maintains that "one variation stands out—all roads led to the White House, not to a War Resources Administrator."[58]

The measure of the WRB legacy would be the extent to which the Baruch faith in super-agencies prevailed in World War II. The man himself would be an issue because he became a symbol of that policy conflict.

Baruch's proximity to the White House was a source of concern to liberals. During the war, if Baruch, his acolytes, or their sympathizers prevailed in the management of mobilization or stabilization, it would be interpreted as a setback for the New Deal. More than ever, the image of Baruch as a manipulator took on considerable significance.

THE CAMPAIGNS OF 1940

The winter of 1939–40 was the time of the "phony war," the *Sitzkrieg*, as Europe awaited Hitler's next move. Poland had been swallowed by her neighboring giants, Germany and Russia, an aggression that brought declarations of war against Germany by France and Britain. In the United States, Congress repealed the arms embargo in November, but cash-and-carry remained the terms of sale. Americans were still determined to keep out of the war. It was not quite armed neutrality, Baruch grumbled, because the people and the administration were unwilling to arm. The surprising standstill in Europe, broken only by the Russian invasion of Finland, encouraged the hope that the dictators had all they wanted. Then, in the spring, Hitler swiftly lunged for Denmark and Norway, and soon followed with a *Blitzkrieg* upon the Netherlands, Belgium, and Luxembourg. Then he turned against the Maginot Line and swept toward Paris, with France surrendering on 22 June. There was war in Europe after all, but it remained to be seen how it would involve the United States.

It was a season of disappointment for Baruch. Following the cashiering of the War Resources Board, Roosevelt conducted his own *Sitzkrieg* against Baruch. The president had no wish to dispel the illusion of neutrality or to incur the wrath of Congress and the public with rearmament, unless the situation warranted it. With Baruch's views on preparedness so well known, the speculator found himself all but ignored at the White House. When Hitler first cast covetous eyes upon Czechoslovakia in 1938, Roosevelt had told Jimmy Byrnes that Baruch "was nuts on Army preparation." With considerable self-pity, Baruch in 1940 believed that in the administration he had "become persona non grata because of my continual cry for preparedness in the last four years." Indeed, Roosevelt could not encourage Baruch without offending Americans who wanted unarmed neutrality. However, with the 1940 election in sight, he had to give Baruch enough of an ear to prevent him from "getting off the reservation." After all, most of Baruch's sidekicks were renegades already and, although it was clear that Baruch had no wish to join them in exclusion from the White House, Roosevelt had to be careful not to give the old Democrat cause for disaffection.[59]

Roosevelt need not have worried. Baruch's chief indictment of Roosevelt, although he would never invoke the president's name in his bill of particulars, was that he led by misdirection. On the one hand, he claimed neutrality and backed it up with a refusal to arm; yet, as men informed in economic diplomacy could see, the United States remained on a collision course with Japan in the Pacific while it waged economic war against Germany in Europe and in the Americas. In London, Joe Kennedy verged on abandoning Roosevelt for the same reasons Baruch stayed with the president—the inevitability of war.

As Kennedy put it: "Every country in the world is, to all intents and purposes, in a state of war as far as their economic well-being is concerned. They are all arming, they are all standing ready, they are all losing their export business. They are all faced with internal problems and when it is all over, everybody will have found out they have gained nothing. It is just too terrible to contemplate." Essentially, Baruch agreed with his "Little Chairman." However, Baruch insisted that Hitler's intentions left the United States little recourse but to wage an economic war that must by itself yield a state of belligerency with Germany. While Kennedy and others deplored rearmament, Baruch bemoaned the psychological and military state of unpreparedness that left the United States defenseless against Germany. As he told Senator Wagner shortly before France surrendered, "If Hitler goes after us (and mind you, *we have practically declared war on him*), we have not much with which to fight."[60] Although Kennedy envisioned anything beyond a two- or three-year war as catastrophic for all, Baruch argued that a well-conceived mobilization and stabilization program would enable the United States to triumph on the battlefields *and* in the postwar markets—and that the time was approaching when the president would need that program.

In the meantime, Baruch carefully advocated preparedness strictly for the defense of hemispheric markets. Like Roosevelt, he publicly insisted that America should not embroil itself in Europe's war unless attacked. Thus, he perched himself precariously between defense preparedness and warmongering. "Nobody wants a war and nobody gains in the end," he told reporters following a White House visit in 1939. He depicted an armed America as the most effective deterrent to the aggression of totalitarian powers. But America was "seriously unprepared" for a possible two-ocean war, could no longer rely upon the British navy to control the Atlantic, and faced the real possibility that "a combination of powers . . . might try to take our vast resources from us" (an oblique reference to Latin American raw materials); and in case of invasion the United States would depend upon an army that was "pitifully small, untrained, lacking modern arms and up-to-date munitions." During the phony war he confined his counsel to sympathetic listeners in Congress and in the War Department. Even in the latter he found "procrastination" induced by "pressure brought to bear to keep down expenditures."[61] In an election

8. "Big Chairman" and "Little Chairman" relaxing in the 1930s—Baruch and
Joseph P. Kennedy. (Courtesy Seeley G. Mudd Manuscript Library, Princeton
University)

year, the president wanted no harbingers of higher taxes. As good politicians, the civilian secretaries in the War and Navy departments dutifully complied.

The military were not restrained by such electoral considerations. Army Chief of Staff George C. Marshall invited Baruch to training exercises at Camp Jackson, South Carolina, and detailed a colonel to serve as Baruch's personal aide during exercises that demonstrated how woefully unprepared the army was for a big fight. Then Marshall tactfully inquired if Baruch might "say a word to the President in support" of an appropriation of $11 million for an air base at Anchorage, Alaska. Baruch responded with a lesson in politics: take what you can this year and come back for more later. He took Marshall's case for Anchorage to Pa Watson in the White House, urging him to restore $4 million for the air base. Then he prevailed upon Jimmy Byrnes to host a dinner for some Democratic senators at which Marshall presented an eloquent description of an army ill prepared for modern warfare. Marshall got the money. In the words of Marshall's biographer, Baruch proved valuable to the army as "a pipeline to the centers of influence."[62]

But Hitler was more useful to the army than Baruch. General Marshall's pleas for increased appropriations began to command greater respect at the White House. Roosevelt began a May budget conference by estimating an increase in defense spending to about $500 million and concluded it by authorizing over $1 billion. Even so, when a luncheon conference with Baruch touched off rumors of an impending mobilization, press secretary Stephen Early quickly denied them. For the time being, preparedness had to be a covert operation.[63]

Moreover, any mobilization would be without 1918's mobilizer. While Baruch sat in Lafayette Square and "dreamed of old times" and awaited a call to head a new WIB, on 25 May the president without fanfare issued an executive order creating the Office of Emergency Management, through which the White House would channel all mobilization. Then, as he had hinted previously, Roosevelt invoked the Defense Act of 1916 to create his own Advisory Commission to the Council of National Defense, which reported directly to the president. On it were General Motors President William S. Knudsen, Stettinius, union leader Sidney Hillman, New Deal economist Leon Henderson, former AAA head Chester Davis, railroad head Ralph Budd, and consumer expert Harriet Elliott. Each would advise in a special area, but otherwise each would be impotent. As Budget Director Harold Smith observed, "What we were trying to do was to avoid setting up a super-government for the emergency." The body even lacked a chairman. "Who is the boss?" Knudsen asked Roosevelt. "I am," came the crisp reply. Even Roosevelt conceded that his defense coordinators had overlapping functions that depended upon jealous departments in the executive branch. The word most often used to describe the Advisory Commission would be "monstrosity."[64]

Apparently, Baruch knew beforehand that something like the Advisory Commission was in the offing and told the White House that what mobilization needed was a "coordinating committee" instead of a "super-board." But, he confided to Byrnes, it had to be led by a strong and knowledgeable preparedness advocate like Louis Johnson. Roosevelt had other plans for Johnson: he fired him. It was small consolation to Baruch that the president also sacked Woodring and Edison. Before long the word was out that Baruch was "raising hell" at the White House over Johnson's dismissal. As Roosevelt had planned a year ago, he now brought two Republicans in as secretary of war and secretary of the navy, former Secretary of State Henry L. Stimson and 1936 GOP vice-presidential nominee Frank Knox, publisher of the *Chicago Daily News*. At Stimson's insistence, Roosevelt appointed Wall Street Republican Robert P. Patterson to fill Johnson's place as assistant secretary of war, the position charged with responsibility for industrial mobilization. Patterson, as Baruch would fondly recall a decade later, proved to be "the most driving man in the outfit . . . with whom I worked in full accord." Two months later, Roosevelt made James V. Forrestal, a Wall Street Democrat, undersecretary of the navy. He also would become a wartime favorite of Baruch. Nevertheless, in mid-1940, Baruch was known to be disappointed that all these appointments were made without his consultation.[65]

For Roosevelt the primary consideration in the Stimson-Knox appointments had been to make mobilization an occasion for a political coalition. Faced with the political prospect of being branded a warmonger if he took the route of the WIB, as well as being accused of weakening the New Deal coalition by antagonizing organized labor, he created a powerless civilian Advisory Commission. To counter charges of indifference to preparedness, he appointed preparedness advocates Stimson and Knox. Not yet prepared for a military campaign, at least the Roosevelt administration was prepared for another political campaign.

Baruch had seen the third-term effort coming. In the summer of 1939 he had told Corcoran and Cohen that he would support Roosevelt again because no other Democrat could be elected president. At a White House dinner in early 1940, Roosevelt suddenly inquired of Baruch, "Who do you think would make a good candidate for the Presidency?" "Mr. President," Baruch responded, "are you trying to kid me or kid yourself?" Roosevelt laughed and the subject shifted to vice-presidential possibilities. Still, both men played a cagey game during 1940. When Swope sent FDR a florid letter begging him to run again, the president read it very carefully and declined to comment.[66] It would be up to the Democratic convention in Chicago to "draft" Roosevelt.

Baruch disliked the breaking of the third-term tradition. When a New Deal senator asked him to endorse Roosevelt before the convention, Baruch asserted that he had not made preconvention endorsements since 1924, but always supported the convention's nominee. And so he did again, while covertly keeping his lines open to the Republican camp via George Peek. Peek had returned to the Republican fold since leaving the New Deal and conferred with GOP presidential nominee Wendell Willkie on 20 July regarding farm and trade issues. Less than two weeks later, Baruch suggested to Peek that the Republicans ought to brand Roosevelt a tool of the big city bosses. Baruch also contributed $4,000 to Senator Harry Truman's primary campaign against White House support for challenger Lloyd Stark. In the fall, Baruch helped campaign for FDR in Tennessee, quietly complaining as usual about the administration's lack of military preparedness. Baruch had a talent for having it both ways. An old Baruch watcher and Roosevelt hater like Frank Kent thought that the speculator carried the great game of politics too far. "That, it seems to me, is the one thing in which you fail," Kent scolded. "You know [Roosevelt] to be incompetent, unsound, hypocritical, insincere, disloyal to his friends, ungrateful and dangerous. . . . You know a change in direction is what we need. And you are too highly intelligent to fall for the silly swapping horses while crossing the stream twaddle and certainly the doctrine of the Indispensable Man must revolt you. And yet, you 'go along' against your judgment and your instinct. I weep. I wail. I tear my hair."[67]

Surely, Kent understood why Baruch had to "go along." It was just good politics for a man of seventy years whose greatest ambition was to repeat his triumphs at age forty-eight. If the Republicans should, by some miracle, win the White House, then Willkie would need Baruch for "consensus" leadership much as Hoover had needed him in 1932. But if Roosevelt won again without Baruch on the bandwagon, then an apostate Democrat would never be forgiven. Besides, Baruch shrewdly recognized that he had great utility for Roosevelt as "that rare bird of a rich and successful businessman who is still loyal to the President"[68] and still commanded a large following in the public and in the Congress.

Preparedness for war advanced Baruch's interests and the public's. Despite his three score and ten years, and recent bouts with assorted ailments, he shrugged off accounts of his various infirmities as a New Dealer conspiracy to suggest that he was "not available for the part in the present defense program that some of the public believe I should take." He left no doubt in the minds of friends that the only appropriate defense program would be one headed by Baruch. At every gathering with Democrats he impressed them with his acuteness of mind and physical vigor, his grasp of data on raw materials needed for war, and his familiarity with the army's dearth of weaponry (having absorbed the latter information directly from War Department sources like Louis Johnson and George Marshall). All the while, his conferences with Roosevelt at Hyde Park or at the White House were noted in the *New York Times* and elsewhere—reminders to the public that Bernard Baruch remained a presidential advisor on economics and preparedness. By now the Battle of Britain had commenced. Roosevelt would have to abandon his obdurate insistence upon confining all mobilization activities to the White House and the cabinet. Industry, intent only upon reaping the long-awaited profits that accrued from expanded government spending, resented the government's confining defense contracts. The press began to talk of "defense bottlenecks" and the need for a mobilization coordinator. It sounded like the winter of 1917–18 all over again. Would 1941 bring "another Baruch?" Would it bring the return of Baruch?[69]

Belaboring the obvious, Baruch harped upon the mobilization chaos. "The voting of money is not enough. There must be someone to see that it is spent wisely," he reminded Byrnes. "The principal objection to the present setup is that there is no coordinating head to the whole enterprise," he told Leon Henderson, Roosevelt's advisor on price stabilization. Though it would be presumptuous to attribute Henderson's thinking to Baruch's influence, from his notes we can detect a strong similarity in Henderson's language and argument on current defense needs: "Overall coordinator . . . Quick translation of new appropriations into orders . . . Advance trouble shooting on bottlenecks . . . Access to F. D. R.—perhaps thru # 1 . . . Real knowledge by someone representing F. D. R. of what is going on." Moreover, the Defense Commission listened respectfully when Baruch appeared before it to preach his doctrine of comprehensive and coordinated mobilization. More than anything else experience was Baruch's ally—not necessarily his own experience, but rather that of the mobilizers, through which they discovered the practical lessons to be learned from Baruch.[70]

But Roosevelt and the New Dealers were not yet prepared for either Baruch or "another Baruch." Announcing in December the creation of the Office of Production Management (OPM), Roosevelt stipulated that it would have the hydra-headed leadership of William Knudsen for production and Sidney Hillman for labor. Initially the press mistook Knudsen for the powerful industrial mobilizer it had anticipated; Krock immediately hailed him as "the Baruch" of Roosevelt's mobilization effort. However, Baruch knew better. Hearing rumors of Roosevelt's plan, Baruch sent the White House a warning that it "would be considered a makeshift and [would] not impress the American people." Also, he privately took a swipe at Knudsen, calling a recent public utterance an example of how the General Motors man "was not quite playing ball." But OPM had the backing of Stimson and Knox. The navy secretary conceded that it was not "the equal of a single-headed authority," but he begged Baruch to remember that "we are still at peace" and that political realities still took precedence over emergency exigencies.[71] Even so, Roosevelt had called upon America to become an "arsenal of democracy," offering lend-lease aid to the besieged victims of Nazi Germany.

How could the United States lend-lease military hardware it possessed in grossly insufficient quantities? Here the political logic of Roosevelt's tactics became apparent: House bill 1776, lend-lease, would be his chief device for promoting defense mobilization *sans* European intervention. At the same time, OPM's strong labor representation would assure liberals that preparedness would be a New Deal enterprise. However, on the other side of the aisle, Republican Senator Warren Austin of Vermont, recalling the "industrial miracle" of 1918, asked where in OPM was "the principle of centralization of responsibility and decentralization of authority" that had succeeded so well in the WIB.[72]

The winter of 1940–41 must have seemed different to Baruch from that of 1939–40. True, he was no closer to repeating his WIB performance; and Roosevelt had moved only modestly toward the defense arrangement of Baruch's dreams. The difference lay in the fact that the president, having taken a momentous step toward arming both the United States *and* Britain, had to convince industry and Congress that OPM meant business, that despite ambiguous lines of authority it was intended to mobilize for defense. Otherwise, Roosevelt ran the risks of an impotent OPM and no lend-lease approval by Congress. To achieve his goals he needed to obtain Baruch's backing without having to confer power upon him.

Again it was public relations time. In January, Baruch hailed OPM as "a long forward step," even though he wished it had a single chief. In February it was announced that OPM would include a Production Planning Board headed by industrialist Samuel R. Fuller, a friend of Baruch. At the same time the White House let it be known that Baruch had begun to lunch with the president on a weekly basis and that the New Dealers in the mobilization program paid him close attention. In March lend-lease sailed through Congress while the Capitol buzzed about the contradiction of Baruch's increasing presence at the White House, his expanding influence among defense planners, and his open criticism of OPM's ineffectiveness. As Krock pointed out, Baruch continued to give advice, and received a respectful hearing, but his words went unheeded. Priorities remained a jumble, prices were rising swiftly, and production was hampered by untold bottlenecks. The Senate, at the instigation of Missouri's Harry Truman, initiated a special investigation of the defense program under the leadership of this recent beneficiary of Baruch's funds. It remained to be seen how long Baruch and his admirers would settle for the enhanced prominence of Baruch and defense mobilization without substantial power for both.[73]

PREPAREDNESS WITHOUT PRIORITIES OR
PRICE CONTROLS

Baruch was an unhappy soothsayer as he surveyed Roosevelt's defense program in 1941. Sometimes he claimed that the White House had ignored him; but nobody, not the Office of Production Management, the Department of War, or the Office of Price Administration and Civilian Supplies (OPACS) created in April under the leadership of Leon Henderson, could afford to overlook his experience or his presence. They were engaged in an enterprise that had but a single recent precedent; Baruch had written the book on that. The various departments and agencies studied the histories of the WIB, taking from them what lessons they wanted to find and discarding much as irrelevant to their time and circumstances. Baruch agreed that the WIB had made mistakes in 1917 that ought not to be repeated; however, by the summer of 1918 it had developed mobilization and stabilization plans that its successors in 1941 could build upon.

The incessant repetition of his message might have frustrated less-motivated men. He knew that his admonitions were tiresome and didactic. He also believed that his time had come, that history had prepared him for this moment. He no longer sought a position of leadership for himself. He conceded that he was too old for the demands of daily administration. Through his contacts and his writings he would inform those for whom history had begun in the follies of the 1920s or the despair of the 1930s. Beginning in 1940, a series of publications recounted the mobilization shortcomings and triumphs of 1917–18. Baruch reissued the WIB report twenty years after its publication. Ever the master publicist, he saw to it that copies of every recent article or book written about the WIB, whether by himself or by others, were circulated throughout Washington.[74]

He referred to himself as a "hair shirt." If he had not been such a powerful influence upon public opinion and conservative congressmen, the new mobilizers might have been able to dismiss him as a public nuisance. He harassed OPM with complaints that it moved too slowly in motivating industry to convert to war production. The essence of mobilization was priorities, the distribution of a finite quantity of society's materials among competing civilian and military sectors. Priorities had to be the "synchronizing force" of the war effort, and OPM would have to become the ultimate arbiter between those who sought to produce for the civilian market and those in Washington who demanded first call upon manufacturing for war. Yet the mobilization of 1941 was marked by bureaucratic conflict instead of the harmonious priority allocation needed if the United States were to become the arsenal of democracy. Defense mobilization called for coordination of complex market forces involving not only the distribution of materials but the control of prices that soared as a consequence of the extraordinary demand for everything. But Washington had compartmentalized production, purchasing, priorities, prices, and civilian supply—a proliferation of responsibilities that defied rational relationships among people or economic forces. When so many bureaucrats had authority, nobody had ultimate authority. All the mistakes of 1917—18 were being repeated. Too smart to indict the chief executive, Baruch attributed indecision and mistakes to a universal irresolution that infected Washington. Never mentioning the president, he criticized the agencies charged with organizing the chaos.

Meanwhile, Roosevelt remained adamant against endowing any mobilization czar with powers that only a president should wield, for the distribution of the resources of war, he realized, could involve the distribution of economic power for generations. Those decisions ought to be made in the White House. Moreover, if they were made in 1941 they would influence foreign policy at a time when the nation was nominally at peace. Both the appearance and the reality of defense procrastination were preferable to the alternatives of industrial cartelization for defense or the politically unwelcome step of a virtual declaration of hostilities by total mobilization. Washington in 1941 was a battleground for the forces of public enterprise, private enterprise, organized labor, and the military. The lines of battle were confused and somewhat ironic. All claimant groups agreed on the need for mobilization, but they disagreed on its speed, its thoroughness, and its leadership. The military wanted all the mobilization it could accomplish as soon as feasible. New Dealers were ambivalent: some popular front advocates wanted an all-out war against Fascism and decried the "business as usual" attitudes apparently prevalent at high levels in the War Department and in OPM; others feared government regimentation of labor and loss of union gains. Liberals chafed over the priority muddle that so generously benefited big business. Nevertheless, the liberals believed in the profit system. All-out mobilization must be a public enterprise that sustained private enterprise. But it was not clear how America could fight a war and preserve a free marketplace.

Big industry in 1940—41 wanted to produce as little for the government as it would allow. Baruch had warned the Advisory Commission's Donald Nelson as early as July 1940 to expect that mobilization would create scarcities requiring priority rulings and price-fixing to avoid inflation. He had outlined his full scheme before the entire commission in November. But the big push for defense orders did not develop until after lend-lease and the creation of OPM, and then both the steel and auto industries refused to take it seriously. Pittsburgh and Gary remained unconvinced that military orders would justify the expansion of capacity sought by Washington. Most available steel went to Detroit, where the automobile plants turned out a record-breaking five million cars. OPM chief Knudsen ignored calls for a sharp curtailment of that civilian production because, he said, the War Department's needs were not substantial enough to warrant civilian displacement. The 1941 experience with voluntary cooperation caused a mobilizer to conclude, "The automobile situation has demonstrated that conversion appears to commence when you compel it, rather than in response to exhortation."[75]

But who would do the compelling? With prices and civilian supply in the hands of one administrator and defense production in the clutches of another, and the question whether either had authority to give priority orders unresolved, mobilization floundered through mid-1941, torn between "all-outers" and those who wanted preparedness diluted with "business as usual." Foremost in the first category were the New Dealers who administered civilian supply and doubted big business's commitment to the fight against Fascism. OPACS head Leon Henderson's public demand for a 50 percent slash in automobile production in July served to sharpen New Deal-Wall Street differences, with Forrestal of the navy and of Wall Street remarking that the New Dealer really sought "to fight a social as well as a military war." However, according to Henderson, OPM's labor chief, Sidney Hillman, was no more supportive of priorities than OPM's industrial head.[76] Meanwhile, Roosevelt encouraged a standoff between OPM and OPACS.

Although Baruch hoped that Roosevelt would create a great coordinator of the priority and price functions, he nevertheless accommodated himself to the defense conceptions of 1941. If the president desired a war administered by New Dealers, then Baruch saw no reason to disagree. Besides, even without portfolio, the Old Man remained one of the most visible personages in the defense operation. The president entertained him for lunch once a week through the winter and spring. Visits with the once-hostile Harold Ickes became frequent and almost regular. Leon Henderson and the young New Deal economists and lawyers of OPACS sought his advice on handling the price problem. Perhaps never before had Baruch been so close to New Dealers. Like them, he sought all-out mobilization and deplored the recalcitrance of OPM and big industry. He supported Henderson fully and went out of his way to pass the word that he believed that here was a man of "ability and courage" who could keep prices in check. Knowing that industry would take advantage of rising prices to inflate its own profits, he sincerely preferred a strong liberal in price administration to a businessman with an indifferent sense of the public interest. *Time* magazine and columnist friends such as Krock and Kent assured their readers that Henderson's mind was receptive to Baruch's practical wisdom. His admirers in Congress were told that Henderson was a New Dealer they could trust.[77]

In May, Baruch told the president that he found OPM noticeably improved and priorities operating "satisfactorily," but he confided to TVA head David Lilienthal that the defense setup was "rattled." New

Dealers grudgingly gave Baruch their respect. In the matter of priorities, he left no doubt in their minds that they were "really at the feet of a master at that game." Despite his years, or maybe because of them, he convinced them of his wealth of understanding of economic relationships, and current problems and data. And he shared their doubts of Knudsen's disinterested leadership of OPM. By June, Baruch carried his complaints about Knudsen to Roosevelt while disclaiming interest in the post for himself. He had had some recent health difficulties, Baruch told Ickes. Nonetheless, Ickes concluded that Roosevelt would soon replace Knudsen with Baruch and sent the president a letter with that recommendation. A change was in the offing, but Ickes had bet on the wrong horse.[78]

The major push for reorganization came from Henderson's office and the Bureau of the Budget. Shortages in the metals markets became evident in January, and prices began to reflect hoarding by industrialists. Henderson's people sought civilian rationing as a means of accelerating the military buildup without a corresponding acceleration in civilian prices. They candidly challenged business control of priorities in OPM and in the War Department, expressing doubt that "these businessmen and military representatives have the breadth of economic and social vision properly to carry out such an important program" of military priorities and civilian rationing. As Baruch had forecast, government expenditures for the military had risen because of the lack of priorities management, and the liberals were accordingly encouraged to take their case for rationing to Treasury Secretary Morgenthau. They argued that "the military-business group" had natural conflicts of interest between their public offices and their private attachments. Although price control could stymie exorbitant profits, only control of priorities would assure a quick and fair mobilization. The liberals prevented the power of priorities from being lodged exclusively in OPM and enabled OPACS to become the ostensible voice for the public's interest in price stabilization. A murky arrangement was established in which the distinction between materials for military and civilian allotment remained undefined. All OPACS could do was to "jawbone" against higher prices and "business as usual."[79]

The New Dealers renewed their efforts to speed mobilization during the summer of 1941, with the executive office of the president spearheading the effort to break bottlenecks that advantaged certain industrial groups. Like Baruch, the Bureau of the Budget argued that OPM needed to show business that defense had greater priority than "business as usual" and that this could most effectively be done by greater coordination and centralization of powers. Applauding OPACS for having "consistently represented the governmental or public viewpoint in contrast to concern for private interests," the bureau nonetheless conceded that "the growing need for unification of responsibility for the supply function" could not enhance OPACS' powers. The White House faced a Hobson's choice for liberals: either it could strengthen the heretofore ineffective OPM and its business cronies, or it could create a new agency to supersede OPM, without any assurance that it would be an improvement. Still, the bureau recommended a new "Emergency Supply Board" to direct general policy for a subordinate OPM. As a concession, OPM would receive all civilian allocation work then performed by OPACS, a transfer that would make the latter more clearly a civilian price agency. To head the new board, the bureau called for "a vigorous chairman" who would bring to mobilization "a governmental or general social outlook." Though refraining from adding its voice to those calling for a mobilization "czar," the bureau significantly declared, "This proposed plan for the determination of priority policies and the administration of priority activities is supported by World War experience. . . . The key to the successful working of the World War plan was the strong hand who served as chairman of the War Industries Board."[80] In other words, an expeditious mobilization operating in the public interest called for another Baruch—preferably working out of the White House.

In some quarters in Washington, Baruch remained an anathema, but increasingly his writings and lectures on mobilization were becoming required reading for the new mobilizers. Surviving veterans of the WIB were sought out for their recollections of how they had handled priorities in 1918. By no means, however, had Baruch and his doctrines won acceptance. For years afterwards the legal counsel of OPM would be among those who maintained that the value of the WIB as a precedent "is somewhat exaggerated."[81] In the summer of 1941 the most important holdout against any new WIB with another Baruch was the president, reinforced by some New Dealers led by Harry Hopkins and businessmen intent upon profits without controls.

Roosevelt's solution to the priorities muddle took Baruch and others by surprise. In late August he announced the formation of the Supply Priorities and Allocation Board (SPAB) as OPM's policy-making superior with OPM's purchasing director, Donald M. Nelson, as its executive director. If SPAB resolved the priorities confusion, it would have to overcome the compounding of administrative confusion; Nelson remained Knudsen's subordinate in OPM, but became his superior in SPAB; Henderson remained Knudsen's subordinate in OPM, but was his equal at SPAB. Other members of the new board were Henry Wallace and Harry Hopkins, appointments suggesting that the New Dealers had come out on top in this latest skirmish for the soul of the mobilization effort.

On the advice of White House counsel Sam Rosenman, Roosevelt had adopted the Bureau of the Budget's proposals. The new mobilization chief, Nelson, a Sears, Roebuck vice-president, had a reputation as a "New Deal businessman." He was also a political protégé of Harry Hopkins, a fact that annoyed an old Hopkins antagonist and new Baruch friend, Harold Ickes. Baruch had believed for some time that Hopkins was hostile to him, and so he was receptive to Ickes's interpretation that he "had been pushed aside." Hopkins had become the Rasputin of Roosevelt's third term.[82]

A week after the SPAB announcement, Baruch went to the White House for his regular luncheon with the president. SPAB notwithstanding, Baruch pressed Roosevelt to put the defense mobilization in the hands of an industrial czar. Obviously expecting Baruch's recommendation, which he had heard so many times before that the two probably had lost count, Roosevelt pulled out recent figures showing armament output at twice what it had been in the last year of World War I. Furthermore, he asserted, Nelson had all of Baruch's WIB powers and more. Leaving the White House, Baruch found reporters wanting to know what he thought of SPAB. "No one has final authority," said the industrial czar of 1918. "It always gets back to that. You have seven excellent men there, any one of whom is capable of doing a swell job, but none has the final word. It's a faltering step foward." Baruch continued on with kind words for the board and Roosevelt himself, but "faltering step forward" was seized upon by the newsmen as the strongest criticism of SPAB yet heard. Did he mean it? Baruch shrugged: "Well, it's been storing up here for eighteen months. Go ahead and get me in trouble."[83]

The White House moved immediately to patch any possible damage Baruch might have inflicted upon the public's perception of the mobilization program. That very day, Pa Watson told Baruch he had "over talked himself" and requested that he issue an endorsement of SPAB. Baruch visited Donald Nelson and told newsmen that the SPAB chief had "a thorough grasp of the problem" and deserved full backing on priorities control. The incident marked one of the few times that Baruch had publicly criticized the president, and he hastily endeavored to close the breach. Accordingly, in a column entitled "The Unproud Father of a Changeling," Arthur Krock depicted Baruch as the author of a SPAB that had been altered by the White House and reminded Roosevelt of Baruch's steadfast loyalty in spite of many rebuffs. Baruch assured Roosevelt of his "affectionate loyalty" while reserving a face-saving right to avert "subservience or no honest criticism." The White House said nothing further regarding the incident and Nelson expressed appreciation for Baruch's public blessing.[84] Even so, the administration had reason to worry whether the hitherto supportive Baruch would go "off the reservation."

SPAB's creation had altered Baruch's relations with the administration. Feeling unheeded by Roosevelt and "in the dog house" as a consequence of his outburst on the White House steps (the last place anyone could assail the president and get away with it), Baruch had less to lose by frontal assaults upon the administration. In the words of an old Wilsonian, "Formerly Baruch wanted recognition—officially. Now he spurns it—

theoretically."[85] As Roosevelt had recognized before, a Baruch without any influence in the administration amounted to a loose gun on the ship of state. Only once before had Baruch confronted Roosevelt so directly— on the 1938 tax bill. But then he had retreated before any serious disruption between them developed. In the current confrontation, Baruch already signaled another attack to come.

"I'm going to knock the everlasting life out of it," Baruch promised reporters who asked how he would testify on the administration's price control bill before the House Banking and Currency Committee on 19 September. The bill would exempt wages that had fallen behind rising prices. Baruch wanted no exemptions from controls: "Everybody knows what my views are on prices. I've been writing them for twenty years. I stand on my experience." As he evidently believed, he could afford to pit his reputation against the administration on price controls. Who better espoused "taking the profits out of war," putting the general interest above any special interest? At a time when Baruch had joined New Dealers on the "all-out" side of the defense mobilization issue against the selfishness of industry's "business as usual" attitudes, they could ill afford to be painted by Baruch as the parochial defenders of free enterprise for wage earners and controls on industrialists. Sounding like the Wall Streeter he was, Baruch suggested that the New Dealers' resistance to comprehensive controls in 1941 veiled another struggle: "We can't fight two wars successfully at the same time: The war against Hitler and the internecine American war of personalities and social-economic theories." In effect, Baruch's dissent on the price control challenged liberals to choose between fighting business and fighting the Nazis.[86]

Baruch's comprehensive program for industrial mobilization had anticipated the inflation dilemma now confronting New Dealers. Consistently he had advocated plans that included stockpiling strategic materials as a hedge against their rising prices, higher taxes to mitigate consumer demand, and price controls—inflation restraints that would have made labor's wage demands unnecessary. The price conundrum besetting the White House in the fall of 1941 was a result of what administration economist Isador Lubin called "our failure to control the cost of living at an earlier date." On the other hand, although he saw no immediate need for price controls in 1940, Baruch had urged the National Defense Council's Advisory Commission to prepare plans "to adjust prices when necessary." Yet Brookings Institution economists preferred a free market to the administrative headaches of controls. Baruch was not in the least disturbed by the paradox of New Dealers defending free markets while he demanded government intervention. After all, he reasoned, when the government intervened in the marketplace as a massive purchaser of defense materials, the law of supply and demand no longer functioned normally anyway, and therefore Washington's controls were in the public interest.[87] For Baruch, maintenance of a stable price structure during a war was a sine qua non for victory.

The prices businessmen could charge in 1941 outraced wages demanded by their workers. Although the government worried about the defense program's rising costs, it was handcuffed by a business-labor consensus favoring voluntary cooperation. Baruch's sermons on across-the-board price controls endeared him to few people. When the navy attempted to check its labor costs, Baruch lectured Frank Knox, "Nothing could be more unfair or unreasonable than to put a ceiling over wages, unless you put a ceiling over the things which the workers buy with their wages. And, if you put a ceiling over shipworkers' wages, why not over the wages of other people and the things they buy with their wages?" With prices increasing at about 1 percent per month in 1941, the administration began to pay closer attention to the problem. Even then, the administration had grasped the relationship of priorities to prices too late to prevent unnecessarily high prices. In the words of the Bureau of the Budget's history of the war, "Ideally, a general ceiling should have been issued early in 1941, coincident with the development of priorities machinery for dividing up supplies of scarce raw materials."[88]

Organized labor had resisted price controls. In response to an invitation from Baruch, OPM director and CIO labor leader Sidney Hillman, OPACS chief Leon Henderson, OPACS economist John Hamm, OPACS counsel David Ginsberg, and White House aide Wayne Coy conferred with him at his Carlton Hotel suite in April. The conferees took three positions on controls. At the extremes were Hillman and Baruch. According to Ginsburg, Hillman wanted no stabilization of wages, a stand he made "specific, emphatic and unshakeable." Baruch also would not compromise on excluding wages in any price control bill, although he stressed that he could not endorse a freeze that prevented "any upward adjustments" in the lower wage brackets. The OPACS leaders took a middle position that conceded to Baruch the economic and political logic of including wages in any price control package but sided with Hillman in support of voluntary cooperation to stabilize wages until blanket controls could no longer be postponed. Importantly, however, Henderson, Hamm, and Ginsburg felt that prices and wages should be separately administered. That contradicted Baruch's dictum that any price control bill that did not include "all goods, services, wages, rents—everything!" had to fail.[89]

Of course, Baruch considered the administration's September price control bill "piecemeal." The outburst on the White House steps was unfortunate for him because, he said, "I do not want to appear as a disgruntled advocate of anything." He genuinely sought to aid OPACS in what he appreciated was a politically difficult task. But now he found himself pitted against the president. Despite his weekly luncheons with

9. According to David Ginsburg, "a newspaper photographer just happened" to come upon this group during the late summer of 1941. On his park bench "office" in Lafayette Park across from the White House, Baruch listens to Price Administrator Leon Henderson make a point while OPA counsel Ginsburg and Henderson's deputy, John E. Hamm (seated on the ground, left and right), and John Maurice Clark, then professor of economics at Columbia University, listen and look on. Note Baruch's plain high-top black shoes, which he wore and promoted as part of wartime austerity. (Courtesy Seeley G. Mudd Manuscript Library, Princeton University)

Baruch, Roosevelt at a press conference denied that he had ever heard of a Baruch plan for price controls. SPAB chairman Donald Nelson argued that comprehensive controls would be impossible to administer. Adding to the confusion of the price control struggle were the demands of farmers and their representatives for 110 percent parity, which Baruch branded "a disparity of parity." OPACS assigned its assistant administrator in charge of the price division, agricultural economist J. K. Galbraith, to explain the importance of selective price controls to farmers.[90]

Baruch was careful not to attack OPACS when he testified before the House committee. After all, Henderson in his appearance before the committee had shrewdly declared that he owed his OPACS post to Baruch's support. Also, Baruch carefully kept his dissents on a policy level, reserving his evaluations of personalities administering those policies for private conversations. He merely argued that Henderson's proposals would not stop inflation, "but may lessen" its pace. Asked at what level he thought the price structure should be stabilized, Baruch drew laughter with his response, "As far back as you think you can get away with it." Although he disliked being pinned down for a price level date, he endorsed the principle of a price rollback to levels that prevailed in the early part of 1941—"the earlier the better." He reminded the legislators that the bill's antiinflation potential was inherently limited because taxation would enervate much of the demand that hiked prices, and taxation remained the province of another committee, Ways and Means.

It was politically improbable that Baruch could win on comprehensive controls before the United States went to war. In a nation that prized its individualism, competitiveness, and liberty, Baruch had devised a total operation in the name of defense, a "practically unitary system under which all producers will cooperate, sharing trade secrets, pooling patents, resources and facilities." It amounted to nothing less than a gigantic national corporate trust justified by the threat of war. The only difference between the United States and its Fascist adversaries would be a heritage of freedom. Before Pearl Harbor, about all his proposition could accomplish would be an intensification of the struggle among interest groups to prevent antagonistic interests from winning decisive power.

The price control debates aggravated the social conflicts of the 1930s. The United States Chamber of Commerce dismissed Baruch's scheme for price controls as without justification and saved its heaviest fire for the administration's proposal, accusing it of intentions "far beyond accomplishments through price control." Like workers and farmers, businessmen wanted exemption from the stringent measures of war mobilization. Even the military was chary of price controls. Rapidly becoming a major purchaser and claimant group in the economy, the War and Navy departments also sought exemption from blanket controls on the grounds that arms development had no cost precedents. Roosevelt denied the military's request, which evidently would have benefited big business contractors. In the weeks before 7 December, Henderson argued that blanket controls were theoretically correct, should have been implemented a year before, but now threatened gargantuan administrative headaches owing to higher prices. Moreover, only the wages of selective and strategically placed workers would improve, while government spending crippled small businesses and enhanced monopolies. Taxation, he asserted, would serve as the most effective deterrent to inflation.[91]

In October the Baruch plan acquired a congressional champion. Representative Albert Gore, a Tennessee Democrat with populist inclinations, introduced his own price control bill styled upon Baruch's comprehensive plan. Likening the administration's bill to "a man who is trying to keep the grass from growing in a 10-acre lot by sitting down on it," Gore assailed it as "weak-kneed piecemeal legislation." His bill called for ceilings on wholesale prices, wages, and rents and an 8 percent limit on profits from defense contracts. Although Baruch had maintained that the only proper way to take profits out of war was through taxation, Gore apparently had little faith in the administration's and Congress's pursuit of an equitable tax bill. Without even studying Gore's measure, Baruch endorsed it and a month later sent the Tennessean a letter reaffirming his stand on blanket controls and allowing him to use it in public debate on the bill. In November the price control bill hung in limbo. By then, Baruch was advising his publicity outlets "to mention me only occasionally and refer to the Gore plan which is about what I have suggested."

The administration was on the defensive. Canada had just adopted ceilings on wages, rents, and commodities, a measure described as "virtually the same" as Baruch's plan. Henderson promptly sent aides north of the border to study their setup. The House of Representatives fell into disarray, its leadership torn between accommodating agricultural, labor, and business resistance to controls and facing the 1942 campaign amidst a possible 25 percent rise in the cost of living. Just before Thanksgiving, Baruch made a second appearance before the House Banking and Commerce Committee. This time he came under very different circumstances: that very day the House Rules Committee decided that the full House was not limited to considering the administration's bill, but was free to write its own. That move placed Gore's bill on a par with the White House's.[92]

Significantly, the House leadership was intent upon defending corporate interests. Included in the House leadership's rule was a provision that the Gore bill's section limiting defense profits to 8 percent was not to be germane to the price control debate. Also, it was rumored that the House leaders were thinking of antistrike legislation, which would effectively limit labor's bargaining power even if it won exemption of wages from controls. Conservatives were intent upon imposing their own version of controls. Baruch implored Senator Carter Glass to keep in mind that "all segments of society should be treated alike in order that the status quo remains." Assured that war would bring about enormous public and private demand, many businessmen were being won over to controls without a curb upon defense profits. Baruch's scheme for maintaining a low price structure began to look like cost control for producers rather than price control for consumers. But when the Japanese struck at Pearl Harbor, the United States still lacked both the priorities coordination and the price controls Baruch considered essential to making the enterprise of war worth the national undertaking.[93]

10. Baruch's recommendations for price controls in late 1941 are seconded by Seibel in the Richmond Times-Dispatch. (Courtesy Seeley G. Mudd Manuscript Library, Princeton University)

"OUR OWN LACK OF PLANNING
MIGHT WELL WRECK US"

Baruch, like most successful public men, had based his whole career upon his ability to anticipate future developments and his commitment to influencing them. Thus, he was both a speculator and a promoter even where watersheds like war and peace were concerned. He anticipated war and did his best to prepare his country for it adequately. Moreover, even as he publicized his idea that war ought to be based on an orderly and equitably planned mobilization, he stressed the relationship of war policies to the nature of the postwar world. Well-conceived preparations for war were well-conceived preparations for peace. He approved of Franklin Roosevelt's intent upon controlling forces, to the extent that domestic politics allowed him to, in order to protect American power and interests. Roosevelt had demonstrated that within the limits of politics he possessed a philosophy of history that, though not always compatible with Baruch's, was essentially committed to upholding Wilsonian liberal values throughout the world.

At heart, Baruch was an elitist in the defense of an established order against leveling forces at home and abroad, an individualist and capitalist resisting the forces of collectivism and socialism, a nationalist in quest of an American open door in the world against imperialist rivals. He recognized that "the masses have been on the trek. They have decided they are going to have a larger share of what is being produced and enjoyed in the world." It was a phenomenon that took different forms in Germany, Italy, Russia, England, and America, but whatever its form the response had to be a promised improvement in standards of living. That is how Baruch interpreted the New Deal. Confronted with a crisis that threatened to topple the system, Roosevelt had "met it well." Perhaps haste and politics had intruded in the expenditure of government funds for public works, but much of the money "was well spent." Roosevelt had shrewdly integrated European collectivism with American individualism on a scale never before attempted. The most unfortunate consequences of the New Deal were the growing number of Americans who did not work for a profit-making enterprise and the New Deal's tendency to engender class conflict or fears of it. Still, Baruch appreciated Roosevelt's efforts to preserve American individualism and even to extend its frontiers. By the end of the 1930s, however, the world had reached a crossroads between state and private enterprise. Baruch was not an inflexible ideologue; his concept of free enterprise valued an interested role for government—a public investment function in "self-liquidating enterprises" and in societal needs like roads, schools, and hospitals. "Indeed," he said, "I think we were too parsimonious in previous spending in reference to great public enterprises."[94]

As he had in his Wilsonian days, Baruch in 1940 subscribed to the overproduction thesis. The greatest dangers America faced in the world were the German and Japanese ambitions to close markets to other nations through conquest and economic warfare. "Here we have mass production with consumption, superior skilled labor and [business] organizing ability. We can make things in quantity and quality and sell them cheaper than anybody else." But the totalitarian nations sought to deprive the United States of overseas buyers and raw materials. With its growth-oriented society, America had little choice but to "produce and produce and sell and sell." All it wanted were rules of "fair competition and only that part of the [world] trade which rightly belongs to her." It did not need all markets, but Baruch was particularly anxious over the German and Japanese invasion of Latin American markets for raw materials. As Henry Wallace observed of Baruch, "He thinks Tropical America is our new frontier." Because American exporters had to work harder during the war to find their customers, Baruch urged upon the administration a tax credit for them. But even that would not be enough governmental assistance if American manufacturers lacked vital raw materials or were compelled to pay exorbitant prices for them. To sustain output at low prices, and to protect industry's capacity to produce for war when American lines of trade had been disrupted by the Axis, Americans would have to resort to producing synthetics. That would frustrate the Axis design. America had the technical ability and manufacturing capacity to produce large amounts of materials at low prices that would drive Axis products from any free markets in the world. Then, Baruch promised, America "will make puny the efforts of those who will destroy the opportunities of the whole world for a place in the sun. We will create and make substitutes that will make it impossible for other nations to live against that competition."[95]

The chief dilemma lay in the fact that competition would give way to war and all parties would be losers whatever its outcome. As the defense mobilization accelerated in 1940–41, Baruch insistently cautioned that preparations be made consistent with American enterprise's postwar interests: "All must be done without losing sight of our condition after the war—not merely to fight and win the war, but also to survive it economically, with a low price structure and an industrial system dislocated to a minimum degree, well prepared for post-war conditions in the international markets." To emerge from the war with a high price structure would be "a terrific blow at the capitalistic system." No matter what was done, Americans had to anticipate that "when this show is over, there are going to be difficult social and economic conditions to face." But the degree of hardship would depend upon the foresight of American leadership. It had to demand of industry sacrifices in order to preserve the price structure necessary to compete against the "sweated" labor products of other nations. Baruch argued for enlightened industrial self-restraint in profit making. Profiteering could always withstand future congressional investigations, just as World War I's "merchants of death" emerged from the Nye investigations with nothing lost save honor. More serious was the inflation encouraged by profiteering. "Except for human slaughter and maiming and all that goes with them," Baruch told the House Banking and Commerce Committee, "inflation is the most destructive of the consequences of war." He tied America's influence at the peace table to its capacity to command world trade:

> If ours is a high-price structure the lean and gaunt nations, which have learned to do without, even if defeated, will be able to undersell us in the markets of the world. The economic and social dislocations that would result in this country might destroy all the freedoms for which we say we are fighting.
>
> With a low price structure, America can hold her own and demand as a price for economic collaboration just terms of peace.
>
> If we have such a low-price structure we can insist upon living standards everywhere being raised so that our own shall not be destroyed and we shall not be forced to undersell everybody. . . .
>
> But with a high-price structure we shall be powerless to write a peace treaty that will protect our own standards of living from attack by other nations. We will lose our foreign markets and to protect our home workers will have to take refuge in artificially high trade barriers.
>
> The disparities between various segments of our economy, between farmers producing for export markets and industries producing for home markets, will be aggravated. We will be unable to provide for full employment for all our workers. Such a situation created by our own lack of planning might well wreck us.[96]

To those who argued that Baruch's chief concern was the prosperity of the investor class, he responded that the accuser knew not how inflation worked or whom it affected. Workers would not be better off after the war if prices rose sharply. They would have to spend a higher percentage of their income on necessities. Social services would either be curtailed or cost the taxpayer more. Because most of those services were supported by taxes paid by modest homeowners and regressive taxes paid by consumers, the rich lost less to inflation than did the lower classes.[97]

Baruch articulated his interpretation of the public interest. However, the mobilization issue exacerbated social conflict instead of occasioning the consensus for planning he sought. The brief debate over the War Resources Board had been the opening round in this fight, and the *Wall Street Journal* left no doubt in its readers' minds that socialistic New Dealers had won it. So the principal issue from the start was who would plan governmental expansion. Unavoidably the government had to embark upon industrial enterprises. Cut off from raw material sources such as rubber, faced with plant capacities inadequate for the production of all the aluminum and other metals needed in armaments, lacking enough plants and shipyards to produce all the planes and ships needed by Britain, the Soviets, and the United States, Washington had no choice but to launch great enterprises that dwarfed all other undertakings if the United States truly were to become an arsenal of democracy. Beginning in August 1941, the leadership for this enormous expansion was bestowed upon the Reconstruction Finance Corporation (RFC) under the command of Baruch's crafty Wilsonian comrade, Texas banker Jesse Jones. The RFC created a subsidiary for the task, the Defense Plants Corporation. Jones's responsibility would be to finance the building of the rubber, aluminum, aircraft, and other plants needed for the conduct of war. As the conversion to war production commenced in 1940–41, so did the debate over reconversion to peace. Both the New Dealers and the businessmen who came to Washington for the defense effort appreciated this. In the words of an OPACS memorandum, *This power to determine the growth and survival of American industry is tremendous. It is unquestionably the most far-reaching authority which the Government will require during the defense program.*[98]

For the time being the unproductive enterprise of war was in public hands, but New Dealers and businessmen were not unmindful that these same facilities could find productive use in peace. But who would decide who would control that peacetime production? Would it be the public developer or the private operator? Appraising the situation in January 1941, the chairman of the Army-Navy Munitions Board, Wall Street broker Ferdinand Eberstadt, wrote: "There is no question that government funds are handling the major part of the expansion financing of the defense program. This means that at the same time the government will have to liquidate its holdings or take over the plants after the [war]. . . . Consideration of a program in this connection would seem to me to constitute an important part of preparation for return to a peacetime economy. A lot of manufacturers are thinking, and some talking, about the time when they will purchase these plants for a song."

However, what disturbed Eberstadt and other speculators was the very real possibility that American industry would not be able to find productive postwar employment for these plants because of insufficient customers for their aluminum, aircraft, and synthetic rubber. The maintenance of postwar international stability would depend upon the ability of every nation to find productive uses for its plants in such a way as to raise the standards of living for its people. The thoughtful Eberstadt, who had participated in the European debt negotiations of 1929, noted in 1941:

The present world situation is due to the fact that neither Democracy, nor Fascism, nor Bolshevism, nor Naziism for that matter, have been able to use their equipment in such a way as to sustain and raise the standard of living in [*sic*] their respective populations. . . . [The basic problem will be] turning over into productive use and occupation at the end of the war, the hundreds of millions of people and the mass of facilities which have been employed in non-productive use. The permanent answer to this lies along the lines of raising the general standard of living.

Just as American production would decide the war, so must it decide the terms of peace. The United States would assert its economic might to decide prices in the markets of the world and thereby assure that the world's living standards were no lower than the American. "It is a job similar to what was done at the Conference of Vienna," wrote Eberstadt. "If we are able at the end of this conflict, to do as well [as the victors at the Conference of Vienna], we need not be concerned about . . . criticism which will be heaped upon us a century later."[99]

Planning of the economy after the war required control of it during the war, a necessity that intensified the conflict between the respective partisans of public and private enterprise. Priority control meant nothing less than determining the extent of economic concentration after the war or, in the words of an OPACS memorandum written in February 1941, "what firms and industries shall continue to exist and prosper and what firms and industries shall be eliminated and reduced." In the Departments of War and the Navy, the leadership beginning in 1940 was dominated by Wall Street lawyers and brokers and the planning was naturally corporate-minded. They disdained the pluralistic approach of the lawyers, economists, union leaders, and civil servants in OPACS, the White House, and the other departments. Undersecretary of the Navy Forrestal, for instance, saw Leon Henderson's insistence upon all-out mobilization as a power play in behalf of the advocates of public enterprise and hoped "that his activities will be brought under proper control."

In this conflict, Baruch presented himself as a noncombatant whose sole interest was a patriotic prosecution of the war mobilization. Before Pearl Harbor he appeared plausibly sympathetic to the New Dealers' perspectives on most issues except controls on wages. Like them, he sought a greater mobilization effort than was deemed economically desirable by the big business leadership in OPM and in the military departments. As recalcitrant as it had been in 1917–18, big business resisted the enormous planning that went into Baruch's priorities and price controls. No New Dealer could decry "business as usual" as effectively as Baruch. Harold Ickes put it well: "A man like Baruch can go on the witness stand and insist that all profits really ought to be taxed out, where a more radical person would only arouse the feeling that he was attacking business as such."[100] The fight against Fascism in 1941 was the fight for the New Deal.

But following 7 December it was no longer a New Deal war. With national survival at stake, all-out mobilization had to prevail. Big business had to be enlisted in the effort. Then the New Dealers and the business mobilizers switched roles, the New Dealers fearing the end of competition and the concomitantly enhanced position of big corporations, while the business mobilizers argued that there was no such thing as too much mobilization. Through it all, Baruch remained constant in his advocacy of a comprehensive and consolidated mobilization, thereby becoming an effective ally of Wall Street comrades in the military departments. More than ever, Baruch himself would be an issue in the bureaucratic politics of Washington.

CHAPTER EIGHT
PARK BENCH STATESMAN

Incredible as it would have seemed to Baruch a few years before, the United States entered World War II without his official guidance. Not only was he not a member of the mobilization apparatus, but Pearl Harbor had been struck by the Japanese at a time when the war effort was still run by an unwieldy committee called SPAB. By then, Baruch had come to accept and even prefer his role as a bureaucratic busybody. It did not surprise him when Roosevelt created the War Production Board (WPB) in early 1942 with only a perfunctory courtesy request to him to recommend its chairman. Submitting five names, Baruch carefully omitted everyone currently identified with the mobilization setup, including the head of SPAB, Donald Nelson. But Roosevelt chose Nelson as the Baruch of World War II. At least the seventy-one-year-old former mobilizer could take comfort that the president finally had conferred upon a businessman the supreme authority the task demanded. Moreover, Nelson wisely deferred to Baruch. Not only would Baruch's visits and advice be welcome at the WPB throughout 1942, but Nelson would go out of his way to spend some weekends listening to his voice of experience. However, it remained to be seen whether the Baruchian wisdom would be heeded.

Baruch was everyone's consultant, but nowhere in the capital was he more welcome than at the War Department. With Roosevelt's blessing, General Levin H. Campbell, Jr., chief of army ordnance, appointed him a member of his industrial advisory staff, thereby involving him with procurement. With three prominent industrialists, Baruch served on the service's board of directors, was consulted upon its management, advised of its problems, but made responsible for nothing. It amounted to a license to be an insider. He was grateful for that.[1]

His principal means of public visibility lay in his continued demands

for price control. Because the government had become the major consumer of production for the war period, it behooved Washington to take
price-fixing authority from the mobilization agency, as had been the case
in 1917–18. But with inflation pressing steadily ahead, Roosevelt remained reluctant to take steps encompassing the entire pricing system.
The Office of Price Administration (OPA—so renamed after relinquishing
civilian supply to the WPB) announced the General Maximum Price
Regulation ("General Max"), which froze all retail prices at their highest
price levels of March 1942, a step Baruch endorsed as a partial effort at
stabilization. In general, Baruch remained through early 1942 strictly a
kibitzer on war administration. A *Fortune* magazine poll of May 1942
said that only 9.9 percent of its respondents listed Baruch as a public
figure who should be given an important position in Roosevelt's war
administration. Seven other men were preferred over him.[2]

Nevertheless, in August, Baruch again became the center of national
attention when the president announced that the speculator would head a
committee chosen to study the nation's rubber shortage for the purpose of
recommending remedial measures. Along with Baruch, James B. Conant
and Karl T. Compton, presidents of Harvard University and Massachusetts Institute of Technology, would determine "such action as will best
produce the synthetic rubber necessary for our total war effort, including
essential civilian use, with a minimum interference with the production
of other weapons of war." Moreover, Roosevelt vetoed a bill for producing rubber from grain-based alcohol, denouncing the creation of a
synthetic rubber industry "by legislative fiat." Thus, Roosevelt served
notice that this vital aspect of mobilization and stabilization would be
controlled by the White House by commissioning Baruch to lead a "quick
but adequate survey of the entire rubber question."[3]

For many reasons, Baruch was a logical choice for the assignment.
Since 1903 he had been involved with the quest for a western hemisphere
source of rubber. He had possessed knowledge of the strategic value of
rubber and other raw materials since 1917. Also, except for State Department economic adviser Herbert Feis, there was no earlier or more insistent
advocate of stockpiling rubber in the 1930s than Baruch. He had been
active in promoting the rubber-for-cotton barter arrangement with Whitehall in 1939. Politically he enjoyed the confidence of Congress. He was
an experienced hand in delicate public relations. It was a stratagem that
appealed greatly to Baruch: the committee possessed a quasi-judicial
mandate, impossible to achieve in peacetime, to rule on an economic
conundrum that apparently defied ordinary legal channels—it was a high
court of commerce of three wise men!

The rubber crisis of 1942 bore several similarities to the nitrate crisis
of 1917–18. In both instances the United States confronted a shortage of
a raw material essential to the war effort that could not be produced

domestically except by a synthetic process requiring a large initial federal investment. In both wars the Germans were prepared to produce the material synthetically. Both situations involved agricultural interests who exercised their influence via the legislative process. But in World War II's rubber crisis there were significant differences relating to the farm bloc in Congress: now farmers sought to be producers, not consumers; and the outcome would show that Roosevelt outwitted agrarian claims more successfully than had Wilson.

America's automobile culture made the United States the world's greatest buyer of rubber grown in colonial regions of the world. The War Department showed an interest in the strategic value of rubber in 1930 when Baruch's most apt pupil in the military, Dwight Eisenhower, urged the growing of guayule rubber in the western hemisphere. But interest in this highly adaptive strain of crude rubber continued to lag despite Baruch's best promotional efforts. As Nazi Germany embarked upon a course of self-sufficiency via production of synthetic rubber, both the army and Baruch began to agitate for American purchase of stockpiles from an Anglo-Dutch cartel.

But neither the British nor the Congress appreciated the strategic significance of rubber stockpiles. The British saw the Americans as customers rather than allies; U.S. stockpiles could be inimical to their commercial interests. And the Congress proved more concerned with the expense than with the preparedness value of stockpiles. Guayule rubber and synthetic processes were unfeasible because the cartel's rubber was so much cheaper. Besides, the leading synthetic process would have violated patent rights Standard Oil had conferred upon a German corporation: business came first. While the Soviets produced their own synthetics, the United States remained a good customer of the cheaper British crude production. By the late 1930s, the State Department pursued a stockpile of British rubber, the War Department sought a synthetic alternative, and the Agriculture Department encouraged guayule production in Latin America. But not until the cotton-rubber exchange of 1939 did America accumulate rubber for strategic reasons.[4]

The imminence of war made the deal possible. The British horde of rubber and its high price seemed less important to Whitehall than America's capacity to be an arsenal of democracy. In 1940, Congress created the Rubber Reserve Company, a subsidiary of Jones's Reconstruction Finance Corporation, charged with accumulating America's stockpile of crude rubber. Although part of the Rubber Reserve's responsibility was the erection of plants for synthetic rubber production, Jones had little to show the public a year later.

At a time when the State, War, and Agriculture departments pressed for swift development of the nation's rubber resources for strategic reasons, Jones moved with the deliberation of a banker confronted by a risk-laden borrower. He wanted the rubber companies to finance their own expansion, and they wanted his Rubber Reserve to do the job with capital from the Treasury. Meanwhile the British were aghast at the prospect of American construction of synthetic rubber plants, which presaged the ultimate loss of the American market for British natural rubber. The British encouraged Jones's trepidations that the plants would involve government financial losses before a competitive product could be manufactured. But the British ran into shipping difficulties in early 1941 and could not deliver the natural rubber Jones counted upon. At the same time, 1941 proved to be the best automobile production year since 1929, and civilian markets competed with the military stockpile. The increased civilian demand drove the rubber price up beyond what Jones's company wanted to pay. Finally, the Japanese advance into southeast Asia imperiled control of the west's chief growing area. Jesse Jones had bet on natural rubber instead of synthetic plants. "Our friend Jesse is going to come in for a good deal of criticism on that rubber thing," Baruch observed in May 1941. "The [synthetic rubber] factories should already have been built."[5]

That may have been the case, but a variety of interests encouraged Jones to focus upon natural rubber production. Standard Oil threatened suits against Goodrich and other rubber manufacturers who dared to infringe upon its synthetic rubber patents. Baruch, while supporting synthetic production in the United States, encouraged Jones to grow guayule rubber in Latin America.[6] Come Pearl Harbor, the rubber situation would finally earn the public attention it deserved, and then the blame for its insufficiency would fall comfortably upon Jones's shoulders.

The impending rubber shortage exploded upon Congress and the White House in the spring of 1942. In May the president labeled it "one of the most serious materials shortages which this nation now faces." The Truman committee called for the creation of a rubber czar who would "take all necessary action to provide such rubber as is necessary to the war program." Senator James E. Murray of Montana assailed the oil companies for "outrageous trafficking with the enemy" by preserving a patent monopoly that inhibited synthetic rubber development for war. Agricultural interests, encouraged by Vice-President Wallace and the internationally reknowned chemist Dr. Chaim Weizmann, called for rubber development from alcohol instead of oil. And Petroleum Administrator Harold L. Ickes, in an effort to forestall gasoline rationing, pushed for rubber conservation as a means of extending its supply. With so many political pressures and economic interests involved, the White House began to look for a solution worthy of Solomon.[7]

Simultaneously with expanding the supply, the administration had to curb the demand for rubber. Rationing the civilian supply of rubber was the subject of a war administrators' conference at the White House on 5

June. The president began by reporting that there had been "a considerable protest" against the prospect of gasoline rationing. Public opinion,
he noted, was confused and in need of education on conditions. Speaking
for the WPB, Nelson called for a mandatory program for rationing gasoline. But Roosevelt discerned political dangers in a coercive program
for which the public had not been prepared. Ickes, admitting that he
approached rationing "from the point of view of a singed cat," allowed
that if the WPB were correct on its figures concerning America's supply
of rubber, then rationing was desirable. But the president had not yet
crossed a *voluntary* rationing program off his list of alternatives and was
searching for means with which "to lay the groundwork with the public";
after all, asking Americans to change their driving habits "was so much
political dynamite."[8]

The next day, Baruch called the president's press secretary, Steve Early.
He probably knew of the meeting, for he blamed everyone in the war
administration who had allowed the responsibility for rubber to be laid
at the doorstep of the White House. He recommended that Roosevelt
appoint Justice Jimmy Byrnes or Justice William O. Douglas "or some
one of their caliber to investigate the rubber-gas situation—[and] that
the investigator report and make his recommendations to you."[9] The
scheme had great appeal: it shifted the initiative for a solution away from
the White House while keeping it away from Congress. The Supreme
Court had the aura of being above politics, and a pronouncement for
gasoline rationing from its ranks would carry weight with the public.

However, according to James MacGregor Burns, Roosevelt "seemed
to lack his usual sure grasp of a policy question." When he asked Chief
Justice Harlan Fiske Stone to lead the rubber survey for him, Stone
declined. Perhaps Roosevelt did not want to jeopardize the popularity of
Byrnes and Douglas on the sensitive rationing issue. Rumor constantly
had it that their talents would not long be wasted on the Court, that he
would find places for them in the war administration as needs developed.
Meanwhile the Congress forced his hand by passage of a bill for setting
up an independent rubber supply agency to be headed by a czar appointed
by the president with Senate approval—and mandated to produce synthetic rubber from alcohol.[10] Not only would this bill detach the rubber
question from the WPB, which had authority for its supply, but, as Ickes
fretted, "It could create hell generally and the worst of the bill is that it
could set a precedent by which Congress might set up any number of
separate authorities with respect to the war." Ickes feared the loss of his
control over petroleum; Roosevelt feared the loss of his control over the
entire war effort. It had to be vetoed.

All that remained to be decided was who had a reputation secure
enough—or who was expendable enough—to take charge of promoting
gasoline rationing. On 29 July, Ickes phoned the president and proposed

that he commandeer Bernie for this job. I pointed out that Bernie had the confidence of the people. He isn't a government official and he commands the respect of Congress on the whole more than any man in public life. He has far more prestige than most men in public life. He also knows how to get results. The President thought well of the suggestion and asked me what I thought of associating with Bernie President Conant of Harvard and Lyman J. Briggs, Director of the Bureau of Standards. I thought that this would work out all right.

Roosevelt was so far ahead of Ickes that he already had considered whom he wanted to surround Baruch. By 3 August "it was in the wind" throughout Washington that Roosevelt would ask Baruch, Conant, and Compton to undertake the rubber survey. The next day, Roosevelt sent Baruch a handwritten note saying, "Because you are 'an ever present help in time of trouble' will you 'do it again'?" And then he added, as if to remind Baruch that the idea had been his, "You would be better than all the Supreme Court together!" That evening, Baruch went to Washington.[11] Then came the 6 August veto and the White House announcement of the Baruch committee.

A little over a month later the Rubber Survey Committee made its report. Its deliberations, findings, and recommendations ought never to have been in doubt. Some New Dealers in the WPB suspected that the report would recommend an agency independent of Nelson's jurisdiction. But that would have been out of character for Baruch, whatever his doubts concerning Nelson's abilities. He was committed to centralizing authority for all production with Nelson. In July, on the matter of raw materials, Baruch had made it plain to Nelson that "you must be the boss and when you say anything about rubber, tin or anything else, it just has to go. . . . Otherwise the authority you have been given will be worthless and had better not have been given." The Rubber Survey Report, although it criticized both the WPB and the Rubber Reserve Company for mistakes that brought on the crisis, recommended that all production authority be put into the hands of a rubber administrator who would be appointed by the WPB chairman, from whom he would draw his authority. The Baruch report applauded all efforts to expand rubber supplies, but its first recommendation was for expanded capacity in the existing synthetic plants, with the construction of another by 1944, using petroleum as its raw material. "Charge off the capital expenditures [for producing raw materials] to the cost of the war," he had advised Nelson. "If we do that, the cost of [raw materials] . . . will be low enough to permit us to compete with the rest of the world and *we will have it in this country*." No longer would the United States be a "have-not nation in rubber."[12]

On the toughest political issue of 1942 the committee was unequivocal.

Written by Samuel Lubell but sounding very much like a Baruch sermon, the report exhorted the nation on gasoline rationing in order to conserve rubber. It recommended a speed limit of thirty-five miles per hour, reduction of the average mileage per year from 6,700 to 5,000, and enforced rationing of gasoline on the nationwide basis. It assumed the role of a national conscience, one that suited Baruch perfectly: "Let there be no doubt that only actual needs, not fancied wants, can, or should, be satisfied. To dissipate our stocks of rubber is to destroy one of our chief weapons of war. We have the choice!"

Roosevelt wasted little time in invoking rationing with the moral authority of the Baruch report. Yet the president seemed fearful of its political repercussions; he denied to reporters that rationing required new legislative authority. He scolded newspapers for headlines that proclaimed the imminence of gasoline rationing, preferring to call it "mileage rationing."[13]

Generally speaking, the report rallied the nation behind rationing, as it was supposed to do. Of course not everyone liked it. The agricultural interests in the Senate complained that it skirted the issues raised in the bill vetoed by the president, but they conceded that sentiment was now with the White House. Chaim Weizmann believed that the Baruch committee had been intimidated by the oil industry and that alcohol could have produced more rubber six months sooner. He disparaged Baruch as a man "so immersed in his own vanity and in the past that it was impossible to make him see the light." Roosevelt swiftly invoked almost all the recommendations. Ickes took special delight that the report, without naming names, "certainly kicked the daylights out of Jesse Jones and his Rubber Reserve."[14] For that there was more than a little gratitude among war administrators who were relieved not to be scapegoated and happy to see a finger directed against the tightfisted and crusty Jones.

Public opinion swung sharply toward gasoline rationing. As a political scientist observed, "the incantations of a prestigious authority" had been invoked to win public acceptance of a policy on which it had been sharply divided. The American Institute of Public Opinion (the Gallup Poll) asked Americans before and after the Baruch report, "Are you in favor of nation-wide gasoline rationing to conserve tires?" The results were:

	Favor	Oppose	Undecided
Before Baruch Report	49%	44%	7%
After Baruch Report	73%	22%	5%

Rumblings against rationing were not stifled, but complaints were seldom voiced against the report. In fact, the complainers, especially numerous in the west where distances were long and dependence upon gasoline was great, frequently demanded a "Baruch report" on their concerns.* Hardly had the rubber report been made public when grocers were calling for a similar investigation of "chaotic" conditions in the food industry. Both Baruch and the White House deflected such requests in favor of letting the agencies in charge perform. Yet the public relations value of the "Baruch committee" blue-ribbon court solution could not be denied. The Baruch committee had succeeded in its purpose. Nearly a year later, Vice-President Wallace reminded Roosevelt that "the Baruch Committee . . . met the issues, restored public confidence, and relieved you of what threatened to be continuing embarrassment."[15]

THE LIBERTY SHOE IN WORLD WAR II

The Baruch committee on rubber served to mobilize opinion for conservation and rationing in wartime better than any law or executive order. That was as Baruch and the president had intended. But beneath the public acceptance of gasoline rationing for conservation of rubber raged a policy controversy concerning the principle of rationing itself. That Baruch himself was conscious of the internal debate is evidenced by his comment to an old detractor, Felix Frankfurter: "So many men are so anxious to carry forward their own ideas whether they be economic or social that they lose out entirely. The first thing to do is to win the war."[16] The policy debate was related not directly to the problem of winning the war, but rather to the nature of the peacetime economy. Baruch was in the midst of a power and policy struggle for direction of the home front.

In war, he believed, the military ought not to be the only Spartans. If Baruch had his way, civilians would share hardships nearly to the extent of wearing uniforms and consuming rations. Something of this is suggested by his 1942 proposal "that no family or home operate more than one car." It was not included in the report and we can only conjecture why. Certainly for the overwhelming majority of American families the idea would have worked no hardship if it had been implemented. What it promised was the reduction of American life during war to its simplest needs and the symbolic equalization of civilian and military sacrifice. Sacrifice there would be if U.S. military needs, or the needs of allies, competed with those of civilians. Noting that materials shortages had

*Immediately following the release of the report, another Gallup Poll found that 67 percent of all Americans thought that this committee or one like it ought to investigate other domestic problems related to the war effort; 13 percent opposed this method. However, another question revealed that only 37 percent had read or heard anything about the report.

developed in the war economy, the rubber report urged "conservation, inventory control, standardization, and simplification," in the industrial system.[17]

The recommendations were distinctly Baruch's. They came directly out of the War Industries Board plans of July 1918. At that time the WIB's Priorities Division had served notice to America's industries that wherever shortages of materials, facilities, or labor existed, procedures of conservation, substitution, inventory control, standardization, and simplification were to be followed. This came back to the "essentiality" dispute of the First World War: whatever could not be justified as essential to the war effort or civilian needs was liable to curtailment for the duration. In the case of the clothing industry, whose product went for European needs as well as American, priorities planners had dreams of restricting manufacturers to ten models of men's suits per season in order to effect a saving of 12 to 15 percent in yardage. Also, packaging would be simplified and colors standardized. Baruch's planners honed in on the shoe industry in particular:

> A very exhaustive investigation was made here, far-reaching plans inaugurated, and schedules issued. The schedule provided that shoe manufacturers should be restricted to three colors—black, white, and one shade of tan. New lasts were forbidden; heights of shoes were limited; and certain other features requiring an unnecessary amount of leather were eliminated. . . . This schedule effected savings in leather not only in stock carried by retail stores but in shoes standing in the homes. It saved capital, packing boxes, labor, and transportation in amounts very large. . . . One tanner reduced his lines from 81 colors to 3 colors. Most manufacturers reduced their styles by about two-thirds, and retail stores by greater amounts.[18]

Standardization and simplification during the First World War threatened to straitjacket—or Mao jacket—the American fashion industry. The Model T had made inroads on Seventh Avenue by WIB fiat. War had made Baruch an arbiter of fashion, and he had ruled that design was a waste of resources. As the industrial mobilization plan of 1931 noted, "Had the war gone on another year, our whole civil population would have gradually emerged (as wardrobes and inventories became exhausted) in cheap but serviceable uniform." What saved the American scene from taking on this Baruchian gray quality was the Armistice. On 7 August 1918 the priorities commissioner had issued an order that any shoe manufacturer wishing a place on the preference list for fuel and transportation had better take the pledge to reduce his output to styling approved by the WIB. Moreover, the WIB thought carefully about a single-style "liberty shoe." The shoe manufacturers fought that liberty-limiting proposal, and finally settled for regulations that stipulated four different categories of shoes and prices.[19]

Baruch, who wore black high-topped shoes, espoused the liberty shoe in 1918 with almost evangelical enthusiasm. It conformed with the spirit of equal sacrifice among all classes that symbolized the war to make the world safe for democracy. But Baruch was too practical a man to undertake such a monumental task as standardization solely as a gesture of solidarity with the men in the trenches. Obviously demand had something to do with savings inherent in the liberty shoe scheme. Notwithstanding Napoleonic maxims, armies march on their feet as well as their stomachs. Leather was exhausted at a more rapid rate than ever, and much of this good American cowhide was needed for European feet as well. Were these the only considerations, however, it is doubtful that Baruch would have sought anything but expansion of the industry's output. What made any risky enterprise worth the effort was *price*, and so it was with the liberty shoe.

It was a cheap shoe. The public paid only for it—not for the myriad of styles, colors, and lasts also produced, or the packages and advertising that helped sell it. Advertising and salesmen created "unreasonable demands" for which "the public ultimately pays the bill." Like a "small is better" tract of the 1970s, the WIB report argued that Americans had to reduce waste in order to improve the quality of their lives: "We may well draw from this war experience a lesson to be applied to peace, by providing some simple machinery for eliminating wasteful trade practices which increase prices without in the remotest degree contributing to the well-being of the people." It is also well to remember that this report was written during the roller-coaster years of 1920–21, when a brutal inflation dissolved into a major postwar depression. At the peak of the inflation, Baruch publicly recalled the liberty shoe experiment and wished anew for the industrial planning that stabilized shoe prices under government supervision, "rather than unnecessarily multiplying [shoe styles and colors] to appeal to the fads and fancies of a consuming public prodigal in their expenditures."[20]

Was the liberty shoe a genuine expression of Baruch's concern for the American standard of living? Partly so, to be sure, but to some extent that living standard depended upon customers overseas. The WIB price-fixers were keenly aware of Great Britain's efforts to stabilize its costs of living, both to satisfy its workers' demands for better wages and to find overseas markets in the postwar world. Only Washington's arbitration had kept U. S. wages somewhat ahead of prices during 1917–18. Price stabilization was required for the sake of both domestic harmony and postwar overseas opportunities. Baruch had somewhat patronizingly lectured shoe industry representatives on their shortsightedness in resisting conservation measures. WIB policies were developed not only with the wartime expediency in mind, he had told them, but with a view toward "protecting the various industries so that they will be in a position to speedily readjust themselves. . . . Perhaps I am entirely too radical in this," Baruch flattered himself, "but I believe we are going to get further with the public and get a bit further with the large masses and I believe we will greatly help the war program if you will stabilize the price of shoes and standardize the styles."[21]

The liberty shoe embodied the principle of rationing. Baruch really did not advocate a single type of shoe for all; he believed that four categories of shoes were more tolerable than one. Less than three weeks before Pearl Harbor he revived his prescription of leather rationing for stabilizing the cost of living. He argued that the current supply of shoes should be exhausted and then "only the standardized shoes made on government specifications would be sold. This step should be taken now in order to break the continuity of rising prices for the bare necessities." His solution to potential shortages in commodities like leather and the concomitant rise in prices was conservation through standardization and simplification of products. These essentials could not be done without, so they had to be stretched.[22]

Although the Bureau of the Budget and OPA recognized the definition of priorities for civilian supply as imperative, some doubt remained in the White House. But on 27 April 1942, when Roosevelt outlined for the Congress a seven-point economic stabilization program, he included civilian rationing; and he reaffirmed it the next day in a Fireside Chat to the nation. Calling rationing "the democratic, equitable solution" when articles or materials were scarce, the president sounded a bit like the WIB report as he warned that Americans "will have to give up many things to which we are accustomed. We shall have to live our lives with less in the way of creature comforts than we have in time of peace. Our standard of living will have to come down."[23]

It remained for the War Production Board to translate rhetoric into practice. The WPB did not favor an acute curtailment of civilian supply. OPA could not enforce price controls unless the WPB, through industrial committees, practiced production controls. In July, Baruch cajoled Nelson, "Standardization and simplification must be undertaken with more drive," and urged him to find an executive for the task. That same day he reminded OPA chief Leon Henderson of the importance of that aspect of price control, assuring him, "I think Don is going to make some changes there." Baruch wanted Nelson to get rid of Lessing Rosenwald, chief of the WPB's conservation section, but the change was not forthcoming. Neither was the extensive conservation envisioned by Baruch.[24]

The rubber crisis served to focus administration attention on the larger problem of civilian conservation. "Rationing on a large scale draws ever closer," warned a White House memorandum; "it would be more than unfortunate, for example, to repeat the history of the rubber crisis in connection with the rationing of wool clothing. Price control is in a most critical phase." In September the WPB announced restrictions upon the shoe industry that would reduce the number of shoe styles and permit only six colors and no multitoned footwear, in an effort to curtail consumer demand, conserve leather, and check price rises. However, the order would not take effect until the following spring, and other types of clothing were unaffected.[25]

Baruch was unimpressed by the WPB's limited and delayed commitment. Americans still indulged themselves in "bigger and better frills." Returning to shoes, Baruch presented his case for industrial efficiency to Roosevelt: "Simplification and standardization will result, not alone in manpower savings, but also will reduce prices and make it easier to regulate them. (Take your example of a $6 top-price shoe.)" Between Baruch and Roosevelt the matter of cheap shoes became an *idée fixe*. Several times during 1943 they discussed the concept of simplification and serviceable shoes, but it was not an issue that could be resolved by the president. "What can I do about this? Bernie is dead right," Roosevelt told Director of Economic Stabilization Jimmy Byrnes in response to a Baruch memorandum. But the president had more important things to worry about than the price of shoes.[26]

It was the province of the WPB to regulate the civilian economy. If Baruch pestered Roosevelt with the stabilization need for inexpensive shoes, it was because Nelson and the WPB gave the idea lip service. Baruch had Nelson's ear. In January 1943, Nelson told the press that he agreed with Baruch's recommendations for a wide variety of "victory" lines of goods. He had studied the WIB's plans for simplification and agreed that the WPB ought to follow a similar course; indeed, it was working on such a plan. "Take shoes as an example," Nelson said. "We know many pairs will be required for the Army, Navy, lend-lease and civilian needs. We know also the amount of leather available and the manpower and productive facilities on hand to make shoes. The simplification of styles and standardization of production methods will make it possible to turn out more civilian shoes from a given supply of raw materials than was possible a year or so ago." Although Nelson listened to Baruch, he disagreed on the need for additional conservation measures. The speculator wanted further cuts in the amount of raw materials used in manufacturing, whereas Nelson had "the feeling that not much more in the way of worthwhile savings" could be attained.

There would be no further simplification orders for the shoe industry. In May 1943 the WPB reaffirmed its position that further rationing of wearing apparel was unnecessary and that the discussion of shoe rationing only incited runs on stores and hoarding in closets. That might have ended Baruch's agitation for a "victory" line of shoes and clothing but for the fact that by autumn the WPB itself conceded that shortages of leather were evident. In early 1944 the Foreign Economic Administration reported that "our inability to get adequate supplies to foreign countries is all the more embarrassing in view of the fact that civilian consumption in the United States is at an all-time peak." It singled out footwear as an especially "critical" problem. At the same meeting OPA complained that the textile industry concentrated upon higher-priced merchandise. The army buttressed that point with the report that when it asked for bids on 170,000 uniforms, it got back bids on only a tenth of that requirement.[27]

Whatever their cost, Americans bought those higher-priced shoes because they had sufficient disposable consumer income to satisfy their tastes. America's commitments to its armed forces, Nelson assured the generals, would not be ignored because they could always be filled with mandatory orders. As Baruch had feared, the American standard of living had not been reduced, consumer prices were higher than they ought to be, and even though troops were not about to go barefoot into battle, the scarcities would affect civilians in Europe and mean higher postwar prices. Whether further simplification, as Baruch had stressed, could have averted the shortages of 1943–44 remained a moot point. In any event, planned civilian scarcities were a controversial issue in this war. But so was the entire matter of price stabilization.

KEYNES, KEYNESIANS, AND THE BARUCH PLAN FOR STABILIZATION

Simplification and conservation during the war were issues that sharpened a fundamental conflict over economic policy. At stake was the size and division of the economic pie; the debate over its portions (priorities) obscured a demand from the combined interests of disadvantaged civilians for a larger pie. Big manufacturers and the military were symbiotically earning the largest portions because only the former efficiently delivered the latter's needs. Expediency, the necessitarian view, and patriotism required that the largest allocations of materials and manpower be reserved to those in manufacturing who carried the war to the battlefields. Civilian producers and civilian consumers received the leftovers. But if the pie were enlarged, assuming a predictable military portion, liberals argued, then both the military and civilians might prosper together. Unresolved were these questions: Could the pie be enlarged? What would be the wartime and postwar price consequences of its enlargement? In 1942 no answer to the first question was a certain one, but in 1943 a consensus answered in the affirmative. However, those who took a pessimistic view on the second argued that the first question should be framed, "*Ought* the pie to be enlarged?"

For the sake of a clearer understanding, we will label the advocates of enlarging the pie "expansionists" and their opponents "stabilizers." The expansionists had a depression-bred fear that the war would offset the social gains of the New Deal. Wartime expediency put big business back in power and regimented everyone else in the name of patriotism. In order to guarantee big investment and manufacturing cooperation, the money changers and economic royalists were given places of honor. Only a "guns *and* butter" economic policy could preserve the social gains of the New Deal. The needs of small business, workers, farmers, and consumers had to be given special attention or else democratic America would emerge a postwar plutocracy. On the other hand, the stabilizers framed the proposition along the lines of "guns *or* butter." In public they disingenuously used patriotic arguments to insist upon exclusive production for the military. Privately they worried about postwar overproduction resulting from wartime-induced excess capacity. As had been the policy in 1917–18, the stabilizers would starve civilian markets in war in order to induce postwar demand. To be sure, the man who best articulated stabilization concerns was Bernard M. Baruch. On the other hand, the intellectual godfather of the expansionists was John Maynard Keynes.

This was, of course, the same economist-speculator-government official whose polemic *The Economic Consequences of the Peace* so enraged Baruch in 1920 because of its assault upon Wilson. For that slander alone, Baruch was unforgiving toward Keynes. In the 1920s and 1930s, Keynes acquired American admirers in academic circles for his attacks upon monetarist support for the gold standard and orthodox fiscal policy. The depression broadened his American following to include some well-read proponents of compensatory spending for public works. Even before the New Deal a Philadelphia publisher named J. David Stern proclaimed Keynes his authority for the notion that $5 billion spent by Washington on public works projects would have a salutary impact upon employment, federal deficits notwithstanding. Harvard law professor Felix Frankfurter was an admirer of Keynes's iconoclastic intellect, as were many of Frankfurter's disciples, who had been placed strategically throughout the New Deal structure.[28] More significant for the war period, another Harvard adherent was economist Alvin Hansen, who would join his students in policy-making positions throughout the government.

Keynes did not so much teach his adherents as rationalize what they advocated. That was the chief effect of his publication of *The General Theory of Employment, Interest and Money* in 1936. Amidst the reigning New Deal depression, it made sense that Washington ought to establish a social goal of full employment with federal spending as its economic means. In 1938, Hitler provided both the British and the American governments with an excuse for investments in job-creating defense installations. Keynesians seized the opportunity of impending war to advance the cause of public works planning that Keynes had articulated, a replacement of the stagnant peace economy with an *expansionist* defense economy.[29] In 1939, however, Britain went to war; in 1940, Keynes published a pamphlet, *How to Pay for the War*, whose principal theme was that social equity and economic efficiency in wartime economy required a stringently planned scheme for *stabilization*.

Keynes argued that the time for planned civilian expansion was past; war inspired expedient military expansion. The increased demand for materials and money called for a planned curtailment of the civilian market. Keynes's civilian product—to continue the pastry-shop metaphor—would be finite and divided beforehand:

> In peace time . . . the size of the cake depends on the amount
> of work done. But in war time the size of the cake is fixed. If we work
> harder, we can fight better. *But we must not consume more.*
> This is the elementary fact which in a democracy the man in the
> street must learn to understand if the nation is to act wisely—that
> *the size of the civilian's cake is fixed.*

Keynes prescribed austerity for Britain: "Civilian consumption at home will be equal to what is left [after expenditures for war]."[30]

In order to counter inflation, Keynes recommended broad-based compulsory savings, a drastic move that he justified socially on the grounds that a majority of the national debt would be obligated to the masses of Britons. To allow civilian consumption would invite high prices that would "be to the clear advantage of the richer class and will result in the class bearing not more, but less, than their fair share." Broad-based taxes reaching the poorest workers were fairer than the unproductive tax of inflation. A comprehensive antiinflation program would incorporate price and wage controls along with consumer rationing. Because the poor would have their purchasing power more drastically reduced than the rich without it, Keynes insisted that his plan "certainly uses the opportunity of war finance to effect a considerable re-distribution of incomes in the direction of greater equality." Wage increases would be deferred in the name of a controlled cost of living, a provision that compelled Keynes to assure trade unions that capital would not benefit from wartime social discipline.[31] Subtitled *A Radical Plan for the Chancellor of the Exchequer*, his presentation had as its most radical aspect his justification of strict social discipline in the name of social justice. Yet tory Prime Minister Winston Churchill took Keynes and his radical plan into the wartime government.

Keynes's American admirers were not ready to prescribe his restrictive diet for civilian consumers during the defense days of 1940–41. In 1940 they argued that inflation posed less of a social hazard than unused capacity in industry. Presidential economic adviser Lauchlin Currie and

OPA's Leon Henderson urged the delay of civilian restraints until the defense economy had advanced further toward full employment. That, they believed, would not come for at least another two years. Keynesians, led by Alvin Hansen, argued in early 1941 that output and employment were at only 80 percent of potential capacity, so that inflation could still be absorbed. But Hansen acknowledged that Americans could not wait until full employment to institute an antiinflation agenda: "Inflation is more serious and insidious than unemployment, and it should not be allowed to get started in any area." The time was right to consider antiinflation devices such as taxation, saving, and rationing. Hansen assured his readers that 1941's economy could handle wartime inflation "from a stronger vantage ground than in the first World War. But this fact should not cause us to relax our efforts to the utmost. Our economic structure cannot endure either deflation or inflation." Hansen's comments excited academic debate concerning the timing and choice of inflation controls, the most prescient observation coming from a future OPA deputy administrator, J. K. Galbraith, who argued "that the important decisions in price policy and fiscal policy will have to be made long before full employment is reached."[32]

Both Hansen and Galbraith were alert to the fact that political markets were more concerned with inflation than was the insular academic market. After all, Washington in 1941 had already debated the Baruch proposals for stabilization. Although the Keynesian objective of full employment was still two years away, Hansen sought to promote antiinflation planning:

> I am disposed to think that economists have not given sufficiently serious consideration to the Baruch plan of freezing prices, permitting, however, individual readjustments where these are deemed necessary or desirable. The argument made against the Baruch plan is that it interferes too much with the flexible functioning of the price system. This is true, but under war conditions admittedly the price system functions very badly, and too often in the really important areas control measures lock the stable after the horse is stolen. The Baruch method at any rate prevents the stealing of the "horse," though it may make the "horse" a little less useful than an ideal functioning of a flexible price system would make possible. I do not know whether the merits of the Baruch plan outweigh the demerits, but I do wish to suggest that it deserves more examination and consideration than economists seem to have given it thus far.[33]

In his usually evenhanded way, Hansen cautioned his fellow economists to pay attention to the speculator's Washington campaign for controls in pace with expansion. It was more than J. M. Clark could bear. Baruch's plan "has been and is being seriously examined as Hansen suggests," Clark insisted. But it was inherently inequitable: "It rests among other things upon a general wage-ceiling, which hardly accords with Hansen's expressed views, or with what has already happened to wages."[34]

Baruch probably could not have cared less whether Clark and other economists thought well of his stabilization plan or not. He was intent upon persuading Washington rather than Cambridge, Massachusetts. However, that does not mean that Keynes's proposals for wartime controls were unknown to Baruch, for an alert newspaper friend brought them to his attention. As early as April 1940, only two months after publication of *How to Pay for the War*, Baruch dismissed Keynes's proposals as "nothing more than [what] our War Industries Board has recommended time and again." Significantly, Baruch conceded grudging agreement with Keynes—or rather, conceded that Keynes's proposals agreed with Baruch's experience. As he testily put it: "The only difference [between us] is that Keynes has never had any experience but is endeavoring to improvise on what somebody else did. I consider him a very impractical and shallow fellow. Just like most of our economists in Washington, who do not have two nickels to rub against each other, yet they tell everybody how it should be done."[35]

Significantly, the debate on stabilization was jointly defined by Keynes and Baruch—a fact that Hansen recognized, Clark deplored, and both Keynes and Baruch ignored. Keynes came to Washington in June 1941 as an official of His Majesty's government and discovered that at a time when defense expenditures pushed demand and consumer prices upward, the "Keynesians" were unprepared to heed his call for controls. Still enamored with the expansionist *General Theory*, they doubted that it was yet time to apply the restrictionist *How to Pay for the War*. "Using similar analytic approaches, Keynes and his American disciples differed on forecasting empirical relationships, and perhaps on the goals of policy. Keynes wanted war goods for Britain while the Americans were still worried about persistent unemployment."[36] The cost of lend-lease bundles for Britain would be high unless Americans brought their inflation under control. But, ironically, Keynes's own adherents preferred to view the inflation as expansion toward full employment and to call Baruch's cry for controls subversive of gains made in reemployment. As Keynes had written (and the Americans had confirmed), "We have become so accustomed to the problem of unemployment and of excess resources that it requires some elasticity of mind to adapt our behaviour to the problem of full employment and of resources which are no longer adequate to supply our needs. In war we move back from the Age of Plenty to the Age of Scarcity." That unemployment continued while inflation soared was attributable to the lack of planning. "It means that the Age of

Scarcity has arrived *before* the whole of the available labor has been absorbed. . . . It is not true that we can postpone action until after full employment has been reached."[37]

Nevertheless, the Keynesians operated on the premises of the depression: broad expansion was preferable to constraints. That Baruch argued for the latter confirmed their faith in delaying the passage to the Age of Scarcity. They knew it would arrive and they sought to postpone it. Their stress was upon the timing of controls. Having argued that it was *too soon* to apply them in 1941, they would be able to argue later that it was *too late*. The dialogue between the expansionists and the stabilizers would continue through the war long after the Age of Plenty ought to have adjourned in favor of the Age of Scarcity.

But that did not mean, as Baruch inferred, that the expansionists were ignorant of or indifferent to the experience of the First World War. On the contrary, no government official or economist could afford to ignore it, a fact shown in their writings and everyday activities. By and large, with certain reservations, they admired what the mobilizers of 1917–18 had accomplished. New Dealers interested in planning could not fail to appreciate the designs of the war period. But they still operated within the context of the 1930s. That meant suspicion of deflationists like Baruch, conservatives like Baruch, and friends of big business like Baruch. Even if his prescription for stabilization coincided with Keynes's, they evaluated the experience of Baruch in the context of the *General Theory* and their own more limited experience. They fought the depression in World War II.

Nothing interested the American Keynesians in 1941 more than Baruch's exposition on the planning of priorities. Priorities offered the advocates of business expansion and full employment a tool for guaranteeing the survival of less-essential enterprise. As Henderson told Roosevelt, "No one was interested in the change-over or the maintenance of existing civilian production except ourselves." An aide in Harry Dexter White's Monetary Research Division of the Treasury Department reviewed Baruch's *American Industry in the War* and singled out priorities as his "strong point" and one that "definitely merits reading." Written by an American Keynesian while Keynes himself was in Washington, the critique has significance:

> For the greater part, however, this book is now merely of historical interest. It does *not* stand on the frontier where new ideas are being suggested for expanding our defense effort and improving its administration. It *does* have some strong points, particularly in its emphasis on the necessity of priorities, price controls and centralized administrative responsibility for defense output. But the book's strong

points are much more than counterbalanced by the following grave deficiencies:

1. It has no conception of the possibilities of expanding our defense production through increasing employment and plant facilities.

2. It is timid and unimaginative in its proposals for diverting industrial resources from civil to military resources.

3. It approaches but does not reach the basic idea that what is needed for an efficient war economy is centralized government production planning for the whole economy, with authority—under proper legal and political safeguards—to carry out the plans.

4. Its ideas about the proper reorganization of the government agencies charged with administering the war economy are unjustifiably conservative.

Later in his review the economist wrote: "The limits on the justifiable self-congratulation of the War Industries Board are very narrow. *The Board never succeeded in expanding production*; it merely diverted production from civil to military purposes."[38] Paradoxically, the author celebrated Baruch on priorities without appreciating that the goal of priorities was to divert production in order to avoid expansion.

Keynes and Baruch believed that mid-1941 was the crucial time to dampen civilian supply. Inflation threatened the entire economy, whether it had reached full employment or not. Military needs would ineluctably bring full employment—and high prices. Discussing the 1942 federal budget, Harold Smith advised Roosevelt that "unless an effective and integrated program of anti-inflationary devices is soon adopted, the inevitable price rise may disrupt the national economy and aggravate post-defense difficulties." No longer could the administration afford the luxury of debating the timing of an antiinflationary program: "We must prepare now to control inflationary forces." Smith was no fan of Baruch's and it is uncertain what he knew about Keynes, but he knew what the British were doing in order to curtail prices: "A coordinated anti-inflationary program must utilize priorities, rationing, other production and inventory controls, and extensive price regulation. It must provide also for absorbing consumers' redundant purchasing power through taxation, stimulation of savings, and expansion of types of production that do not compete significantly with the defense effort." In his own bid to have direction of the war economy conferred upon him, Smith had neatly synthesized Baruch's plea for comprehensive stabilization planning and controls with the expansionists' plea for a viable civilian market that coexisted with military demands.[39]

A consensus for planning had evolved, but it remained to be seen *when* it would be implemented, *who* would implement it, and *how* comprehensive it would be. The three questions were interrelated. Politically, Roosevelt could not plan the economy before a declaration of war, a fact that made the concerns of Baruch, Keynes, and Smith relevant but secondary. That settled the first issue by default. As to the second, Smith wanted stabilization leadership to be located in the Bureau of the Budget, OPA wanted it out of the hands of mobilizers in either OPM or the War Department (a desire that led to the creation of SPAB),[40] and Roosevelt hesitated to use taxation as a stabilizing device lest he deprive the Treasury of its role or allow Congress to put through its own tax package. Stabilization in 1942 was piecemeal after all. Americans in World War II, notwithstanding rationing of gasoline, never learned that the Age of Plenty called for an ensuing Age of Scarcity. Americans did not fight World War II according to the dicta of either Keynes or Baruch.

DEVELOPING A STABILIZATION STRATEGY

The debate over the need for stabilization ended at Pearl Harbor, but the debate over the timing and selection of controls never ceased. Mobilization and stabilization were not yet two sides of the same coin in Roosevelt's eyes. The president saw rationing of rubber as conservation of a material; Baruch saw it as that *and* stabilization of a price. Most of the administration swung behind the idea of comprehensive controls espoused by Baruch, but where pressure for exemptions from controls remained, Roosevelt was reluctant to make enemies.

Baruch knew that the Canadian program of full controls and the war itself had convinced OPA that even wages and farm prices would have to be brought in line. Moreover, the refractory behavior of agriculture and labor had driven the point home. Leon Henderson pleaded with Baruch to use his influence with Congress to head off the agricultural bloc's drive to obtain 110 percent parity and a veto for the secretary of agriculture over OPA's control of food prices. Labor's hostility to the Little Steel wage formula demonstrated to Baruch—and he hoped that it was clear to the White House as well—that wage demands could not be assuaged by promises to prevent further increases in the cost of living. Prices were escalating. Something had to be done. Baruch had defined the issue as between a general ceiling on all prices or piecemeal price-fixing. In 1942 it seemed reasonable to most of the administration that it could no longer afford the luxury of a partly planned market.[41]

The Price Control Act of early 1942 gave OPA broad powers to curtail inflation with limitations in the area of agricultural commodities. Yet no broad antiinflation strategy had been adopted. It remained to be seen how the government could finance the enterprise of war without resort to a comprehensive prices program. In his January budget message, Roosevelt emphasized an antiinflation program combining controls and voluntary cooperation. That this amounted to the absence of any real antiinflation scheme quickly became evident. On 16 March, Budget Director Harold Smith informed the president, "The nation drifts swiftly and surely toward inflation. I am convinced that unless the upward surge of prices is checked the war effort will be greatly impaired. What is needed is a unified and far-reaching fiscal, monetary, wage and price control policy."

As part of his Bureau of the Budget duties, Smith had canvassed agency heads, and he was thereby enabled to articulate a consensus of opinion. It was his personal judgment that no single official could undertake a successful antiinflation effort without White House coordination. Meanwhile, prices were increasing government expenditures beyond the budget's projections, and "revenue policies still pursue peacetime patterns at a peacetime pace." He wanted Roosevelt to educate the public on the imperative of a comprehensive antiinflation program through a message to Congress and a Fireside Chat to the nation. Smith showed Roosevelt figures on inflation in 1915–16 that suggested that a fifteen-point rise in the cost of living could be repeated in 1942. The analogy might have been specious, but it stirred Roosevelt to think how he could dramatize the First World War's unfortunate experience in a Fireside Chat. He finally agreed to warn Congress and the public that the situation was "explosive" and "requires vigorous methods if disaster is to be avoided." By 13 April the White House was telling the press to expect a broad antiinflationary program within two weeks. The initial Senate reaction suggested support, Vandenberg of Michigan endorsing "all-out price control on a rational basis along the lines of the Baruch plan."[42]

The swift events of April 27–28—Roosevelt's Seven-Point Economic Stabilization Program, his Fireside Chat, and OPA's issuance of the General Maximum Price Regulation—gratified Baruch. At lunch with Breckenridge Long on 30 April he took credit for the developments without any pretense of modesty. Although he foresaw the need for adjustment and continuing readjustment of price controls, he was elated that the administration had finally acted according to his prescription. And well he should have been. More than any other person he had publicized the need for an antiinflation program to accompany the war effort; he had indoctrinated Congress before Smith found acceptance of full controls in the White House. "The problem is becoming acute," observed Walter George, chairman of the powerful Senate Finance Committee, two weeks before the administration acted. He added that "probably we shall have to go . . . to a general ceiling such as that recommended in principle by Bernard M. Baruch." John Kenneth Galbraith has commented, "We came to his design less because of his influence than because of the absolute force of circumstance. But I expect that the fact that Baruch had urged the course had something to do with our tendency to proceed. It gave a certain reassurance."[43]

But Baruch should not have engaged in an orgy of self-congratulation. First, he was hardly alone as an advocate of broad controls. Second, parts of his agenda, such as standardization and simplification, would never win the acceptance he sought—as we have already seen. Finally, the 1942 consensus favoring stabilization still contained strong pockets of resistance that would resurface the next year in a drive for expanding the civilian sector of the wartime economy.

Opposition to Baruch's prescription for stabilization stemmed from the fact that some groups considered stabilization a euphemism for something odious. As the labor unions and their advocates in the war agencies argued, "The term stabilization has often been used when the speaker really meant wage freezing."[44] Undoubtedly this was the case. Strong conservative support for government planning reflected a considerable desire to put a clamp upon wages in the name of national security. Baruch avoided that pitfall by insisting upon a "ceiling" to which wages, assisted by continued collective bargaining, would be allowed to rise. It was half the distance to a wage freeze.

Advocates of competition likewise considered stabilization a camouflage for something more notorious. Assistant Attorney General Thurman W. Arnold publicly forecast an age of consumer plenty because the war was "forcing us to produce to the fullest." At a time when the concept of rationing and controlled materials took hold, Arnold foresaw a cornucopia, not scarcity: "The opportunity for new business and new opportunity should be the greatest in the history of the nation, but it will come only if we get over the idea of stabilized process and production." Arnold prescribed antitrust litigation for bringing about expanded opportunity. But Roosevelt would find a judgeship for Arnold rather than wage simultaneous wars against big business and the Axis.[45]

During the summer of 1942, OPA and the Bureau of the Budget launched a drive for centralizing stabilization authority in a single agency. Assistant Director of the Budget Bureau Wayne Coy argued that a truly comprehensive program would avoid the appearance of discriminating against workers. Also, Coy shrewdly noted rising congressional opposition to Roosevelt and suggested that individual legislators who took pleasure in defeating him on domestic issues might think twice if they had to confront an "economic stabilizer" respected by the Congress. Responsible to the chief executive, the economic stabilizer should be known as a strong figure who was free from identification with agencies or interests involved in stabilization. Following the overwhelming public acceptance of the Baruch rubber report, with its clear admonitions on the need for rationing to achieve price stabilization, Congress appeared more amenable to the concept of a single price administrator. After research into 1918 precedents, the White House decided that it had legal authority to create the Office of Economic Stabilization (OES) with a director who would "interpret and re-interpret the program as rapidly as questions arise . . . , harmonize the conflicting views inside the Administration and among the major pressure groups, and . . . command the respectful attention of the Congress."[46]

What Coy had in mind amounted to a trusted politician-publicist with expanded executive powers: Baruch. White House legal counsel Sam Rosenman sounded him out for the job in September, but Baruch turned it away for personal and policy reasons. On Byrnes's recommendation, Baruch would conserve his energy while using his prestige as an independent sage to promote programs with the public. This choice effectively eliminated Baruch from any official capacity of an indefinite duration. Moreover, he did not want responsibility for fighting inflation without the Treasury portfolio. Taxation was a crucial weapon in the stabilization arsenal, and he knew that Roosevelt would not replace Morgenthau, with whom Baruch could not agree on fiscal policies.

According to Baruch, Harry Hopkins then visited him to discuss possible choices for director of the proposed Office of Economic Stabilization. He wanted to know what Baruch thought of Averell Harriman or John G. Winant for the post. Baruch thought neither Hopkins acolyte was fitted for it. Hopkins then allowed that he would accept Baruch himself in it, and Baruch declared that Jimmy Byrnes would be a good choice. As Hopkins and Baruch discussed whether Byrnes would leave the Supreme Court for this post, Byrnes arrived and answered the question in the affirmative. Later, Rosenman made the offer official. Byrnes was unclear about what powers were entailed in the position, but Baruch urged him to secure White House assurances that he could influence tax policies. Byrnes responded that if he could not get along with Morgenthau he would have finally found a man with whom he could not deal. A year later Stabilization Director Byrnes and Treasury Secretary Morgenthau publicly squabbled over who had jurisdiction over the tax bill to be presented to Congress, and Byrnes bitterly recalled Baruch's admonition not to direct the stabilization office without control over taxation.[47]

But personalities were important only as they affected policy. Like Keynes, Baruch had pointed to taxation as the most effective weapon in antiinflationary policy making. Without it, price controls would never be truly comprehensive. Without broad-based taxation, the administration's stabilization policy was inherently limited.

It is most unlikely that Roosevelt would have allowed Baruch any influence on wartime tax policy. Baruch had been told that Morgenthau had begged the president not to let anyone else contribute to the making of tax policy. At any rate, Roosevelt would not have followed Baruch's fiscal advice. They had differed over the sales tax in 1932, and Baruch's public opposition to the administration's tax bill in 1938 must have been fresh in the president's mind. In 1939, Roosevelt had chided Morgenthau for the Treasury's proposal to reduce corporate and income taxes because it agreed with Baruch's ideas. Morgenthau sheepishly conceded that for once they did concur on taxation. "Well," Roosevelt said, "are you willing to pay usury to get recovery?" The question amounted to a presidential commentary on Baruch's tax advice.[48]

Yet the idea of stimulating economic recovery in 1939 by cutting taxes appealed to others besides Baruch and Morgenthau. Harold Smith was then endeavoring to involve himself in fiscal policy, and over a dinner enlivened by liberal quantities of scotch and soda, he heard Beardsley Ruml, treasurer of Macy's department stores, denounce the administration's fiscal policy as "stupid." Smith found it fascinating "that a business man should have come to the compensatory budget idea as a solution to our national economic ills." Of course, Ruml's arrival at such concepts approximated Marriner Eccles's embrace of government spending—a matter-of-fact practical Keynesianism. The paradox that bemused Smith was that Roosevelt was married to an orthodox budget policy, whereas Ruml espoused what sounded like economic heresy. As Smith would learn by 1942 when Ruml launched the Committee for Economic Development, a business group dedicated to remodeling the federal tax structure, Ruml was a publicist for governmental policy who could rival Baruch.[49]

The "compensatory budget idea" made even more sense in war. After all, taxation was the easiest and least controversial method of restraining prices. Through broad-based taxation, Washington simply diminished demand that boosted prices. That was partly what Ruml had in mind when he ridiculed fiscal policy. In war the Treasury had to provide investment incentives for capital while paying for public enterprise from the improved incomes of the poor. Moreover, this regressive taxation could be justified morally, on the grounds that it spared the masses the harsher burden of inflation. A higher cost of living would cruelly defeat gains in income made by workers. Inflation was an unproductive social tax. A wise and even altruistic policy called for planning whereby the government captured surplus income during the war through taxation and forced savings; it was returned as rebates or reductions after the war when public spending receded. In theory at least, the government equitably paid for its war through taxes on enhanced corporate and personal wealth. Baruch, ever a good progressive in war, preached the ethical need for very high excess profits taxes; but as Morgenthau knew, because his aides had studied the speculator's writings on wartime taxation, the excess profits tax was itself inflationary: corporations would pass the tax along to consumers—unless prevented from doing this by price controls! Baruch's advice to Byrnes made sense: stabilization without any influence upon taxation was as ludicrous as taxing profits without recourse to price controls. Either an antiinflationary program was comprehensive or it was a failure. As Galbraith had conceded, "Baruch was right on price policy—to his credit."[50]

Nowhere in the administration was this point better appreciated than in the Bureau of the Budget, where the views of Keynes and Ruml were respected and those of Baruch tolerated. But the stumbling block to a consensus was Morgenthau. He refused to approve an administration recommendation for broad-based taxes and compulsory savings that hit lower-income groups hard. Recognizing "radical points of difference between our conclusions and those of Harold Smith's group," Morgenthau blamed the conflict on Keynesian economists (of which Treasury had its share): "First they want inflation . . . and they don't want any rationing or anything sensible about finances. They think that the Government can do the thing one day by pumping money in, and the next day they think the Government can do the thing by putting the brakes on the lower income groups, but I have yet to see a single one of them make a success of anything that they have undertaken."[51] (The latter disparagement would have drawn a nod of agreement from Baruch.) But it was the Keynes of 1940, whom his adherents had finally caught up with in 1942, who set the tone of the fiscal debate. Morgenthau adamantly opposed Keynes on compulsory savings because he would have little to do with a savings scheme that was not voluntary.

Yet nobody in the administration was clear on the lines taxation ought to take. Roosevelt seemed disposed to allow the Treasury and the House Ways and Means Committee to work things out in an ad hoc fashion. Smith was horrified by this lack of direction: "It would be fatal not to ask Congress for an additional tax program to undercut purchasing power." The president had politics on his mind. He did not want rationing blamed on himself; he sought euphemisms for sales taxes ("general excise taxes") and inflation (a "naughty word") with which to sell the electorate on his stabilization program. The administration went on the record in April for lower income tax exemptions, "universal savings," and a "war consumption tax."[52]

But the proposal that sparked the greatest public furor was Roosevelt's suggestion that nobody have a net income in excess of $25,000 per year during the war. It never had a chance in Congress. Baruch probably knew this and therefore it cost him nothing to approve it in principle. He also believed that equity required that wealth be subscribed to the war effort. In fact, he took exception only to efforts to cut the gift tax annual exclusion and exemption on the grounds that it would be a hardship for those whom he helped every year. At the end of 1942 he contributed a million dollars to many servicemen and refugee organizations. After first assuring Morgenthau that these gifts would be made "quietly through ordinary channels," he later made them public enough for the *New York Times* to emblazon them on the front page. His principal objection to the gift tax was that it did not allow rich men to direct as much as they wanted to recipients of their choice.[53]

Without Robinson, Pittman, Harrison, and Byrnes in the Senate, Baruch's influence upon the tax bill of 1942 was negligible. And organized labor's contributions to Democratic war chests further reduced his importance in Congress. The Old Man barely knew Senator Walter F. George and Representative Robert L. Doughton of North Carolina, the principal architects of revenue bills in their respective chambers. He took no part in any public discussion of specific tax proposals.

However, the Baruch antiinflation program created the necessary environment for the Revenue Act of 1942. It was Ruml who publicized the specific provisions that eventually revolutionized taxation in the United States. Already the principle of reducing exemptions to snare money from lower-income groups had been adopted by the Congress and the Treasury as preferable to sales taxes that would not stifle spending by consumers with incomes high enough to absorb higher costs. Besides, sales taxes were inflexible in adjusting to changing economic conditions. Passed along to consumers by manufacturers, they would add to inflation rather than reduce it. But even the lowered exemption rates would not sufficiently slash demand. Only about seven million Americans filed returns in 1941, though with exemptions lowered to $500 in 1942, more would follow suit. The problem lay in the government's method of collection, which relied upon individuals' filing returns for the taxable year during the following year. Would those who had never filed know how to do so? Would they save their money to pay taxes? Or would they have already spent it and thereby increased inflationary pressures? Ruml's contribution to the American tax system was the "collection-at-the-source" tax that withheld the workers' earnings before they could be spent. First broached to the Senate Finance Committee in July as the "Pay-as-you-go Income Tax Plan," it caught on quickly. Although it did not become part of the Revenue Act of 1942, the fact that the Treasury embraced it in August practically assured its passage the next year. In 1944, forty-two million Americans would pay income taxes.[54]

The consequences of war taxation policies are imposing. Prior to the adoption of the withholding tax in mid-1943, even Roosevelt acknowledged "that we had not done nearly so good a job in stabilizing the cost of living as either the Canadians or the British."[55] The tax permitted what rationing and controls did not: the removal of spending money from wage earners' pay envelopes. To the extent that it limited inflation, wartime taxation conformed with principles of social justice.

But there was no real equity in wartime taxation, although that was not Roosevelt's fault. He could not foresee that Congress would care more for the greedy than for the needy or that the withholding tax would not be ephemeral. And excess profits taxes did not mean that there would be no excess profits. The Department of the Navy had figures that showed profits for randomly selected corporations performing war work at 233 and 350 percent of their average profits for 1937–40; Undersecretary of the Navy James Forrestal was prompted to comment, "Both these individual cases and the Treasury over-all figures seem to me to preclude any possibility of showing that wartime profits are only 'normal.' "[56] Clearly this was inequitable to laborers who never saw a portion of their gross incomes.

Finally, who would pay the national debt accumulated from the war? Keynes had argued that through compulsory savings the poor might own a fair share of the national debt. But Morgenthau preferred to elicit voluntary savings with a Madison Avenue pitch. Baruch, who did not need incentives to purchase his share of the debt, had urged a scheme of deferred payment for war bonds but was rebuffed by Roosevelt. The closest the United States came to compulsory savings was the Victory Tax of 1942, which it abandoned the next year. The debt and postwar tax policy were never far from the minds of policy makers and legislators as they deliberated taxes in 1942.[57] Late in the war, Roosevelt privately envisioned reducing taxes and retiring the federal debt in about twenty-five years. "Wow, Mr. President!" exclaimed Harold Smith, who avoided further comment by promising to study the matter. In his notes, Smith commented, "I was tempted to say that this sort of fiscal policy would go a long way to ruining the country."[58] Baruch would have agreed with Smith.

INFORMAL LIAISON

The apogee of Baruch's fame and prestige came during the first year of America's participation in World War II. The crisis politics of 1942 were made to order for Baruch, who was hardly a stranger to such things. First, there were his credentials. Innumerable news reports reminded readers that Baruch had been chairman of the War Industries Board in the first war; nobody else could speak with such authority on the issues of mobilization and stabilization. Baruch exploited this distinction systematically. The Byzantine nature of wartime Washington, reminiscent of 1917–18, with its cabals and constant plotting of individuals and agencies against one another, was well suited to his peculiar style of performing *pro bono publico* (in Herbert Swope's words), as a freelancer without portfolio (in Baruch's own words). Without authority or responsibility, Baruch possessed more public trust than any government official except the president himself. He became the "park bench statesman," the sage of Lafayette

Square who, without an official title, dispensed wisdom to reporters and others. With a reputation for insight and interest beyond ambition or faction, he intrigued with a deftness that earned him at least some fear, if not respect, from insiders. About him there was an aura of mysteries, not the least of which were the real purposes of his activities.

He was seventy-one years old, a widower, virtually deaf in one ear, suffering from gout, and susceptible to numerous ailments that frequently afflicted him. Among his contemporaries he was a survivor; his principal congressional cronies of a decade before—Joe Robinson, Pat Harrison, and Key Pittman—were dead and Jimmy Byrnes had moved temporarily to the Supreme Court before being installed in 1942 as economic stabilizer for the war effort. No longer could Baruch call the tune for certain pieces of legislation through his Senate contacts. He had to make new political alliances and find other worthy collaborators for his governmental forays. Most of his international friends were gone from the scene, too—a fact that could be overlooked only because his closest comrade in England, Churchill, was about to become the greatest Englishman of the century—and every visit by the prime minister to U.S. shores reminded Americans that wise old Baruch was a friend of some twenty-five years standing. But Baruch's summers were now spent in a Long Island home rented from Cissy Patterson instead of a Scottish manor leased from nobility. However, Baruch himself preached the need for democratic austerity during the war—although guests at Baruch's "Little Hobcaw" at Kingstree, South Carolina, his Fifth Avenue home in New York City, or his suite costing $1,000 per month at Washington's Carlton Hotel, found little that was austere in Baruch's new manner of entertaining.

The war gave him a new base of influence. It brought numerous businessmen who spoke his language to positions of responsibility in the War Department and the emergency agencies. Few of the businessmen, lawyers, and assorted career government officers who ran the war effort could discuss the extraordinary problems that confronted them with the sort of experience and expertise Baruch exhibited. Those who were not neophytes in government confronted policy and administrative issues unlike anything they had experienced before. Yet this ubiquitous old man with the white thatch and a hearing aid could discourse on their difficulties with a familiarity that demonstrated reflection. In myriad ways he sought to be useful; and he was useful—even to those who maintained an unrelenting distrust of him. He proved his worth by refusing to retire gracefully. He was certain in his own mind that he alone possessed the understanding of what war called for in the way of mobilization and stabilization policies; patriotism—if not ego—required that he not remove himself to the sidelines at such a critical juncture in history. Besides, his charm and personality had not deserted him; he retained the capacity to create new alliances. And one person above all in wartime Washington knew how helpful Baruch could be—Franklin D. Roosevelt.

"The President does not easily readjust personal relationships that he has once established," Harold Ickes once cogently observed. For Baruch that characteristic of Roosevelt's worked two ways. It frustrated Baruch and his admirers, who believed that Roosevelt ought to heed the speculator's counsel on great issues; and it disappointed his antagonists, who would have rejoiced to see Baruch banished from the White House once and for all. Although Roosevelt nourished an old alliance that allowed Baruch to draw upon the open door at the White House for prestige when he gave unsolicited advice, the president would never overcome his suspicions that Baruch operated fundamentally for his own personal aggrandizement in matters both of finance and of prominence and power. Morally and ethically, Roosevelt believed that he was Baruch's superior; perhaps he was. At any rate, he treated Baruch as a handy conniver who, although unworthy of public trust, could be of personal service if dealt with carefully, or a public nuisance if unnecessarily alienated. They were friends out of convenience and associates out of necessity. The president defined the relationship.

Roosevelt continued to treat Baruch's money, public relations, and zeal for governmental meddling as disreputable, but serviceable to his own interest. On the one hand, Baruch had been troublesome when he helped finance the campaigns of Roosevelt's intended victims of the 1938 Democratic purge, but he also knew that Baruch would contribute to Roosevelt-designated candidates for the Senate. Moreover, Baruch money could be relied upon for causes that kept Eleanor Roosevelt involved and happy. It would require an accountant's efforts to discover all the White House channels for Baruch's money, but Ickes's discovery that Baruch contributed to Harry Hopkins's income in 1941 suggests that not all of them were regular. Even the Nazis suspected that Roosevelt used Baruch financing to undermine the isolationist America First Committee.[59] In return, Roosevelt proved quite willing to appease his wealthy friend's "strong taste for lunching at the White House regularly." The frequency of those visits was spasmodic. They increased during the mobilization speedup of 1941–42 when it seemed reassuring to the Congress and the public for the president to appear in consultation with the First World War's mobilizer. Even then the regularity of the luncheons was interrupted by Baruch's impolitic description of SPAB as a "faltering step forward." Then too, in October 1941, the *New York Journal-American* published on page 1 a letter from Baruch to its publisher, William Randolph Hearst, commending him for an anti-America First editorial and urging his support for a comprehensive price control bill made all the more necessary "due to procrastination and improper organization" by the administration. The letter "disgusted" Roosevelt; Hearst was "associated with the worst elements in the country." He instructed press secretary Steve Early to ask Baruch if he really had sent the letter to Hearst, a query that Baruch interpreted correctly as a Roosevelt effort to intimidate him into silence.[60]

However, their meetings resumed, both parties content in the knowledge that publicity about them suited their purposes. In private, Roosevelt spoke of "Old Bernie," employing the term with both affection and resentment of the aura attached to that indispensable nuisance's fame, which he was compelled to enhance. They were so alike in certain respects that they had to be jealous of one another. Prima donnas who basked in the warmth of press attention, Baruch came across as a statesman above politics, Roosevelt as a statesman in politics. Once, in the wake of the furor following his "quarantine" speech, Roosevelt asked Baruch why "you can talk like a Dutch uncle to the public, and if I do the same all hell breaks loose?" When Baruch gained fame as the wartime "park bench statesman," Roosevelt would snipe, "There's Bernie on the bench, the star on stage." With each other and about each other they gossiped and wagered, women figuring prominently in their talk. Clare Boothe Luce had once been "Baruch's girl," and, according to Roosevelt, Baruch surrounded himself with beautiful women; when he heard that the ailing Baruch had a new nurse, Roosevelt's immediate response was, "I bet she's pretty." Their conversations frequently had a clubhouse quality. Roosevelt, son James remembered, likewise appreciated attractive women: "He had few homely women working for him; that was not his style." During the war, Martha, the refugee princess from Norway, spent much time at the White House as a guest of the president. "She's a pip," Baruch once exlaimed in appreciation of the president's tastes in royal women, jocularly adding, "I'm going to ask Roosevelt how he does it." In 1944, Roosevelt took a vacation at Hobcaw that amounted to a tryst with Lucy Mercer Rutherford, who drove over from her nearby home at Aiken. Not until the president died a year later would Eleanor Roosevelt learn that her good friend Baruch had kept a personal secret from her.[61]

But Baruch was no mere crony or hanger-on whom Roosevelt kept at arm's length when involved in the serious matters of state. Baruch turned up in some of the most unlikely developments simply because of his fame as somebody who knew his way around the White House. In the days immediately preceding Pearl Harbor he served as a go-between for the Japanese special envoy, Soburo Kurusu, who endeavored to give Roosevelt a message directly without State Department intermediaries.[62] But Baruch seldom involved himself in diplomacy. He polished his self-defined role as watchdog of mobilization and stabilization during the war. Roosevelt could not repress a Baruch opinion on policy and organization; so it was evidently in the president's best interest that Baruch have access to the White House for venting his judgments. Roosevelt could tolerate his friend's omniscience as long as he did not go public with his opinions. He would much rather give Baruch an ear, with the understanding that adverse comments were to be kept within the family of the administration, than have Baruch rallying opposition with an authoritative voice. For that matter, Baruch, too, disdained a role as critic of the president. He believed that he worked better "in the tall grass," "mixing medicine" in the corridors of power. He went public only when he found Roosevelt unresponsive to an increasingly desperate situation—desperate by Baruch's definition.

Roosevelt valued a ubiquitous troubleshooter. The problems of the presidency at war were complex, and Roosevelt was intent upon hoarding as much power and authority as he could. He needed extra eyes and ears about him to avoid various domestic pitfalls. He took Baruch's eclectic mission seriously. Memoranda from Baruch were given careful attention and follow-ups. Baruch took it upon himself to become a one-man personnel agency, a bird dog for executive talent for the war organizations that grew out of the White House or the War Department.[63] His contacts in Congress may have been depleted by death, but the White House frequently requested the prestigious Baruch to call a wavering congressman on a crucial bill. And who else would have dared to call the White House in 1941 to challenge figures on airplane production distributed by the War Department? When it became evident that two agencies were duplicating economic warfare activities, Baruch's mention of the fact to Roosevelt brought the conflicting bureaucracies together. At the same time, Roosevelt often tried to keep the identity of his source of information and advice a secret. Thus, a Baruch memorandum on international gold and silver markets resulted in a Roosevelt message to the Treasury asking for its "slant" on these matters, followed by two paragraphs beginning with anonymous references: "It has been suggested that . . . " and "I am told that . . . "[64]

When Harry Hopkins went into the cabinet as secretary of commerce and then into the White House as a star boarder (to protect his frail health), he ironically increased Baruch's importance to the administration. For conservatives, Hopkins was the symbol of the New Dealer's quest for public dominance over private enterprise. His bureaucratic rivalry with Interior Secretary Harold Ickes was legendary, even if Ickes's loyalty to Roosevelt and the New Deal was beyond question. Hopkins spurred resentments for no other reason than his proximity to the president and his assumption of responsibility for the president's mistakes. Even Eleanor Roosevelt resented his presence in the White House. Thus, Hopkins enhanced Baruch's role as an alternative policy influence who, while not balancing Hopkins, at least presented the president with another viewpoint.

Baruch blamed Hopkins for everything wrong with the war administration, including his own absence from it. But neither man dared to
estrange the other. Their relations were always cordial and correct. They
were smart enough to keep their mutual antagonism sub rosa. The news
that Baruch's gift to Hopkins upon his marriage to Louise Macy in 1942
was a party for a select group of sixty surprised and appalled many of the
speculator's friends. They considered it an obsequious gesture. But it
turned out to be an embarrassment for Hopkins. The guest list was
drawn up by Hopkins and his bride and consisted of the rich and powerful of New York and Washington (Ickes and Wallace excluded). According to Ickes, who savored such gossip, about half of the guests were
"economic royalists from Long Island," and only a tenth of them were
known personally by Baruch. The host had chosen the party's lavish
style. At a time when Americans were being told by their government to
conserve food that might feed the hungry children of Europe, guests at
the Hopkins wedding party feasted on pâté de foie gras, lobster in aspic,
terrapin (Baltimore style), and other delights served by attentive waiters
who freely poured vintage champagne. In peacetime, "the ordinary citizen
would have not given it a second thought," a Hopkins biographer has
written. "Now it became a first-rate scandal. And oddly enough, Hopkins
got more blame than Baruch."[65]

In wartime Washington, many New Dealers who had fought businessmen now fought to survive. Like others, many of them set aside their
idealism and gave some attention to future personal security and how
their associations with businessmen might enhance it. Ickes, an old progressive who had fought privileged wealth and looked upon Baruch as an
apostle of corporate cartelism, began a reorientation toward him in 1940.
He had met Baruch a few times before, but somehow they had never had
an opportunity for conversation. Then, during a swing through the upper
South in the third-term campaign, Baruch spent some time impressing
the interior secretary and his wife, Jane, with the wisdom of his mobilization doctrines. When he discovered that Baruch detested Hopkins, Ickes
knew that the speculator had to be a kindred spirit after all. Of course
there were other things that recommended Baruch to Ickes: in addition
to commending Ickes as the best administrator in Washington, Baruch
stated that he considered donating his coastal estate to the Interior Department, that he enjoyed giving gifts to individuals he liked, and that the
Ickes family would be welcome to vacation with him in South Carolina.
Four days after Pearl Harbor, Ickes wrote President Roosevelt: "I wish
that you could be persuaded to recall Bernie Baruch and give him the
authority that he so well carried out twenty years ago. I believe that this
would be particularly reassuring to the country at this time, and in all
frankness I don't believe anyone can do the job so well as he."[66] Ickes
attributed his war position as petroleum coordinator to Baruch's recom-

mendations to the White House and appreciated his friend's continuing campaign to have Ickes administer all energy resources. For much of the early part of the war they would meet once a week for lunches at which they would exchange gossip and gripes. Both men had a penchant for picking up rumors before they became fact, as well as promoting causes and careers before they became successful. As an intermediary with corporations vital to the Interior Department's operations, such as Alcoa, and with military agency heads, Baruch proved quite useful to Ickes.

Ickes's diary gives us an insight into Baruch's manner of winning over an old adversary. He charmed Ickes's wife, generously praised the abilities of his assistants, and casually impressed him with evidence of his wealth, noting, for example, that it cost him between $150,000 and $200,000 a year to maintain a staff and facilities in New York and Washington for his public activities. He assured Ickes that his public service was possible because he never had difficulty making money, although he no longer had any business interests. From time to time he would mention the widow of a public figure who had benefited either from his financial advice or from benefactions that took the place of pensions. "I love to make presents," Baruch once declared during a denunciation of the gift tax. "I am always giving to my friends. I suppose that every year I give away from $50,000 to $100,000, not to charity but to people who need a little help." (It was not a hollow boast; but, in the words of a cynical friend, "He was always generous to the deserving rich.")[67] With magnificent indirection, Baruch insinuated that his friendship could be worth more than an annuity or a life insurance policy. Ickes, a man about to pass the age of seventy, with two young children, various debts and tax problems, a young wife who shared his anxieties, and assorted animosities and ambitions, could not afford to ignore Baruch. In June 1943, Jane Ickes would enlist Baruch's advice on their personal finances. While it lasted, there could be no doubt of the genuine admiration between Baruch and Ickes. "Baruch is a very great man and completely disinterested," Ickes assured Henry Wallace, as if to reassure himself that the New Deal picture of the speculator as a predator was an injustice.[68] However, as the war came to a close and policy differences over reconversion became evident, their friendship would go the way of most wartime flirtations. By V-J Day all Ickes would recall would be the number of times he bought lunch for the rich man, the invitations to Hobcaw that were not forthcoming, the favors he had done Baruch, and the increasing infrequency of the great man's visits. Jane Ickes would not be on Baruch's list of most-favored widows.

Throughout Washington bureaucrats would warn each other that Baruch was a "slick operator," but most of them enjoyed being operated upon by the Old Man. He was nonpartisan in the objects of his attention; New Dealers were good men, too, if they were capable and, by Baruch's lights, apolitical for the duration. Rank mattered little as well, for in a bureaucracy even a junior officer usually had access to useful information. Baruch came across as exceptionally kindly and encouraging and wise. When a conversation climaxed with the other party gaining an insight into a topic of which Baruch was a master, he would be lavish in his praise—as any teacher ought to be with a pupil. And praise from Baruch could be heady medicine, even if all knew it was applied with a bit of excessive stroking.[69] Of course there were many who detested his manner. "Baruch was a polished flatterer, particularly of women," Jimmy Roosevelt observed, resentful of the speculator's close friendship with his mother. Yet even the eldest Roosevelt son conceded that his wily father, who could not be fooled by empty praise, allowed Baruch to "play up to his fancy" by accepting presents of game birds that he ate with pleasure. (But, knowing little else of Baruch's technique and disliking him intensely, Jimmy erroneously insists that Baruch "got to father through mother." Had Eleanor possessed such influence, Joseph Lash might have been a presidential advisor and Harry Hopkins a biographer.) Baruch performed personal favors on a scale that could only be imagined, showing some partiality for women. "If you ever get into a jam, come and I'll take care of you," he once advised Frances Perkins. "There's no reason for women to lose their money. They should increase their capital all the time." He was a Victorian protector of womanhood; Perkins, as a New Englander and a New Dealer who wondered about the propriety of an officeholder's accepting his succor, attributed no other motive to his munificence than that he "likes to be a benefactor."[70]

The war made Baruch one of the most celebrated Americans of his time. As the mobilization muddle was confirmed by the Truman committee report in 1942, and the administration took a major step in the direction of stabilization that Baruch had been calling for, and the bureaucratic infighting and rivalries escalated into 1943, and the president felt called upon to give Baruch special assignments with high press visibility, Baruch emerged as "the grandfather of modern war economy." By 1944 a Hearst columnist would declare that "Baruch today is without doubt the most respected individual in the country." When the Carter Field biography of Baruch, *Park Bench Statesman*, appeared, the advertising for it heralded the subject as "one of the least-known and most talked about men of our century."[71]

Baruch himself orchestrated the publicity campaign. His chief agent was his old columnist friend Arthur Krock of the *New York Times*, whose prestige during the New Deal had been boosted by exclusive interviews granted by Roosevelt. According to Gay Talese, "Krock knew every important figure in Washington, [and] was possibly more influential in the nation than the Secretary of State." Certainly more politicians, bureaucrats, and policy makers read Krock with their breakfast than

MR. BARUCH'S SUCCESS AS A PARK BENCH ORACLE SHOULD ENCOURAGE
OTHER PROMINENT DISPENSERS OF ADVICE TO ENCROACH ON HIS TERRITORY

*11. At the height of his fame as a publicist of issues in 1943, Baruch is
depicted with potential imitators Wendell Willkie and Eleanor Roosevelt by
Parrish in the antiadministration* Chicago Tribune. *(Courtesy Seeley G. Mudd
Manuscript Library, Princeton University)*

read Cordell Hull. Frequently a Krock column was little more than a
rehash or celebration of Baruch's wisdom. Sometimes its newsworthiness
was enhanced by tips on the inadequacy of American mobilization from
a "thoroughly reliable source." Krock deferred to Baruch as an unimpeachable authority on mobilization and economics. If Baruch said that
the delay in war preparations cost the lives of at least one hundred
thousand soldiers, then that estimate was a fact for Krock.[72]

Krock was not alone among journalists in idolizing Baruch. At any time during World War II the administration could have dozens of editorial writers and columnists assailing it for ignoring the mobilization and stabilization principles of B. M. Baruch. Besides Krock, Baruch counted among his journalistic friends columnists Marquis Childs and George E. Sokolsky; publishers Roy Howard, Cissy Patterson, and Henry Luce; editors E. D. Coblentz of the *San Francisco Call-Bulletin* and Charles McCabe of the *New York Mirror*; Washington reporters Blair Moody, John N. Wheeler, and Walker Stone; and editorial cartoonist Jay N. "Ding" Darling of the *New York Herald-Tribune*. And there were hosts of editors and reporters across the land who took the word of Baruch before that of the president.

Jimmy Byrnes played no small role in Baruch's schemes. Since 1939 the petulant and ambitious South Carolina senator had been lobbying for a Supreme Court vacancy through Baruch and others. In increasingly poor health as he entered his sixties, Byrnes believed that a seat on the Court promised a less demanding role than one in the Senate, with no diminution in prestige. Following the death of Joe Robinson, Byrnes had assumed the task of managing Baruch's relations with the Senate, advising the speculator which bills and candidates to throw his fame and fortune behind. Baruch apparently disregarded the warning of another old friend that Byrnes's sole concern was "the stocks he is carrying." Baruch expected to be used to improve his friends' portfolios and quests for power, as long as there was a quid pro quo. Although he must have regretted Byrnes's desire to leave the Senate, he respected his wish for a life "which will be longer if not happier." As was to be expected, the Court did not suit a man accustomed to political dealing and still nursing ambivalent quests that included the presidency itself. After a little more than a year on the bench, Byrnes moved into the White House as director of economic stabilization.[73]

The focus of Baruch's influence shifted to the executive branch during the war. The War Department became practically a Baruch fan club. The generals knew him as the prime civilian spokesman for their requirements. The new civilian leaders of the military learned what the generals already knew. Soon after he became secretary of war, Stimson sought and got "a very satisfactory and useful talk" with Baruch. They agreed on the need for a production autocrat who would get the military what it wanted as rapidly as possible. Drawing on his Wilsonian background, Baruch recommended a "conspectus" on war materials—where they came from and in what quantities and where they would be used—and drew a flow chart for Stimson that simplified the procurement puzzle. In retrospect it almost strains credulity to find that the War Department leadership in late 1940 approached mobilization at about the same level of understanding as the War Industries Board in the winter of 1916–17. Yet Stimson found Baruch's suggestions for the flow chart analysis and materials inventory a revelation. "As soon as he went away," Stimson called in his assistants "and told them that I wanted such a conspectus and asked if they could get one together for me. I have been trying ever since I have been here to get such tables."[74]

Baruch was valuable as something more than an itinerant advisor, a perambulating and pedantic reference source on the previous war's civilian experience. Familiar with the way in which bureaucratic rivalries infect war organizations, Baruch served as a self-designated broker between competing agencies. It was a welcome and necessary function—particularly if agency leaders found him on their side of the struggle. He became a much sought-after factotum in the ineluctable interdepartmental conflicts that beset wartime Washington. Roosevelt indirectly made his ombudsman service imperative by his emphasis upon his own ultimate control. The president calculatingly had established no other arbiters of power but himself. But the "bring it to Papa" approach had drawbacks in that Roosevelt himself disliked settling disputes. And the war lords were reluctant to bring him problems that revealed their own weaknesses, made them appear petty for imposing upon him at a time when vital concerns demanded his attention, and placed them in jeopardy of losing the argument should he rule against them—if he could decide at all. So the bureaucratic battles were fought in the corridors, in the Congress, and in the newspapers. If a controversy ever went as far as the fourth estate, the legendary Baruch was an important ally.

As a troubleshooter for favored bureaucrats, Baruch made a comfortable and discreet niche for himself in the history of World War II. Not only did he fight Ickes's battles for an empire of energy materials, he also assisted Henry Wallace's efforts to secure financing power for the Board of Economic Warfare from Jesse Jones's Reconstruction Finance Corporation. When David E. Lilienthal wanted scarce diesel electric locomotives for TVA, Baruch went directly to the president of the Association of American Railroads, who was enthusiastic about "getting in good with the government" and eagerly cooperated. Having no portfolio, Baruch could afford to be no respecter of bureaucratic protocol and red tape. Though agency heads might be befuddled by the complexity of competition and procedure, Baruch concentrated on the desired results. He owed nobody his job, his allegiance, or his livelihood. He could afford the impudence of intervention. If the intervention was welcomed, it was meddling at its best. When Admiral Emory S. "Jerry" Land, chairman of the Maritime Commission, wanted a larger allotment of steel, he called in Baruch. As he told it later, "The greatest asset I ever had in my maritime career was Mr. Baruch, who knew the setup of the [War Production] Board, knew the man who was in the steel allocation part of it . . . and when I got in a hell of a jam, I told Mr. Baruch and Baruch told this fellow, 'See that Maritime gets a fair break,' and we got it."[75]

Not everybody, of course, was so appreciative of Baruch's interventions. The War Production Board had many New Dealers who would have been content with Baruch's retirement from Washington when their conflicts with the War Department heated up. The most frequent complaint, first sounded by allies of the WPB like Justice Frankfurter, was that Baruch's power was exercised "without the necessary responsibility and often without the adequate knowledge for exercising judgment." Moreover, his prestige was intimidating because few people were certain of his fixed role in the wartime structure. Did Baruch's unofficial voice carry the weight of official authority? Director of the Budget Harold Smith, who revered clear lines of bureaucratic domain and jealously guarded the White House's control of everything, informed Roosevelt:

> I have heard a number of times that Mr. Baruch had lunch with you and that he then talks with subordinates in the Office of Production Management, with his conversation carrying the assumption, if not openly stated, that his views are in accord with those of the President. Even sophisticated persons are likely to make some point of the fact that they have just seen the President and he said so and so.
> Such informal liaison should be reduced to a minimum.[76]

In Baruch's case, such informal liaison already was at its minimum in 1941.

A bureaucrat-businessman who benefited by his forays described the Old Man's second war legacy: "When the final history [of World War II] is written, [it] will tell how Bernard Baruch has been the confident adviser of factions within the Government, and how even those who have received no soft words from him have gone to him for advice, harsh as it may be. It will show how he has been able to maintain the confidence of strong, earnest men while telling them that the men against them were equally fine." Always he operated as part scold, part cheerleader, part solicitor, part mediator, and part arbiter. His specialties were problems of economic production and their consequences. But also of value were his acknowledged talents as a publicist and bureaucratic politician. Sometimes he volunteered his services and sometimes they were solicited. "I suppose that nearly everybody in top Washington officialdom during the war could say that Baruch was of assistance to him at one time or another," recalled White House counsel Sam Rosenman, whose appreciation of Baruch was belated and perhaps stimulated by the retainer for legal services Baruch gave him after the war. Still, as Rosenman writes, "he was a kind of Mecca for troubled officials who wanted some wise and experienced but sympathetic soul to whom they could pour out their troubles."[77]

THE WAR LORDS OF WASHINGTON

On the cost-of-living issue, Baruch functioned effectively as a publicist; but on war production he was a behind-the-scenes operator because he disapproved of open controversy in the war effort. Indeed, he reproved friends or anyone who by dissent with the War Production Board leadership appeared to obstruct the mobilization process. When an old WIB comrade, working for the WPB in 1942, blasted Donald Nelson for surrounding himself with antibusiness New Dealers, Baruch sharply rebuked him. "I regret your role of a *public critic*," Baruch scolded. "There is no reason why you should not have said what you wanted to, to him within the organization, and that is what I would have preferred you to have done."[78] He would have nobody give the appearance of partisan politics in wartime. This is not to say that he sublimated policy and personnel disputes. On the contrary, Baruch had a talent for crystallizing them within the confines of the war bureaucracy.

The basic issues of mobilization in 1942 had not changed at all since the fight over the War Resources Board in 1939. Policy conflict over the nature of war production began with resistance to the Baruch concept of economic organization. It asked the fundamental question how the capitalist system could mobilize and stabilize itself without effectively reducing or eliminating competition through industrial cooperation tending toward cartelization. Thus, stabilization required fewer units collaborating in a planned market to control civilian supply and demand. Put simply, as New Deal economist Tom Blaisdell, Jr., explained it, "The struggle got to the point of one between big cartels in the formative stage and the American system of free enterprise."[79]

Obviously that is too neat an explanation. Washington's wartime fights involved other issues as well. Civilian wartime administrators suspected army supply chiefs of plotting a coup d'etat against democratic processes. New Dealers were certain that big businessmen were intent upon eliminating smaller competition. Businessmen believed that liberals sought to carry on their social crusades besides fighting the Nazis and the Japanese. Sometimes the political conflicts were predicated upon personality, civilian occupation, or class background. To begin with, wartime administrators often characterized each other with words like "ruthless" and "ambitious" because so many of them were ruthless and ambitious to win power in the war setup. But that was nothing new in the bureaucracies of government, business, or academe whence they came. Career government officials tended to disparage the abilities of businessmen who wandered through their bailiwicks during the emergency. Academics, mostly economists, agreed that businessmen usually brought a narrow focus into government. Even lawyers sneered at businessmen. Some discerning observers realized that not all businessmen could be lumped together and began distinguishing between "production men" from the corporate world and "bankers" from Wall Street. Finally, even the old school tie mattered in making alignments. Princeton and Yale men dominated the War Department leadership and obviously felt quite comfortable with one another. Most were either Wall Street brokers or lawyers who moved easily in financial circles. They tried not to discriminate along such lines, but a man from Cornell was easier to respect than one from the University of Missouri.[80]

An acid test for the nature of wartime mobilization was Baruch's insistence upon industrial committees and the WPB's resistance to anything that abridged the antitrust laws. Baruch was unrelenting in his argument that mobilization could not be effective until businessmen upon WPB industrial committees achieved conversion by "a voluntary cooperation instead of a driven, forced acceptance." Baruch argued that the committees were essential to achieving priorities and stabilizing prices. Industrial committees in government would carry a clearly stated immunity from prosecution for time collusion. Following Pearl Harbor, Baruch pushed hard for the suspension of antitrust laws and all trust-busting activities for the duration. "His plan," WPB counsel John Lord O'Brian believed, "if followed, would have operated to promote the cartelization of industry."[81]

Baruch often boasted that he could play rough in bureaucratic politics to get his way; this is what he did in thwarting antitrust activities during the war. When Nelson was about to appoint Charles E. Wilson of General Electric as the WPB's top production man, Baruch telephoned Wilson's GE superior, Owen D. Young, and got him to agree that Wilson would not go to Washington unless Nelson could give them assurances that antitrust prosecutions would be stopped for the duration. Then he informed Nelson of this, making it clear that he expected the WPB to add its voice to those telling the White House to call off the Justice Department's antitrust crusaders. Baruch later reported to the head of General Mills that he need fear trustbuster Thurman Arnold no more. But Baruch and his friends remained wary about possible antitrust prosecutions for the rest of the war. In December, Nelson was pressed to secure a waiver of the antitrust laws for the remainder of the war and six months after. As late as 1944, Baruch warned Roosevelt that Wilson would be asked to return to GE if the Justice Department instituted an antitrust suit.[82]

The key figure in blocking or implementing Baruch's recommendations for organizing the war effort was the enigmatic Donald Nelson. Along with Averell Harriman, he constituted Harry Hopkins's principal link to the business community. The Hopkins connection alone aligned some New Dealers with Nelson, just as it aligned some businessmen against him. Notwithstanding the antipathies of their friends, Nelson and Baruch cultivated their friendship as Nelson moved up the defense organization ladder. Yet when Baruch was consulted on his choice to head the WPB, Nelson was not the man. The key to Roosevelt's selection of Nelson was probably his demonstrated loyalty and deference to the president. During the 1940 campaign, when other businessmen in the defense setup had quietly supported Willkie, Nelson let it be known that he was a Roosevelt man. In March 1941 he had told Roosevelt that he desired to return to business, but the president would not allow his departure. Even among New Dealers, doubts concerning Nelson's administrative and organizational abilities abounded late in 1941, but once the decision to create the WPB was made, administration leaders decided, "It was probably preferable to take him with his known limitations than to take a new man whose positive or negative qualities were unknown."[83]

During the next year, Nelson alienated his doubters and disappointed many of his friends. As top dog in mobilization, he had to organize its apparatus. But by his habit of procrastination when it was apparent that action was called for, or his unpredictability when a move was finally made, Nelson managed to encourage a consensus of opinion, to which even his sympathizers subscribed, that he was "incapable of exercising with decision and dispatch the authority which has been given him." Such critical judgments were arrived at reluctantly because practically everyone who came in contact with him found him likable and intelligent. A subordinate said of him in 1942, "If I were to point out characteristics of Mr. Nelson, I would say that the first outstanding characteristic of his is patience; the second is patience; and the third is patience; and, after you get through with all of these, throw them away, and the fourth and most important one is patience. His willingness to listen, his willingness to learn, and his willingness to be slow in taking drastic action."[84] Admirable in peacetime administration, such traits were viewed as signs of weakness in war. All factions wanted drastic action. Nelson was constantly being called upon to dare to make a mistake, to dare to antagonize somebody with a decision for greater authority over the war effort. Evidently he wished to avert any of these choices.

Baruch, who even in peace wanted "an autocrat" in defense production, obviously had to be impatient with Nelson's methods. Moreover, Nelson's first major decision was perplexing. Empowered to do anything necessary in the interests of the war effort, Nelson chose to leave the power of procurement with the military. That went counter to Baruch's contention that the War Department was "not organized to *place business*" in 1942 any more than it had been in 1918. Although Baruch's concern was assuaged by the increasingly dynamic leadership of the Army-Navy Munitions Board (ANMB) chairman, Ferdinand Eberstadt, the mobilization structure still went against his principle of centralizing power in a civilian board.[85]

Otherwise, Nelson proved himself politically adept. In March he set up labor-management committees that immediately drew Baruch's dis-approval. Labor involvement in war production would "cause lots of trouble," the Old Man forecast. Nelson did not recant; rather he talked the matter over with Baruch, and it is noteworthy that the committees never really involved labor in major WPB decisions.[86]

"I have not yet made up my mind about Nelson," Baruch told a friend early in the life of the WPB. He defended Nelson against criticism:

> Mr. Nelson's job is not quite so simple as it appears. He inherited an organization which, no one knew better than he, had to be revamped. . . .
>
> Donald Nelson and his men have been consulting me rather freely about men and organization. . . . He is getting the thing under way, perhaps too slowly from your or my viewpoint, but the head of an organization has to handle it the way he sees fit just as each golf player has a different stance.

Baruch's patience with Nelson was predicated upon patriotism and politi-cal common sense. Nelson would have to break himself upon the crucible of war before Baruch would join any foolish mob of businessmen calling for his head. Even when he began to concede that the WPB was "not what I would like to see," Baruch still praised Nelson for his "unfailing courtesy and willingness to listen." It was difficult not to be charitable to Nelson. In July, Nelson initiated a reorganization of WPB and Baruch told a doubting journalist friend:

> He has had to face great difficulties in getting the men he wanted. . . . He is not a colorful man who makes a big noise, but he is much harder and determined than people think he is. Some think he is a little too polite and considerate at times. I have seen no evidence of any selfish interest on his part. He has kept his poise and temper in very trying circumstances. No one could have been more courteous or generous, or could have sought more frequently advice and suggestions than he has from me. Naturally he does not always agree with me but I have always found him open-minded.

Conceding that Nelson might not be the best man for the job, and that he might even have drinking and financial difficulties, Baruch insisted, "We all have to follow our leader."[87]

By contrast, Baruch was enthusiastic about a newcomer to Washington, Ferdinand Eberstadt. Eberstadt was the sort of "driver" Baruch liked—a man almost without introspective doubts about either his abilities or the choices before him. Intellectually brilliant by all accounts, Eberstadt ad-mired men who were able, dedicated, and ruthless; and these were adjec-tives often applied to him. In the 1920s he had been a Wall Street lawyer before joining the brokerage firm of Dillon Read, where he made a reputation as a specialist in corporate mergers. He struck out on his own in the latter part of the decade, participated in European debt negotiations of 1929, suffered a reverse in Wall Street early in the depression, but soon earned a reputation for reorganizing small and middle-sized companies. Later in the decade he created a mutual fund that focused upon chemical companies; the Chemical Fund's assets would grow handsomely. *Fortune* described him as an "autocrat" and a "lone wolf." What undoubtedly made Eberstadt eminently qualified in Baruch's eyes for a prominent role in mobilization was the fact that he was a superb scholar of business. He extensively studied corporations and maintained a "good man" list of especially talented executives. As Baruch knew from World War I, that sort of knowledge was invaluable for organizing the enterprise of war. Eberstadt's old friends from Wall Street, now ensconced in the War and Navy departments, brought him to Washington in 1941 for the purpose of studying ways to revitalize the Army-Navy Munitions Board. Eberstadt immediately turned to the Industrial Mobilization Plan of 1939, which had called for the War Resources Board dropped by Roosevelt. He recommended that the ANMB be reconstituted as "the simon-pure all-out advocate of the requirements of the services," a suggestion with obvious appeal to the men who had commissioned the study. They immediately offered him the ANMB's chairmanship, and following Pearl Harbor he accepted it.[88]

To the delight of the military and the consternation of some civilians he made a superb advocate for the ANMB. Often dubbed a Prussian, Eberstadt became known as a tough and indefatigable administrator whose views on policy and organization were original and frequently in conflict with those of the WPB. He aligned himself so easily with Baruch that Eberstadt soon became known as his "protégé," even though they had struck up a friendship only after Eberstadt reached Washington. He knew how to defer to Baruch as "Boss" and gave old J. Leonard Replogle, the WIB's steel man, a job in the ANMB—even if nobody else would take him on as Baruch requested. "Eberstadt has more overall brains than any there," Baruch soon enthusiastically proclaimed. "If we had him before!"[89]

"Eberstadt was an exceptionally capable executive," Henry Wallace remembered years later. "He was probably a genuine reactionary, but the kind of man who can be useful in time of war."[90] The New Dealers had good reason to be leery of Eberstadt, although they could not dispute his talents. Among those talents was a capacity for sharpening issues between stabilizers and expansionists. Military-civilian priorities always went to the heart of the struggle; in 1942 the military had a decisive priority over civilian needs, but the proportions to be allocated remained in dispute. How much of the economic pie could be diverted to military use before civilian scarcity would impinge upon home-front morale? This was a problem that called for a careful division of materials and manpower so as not to limit the military's capacity to fight or the civilian's capacity to produce. Fearing that Wall Street stabilizers would distribute resources in a way that would allow military production and unemployment to co-exist, New Deal expansionists argued for the allocation of materials in a manner that permitted a strong civilian market to supplement military production. They believed that Eberstadt, Baruch, and the military leadership would sacrifice labor and small business to the cause of victory through cartelization. Only by expanding the civilian's fair share of resources could they preserve a measure of economic equity. On the other hand, the stabilizers retorted that the New Dealers put social objectives ahead of winning the war. Against that impugning of their patriotism the New Dealers knew that they were helpless. For the first year of the war they could only hope to prevent the military from conscripting everything for its purposes.

New Dealers sometimes interpreted the conflict as resistance to a military putsch. Such jitters among liberals were encouraged by examples in Germany and Spain. Also, the army's head of supply services, General Brehon D. Somervell, had an appetite for control that seemed to have no limits. Some liberals often assumed that Eberstadt's "Prussianism" ran interference for Somervell. Actually, however, because Eberstadt followed Baruch's mobilization scheme with its defined supremacy for civilian industrial leadership, he prevented the army from running amok. Somervell's quest for an inordinate amount of power encouraged the illusion of a civilian-military conflict, but the bull never got into the china shop. In fact, Nelson's initial decision to leave the procurement power with the services, which ran counter to what Baruch and Eberstadt prescribed for the WPB, encouraged the notion of military ascendancy. Accorded such authority by the head of war production, Eberstadt and the ANMB saw little choice but to use it. But he and Baruch would have preferred to see Nelson exercise complete power over production in behalf of stabilization.[91]

Eberstadt's task as chairman of the ANMB called for coordinating procurement among the services, securing raw materials for munitions, and advocating military requirements before the WPB. That meant pushing the WPB toward conversion of industries and plants more quickly than some people thought desirable. Industrialists such as tool manufacturers encouraged delay because of their fears of wartime overexpansion with postwar contraction. Eberstadt's major accomplishment with the machine tool industry was in eliciting greater production without an increase in plant capacity. That required standardization of tools among the services and heavy pressure upon the industry to deliver what the ANMB wanted when it wanted it.[92] It is not surprising that Eberstadt quickly became a favorite of Baruch and the War Department.

But free enterprise prevailed in America despite the best of mobilization intentions because the priorities system had broken down at the inception of the production process. As the system originally worked, a high priority rating did not guarantee anything but a "hunting license" for a manufacturer seeking materials he needed to fulfill a war contract. But the manufacturer had to find the materials before he could flash his license and claim them. Moreover, the number of licenses proliferated. Eberstadt's major contribution to the war effort was devising the Controlled Materials Plan, which the WPB adopted and modified through late 1942 and into 1943. That converted the various services and other agencies into claimants upon the stock of materials. They in turn had responsibility for dividing the stock among prime contractors, who passed a "warrant" for materials along vertically to subcontractors. This method immediately drew apprehension from liberals, who viewed it as a shift of production authority to the military and claimed that it would permit materials to be controlled by giant corporations acting as prime contractors. The WPB's Planning Committee, a liberal stronghold, swung behind Eberstadt's Controlled Materials Plan in September after receiving assurances from expansionist economists "that there is a plentiful supply of material to carry out everything which we want to do, including adequate civilian supply." Nelson already had decided to implement Eberstadt's scheme and had asked him to join the WPB for that purpose. But Eberstadt declined to take a third-level position of authority. Once the Planning Committee offered assurance of nonobstruction, and Eberstadt understood that he would be second in the WPB organization only to Nelson, he accepted.[93]

Baruch played an influential role in the events that brought Eberstadt to the WPB. With Baruch's encouragement, Eberstadt demanded "clear and final authority" in the WPB, which meant that he would "report directly to Don." Baruch personally gave that message to Nelson. On 19 September, Eberstadt wired Baruch, "Personal deal with Don for which you principally responsible closed this morning on satisfactory basis."[94] It seemed that the Baruch method of mobilization-stabilization had triumphed in late 1942.

"I WOULD APPOINT BARUCH"

"The summer and early fall of 1942 were unquestionably the lowest point of the war in terms of morale on the war production front," writes a historian of mobilization. "Production was rising but fell far short of the goals established by the President and the armed forces."[95] In part the problem lay not in production but in the goals sought by the military. Nobody had any concept of what quantity of war goods would win the war. Thus, military demands that the services receive all that the economy could produce without destroying civilian morale seemed reasonable. Of course that left undefined the point where production satisfied military requirements for victory or the point where the civilian sector screamed in protest. Alarm and doubt began to spread in the summer of 1942 as it became evident that output quotas would not be filled. War production was proceeding apace, but not reaching the targets set by the mobilization's leadership. Partly at fault, went the consensus of judgment, was the distribution of essential war materials. Eberstadt's Controlled Materials Plan was expected to remedy that structural dilemma. But the WPB's Planning Committe began to argue that military expectations for production distorted war and economic realities.[96] The stage was set for a bureaucratic power struggle involving Baruch's "informal liaison."

Baruch's "protégé," Eberstadt, drew the fire of New Dealers in the war agencies. First, they sought to "counterbalance" his sudden ascendancy to power in the WPB with the appointment of General Electric's Charles E. Wilson as WPB program vice-chairman and head of the Production Executive Committee. It was not that Nelson and the WPB planners expected Wilson to side with them in reducing the military's bite of the economic pie. Rather they were counting upon the bureaucratic imperial impulse of a successful production man to neutralize Eberstadt's financial genius. It was a calculated gamble that the production man would side with advocates of an expanding civilian economy against the financial-military combine of Baruch, Eberstadt, and the Pentagon. It worked. Barely two months after they arrived at WPB, Wilson and Eberstadt were squabbling over scheduling requirements; and Wilson was demanding from the War Department procurement powers to which Nelson had relinquished the WPB's claim.[97]

As anyone could have predicted, the military was not about to give up procurement without a fight. It carried its case straight to the president, who, as was his custom, advised both parties to work out their differences amicably. This Nelson did with Secretaries Stimson and Knox. But some New Dealers feared a military "putsch" against civilians. "Wilson is now carrying the ball for civilian control," went the analysis of economist Mordecai Ezekiel. "He is a symbol of American democracy and of proved ability in industrial management. . . . He is a big-business man who—fortunately—is on the side of the angels. If we let him go down, there will be nothing left to stop the Army-Eberstadt-Baruch clique from obtaining complete power and control over the organization of industry for the war, and probably for the peace as well." Ezekiel apparently did not know that the War Department considered Wilson "one of the two strong men we have placed under [Nelson]."[98]

But the bureaucratic imperative prevailed. Wilson demanded jurisdiction over industrial divisions then under Eberstadt's authority. Nelson delayed making a decision but Wilson persisted. Finally, Nelson approved an order for the transfer in February.[99] That month, Nelson also fired Eberstadt.

Though the two events were not unrelated, the firing of Eberstadt had less to do with Wilson's jurisdictional claims than with the ominous shadow over Nelson of Bernard Baruch. Baruch had earnestly sought to avoid any personal conflict with Nelson. They saw each other frequently, Nelson always careful to give Baruch the "Boss" treatment even when deference did not necessarily signal agreement. It was a correct relationship. Nelson needed Baruch as an ally as much as Baruch wanted Nelson to succeed. Baruch enjoyed the role he played in 1942, freelancing through the bureaucracy, appearing before congressional committees, heading the rubber committee, dispensing, in the words of Felix Frankfurter, "occasional wise advice of a general nature." Promoting policy and bureaucratic rivalries appealed to him more than front-line administration. However, Nelson's indecisiveness frustrated Baruch's quest for a mobilization czar who organized everything. The appointments of Eberstadt and Wilson he took as omens that Nelson "at long last" had embraced his concepts of mobilization.[100] But Nelson was fated to disappoint even his closest allies.

It was not like Baruch to be part of a cabal to overthrow somebody in power. He liked to be on the winning side in any fight. He gravitated naturally to people in power, rather than to complainers. He was eclectic in his alliances. Liberals like Ickes and Mrs. Roosevelt were his warm friends during the war years; their shared distaste for Harry Hopkins undoubtedly had something to do with that. Still, his association with Nelson demonstrated that he could go along with a Hopkins favorite. Although he clearly sided with the War Department in its disputes with Nelson, he believed that the military lacked the economic intelligence required for running mobilization. He feared that its appetite for weaponry outpaced what the society could reasonably produce. Stabilization required that the military scale down its expectations. He reminded General Somervell that the army's needs had to be filled "with the least dislocation of civilian life," which meant that the WPB had to "see that the minimum requirements of the civilians are met in order that the programs of the armed forces can be carried out." The military ought to appreciate that Nelson had an obligation "to see that the armed forces do not ask for more than our economy can produce."[101] Just as the designs of liberals would, he feared, produce undesirable overexpansion so too would the military's claims. He preached a gospel of economic restraint.

Baruch allied himself with the War Department for many reasons. To begin with, the department was more receptive to him than was Nelson, sincerely listening and learning from him. The finance men of the War Department agreed on a concentrated economic organization for war.

Also, Baruch liked strong men who could reach for power and exercise it with an authority that commanded respect rather than hostility. Patterson, Forrestal, and Eberstadt were determined men without immobilizing introspection; they must have reminded Baruch of Summers, Legge, and Peek. They could be autocrats; Baruch wished for such qualities in Nelson. Even so, he did not yet agree with the War Department's view that the war effort would be served by the replacement of Nelson with himself.[102]

On the other hand, New Dealers appreciated the fact that civilian supply had no spokesman with the prestige of Baruch who could publicize demands for horizontal expansion. New Dealers yearned for a spokesman with "the quality above all of enlisting public support and identifying public feeling about him[,] . . . a man with a strong flair for begetting and holding confidence." Names like Nelson and Wallace were bandied about, and even that of Baruch "(somewhat ironically proposed)," a tribute to his reputation as the master publicist.[103]

In early 1943 a consensus in favor of Nelson's removal began to take shape. Of course the War Department considered him incompetent, a judgment that the WPB Planning Committee began to share. At a time when they looked for a champion around which they could rally, liberals realized that Nelson was "an utterly weak man incapable of exercising authority or making decisions if contending forces about him have to be composed." But who could they trust to resist the War Department? At least, Nelson's penchant for tergiversation had prevented the triumph of the War Department, if nothing else. Wilson's greatest virtue was that he had disappointed his War Department sponsors. Liberals knew the War Department had visions of Baruch as chairman of the WPB with Eberstadt running the operation. To get rid of Nelson without enthroning Baruch and Eberstadt, liberals sought a conservative compromise.[104]

At the same time, Congress was politically sensitive to the public controversies swirling about the WPB. Congressional calls for a production czar were heard with greater frequency, and it was not uncommon for Baruch to be mentioned as the super-mobilizer. In January, Senate liberals introduced a bill calling for an agency to supersede the WPB. With Congress threatening to grab control of production from him, Roosevelt began seriously to consider an overseas assignment for Nelson while Wilson ran the WPB. Nelson's ouster would satisfy his detractors and head off a Baruch boomlet. But Roosevelt, as was his wont, temporized. To confuse the situation further, Wilson was threatening to resign. Roosevelt appeared about ready to send Nelson to Australia and put Wilson in charge of the WPB when on 5 February, Jimmy Byrnes wrote the president a letter.

In essence it was a brief for Baruch. As director of economic stabilization, Byrnes was an arbiter of claims to materials needed in production. And now the former Supreme Court justice made a case for Baruch as the safest political choice to lead the WPB. "I would appoint Baruch," Byrnes advised the president:

> You would be taking no chances. He knows that organization better than anybody in it. For the past year he has spent four or five days each week in Washington, and the heads of the various divisions have taken their problems to him. Without any power he has accomplished miracles in straightening out controversies and in securing the cooperation of manufacturers. Mr. Wilson, Mr. Eberstadt and every other leader in the organization would welcome the appointment of Baruch. Baruch likes Wilson; he could appoint him as his vice chairman. Eberstadt would gladly follow him.
>
> Every agency of the government doing business with WPB would applaud the appointment. Both the Army and the Navy have asked me to make this statement to you. . . .
>
> You and I know his appointment would be welcomed by the Congress. [Senator] Hill telephoned me today that the agitation for the Pepper bill [for a super-agency] was due entirely to their belief that WPB was not performing; Truman is of the same opinion. They believe that the appointment of a strong man would kill the Pepper bill. When they say strong man, they do not mention Baruch, but I know they would throw up their hats for his appointment. The press would welcome the appointment. There are a number of leaders of the press who would criticize Wilson's appointment, but will applaud Baruch. Some of your severest critics would find it difficult to shoot at WPB when Baruch is in charge. . . .
>
> Baruch would like the appointment. He has never told me this, but I know him well enough to know that his heart is in the production fight. He would rather do that job than anything else on earth. . . .
>
> If you get rid of Nelson and appoint Wilson, his subordinate, Nelson and his friends will certainly resent it. . . . We know that Nelson would not feel so bad about it if his friend Baruch was appointed.
>
> Last but not least, he is loyal to you. For a year he has worked as hard as if he were on the payroll. . . . You would be appointing not only the best man for the place, but appointing one of your best friends.
>
> Harry Hopkins told me to say to you that he concurs heartily in my suggestion.[105]

The last sentence was the clincher. Roosevelt had no choice but to go with Baruch for the sake of production harmony; even Hopkins, who had resisted anything politically associated with Baruch, had capitulated. Not only could Baruch silence Congress, the War Department, the press, and business critics of the WPB, but he would be tolerant of New Dealers in the war establishment. After all, Baruch had recommended Ben Cohen, one of Frankfurter's protégés, for the post of Byrnes's OES counsel. Although there was no mistaking Baruch's passion for stabilization along lines favorable to giant corporations, New Dealers might agree with I. F. Stone that "he has more understanding of social issues than is common in one of his class and background." Baruch offered Roosevelt a public relations miracle; he offered liberals survival within the war apparatus.

According to Byrnes, Roosevelt asked him to draft a letter offering the WPB to Baruch. Byrnes did it immediately, returned to the president for his signature, and then personally delivered it to Baruch at his hotel. Baruch read it and told Byrnes he was leaving for New York that evening and would give him a reply the next day. Byrnes did not hear from Baruch for several days, the Old Man later claiming to have taken sick on the train to New York. When he returned about ten days later, Roosevelt acted as if no letter had been sent. Significantly, by that time, Nelson, in an unusual display of decisiveness, had fired Ferd Eberstadt.

Why didn't Baruch take the post as soon as Byrnes brought him Roosevelt's offer? "The proposal came as a bolt from the blue," Baruch claimed in his memoirs. If that be so, then Baruch must have been the only surprised man in Washington. Rumors of the impending switch were rife throughout the capital. Baruch was too good a rumormonger himself to have missed that one. On the very day Byrnes swung into action a New Deal senator reported to Henry Wallace: "Baruch is certainly on a high these days with everybody coming to his place at the Carlton. . . . There is a movement of foot [sic] to have Baruch reorganize production and quite a few people may go to the President soon. . . . The argument is that Baruch has great prestige in the country and that Nelson is fading fast and he is too weak." Moreover, two days before Baruch received the offer, Eberstadt had shown Baruch a letter of resignation he planned to give Nelson. Baruch pleaded with Eberstadt not to send it because "certain developments had taken place" of which Eberstadt was ignorant. Baruch had to recognize that a showdown was approaching in which one of the three—Nelson, Wilson, or Eberstadt—would be ousted.[106]

But Byrnes ought not to have been surprised by Baruch's apparent reluctance to lead the WPB; he had been the political tactician who had convinced Baruch that he could best operate without a portfolio. On the basis of that strategy, Baruch had launched his career as a "park bench statesman," a masterpiece of public relations that brought him power without accountability. Meanwhile the moody Byrnes estranged himself from Baruch until that 6 February. Then Byrnes expected a seventy-two-year-old man who was deaf in one ear and required afternoon naps to get him through the day to take on the most vital task of the war effort. As Baruch wrote an intimate friend later that year: "My increasing deafness saps my physical and nervous system and it is making me more of a recluse—not by wish—but because of the strain in carrying on my work.

The ordinary amenities, contacts, meals at which several persons are present are entirely denied to me. I recognize that I can preserve a certain amount of usefulness, but when evening comes I am tired. I still am able to function as well, and even better than I ever did, up to late afternoon." Obviously, Baruch at the WPB would be an arbiter of policies and responsibilities, while the routine administrative assignments would be done by others. (That was how he had operated even a quarter of a century before.) And that in itself presented a problem for Baruch. For though everyone assumed that Baruch's chief lieutenant would be Eberstadt, Baruch wanted his old WIB comrade, John Hancock. Hancock's wife had suffered a heart attack in 1942, however, and he was afraid to leave her for a Washington assignment. Baruch was too dependent upon old associates like Hancock to risk any job without them.[107]

Why did Nelson fire Eberstadt and what did he accomplish by doing so? The answers lie with the key war role played by the Bureau of the Budget. The bureau's position on the WPB's upheaval was distinctively anti-Baruch. Although they usually concurred on stabilization questions, Director Harold Smith did not like Baruch's activities. However, Smith was among those disenchanted with Nelson. When Nelson would not be budged gracefully into the Australian portfolio if it meant relinquishing the WPB to Baruch and Eberstadt, Smith and Assistant Director Wayne Coy counseled Roosevelt and Nelson to maintain the status quo until a groundswell for Wilson materialized. But tensions were so high that such temporizing would no longer work. Coy finally went to Nelson with the recommendation that he save himself and Wilson by firing Eberstadt. That Nelson did so, was, Smith observed, "the first evidence on [sic] any real intestinal fortitude on the part of Nelson." Thus, Nelson saved his own position at the WPB. Had Roosevelt then removed Nelson, it would have suggested to the public confusion at the WPB and retaliation for the firing of Eberstadt. (And Roosevelt personally disliked Eberstadt.) Nelson had to stay for a while. Baruch had done Roosevelt a favor by not leaping at the offer of the WPB and allowing it to die.[108]

Nelson survived only as long as Baruch was the alternative to him. In the struggle of factions, Baruch was too closely identified with the War Department. In Washington it was widely believed that if Baruch got Nelson's job, it would mean the expansion of War Department power through Eberstadt and further contraction of the civilian economy. Hardly anybody outside the Pentagon wanted such a clear-cut political decision. Wilson, having just inherited real authority in the WPB, threatened to resign if Baruch were appointed his superior. He sensed that a Baruch appointment would reverse his triumph over Eberstadt. Harold Smith went out of his way to inform Roosevelt that "Nelson's removal in favor of anyone other than Wilson would indicate that he had been removed because of his dismissal of Eberstadt." To the relief of New Dealers,

Nelson vowed to resign only if replaced by Wilson, not Baruch—whom he considered a "calamity (not because of Baruch as a person but because the situation needs somebody like Wilson and not somebody like Baruch)." Felix Frankfurter admonished White House counsel Sam Rosenman that Roosevelt could ill afford a WPB head accustomed to leaking stories to Arthur Krock and David Lawrence and hobnobbing with arch-conservative Clare Boothe Luce:

> I told him . . . that the man at the head of WPB must be one who is actually capable of running the organization ten hours a day for six days, and that Baruch certainly is physically and psychologically not capable of that. The war production process cannot be run by intermittent flashes . . . which is the function that Baruch has been exercising and could only exercise if he were formally made head of WPB. . . . In a single word, my view was that while Baruch's appointment would result in what is called "a good press" for a short honeymoon period, honeymoons are notoriously brief and the problems of production are technical, humdrum problems not to be solved by glamour and a good press. Sam said "You are speaking words of wisdom."[109]

The intrigues of February did not pass. On Washington's Birthday, Stimson went to the White House to "push for Baruch." The secretary of war belatedly heard from the president that Baruch had been offered the WPB; but, Rooosevelt told him, "Baruch had asked for a little delay to see how the thing would go." As Stimson left he was followed by presidential assistant "Pa" Watson, a Baruch admirer, who advised Stimson that Roosevelt was the one who was delaying and needed a push. Back at the Pentagon, Stimson sent for Baruch and exacted a promise that the next time he received a presidential offer he would accept on the spot. Stimson then passed that assurance along to Watson. Yet he sensed that Roosevelt already had decided as firmly as he ever decided anything not to give the nod to Baruch.[110]

Writing in a February issue of the *Nation*, I. F. Stone declared, "Now it looks as though Baruch's moment has come." Stone could not know it then, but Baruch's moment had passed. The climax to the WPB-War Department struggle was history—although a significant denouement still awaited. But to Stone's credit he understood that the fight represented more than a conflict of personalities or government agencies: "This current quarrel can easily be over-simplified and over-dramatized. It is only superficially a military-civilian struggle. Only 9 per cent of the men in the War department's services of supply are regular army officers; the rest are businessmen in uniform. It is a clash between two groups of big-business men, one linked with the military bureaucracy, the other somewhat tenuously allied with New Dealers and labor." The struggle had no heroes. If Eberstadt was, as Stone believed, a "Wall Street monopolist," then it had to be remembered, too, that "Nelson, a very weak man, fired Eberstadt and delegated all power to Wilson from fear as much as from conviction."[111]

The importance of Nelson declined significantly, and Jimmy Byrnes's star seemed on the rise. Nelson and Wilson reorganized the WPB with changes that weakened its New Deal influence. That process did neither man any good. Nor did Wilson's shift from support of Nelson to antagonism help matters. Wilson's star began to fade. Although he had once boosted Wilson for the WPB, Baruch had come to consider the former GE executive "sly, tricky, and undependable." Clearly he was not the man who could bridge the gap between the factions. Nelson's remaining support seemed centered on Capitol Hill, where the Truman committee was his staunchest backer. With such political support, and because it would not have looked good for another major switch so soon after the WPB reorganization, Roosevelt in May 1943 opted for the creation of the Office of War Mobilization (OWM) in the White House under Jimmy Byrnes. It was an artful compromise that satisfied Stimson, subordinated Nelson, and silenced liberals in Congress.[112] It was the last major administrative change of the war and represented the culmination of Baruch's efforts to secure concentration of mobilization and stabilization. Byrnes had emerged as the Baruch of World War II.

BREACH WITH BYRNES

On the day before Byrnes's appointment as director of the Office of War Mobilization was announced, Byrnes—with Roosevelt's approval—offered Baruch the position he was vacating, director of the Office of Economic Stabilization. It was the second time it was offered to Baruch; for a second time he rejected it. That, combined with a hesitation that suggested reluctance when he was offered the WPB chairmanship, gave considerable credibility to the Baruch reputation of World War II—that he desired influence over policy without responsibility for its implementation.

There is an element of truth in the charge, but the accusation—whispered by longtime detractor Felix Frankfurter, promoted by Frankfurter acolytes, and accepted by Baruch biographer Margaret Coit[113]—is too facile and simplistic. It should also be recognized that Baruch was still critical of a basic shortcoming of stabilization policy, which Frankfurter New Dealers defended—separation of controls from taxation. Without their central coordination, stabilization was not comprehensive—it was incomprehensible. Secretary of the Treasury Morgenthau still held sway over fiscal affairs, and as Baruch predicted when Byrnes took the stabilization assignment, Byrnes clashed with Morgenthau over taxation policy. It was said that Baruch wanted Morgenthau deposed; certainly Baruch did not hold him in high regard. But it is unlikely that Baruch himself would have taken the Treasury Department in the even more unlikely event that it had been proffered. He wanted Byrnes to remedy the mobilization-stabilization muddle by asserting the need for a compatible fiscal policy. All Baruch told Byrnes was that the stabilization office lacked definition.

But it is noteworthy that Baruch gave no final answer before he called John Hancock, both for his advice and to see if Hancock were available to assist in OES if Baruch took it. The Lehman Brothers partner responded that his work would allow him to come to Washington, but he could not recommend that his friend take the job because he "was *not* experienced" in stabilization management! Baruch apparently did not dispute this. In fact, the Old Man was "profuse in his thanks" for reinforcement of his decision to turn down OES. Hancock believed that basic policy still came from the White House rather than the war agencies and that the president was ultimately persuaded by "back door appeals to him," by New Dealers. Thus, the stabilizer lacked power to make stabilization policy. Moreover, existing policy proceeded upon the erroneous assumption "that the mere holding [down] of prices is the whole of the price problem." Like Baruch, Hancock insisted upon "a very well rounded program, integrating price and production policies, with recognition of the distribution function handled collaterally, covering wages and wage policies, taxes and tax policies, possibly enforced savings," and greater controls over food production, prices, and distribution. Needless to say, "selfish pressure groups" were not about to subscribe to Hancock's corporatism. Both labor and agriculture would resist expanded controls; nor would businessmen be happy with the Baruch-Hancock formula for rolling back prices to their levels at the time of the Fall of France in 1940, rather than living with "all disparities" built into the 1942 scheme. World War II was not the executive matter without politics sought by these veterans of 1918.[114]

In 1943 the war effort was still evolving, as was Baruch's place in it. Stabilization policies were still unsatisfactory. That Baruch complained about them is not surprising. The absence of a comprehensive and stringent price scheme drained materials from the war effort and made them unnecessarily expensive, he reminded Nelson and others who had no choice but to listen to him. He could concur with his fellow Wilsonian Herbert Hoover that it was "utterly impossible to separate the price question from the production question," as the Roosevelt administration and Congress seemed intent upon doing. However, when conservatives like Senator Byrd endorsed "the Baruch formula" because it restrained agricultural prices and industrial wages, "which are the very basis of any inflationary movement," then it was bound to be viewed as politically troublesome by the White House. Price control administration had been weakened by the replacement of Leon Henderson with the politically minded former senator Prentiss Brown. Baruch was not unhappy to see Henderson depart, for the scrappy OPA chief had begun to bait the army and incur Baruch's ire. But, significantly, others shared Baruch's belief that as production and battlefield triumphs manifested themselves, the White House began to overlook stabilization shortcomings. OPA counsel David Ginsburg expressed such an opinion, and Budget Director Harold Smith privately and bluntly told the president that the stabilization program was inadequate. Not only did Roosevelt concede Smith's point, he also agreed that Congress needed firm administration leadership on an agricultural subsidy program and "a vigorous tax program to absorb purchasing power." Without such measures, Smith warned, the administration could anticipate new and justified demands for wage hikes.[115]

Ever an advocate of regressive taxation abhorred by FDR, Baruch knew that the war justified a Draconian fiscal policy. Antiinflationary taxes promoted social equity in a nation under arms. As he told the chairman of the Senate Finance Committee, the economics of war distributed burdens unequally:

> If we have uncurbed competition for prices, manpower, and priorities on implements, it can only lead to chaos. If food prices go up, wages must go up. So too must everything else. What happens then to the unorganized people—soldiers' dependents, pensioners, schoolteachers, firemen, policemen, all government employees, and non-union white-collar workers in industry? The incomes of these people have been enhanced very little, if at all, by the war boom. And, again not the least, what happens to the credit of the government—with spiralling prices multiplying the costs of the war? . . .
>
> In conclusion—and I know you will agree—no amount of centralized control through OWM and OPA, and no government guarantees, will succeed in freezing the price level unless we develop a fiscal program to siphon off the excess spending power. If we continue to give more money to our people, they will bid up prices. To the extent they buy things they do not need, we will have to cut down our lend-lease supplies, which would be skimping our allies while fattening and softening ourselves. *We must resort to a drastic program of taxation and savings for a great and necessary levelling*, and to protect the credit of our government.[116]

Thus, he sought to stiffen the president's resolve to control the shape of revenue legislation, as did the Bureau of the Budget and OWM. This campaign would climax in 1944 with the first veto of a revenue bill.

Baruch ought to have been pleased that his political protégé had been granted "super-czar" status. The *New York Times* noted that if Nelson's powers were comparable to those wielded by Baruch in 1918, then Byrnes's authority surpassed any ever enjoyed by Baruch. Also, in an "advisory and consultative" capacity, Byrnes created a War Mobilization Committee equivalent to a "war cabinet," a pet Baruch ploy for coordinating the war machinery. Although the committee lacked both the stature and broad membership Baruch preferred for it, its resemblance to his vaunted war cabinet was unmistakable. Appointed to it were Stimson, Knox, Nelson, Hopkins, and Fred M. Vinson, the new director of economic stabilization. (Vinson had resigned as a justice of the United States Court of Appeals to take the job. Significantly, he previously had been a prominent member of the tax-writing Ways and Means Committee in the House of Representatives.) Baruch had known about the committee beforehand. In fact, it seemed to exist primarily as a lure for engaging him in an official capacity; the committee met often in OWM's early stages, when Byrnes found it useful as a sounding board, but it never really figured in policy making and soon died from desuetude.

Byrnes hoped to avoid direct meddling in the affairs and activities of the various war agencies. He shrewdly appreciated that he would find his role of arbitrator, coordinator, and policy shaper taxing enough without relieving agency heads of their designated responsibilities. To avoid creating a bureaucracy that duplicated existing ones, Byrnes temporarily borrowed experienced hands from the Budget Bureau to confront particular problems, in the process complimenting an existing executive agency whose impact upon policy appeared diminished by Byrnes's ascendancy. Also, the War Department found it easier to swallow adverse decisions if they came from the conservative Byrnes. The confidence of congressmen in their old crony made enhanced White House power more acceptable. The man and the job were made for each other.[117]

Byrnes needed, however, to solve the problem of what to do with Baruch. The fault did not lie alone with the cantankerous older man. Byrnes was proud and ambitious. Solicitous of Baruch's pride and prestige, Byrnes grudgingly deferred to his old friend. They owed much to each other, debts not easily repaid because their value could never be estimated. For much of their association, Byrnes had worked in the senior man's public shadow, even when as senator from South Carolina he was widely recognized as one of the ablest men on the Hill. Now he was hailed in the press as the "assistant president," a prominence he achieved by himself. Some believed that he yearned to drop the adjective in his popular title by 1945 or 1949. Mounting pressures tended to make Byrnes, a man of engaging personality, more acerbic and aloof. Nobody noticed this more than Baruch.

However, the breach between them antedated Byrnes's failure to replace Nelson with Baruch in February. Baruch had expected that his friend would consult regularly with him regarding policy matters. That had not happened, and in early 1943, Baruch was complaining that he had not heard from Byrnes for a long time and interpreting this as evidence that Byrnes was too proud to turn to him. But then Byrnes turned to him to replace Nelson. Years later, Byrnes still recalled, "I was disappointed."[118]

Baruch endeavored to recover from his slight embarrassment over the WPB conflict by increasing his activities and visibility throughout Washington. He busied himself by investigating materials shortages, urging agency appointments for favored businessmen, and making himself seen at the White House. However strained their relations had become, Baruch's activities served as a reminder to Byrnes that he was still a force on the Washington scene to be reckoned with. Important memos regarding administrative policy still flowed out of Byrnes's office to Baruch for comments he scrawled in the margins. Even these occasional invitations for advice did not satisfy Baruch. He dared not barge in upon Byrnes without being asked; apparently he seldom received a call. Once he penned a note to Byrnes, "I have kept away from you because if you wanted me you knew where to find me. If you did not want me I would be a nuisance."[119]

Baruch would not have been a nuisance if he had allowed himself to be used as Byrnes saw fit. But his rejection of a position subordinate to Byrnes suggested that he wanted nothing that abridged his independence or diminished his prestige. Indeed, Baruch quickly signaled friends in the War Department that he sought to enlarge his personal staff. In OWM, Baruch would be, in Stimson's words, "the backstairs operator." Byrnes needed to find an official capacity for Baruch if he were to control the Old Man's activities. Baruch was telling Krock—for public consumption—that he refused the OES portfolio because he considered OWM's vaguely defined role as unpromising for the super-agency. To counter Baruch's hints of Byrnes's bureaucratic impotence, and to bring Baruch under his supervision, Byrnes announced on June 9 that the "hitherto itinerant adviser" would become his personal advisor. Without title or salary, Baruch would perform tasks not yet known. He was officially "on call." Krock hailed this as "an event of the highest consequences," for no other reason than that it supposedly enhanced Byrnes's public image. "I am delighted always to remember that you are my boss," the touchy Baruch assured the touchy Byrnes.

So Baruch in 1943 had a license to give advice, something he had never needed before. In his first month on the job it was evident that he wanted nothing less than to give counsel that Byrnes should act upon; and it already was even more evident that Byrnes did not follow his counsel, for each succeeding memorandum repeated recommendations that apparently had not been enacted. Moreover, Baruch had brought Hancock along as his ever-faithful associate, thereby doubling the paper flow toward Byrnes. It was, in the words of OWM's historian, "a unique arrangement." One anonymous observer later recalled Baruch as "a free-wheeling genius in the house." To some extent his genius went unappreciated by OWM's chief.[120]

Though Byrnes could ignore Baruch's advice, he could not ignore Baruch. The Old Man's prestige in wartime Washington made him useful. For instance, because it was Byrnes's responsibility to resolve bureaucratic squabbles, he commissioned Baruch to mediate squabbles before they reached Byrnes for adjudication. To some extent, Baruch already served as a go-between in these conflicts, with the grateful appreciation of the participants. When the Board of Economic Warfare contended for overseas financing authority that Jesse Jones's Reconstruction Finance Corporation was unwilling to share, the board's Milo Perkins took his

MR. BYRNES CONSULTS THE ORACLE

12. *The Baruch–James F. Byrnes relationship in* 1943 *as viewed in the press. (Courtesy Seeley G. Mudd Manuscript Library, Princeton University)*

fight to Congress and invoked the name of Baruch on his side. "On several occasions Mr. Bernard Baruch has helped us break log jams on this front," Perkins told an investigating Senate committee. "I have sought and been helped by his counsel and advice and have seen him on an average of once a week for more than a year now." Clearly that won the approval of the senators. Baruch's name was a talisman for practical administration.

Baruch remained without an office in the White House, but he did not need one. His suite at the Carlton served as headquarters for a staff that included Hancock, writer Samuel Lubell, and publicist Herb Swope. Government officials trekked to the Carlton, but Baruch received the press at his bench in Lafayette Park. Little had changed except that now the freewheeling Baruch operated semiofficially—as a publicist under Byrnes's reins.

It would be almost two years before Baruch would talk about his ruptured partnership with Byrnes. Then he would bitterly recall, "For months I hung around without anything to do, not knowing anything that was going on." By 1945, Baruch would be telling everyone that Byrnes no longer confided in him. Angrily he would assail Byrnes as "power crazy" and merely a "fixer" devoid of the knowledge of good administration. He resented the lack of deference from Byrnes's ambitious assistant, Donald Russell. Even newspapers would be noting signs of a rift between them.[121]

Still, that belonged to a time when both men could afford public recognition of the rift. In 1943 they artfully cultivated illusions of collaboration. On important issues like the manpower question, Byrnes still valued Baruch's talent for drumming up public approval of controversial policy. And when the WPB and its allies in Congress launched the reconversion planning debate, Byrnes could control it only by assigning Baruch the task of making recommendations that would carry the White House's imprimatur. Ironically, Byrnes would make possible Baruch's final public relations coup of the war. More significantly, he would enable stabilizers to stage a counteroffensive against Keynesian expansionists in the ongoing struggle to define the postwar American economy.

CHAPTER NINE
"SECOND ROUND TRIP
INTO WAR, PEACE,
AND THE AFTERMATH"

Whether the United States would embark upon a policy of stabilization or one of expansion in the postwar era was a basic issue in the manpower controversy of 1943–45. In his memoirs, Baruch suggested a part of the complexity of the matter:

> One of the thorniest problems of the war was manpower, particularly the control of labor. This was so because, first, the effective use of manpower is one of the crucial factors in the conduct of the war; and, second, manpower is not nearly as susceptible to clear-cut control as are other economic elements, such as raw materials, transportation, money, and credit.
> Here, again, one comes up hard against the human equation. Because manpower decisions affect immediately, and directly, the lives of countless human beings, it is an emotion-charged issue. Every decision in war, of course, affects human lives. But a ruling to give high-octane gas priority over steam valves is essentially impersonal, and of a very different kind from a decision on conscription quotas, or collective bargaining principles, or labor controls. Moreover, manpower issues usually involve philosophical as well as purely practical considerations, which serve to complicate them.

Stabilization administrators had been endeavoring to create civilian scarcity markets; but, in the case of manpower, by 1943 they had succeeded too well. The surplus labor force of the 1930s had dwindled to less than one million jobless nationally, "about the irreducible minimum."[1] By then administrators no longer debated whether they required more personnel but rather how were they to use the personnel they possessed. It was a variation of the old "essentiality" issue of the first war, now the priority issue of the second. Employment statistics revealed a new social condition: women filled vital places in plants because there were severe civilian shortages of workers. Except for military conscription, which almost indiscriminately took young men out of the labor force, manpower organization depended chiefly upon voluntary cooperation with wage incentives for war labor. After a year and a half of war, shortages of workers called for a more disciplined system.

The administration had no real manpower policy. The military was content as long as it drafted its quotas. The War Production Board did not complain as long as it found workers to fill war plants. The War Manpower Commission was almost incidental to the war effort while labor was still abundant. That was as Roosevelt, Baruch, and others had intended. In 1942 the president had asked Baruch to give some thought to the manpower situation. The essential question in Roosevelt's mind was whether the country needed a national service law that would direct the flow of labor much as it controlled the uses of petroleum. Baruch's counsel was that the president had all the powers needed vested in the offices of production and stabilization. Roosevelt summarized Baruch's points in a White House memo:

I like B. M. B.'s conclusions:
1. No further laws.
2. Voluntary cooperation.
3. Central authority.
4. No further enlistments. (I question this)
5. Improved administration.
6. Length of work week.

Baruch's point four had been a warning that "airplane factories and other essential industries are losing too many trained men by enlistments." Because of worker mobility and the use of women at an unprecedented rate, Roosevelt challenged the speculator's trepidations at the time—but not in 1943. Labor problems became so widespread in West Coast aircraft factories by August that Donald Nelson could define the issue simply— "do we want men in the army or airplanes for the army?"[2] In a tight market, claimant agencies of the government were reduced to squabbling over bare bones.

Baruch would have brokered the issue through a war cabinet composed of agency heads—much like the one that existed in 1918. It was a corporate solution designed to depoliticize a volatile issue, but Roosevelt was not about to share his authority with a "super war cabinet." He allowed Byrnes to form a "clearance committee" composed of Baruch, Hopkins, Admiral Leahy, and Rosenman, with Byrnes as chairman. It met a few times in 1942 to discuss manpower problems, but it had no formal powers and was unlikely to be granted any by Roosevelt. More-over, a planned resolution of the manpower problem would necessarily concede that a free market, desired by both businessmen and unions—and the ideology of voluntary cooperation—were dispensable in war. The committee was forgotten and the situation awaited a crisis.[3] The West Coast manpower shortage was that crisis.

The resolution of the shortage demanded bureaucratic mediation and public relations manipulation—a job for Baruch. It was not too different from the rubber survey situation. The newly installed head of the Office of War Mobilization turned to his resident sage for a predictable judgment. With shipping yards and aircraft plants from Seattle to San Diego behind on production schedules, who could better tell the military that it had enough manpower to fight with than Baruch? And who could better sell the idea politically than Baruch? Byrnes knew what policy recommendations to expect from Baruch; as the speculator had written him:

> Germany made a mistake in the first World War, as all of her military experts and war agencies have said, in taking too many men from industrial and farm activities and putting them in the army. They devoted too much time to munitions, and not enough to the home-front. Ludendorf [sic] complained [that] his homefront crumbled first. We are facing the same mistake.[4]

So Byrnes appointed the knightly Baruch, along with his Sancho Panza, Hancock, to slay the West Coast dragon in August 1943.

Byrnes could have written the Baruch-Hancock West Coast Plan himself, but he had enough political sense not to do so. Besides, he could pick and choose from Baruch's suggestions, taking what he wanted and ignoring what was politically hazardous. What he wanted was not original with Baruch and what was politically hazardous was typically too corporatist for Byrnes, Congress, and the claimant agencies. He wanted a program such as the one developed by the local War Manpower Commission director in Buffalo and successfully applied there. That is what Baruch gave him. The Baruch report called for local commissions "headed by an outstanding citizen of the community" that would implement, among other things, deferments of aircraft workers, cost reductions and wage incentives for managements and labor, denials of additional military deferments to agricultural workers, and furloughs to drafted workers from aircraft plants. Baruch presented the report on his seventy-third birthday, but it was not until 4 September that Byrnes felt confident enough to announce its adoption in principle. The report, when implemented, accomplished its purpose. Labor turnover was considerably curtailed. In the words of WPB historians, the West Coast Plan "established the pattern of manpower control for the remainder of the war." By the end of the year the manpower situation was satisfactory, and aircraft production on the Pacific slope was running on schedule.[5]

The War Department and its friends did not want the West Coast Plan to be the last word on manpower. Henry Stimson considered the plan "enough of a red herring to block the President's approach . . . to what I consider to be the only effective solution of the manpower problem, namely a National Service Law." To the military and to the White House, a civilian counterpart to Selective Service seemed a logical part of a comprehensive scheme to insure production and equity of service. Comprehensive, showing little faith in the efficacy of voluntary cooperation, national service sounded like something Baruch might have promoted or at least subscribed to. Indeed, it came from an old leader of the preparedness movement of 1915 to which Baruch had belonged—Grenville Clark. James W. Wadsworth, a New York GOP congressman whom Baruch had long admired for his public interest views, was a cosponsor of the Austin-Wadsworth bill for national service. Appealing to Baruch's conviction that America needed comprehensive mobilization, Clark touted the respected James B. Conant and Robert P. Patterson for administrators of national service.

With such agreeable people pushing national service in 1943, Baruch and Roosevelt both waffled on the issue. It was loathsome to organized labor and might prove to be more political trouble than it was worth. "As you know, I have not been in favor of a National Service Act up to this time," Baruch advised Clark in August 1943. However, "I must admit that the arguments being advanced in support of it are growing stronger every day, and it is not beyond the realm of possibility that I will be a supporter of the general plan if conditions continue to drift." But he was skeptical that the law could be made to work any more than individuals could be made to work without wage or profit incentives. Yet, that was the difficulty: as the prospects for victory grew, workers did not want to remain in ephemeral war production when there was greater security in civilian peace production. "As the talk is more and more centering on postwar problems," Herb Swope reminded Baruch, "it becomes increasingly necessary to hold labor to war work." Swope was then performing publicity chores for the War Department and probably reflected its concerns. But Baruch was not about to be stampeded from a position he had held since 1918 (and one repeated by opponents of the Austin-Wadsworth bill) that "drafting a man to fight for his country was not the same as drafting him to work for an employer in business for a profit."[6] He put Sam Lubell to work researching the issue.

Forecasting "a new high in buck-passing and blaming of the other fellow," Lubell argued that a national service law would be an administrative monstrosity. The fault in production lay less with a short labor

supply than with inept military placement of contracts with manufacturers who profited without full utilization of labor. Also, "there is serious
question whether the requirements of the armed forces are not exaggerated." Finally, Lubell repeated his employer's quarter-century-old argument that conscription of workers was slavery and a harbinger of profit
conscription. Indirect controls, incentives, and freedom were preferable
to national service. As Baruch had once told the National Industrial
Conference Board, "The government cannot say, 'Work here, work there'
or 'Work for Mr. A.' But it can say, 'Work or fight.'" Thus, Baruch
strongly urged the White House to reform allocation of materials and
contracts rather than drafting labor.

In late 1943 a series of strikes gave the War Department an opportunity to push national service. The administration was anguished and
outraged over the strikes, which slowed up production anew. Stabilization Director Fred Vinson was "despondent" over the prospect of granting
wage increases to miners and thereby opening the floodgates to a torrent
of demands for higher prices and wages. Byrnes and Roosevelt were also
irate over threats to the fragile stabilization equilibrium. Needless to say,
Baruch, who preached patriotism before profits for management, opposed higher wages for workers already paid fair wages.[7]

But Budget Director Smith resisted national service proposals, as did
Baruch. Stimson anxiously wanted this superb publicist and lobbyist to
endorse national service, but, although he was "wobbling a little bit
in his opposition," Baruch was unmoved by the secretary's arguments.
Baruch thought the administration of Selective Service exacerbated manpower problems by depleting it regionally; he bluntly told Stimson that
its director, General Lewis Hershey, was a "bungler" who ought to be
removed. How, Baruch asked, could a national service law prevent strikes
in America when it had not in an England that lived under German
bombs. "Force," he declared, "will not prevent a man from doing something if he treasures a wrong or a grievance."[8]

The War Department marshaled all the forces at its command, but it
could not even get the Austin-Wadsworth bill out of committee. Not
until the American prospect of victory in Europe was set back by the
Battle of the Bulge late in 1944 did the military again push for the
national service bill. Conflicting bills passed both Houses of Congress in
early 1945, but the conference report was rejected by the House. Victories
overseas negated the rationale for a draft of civilians at home.

Baruch contended that no real need for national service ever existed.
Moreover, "there must still be a legal question as to whether the government has the right to order a man to work in a plant producing for a
profit." What effect his endorsement of national service legislation would
have had upon public opinion and Congress is moot. However, Roosevelt
could not expect Congress to approve something both the unions and

Baruch opposed. Baruch enjoyed the irony of siding with the unions against the New Dealers in the White House who abetted the War Department's cause. His stubborn pursuit of stabilization for capitalism had not included the ultimate regimentation of free labor and free capital.[9]

THE FIGHT AGAINST THE NEW DEAL IN 1943

The West Coast manpower crisis directed attention to a larger controversy: planning for peacetime reconversion of the economy. What the manpower issue did was to raise the prospect of control of labor—for what purpose and by whom? Economic expansionists argued the need to create as many civilian jobs during the war as needed to insure postwar full employment; stabilization advocates and their allies in the War Department took the optimistic line that the war had proven America's ability to produce and that the scarcity civilian sector would provide enormous postwar demand, no matter when reconversion was instituted. In the meantime, the military was determined to prevent any channeling of labor away from war work until peace was won.

The old war between the War Department and the War Production Board liberals resumed, with Robert Patterson defining the issue as one of "all out for victory" against Donald Nelson's "business as usual" position. Yet, what the military feared was not a manpower crisis but a *prospective* shortage that would result from any hint of peace, or any expansion of the civilian sector that would lure workers from war plants into more secure jobs. The military wanted a national service law that drove them back into war production. The military's appetite for materials and men clearly could not be satisfied. It resisted any planning for demobilization it could not control.[10]

Moreover, the issue involved small business competition with corporate giants. The big corporations, though prosperous during hostilities, feared that smaller companies without war work would get a head start in civilian production and reap a postwar advantage. Stabilization preserved the wartime status quo. But liberals demanded that the government encourage postwar economic growth by allowing smaller enterprises to produce for the civilian market before peace arrived.[11]

Donald Nelson initiated the reconversion debate in April 1943, when he commissioned a report that the WPB could use to develop its economic reconversion policy. In June the Kanzler report argued for concentrating demobilization control in the WPB. It was a brief for postwar full employment that began with quotations from addresses by Henry Wallace and reminded readers of a manifesto published by the National Resources Planning Board shortly before Congress killed the board that spring. Also, about this time liberal economist Robert R. Nathan wrote a controversial book that forecast enormous unemployment after the war unless conversion planning began soon.[12]

Pressure upon the White House to assert its leadership in demobilization planning began to build. Of course the War Department denounced any such discussion as bordering upon treason. But the influential Bureau of the Budget argued that it ought to take up where the defunct National Resources Planning Board left off and lead the economic planning for peace. The Treasury initiated a study of conditions following World War I, predictably found them deplorable, and prescribed that one department (why not the Treasury?) "bring together the scattered activities of the several Government agencies and try to develop a consistent over-all policy" for demobilization. Liberals in the White House, perhaps afraid to depend upon the uncertain leadership of Nelson or wary of the corporate power in the WPB's Production Executive Committee, proposed a special planning and operating agency to supersede existing war agencies on the grounds that the problems of peace would not resemble those of war. White House counsel Sam Rosenman acted as a clearinghouse for all these ideas.[13]

Congress would not be left out of planning for peace. Two Senate committees, the Special Committee Investigating the National Defense Program—the Truman committee—and the Special Committee on Post-War Economic Policy and Planning chaired by Walter George of Georgia, began to prepare their own recommendations for demobilization. Other committees in the House and Senate also found virtue in planning for the revival of peacetime free enterprise. With American armed forces established on the European continent, thinking of victory and the problems of peace was irresistible—despite military injunctions to the contrary. In the words of one history of the period, "Indeed, there were few organizations, Government or private, which did not find it possible and desirable to assign small staffs to work unobstrusively on such problems."[14]

On 11 October, Jimmy Byrnes, trying to anticipate the massive reconversion headaches that awaited the government, began conferences with agency heads. Four days later, Roosevelt authorized Director of War Mobilization Byrnes to create a special OWM unit on postwar adjustment problems. Byrnes asked Baruch to study them informally for him, but it soon became apparent that something official and more elaborate would be in order.

Baruch hesitated to commit himself to the task. Having followed the reconversion controversy closely, Baruch wanted to promote certain principles as guidelines for demobilization. To begin with, he could not divide mobilization and demobilization into wholly distinct spheres because "in all of the demobilization problems it is most important to determine how to make a start towards solving them as part of the continued prosecution of the war." Then there was the bureaucratic question of who would do the planning: OWM should act only as a policy maker and bureaucratic broker in reconversion. Expecting his unit to function in an "atmosphere of distortion, half-truth, and hostile interpretations," Baruch wanted certain assurances that Byrnes would support his reconversion recommendations: "It is vital that we get the country behind one plan that all of us can carry out." Byrnes responded that he foresaw no difficulty; after all, he recalled, "we have never yet failed to agree on important matters."[15]

At age seventy-three, Baruch was not about to perform single-handedly something he could not have done twenty years before. He bestowed equal status upon his old sidekick John Hancock, an act of magnanimity and a gracious appreciation of the fact that Hancock was the operating liaison between the OWM postwar adjustment unit and all war agency and government departments considered vital to planning. Sam Lubell extracted the agency and departmental plans from them, integrating them with Baruch's concepts into the final report's sharp, promotional prose. But the process of putting it together was, as Baruch anticipated, hardly tranquil or deliberative; political infighting and public controversy marked the unit's operations.

Personalities and policies were interwoven into demobilization's political tapestry. First, there was the survivor, Donald Nelson, whose WPB still ran anything related to war production's timing, quantity, and disposition. To Nelson, reconversion heralded a slack in the economy unless the government took measures to create jobs. He articulated the liberal concern that "we have never really reached the capacity of our productive machinery in this country." That would not be achieved even in World War II unless the civilian sector of the economy received a higher production priority than it enjoyed under the current regime. Moreover, knowing Baruch's penchant for a scarcity civilian sector, Nelson did not expect any Baruch recommendations for an early reconversion to domestic production. His trepidations reflected those of the liberal planning division of the WPB, where two cogent questions were raised: To what extent would postwar planning include ideas from farm, labor, and small business groups and their allies in Congress? And to what extent would OWM consult the WPB on policy and then use the WPB as its implementation agency?[16] Rather than wait for answers to these questions, Nelson resolved to present Baruch, Byrnes, and OWM with his own reconversion fait accompli.

On 10 November, four days after Byrnes announced the creation of the Baruch unit on formulating reconversion policy, Nelson told a Senate subcommittee that the time was fast approaching when "more and more [plants and materials] can be released for essential civilian production" of transportation equipment, farm machinery, washing machines, refrigerators, and some household "essentials." A few days later, Nelson conferred with Baruch and served notice that the WPB would not be of "secondary importance" in the transition to peace. Baruch assured him, "I have always felt that the WPB should be the archstone of industry for the conduct of the war, and it should be the archstone in the adjustment and the final demobilization for peace." Baruch repeated this to a closed meeting of the WPB's Steel Industry Advisory Committee, adding that no industrialist would be allowed "to beat the gun" in converting to civilian production. The next day the essence of his remarks was reported in the press, an embarrassment to Baruch because it suggested that he had reached premature conclusions on reconversion. Blaming the WPB for a press "leak" (it retorted that Baruch himself had spoken to reporters following the meeting), Baruch depicted the incident as an attempt by the WPB's press section to manipulate the outcome of his unit's deliberations.[17]

It was natural for the old publicist to blame the WPB's publicity apparatus. It was decidedly liberal and loyal to Nelson. The armed services monitored its output in every dispute. Shortly before this incident, Nelson had allegedly told Baruch, in a moment of fatigue and exasperation, that his response to bureaucratic infighting would be to hire the best "whisperers" and "connivers" he could find. Baruch never forgave Nelson for that remark—or the WPB's press section. It was headed by Bruce Catton—"a first-class troublemaker," Ferd Eberstadt called him, an opinion confirmed when Catton went to work for Henry Wallace in 1946 and later wrote *The War Lords of Washington*, a strongly antimilitary history of mobilization.[18]

But propaganda would not make policy and Nelson was determined to establish the correct one. On 30 November he put reconversion on the WPB's agenda and, following a very satisfactory production report by Wilson, announced that "hereafter as manpower, facilities, and materials become available in any given area, it shall be the policy of the War Production Board to authorize the production within that area of additional civilian goods, provided such production does not limit production for programs of higher urgency."

Nelson had taken the War Department by surprise, but he could be certain that it would counterattack quickly. It was not long before the Pentagon joined forces with Wilson to insist that any reconversion program be developed by Wilson's Production Executive Committee. Confronted by this military-industrial alliance, Nelson decided that he was weary of Washington intrigue and would resign as soon as possible, leaving reconversion, because "that is Baruch's job."[19] Despite such talk, Nelson remained in the WPB, as determined as ever to shape reconversion policy.

At a 22 December meeting with Baruch, Wilson, and Hancock, Nelson announced that expanded civilian output had begun on a "piecemeal" basis, as materials allowed it. Wilson interjected that he was worried by potential siphoning off of war labor, although materials for expanded civilian production were ample. Baruch repeated his assurance of a large role in demobilization for the WPB, and Nelson agreed that there was no question of Baruch's attitude. But Baruch later made it clear that he intended to "tighten up the war mobilization machinery" by increasing the authority of the Production Executive Committee under Wilson.[20]

Cordiality aside, Baruch joined with the Pentagon in its campaign to oust Nelson. In January he informed Henry Stimson that he would ask Roosevelt to replace Nelson with Wilson, and the next day he sent his recommendation to the president. On 11 January the Pentagon seized upon the issue of facilities usage to make its case that any conversion of plants to expanded civilian production could convey a false sense of security and thereby relax the national commitment to victory. The WPB meeting unanimously upheld the military's position, a setback for conversion to civilian output that Nelson himself affirmed.[21] Although Nelson temporarily clung to his job, reconversion policy making had effectively been returned to Baruch.

The shape of demobilization was set in his mind. With or without Nelson—preferably the latter—the WPB would implement reconversion. But Baruch, despite Byrnes's continued entreaties, would not administer the WPB. "I just cannot do the job at my age, George," he told that old warrior of 1919's reconversion, George Peek. And he added, gloomily, "We will be in for hell's-a-popping with these great productions and the long-haired boys around. If business men leave Washington—the good ones—they can't blame anyone but themselves." His mission was to block New Deal public works projects designed to achieve full employment. Beholden to nobody except the public interest as he defined it, Baruch assured business friends that he would not tolerate "pressure group" influence upon reconversion. His task was to reassure everybody that nothing drastic would be recommended or attempted. He touched base with all policy groups, but the policy would have his own stamp on it.[22]

He left very little to chance or other influences. A prime issue was the disposition of surplus property—both the materials and the plants owned by the government. Baruch envisioned an agency that would stockpile nonperishable raw materials while selling off plants not needed by the military—"No government in business," he said. That appealed to the big corporations operating plants for the government. Liberals wanted easy terms for businessmen, too—in the hopes of opening up competition in major industries. The House of Representatives had begun consideration of a surplus property bill, but Baruch objected to any White House stance on it prior to his own public proposals. To head up the proposed Surplus Property Administration, White House liberals Jonathan Daniels and Sam Rosenman wanted the Brandeisian lawyer and chairman of

TVA, David Lilienthal. But Baruch prevailed upon Byrnes to push Will Clayton, then assistant secretary of commerce and a Texas cotton broker he had brought into government during WIB days. Roosevelt remembered Clayton as a member of the anti-New Deal Liberty League; liberals considered him "an unbeatable bulwark of privilege." Still, the president was unwilling to defy Baruch in 1944. The announcement of Clayton's appointment would not come until after Baruch's reconversion report was made public, but that merely ratified a decision made weeks before. "The President was therefore presented with the necessity of bucking Baruch, in effect repudiating him," Lilienthal wrote. "So he went along, not wanting to risk it. . . . The story shows how much the President has become the prisoner of his own generals!"[23]

But both Roosevelt and Baruch were being monitored carefully on the reconversion issue by Congress. It was a Balkanized Congress, deeply suspicious of anything but its own prerogatives. In 1943 it had dismantled the remnants of the New Deal and now it was completing a tax bill that would have the distinction of being the first to be vetoed; compromises were no longer easily made. Senator George led the legislative attack upon executive authority. Senator Murray fought for full employment. Senator Truman listened to WPB staffers. Even as Baruch prepared the ground for his own ideas on reconversion, they planted theirs. On 5 November the Truman committee issued broad principles on reconversion, and thirteen days later the George committee publicized its outline. The president set forth his own philosophy of reconversion in his January budget message, taking care to acknowledge the leadership of OWM and its Baruch unit. It would be Baruch's turn on 15 February.

"THE PEACE JITTERS"

The Baruch-Hancock report was intended to be a consensus manifesto. It borrowed liberally from the WPB, paid its respects to Congress—and then rejected public works proposals for full employment and affirmed the leadership of OWM in guiding reconversion. With something for everyone to like and dislike, in the best publicist language Samuel Lubell could write, it set forth the terms of the 1944 reconversion debate. The Baruch-Hancock Report on War and Post-War Adjustment Policies served as a public reference point for reconversion discussion during 1944–46. It reinforced conservative principles on stabilization and countered New Deal heresies.

The form and style of the report were vintage Baruch. Contemporary terms like "reconversion" were eschewed in favor of the Wilsonian "re-adjustment." Others knew how to write a public document designed to influence opinion, but Baruch put a quarter century's experience into his, along with no spared expense in printing and disseminating it. It was a masterpiece in the art of public relations. An official government document, it set forth the philosophy of its authors in large and bold type that summarized the report's numerous proposals. Large italicized type announced a topic that was seldom discussed in more than two paragraphs. Type styles varied, with key phrases or words italicized in bold print. Considering that the report was larded with homilies and exhortations that wore thin in the third year of war, boredom might have overcome even an interested reader. But it was not written to be read word by word. It was a tabloid intent upon a quick dispensing of Baruchian wisdom.

The public response to the report was predictable. In principle, liberals denounced it, conservatives cheered it; in practice, Congress, Byrnes, and all the involved agencies would implement the philosophically acceptable and the politically possible. Its injunctions could be disobeyed, but not ignored. The press and public officials—and, to some extent, historians since then—used the Baruch-Hancock report as a yardstick that measured reconversion. Nothing else, except its total adoption, could have given its authors more satisfaction.

The assault on it from the left proved useful in defining its purposes and limitations. It united old New Dealers Harry Hopkins and Harold Ickes in its opposition. "Although I haven't read the report in full, from what has appeared in print, I have very grave reservations with regard to it," Ickes wrote. "It looks to me as if it is a build-up for big business, although conventional things are included about the 'little business man.'" The report's blanket proclamation that the mission of reconversion was "taking the Government out of business" bothered liberals who correctly attributed recent prosperity to putting the government into business— albeit principally the war business. The report was intent upon restoring the supremacy of private enterprise; New Dealers were reminded of Wall Street, Herbert Hoover, and the follies of the 1920s that preceded the debacle of the 1930s. "I am persuaded that the Baruch Plan will not do as a pattern," Harry Hopkins told Eleanor Roosevelt, "largely because it completely ignores all the human aspects for whose benefit our great industrial system should be organized." Ignorance of the "human aspects" would be a common complaint among liberals—a polite way of observing that, beyond proposing an ambiguous "work director" and recommending a reserve of public works projects in case of unemployment, the report relied solely upon the private sector for the creation of jobs. However, a WPB historian later concluded, after close analysis of reconversion documents: "One cannot fail to note that close similarity of parts of the Baruch-Hancock report and the [WPB] Planning

Division's study." On issues such as contract termination and surplus property disposal, Baruch and Hancock virtually echoed earlier WPB recommendations.[24]

Careful critics of the report on the left were disarmed by it. I. F. Stone astutely concluded that it proved "(1) the hold that the idea of planning has taken on the entire community and (2) the determination of Wall Street and big business to do the planning." *New Republic* editors went through the report with a fine-tooth comb before they announced disagreement "with the Baruch suggestions on only one main point"—the sale of government-built plants, which they saw as potential yardsticks for measuring real corporate competition. On the other hand, Max Lerner knew his enemy and was not about to fall for Baruch's exhortations and generalizations:

> The report can best be summed up as an attempt to solve a crisis situation by the formula of surrender plus a slogan. . . . The surrender is the surrender by the American people to the big corporations and the petty congressional reactionaries. The slogan is that all will be for the best in the best of all possible postwar worlds if only we keep free enterprise and private initiative.
>
> [Baruch] has done a perfect job for everyone who has a war contract and for every prospective buyer of war materials and government-built war plants. He had done a perfect job for the big corporations, the monopolists, and the carteleers. . . .
>
> . . . He has put corporate demands ahead of full employment, and money and profit [are] valued ahead of production values.

Though somewhat hyperbolic, that was a fair assessment. Another *New Republic* writer characterized Baruch's forecast of an "adventure in prosperity" after the war as "the imposition of a set of pious hopes upon a hardcore of reactionary realities. It is Victorian both in its economics and its optimism—and in its gentlemanly refusal to call a problem a problem." The problem he referred to—Lerner's impending "crisis"—was the unemployment of millions of Americans unless the government maintained the expanded apparatus of the nation. For Baruch, of course, that amounted to ideological idiocy.[25]

But there were also plaudits for the report. *Time* conceded that to some people "the report seemed disappointingly obvious"; nevertheless: "This, too, could be construed as a triumph for the Baruchian wisdom, which is platitudinous as most wisdom in that it concentrates on the all-too-often-forgotten obvious things, which are so often the fundamentals." Praise of Baruch tended to be less analytical than damnation of the report. The editorial by Baruch's old friend E. D. "Cobbie" Coblentz in the Hearst *San Francisco Call-Bulletin* was a model of celebration:

Mr. Baruch's program of reconversion is not basically a new program.

It is certainly not a New Deal program.

It is sound and sensible, a long tried and always proven AMERICAN program, expressing faith in American ideals and institutions, counselling safeguards for those ideals and institutions.

It is the forthright, informative and constructively patriotic program of a man determined to see that "the human side" of demobilization is not forgotten.[26]

The test of all these epithets and encomiums would come when Byrnes and Congress began to implement the Baruch blueprint. The real nature of Baruch's prescribed reconversion was revealed when Byrnes announced his choices for surplus property administrator and work director, Will Clayton and Brigadier General F. T. Hines. Liberals were furious. I. F. Stone branded Clayton "a triple-plated guaranty" that government-owned war plants would not be used to disturb existing monopolies, whereas Hines was "a mediocre reactionary, a hangover from the Coolidge-Hoover era, and notorious in Washington for his opposition to work relief. His appointment makes the job a kind of cruel joke." Was Hines, like Clayton, another reactionary Baruch had foisted upon Roosevelt? Apparently not. As Baruch told a friend, Byrnes had offered the job to him, but "I would not be up to the job." Baruch's candidate for work director was businessman William Jeffers, who had won Baruch's admiration with his single-minded and outspoken administration of rubber. Byrnes would not take the brusque Jeffers and opted for the cautious Hines. But Baruch was content with the Clayton selection. "I, alone, am responsible for the Clayton appointment," he boasted to Marquis Childs.[27]

But Byrnes did not take Baruch's charted course of turning OWM into the corporate architect of the postwar economy. He mostly made administrative adjustments that shifted responsibility from OWM to the president's office. Even before the publication of the Baruch-Hancock report, Senator George had moved to assure that Congress would take the lead in reconversion, a fact to which Byrnes paid respect. Although it is true that between Senator George and Baruch there was agreement on the need to liberate private enterprise from government restraints as soon as possible, there were serious political conflicts between them. While paying lip service to congressional consultation, Baruch wanted no role for Congress in reconversion other than rubber-stamping the Baruch-Hancock report and OWM's leadership. Involving Congress meant involving "pressure groups" such as unions, farmers, and small businessmen, about the last elements Baruch ever wanted in serious economic planning. The conflict between Baruch's corporatist way of doing things and the Senate's assertion of its prerogative might not have developed in Joe Robinson's day, but the current Senate leadership was more mindful of influences other than Baruch and the war agencies.[28]

Although everyone called for speedy planning for reconversion, congressional debate was deliberate. France was under Nazi control and the Russians were still a long way from Berlin; "there was no demonstrable need for the [reconversion] legislation at that particular time." However, even after D-Day, Congress's pace suited none of the planning advocates, and its final product satisfied most of them even less. Liberals in the Senate sought a commitment to public works planning that the more conservative House resisted. By September conferees from both houses agreed on four reconversion bills—a War Contracts Act, a Surplus War Property Act, a GI Bill of Rights, and a War Mobilization and Reconversion Act—with the House playing a role decidedly favorable to Baruch's conception of reconversion. The surplus property law, written largely under the influence of Will Clayton, was "an amazing compilation of platitudinous prescription which formed no clear guide for an administrator in formulating policy"; one man would make policy with congressional carte blanche. It satisfied Baruch: "In general terms, it seems to me the House has proceeded with the sounder method of approach."[29]

In effect, reconversion was what Byrnes made of it. Congress transformed the Office of War Mobilization into the Office of War Mobilization *and Reconversion*. Following Baruch's lead, Byrnes communicated no sense of potential crisis. "Notwithstanding what we may do to facilitate reconversion, we are bound to have some unemployment," Byrnes had forecast. "I do not think that Congress should revive the Works Progress Administration. . . . I believe that unemployment insurance should be our first line of defense." Until the transition to peacetime production reached an effective scale, "there is no other place where people can get work so quickly as in the present war plants," John Hancock declared. Baruch paid homage to the principle of a shelflist of public works measures, but he paid little attention to whether one existed—just as long as unemployment insurance covered the "human factor" until those war plants began turning out cars and refrigerators again. This reliance upon the private sector to avail itself of the federal war bounty amounted to a policy of *negative* federal planning. Baruch was not a man of any uncertainty: "I am not afraid of the outlook for 1945, as business will be booming by then in spite of all we are doing now."[30]

A more legitimate controversy, to his way of thinking, concerned the timing and extent of conversion to civilian production. In the summer of 1944 a sharp difference of opinion existed on the question when reconversion ought to commence—and the friction increased in proportion to the amount of civilian output proposed. Both sides tended to state their cases in cataclysmic terms. Robert R. Nathan forecast a postwar unemployment of more than eighteen million people unless civilian production expanded immediately. Though not so extreme in their prognosis, many industrialists endorsed reconversion measures begun as soon as possible. All of this prompted War Department leaders to liken the situation to the "business as usual" days of 1940–41. Actual reconversion amounted to subverting our armed forces in battle. Certainly the country had a bad case of what Baruch called "the peace jitters."[31]

In 1944 the government terminated some war contracts, sometimes creating local unemployment and heightening national trepidations that America faced peace unprepared for reconversion. Certain groups in Congress, notably the Truman committee and full employment advocates, persuaded Byrnes to have the WPB at least make a meaningful gesture in the direction of reconversion. Nelson, ever malleable under pressure, ordered preparation of reconversion plans. No threat to war production was intended; after all, as Ferd Eberstadt expressed it, "To put the matter paradoxically, the function of the War Production Board should be to demobilize in such a way as not to impair war production." But Patterson and Stimson were adamant against even a hint of reconversion while battles were fought in Europe. Caught between a determined army and an uncertain WPB, Byrnes naturally chose the course of least resistance, and probably the one closest to his own sympathies. Noting that "there is a public psychology in this country that the end of the war is near at hand," Byrnes took the Pentagon line that "no man knows when the war will end. We must produce until the last shot is fired." At last, Roosevelt mercifully removed Nelson from the military's line of fire by sending him off to China. Julius Krug became the WPB's second chairman.[32]

As Patterson later recalled, the army "never had trouble with Krug." Other WPB changes followed, much to the satisfaction of the military. The service secretaries virtually controlled the tempo of demobilization and reconversion; demobilization was nonexistent and reconversion was selective. "When this war is over we will have a terrific surplus of arms," Forrestal once confided, but he rationalized the excess as preferable to risking the unnecessary loss of lives. In October, Forrestal was satisfied that the "peace jitters" of August had subsided; "my own maxim is to keep shoving as if the war might go on forever." The service secretaries bureaucratically thwarted reconversion while paying homage to its planning in the press. Only the White House could overrule the military's continued mobilization impetus.[33]

Roosevelt was not about to take that step before the election of 1944. He agreed with the argument that no substantial reconversion could proceed until Germany was beaten. "Suppose it would require 12 months," he told Harold Smith. "All of our current calculations on supply would be upset." The president could not risk disregarding military judgment that peacetime production was "vicious business . . . before we have won our victory." Planning for peace would require a guarantee of peace itself.[34]

But the final blow against advance planning for reconversion came in the December snows in Belgium—the Battle of the Bulge. Roosevelt had worried that an invasion of Germany would stiffen enemy resistance and prolong the war, and now his fear seemed to be borne out by events. Intent upon initiating his own drive for reconversion planning after the election, Budget Director Smith had asked agencies for submission of budget estimates based upon the need to fight only a Pacific war. On 21 December, President Roosevelt called Smith to talk over budget policy. What was said is unreported, but the Bureau of the Budget's history of the war notes that the Battle of the Bulge "forced an upward revision of military requirements. Discussion of reconversion disappeared."[35] That was the coup de grace to pre-V-E Day reconversion planning.

New Dealers in 1945 promoted planning for full employment and financial aid for Britain; Baruch preferred ideological consistency: free enterprise at home and abroad. The ideological tone of the argument for full employment through government planning and spending, along with Britain's somewhat surprising turn to Labour and socialism, inspired Baruch's fervent defense of the business system. Many of the full employment adherents were free enterprisers themselves—full employment through competitive enterprise was their line—but others were assorted planners who doubted the commitment of businessmen to anything but their profits, and they included progressive-minded businessmen of the Committee for Economic Development variety down through varying shades of socialists. Baruch was an advocate of rational planning, too, just as long as it pragmatically operated within the eternal verities of market supply and demand, and as long as the planners were entrepreneurs or investors with a stake in cooperation. Pessimism pervaded the utterances of the full employment promoters; Baruch in 1945 was unusually bullish. He believed that five to seven years of economic expansion were practically assured if the United States merely followed the most sensible policies of price restraints at home and market development abroad. Government had a place in the economic system when it organized the resources of free enterprise and succored the have-nots; but government did not bestow enterprise upon entrepreneurs or jobs upon workingmen. And that is where Baruch differed with most full employment supporters.

He was not against full employment or hostile to the measures that eventually became the Employment Act of 1946. "As a slogan, full employment became almost irresistible by the end of the war, surpassing even free enterprise, which had enjoyed a significant revival of its own."[36] An inveterate publicist, Baruch appreciated potent slogans. Opposition to full employment could be akin to endorsing starvation, and Baruch never liked the reactionary side of any issue. Therefore, he was careful to wage a campaign for alternative thinking, rather than one against creating public employment. He merely contradicted the liberals' pessimism with his own assurances of impending prosperity. He had hoped that his forecast in the Baruch-Hancock report of a postwar "adventure in prosperity" would capture the public imagination better than it had, but it was worth repeating.

The headline on the front page of the *New York Times*, "Baruch Sees Five-Year Prosperity after War as Certainty for U.S.," served as the best rebuttal to doomsayers who forecast lengthy breadlines without a full employment law. When the veterans returned, Baruch predicted, "there will be more work in the United States than there will be hands with which to do it." This miracle would occur not because of anything the government would do, but because of all it already had invested in behalf of victory for free enterprise. Postwar capital and incentives would be plentiful. He admonished a powerful senator, "And don't let anybody think there will not be jobs for everyone. For five to seven years, *no matter what they do or do not do, there will be work for all.* The cupboards of the world are bare and the ruins rebuilt [*sic*]. They will be rebuilt and the people will demand much and will get what they want, if they will only work."[37] All that Washington had to do was to facilitate liberal unemployment insurance laws and speedily sell off federal surplus property.

Full employment's principal advocate within the administration was Harold Smith. The budget director was a cautious economist not given to fanciful programs, especially if they were expensive. But when Smith sent the president a nine-hundred-word draft on full employment for inclusion in his 1945 budget message, and Roosevelt included it, it signaled a departure in Smith's fiscal approach, a point Smith himself acknowledged in a postscript that accompanied the draft: "Incidentally, I'll bet you did not hear talk like this out of the Bureau of the Budget a few years ago." Henry Wallace promoted "Sixty Million Jobs" and the president talked about a "nation's budget," but, as Smith observed, "actually almost nothing is being done about it." Less than a week after the death of Roosevelt on 12 April 1945, Smith conferred with President Truman, an erstwhile Senate supporter of reconversion planning. With the swift advance of Allied armies into Germany, Smith pointed out, "for all practical purposes . . . V-E Day [has] passed"; he found Truman in agreement with his suggestion that battlefield successes called for discussion of budget changes with the service secretaries. Still, Smith's reconversion plans did nothing for full employment.[38]

Baruch made the connection between reconversion and full employment. The problem, as he saw it, was that nobody had implemented the agenda outlined in the Baruch-Hancock report; Byrnes had not "followed my ideas." As the war in the Pacific reached a climax, Baruch believed, "We are as unprepared for peace that we know is surely coming, as we were for war which we hoped would not come." Of course his support of military resistance to reconversion planning partially accounted for that failure. Also, some of his own proposals had been halfhearted, mostly intended for public applause rather than implementation. Nevertheless, an inept veterans' program encouraged Baruch to repeat his call for a "work director," which the less discerning American could construe as Baruch's plea for full employment. More constructive was his linkage of reconversion to jobs via the swift sale of surplus property.

"When there is any doubt—sell," he advised members of the Surplus Property Board; "sell, sell, sell." The plants would employ veterans and war workers in manufacturing items demanded by consumers. Liberals charged that the hasty sales of plants and materials would play right into the hands of all the institutions and individuals who had surplus capital from war profits to invest in postwar production. Baruch conceded the bias in favor of big business; but he reminded critics that the longer the government held war property the longer it would be nonproductive, with all the loss in working hours that that entailed. Besides, even sales to big business would assist in creating small new businesses.[39]

At a Washington party to celebrate his seventy-fifth birthday, Baruch delivered a discourse on the virtues of free enterprise as opposed to collectivism, whose current popularity he ascribed to "political emotionalism." Again he asserted that prosperity was certain, but his words took on a more ideological coloring than ever before: "We can't marry our system to another and keep our strength. If we do, there will be a divorce and somebody will wake up dead. . . . I'm never afraid of the future of America. I have boundless faith in Americans taking care of themselves, if they are told what to do and why." He did not say who would instruct this nation of individualists, but it was the sort of Dutch uncle, upbeat talk reporters expected of Baruch. "Prosperity Ours for the Making, Baruch Says on the Eve of 76th Year," the *Times* headline assured Americans.[40] If jobs were no worry for Americans, did they have any worries?

OMBUDSMAN TO AMERICA

Baruch aged noticeably during the late war years. Although many people professed surprise that a man in his seventies could be as ubiquitously active as Baruch, friends observed signs of his age. Most obvious was his hearing problem—an old injury that time worsened. It made conversation with him difficult and unreliable. Also, his use of homilies and aphorisms, punctuated with southern colloquialisms to make points—

many of which had been appreciated by the Democratic leadership on Capitol Hill a generation before—was not understood by the Yankee academics and businessmen who infested the wartime bureaucracy. However, his speech patterns added to his color and reminded administrators that his power in Washington had originated in Congress. More disconcerting was his conversational habit of jumping from one issue to another without a signal for a change in topic. In his mind most topics were related—a fact others would recognize later, as they came to appreciate the deftness of his mind. But sometimes his talk seemed to be the ramblings of an old man who had difficulty sticking to one issue at a time. Compounding this feeling was the fact that he obviously was weakening physically. He could not hide his numerous and evident infirmities. He kept a strict routine that called for more rest than Washington figures usually get. A nurse became a very important part of his retinue. With the exception of Henry Stimson in the War Department—who left the operational role to Undersecretary Robert Patterson—and a few senior members of Congress, men of Baruch's age were not active in Washington. Nevertheless, even more evident than Baruch's age was his intense ambition to shape postwar economic policy.

He reminded Forrestal, and undoubtedly others, "This is my second roundtrip into war, peace and the aftermath"; he was among the few Americans who had contributed to policy debates in both epochs. But the reminder had motives other than ego gratification. Believing in the moral and material improvement of the human condition and the superior qualities of western civilization and capitalism, and retaining a patriotic faith in the greater glory of the nation, Baruch genuinely conceived it as his duty to use his influence and power to assure that American policy did not repeat the mistakes of 1917–19.

To borrow one of his minted clichés, America had to win the peace as well as the war. In Baruch's mind that meant a Pax Americana in which a stable and prosperous United States would lead the world. He would achieve this through a planned economic reconversion to free enterprise without the debilitating cycle of inflation and depression that followed World War I. In a world liberated from the restraints of British imperial preference and German cartels, mankind would find more abundance than ever. This called for wise leadership that put the practical idealism of American business interests ahead of the sentimental altruism of internationalists and New Dealers. That was his personal and public mission.

The elder statesman was still powerful and influential in Washington and with public opinion. He remained useful in brokering between wartime agencies or in promoting legislation. Bureaucrats with problems still sought him out as a troubleshooter. Late in the war, for example, J. A. "Cap" Krug, Nelson's successor as chairman of the WPB, told Baruch that a housing shortage for foundry workers threatened military production unless a million dollar allocation for housing was made. The next day, Baruch telegraphed Krug that money would be advanced from army sources, and soon Krug had $565,590 promised to him for housing foundry workers.[41]

On the face of it, Baruch's prestige cut red tape when it resisted men in authority. That is the image Baruch wanted to convey. But, in most instances, he served as a capstone to a campaign, as the heavy gun used to decide the outcome. Throughout Washington it was thought better to have him as an ally than as an enemy. His friends knew how valuable he could be to their plans. Eleanor Roosevelt admonished Harry Hopkins that they needed Baruch on their side in the coming struggle over reconversion: after all, "he does have more influence at the present time than any of us. We do have to work with Congress, you know, and he has more influence than you or I or the CIO, or most people who feel as we do." Planning for the Bretton Woods conference, a Treasury Department official advised Secretary Morgenthau, "If Baruch were with us, he could be a lot of help. He is too big for anybody else around here. . . . I think it is desirable also that you have a talk with Bernie Baruch and see if we couldn't get his help." Morgenthau did just that.[42] It undoubtedly annoyed Hopkins and Morgenthau that Baruch wielded such ineffable and illegitimate influence in Washington, but it was a fact of their lives that they had to deal with.

Nowhere were his unofficial efforts better appreciated than in the Pentagon. After the war, Undersecretary of War Patterson personally wrote Baruch,

Dear Chief—
    I am thinking of you this Christmas Day, and of the great help you have so freely given me for more than five years, ever since I came to the War Department. I made many mistakes,—mostly when I did not follow your advice or when I acted without getting it. I cannot recall a single case where you gave me a bad steer. The thought that you would give an approving nod has always been a great source of strength.

For favors received, Patterson rendered favors—the sale of a surplus plane for Baruch's personal use when they were still scarce, or the award of the Medal of Merit for wartime service to Herb Swope ("I promised Mr. Baruch. . . . It is not a strong case but . . .).[43] It was well known that his suite at the Carlton was a gathering place for the desk admirals and generals who found Washington a bewildering battleground.

In the twilight of his life, Baruch may have seemed genial and generous, but in fact he grew more determined to have his way and settle a few old scores. He doted on the public worship that came his way, but in Washington, he told a friend, "I'd rather be strong and be hated than be weak and be loved!" Seldom did he reveal that hard side of his personality, although it was memorable when he did. Early in the war period, he told Leon Henderson that if William Knudsen should "get tough," Baruch would do likewise. Many in the war establishment expected him to be devious and cunning, but few expected such direct confrontations. By the end of the war the Old Man was brimming with animosity. Harry Hopkins had never been a favorite during New Deal days, but a Hopkins comment during the early war mobilization period that he did not want any World War I stuff was unforgivable. John Maynard Keynes, detested since 1919, was damned incessantly. Leon Henderson fell out of Baruch's favor, and as Morgenthau told his aides, Baruch hated Henderson so much that he prevented him from speaking for Roosevelt during the 1944 campaign. However, in the case of Hopkins and other prominent New Dealers, Baruch both gave and commanded civil deference—at least for the duration. As he told a British conservative, "I guess we have to overlook everything until we beat our outside enemies. Then we will have to turn and take care of the ones inside."[44]

But Baruch was not merely ideological, for he confounded liberals with his unyielding criticism of the conservative Jesse Jones. The Rubber Survey Report, though not mentioning Jones directly, blamed him for the shortage and blocked him from control of synthetic rubber development. Jones's fight with Henry Wallace's Board of Economic Warfare provided Baruch with another occasion for rebuking Jones while pleasantly flabbergasting Wallace and his followers. Moreover, as the war's end neared, Wallace observed that "Baruch is doing everything he can to prevent Jesse Jones from taking on the job [of demobilization]." He even advised Roosevelt to remove Jones as head of the Reconstruction Finance Corporation. Baruch constantly deprecated Jones as a tricky and untrustworthy conniver. When Jones claimed that in the matter of disposal of government property he would have two votes, one as commerce secretary and one as Defense Plants Corporation head, Baruch, as Baruch told it, sternly rejoined, "You will have one vote." To make certain of that, Baruch successfully worked to get another Texas conservative, Will Clayton, put in charge of surplus property sales. In conversation with Wallace, Baruch called Jones a "rascal . . . lying [in] the grass with a long knife" and boasted of how he had pushed synthetic rubber operations over Jones's protest by telling him, "Get out of the way or I will cut your throat."[45] Baruch may have been settling an old score that dated back to his clash with Jones during the campaign of 1924.

Baruch had developed a penchant for threats. Indeed, when Clayton disagreed with him on the disposition of postwar Germany, he told Morgenthau—with "fire in his eyes"—"I will cut his heart out if he doesn't behave himself, and he won't be able to stay around Washington after I get through with him. He either is right on this German thing or he will leave town." Baruch once said Hopkins had a "mean, hard nature"; many in Washington could have said that of Baruch.[46]

Baruch was usually circumspect about his threats, but once he stumbled into an indiscretion. And then the threat frightened Baruch more than anyone else. Interviewed in England by *Stars and Stripes* reporter A. Victor Lasky in April 1945, Baruch assured the young correspondent that veterans could look forward to plenty of jobs for at least five to seven years after the war. He was quoted as saying:

> What happens after those five or seven years depends on the peace the big boys are preparing for us now.
>
> And one reason I am over here is to hold the big stick over the big boys to make damn sure they're not going to foul up the peace.

The statement is consistent with Baruch's image of himself as a guardian of the public interest; but one of Baruch's guardians of his public image, Samuel Lubell, accused Lasky of writing the story "as if he was covering a fire" and denied that Baruch had ever made that last intimidating statement. Moreover, because the Associated Press had picked up the story and the *New York Times* had put it on page 1, Baruch cabled the White House that his deafness and the reporter's imagination caused the story: "I did not make any such statement. I am quite aware of how delicate is situation to make any such statement that might appear as offensive as this."[47]

He worried that Washington would learn the true nature of his relationship with "Assistant President" Byrnes. At the 1944 press conference announcing the creation of the Surplus Property Administration, a recommendation of the Baruch-Hancock reconversion report, reporters twice raised questions of new assignments for its seventy-three-year-old author. No, said Byrnes, Baruch would not take the leadership of a reconversion agency because he did not want to work a six-day week: "We are such good friends that I could not insist upon it and I told him I would find something else for him to do before very long." Byrnes had more important matters on his mind than Baruch. To Baruch's consternation, he found Byrnes's office a barrier to reaching him. On one occasion when they could talk privately, Byrnes called the old man a fool for recommending that he seek relief from OWM pressures by taking an overseas assignment. Not until 1945 did the breach become public knowledge. A reporter called Byrnes and asked directly if Baruch were still his adviser; Byrnes responded that Baruch no longer served OWM, and Baruch confirmed the statement. He drafted a letter to Arthur Krock interpreting the Byrnes relationship in the best possible light, glowingly describing their qualities of enduring friendship, but conceding, "I'll admit he has made me unhappy." The letter rambled somewhat incoherently, and perhaps for this reason, Baruch put it in his files rather than sending it. Publicizing his rupture with Byrnes could do neither of them any good.[48]

Both men had been disappointed when Byrnes failed to capture the vice-presidential nomination in 1944. To preserve a Roosevelt presidency, the quest for a viable alternative to Henry Wallace took Byrnes into consideration. But liberals argued that the South Carolinian would alienate labor and Negroes—thereby hurting the ticket more than he could help it with business and in the South—and big city Democratic leaders feared that Byrnes's conversion from the church of his birth would offend their Catholic constituents. Of such negative factors was the ultimate presidency of Harry Truman made.

For months after the 1944 convention, Byrnes brooded upon the denial of his ambitions. That fall, Baruch consolingly wrote him, "I am well aware of the hurts and rebuffs you have experienced, undeserved as I know them to be. In times like these, however, none of us can think of himself. Indeed, the longer I live, the more I feel that no one of us can enjoy the luxury of a personal grudge or injured feelings." It did not improve their relations. Baruch sent him another handwritten message some months later: "What you have in your mind or heart about me I do not know. I am unhappy, very unhappy, because you have something. There is no cause to ever doubt my loyalty, confidence and affection. I know you have had a hard road and I know how hurt you have been. You were so hurt and mad I fear you made it all inclusive without the slightest reason except an imaginary one." Byrnes's coolness remained, and it was then that Baruch began to drop little deprecating remarks about his former crony. Truman made Byrnes secretary of state in 1945, but Baruch damned Byrnes as a politician without administrative talents. Later that year, Byrnes made overtures of reconciliation with Baruch. Their rapprochement would warm when both were in their dotage, though they never wholly recovered from the earlier conflict. Baruch would ever after consider Byrnes a political parvenu who was jealous of the press's celebration of Baruch. As Ickes once observed, breaches between old friends never fully heal.[49]

During the war, Baruch began to show some political independence. In 1942, Clare Boothe Luce was elected to Congress as a Republican from Connecticut. Her virulent anti-New Deal attacks and Baruch's contributions to her election were apparent, as was his pride in his political "protégé." The election of Thomas E. Dewey as the Republican governor of New York brought a warm congratulatory telegram from Baruch. In 1943, Baruch talked about how he would take a politically independent stance following the war. He disliked the growing Democratic dependence upon the political funds of organized labor. As for a fourth term for Roosevelt, he believed it was likely, but he liked it no more than the third term. Democrats still looked to him for contributions to Senate campaigns; in 1942, Edwin C. Johnson won by 3,642 votes in a very light turnout and thanked Baruch for his "generous support" that saved a Colorado seat. But for Baruch the Senate was not what it had been. Except for a few southerners like Harry F. Byrd of Virginia, most of the Senate Democrats were too liberal for him. Even an Alabamian and a Floridian, Lister Hill and Claude Pepper, were New Dealers. Yet they were the ones Roosevelt asked Baruch to help in their 1944 primary fights. Baruch grumbled about it, but gave.[50]

There was little about the Democratic party in 1944 that he liked. Its failure to put Byrnes on the ticket disappointed and disgusted him. The apparent prominence of Russian-born labor leader Sidney Hillman in the vice-presidential selection process was ominous; Hillman "may know something about institutions," Baruch commented, "but they are not American institutions." He told a fellow South Carolinian that Byrnes lost out because "the C.I.O. and colored folks did not want him." "My gorge rises and it is very hard for me to swallow these things," he told Ickes. To columnist Frank Kent's question what sort of man Harry Truman was, Baruch responded: "He is nine pounds lighter than a toy balloon." On the other hand, he was most enthusiastic about GOP nominee Thomas E. Dewey. In August, Drew Pearson reported this description of James M. Cox's conversation at a Democratic gathering:

> "Bernie Baruch has been trying to tell me what a great man Dewey is and what a fine President he would be. I used all the arguments on him, asking him to tell me how Dewey would be able to negotiate with Stalin and Churchill. But I couldn't convince Bernie. He had almost a fervor in his eye when he talked about Dewey."
>
> "Yes," replied Albert Lasker, "that's exactly what Baruch has been trying to tell me."[51]

But certain Baruch habits prevailed. He never spoke ill of Roosevelt, even if he spoke well of Dewey. He had an understanding with Roosevelt, even if they did not always see eye to eye. Roosevelt knew his value, both in public relations and in political contributions. And Baruch understood that it was better to be on the prudently progressive side of social issues than to be tabbed as an unrepentant tory. They needed each other, they used each other, they were comfortable with each other. Roosevelt probably resented Baruch's insistent intrusions with prescriptions that offended him and alienated liberals; and Baruch certainly detested many of the New Dealers and labor leaders the president surrounded himself with— but all of that was ancient history in 1944. Roosevelt was not about to cease calling upon Baruch for aid in holding the Democratic coalition's conservative wing in place, and Baruch believed enough in what Roosevelt espoused—and liked well enough the occasional public assignments that came his way from the White House—to continue in his role as a presidential advisor and friend. He identified himself with the Democratic party's successes. As he told Mrs. Roosevelt following the fourth-term victory, "I feel I did my duty—Just glance at the congressional (both sides) results."[52] Despite his conflicts with Democrats and his flirtations with Republicans, a Democratic president would have to throw him out of the White House before he would openly back a Republican.

Amid the increased political bickering that marked 1943–46, Baruch's influence was based upon his hold upon public opinion. It was awesome and even frightening. A Baruch dissent was capable of bringing a torrent of constituent letters and outraged editorials down upon the heads of Washington officials. Harold Ickes, among others, marveled at the Old Man's achievement; despite the best efforts of Hopkins and others in the White House to reduce Baruch's influence upon the war administration, "here was Bernie right in the center of the stage and in the full confidence of the country." "His prestige is very great," remarked David E. Lilienthal. The British ambassador, Lord Halifax, reported to Whitehall that Baruch's assignments from the White House were a tribute to his "unique position as the elder statesman of war production." A Hearst columnist in May 1944 maintained that "Baruch today is without doubt the most respected individual in the country." Advising his staff to treat Baruch more gently than White House economist Isador Lubin had been doing, Henry Morgenthau, Jr., exclaimed, "This is a very powerful fellow, and he just runs circles around Lubin." According to the Gallup Poll, 2 percent of all Americans polled listed Baruch among those who had not held elected office but who might make good presidents.[53]

"Mr. Baruch, in short, has become a national oracle whose utterances exert a strong influence on public opinion," averred one writer in late 1945. His detractors feared his influence with the public. When Walter Lippmann assailed Baruch for his outspoken opposition to a proposed American postwar loan to Great Britain, Felix Frankfurter rushed to second "your piece this morning on Baruch's recent very mischievous outgivings. It was high time that someone with an effective pin pricked that inflated balloon." (What made Frankfurter's note all the more remarkable was that he and Lippmann had not had a kind word for each other since 1933.) At Franklin Roosevelt's funeral, Baruch was a very prominent mourner, as Henry Wallace recalled: "Jim Farley, Bernie Baruch, Robert Hannegan, and Ed Kelly from Chicago all very tall and impressive edged to the front and stood together side by side, symbols of the composition of the Democratic party."[54]

Baruch's power came from the people. Throughout the war commodity shortages evoked demands for the president to appoint "a Baruch committee" in the manner of the Rubber Survey Committee. The automobile clubs and their friends in Congress beat a steady tattoo for an investigation of the gasoline situation. A Gallup Poll showed that 67 percent of Americans believed that food problems could be remedied by a food committee. Baruch himself was amenable to a gasoline committee, though he eschewed one on food. Even after the war he was sought out to resolve special problems. In early 1946, 487 soldiers stationed in the Philippines cabled Baruch to help them win discharges: "Demobilization policy now a farce. If you would locate and place the facts before public and proper people it would help to get us home quickly. We have faith in you."[55] That said it succinctly: the American people had faith in Baruch to correct any social problem if he were assigned to investigate the facts: his report would put pressure upon ignorant or incompetent government officials to make the necessary adjustments of policy. (It should be noted that Baruch referred the soldiers to Secretary of War Patterson.) Baruch was ombudsman to America.*

That was as he intended. "He saw himself as an iconic father figure to the nation," Helen Lawrenson writes. He sought the role of public problem arbiter—sometimes too zealously for the tastes of others in the spotlight. White House counsel Sam Rosenman remembered that "the President's sole reservation about Baruch was the great publicity that attached to his name. It was a publicity that Roosevelt thought Baruch sometimes courted, but on most occasions could not avoid." Baruch could bring reporters running to him by calling the *New York Times,* but more subtle publicity was his through the efforts of the ever faithful Herb Swope. Swope depicted the war as a Baruch triumph. "Unquestionably," he once told Drew Pearson, "at the end of the war the President wanted Baruch and his group to take hold of practically everything." On the Baruch payroll was journalist Samuel Lubell, a shrewd student of politics and economics, who researched and wrote most of Baruch's public papers. It was also Lubell who saw to it that Baruch's wisdom on foreign affairs, articulated before the Senate Military Affairs Committee in 1945, was bound and disseminated to 10,261 libraries, 1,772 high schools, 1,727 university presidents, 1,700 daily newspapers, and 10,000 weekly newspapers throughout America. It was just part of his circle's effort to propagandize what John Hancock called "the same old philosophy . . . which we have joined in trying to sell to America."[56]

As ever, Baruch was his best publicist. Age and ailments would slow him, but never inhibit him. His causes and his friends needed his efforts. "A public statement by B. M. . . . would do more than anything else to

---

*Nobody called Baruch "ombudsman to America" because the word is too current in usage. Indeed, the reader is hard put to find it in any but quite recent dictionaries. *Webster's New World Dictionary and Thesaurus of the American Language* (1970) defines "ombudsman" as a "public official appointed to investigate citizens' complaints against local or national government agencies that may be infringing on the rights of individuals."

give the public a true perspective" of an issue, Robert Patterson once wrote. Indeed, on that issue, Baruch assured Patterson that he "would do a little talking around in semi-public places from time to time and that otherwise through the discreet expression of his own viewpoint he would try to stimulate public discussion." *To stimulate public discussion*: that was his function in public life. "I will put in my oar," he comforted lobbyists for a cause.[57] A word from Baruch was trusted by the people, both prominent and ordinary.

THE MORGENTHAU PLAN

Baruch in 1945 was an old man with grievances and goals. He had lost much of his former power and influence, although his name was certain to be given respect and deference by Congress and the press. Byrnes was aloof; his friends in the War Department had their importance diminished by peace; Roosevelt's death in April brought a turnover of White House personnel. Though Truman retained Sam Rosenman, the new chief executive and his entourage were less tolerant of Baruch's intrusions in policy debates. As Henry Wallace observed in July, Baruch "today feels a little bit out in the cold." About all Baruch had left was his command over public opinion, which was very considerable. It still opened doors that were closed to less prestigious men. His testimony on economic questions was still welcomed on Capitol Hill, and a Baruch dissent on policy could still produce an outpouring of constituent mail. He played public opinion for all it was worth, for he was determined to shape postwar policies. He was not about to let anyone forget that the issues of 1945–46 bore a resemblance to those of 1919: "I can tell you that already I see nothing but a repetition of what took place after the last war."[58]

Aside from the matter of postwar price stabilization, foreign policy settlements with vanquished Germany and America's British and Russian allies captured Baruch's attention. It was evident that there would be no repeat of the Paris Peace Conference after this war. For one thing, the Allies were intent upon defeat of Germany and its unconditional surrender, a goal agreed upon early and reaffirmed in wartime conferences among the Big Three—the United States, Great Britain, and the Soviet Union. Postwar arrangements received increasing attention as the Allies drove toward Berlin. Roosevelt showed no more need for special economic advisors in making peace than in making war. Baruch was relegated to his familiar role of kibitzer. Yet he was certain that the issue of reparations would be revived as discussions focused upon Germany's postwar fate. Then, as it had on the matters of mobilization and stabilization, his experience would tell.

But the Morgenthau Plan for postwar Germany upstaged Baruch on reparations. For that matter, the secretary of the Treasury upstaged everyone else in the administration with the proposition, conceived in the summer of 1944, independently of the State Department, that Germany after the war ought to be deprived of its industrial potential to make war again. At its worst, the Morgenthau Plan was nebulous—politically shortsighted and economically improbable. It invited characterization as a scheme to reduce Germany to a pasture and its people to abject poverty. Although even its detractors conceded that the Morgenthau Plan had a plausible moral justification on the grounds that Germany had to be punished for its transgressions against Europe in the last quarter century, the penalty and its possible consequences were considered excessive. Churchill reasoned that Britain needed an economically healthy Germany to repay it for war damages and perform as a viable trading partner. Besides, would a pastoral Germany be an effective bulwark against Bolshevism? The State Department also argued that postwar prosperity for all Europe was keyed to an industrial Germany. The War Department, envisioning itself as the administrator of a militarily occupied Germany, seconded these arguments. Even within the Treasury Department leadership there were those who questioned the soundness of the plan. Roosevelt was sympathetic to it, but uncommitted. It had minimal congressional support.[59] Thus, considering the coalition building against it, Morgenthau was surprised to receive encouragement from Baruch.

Coming from a man known for his political sagacity and his determination to avoid losing sides, Baruch's support of the Morgenthau Plan is surprising. Not only did he endorse an unwinnable position, but his timing was faulty. While the Morgenthau scheme had had the initiative in 1944, Baruch's support was relegated to behind-the-scenes memoranda, letters, and phone calls. "We can't—Henry, we won't let the Germans get away with anything this time," he assured Morgenthau. Baruch wanted to destroy the Reich's cartel system that had waged economic warfare against the United States for much of the twentieth century. In his eyes, before the war, Germany's "sweated labor and subsidized exports . . . flooded the export markets of the world everywhere, reducing prices and profits and causing reduction in scales of wages and standards of living." Baruch linked German and Japanese autarchy to their capacity to make war. He would substitute American control of their trade for their own cartel system: "If we do that, oh boy, oh boy, what long-time prosperity we will have."[60] But he did not speak out publicly for a punitive German settlement until the spring of 1945, by which time the Morgenthau Plan was decidedly on the defensive as the sort of Carthaginian peace that would recycle the depression and war of the 1930s.

Baruch seems to have been unaware of the bureaucratic controversy stirred up by the Morgenthau Plan. In March he called upon Henry Stimson for the first time in quite a while, and the discussion between the septuagenarians ranged over reparations and Germany; on both topics, Stimson recalled, "we were on all fours. . . . He was not so clear about how the thirty million extra people in Germany were going to live with their foreign trade drastically curtailed. I pressed him pretty hard on that subject and he agreed that they must be allowed to have enough non-military foreign trade to live." In preparation for an upcoming trip to England, Baruch then visited Secretary of State Stettinius, but he was not more circumspect about revealing his own opinion on reparations and Germany. He may have been encouraged to believe that the issue was far from being resolved by Roosevelt's determination not to be rushed into decisions regarding Germany. The president was telling people that the Germans needed a firm American hand and that he relished the idea of sending economic advisor Isador Lubin to Moscow to negotiate reparations, because "it would do the Germans good to know a Jew from Russia was handling the American part of reparations." Roosevelt appeared as oblivious to the German controversy as Baruch.[61]

Realizing that he was out of touch, Baruch asked for a brief on reparations from John Foster Dulles and put Sam Lubell to work investigating department positions on German reparations. Lubell went to the State Department to find out what had transpired on the question at Yalta and found that Roosevelt had agreed with the tough Russian position. Lubell next spoke to Treasury Department aides, who were anxious to sell him on the Morgenthau Plan, even if it meant, as Morgenthau put it, that Baruch would "be calling it the 'Baruch Plan' pretty soon." It was with some relief that a Morgenthau aide reported from his conference with Lubell that "Baruch was in general agreement with Secretary Morgenthau on the treatment of Germany, and insofar as he could gather the President was also in agreement." The importance of the Baruch position was heightened by the Old Man's forthcoming visit to London, where he would discuss reparations with Churchill. As Stettinius said, "You know, he's got a great influence with the Prime Minister."[62]

Aside from providing a chance to score points with Churchill on German reparations, Baruch's 1945 trip was an exercise in public relations: he was intent upon building his position as a lay spokesman for popular concerns. Armed with War Department polls on GI postwar interests, Baruch concentrated upon telling the press in England and Europe that postwar prosperity was assured and that he was there to make sure that the important people did the right thing by the prospective veterans. Lubell conferred in London with Ambassador John Winant's political aide, Philip Mosely, who was most unsympathetic with the Morgenthau Plan. That set the stage for Baruch's meetings with Churchill and other British officials—he went not to influence them on German reparations as Morgenthau hoped he would, but to sound them out on just where they stood; for Baruch, despite the trappings of the president's plane and a military aide, had no official commission to discuss German reparations with the British. What he found in London was a controversy similar to the one in Washington, except that the issues were even more keenly felt by the British. They were torn between seeking an industrially weak Germany that could not resist British trade expansion and desiring a strong Germany that would resist Russian expansion. But Churchill's economic advisors sought to persuade Baruch that Britain needed a revived German trade. On 11 April, before he left London, the park bench statesman sat in Regents Park telling reporters how he had defied Nazi "Werewolves" who had sworn to kill him in Frankfort.[63] The next day, Franklin Roosevelt died.

In the uncertainty that followed FDR's passing, Baruch stepped up his efforts to obtain a German deindustrialization policy. "It would be a grave mistake to let Germany industrialize until a new German people has arisen from the present wreckage," he told General Eisenhower. "We have had to pay twice. Let us see that it does not happen again." (Eisenhower said he agreed.) With tears in his eyes, Baruch told Morgenthau, "All I have got to live for now is to see that Germany is deindustrialized and that it's done the right way, and I won't let anybody get in my way." Morgenthau was heartened by Baruch's attitude, but not by the news that Jimmy Byrnes, soon to be secretary of state, wanted a strong Germany. Nevertheless, on the issue of Germany, Baruch assured Morgenthau, "We can't lose on that one." He sent President Truman a detailed memorandum on his visit to England and received a polite response that promised further discussion of it. But by the end of May, Baruch must have felt that the situation was deteriorating, for he leaked a memorandum on Germany to Krock, and it eventually found its way to the front page.[64] Events were moving swiftly now, and they were not going as Baruch forecast. But he had gone public on a very volatile issue.

On 22 June, Baruch appeared before Senator Elbert Thomas's Military Affairs Committee to call for a curb on Germany's ability to wage war. It was Baruch's most definitive public statement on the subject. Declaring that Germany was the key to American relations with Britain and Russia, he called upon Americans to make certain that this would be the last German war by rendering the foe industrially incapable of waging another. "I have not thought in terms of a hard or a soft peace," he insisted. "I seek a sure peace." A certain peace entailed a settlement that would "break once and for all Germany's dominance of Europe. Her warmaking potential must be eliminated; many of her plants and factories shifted east and west to friendly countries; all other heavy industry destroyed; the Junkers estates broken up; her exports and imports strictly controlled; German assets and business organizations all over the world rooted out." But Baruch was vague. What could Germany trade with the world? Her labor, said Baruch. Would that entail slavery? No, it would be a temporary control of Germany and repayment of her debts to Europe. For how long? "Until Germany has a rebirth." At any rate, he took Morgenthau's approach that German industry was cartelized and waged economic war against America's free enterprise, and he argued that, "in the end, you cannot industrialize Germany and keep her from being a war agency." This dismal view required strict Allied control of a potentially resurgent Germany. Among New Dealers on the committee, Baruch's statement was warmly received, Lister Hill congratulating him on his "very magnificent contribution."[65]

But Congress did not make foreign policy and there were others in Washington and elsewhere who thought less of his position. The conservative *Economist* of Britain deplored Baruch's plan for Germany as "immoral, uneconomic and unworkable." That opinion found agreement in the Departments of War and State. Moreover, President Truman bracketed Baruch with Morgenthau as men who "couldn't keep from meddling in" German questions. Truman took Stimson with him to the Potsdam Conference and deliberately left the Treasury without a representative in the America delegation.[66] Morgenthau submitted his resignation, and Truman replaced him with Fred Vinson, already a member of the American Potsdam delegation.

Baruch began to tack. He still distrusted an industrialized Germany, but he restricted his comments to conversation and correspondence. In November he complained of the illogic of dividing Germany and thereby depriving Europe of Germany's manufacturing and distributing capacity. He appreciated the fact that his advocacy of "control" of Germany contradicted Wilsonian equality of opportunity, but he was torn between his desire to restore Europe, with the knowledge that that also required a revitalized Germany, and his conviction that the Germans were unrepentant corporatists who needed war to fulfill their ambitions of hegemony. Although the Morgenthau Plan had a visceral appeal to him, he was now mindful of its political liabilities and aware that a consensus was evolving in London and Washington in favor of restoring a devastated Germany against the onslaught of victorious Russians in central Europe. Baruch modified his statements on Germany, but not his views. As he put it in his memoirs, "For a time I even sympathized with Henry Morgenthau's radical plan to reduce Germany to a pastoral economy, but I soon saw that this was not practicable." He conceded that the perceived Soviet menace had altered American attitudes toward Germany, something he called "one of the bitterest ironies of our time." He would not be happy with the resurgence of Germany; "the bitter memories and the mistrust have not yet been entirely eradicated." The revival of the German and Japanese economies, he forecast, would ultimately pose a threat to American prosperity. Liberal economics aside, the United States had to remember the power of economic nationalism in the world. And morally, he told Churchill, he could not forgive the German industrialist Krupp, "whose steel helped to kill so many of your boys and my boys. He also established those terrible labor camps." As late as the gathering crisis over Berlin in the early 1960s, he would write: "I do not happen to be one of those who favor the restoration of a reunited and a rearmed Germany. I understand the fears of Russia in that respect but I also understand our fears."[67] The world was changing, but Baruch believed that certain verities remained—distrust of Germany being one of them.

THE BRITISH LOAN

Baruch argued that a German settlement was the key to the reconstruction of Britain and her ability to stabilize the empire. Monetary stability and a second phase of lend-lease were midwar issues that cropped up in Anglo-American discussions. Baruch, ever suspicious of British intentions, opposed any agreement that made London the beneficiary of Washington's altruism. Rather, he insisted that Britain seize German resources and markets as just compensation for its wartime economic losses. Thus, he argued, a weakened Germany would yield a strengthened Britain.

Baruch was not a postwar liberal internationalist. He lived in a world of imperial competition and, although he resented the British imperial preference system that closed the door on competitive trade, he welcomed the British Empire as a force for order in the world and as a reminder to Americans of the realpolitik of nations. Thus, in reaction to the "one-world" anticolonial liberalism of a Wendell Willkie or Henry Wallace, Baruch cheered Churchill's declaration that "he had not been made His Majesty's servant to liquidate the British Empire. That stopped a lot of globaloney." Of course, "globaloney," coined by Clare Boothe Luce, was derisive of liberal internationalists and resounded of isolationism. Baruch's perspective of international relations had not changed much since 1919, and it was not likely to advance much beyond that momentous year as long as the British Treasury sent John Maynard Keynes to Washington as its representative almost every year of the war. They clashed at a dinner hosted by Churchill in London in 1945, Keynes finding Baruch "stone deaf, though . . . in other respects in rather remarkable form." (Baruch turned his hearing aid off when he did not care to listen to someone.) Whatever Keynes proposed, Baruch received with unconcealed suspicions. To him, Keynes was "a menace," "a pretty slippery one" who really "represents the Bank of England." The Bretton Woods agreement of 1944 to establish an International Monetary Fund dominated by American capital was looked upon by Baruch as inadequate for guaranteeing American businessmen free access to British markets—even as it was resented in London because it opened British markets to American capital! As for a proposed multibillion dollar loan to Britain, Baruch suspected that it would only strengthen British economic imperialism at the cost of American liberal trade. He warned both Morgenthau and Stettinius, "You will certainly drive Wilsonites like myself into the position of looking like isolationists."[68]

His strategy was to insist that a German settlement precede any agreement with the British. He counted upon the British to extract what they could from a prostrate Germany, thereby considerably lessening England's dependence upon American postwar economic relief. "This German reparations policy has got to be settled . . . before the Bretton Woods matters can be definitely decided," he told Morgenthau; it would be "a great mistake to push Bretton Woods before reparations is settled." Morgenthau found Baruch's conversation discursive; he darted from topic to topic, from Germany to Britain to American inflation, without any apparent connecting thread of an idea. In part, the fault lay with Baruch's occasionally diffuse and elliptical patterns of argument. In part, it lay with the fact that he opposed plans dear to Morgenthau's heart: the secretary of the Treasury had no trouble understanding Baruch's approval of the Morgenthau Plan. But another problem lay in the fact that Baruch saw economic concerns as parts of an interrelated political economy; most listeners could not conceptualize more than a couple of distinct issues at a time. To Baruch, everything hinged upon maintenance of the American standard of living by resistance to anything that inflated domestic prices. Although "the problem of inflation has permeated every single one of our policies," Washington tended to divide its political economy into neat bureaucratic segments, "instead of having all the elements pieced together." Thus, his insistence that aid to Britain wait upon a German settlement did not make sense to Morgenthau; least of all did Morgenthau understand how such aid would be inflationary for the United States.[69]

During his mission to London in early April 1945, Baruch hoped to deflect British financial interests from coveting a share of America's wealth to preparing to strip Germany of her resources. As Baruch later reported to President Truman, he found the British pessimistic concerning their economic future, but "I left them prepared to do more for themselves and to ask less of us." The British had to realize that they were "heirs to much of the former German and Japanese markets," which would assure their future prosperity. Still, while the British took markets from their defeated enemies, they could not shut their great American friends out of their own imperial markets as they had done before the war. He had told the British that American financial aid should not subsidize colonialism. Britain had to choose between filling the economic needs of her colonies and satisfying her domestic market; the latter choice would justify American entry into colonial trade. After all, Baruch declared, "Preferences are of no avail without the goods to sell." Only America had the goods for both overseas and domestic markets. Baruch urged Truman to recognize that his greatest difficulty lay in balancing "domestic demands (stimulated by accumulated savings) with needs abroad." Without that managed balance the United States could run into a destabilizing inflationary spiral.

The greatest obstacle to making the British appreciate his logic was their fear of Russia: "British officials are wavering between an economically weak Germany and rebuilding a strong Germany as a buffer against the Soviets"; hence his first premise, "Germany is the key to the whole peace." Churchill understood Baruch's point, but countered by demanding "an Anglo-American military alliance" that would guarantee collective security against a Soviet onslaught. Baruch could only respond that Churchill knew that that "was foreign to our traditions." In sum, Baruch urged Churchill not to ask for anything that weakened the American economy as a bulwark of western prosperity.

Truman received the report with enthusiasm and then, to Baruch's everlasting disappointment, put it away.[70] It had been intended as a comprehensive guide to postwar foreign policy, but it clearly contradicted prevailing instincts in the State, Treasury, and War departments.

To some extent the question of the British loan depended upon Britain —its perceptions of its interests in Europe and who made British policy. Following British elections scheduled in 1945, Churchill and the Conservatives could be replaced by a Labour government. Would the United States extend its credit to a British government intent upon socializing major industries? Baruch thought it should not. He was concerned that Congress might approve the Bretton Woods agreement before the British elections. If he had his way, there would be tough terms in any British loan, but probably no loan at all to a socialist government. Labour won in July.

At stake was nothing less than the survival of the free-enterprise system. America was living in a world that was increasingly "totalized." After defeating the totalitarian systems of Germany, Italy, and Japan, it would be a bitter blow to discover the viability of America's private enterprise limited not only by the Soviet Union but by England as well. As Baruch told a U.S. senator:

> There is a much graver danger to the American system than the Bretton Woods Agreement, and that is the nationalization of England's industries. They probably will start with steel, railroads, coal and textiles. Now what does it all mean? It will be done only for the purpose of raising their wages, but that will raise the cost of their

production. England is interested primarily in exports and in importing food. With a higher cost of production she will not be able to export in competition with other countries, so she will have to subsidize those industries. Are we to transfer billions of dollars to England to enable her to carry out this theory of Professor Laski, et al? Totalization and nationalization by other countries will certainly threaten our industry and our institutions.[71]

Byrnes was secretary of state now, with Will Clayton his undersecretary, but neither man paid Baruch much heed. Both were intent upon integrating Britain into a western system dominated by the United States, writing off the British debt in return for assurances that American businessmen would have freedom within Britain's sphere. To the argument that the loan was unwise generosity that would cost America a measure of her own prosperity, Clayton replied that it would "enable the British people to open up their commerce to the United States . . . instead of confining it to the British Empire." For that matter, President Truman privately observed "that the loan would be principally of value to our own country, since the money would be spent here."[72]

But Baruch maintained that America could not absorb British spending without inflating domestic prices. As he put it, "What sense is there in lending money to people to purchase in a market as bare of goods as this market is?" With U.S. demand soaring through 1945–46, Washington proposed to subsidize foreign buyers. "Are the American people to stand for that, when there are huge amounts of money bulging out of their pockets?" Baruch asked. "We recognize that there is a minor amount of inflationary pressure in this," Secretary of Commerce Henry Wallace responded, "But we feel that this has to be endured in the interest of establishing the kind of international relations necessary for future peace and security and in order to establish markets we shall need later, when the immediate pressure of deferred demand has been worked off by several years of high-level production." Baruch was not convinced by this claim to farsightedness that challenged his own. To him, the long run included an inflationary trend that would inhibit future expansion of America's export trade. For now and later, Baruch contended, the loans could benefit only American financiers. "The bankers are in favor of loans to everybody. Why? Because that is good business for them. But where is the stuff this money can purchase?"[73] He would endorse a modest loan to the British to enable them to feed their people, for that was both morally correct and economically tolerable.

"Of all the opponents of a large British loan, Baruch was perhaps the most effective," historian Lloyd Gardner has written. Eleanor Roosevelt urged President Truman to give credence to Baruch's arguments and repeated his contention that anything but a small loan would boost inflation at home. Baruch took his case to Clayton, who was negotiating the loan, stressing his fear of the size of the loan and the possibility that it encouraged socialization of British industry. Clayton's opposite number, British negotiator R. H. Brand, met with Baruch and vainly sought to neutralize him. Baruch could not be persuaded. "In the main he certainly wishes us well," Brand reported, "but he certainly does not wish that we should get away with anything that we are not entitled to."[74]

The State Department in 1945–46 was eager to have Baruch sell its policies to the public, but Baruch could not buy the British loan. Clayton sought to soften the sting of Baruch's opposition by asserting that the loan would "help to slow up or prevent further nationalization of industry and commerce by Britain" because, without it, London would have to adopt more stringent nationalistic measures. The terms arranged were as favorable to American trade interests as Clayton could possibly make them. The United States would loan the British $3.75 billion at 2 percent interest, forgive most of the lend-lease debt, and be assured that the Sterling Bloc was broken, as was the practice of imperial preference. Baruch was beaten, but not mollified. Noting expanded nationalization of British industry, Baruch told Clayton, "There seems to be hardly any need for further discussion between us because it is hard to come to or stay on any common ground."[75] Indeed, it remained to be seen whether Baruch could find any common ground with the administration in its dealings with that other wartime ally—the Soviet Union.

FOR A "LOOK-SEE" AT THE SOVIETS

Baruch was a thorn in the sides of Truman and Byrnes. At a time when the new administration was preparing to dump Morgenthau and his plan for Germany, Baruch was promoting the scheme on the front page of the *New York Times*. As Washington pushed to restore the British economy via a loan, Baruch was marshaling public opinion and lobbying with Congress against it. Considering that Baruch allied himself with old conservatives like Herbert Hoover and Jesse Jones in denouncing the loan for encouraging the trend to statism and socialism, he should have been ideologically comfortable with the Truman-Byrnes policies of toughness toward the Russians. But even there, Baruch dissented in 1945. His scheme for reorganizing the postwar world called for American-Soviet cooperation in dismantling Germany in order to insure Britain's prosperity and guarantee Soviet security. The Soviets, according to the Baruch formula, would be accorded American approval of their claims for German reparations. In turn, the dreams of American business expansionists would be realized, as the Soviets would be induced by American generosity to admit Yankee traders. New Dealers who looked forward to opening Russia to American trade after the war were flabbergasted to find that Baruch was not a fervent anticommunist like his good friend Churchill. "Baruch came in on the Russian side," Henry Wallace observed; Baruch was "right" on Russia, commented an elated Henry Morgenthau.[76] Although Baruch was obsessed with the European spread of "totalization" that endangered America's free enterprise system, in 1945 he was *not* obsessed with the Soviet menace.

Since the Bolshevik revolution, Baruch had advocated a Wilsonian policy of benevolence toward the Russian people and hostility toward the Soviet government. In 1918 he had recommended a gesture of sending Herbert Hoover on a mission to Moscow to show the Russians that Washington was concerned with famine in their land. During the Paris Peace Conference he expressed a willingness to help "the masses of Russia." He was not a counterrevolutionary, for he felt sure that "the American people would never stand for putting back in power the reactionary element." Baruch's apparently enlightened attitude toward the Soviets drew progressive journalists to him; apocryphally it was Baruch whom Lincoln Steffens sought out with his famous exclamation, "I have seen the future and it works." In 1920, Baruch told an interviewer that "the Russian people have a right, it seems to me, to set up any form of government they wish. The world has no right to impose any system of government upon any people." Baruch's position espoused self-determination: "Russia has the right to work out her own salvation in her own way."[77]

But nobody could mistake Baruch for a communist sympathizer. He made it evident that he hoped American cordiality toward the Russians would open their markets to trade and investment—thereby assuring, he felt, a Soviet demise and a restoration of the profit system. Indeed, because he considered the Russian market potentially rich, he told socialist John Spargo that, instead of blockading the Soviets, "we should see that no one attempts to fasten any carpetbag financial or political Government upon her in order to secure special advantages"; he advocated, then, an open door for Russia. To restore capitalism to Russia, Baruch in the 1920s suggested that the Germans undertake "economic penetration" of eastern Europe, including Russia. When the *Berliner Tageblatt* sought out fifteen American opinions on the Dawes Plan, Baruch's was the only one specifically to mention the importance of the Russian market for the Germans.[78] In 1925, through an American newspaperman who served as intermediary, Baruch met at Versailles with the Soviet commissar for foreign trade, Leonid Krassin, who was sounding out Baruch about organization of Russian industry. Baruch listened to Krassin expound upon Russia's economic troubles and then prescribed concessions to western investors for industrial development. He never heard again from Krassin.[79]

Baruch wanted business with the Soviets, confident that "Bolshevism would soon break down" following these commercial contacts; but he opposed diplomatic recognition of the Soviet Union. "I am one of the staunchest opponents of recognition," he reminded a newspaper reporter who dared to suggest that he conspired for United States-USSR relations in 1933. Ideologically—and, he believed, practically as well—communism had to fail because it denied to the multitude the liberty and incentive needed to create prosperity. "In Russia you see one extreme—all people are equally miserable," he told Churchill, who was certain to agree with him. Yet he was respectful of Russian production of gold and synthetic rubber, ever willing to give credit when he believed it was due. In 1942 he contributed $100,000 to Russian war relief. His respect for the Russians grew tremendously during the war. "You know, I was wrong when I told you that if the German army ever invaded Russia they'd go through it like a hot knife through butter," he told Helen Lawrenson. "When it comes to talk peace terms, all Joe Stalin's got to say will be one word: 'Stalingrad.'"[80]

Toward the end of the war, Baruch turned to a scholar who had written admiringly of Woodrow Wilson's perspective on international relations, D. F. Fleming, for research and advice regarding a peace settlement. The Vanderbilt University political scientist, who would later emerge as the first Cold War revisionist historian,[81] had a conception of world power relations that appealed greatly to Baruch. In February 1945, Baruch sent President Roosevelt a Fleming paper on the need for European unity. Truman was president for only a week when Baruch sent him a Fleming memorandum entitled "Why Are the Russians Slow to Trust the Western Powers?" He put Fleming on a monthly retainer in May and constantly touted him to everyone as someone "who knows more about international relations than anyone else I know." During the summer months of 1945, Fleming moved to the New York area and produced position papers for Baruch on international affairs.

Fleming stressed the importance of cooperation with the Russians in order to reduce their trepidations about capitalist encirclement. He argued that Russia ought to have earned the confidence of the west by its resistance in the League of Nations to Fascist aggression, which made Russia "the best Great Power member that the League ever had." Reasoning that "there was bound to be some shock when we at last stood face to face with the Russians" in devastated Germany, Fleming foresaw difficulties ahead if the west began to "concentrate on standing up to the Russians." War between the leading exponents of capitalism and communism was not inevitable: "There will be sharp competition between the two surviving systems for the favor of mankind, . . . but both are plainly in evolution and there need be no irreconcilable clash between them." He called for "firm, tenacious cooperation with Soviet Russia."

The first decade of the postwar era would determine, as had the first decade after World War I, whether there would be yet another great war. Fleming never discussed economics. Baruch used him to supply historical background and international relations concepts. Essentially both men were Wilsonians living in an age increasingly removed from the man they so intensely revered.[82]

Fleming's influence showed in Baruch's June testimony before the Senate Military Affairs Committee on German deindustrialization. "America's role in dealing with Russia should be one of tolerance and fairness," he declared. "Cooperation is a two-way street. I would like to see this simple rule laid down: What we permit the Russians to do, they should permit us to do. There should be a free look-see for all the United Nations throughout Europe." This meant that businessmen would enjoy freedom of movement and enterprise throughout eastern Europe and that the Soviets would open up their own society to capitalist scrutiny on the basis of mutual goodwill. Mindful of Fleming's warning that much of Latin America had no relations with the Soviets, Baruch also urged that "the United States should use her offices to persuade those nations who still refuse to recognize Soviet Russia to do so." That was quite a turnabout for a man who once had boasted that he was the arch-opponent of American recognition of the Soviets. However, stressing the bitter legacy of the past thirty years, Baruch reminded his fellow Americans that "any nation which has undergone such experiences is bound to be security-conscious to a very high degree." Like France after World War I, Russia now needed to have her fears of Germany respected by the west. In response to questions, Baruch elaborated upon his proposed policy of cooperation and open borders:

> Let us be very frank about it. I mean Americans should be permitted to go into Poland, Bulgaria, and all of the other countries that have been occupied by our associates in the war. . . .
>
> If we allow the Russians in here to have a look-see, I want the same right. I do not want to pry into anyone's political methods; I want to keep my nose out of their politics, but I think it should be a 50-50 proposition.
>
> . . . If I were a Russian I would want to get every impregnable or semi-impregnable wall to protect myself. I would do what she is trying to do—to have all along her border countries under Russian influence.
>
> Mind you, I am not advocating that, I am trying to answer your question of what I believe the Russians want to do. Do not forget that Russia has long had a desire to get warm-water ports. Maybe she will make some demand about Kiel. I do not know what is in her mind because I have not seen any Russians since the war.
>
> They may want to get to the Mediterranean and undoubtedly are

casting eyes toward the Persian Gulf and watching interestedly
proceedings on the Chinese and Russian fronts.[83]

Thus, Baruch was neither subscribing to the popular front nor prepared
to launch the Cold War. He would offer the Russians a quid pro quo:
political hegemony over eastern Europe in return for free trade there for
the west. For that matter, his policy toward Britain also called for recognition of its sphere of influence in return for equality of opportunities.

Baruch on the Soviet Union was a philosophical Wilsonian liberal. In
1945 he viewed all international relations as part of "the contest that
looms between totalization and the American competitive system." He
wanted American loans to be used for "the opening up of their borders to
our commerce, trade and look-see." He made it clear this did not refer
solely to the Russians, but to all European nations where nationalization
of industries was in progress or even contemplated. American businessmen should not have to trade with cartels or government corporations.
He would use America's wealth to demand equal opportunity throughout
Europe now before the trend toward totalization succeeded. Ideological
competition with the Soviets was welcomed as long as it did not hinder
economic freedom.[84]

Baruch did not want the United States to make any bilateral loans
without first attempting to erect a "supreme peace council" through
which postwar aid to Europe would be administered. He would deal
with Europe as a unit through the council, thus allowing America to
make one demand for restructuring the Continent along lines acceptable
to her. The Soviets would be treated there as equals and would give the
Americans freedom of trade corresponding to the aid given in return by
the United States. If the United States of America did not choose to
demand a "United States of Europe" for the reconstruction of the Continent, then Baruch prescribed only modest loans to each country, which
would allow America to husband her resources. He would not treat any
nation differently from another. If the United States loaned money to
Britain, fairness required that it loan money to the Soviets—and he
seemed to suggest that Moscow was a better risk for the United States
than London. But the issue of a Russian loan never materialized to the
extent of the British loan controversy. The Russians had come in belatedly with a second-round application for lend-lease. The consensus in
Washington early in 1945, with the war's end apparently in sight, was
that lend-lease really amounted to postwar rehabilitation. Jimmy Byrnes
and others did not favorably view the Russian request for "industrial
equipment and machinery, postwar in usefulness." In May, Truman ordered all lend-lease to Russia cut off. The Russian application for a loan
would be "lost in the shuffle." Baruch considered this as contributing to

poor relations between the two nations and as a lost opportunity to integrate the Soviet economy into that of all Europe.[85]

Baruch's insistence upon fairness to the Soviets was something that, as he knew, many old associates did not share. He knew that Churchill was rabid on the topic of the Soviets, having advocated all-out intervention in Russia in 1919 on the side of the White Army. Only the Nazis could have forced Churchill into an alliance with Stalin. Otherwise, Baruch told his radical-minded girlfriend, Helen Lawrenson, "It's his dream that England and Germany unite to crush Soviet Russia. He's not one of your anti-Fascists, my dear. He admires Mussolini and, between you and me and the lamppost, if Hitler had stopped at just killing Commies and Jews, I don't think Winston, like a lot of other people, would have any quarrel with him." Roosevelt is supposed to have asked Baruch on one occasion to try to tone down Churchill's anti-Soviet comments. Churchill was "all for letting the Germans and the Russkies fight it out together." Churchill's ouster as prime minister in 1945 did not eliminate him as an influence in postwar international politics. Baruch appreciated the irony that Churchill's Labour successor, Clement Atlee, "is able to take the position Winston took with the Russians and get away with it when Winston might not have been able to do so." But Baruch remained throughout 1945 a strong advocate of patient and tolerant cooperation with the Soviets. As late as Christmas he told Fleming, "Our friends in Washington would have done well to have heeded some of the things we told them, especially the memorandum on 'How I would feel if I were a Russian.'" But Fleming would return to the campus, his hopes of shaping policy unfulfilled, his influence with Baruch dwindling. Increasingly an outsider in Washington himself, Baruch had no more use for Fleming. On the other hand, Churchill was an old friend and a man who, Baruch knew, "is idolized here." His relationship with Churchill drew Baruch back into the limelight, sometimes even into the White House. In early 1946 hostility to the Soviet domination of eastern Europe was increasing. Baruch was easily susceptible to such thinking himself. The American way of liberalism was being rejected in Europe. As he commented to another longtime anticommunist colleague, Herbert Hoover, "Certainly Statism marches westward. It beats upon all our shores. There lies the greatest fight to preserve our form of government which is the only one where men still have some freedom and some dignity." In February, Churchill came to the United States and Baruch met with him and Byrnes in Miami. A news dispatch noted that the three men were reluctant to discuss the nature of their conversation, but parts of it "would be revealed March 5 at Fulton, Mo., where Mr. Churchill is scheduled to appear with President Truman for a formal address." That would be Churchill's "Iron Curtain" speech.[86]

THE BARUCH PLAN FOR INTERNATIONAL CONTROL
OF ATOMIC ENERGY

Less than two weeks after Churchill's Iron Curtain speech, the White House announced that it was nominating, as the American representative at the United Nations Atomic Energy Commission (UNAEC), Bernard M. Baruch. Explaining that he felt it his duty to accept the assignment, Baruch said that he would be assisted by John Hancock, Ferd Eberstadt, Fred Searls, and Herbert Bayard Swope. "You know I never do any work myself," he joked with reporters. It would be Baruch's responsibility to define a policy on the international control of atomic energy and to negotiate it at the United Nations. Considering the distrust of the Russians, the misgivings of the British allies with whom the United States would not share its atomic power, and the apprehension of some congressmen that the United States would unwisely surrender its monopoly, Baruch again found himself at the center of controversy. "I certainly have a hot potato in this foreign policy on the atomic bomb," he told a friend about three weeks later. "It is a mystery to me why they took me out of the domestic and international fields of economics where I had such vast experience, and put me in another field where I know nothing."[87]

It was a mystery—although his nomination for the post was widely acclaimed and assured of overwhelming approval by the Senate—not only why President Truman and Secretary of State Byrnes wanted this seventy-five-year-old man for a difficult diplomatic task for which he had no background, but why Baruch agreed to take it, feeling, as he freely confessed to friends, that he knew nothing about atomic energy.

It was no mystery to Truman or Byrnes. Throughout the war the White House had used Baruch for public relations whenever it held a "hot potato." But those difficulties involved matters of economic stabilization for which Baruch claimed expertise, rather than the virgin field of atomic diplomacy. No matter; former senators themselves, Truman and Byrnes knew the value of Baruch's name on Capitol Hill. They were already in trouble enough with Congress on atomic energy policy; partly to overcome those domestic difficulties, the State Department hastily fabricated a plan that created the diplomatic illusion of international magnanimity at a time when the administration itself fostered an apparently contradictory hard line toward the Russians. They needed somebody with enormous integrity who could negotiate and explain policy satisfactorily to the American people. At about this time, Democrats with ties to fund raisers were said to be pressing Truman to "put some men like Bernard Baruch in the Administration so as to get public confidence." Even within the administration there was a feeling that it was handling public relations poorly: Forrestal was telling Byrnes that he believed "the American press should be an instrument of our foreign policy."[88]

However, Truman wanted no part of Baruch. He had called the Old Man a "meddler" in the German question, did not relish his opposition to the British loan, had received Baruch memoranda urging a softer line on the Russians, and reacted to pressure to take him into the administration by complaining that Baruch would be holding press conferences in Lafayette Park. Yet, as Byrnes knew from experience, Baruch on the inside was as useful to an administration as he was threatening on the outside. Moreover, during the Churchill visit to the United States, Byrnes had had enough discussions with Baruch to be assured that no substantive differences on Russian policy existed. As for the German and British questions, as well as domestic economic issues, if Baruch enjoyed an official capacity he would reinforce policy he agreed with and be silent on policy he disagreed with. Public relations logic dictated Baruch's appointment as the American delegate to the UNAEC.

Byrnes and Truman could not be certain that Baruch would accept the assignment. The Old Man had turned down wartime assignments and, in fact, was reluctant to take Byrnes's latest tender. After a weekend of thinking it over, Baruch said that he would take it if they could reach an understanding on certain matters. He felt that a younger man should have the job, that "he wasn't much on technical scientific stuff, but he could smell his way through it."[89] Baruch's hubris dictated his acceptance, and foreign policy held a great attraction for him. Although he lacked any real understanding of atomic energy, he viewed it as simply another political or ethical question concerning the development of a vital raw material that governed the relations of nations. Because he had been frozen out of the other postwar international discussions, this might be his last opportunity to play any role in historic settlements—his 1946 version of the Paris Peace Conference. Assuming that he would have the assistance of the State Department's technical consultants on atomic energy for his own political staff, much as he had used technical assistants in business and politics all his life, he would muddle through the issues.

"This is a very important matter and I do not want to say No," Baruch told Byrnes in his letter of acceptance. Yet, besides his ignorance of atomic energy and his inexperience in negotiating international agreements, his age handicapped him. At seventy-five, Baruch required the services of a full-time nurse-housekeeper-companion. He was practically deaf in one ear. His routine was inflexible. "I can only work between the hours of 10 and 12 in the morning and from 2:30 to 4:30 in the afternoon," he warned Byrnes. "I cannot go to any night sessions." After 4:30 he "sagged badly" and wanted to retire while younger men pressed on.

That schedule was hardly conducive to strenuous diplomacy, but he would depend upon his seconds for that. Though his task was to articulate American policy on atomic energy, he reserved the right to speak out on other issues. "In view of all this, if you still want me to serve I will accept."[90]

Baruch then believed that he would have a hand in defining the policy that he would bring to the United Nations, but he soon realized that Byrnes and Truman wanted him only as a spokesman. Policy had been formulated by a select committee headed by Undersecretary of State Dean Acheson and Tennessee Valley Authority head David Lilienthal. Convened in January, the Acheson-Lilienthal committee* was a blue-ribbon panel selected by Acheson. Like Baruch, it was impressed with the magnitude of its responsibility. The announcement of Baruch's appointment in mid-March, just as the committee completed its deliberations and report, was a surprise and a disappointment. The Acheson-Lilienthal committee believed that it had devised a set of policy guidelines for the international control of atomic energy and expected that its interpreter and advocate would be a skilled diplomat; instead, its statesman was a publicist.

In a rational world where pride does not intrude, policy would have been the paramount consideration of everyone involved. However, vanity and resentment prevailed. Undoubtedly peeved that Byrnes chose Baruch without consulting it, the committee began to leak its report to the press before Baruch could see it. That action suggested to Baruch that the committee considered him merely its "messenger boy." In a year when trust between the United States and the Soviet Union deteriorated, trust among the formulators of American atomic control policy was almost as elusive. Aside from the antipathy that developed between Baruch and the Acheson-Lilienthal group, mistrust among Baruch, Byrnes, and Truman was also considerable. Baruch still complained that Byrnes "would not take any advice," and after he completed his U.N. mission he would comment about Byrnes, "I have known him all his life, but he never would talk things out with me. Never told me what was in his mind." And Truman was said to have no confidence in either Baruch or Byrnes.[91]

The Acheson-Lilienthal group had its share of bruised egos. Acheson and Lilienthal were friends and disciples of Justice Felix Frankfurter, whose dislike for Baruch dated to 1917 and had intensified since then. Acheson and Lilienthal adopted Frankfurter's biases as their own. Ache-

---

*It consisted of scientific advisor Vannevar Bush, Harvard University President James B. Conant, General Leslie R. Groves, Assistant Secretary of War John J. McCloy, Acheson's special assistant Herbert S. Marks, atomic scientist J. Robert Oppenheimer, Vice-President of Monsanto Chemical Company Charles A. Thomas, General Electric Vice-President in charge of engineering Harry A. Winne, President of New Jersey Bell Telephone Company Chester I. Barnard, and Bush's aide Carroll Wilson.

son loathed the patronizing avuncular manner of inferior intellects such as Baruch or Franklin Roosevelt, and he also considered lawyers the intellectual and moral superiors of businessmen. In public policy development, Baruch was an anathema. Yet here was Byrnes "unflatteringly" telling Acheson that Baruch would go to the UNAEC "'for the task of translating the various proposals stimulated by the Acheson-Lilienthal report into a workable plan.'" Acheson bristled: "I protested, distrusting Mr. Baruch's translation and dissenting from Mr. Byrnes's—and the generally held—view that this so-called 'adviser of Presidents' was a wise man." Acheson, believing that the State Department could publicize its atomic proposals without Baruch's reputation, approved their release to the public. The resentments would smolder for months, flaring in an accusation Baruch made against Acheson—that Acheson was secretly recording their telephone conversations—which Acheson heatedly denied. Baruch considered the assistance of Lilienthal and his technical consultants a key to the entire mission. But Lilienthal's reaction to the news of Baruch's appointment was, "God! Isn't *this* something!" Instead of a vigorous young advocate of international cooperation, Byrnes had appointed an old and notoriously vain man who surrounded himself with cronies who made Lilienthal sick to contemplate: "This is the hottest seat B. B. has occupied since World War I. He has responsibility this time, and not just a chance to kibitz."[92]

Following release of the Acheson-Lilienthal report, Baruch telephoned Lilienthal and asked if he considered it binding upon the U.S. representative. Lilienthal responded that it had no official status other than as an exploratory discussion. Baruch expressed the hope that he would have the assistance of Lilienthal's advisory scientists. For that matter, Baruch told Lilienthal, "Don't think, young man, you won't be pulled back into this. When are you coming to Washington to go over this with me?" But Lilienthal "dodged, feeling . . . torn between a desire that this terribly important matter not be left to the judgment of an old man and my intense desire to stay on the TVA job." Lilienthal's responsibility in this situation called for aiding the Old Man, but both resentment at being upstaged and fear of being co-opted—with Baruch's ill-formed notions on atomic control superseding his own—played a strong role in Lilienthal's sulking resistance to Baruch's blandishments. Through the spring of 1946, Baruch would plead with Lilienthal for assistance in persuading the key technical advisor, Dr. J. Robert Oppenheimer, to become Baruch's advisor. But, like the rest of the Acheson-Lilienthal group, Oppenheimer treated Baruch as if he were a Typhoid Mary. To his face, Baruch called Lilienthal "sour" and uncooperative until the younger man finally agreed to call a meeting between Baruch's advisors and his own group. He knew that Baruch's people were floundering in a field strange to their experiences. Yet he had to be cajoled into consulting with them. "I hate to have to undertake this [meeting], but perhaps we must," Lilienthal wrote resignedly. Yet meetings between the two groups changed little. Baruch sought nothing less than the absorption of Lilienthal and Oppenheimer into his group, but they would not join a bunch they considered political adversaries. In conferences Baruch initiated, he told Oppenheimer that he was angry with the intransigent Lilienthal. He "ought to be up here working with us, but he won't cooperate," Oppenheimer reported Baruch as saying: "He will regret his attitude."[93] Baruch and his group respected Lilienthal and Oppenheimer and defended the liberals against political smears in the early cold war years.*

Baruch knew that he had been chosen to present the American plan to the United Nations because he was insurance against domestic right-wing hostility to proposals that the United States share its secret atomic information with an international Atomic Development Authority. Therefore, he felt safe in demanding that his views prevail without any slavish adherence to the Acheson-Lilienthal recommendations. Any time it appeared that he was not in control of policy, he could merely suggest that his resignation would be forthcoming. Even before he was confirmed by the Senate he was hinting to Truman and Byrnes that he would not be bound by all the Acheson-Lilienthal guidelines. Although there would later be some disagreement as to what transpired when Baruch met with Truman on 26 March, the consensus among historians accepts the Baruch version that when he asked the president who was drafting the American proposals, Truman quickly responded, "Hell, you are.!"[94]

Byrnes and Truman needed both sides. The secretary of state appealed to the Acheson committee to be generous in its advice to Baruch because the Old Man appreciated his limitations and was "quite earnest" in seeking the committee's policy input. On 18 April, Byrnes conferred with Baruch for the purpose of defining responsibilities, reminding him that only the president could make policy, with the advice of the secretary of state, and that though he was "favorably impressed" with the Acheson report, he did not believe that it was "the last word on the subject." He

---

*Ferdinand Eberstadt considered Lilienthal's 1946 behavior "decent and fair and reasonable" and "his competence . . . beyond question." Excerpts from James Forrestal-Ferdinand Eberstadt telephone conversation, 13 February 1947, Clark Clifford Papers, Box 1. Baruch did not push Lilienthal for chairman of the United States Atomic Energy Commission, but he did not oppose him either. Their relations warmed in later years, and Lilienthal grew to respect Baruch and even concede that he had formed a new opinion of the Old Man, "a long way from the brash kind of judgment of him as a hopelessly vain and antiquated dodo I made years ago when the Acheson-Lilienthal Board was at work." David E. Lilienthal, *The Journals of David E. Lilienthal: The Harvest Years, 1959–1963* (1971), p. 519. By then, Lilienthal himself was a businessman, a change that moved Baruch to comment: "He is one of those Liberals who as soon as he has to make a living, goes into big business and soon becomes their defender. He is in the big money now." Baruch to Herbert Bayard Swope, 25 February 1953, Selected Correspondence, Baruch Papers.

assured Baruch of "careful consideration to any views that may be presented by you." As long as Baruch's actions were consistent with presidential directives, he would have "discretion" to exercise his own judgment. Congressional debates on the nature of the pending U.S. Atomic Energy Commission (USAEC) were on Byrnes's mind, and so Baruch was of special service to him. As interpreted by Baruch's right-hand man, John Hancock, Byrnes gave them reason to believe that "there is no stated United States policy at this time" and that "Mr. Byrnes will look to Mr. Baruch" to determine it. Conceding that he might be too old for the job but affirming that at least he was not senile, Baruch renewed his pleas to Lilienthal, who thought that he was fishing for "goose grease" compliments. In their discussions of the State Department report, Lilienthal found it "significant that at no time did [Baruch] say he approved our report, thought it a sound policy, etc. The most he said was that it was 'thoughtful.'" It is obvious that younger men have egos that yearn for a little "goose grease," too. Lilienthal withheld any commitment; no cajoling, not even a thinly veiled offer of Baruch's endorsement of Lilienthal for the USAEC chairmanship could bring him on board as an official advisor. Baruch stubbornly would not swallow the Acheson-Lilienthal report whole and Lilienthal stubbornly would not assist Baruch.[95]

In May, because neither group trusted the intentions of the other, it was dawning upon Acheson and Lilienthal that a tragedy was in the making. The Baruch group was talking about a much harder line, one that it freely conceded would invite a Russian veto in the Security Council. By 9 May, Acheson acted to bring the two sides together for a conference to clarify issues. Baruch agreed to the conference, but when Acheson proposed that they use the Acheson-Lilienthal report as a working paper for American policy, Baruch again threatened to resign.[96]

Now armed with his own scientific advisor, Richard Tolman of Cal Tech, Baruch and his group met with the Acheson committee at Blair-Lee House across from the White House on 17 May. The urgency of the situation was heightened by the approaching June meeting of the UNAEC, for which the United States still lacked concrete proposals on control. Hancock initiated discussion by proposing a world survey of uranium ore, something that the Russians would oppose as an infringement of their sovereignty and something that Baruch considered an opportunity for a "look-see" in Russia. Acheson countered that it was too early in negotiations for the proposal to be anything but disruptive. Other issues were then discussed, but it took another Wilsonian—Swope—to direct attention to the matter of enforcement. How would the proposed treaty of cooperation deal with a transgressor who held a veto on the Security Council? This introduced two ideas that were to become major changes from the Acheson-Lilienthal plan—and were strongly opposed by the State Department group—punishment for violators of the treaty and abrogation of the veto power in matters of atomic energy. Acheson responded that any treaty was unenforceable without the good will of its signatories. Otherwise, the discussions revealed that the Baruch group had little more to add to the Acheson-Lilienthal plan.

To Baruch, Swope's call for incorporating punishment of treaty violators into the treaty itself was reminiscent of article 10 of the League of Nations Covenant, which, Baruch recalled, Wilson had considered the "heart of the League." To Acheson, procedures for enforcement of the treaty waited upon an agreement on a treaty. Coupling sanctions with the treaty would guarantee Soviet rejection of the treaty itself; if sanctions were advisable, Acheson's lawyerly mind preferred that they be discussed at a later stage of negotiations. Baruch's penchant for a comprehensive scheme that did not rely upon the voluntary cooperation of participants sought enforcement even at the price of the treaty itself. Lilienthal, seated at Baruch's side by the Old Man's command, waspishly thought the discussion was "evidence of how little they understand the purpose or spirit of our Report."[97] Events would prove that Baruch's group understood it very well.

Was "all this bucking and argument . . . just part of the window-dressing" before Baruch brought the Acheson-Lilienthal report to the United Nations? As the next day's meeting between the two groups revealed, Baruch had no policy to substitute for it, but he nonetheless might choose not to embrace it. Having been treated with condescension and indifference by Acheson's consultants for two months, Baruch was more than ever determined to demonstrate that he would not be their messenger boy to the United Nations. Acheson wanted to know what was the American position. The Senate Atomic Energy Committee waited to hear it before Baruch brought it to the United Nations on 14 June. "I'm not ready to say," Baruch responded. "This hasn't jelled in my mind yet . . . I am not going to say anything until I understand all this." Putting his hand on Lilienthal's knee, Baruch went on: "The gentleman here at my left told me quite frankly over the telephone back in March that it would take me eight weeks of study to understand this subject, and it is going to take even longer." Acheson's mouth dropped open, but he said nothing. Baruch went on to request elaboration upon the Acheson report before the flabbergasted Acheson resignedly said, "All right, Mr. Baruch." The Old Man wanted to talk personally with the Russians, even with Stalin. "Another Colonel House," thought Lilienthal. "This kind of informality can become very confusing indeed." The two groups parted, their adversary relationship firm. When Baruch conferred with Oppenheimer on 19 May, he conceded that the Acheson report remained the heart of any American plan, that many of his own group's ideas were "nonsense," and that he "had no thought of deviating" from the prin-

13. Byrnes, Dean Acheson, Robert Hannegan, and Baruch, 18 May 1946.
(Courtesy Seeley G. Mudd Manuscript Library, Princeton University)

ciples of the Acheson report. Yet Lilienthal interpreted these conciliatory words as a Baruch plot "to dissever Oppenheimer from our board and begin the process of breaking it up."[98]

Stressing that the Acheson report was still the foundation of American proposals, Baruch insisted that it needed an enforcement mechanism and, perhaps, even needed to be broadened to include general disarmament. Lilienthal softened; the Old Man had to be made "more receptive to our ideas" because "for better or worse B. B. is the vessel, and we must try to help as much as we can." Baruch was firm in demanding punishment for violation of a treaty, a point Acheson vigorously challenged. Byrnes took the issue to Truman and reported that the president approved Baruch's stand on penalties for transgressors. On 7 June the president formally approved the concept of penalties, commenting that if Henry Stimson could have punished Japan's 1931 aggression in Manchuria, World War II could have been prevented. Baruch had put his stamp upon the Acheson-Lilienthal plan. As the historians of the USAEC comment, "It had been a long fight, but Baruch had won."[99]

Baruch prevailed in part because he had threatened Byrnes with resigning and informing "the Congress or the American people" that the Acheson report "had a lot of loopholes." As written, he said, the Acheson report "would not do anything except hold out false hopes. That is what I have been trying to tell you . . . and will tell the Senate Committee, if I am asked." It was then that Byrnes brought Baruch to Truman and Truman approved the principle of punishment. The wily Baruch knew that they were afraid of a right-wing Senate reaction against the American plan. Toughening the American position would be appreciated in the Senate. Indeed, when he finally presented the American plan to the Senate Special Committee on Atomic Energy, "newsmen concluded the senators were highly pleased with Baruch's testimony, especially what he had said on the veto." Like Roosevelt, Truman had to a degree become a prisoner of Baruch's prestige. Byrnes is supposed to have told Acheson, "This is the worst mistake I have ever made. But we can't fire him now, not with all the other trouble."[100]

As for Baruch, 1945's advocate of firm cooperation with the Russians had become a 1946 strategist of confrontation. The principle of punishment was a calculated strike against a veto power that protected the Soviets from a capitalist majority in the Security Council. "The essence of . . . penalties is that this may be a way of getting around the veto. There isn't any use in blinking that fact," Hancock had written. Baruch had told Byrnes, "When you talk about penalty, you know what it means — . . . the abrogation of the veto as far as that particular thing is concerned."[101] "That particular thing" was then atomic energy, but Baruch was attempting to broaden discussion to include general disarmament. However, the administration was convinced that the Russians would never accept a reduction in Red Army divisions while the United States possessed a monopoly in the atomic bomb. Thus, Truman conceded Baruch the veto, but not general disarmament.

From policy making, Baruch turned to public relations. Swope, pressed into service as Baruch's speechwriter and more attuned to creating public images than researching issues, knew that sanctions appealed to Baruch because they generated a Wilsonian idealism in international arrangements. The maudlin Swope's whole existence was now linked to Baruch's activities and to selling the atomic energy plan that would bear his name in the history books. "It is the biggest thing in his life—and in mine, too," Swope declared. On 14 June, Baruch would give the United Nations the American plan—the Baruch plan—on the international control of atomic energy, and Swope wanted to craft the address with words that would be repeated for generations to come, words that would move the nation to close its ranks behind his old comrade, words that would persuade the leaders of the world. At the temporary home of the United Nations Atomic Energy Commission, the Hunter College auditorium in Manhattan, Baruch delivered a stirring reading of Swope's melodramatic words:

14. *At the United Nations in 1946 with Herbert Bayard Swope and Secretary-General Trygve Lie. (Courtesy Seeley G. Mudd Manuscript Library, Princeton University)*

My fellow members of the United Nations Atomic Energy Commission and my fellow citizens of the world, we are here to make a choice between the quick and the dead. That is our business.

Behind the black portent of the new atomic age lies a hope which, seized upon with faith, can work our salvation. If we fail, then we have damned every man to be the slave of fear. Let us not deceive ourselves: We must elect world peace or world destruction.

Science has torn from nature a secret so vast in its potentialities that our minds cower from the terror it creates. Yet terror is not enough to inhibit the use of the atomic bomb. The terror created by weapons has never stopped man from employing them. For each new weapon a defense has been produced, in time. But now we face a condition in which adequate defense does not exist.

Science, which gave us this dread power, shows that it can be made a giant help to humanity, but science does not show us how to prevent its baleful use. So we have been appointed to obviate that peril by finding a meeting of the minds and the hearts of our peoples. Only in the will of mankind lies the answer.

It is to express this will and make it effective that we have been assembled. We must provide the mechanism to assure that atomic energy is used for peaceful purposes and preclude its use in war. To that end, we must provide immediate, swift, and sure punishment of those who violate the agreements that are reached by the nations.[102]

Laying out philosophical dichotomies that emphasized the problem's ethical and political nature, Baruch proceeded to demand penalties against violators of an agreement on control before one existed.

The speech was the main thrust of a public relations blitz. Baruch personally requested of Acheson that it be reprinted and distributed to every representative of the U.S. government around the world for dissemination. Comment in the United States, monitored by Baruch's staff, was overwhelmingly favorable. *Newsweek* applauded the "clear choice between effective disarmament or an atomic-weapons race" with which Baruch had confronted the Russians. Most editorial opinion celebrated both the relinquishing of America's monopoly on international control and the dilemma that it imposed upon the Russians, who surely yearned to break the monopoly. Yet it troubled the *New Republic* that Baruch demanded punitive terms and the breach of the veto, gauntlets thrown down that the Russians were dared to retrieve. These misgivings were not with the challenge, but rather with its timing.[103]

That essentially was the position of the Acheson group—which was itself busy influencing the writings of Walter Lippmann, Joseph Alsop, and Raymond Gram Swing. Gratified that what Baruch had presented to the United Nations was nothing less than the Acheson report in toto with

Baruchian twists, the Acheson group gave its approval of punishment, but only after a treaty had been negotiated. As the erstwhile law professor Felix Frankfurter lectured Swope, "The mark of a wise lawyer [is] to decide what issues to present when." Baruch was guilty of putting procedural questions ahead of substantive law. Nevertheless, the Old Man had put the Acheson group in a bind. It had to cheer the Baruch plan because it was the Acheson-Lilienthal report. And if penalties put the political cart before the legal and diplomatic horse, politics was undeniably at the heart of diplomacy, and penalties made good propaganda in the press and in the Congress. Typically, Lilienthal was torn between exultation that what Baruch had presented was his own work and despair that the injection of sanctions would give the Russians a good excuse to reject it. But he reasoned that although Baruch's sanctions were "contradictory to the spirit of our Report," they would not "affect [the] operability of the plan itself." So the American factions closed ranks and awaited a Soviet response. Acheson even suggested that President Truman send Baruch a telegram expressing his full support of the Old Man and confidence that the American mission "is in good hands."[104]

The Soviet response on 19 June was delivered by its delegate to the UNAEC, Andrei Gromyko, who was then less than half Baruch's age. Gromyko countered Baruch with a call for the United States to destroy its arsenal of bombs, to cease building them, and to share the secret of atomic energy with other nations for the development of its peaceful uses. He hinted that he could approve sanctions against violators of an agreement, but stipulated that any implementation of a plan would have to conform to the U.N. Charter and come under the jurisdiction of the Security Council—in other words, allow the Soviets to exercise the veto. Other speeches from the twelve nations on the UNAEC revealed that the Soviet position could command support only from Poland; the American position had varying degrees of support from the rest. The Council established, at Australia's suggestion, a working committee that would negotiate details.

The summer months passed amid an apparent stalemate on Baruch's procedural issues—sanctions and the veto. Lilienthal and Oppenheimer interpreted the protracted U.N. debate as confirmation that substantive action had been sidetracked by the issue of enforcement. They fretted over Baruch's boast that the American position was assured of a 10–2 majority and a propaganda victory. Baruch, intent upon firming his American support and isolating his domestic opponents, made another effort to bring Lilienthal into the fold. Lilienthal, having decided that he wanted the USAEC chairmanship, agreed to confer with Baruch at his weekend retreat, Camp Uncas on Raquette Lake in New York's Adirondacks. There, on 28–29 July, Baruch made it clear that Lilienthal could have his powerful support for any position he wanted if the younger man could deliver the support of the Acheson technical consultants. Amid relaxed surroundings and attended by Baruch's retinue of servants and lavish hospitality, Lilienthal now found the Old Man "exceedingly interesting . . . a most gracious host, and very entertaining." Lilienthal was wooed and won.[105]

In the meantime progress at the United Nations was seemingly nil. At an American staff conference on 1 August, Baruch professed that he had "no real cause of disappointment" over the lack of developments. The American strategy was to "avoid at all costs any humiliation to the Russians," even if it meant small American embarrassments. In this way, the Americans later could put the blame for any breach in negotiations upon the Russians and "make it crystal clear that we have explored every avenue of agreement." With generosity, justice, and power on the American side, Baruch was confident that the Russians would come around "when they had had an opportunity for complete understanding of our proposals." Until then, said Hancock, the Americans had to build support for their proposals among other delegations by employing Lilienthal and his consultants to explain the American plan. The first month had been dominated by discussion of the American plan, the second—by American design—by an exposition of Soviet ideas. Eventually, with some careful educational attention given to foreign scientists by American scientists, the U.S. delegation hoped to win a unanimous UNAEC agreement or—failing that—to isolate the communist nations and settle for a propaganda triumph. Although Baruch still favored giving the Russians as much time as they needed to make a complete study of American proposals, he was mindful that three nations on the UNAEC would be replaced on 1 January, with uncertain consequences for his majority.[106]

The quiet of this period of waiting upon the Russians was disrupted on 18 September by the front-page disclosure of a letter written by Secretary of Commerce Henry A. Wallace to President Truman back on 23 July. Wallace attacked American policies that appeared intent upon a confrontation with the Soviets instead of encouraging their cooperation. At a time when many in Congress still suspected the atomic proposals of excessive generosity to the Russians, Wallace assailed them because they gave the United States "unfettered discretion" over its atomic information and atomic bombs. As for Baruch's abrogation of the veto, that issue was "completely irrelevant" because any nation that did not permit inspection for possible violations ought to expect automatic reaction that included even war.

Baruch was enraged. He could not tolerate Wallace's misinterpretation of the American position—especially if it eroded support on the American left. (It is significant that in endeavoring to preserve an American consensus behind the plan, Baruch sought out the assistance of Eleanor Roosevelt and liberal lawyer David Ginsburg.) Baruch charged that Wallace was just plain wrong on the unilateral discretion of the American position. He immediately conferred with Wallace, but no correction of Wallace's statement was forthcoming. Baruch would not let the matter die. After setting his staff to work on a "refutation" of Wallace, he called the former vice-president and invited him to New York for another conference. Wallace agreed; but the next day, Truman, faced with a threat by Byrnes and Baruch to resign if Wallace spoke out again, fired Wallace. Baruch still would not leave Wallace alone until he felt that any distortion of the U.S. plan on atomic energy had been rectified. He wanted a retraction and feared that an attack on Wallace would only martyr him. He urged Wallace to confer with him at the earliest convenient time; on 21 September, Wallace notified Baruch that he would meet with him on the twenty-seventh at the U.S. delegation's offices in the Empire State Building.[107]

As Wallace later put it, "This was the beginning of the row with Baruch where he tried to lure me off base and get me to say things that I didn't want to say." Wallace arrived with his aide Philip Hauser, who had directed the drafting of the 23 July letter to Truman. Baruch was joined by Hancock, Eberstadt, and other aides, one of whom took notes on their discussion. The Baruch group explained the American position vis-à-vis the Soviet stand, insisting that it was not Wallace's right to express himself that they challenged, but his misstatement of policy. Wallace responded that the Baruch plan was only symptomatic of the greater problem of mutual Soviet-American distrust and that he hoped that they would find a way for the Russians to save face and reach an agreement. Asked by Eberstadt to recommend a face-saving move that would not entail considerable risk for the United States, Wallace conceded that the time was not ripe for such a move, but insisted that the United States should think along those lines. As Wallace prepared to leave, he commented, "It is obvious that I was not fully posted."[108]

Realizing that he could not secure what he wanted from Wallace— partly because Wallace, seeming not to understand what Baruch did want, was clear only that he did not trust U.S. foreign policy or Baruch— Baruch assailed Wallace at a press conference on 2 October for giving the American people "misinformation" and not correcting it. Wallace retorted the next day that Baruch refused to deal with "the central issue" of a confrontation foreign policy and had taken a "stubborn and inflexible position" in his negotiations. As watched by Baruch's office, the American press clearly gave Baruch the better of their dispute. For instance, in a story entitled "Statesman and Reformer," *Time* captioned a photograph of Baruch with the word "Facts" and one of Wallace with "Fancy."[109]

In one respect, Wallace was undoubtedly correct: they battled over the whole tenor of American foreign policy, a point Swope alluded to when he observed, "The Wallace episode goes deeper than is indicated by surface appearance." Regardless of that, Baruch focused his defense of American policy toward Russia on the issue of his atomic energy plan. At a dinner where he received Freedom House's award for outstanding service in the cause of peace, Baruch reaffirmed his rejection of the veto and called for "some diminution of national sovereignty [through] free access for international inspection"—a "look-see" beyond Russian borders. He proclaimed the plan nothing less than Wilsonian "enlightened selfishness." The Baruch plan's international atomic development authority would bring to Russia "free initiative [and] full opportunity."[110]

Both the Americans and the Russians were bidding for world public opinion, and in the United States the cold war was going against the Soviets. In the fall the Soviets countered the "generous" American plan with their own propaganda for total disarmament. Having counseled patience with the Soviets for months, Baruch in November and December went all out to wind up discussion of the American proposal and get a certain Soviet rejection of it on the record. But before he could accomplish that, the Americans had to count noses on the commission to make sure that the anticipated 10–2 vote was intact and had also to employ the Gallup Poll to see how the American public perceived the issues. The latter findings must have heartened Baruch, because 70 percent of the respondents rejected Wallace's proposal for U.S. cessation of atom bomb production and destruction of its stockpile. All that worried Baruch on the home front was the sniping of "the left-wing crowd" and Acheson's* journalistic admirers, Alsop and Lippmann.[111] Though Byrnes gave Baruch the green light on 13 December to press for a UNAEC vote on the American proposals before the end of the year, Baruch's last remaining concern was whether the British would fall in line.

The problem with the British was that they wanted the United States to share with them the secret of atomic energy. The Americans believed that if they did, they would have to honor the Soviet claim to it as well or else be guilty of hostile discrimination against the Russians. The Americans argued that maintenance of the monopoly benefited the British more than the Russians because the former had solved the theoretical problem

*The antagonism between Acheson and Baruch never abated. Acheson felt it keenly. See David E. Lilienthal, *The Journals of David E. Lilienthal: The Atomic Energy Years, 1946–1950* (1964), pp. 257–58; Dean Acheson, *Present at the Creation: My Years in the State Department* (1969), pp. 154–56; and F. Eberstadt to James Forrestal, 16 January 1947, Forrestal Papers. Later, Baruch wrote to Arthur Krock, "Acheson is the smartest of all as a protagonist, advocate or lawyer but anything to win a case. He certainly tried to sabotage Atomic Energy. He had all the scientists, Lipman [*sic*], Alsops, liberals and State Dep. boys." 8 April 1949, Krock Papers. Baruch especially disliked chief Acheson aide Alger Hiss (whom he called "Algernon"), because he remembered Hiss as an adversary when Hiss was counsel to the Nye committee in 1934. Baruch to Acheson, 18 January 1947, United Nations Atomic Energy Commission Papers, Baruch Papers.

but lacked only the practical know-how; with the Soviets "the assumption is that they know nothing." Therefore, "quite obviously if the President were to decide to grant the request of the British, Mr. Baruch would be in a tough position in answering the certain requests of the Russians as to why we had treated them differently." But the British were not so understanding; Baruch worried that Truman and Byrnes would give in to British pleas for atomic collaboration. In turn, the British schemed in the UNAEC to break the American monopoly. And so, as Baruch later recalled, "the Socialist Government [of Britain] . . . was always playing footie-footie with the Russians and the Poles." On 30 December, as they prepared to vote on the American proposals, the British delegate informed Baruch that Whitehall could not support him. They exchanged "pretty sharp" words, but when the vote was taken, Baruch was relieved to find that the British had joined a solid western bloc. The Soviets and the Poles abstained, giving the Baruch plan a surprising 10–0 "victory."[112]

Baruch's diplomatic days had ended. Just prior to the vote he had received much journalistic criticism for his stubborn insistence upon weakening the veto. Aside from the expected broadsides from Lippmann and Alsop, even *Time* accused Baruch of conducting "inflexible diplomacy." Satisfied that he had "reached the end of the furrow," Baruch informed Byrnes on 3 January that he would resign; Byrnes announced Baruch's departure immediately, only days before he announced his own resignation as secretary of state. The propaganda battle went on, Baruch seeing to it that every library he could reach had copies of the United Nations report on atomic energy.[113]

By the early 1950s it would be evident that the Baruch plan was unworkable. Nagging memories of Baruch's determined injection of the punishment and veto issues attributed the blame for failure of international control of atomic energy to the Old Man. But the passage of time allows a clearer perspective. The problem lay not in what Baruch added to the Acheson-Lilienthal report, but in the report itself. In 1946, Russian signals indicated that it was *not* the sanctions and the veto abrogation that most disturbed them. The Russians could not accept the basic premise that an international development authority would be responsible for control and development of atomic energy.

In late September the left-wing New York newspaper *PM* published a story on Soviet fears that the American proposal for international supervision of nuclear energy was an "entering wedge, by which 'capitalist America and other conservative Powers' would undermine the Socialist economy of the Soviet Union." *PM*'s unidentified Soviet source projected that the United States would use atomic blackmail to "gain a stranglehold on the whole socialist system of production and distribution in the

USSR." An aide to Baruch learned from *PM*'s correspondent that his source was Arkady Sobolev, assistant secretary general of the United Nations. On 19 October, Eberstadt and two other Americans dined with Sobolev to sound him out further. Eberstadt pressed Sobolev to explain why the Russians were so opposed to international control of the American monopoly. The Russian answered "that the United States plan was in essence a plan for world government" for which nobody was ready. Not satisfied with Sobolev's answer, Eberstadt probed the issues raised by the *PM* article. The Soviet Union, Sobolev responded, wanted "freedom to pursue its own policies . . . without interference or control from the outside."[114]

Another Soviet argument against the American plan was that it preserved an American monopoly on atomic bombs and denied to the Soviets development of their own nuclear weapons. Depicting the American proposals as little more than propaganda, the Soviets countered with some of their own on 29 October when Foreign Minister Vyacheslav Molotov proposed in the General Assembly a general disarmament that included atomic weapons. Baruch was angry—not at the Russians, but at Acheson. Recognizing the Molotov proposals as a Russian propaganda offensive, Baruch recalled that he had been constrained by Acheson from proposing general disarmament in July. Reflecting military fears that the American plan left the Soviet Red Army intact, Baruch had argued that he should be negotiating reduction of all armaments, not just control of atomic weapons. But Acheson and Truman had no wish to draw right-wing attention to the Red Army. Baruch backed off then, but members of his staff remained eager to pursue general disarmament for its propaganda appeal to the left. If negotiations failed, the United States would have to expand its atomic arsenal to counter the Red Army, and military planners dreaded the slogan "outlaw the bomb." The Americans believed that the Soviets sought to curtail U.S. atomic bomb production without opening themselves to international inspection, "the real obstacle to agreement." Acheson hoped to retain the U.S. nuclear monopoly by allowing the Soviets to rely upon the Red Army for their defense, instead of calling attention to the army through a general disarmament proposal. Baruch saw that tack as fruitless if it aroused public opinion against atomic weaponry.[115]

Thus, both the Americans and the Soviets saw the nuclear arms race as ineluctable, but they valued negotiation for its propaganda opportunities. The Molotov propaganda offensive riled Baruch. "It is disheartening, to say the least, to see the moves that can and so apparently must be made, only to find that somebody else makes them, and we are fighting rearguard actions," he bitterly complained to Acheson. To Senator Warren Austin, he wrote: "I was stopped by the President and the State Department from discussing general disarmament when I submitted the American proposals." Still, Acheson refused to bite at the Soviet bait. General disarmament would be discussed only after the Soviets subscribed to an international authority that opened their borders to inspection. The Russians were not considered sincere in offering to negotiate general disarmament because they would not weaken their armies, any more than the Americans would destroy their atomic bombs. All that worried the Americans was the Soviet propaganda counterattack. The Russians, as Forrestal exclaimed, were "stealing the show, and . . . selling their particular point of view to our own people."[116]

Seeking to regain the propaganda offensive, Baruch went over Acheson's head and appealed to Byrnes to unite atomic energy and disarmament matters at the United Nations under his command. Failing in that, Baruch had no other choice than to seek a quick decision on the American proposals and depart with a propaganda "victory" confirmed by the Soviet decision to abstain. The Lilienthal group was satisfied with the outcome in spite of Baruch's distracting injection of the veto issue. American popular support for expansion of its atomic arsenal had been firmed up by the magnanimous offer to place it at the disposal of an international authority unacceptable to the Soviets.[117] And the Soviets were still free to pursue atomic parity with the United States.

The Baruch plan had launched an arms race. Baruch and other Americans were beginning to label the post-World War II era the "cold war." "There is no peace," Baruch had told Dwight Eisenhower. "Because peace is delayed and obstructed, we dare not disarm. We need, General, your military capacity."[118] Thus, Baruch's career in Washington had begun and concluded with its emphasis on preparation for war intact.

CHAPTER TEN
NATIONAL KIBITZER

RETREAT FROM PRICE CONTROLS IN THE COLD WAR

The cold war* should have been that surrogate for war Baruch envisioned as a justification for organizing industry for the real thing. The
Soviet hegemony over eastern Europe confronted the United States with
a threat to its interests and its security. Fear that other parts of Europe or
Asia would succumb to the lure of communism made military preparations increasingly acceptable to Americans. Of course, Baruch did not
need actual hostilities to advocate planning for another conflict. Moreover, according to his thinking, any large expenditures on weapons and
armed forces called for organization of the economy to apportion civilian
and military demand so as to inhibit rises in domestic prices. Thus, early
in 1946 he told President Truman that the absence of genuine national
security and peace necessitated national economic planning that stabilized prices; the cold war ought to be treated as a moral equivalent of
war: "For purposes of economic thinking, we are still at war. We certainly are not at peace. In the transition period we will require the same
effort to produce things necessary to meet the demands for food, clothing,
housing and transportation for the world as we did in war."[1] Even without armament production in 1946, the fact that the United States produced the necessaries of life—capital and sustenance—for its allies called
for sacrifices at home that included price controls.

*Baruch and Swope claimed credit for originating the term "cold war," used to describe
the antagonism between the capitalist west and the communist east during the period following World War II. Baruch had used the phrase in a speech written by Swope and delivered to the South Carolina legislature on 16 April 1947; in it, he said, "Let us not be
deceived—we are today in the midst of a cold war. Our enemies are to be found abroad and
at home." But the press did not then pick up the term. For that matter, Baruch and Swope
did not emphasize it until after a rival publicist, Walter Lippmann, gave it prominence in

Nevertheless, it had become apparent that the consensus favoring controls that Baruch had helped foster early in World War II had disintegrated with the surrender of Japan. Little tolerance for price discipline remained following the demobilization of armies and war production. It seemed to make no difference to most Americans that lagging normal production and starved demand generated rising prices that could be checked only by laws decided upon in Washington. Major economic interests demanded emancipation from controls in order to reap higher profits from those higher prices. Tax cuts in 1945 and 1946 actually fueled inflation rather than restraining it. However, this situation had its roots in the late war period when military victories encouraged civilian restlessness with controls while policy makers were uncertain of postwar economic prospects.

Baruch consistently argued that wartime antiinflation policy had been piecemeal and hence a failure and that higher prices, not unemployment, would be the immediate postwar concern. Even the most ardent of stabilizers doubted that controls would be tolerated after the emergency passed. Believing that controls "will have to be continued even if the war were to be over tomorrow," Budget Director Harold Smith insisted in 1943 "that we should bend every effort to do a solid selling job during the war." Price Administrator Chester Bowles bemoaned the evidence that Americans had not replaced their "producer" attitudes with a new consumer consciousness that militated against higher prices. Instead, the tax debates of 1944 showed that businessmen, farmers, and workers cared more for their own peculiar interests than for a common consumer interest. Like Baruch, Bowles forecast that reconversion would "be a period in which inflationary forces are still highly dangerous" and that "the present levels of prices should yield very good peacetime profits in *most* fields of business." However, he conceded that selective decontrol might be in order politically following the defeat of Germany, but not before then. He anticipated that veterans, farmers, and workers were "not likely to accept an economy based on scarcity" and that businessmen would demand freedom from restrictive controls.[2]

---

a series of articles published that year and then reprinted in a book entitled *The Cold War: A Study in U.S. Foreign Policy*. The term was widely attributed to Lippmann, and Swope, who prided himself on being an expert phrasemaker, was particularly stung. Baruch publicly credited his friend with coining the term, even as he claimed for himself the credit for giving it currency. *The New York Times*, 4 May 1950. Lippmann disclaimed authorship, but denied it to Swope by asserting that the term had a common usage dating back to the mid-1930s. E. J. Kahn, Jr., *The World of Swope* (1965), pp. 405–6. Different sources variously attributed the credit to Lippmann, Baruch, or Swope, the *New York Times* settling on Baruch (21 January 1965). For more on the Swope-Lippmann "cold war," see Bernard Baruch, *The Public Years* (1960), p. 388; and Baruch to Richard B. Russell, 8 December 1947, Selected Correspondence, Baruch Papers.

Policy makers were confused during the period between D Day and V-J Day. Though Baruch resented "the hokum about how much better [World War II price administrators] did with prices than we did in the last war," he seemed as anxious to be freed from controls as were most Americans. Never a great believer in the efficacy of voluntary cooperation, in 1944 Baruch told Byrnes that he expected "industry to be governed by its own self-interest in keeping prices down to reasonable levels. . . . I would drop all price controls just as soon as I could see that supply is reasonably in balance with demand." He could not predict what would happen in the reconversion period; he knew only that policy had to prevent "an inventory boom such as occurred in 1919–1920." Still, "more liberal pricing standards would not need to result in a wave of price increases." In 1944 he was for relaxing price controls in order to allow employers to meet 1945 wage demands.[3]

Indeed, the price administrators confronted enormous opposition to controls from leaders of organized labor. The unions again depicted controls as devices to keep wages frozen. But, in the words of one price administrator, "The labor people seem to have little understanding of the pressure we face from the other side." Bowles urgently wrote White House counsel Sam Rosenman, "With the surrender of Japan, . . . we must not make the same mistake we made after the last war, when we took the initial softening of prices as a signal for stripping off all our price controls." Bowles had no intention "of closing up shop before the job is done." However, he could not withstand pressures from business, labor, and consumers when the WPB removed production controls that were vital to price controls and left OPA fighting a rearguard action.

Truman's chief economic adviser, John W. Snyder, a Missouri banker, steadily modified the controls program. It seemed to Bowles that "perhaps the luckiest thing that happened to the country is that Truman once lost his haberdashery store due to the blow-up of 1920!" Bowles struggled to keep the dangers of inflation uppermost in the president's mind, but political pressure for easing controls increased.[4] In January 1946, Bowles judged his task hopeless and submitted his resignation.

Not only was Bowles's resignation refused, but he wound up as director of economic stabilization—partly owing to the intervention of Baruch. The Old Man was never a disinterested observer of matters of price stabilization. Baruch enthusiastically endorsed Bowles's hard line against inflation and let Truman's administrators know that any softening on inflation would leave them open to public challenges by the still formidable elder statesman. No sooner had the price administrator's resignation reached the White House than Baruch had Bowles on the phone; the call was closely followed by one from Byrnes and a visit from Baruch, the message being that Bowles should stay and fight it out. Obviously, Truman had enough troubles without running afoul of Baruch on inflation. "You will find, my dear Mr. President," he told Truman, "no hit-or-miss program that may be suggested to you can be effective, nor is the subject one in which rules can be improvised as we go along." Either the administration waged total war against inflation or else it would lose. He warned the Senate Foreign Relations Committee that no program for Europe's economic revival would succeed unless the United States stabilized its own economy. That meant more production aided by longer working hours for labor, a proposal that did not endear him to unions. That also meant a restoration of the excess profits tax and a moratorium on tax cuts for two years, a proposal that did not endear him to capital. It was radical doctrine for conservative America, and the *Wall Street Journal* responded with an editorial that concluded, "Therefore, to save Europe from totalitarianism and regimentation we are asked to out-regiment her at home." Baruch never had been afraid of temporary regimentation and he anticipated the *Journal*'s charges: "You cannot save free enterprise if you let the system which protects it go to ruin. What makes the police state? What makes totalitarianism? Not the police, but the absence of law behind the police. . . . I have no fears of the restraints we adopt as free men as long as we uphold our laws."[5]

Price control was a conservative measure, Baruch averred; yet it put him at odds with businessmen seeking relief from regulation and taxation. As he told Bowles, businessmen "have no understanding of the problems you have to face." The settlement of a steel strike in 1946 forced a retreat to a higher plateau of prices and wages, but Baruch sought to reinforce Bowles's determination, to steer Snyder into line with Bowles, and to develop a policy for Truman. It would not be the sort of stabilization that would win votes: rationing, controls on wages and prices, and a revocation of the 1945 tax cut. Truman should tell Americans that more dollars did not mean more purchasing power. Truman responded that "labor . . . will balk and I don't know what affect the program will have on industry generally. Neither side seems to be in any sort of cooperative mood."[6] Baruch's influence upon Truman was, at best, minimal; no comprehensive program emerged.

Controls were becoming analogous to prohibition because they were unenforceable statutes that encouraged lawbreaking. Baruch blamed Truman's leadership for the lawlessness, but he struggled to remain in the president's good graces. That his powers as a publicist were respected by the White House is evident by its choice of him to present the American plan for international atomic energy control, even as it dismissed his notions on price controls. Before Baruch went to the United Nations, he used the House Banking and Currency Committee as a forum before which to repeat his formula for curbing prices, this time adding enough equivocation to avoid offending the White House. The result was that it antagonized everyone except some consumers who told the president to adopt it. Its "phoniness" disgusted Bowles, who advised his deputy:

> If you look at it carefully, you will find that he has promised everybody everything.
>
> We are to be rid of arbitrary power, but we are to have a supreme economics council which will settle everything.
>
> We are to bar strikes and freeze wages, but we should not "fail to increase wages where necessary."
>
> We are to continue price controls, but we are to modify them.
>
> We are to allow profits but we are not to have too much profit. (How do you accomplish that without profit control?)
>
> We are to take good care of the white collar workers and see that they aren't squeezed, but we are to do everything calculated to raise the cost of living, etc. etc.

"It certainly is far from profound," Bowles's deputy agreed, "but it has a lot of appeal paragraph by paragraph." Its appeal seemed limited to the uninformed public. On the left the *Nation* labeled Baruch's statement "a curious hodge-podge of economic horse sense and starry-eyed political hokum." *Newsweek*'s business columnist, conceding that Baruch's was "by all odds the strongest and most influential voice" in favor of broadening OPA, insisted that only Baruch's prestige could "offset one of the most inconsistent and superficial arguments ever presented to a congressional committee." Instead of unfettering the economy, he had prescribed a high court of commerce that any businessman or labor leader could detect as "nothing less than a supreme Fascist economic council." Yet that was one of the few clear points evinced in Baruch's argument.[7]

A member of the administration as its representative to the UNAEC in 1946, Baruch was too preoccupied with the Russians to speak out for OPA. By the time he resigned at the end of 1946, Bowles and OPA and all price controls had departed from the scene, a casualty of the peace that was a cold war. There was an astonishing resemblance between 1946 and 1919: inflation, strikes, and escalating anti-Red feelings. When Baruch returned to the antiinflation war in 1947, higher prices were as evident as a year earlier and the commitment to controls had been vanquished.[8]

With good cause, Baruch was "more fearful" of inflation than "at any time during the war." The pace of rising prices was swifter than at any time since 1941, and the President's Council of Economic Advisers, created by the Employment Act of 1946, recommended persuading businessmen to reduce their prices, rejecting further income tax cuts, reducing the federal debt as soon as feasible, and restricting credit where possible. Baruch, speaking to the South Carolina Legislature, called for a twenty-one-month increase in the national workweek to forty-four hours—more production serving as a deterrent to higher prices. Needless to say, such a proposal pleased a tory such as Raymond Moley, inflamed the *Nation* magazine, and generally created more heat than light; it certainly did not win him friends in the unions.[9]

Labor was on the defensive in 1947, and the Baruch forty-four-hour workweek trial balloon was part of the reaction against unions. Baruch sought no-strike pledges and increased hours as the price for higher wages. He believed that the unions possessed a disproportionate amount of power. "We have reached the end of the era . . . when owners and directors direct," he wrote. "Labor is now in the saddle." Profits would shrink and the system itself would erode. Everywhere "the masses are going to demand a greater share of what is produced—I almost said of what *they* produced. But a large number will demand and receive a great deal more of what everybody else produces, even if they do not produce more themselves." The productive value of capital would be limited. Yet Baruch had enough of the Wilsonian liberal in him to spark accommodation and accord. And he possessed the comfort of historical perspective, reminding Winston Churchill: "This ferment of all classes all over the world is nothing new, for we had it after World War I. It is accentuated and fomented, doubtless, by the Communists. But we shall have to look into their complaints and determine whether we can better their conditions from the standpoint of earnings, education, medical care and as great a share in what they produce and still keep the Capitalistic system going."

Labor leaders were not ready to hear such condescension, although Baruch made every effort to talk sweet reason with them. "Inflation is the greatest danger to labor," he admonished the CIO's Philip Murray. "Labor will get the worst of it. . . . It can destroy government and civilization itself, and lay us open to all kinds of old and new isms." This sort of talk had been heard before, but Baruch also sought to remind Murray, John L. Lewis, and Walter Reuther that their unions were heavily invested in capitalism through pensions and assorted insurance funds—and those investments were jeopardizing individual workers' futures through inflation.[10]

By his lights, Baruch served only a general or national interest—for his stand on controls for inflation was opposed by most capitalists. Not even his close friend John Hancock believed that controls had any virtues. A mere government pronouncement that prices were too high was considered by Hancock to be "an unsettling bit of psychology" because wholesale and retail buyers deferred purchases in anticipation of lower prices. Hancock was not as devoted to lower prices as was Baruch: "Of course, from our point of view, we must avoid inflation"—for no other reason than that "if prices are not kept down, wage demands will come again next spring." But Alfred P. Sloan, Jr., of General Motors firmly rejected controls, reasoning that industrial prices had risen hardly at all since the war. Sloan blamed inflation on surplus personal income, hinting that lower wages or higher regressive taxes would do more to restrain inflationary spending than anything else. Any controls bill, he said, should be titled "'An Act to Promote Black Markets in the United States.'" However, Baruch could not join any chorus for free enterprise: "Ordinarily in a free economy, which all want, price is the controlling factor, but now it is not." The 1945 tax cut, he never tired of repeating, advantaged corporations over individuals. Big integrated corporations prospered in an inflation. The sale of government bonds likewise benefited greater concentrations of capital and contributed to higher prices that the rich bore more gracefully than the poor.[11]

Inflation and international relations, even in the cold war, could not be discussed separately, "the two of them being so closely intertwined." Baruch never believed in government-to-government foreign aid that threatened private enterprise. He had opposed the British loan in 1945–46 for that reason and because he feared that it would have an inflationary impact on the American economy. It was not long after his resignation from the United Nations position that Baruch wrote Senator Arthur H. Vandenberg of Michigan, a leading Republican spokesman on foreign policy, that he still disagreed with the administration's strategy for the economic reconstruction of Europe: "I never was in sympathy with Acheson's or Clayton's economic viewpoints—nor am I now."[12] Within days events would enable Baruch to reaffirm that declaration.

On 21 February 1947 the British informed the United States that they could no longer afford to maintain their position in the eastern Mediterranean and would pull out as of 31 March. Because Greece was in the throes of a civil war between the British-supported monarchy and communist-led insurgents, Acheson and Clayton viewed the London decision as tantamount to capitulation to communism throughout the undeveloped areas of the Middle East, Africa, and Asia unless the United States materially and financially replaced the British presence in Greece and Turkey. The chief difficulty lay in convincing Congress and the American people that the Truman Doctrine for intervention ought to be backed by tax dollars at a time when retrenchment was uppermost in their minds. The administration was in a hurry and willing to scare the public with the threat of communist expansion in the face of U.S. inaction. It needed all the help it could muster in selling Americans on this "new" policy, but the White House had neglected that ace publicist, Baruch.

It appears to have been a calculated oversight. According to a third-hand account, Truman had been advised to touch base with Baruch, but the president, more mindful of past experiences than present exigencies, rejected the recommendation. "I'm just *not* going to do it," he declared. "I'm not going to spend hours and hours on that old goat, come what may. If you take his advice, then you have him on your hands for hours and hours, and it is *his* policy. I'm just not going to do it." The "Baruch plan" was on Truman's mind. However, as White House counsel Clark Clifford conceded, "it was causing some members of the Cabinet who depend on the old boy some considerable time and sweat." They believed that the success of any new policy venture was well worth the time taken to "grease" Baruch.[13]

Baruch sensed that he was being snubbed. Asked to testify before the House Committee on Foreign Affairs on the president's Greek-Turkish proposal, Baruch gave David E. Lilienthal a preview of his position during a lunch at his hotel. "We have to go into Greece now because England is out of dollars. Who said so?" Baruch challenged. "How do we know? Suppose we don't. Then what? How many troops does England have in Palestine? 100,000. What about them? Suppose they say they can't keep on in Germany, then what do we do?" In essence, Baruch was asking how limited was our intervention, how drained were Britain's resources, and what would be the consequences of this precedent for other areas. He refused to be panicked by the argument that the action was imperative in order to stop communism's spread. "The Old Man is a tough baby," Lilienthal concluded. "Well, of course, anybody can think up questions, but he puts these things in a dramatically sharp, tough way that is worth observing."[14]

Inevitably the State Department would have to confront Baruch and his questions. The occasion was provided when his brother, Herman, the former ambassador to Portugal, now reassigned to the Netherlands, was sworn in at the State Department and Baruch attended the small ceremony. Acheson requested Baruch to come to his office, where he began by inquiring if it were true that the new policy "disturbed" Baruch. Baruch responded with what amounted to a cross-examination of Acheson. "What is the new policy? Why are the British quitting?" As Baruch later related it, Acheson responded, "They are out of dollars." Baruch shot back, "Don't say that at the Capitol. It is nonsense. They've got three billion dollars left[,] their wool clip, etc. How many troops, by the way, have they in the Near East?" Acheson answered, "They have 8,000 in Greece and 100,000 in Palestine." "Then the whole thing is about oil," Baruch interpreted. "How could they hold 100,000 in Palestine if it is all about dollars? . . . What do we intend to do if we stand alone—if we intend to do anything?" Acheson could not satisfy Baruch, and he probably did not expect to. Never an admirer of Whitehall's foreign policy designs, Baruch was downright contemptuous of the Labour government. Added to that was his mistrust of Acheson and Clayton, the strong men in George Marshall's State Department, whom he now believed were guilty of a hasty response to British manipulations. As he commented a few weeks later, "I never could understand what the hurry was about."[15]

Baruch was correct in expecting extensive developments from the Truman Doctrine. From it evolved the Marshall Plan for the economic reconstruction of Europe. Through the spring of 1947 the State Department made the poor economic conditions of the Continent a major topic of discussion in Washington. The Harvard commencement address of Secretary of State Marshall gave focus and prominence to that discussion. Baruch greatly admired the general and was loath to disagree at any time with him. Nevertheless, he was of two minds on the Marshall Plan: first, he saw it as still another effort to pull British chestnuts out of the fire; but on the other hand, he saw it as a vehicle for something he himself advocated.

For one thing, Baruch, as was his wont, disdained a piecemeal approach to economic planning. He would have pulled 1919's Supreme Economic Council from the pages of history and made it the planning forum through which America dispensed its wealth to its European clients. Moreover, those clients would not be governments like the British socialist government, but private consortiums. Washington should strive to be not a lender but a buyer—preferably of nonperishable raw materials—and thereby to generate trade among nations. But if Washington did bankroll Europe's recovery, he said during the May 1947 discussion of aid to Europe, "we should have a look-see into their budgets and someone representing us overlook the expenditures of the money." Germany was the key to Europe's rehabilitation, although Baruch still preferred a Germany that was exploited by Britain lest it turn into an exploiter again. In any event, Europe had to coalesce to qualify for American dollars. He did not want to provoke the Russians with a direct snub, but if they did not accept American terms for economic cooperation, then "we ought to organize Europe and Japan . . . without them."[16]

The European Recovery Program (ERP) followed several of those principles, but Baruch was not a force in its development, although officials warily recognized that he had the ability to mobilize opinion against their plans unless he was consulted. He bombarded Marshall and Clayton with questions suggesting that a higher American inflation rate would be a consequence of the planned expansion in exports. Clayton, whom Baruch regarded as overly committed to expanded exports by inclination although not by self-interest (he had been a cotton exporter), insisted that American resources and productive capacity were ample enough to meet the demands of ERP. In response to Baruch, Clayton wrote: "The problem is to organize our fiscal policy and our own consumption so that sufficient surpluses of the necessary goods are made available out of our enormous production, and so that these surpluses are paid for out of taxation and not by addition to debt." Thus, consistently with the new

15. George C. Marshall and Robert P. Patterson applaud the dedication of Baruch's bust at the National War College, 13 June 1947. (Courtesy Seeley G. Mudd Manuscript Library, Princeton University)

economic doctrine emerging in Washington, any inflation arising out of foreign aid would be checked by adjustments in fiscal policy—not by price controls.[17]

Baruch was not an isolationist, but amid the new globalism of postwar America, he repeated principles that had an anachronistic ring to them. "I have always felt that we should keep ourselves strong at home before we undertake to carry too many people on our backs," he told a brother. "Europe has everything she needs—not everything she wants," he declared, rejecting the administration's depiction of a continent in distress.

He attributed contrary perspectives on Europe's situation to a British bias among our diplomats; "there are too many Anglophiles, Francophiles and not enough Factophiles." As Lilienthal observed, "He is quite intemperate about the British," quoting Baruch as saying, "They are going the way of Germany and Russia and Italy—'die for dear old fascism'; 'suffer for the Fatherland and Hitler—rah, rah Princeton; rah, rah Socialism.'" "Look out for our Anglophiles," Baruch admonished Krock. "We have Greece, Turkey, Germany, Palestine, China, Korea and Japan on our backs while they have benefits and oil."[18]

It did not make sense to Baruch to extend loans whose repayment was dubious when Europe's productivity could be restored by purchases of its raw materials. Moreover, it seemed practical to him to build a stockpile of raw materials as a hedge against unknown crises. What did make sense to him was the prospect presented by the Marshall Plan of American industrial cooperation to rebuild Europe through expanded exports. (Secretary of Commerce Averell Harriman reassured the Business Advisory Council that he expected Marshall Plan legislation to contravene existing antitrust laws that prohibited such collusion.) Importantly, German policy would be amended and the denazification program sharply curtailed.[19] As long as Britain was not intent upon making gains at Germany's expense, Baruch could agree that a revival of German prosperity made sense in the European scheme of things. His thinking had totally shifted to resisting Russian and communist expansion.

In their endeavor to promote the Marshall Plan with the American people, Washington and Wall Street were careful to give Baruch considerable attention. His views were solicited at a luncheon with Marshall, Forrestal, Harriman, Robert Lovett, and George Kennan. As usual, he doubted their knowledge of European or American resources, suggesting that the first were underestimated and the latter exaggerated; he demanded that all aid be channeled through consortiums. They listened patiently because, as Marshall told him in November, the program had only a 50–50 chance of congressional approval. In December, Senator Vandenberg, chairman of the Senate Foreign Relations Committee, informed Baruch that he would be the committee's first witness when it began hearings in January. A representative of the British information service zealously sought to persuade Baruch of the dire condition of his country's economy.[20] All that was missing in this courtship was an invitation to the White House, and that came four days after Baruch appeared before the Foreign Relations Committee.

Little of what he told the senators had not been heard already by other officials and by some of the senators. But the way he presented it converted discussion of the Marshall Plan into discussion of a Baruch Plan. It was a broad, eleven-point recommendation that the European Recovery Program be accompanied with comprehensive antiinflation controls. He did not oppose ERP; what he sought was to see it led by someone acceptable to him, such as Ferd Eberstadt. That was what he emphasized when he visited the president on the evening of 23 January. It was evident that they were in agreement on the ERP and on the need to forestall a tax cut. About all Baruch could do to suggest disagreement was to urge Truman to apply British and French holdings in this country toward the credits Washington would be extending them and to lecture him on how the British had shifted their imperial responsibilities to Washington while preserving their hold upon Near Eastern oil. Truman listened without comment.[21]

As one correspondent understood it, "Baruch's goals undeniably went further than the Marshall Plan." Baruch's emphasis had been not merely upon European economic recovery, but upon *European economic and military unity*. To his satisfaction, James Reston of the *New York Times* caught the essence of the message that the Senate Foreign Relations Committee ignored. Although not crediting Baruch with originality, Reston applauded the Old Man for going public with

> what astute students of world politics and economics have been saying in private for quite a while.
>
> The Marshall Plan . . . is all right as a starter, but European economics cannot be separated from European politics, European recovery cannot be separated from American prices and wages, and Europe itself cannot be revived unless it unites and receives the economic and military support of the United States.
>
> Put the hard way, . . . without a political, economic and military union of Europe, the stated objectives of the European recovery program could not be achieved.
>
> . . . [Mr. Baruch] put the economics of the recovery problem alongside the political and military strategy of the problem and urged the committee to see it whole, but after a half hour on the hill top, the committee retired into the valley.
>
> . . . Mr. Baruch at 77, instead of becoming more conservative is far bolder in his proposals and far less concerned about classic economics than he was at 48.

Even so, Baruch still did not practice the art of the possible, for "Washington still focuses on one bit of a problem at a time. It is still leery of the big picture."[22]

The military component of European unity needed more of a catalyst than Baruch the publicist could provide. For the benefit of his friends, he pointed the way toward the military complement of ERP: "I would not proceed with the Marshall Plan unless Western Europe engages in a pact against aggression. . . . If such a union is not formed, we ought to come home before we are kicked out of Europe." A European military alliance was essential to its economic recovery and American economic stability: "If they do form a union against aggression, our expenditures to aid them and arm ourselves will be immensely lessened." European productivity needed the assurance of military security.[23] Baruch had outlined his mobilization program in January and early February 1948; on 25 February the communists took power in Czechoslovakia. As had happened a decade before, the question who rules in Czechoslovakia incited war jitters in the west. In March, Congress overwhelmingly approved the Marshall Plan. Truman told Congress that the ERP would not be sufficient to deter the spread of communism in Europe. He asked for a revival of the draft and a Universal Military Training Law. Congress responded with expenditures for the air force that exceeded Defense Department requests. The United States headed toward rearmament and the North Atlantic Treaty Organization anticipated by Baruch.

It was a decided reversal of attitudes on rearmament; a year before, the defense establishment had pleaded impoverishment. Through 1947, Baruch had been lobbying for rearmament, although he would have settled for an initial step of stockpiling raw materials for national defense —just as he had back in 1937–38. The vehicle for the stockpiling of vital raw materials would be the National Security Resources Board (NSRB), one of the agencies created by the National Security Act of 1947. Congress had intended it to be the equal of the National Security Council (NSC), reporting directly to the president—the mobilization arm that complemented NSC's policy planning. It was headed by Arthur M. Hill, who in the autumn of 1947 was already conferring with Baruch and Eberstadt on preparedness schemes. However, from its inception the NSRB was frustrated because "political considerations" militated against any mobilization thinking so soon after World War II.[24]

Nevertheless, European developments in 1948 encouraged planning for rearmament. The Czechoslovakian coup appeared to be the catalyst; it moved President Truman to tell Arthur Krock, "The worst mistake we made was to demobilize, and I helped make it." In this atmosphere of renewed mobilization planning, Baruch, Eberstadt, and Hill worked out policy recommendations for industrial conversion to war production. Still, the principal issue was what Congress would accept in the way of standby legislation. Hill and Eberstadt were willing to settle for a commitment to voluntary restraints on prices in the early stages of an emergency, but Baruch considered that next to useless. "You know, I don't like the word voluntary," he told them. "It chokes in my gullet because I don't think it means anything." Baruch prevailed; by the end of April, the NSRB submitted to the president its recommendation 7, entitled "Steps and Measures Essential to the Fulfillment of the National Security Program," including prescribed powers for the NSRB to establish a price control program.[25]

"If we are going to have controls, let's have them complete and absolute," Baruch told Hill. To a right-wing senator he declared, "No one is a greater advocate of free enterprise than I am, but there cannot be free enterprise if we have war or even the present state of affairs, which is almost war." In other words, cold war mobilization required hot war stabilization. But Jimmy Byrnes was certain that Congress would not approve plans that "covered the waterfront." If Baruch would confine his antiinflation proposals to priorities and fiscal devices, then the Congress might be considerably more receptive to stabilization. But Baruch felt that inflation could not be contained without controls; military spending would buy little if prices were not restrained. He told Secretary of the Treasury John Snyder, "Much has been made of rearming and not enough about the impact it will have on the economy." On 24 May the White House rejected the NSRB recommendation. Presidential assistant John R. Steelman later stipulated that Truman favored stockpiling of strategic and critical materials by agencies and departments normally concerned with the matter; however, Steelman wrote, "The President does not believe . . . that it would be wise to ask the Congress at this time for the authority to impose mandatory controls primarily or specifically for the purpose of stockpiling." To all intents and purposes, controls, which had been debated within the administration, were dead. They were too controversial at any time, but especially so in a presidential election year. Military spending would proceed without the price safeguards Baruch believed essential to stabilization.[26]

BREACH WITH TRUMAN

A writer interviewed Harry Truman in October 1957 at his home in Independence, Missouri. The former president believed that the economy was in a bad way. "Read Baruch," said Truman, probably referring to *My Own Story*, the first volume of Baruch's memoirs and then at the top of the best-seller lists: "An arrogant, opinionated man—but he knows one should never let government bonds go down." Of course, Truman knew well both Baruch's economic judgment and his arrogance. But Truman had not always inclined toward Baruch's economic wisdom; moreover, Truman's own hubris did not easily defer to or cope with Baruch's. The result was that Baruch found himself unwelcome at the White House following 1948.

It hurt Baruch as nothing else could—everyone knew how much he desired entry to the White House, whoever the occupant. Roosevelt had kept him at arm's length during 1939–41, but then, as Arthur Krock reminded Baruch, "F. D. R. knew that you could put him over a barrel. . . . But this President thinks that nobody can put him over a barrel, especially you, I'm told."²⁷ In part, Baruch's status depended upon the temperament in the White House. Roosevelt had feared Baruch's "leaving the reservation" and respected his hold upon congressional and public opinion; besides, he enjoyed Baruch's company and could volley ideas with him. Truman had no time or capacity for genial conversation, was leery of the Baruch reputation, hesitated to disagree with a man to his face, and considered a dissenter on policy either an adversary or an apostate.

Moreover, Truman could afford to court Baruch's ire because the Old Man's hold upon Washington had declined with the passage of time and friends. Although Baruch was still venerated by many in Congress, his only friend in the Senate was Harry Flood Byrd of Virginia. The military still paid him great respect, but otherwise administration officers listened to him with awe, without giving him heed. He was an institution. Congressional committees and organizations of every kind still sought his wisdom and sought to honor themselves by honoring him. His opinions could still call down upon Washington a torrent of constituent mail demanding that he be adhered to or, even at his age, appointed to office. But most of Washington considered him merely meddlesome.

A good deal of Baruch's trouble with Truman lay in his increasing criticism of the president. Seldom had he dared to strike at Roosevelt in public or in private, but Truman invited attack—or perhaps it was the crankiness of age that allowed Baruch to shed caution. In early 1946 he had complained to one Democratic congressman, "The leadership in our party now amounts to a zero and a very little zero too." He did not have to name Truman for anyone to know whom he was talking about, nor did he confine his barbs to politicians. An accidental president, Truman suffered such criticism quietly. He treated Baruch with cordiality, and he initially bowed to quiet pressures from Baruch. In 1945, Roosevelt had made Baruch's brother, Dr. Herman B. Baruch, ambassador to Portugal; a year later, Herman was angling for the Paris post, but, with an assist from his brother, he settled for The Hague.²⁸ No sooner had Baruch left the United Nations than rumor had it that Truman would not even give him an audience (a report presidential aides branded as "really fantastic"). Yet Baruch continued to sense alienation from this White House staff, commenting to Eleanor Roosevelt, "They keep away from me as if I had the plague." And, as we have seen, Truman himself kept Baruch at a far remove during development of the Truman Doctrine. Baruch publicly questioned the wisdom of assuming British imperial obligations and privately fostered Republican doubts. He acted as a tipster when he had information disadvantageous to Truman's policies, admonishing Krock to treat it as background "because it annoys the people down there when you mention my name." A Truman request that Baruch represent the president at a dedication ceremony further strained relations: "The President had absolutely no right to make so snippy and cheesy a request of you," an incensed Swope advised Baruch. "It is as if he were fobbing you off by giving you entrance to his water closet. Resent it."[29]

Baruch visited the White House on 23 January 1948—"the first time in a year," by his count—as part of the administration's campaign for ERP. Yet the ninety-minute session must have been uncomfortable for Truman because he did not enjoy being lectured to, and lecture is what Baruch did. Yet, with his eye on passage of the Marshall Plan and the upcoming elections that year, Truman could weather even a Baruch polemic in order to build a consensus from which Democrats could gaze upon "the crackpots on one side of the fence, and the fellows who want to look backward on the other." But it grew increasingly awkward for Truman to include Baruch in his vital center of the political spectrum. The president rejected Baruch's crony, Ferd Eberstadt, as administrator of American assistance to Europe because he was too controversial.[30] White House rejection of controls planning only confirmed Baruch's opinion that Truman was playing politics with the economy and Truman's opinion that the Old Man cared for nothing but getting his own way.

Apart from policy, neither man could abide the pontifical manner of the other. Baruch took umbrage over a passage in the preface of *The United States at War*, the Bureau of the Budget's history of World War II mobilization, that denigrated the utility of the previous war's administration; he told Truman of his displeasure because the president had written the foreword of the book. Truman's riposte was defensive and included an irrelevant tirade against the Nye committee that concluded, "It seems to me that the volume to which you refer is a step in the right direction even if it does tread on some toes." Baruch considered himself as much of a historian as Truman, but the president abruptly closed the debate, asserting, "The facts which I set out to you . . . are just as they ever were."[31] Compared with Roosevelt's handling of a similar disagreement, Truman's handling of the matter was unnecessarily acrimonious; even so, Baruch had been tactless in bringing the matter to the embattled president.

Truman chose the occasion of Baruch's birthday to request that he serve on the Democratic finance committee for the upcoming 1948 campaign. What followed was reminiscent of Baruch's tiff with Jesse Jones in 1924. However, in addition to refusing to serve on the finance committee, because he just never did that sort of thing, Baruch displayed magnificent chutzpah by requesting that no American representative attend the upcoming coronation of the Netherlands queen except the American ambassador—his brother. Truman's response was tart: admitting disappointment, he declared, "A great many honors have been passed your way, both to you and your family, and it seems when the going is rough it is a one-way street. I am sorry that this is so." In a postscript he told Baruch that two special representatives would be sent to the coronation to supplement the ambassador. Baruch drafted a reply to Truman, but thought better of sending it. When asked for his version of the quarrel with Truman, he quoted Jimmy Byrnes: "Never get in a peeing match with a skunk."[32]

But the affair became a cause célèbre. Because Truman portrayed Baruch as a renegade and an ingrate, Baruch insisted that other information be made public. For one thing, he had resisted the blandishments of liberals who believed that a Truman candidacy that year was doomed and who sought an open Democratic convention that might nominate Dwight Eisenhower for president. Instead, according to Baruch, in the last week of June he went to the White House and urged Truman to call a special session of the Republican Eightieth Congress and challenge it to implement the GOP's platform. That Truman did just that is beyond dispute; that Baruch was the source of the ploy is moot. In any event, Baruch believed that his behavior during 1948 demonstrated loyalty to the party. He contributed to paying the expenses of the Missouri delegation's trip to the convention and as ever made sizable contributions to the House and Senate finance committees. (For that matter, he had assisted Truman in his 1940 Senate race when Roosevelt was soliciting support for Truman's Democratic primary opposition.) This was the history of the 1948 campaign that Baruch wanted told.[33]

Truman had a different version of Baruch's activities that year, as he later recounted it to David Lilienthal: "I've known him a long, long time—he's the same old Bernie," Truman said. "Gave $5000 to Dewey; then day after election and I won, tried to give Bill Boyle money for us Democrats. Nothing doing. . . . He's just a disappointed man." It is not evident that Baruch contributed to Dewey's campaign, but he did send a congratulatory telegram to the Republican nominee as soon as he was chosen by the convention, and followed it with a letter of praise. "The world is confused," he told Dewey. "I hope you will be able to clarify the issues."[34]

Truman was right on Baruch's disappointment. He had had many of them with Truman, one of the more recent ones involving his aspiration to go on a mission to Moscow in the summer of 1948. Mrs. Roosevelt had suggested it as a way of easing tensions with the Soviets. Baruch considered himself the ideal person for that diplomatic task, but, with the exception of Secretary of State George Marshall, nobody else in authority agreed. Nevertheless, in Baruch's eyes, "Truman made that impossible." Truman's victory evidently was more disappointment. The statement Baruch gave the wire services when the result was known avoided mention of Truman and innocuously celebrated the political system. He congratulated Vice-President-elect Alben Barkley on the success of the ticket, "for which you were largely responsible." He told Chester Bowles, the governor-elect of Connecticut, that it was "interesting" how winning Democrats ran ahead of the national ticket and obviously helped pull it through. With Truman back in the White House, the Old Man felt very much of a pariah among Democrats. Baruch maintained that he was still a loyal Democrat and not a "tree-sitter." Yet it was indisputable that "those people closest to the President are not friendly to me." "I see no one in the administration," he confided to his brother early in 1949, "other than Forrestal and some of the naval and military men and Cap Krug. So, I do not know what is going on."[35] Within months, Forrestal was dead, and the isolated Baruch would discover that Cap Krug no longer even paid lip service to his ideas.

On 28 June 1949, Baruch created a mild stir in Washington when he accused the White House of taking "a needless gamble with our national security" by rejecting NSRB mobilization recommendations. The White House responded that Baruch was "badly informed," but Baruch insisted that he knew the facts. The new secretary of defense was Louis Johnson, whom Baruch considered an old ally in mobilization controversies from the late 1930s; but Johnson no longer wanted to be identified with Baruch. "I quite understand that you can take no position because the President has taken umbrage at what I said," Baruch wrote Johnson. "I am right and I will assert it." However, even the devoted Arthur Krock considered Baruch's remarks "very unprecise" and therefore very unwise, because "when you take on a king your weapons must not be blunt at any point."[36]

Cap Krug, known as a Baruch man when he succeeded Donald Nelson as head of the WPB, and now secretary of the interior in the Truman cabinet, also spurned the Old Man's call for mobilization planning. Most crushing of all to Baruch, Krug rejected his historical experience ("we found in World War II that the [industrial] devices which proved so effective for us in World War I were for the most part obsolete"). It did not help matters that Krug argued that the experience of 1941–45 was likewise obsolete. The economy and knowledge of it had altered drastically by 1949, Krug said, whereas Baruch considered certain fundamentals unalterable. "If a man like you feels the way you do," Baruch weakly replied, "I can understand why the present authorities there are so indifferent to . . . doing things that my experience in two world wars make me feel are necessary. Indeed, my dear Cap, it is very discouraging."[37]

A discouraged Baruch was not a relenting Baruch. Nonetheless, he was more politically ineffectual than at any time since he had entered public life. He always had dreaded inaccessibility to the White House and now his worst fears had materialized. It only remained to be seen whether an alienated Baruch could be as dangerous to the president as Roosevelt used to fear he could be. Truman obviously considered Baruch politically weak—as he was. All Baruch could do was rail at the president and wonder if the country now had a "constitutional dictatorship." He cursed the "selfish, disbarring group around the President," "those Fair Deal radicals." When the United States intervened in 1950 in the Korean War, he drafted a letter of support for Truman but thought better of sending it.[38] The United States was at war again, with its old mobilizer further from the sidelines than he had been in 1941.

"MR. BARUCH IS RIGHT"

The events of 1950 demonstrated that Baruch had lost the sort of influence that manipulates policy in Washington corridors, but he still could command the attention of the American public. Journalists valued his copy, even if he no longer received invitations to the White House. The *New York Times* reported all he said publicly, magazine editors sought articles by and about him, congressmen scheduled him for hearings on the economy, and even Fair Deal liberals dared not rebuff his unsolicited wisdom. Baruch was trusted even if Truman was elected. Although biased in the matter of the Truman-Baruch breach, Swope may have been correct in telling Baruch, "After all, he needs you a darned sight more than you need him." Some people in the administration believed that they needed each other.[39] Whatever the value of Baruch to the White House or the White House to Baruch, Truman stubbornly refused to heal wounds and Baruch just as stubbornly refused to restrain his criticisms of policy.

Even as an outsider, Baruch never lost his sense of involvement with history in his time. The events of 1949 had been traumatic for Americans: Russia's explosion of its first atomic bomb, the communist victory in China, and America's first postwar recession. Policy makers had anticipated the Russian announcement for a long time, although they could not be certain when it would come. But it did not startle Baruch to learn that the Russians possessed the "Abomic Tom," as Churchill cutely called it. China was another matter. Baruch was as shocked by the communist triumph as anyone else. It reopened the old question of diplomatic relations with a regime of doubtful character. Moreover, Baruch was outraged by Britain's pragmatic approach to the People's Republic of China. "I would not recognize the bear if we had to over again nor would I recognize the cub who may grow up to be an even greater bear," he wired Churchill, who had wired him, "Diplomatic relations are not a compliment but a convenience. If we recognize the bear why should we not recognize the cub?" Acheson's January statement that the United States should not deflect China's historic animosity toward Russian expansion seemed to Baruch to ignore the fact that the Chinese regime was an enemy of capitalism and the United States. He did not distinguish among communists. A Red triumph in Peking could be celebrated in Moscow; and now the French were fighting Reds in Indochina, and Baruch expected the worst for western interests. "If the rice fields of the Irawaddy go, all of Asia including India is gone. The Russians knew what they wanted." More than ever he preached the doctrine of military strength, telling the National War College that the French must prevail in the Indochinese civil war by drawing their military power from the United States. America had to save Asia from communism.[40]

Baruch certainly did not need the Asian developments to inspire his calls for industrial preparedness for war. With a diminished audience for his doctrines in Washington, Baruch took his message to the nation. Free enterprise needed peace to assure its freedom, he told the U.S. Conference of Mayors, and the peace in 1949 was illusory. In an article for the *Saturday Evening Post*, Baruch warned, "Not so generally appreciated is what revolutionary changes in our habitual ways are being forced by our being neither at war nor at peace." Having lost control over events overseas, Americans should expect that aggression elsewhere would involve them in war—for which they were unprepared. Americans needed self-discipline to organize themselves for an extended test of will with the Soviets. "Peace-waging" required planning and organization for war, less spending for America's civilian standard of living, more expenditures for defense, and careful restraints upon prices for domestic stabilization; "without such organized self-restraint, what the cold war is now taking could wreck us." Excess demand that was not curbed was immoral. A moral society made adjustments in its individualistic behavior for community stability without sacrificing liberty.[41]

Washington was indifferent to such a politically impossible, economically doubtful, and otherwise just plain repugnant dogma. Unfailingly courteous and deferential, Louis Johnson patiently explained to Baruch, "The scene is much broader than in the days from 1937–1940." Compounding the defense mobilization conundrum was the fact that in 1948–49 the economy slid into recession. The administration, Baruch observed, was uncertainly "teetering between whether we are going to have inflation or deflation." When it became evident that it was the latter, Baruch anticipated a reduction of government expenditures to conform to lowered revenues. The administration response—first expecting inflation in 1949, then planning expansion to meet a brief recession, then arguing for voluntary cooperation to meet the inflation in 1949, then planning expansion to meet a brief recession, then arguing for voluntary cooperation to meet the inflation that returned in 1950—confounded Baruch. "A lot of weird economics, morals and ethics are now being promulgated," he told a newspaperman. The president's economic advisors, headed by Leon Keyserling, "are getting to be like lawyers—paid to take up a client's case."[42]

On 6 June 1950, Baruch told a St. Louis audience that Americans would have to discipline their economic affairs if they were to deal with the cold war. Mobilization of manpower to resist aggression required planning for stabilization to restrain prices. The Selective Service Act, he declared, "is the height of immorality when it is not accompanied by a mobilization of property and material interest, and prevention of profiteering. Why youth and not profits? This shows the deterioration of our moral fiber."[43] Three weeks later the United States went to war in Korea.

The Truman administration counted upon a quick victory without a full-scale mobilization. The NSRB, now headed by industrialist W. Stuart Symington, brought in a twenty-one-point stabilization scheme which the Truman advisors recoiled from in favor of the rhetoric of self-restraint. They were confused and uncertain, Louis Johnson saying over and over again, "We don't know whether this is a 1 alarm or a 4 alarm fire." They had answered the alarm but they chose to believe that it did not deserve comprehensive stabilization. In fact, Leon Keyserling, chairman of the Council of Economic Advisers, maintained that increased expenditures of billions more for military needs were of little consequence: "I have . . . consistently taken the view that the American economy could stand, and in fact *had to stand*, whatever expenses and strains for this purpose might be determined upon by the President with the advice of those people primarily in the State and Defense establishments who are his expert advisers in this field." Beginning with the assumption that it was merely the duty of the economy to deliver what the Pentagon wanted, Keyserling, in lawyerly fashion, considered his role as an economist to be that of a defense advocate rather than a seeker of market truths. As he put it, "It is true that a situation might arise, conceivably, where I would want to say as an economist that the size of these programs was more than our economy could stand. But that situation has never arisen, I cannot conceive of it arising, and I have never exercised any influence in that direction. Quite the contrary." Under attack, Keyserling conceded that military spending "must necessarily impose a strain upon the economy." However, the only "means of deprivation" of civilians he would recommend was increased taxation. He did not believe that the American people would tolerate a grand mobilization-stabilization scheme, although he vehemently denied that this consideration was political.[44]

Yet the hoarding of July 1950 proved that Americans had not forgotten the shortages of World War II, nor had they forgotten the planning and controls that distributed goods more equitably than a wartime free market. Baruch helped revive those memories.

Testifying before the Senate Banking and Currency Committee on the

administration's bill for stabilization through taxation and credit restraints on 26 July, Baruch predictably declared that it did not go far
enough; not only was the White House asking for half the taxes it should
be requesting, but it ignored price controls and rationing. Asked by
Senator Paul Douglas when all those should be invoked, Baruch responded: "Right now. Tout Suite [sic]. Today."[45] By no means was
Baruch the only person of the opinion that Truman's program was timid
and unrealistic. But nobody could mobilize support for controls as this
nearly eighty-one-year-old publicist could. Yet it remained unlikely that
Truman would even listen to Baruch. Asked by a senator if he expected to
deliver his message to the White House, Baruch's answer was a crisp no.
That afternoon an old regular Democrat wired Truman suggesting that
he invite Baruch to call. Truman acidly wrote back that Baruch "seems to
have deserted his office in Lafayette Park so I haven't been able to find a
place to put him since that happened."[46]

Other Americans delivered the stabilization message to the chief executive and Congress in numbers that startled Washington. Not everyone
wanted controls; a manufacturer of giftwares, for example, feared "stringent metals restrictions." But he was the exception to the rule among
those who called themselves small businessmen, professionals, workers,
or consumers of every kind. They supported Truman's intervention in
Korea, but pleaded for protection from market hardships that they knew
voluntary cooperation or indirect controls could not prevent. "Please,
Mr. President, put your faith in the advice of a genius for vision and
common sense, Bernard Baruch," a woman wrote. A Memphis physician
was confident that "Mr. Baruch has ably expressed the opinion of the
majority of the business and professional men of the country." A GI
student and his secretary wife listened to a radio rebroadcast of Baruch's
testimony and were moved to write, "Our income is fixed and when we
see prices shooting up as they have in the last month, it really hurts." A
Chicago mother complained that eggs had risen ten cents a dozen in the
past two weeks and wanted a lid on them such as Baruch recommended.
A black man in Miami, living on a salary of $45 a week in a three-room
shanty with his wife and three children, pleaded for the Baruchian mobilization, asking, "If food and necessities continue to rise as they are doing already What are we common people to do?" "White collar workers
are the forgotten people during war years," a Waterbury, Connecticut,
school teacher told Truman: "Please Mr. President, follow Mr. Baruch's
plan." A salaried man in Queens, New York, advised Truman that his
wife could not find sugar on market shelves for the past two weeks
because of hoarding that justified the need for equitable rationing proposed by Baruch. A small manufacturer of office equipment in Chicago
described how rising prices and unpredictable supplies of materials had
turned him to hoarding out of self-protection, and made him feel captive

to the profiteering of his larger distributors—a circumstance that could be rectified only by the controls proposed by Baruch. Relating how "just this week Chicago and Milwaukee tourists have purchased every bed sheet and ounce of pepper in this small town," a Wisconsin man urged Truman, "Please do all you can to put the Baruch plan in full operation *now*." A shoe wholesaler expected sharp rises in the prices of footware unless Baruch were adhered to immediately. It was spontaneous, an outpouring of mail inspired by patriotism and fear of the market chaos people witnessed in their daily lives under the pressure of war. They were for the war and against profiteering and instability in their communities. They wanted social discipline as an alternative to free exploitation by big business. A Chicago woman told how Sears, Roebuck had raised the price of a clock from $47 to $57 and asked, "Why should a company like that raise their price on an article that was there in stock and certainly hadn't cost them more today than it did yesterday?" She concluded, "Mr. Baruch is right when he says that everything should be controlled by the President at once."[47]

Baruch had crystallized public opinion as he had done in the rubber report of 1942. He had rallied Americans against the president's emphasis on voluntary cooperation and modest taxation, and he had accomplished that with an appeal for social discipline. Lashed by letters from their constituents, congressmen converted a mobilization bill into a stabilization measure because they became convinced, in the words of the Senate committee report, "that price and wage controls directed toward stabilization are so closely related that responsibility for both must be invested in a single agency responsible to the President." Bowing to the rising clamor from Capital Hill, Truman agreed to the standby controls. "You performed a miracle in arousing the country in 24 hours to the need for controls," crowed Senator Harry F. Byrd to Baruch. Baruch kept up the pressure on the Senate, admonishing its members not to be swayed by arguments that taxation would absorb enough spending power to obviate the need for controls. After Truman signed the Baruch-inspired Defense Production Act of 1950, Raymond Moley wrote that this "extraordinary reversal" of Truman's leadership was attributable to public confidence in Baruch.[48]

Agencies for stabilization and price controls were created under Symington's coordination, but the administration's antiinflation program emphasized fiscal policy. Priorities were logical to a degree, Keyserling conceded. "But preoccupation with controls should not divert public attention from the truth that production, and still more production, is the greatest of all nonsecret weapons in the arsenal of American democracy." The administration eschewed planned civilian scarcity. Baruch began to grumble publicly about the "creeping" pace of mobilization, scoring the "wait-and-see and trial-and-error" program that treated war

16. Baruch's admonition for action against high prices during the Korean War as seen by Fitzpatrick in the St. Louis Post-Dispatch. (Courtesy Seeley G. Mudd Manuscript Library, Princeton University)

mobilization as a novelty. Despite the summer furor, little happened. The need for a greater mobilization appeared diminished by battlefield victories in Korea that had Americans talking about having the boys home for Christmas. In November, Baruch wrote, "I go through Washington now and then but I do not attempt to say anything because my views are so different from those prevailing [there]." That was mostly self-pity: he did find audiences, as his correspondence with senators, Secretary of the Treasury John W. Snyder, and Symington indicates.[49] But it took the entrance of the Chinese into the war and the ensuing defeats of United Nations troops to suggest a longer war than anticipated and the accompanying need for antiinflation controls after all.

In early December, following the passage of an excess profits tax, Baruch began to sense that the time for adoption of controls had arrived. Congratulating himself for being the "ice breaker" for stabilization, he nevertheless bombarded key senators with telegrams; the one to Paul Douglas of Illinois read, "Voluntary controls is nonsense. Everyone knows that it is the refuge of the weak and the profiteer. Time is running out as Armageddon approaches." On 15 December the president declared a national emergency and announced that a freeze on prices would be implemented the following month. But it was evident in January that liberals had a new attitude toward price controls. "I am deeply disturbed about the indecision and procrastinating of the administration on . . . economic mobilization," Senator Hubert H. Humphrey of Minnesota assured Baruch, hailing him as a "prophet" and a "realist." For a while congressmen were again rushing to Baruch to express their admiration and agreement. A Connecticut congressman wrote President Truman that it was time the country availed itself of the "wisdom and leadership" of Baruch. John Hancock, on assignment in Washington to aid with price control problems, reported that he had "a little better feeling from the improving administration" of prices. Indeed, the new head of the Office of Price Stabilization, former Toledo mayor Michael DiSalle, paid court to Baruch. A congressional fight over a new controls bill shaped up in June, but the panic over prices that existed the previous summer had subsided. "No sense of crisis seems to prevail anywhere," noted Albert Gore, a longtime advocate of controls. Business-minded Republicans wanted to weaken controls. Baruch roused himself to lobby for the tougher version and found himself allied with Truman, who was himself denouncing the "inflation torrent." But the bill that emerged was weaker than the one Baruch sought. He blamed Truman for procrastination, and Senator John F. Kennedy of Massachusetts wrote him, "We should have followed your recommendations at the outbreak of hostilities in Korea."[50]

Baruch and Truman were still at odds with each other, but the national emergency softened their mutual hostility a bit. In May, Baruch received a note of appreciation from the president for a speech he had made endorsing his foreign policy, and on 26 June, Truman took a Sunday afternoon drive, making an impromptu stop at the Leesburg, Virginia, home of George Marshall, where Baruch was the house guest of the general. They had a pleasant chat but it certainly did not heal old wounds. Baruch was convinced that Truman's economic policies were designed to reelect himself in 1952, and that foolish GOP opposition to controls would aid that result.[51]

"I will not again be a self-starter on the dangers of inflation," he decided in September 1951. "Maybe I am the only one who sees it that way. I hope I am wrong and all the others right." A consensus of interests had formed to resist controls. Business, labor, and agriculture all considered price ceilings discriminatory in one form or another. And there were inequities that aroused the speculator's fury against speculators. "I noticed in the newspapers yesterday that a suit is being brought against an automobile dealer who sold an automobile above the ceiling price," he wrote DiSalle. "What has been done to the fellow who paid that big price for nickel? What has become of the people who bought great quantities of materials which were not but should have been commandeered? What became of the people who bought and sold huge amounts of materials above the ceilings?" Controls during the Korean War did not seem to reach to the deeper sources of inflation. Although the sincerity of DiSalle and his staff could not be challenged, they were administering laws with exemptions built in in the form of "escalator" clauses for business, labor, and agriculture that allowed prices to be indexed higher so that each group could keep pace with the other. For producers such an arrangement was most equitable, but it victimized unorganized, white-collar, middle-class groups; their salaries and savings were depreciated. Baruch worried that government employees such as teachers, policemen, and firemen and others then mostly unorganized, such as nurses and white-collar workers, were ripe for unionization against producers who benefited through "escalators."[52]

It was a strange time in American economic history. It confounded officials in Washington—and Baruch. For in mid-1951, despite heavy outlays for war, inflation began to moderate and prices continued to advance at a very slow pace through 1952. In the midst of this abatement erupted the steel strike of 1952, which inspired Truman to seize the plants to maintain production, an action the Supreme Court declared unconstitutional. The comparative lag in prices suggested three things: that the economy would have suffered a full-scale depression without heavy defense spending, that controls were superfluous and merely aggravating to individual interests, and that the economy actually needed more inflation to sustain it against a serious deflation. This generation of Americans would eschew price restraints.[53]

Baruch never changed his mind about the evils of inflation, but in 1951 he adjusted some of his recommended policies to suit current circumstances. Although an octogenarian, he was alert to everything around him; although a very principled man (hidebound, reactionary, and unrealistic, many people called him), he was a speculator and thus had to make plans that conformed to conditions. Long an advocate of high taxes in war, he was "commencing to weaken" on that position. Without a comprehensive program against inflation, taxes promoted higher prices because industry passed costs along to consumers. Moreover, the revenues gained through high taxes did not dampen inflation when they were indiscreetly expended, and the inflation fueled higher prices for the military hardware bought by Washington. What Baruch missed most in this fourth war of his life was a scarcity market for civilians. Profligate domestic spending while soldiers died abroad was itself immoral; the home front refused to sacrifice while its soldiers made the supreme sacrifice. Also, inflation priced American manufactures out of world markets. He temporarily abandoned his usual counsel in favor of stockpiling raw materials because government purchases bid prices higher, and it was clear that American appetites could not be sated. The higher American standard of living was shortsighted. "What is going to happen when Japan and Germany and other economies we have helped get into full swing?" he rhetorically asked Eliot Janeway. "I have always figured on not only winning the war, but winning the peace."

But direct controls were being equated with socialism. Liberals had long since agreed with business that voluntary cooperation was best—ideologically, politically, and even in market realities. Self-restraint was the only bulwark against inflation, a report by the director of defense mobilization declared; "Hokum should know that," Baruch scrawled in the margin.[54] Certain truths about the need for social discipline still had to be articulated despite the voluntaristic shibboleths of the new economics.

THE DOCTRINAIRES OF THE RIGHT

In 1952, Baruch endorsed the presidential candidacy of Dwight D. Eisenhower, the first Republican nominee to earn his public support. The speculator had maintained covert liaisons with previous GOP nominees when disaffected by Roosevelt or Truman, giving the sort of "moral encouragement" to be expected from a staunch Democratic believer in the two-party system. Both the personality of Eisenhower and the circumstances of 1952 combined to flush Baruch out of the grass as a full-fledged enthusiast for the general. "Ike" was an acquaintance of more than a score of years who had been schooled in Baruch's economic concepts. Baruch, since 1945, had increasingly turned away from the "politicos" and put his faith in the capacity of the military to achieve a disinterested corporate scheme that would stem the rapaciousness of all interest groups. Although Baruch had few illusions about Eisenhower, in 1952 he was the logical gamble.

Significantly, Eisenhower held a "deep-seated conviction" that something had to be done to throttle inflation. On that issue, as he later reminded Baruch, "I have sat at your feet for many years and listened to your ideas, and as you know I have, in the main, thoroughly agreed with them."[55] Eisenhower was not a "protégé" of Baruch. Since 1930, Baruch had expanded Eisenhower's economic education during their infrequent meetings, but mostly their relationship had consisted of Baruch's confirming the younger man's insights into the economy and embroidering upon them to develop in him some coherence and an informed background. Eisenhower possessed philosophical principles that found Baruch's deflationary tendencies congenial; but the military man preferred freedom to discipline.

An incident involving Eisenhower that took place at a dinner with business executives and politicians in December 1947 is revealing. Discussion centered upon rising prices and the general surprised his fellow guests by proposing a strategem for blunting them. As one guest recalled his words, he said: "I would like to see some leadership in industry or somewhere some man who had something to lose who would be willing to lay it on the line, somebody like [Benjamin] Fairless [of United States Steel], who would say, 'Now you can put us in the red if you want, and you can ruin us, but this company is not going to raise prices for a year.' " As the general paused, Senator Robert A. Taft interrupted to comment, "Oh, it is not that simple," and then launched into discussion of food prices. A somewhat chagrined Ike later admitted to being outspoken about "matters [on] which soldiers are not expected to have opinions. . . . But I still believe that some really big man in the industrial world has an opportunity . . . by sincere, even dramatic action, to help halt the inflationary spiral." At James Forrestal's suggestion, Eisenhower discussed with Baruch the notion of an industrial leader absorbing wage increases from corporate profits rather than raising prices, and the Old Man heartily agreed with this plan for private corporate restraint; it would break the responsive action that boosted prices through interest-group demands. Baruch had promoted such voluntary action in the 1920s and fervently believed in it during peacetime. The problem was that he did not believe that the cold war was peacetime; and his faith in voluntary cooperation's efficacy was dwindling. But he shared Eisenhower's concern about the "encroaching state."[56]

Eisenhower cultivated his Baruch connection, consulting with him on matters of mobilization and informing newspapermen that he did so.

After World War II the general's name was ineluctably mentioned whenever people discussed presidential possibilities. In the summer of 1951, Baruch toured army installations in Europe and visited with the supreme Allied commander. Returning home aboard the *Queen Mary*, Baruch was asked by waiting reporters to comment upon the budding presidential draft of Eisenhower; he responded that it would be "a great disservice" to put him into the political arena. As he made clear to Eisenhower, all he meant was that the general had a mission to perform —which did not preclude his being drafted while he performed that duty. When Eisenhower flew to Washington for high-level military conferences in November, he discreetly saw nobody but defense officials—except for a visit at his hotel suite from Baruch.[57]

Baruch would not have endorsed any nominee for president in 1952 except Eisenhower. The steel strike of 1952 and Truman's seizure of the plants probably brought Eisenhower's sermon on the need for industrial restraint to Baruch's mind. Rather than blaming the administration or labor alone for the constitutional crisis, Baruch maintained that businessmen also had to accept responsibility for the inflationary round robin. Throughout the Korean War businessmen had profited from spiraling prices. But this did not exempt the administration from responsibility, and when Democrats began to sound a campaign theme that blamed Congress for allowing inflationary pressures, Baruch was outraged by the "lie." The standby controls given Truman in 1950 had not been used until business, labor, and agriculture mitigated their effectiveness in 1951. Baruch agreed with Eisenhower's hope that businessmen would demonstrate restraint. In 1952, Baruch told a longtime business acquaintance, "I hope we will have the proper cooperation from the businessmen and that they will not look upon this as an opportunity to advantage themselves. It would be a magnificent thing if we could continue these high wages and get prices down. In other words, increase productivity." To one of President Eisenhower's first cabinet appointees, Baruch wrote that he should be mindful of the "science of national prosperity" and beware of "the reactionaries and the rightists who think that only profits are involved."[58] He must have hoped that the general could teach his cabinet of millionaires the gospel of enlightened price restraint.

Two other factors governed Baruch's decision to announce for Eisenhower: the state of the Democratic party in 1952 and his old Wilsonian belief in a national interest prevailing over all group interests. "I have been a Democrat for 61 years but . . . I do not know whether I can continue a Democrat," he declared in June. He felt ill treated by Truman, and he believed that the party was fragmented among splinter groups. Eleanor Roosevelt advised Governor Adlai E. Stevenson of Illinois that a visit with Baruch during a trip to New York City was indispensable for the party's 1952 presidential nominee. Stevenson agreed and breakfasted with Baruch on 29 August, the sole topic of conversation being inflation. At that time, Baruch still professed, "I have not made up my mind about the election." But Truman lurked behind Stevenson, as far as Baruch was concerned. Even when the Democratic candidate endorsed price controls, Baruch snorted that Stevenson's stand was "really an indictment of our Party, for none of the things he advocated have been undertaken." Stevenson "is surrounded by wonderful talkers but bad actors," he commented to Albert Gore. He welcomed the party's defeat because of the prominence of liberals such as Hubert Humphrey and Herbert Lehman, whom he labeled demagogues. Baruch announced for Eisenhower on 9 October in a statement that bracketed the general with Wilson and Roosevelt, attributing his decision to the "errors of omission and commission of my own party." The next day, Krock privately wondered, "Maybe B. M. B. has the common failing of liking to be on the winner [sic] when the choice is otherwise not so clear."[59]

That was not Baruch's motivation. On a personal level, he was more at ease with Eisenhower than Stevenson and probably could count upon more frequent and warmer invitations to the White House if the general rather than the governor occupied it. However, on the paramount issue of inflation, Baruch expected little satisfaction from either of them. He could only hope that Ike's prestige and integrity would better withstand interest-group demands that drove prices up. But he had been warned by Eisenhower not to expect price controls during his administration. Controls were for crisis circumstances, in Eisenhower's judgment, and no sufficient emergency was apparent. Moreover, the GOP candidate was intent upon repairing "a complete breakdown in cooperation between the executive and legislative branches of the government" and controls would only exacerbate the breach. Yet he was Baruch's pupil; for should controls be warranted, Eisenhower believed "that the controls must be of the across-the-board variety. If not, I think they simply unbalance our price structure." In rebuttal, Baruch argued that international developments required a greater mobilization than had been undertaken for Korea—and mobilization called for a comprehensive stabilization program. But the general expressed "the hope that the major effects of increased munitions production have possibly been absorbed"; if so, the economy would not need Washington's manipulations for stability. Eisenhower's free enterprise was obviously congenial to his party's right wing. In December, Eisenhower sent "Mr. Republican" Robert A. Taft to Kingstree, where Baruch lectured him on coping with inflation.

Eisenhower undoubtedly wanted Baruch's approval. A Churchill visit in January provided an occasion for Baruch to play host to both the prime minister of Great Britain and the president-elect, an event that kept him on the front pages for days. Would the eighty-two-year-old Baruch be available for duty in the new administration? reporters inquired while the president-elect sat at his elbow; Baruch happily responded that he had always been available to any president. But Ike was not taking his advice. The president-elect, then preparing his inauguration address, eschewed controls. Confronted by an adamantly free-market GOP right wing, Eisenhower was intent upon "removing the subject from the debatable list—it is quite likely to develop a lot of heat." In the words of one history of the period, "Thus the Eisenhower administration took office in 1953 with a commitment to hold inflation and to do so without controls."[60]

Eisenhower had to confront the issue of controls at the outset of his presidency because the patchwork stabilization law would expire that spring unless Congress renewed it. The general's cabinet was portrayed in the nation's press as one of "eight millionaires and a plumber," a sign that he was in the thrall of big business. Baruch did not read the signs differently. Eisenhower's commitment to removing controls, Baruch feared, was a bow in the direction of businessmen and right-wingers who were foolishly motivated by profits and ideology. Unfailingly courteous and patient, the president nevertheless articulated in a long letter a policy of economic libertarianism:

> I definitely believe that the preservation of individual liberty requires what we generally refer to as a free economy. We can for short periods, and we must in great emergencies, apply specific controls to this whole economy to make certain that the over-riding needs of the state are satisfied ahead of any other consideration whatsoever. But to accustom our population to living indefinitely under such controls will gradually bring a new conception of the individual to the state—a conception that would change in revolutionary fashion the kind of government under which we live.[61]

Stalin had just died and the president was eager to bring about a reduction of east-west tensions; on the other hand, Baruch maintained that "ours is a world under siege," a condition justifying increased military expenditures that in turn necessitated putative industrial controls. When he testified in favor of extending the life of the temporary controls bill, Baruch confronted directly arguments that the speed of mobilizations, the nature of modern national economies and international wars, and the efficacy of fiscal restraints upon prices had made the experiences of two world wars anachronistic:

> Those who contend that taxes or interest rates can be lifted high enough so that direct controls will not be needed are confused between economics of war and economics of peace. Under war or near-war conditions, to raise taxes and leave prices uncontrolled is to invite every producer to try to pass on the tax increases both to the

Government and to the individual consumer. This whips on the inflationary spiral of wage and price rises. What you must do is hold your price line stable, even while you raise taxes.

The principle of supply and demand had not been altered by time. Baruch averred that the budding new consensus which would tolerate a modicum of inflation to achieve growth, under an assumption that there existed a "trade-off" between inflation and deflation, did not reckon with the radical influence of higher prices. "These are the times that try men's values," he declared. He and Eisenhower did not disagree on that sense of urgency, but they did clash on the means of preservation.[62]

Baruch was outspoken in his attacks on the administration's abandonment of controls. He argued that it charted a "dangerous" course in world affairs and deplored Eisenhower's "policy of drift." Baruch insisted that the absence of stabilization contingencies weakened American power in Europe and Asia. As he had against liberals of the Truman administration, he railed against the GOP's reactionary right for blocking stabilization planning. "You will . . . have more trouble with the doctrinaires of the right than we had with the doctrinaires of the left," he cautioned a Senate sponsor of controls, who confirmed that forecast three weeks later. Baruch often was "appalled at how dumb and unreasonable our businessmen are about our economy." He did not exempt the administration from blame. The secretary of the treasury, Baruch told Senator Lyndon B. Johnson, "doesn't know whether he is fighting inflation or deflation."[63]

"Disconcerted" with Eisenhower, Baruch judged that "he pays too much attention to the politicians and has too much respect for big business men." However, he knew that it was a mistake to depict the general as mere putty in the hands of others. "Don't for one moment think that Ike is not a politician," he admonished Hedda Hopper. "If he wasn't, he wouldn't be where he is today." Baruch had to blend tactical arguments with those of principle when dealing with Eisenhower, although he found himself reaching desperately for the former when he sought to persuade the president that "the right thing is always the politic thing."

Part of Ike's political genius was his capacity for ignoring differences with Baruch. He invited the Old Man to the White House for a ninety-minute lunch on 23 May 1953, and reporters quickly noted that this was Baruch's first call at the White House in five years. Full of praise for his host, Baruch commented that Eisenhower had "the toughest job any man ever had." Privately, he told Doris Fleeson two days later, Eisenhower "is a very decent, high-minded man, who is such an improvement over the last." Indeed, the White House door remained open for Baruch. When the president hosted a private dinner for fourteen distinguished Americans from assorted fields, the guest list included Baruch. His letters to

17. *A right-wing view of Baruch's advocacy of price controls in 1950. (Courtesy Seeley G. Mudd Manuscript Library, Princeton University)*

Eisenhower got lengthy responses. For that matter, the secretary of state, John Foster Dulles, was an acquaintance of even longer standing who treated him deferentially and opened his door for an impromptu or an appointed chat. Much policy still offended Baruch's sensibilities, but, a year after Ike took the presidency, Baruch could declare, "The great redeeming and alleviating thing is that the P. is honest decent & well mannered."[64]

Always a person with an eye for aphorisms (when he did not attempt to mint them), Baruch on 5 February 1954, found one especially suited to his discontent: "How patient of history to keep on repeating itself when practically nobody listens." He was history—repeating himself when practically nobody listened, or at least heeded. Confessing that he was confused and disappointed concerning developments in Washington, Baruch deplored Eisenhower's unwillingness to "stand up to the pressure groups"—whether business, labor, or agricultural. The general was not the enlightened leader that Baruch had envisioned. Through 1954 he continued to criticize the military posture of the administration, its "Keynesian" economic policies, and the political expediency of nearly everyone but himself and fellow deflationist Harry F. Byrd. "I have no objections to being a brontosaurus," he told himself. Knowing that few people could stomach an omniscient octogenarian, Baruch confined his criticisms mostly to letters to friends. He told Eisenhower and Dulles what he thought, albeit more gently than he used to do with Roosevelt, but he feared becoming a public scold. When he left the White House following lunch with Eisenhower and was asked by a waiting reporter what he thought of the business situation he said, "I think I'll keep quiet"; then, ambling further, he turned and pointed his finger to caution, "That doesn't mean to say it's bad"; finally, outside the gate, he again turned to the pursuing reporter to issue a well-measured declaration, "I'll say this, that fellow in there knows what's going on." Another time he told reporters, "I never speak when I leave the President."[65]

He kept up appearances. Ever eager to impress Churchill with his power and vitality, in December 1954 he told his British friend, "My relations with the President and Dulles are just as good as they ever were. Very confidentially, my political position is stronger than ever; all congressional chairmen are old friends." The Democrats had regained control of Congress. Many of the leaders were men with whom Baruch had corresponded and visited for years. Like Eisenhower, they had long since learned that courtesy to Baruch was not a commitment to his ideas. Occasionally he still received a call or a letter from one of them asking him to lobby for a particular bill. The name of Baruch still had magic in Washington. At a moment's notice he could reach the president or the secretary of state. But the GOP administration was most uncongenial to the old Democrat. It needed neither his money, nor his advice, nor his influence. "I see less of the present administration than previous ones," he confided to Eleanor Roosevelt, "even of Truman's."[66] He was no longer powerful, no longer influential. At eighty-four he was a national kibitzer, a Democratic talisman, a public icon. He was history—repeating himself when practically nobody listened.

MORE GOOD THAN HARM

"With regard to Baruch that is too long a story," Henry A. Wallace wrote following his old adversary's death. He briefly recalled the New Deal struggles and the way Baruch wielded influence both surreptitiously and openly in Washington. Then, as if he realized that no quick summary could do justice to Baruch, a man he had not understood himself, Wallace declared, "He did more good than harm but I doubt if the full truth will ever be printed."[67]

Considering that they were and are so often depicted as politically poles apart, Wallace's simplification concerning Baruch's "good" and "harm" is surprising and intriguing. Baruch considered himself both progressive and conservative; some people considered him only reactionary. These terms are deceptive if Baruch could be all three—and he could! Issues changed; Baruch changed. Some things were immutable. Plans for industrial preparedness for war always seemed rational to him. If national economic planning for a crisis is progressive, then Baruch was progressive. However, his virtues varied from issue to issue.

It is difficult to avoid labeling him a racist. He unquestioningly accepted the social norm of the South as it existed for most of his time. He moved with the times and he resisted them. He prided himself that the hospital built with his money in Camden, South Carolina, was integrated because he had asked, "Why should these people be separated?" However, the decision for integration was paternalistically his, and he resented the civil rights movement, classifying liberals on the race issue as either "sentimentalists" or demagogues. "I think we talk too much of rights and not enough of obligations," Baruch told Eleanor Roosevelt.[68] But he never went public on his view of social relations between the races.

On many issues of the postwar period he sounded like a conventional right-winger. He resisted appeals from the "Committee for Collective Security" to oppose the Bricker Amendment (which would have limited the president's authority in foreign affairs) and gave Bricker his covert blessing.[69] "Communism in America," he declared in June 1950, "is not a matter of red baiting, or red herrings. It is a question of survival." There was "a Fifth Column at work" in America, he advised General George C. Marshall. The farcical anticommunist antics of Senator William E. Jenner of Indiana were considered "wonderful work" by Baruch. He commended Judge Irving R. Kaufman for refusing to reduce the death sentences of convicted Soviet spies Julius and Ethel Rosenberg. He admired the investigations of the House Un-American Activities Committee and deplored those who invoked the Fifth Amendment against its questions. J. Edgar Hoover was Baruch's kind of patriot, as were Barry Goldwater and General Curtis LeMay. Conservatives like Harry Byrd and Carl Hayden warned Baruch that Red hunter Joe McCarthy was mischievous and merely sought attention for himself, but Baruch considered the Wisconsin senator's proclaimed purposes more significant than his methods or motives. McCarthy overstepped himself in 1954 when he assailed two institutions dear to Baruch's heart: the City College of New York and the United States Army. Baruch reproved McCarthy in both instances, but his judgment of the senator's overall record was that he had performed a service in alerting the country to internal dangers.[70]

Baruch was a bit of a militarist. Although he knew that generals and admirals were capable of asking for too much hardware and quite ignorant of the economic consequences of their demands, he remained a staunch advocate of greater military spending as a deterrent to overseas communist advances. "I do not object to being known as a war-monger who desires to keep the armaments firms busy," he told Lord Beaverbrook. "We have to keep them busy if we are to save ourselves." He put defense spending above everything else. The Truman administration's proposed universal military training struck a responsive chord in Baruch. He pronounced it "a wonderful thing for young men. . . . [What they] learn in basic training—physically, mentally, morally and above all else militarily—will be of use to them and to the country."[71] Universal military training fit in with Baruch's grand design for preserving America's place in the world and organizing its society for that task. However, this side of Baruch ironically alienated the right wing and aligned him with welfare state advocates.

For Baruch, the logical complement to universal military training was a national health insurance system. A son and brother of physicians, a longtime benefactor of hospitals and various medical causes, Baruch was not expected to be a supporter of government involvement in medicine. Yet his attitudes reflected to some extent the public health concerns of the progressive era—updated to meet the world and social concerns of cold war America. He drew the line against what was commonly considered "socialized medicine," but he doubted the social justice of the existing medical system. A compulsory national health insurance system had become a social necessity, and all the arguments for a voluntary system could not persuade him otherwise. In an address to the Medical Society of New York in 1947, he declared: "What troubles me most are the needs of the sizable segment of society which does not earn enough to pay for voluntary insurance." And, he added, "I do not fear government taking its legitimate part in medicine, any more than I fear it in education or housing." Coming at a time when a labor-sponsored drive for a national insurance system had stalled in Congress, Baruch's words excited renewed hope. "Mr. Baruch's speech provides a springboard which can and will be utilized by both progressives and middle-of-the-roaders as a base for winning support for practicable national health legislation," its lobbyist exulted. By early 1948 the campaign for national health insurance had modified its goals in anticipation of winning the sort of support Baruch usually appealed to. Baruch notwithstanding, not even a watered-down version of the original concept could pass.[72]

He never sought equity for the downtrodden, but Baruch possessed a sense of outrage that demanded fairness to those who were victims in a "free" market. The Wilsonian qualities of Senator Paul Douglas's "truth-in-lending" bill drew Baruch's warm encouragement in 1961–62.[73] Still, he did not love the common man. He believed that most men were fools. He had not been a New Dealer and he would not be a New Frontiersman. Such programs were useful in bringing order to social progress, but, as he told Jimmy Byrnes, "the trouble is that you and I believe that elevated sentiment is not a sound basis on which to conduct human affairs." He was a Bismarck on issues of social progress. Mass movements and social crusades made him uneasy, especially if they involved dispossessed individuals. In times of turmoil he wished for a "Moses [who] will quiet or lessen the discords that are tearing us apart." Expressions of discontent ought to give way to declarations of community responsibility, he believed.

Yet he did not expect the social stability that he yearned for. He had been in markets too long to anticipate the best from human nature. "Speculation is nothing for an amateur or a dilettante," he once declared. Markets were chaotic and unpredictable because of swarms of ignorant investors. His favorite book of all time was a history of early capitalist speculations published in 1841, Charles Mackay's *Extraordinary Popular Delusions and the Madness of Crowds*. It was at the top of his list of recommended reading—not merely because it concerned speculation, but because it was a classic in the study of mass psychology. Familiarity with the consequences of market disorder made him distrustful of popular crusades. "No one has been more identified with what is called progressive legislation than I have," he once declared, "but I know that we cannot, humans being what they are, go too far too quickly. This is a wonderful country. . . . I dislike to see it being used by sentimentalists to cure all of our human ills—at once."[74]

He was not a democrat; he was a corporatist. Consistently with his experience in World War I and the 1920s, Baruch in the cold war era wanted basic political-economic policies formulated by a few elite individuals rather than by the public's elected representatives. The latter dilatorily moved in concert with the interests of dominant pressure groups in their states or districts; the former, Baruch presumed, expeditiously acted in behalf of a national interest. As it had had to do during the two world wars, America in the cold war had to establish its priorities —a task that demanded planning and control. Only people inspired by devotion to the community—not by the selfish interests of any economic or social faction—could set national priorities. Public life in America ought to be concerned with national goals above personal quests. Baruch admired Eleanor Roosevelt because, he once told her, "you happen to be, and I hope I am, one of those who give something to politics and do not try to get something." Indeed, Baruch was entranced by individuals who, he believed, "rose above politics." He identified with them. Of André Tardieu he once wrote,

> It always seemed to me that Tardieu was both fascinated and repelled by politics. This is not uncommon among men who are both ambitious and high principled. He was anxious to serve his country and yet he was often distressed at the seamier aspects of political life. . . .
>
> When he had to choose between his political convictions and his political life, he chose the former, refusing to join the extremists of either right or left to remain in office. The middle of the road, or rather, reason, is hard to follow in unquiet times and yet that path, which Tardieu followed in French politics, is the only one which leads to stability and progress.[75]

Any nation would have done well to have trusted power to a Tardieu. In a sense that was why Baruch esteemed the military: in their careers they served only the nation and no particular interest.

Churchill had once whispered to Baruch, "If only they would let you run the economics and me the politics, we would soon have this straightened out." That would have been the ultimate in corporatist direction. Yet, as much as the notion enthralled Baruch, he would have settled for other corporatist strategies of his own devising. He liked the concept of the National Security Council, a select executive body charged with responsibility for America's global strategy. Even that body, he once suggested to Dean Acheson, ought to be augmented by an advisory council of elder statesmen such as George Marshall and Herbert Hoover (he was too modest to propose himself), whose only duties would be to read, think, and propose policy. A prestigious body of sages with no political axes to grind, "composed of five, or at the most seven, could recommend any policy that the President carried to the public, [making it] very difficult for any opposition to prevail against it." Of course, if such a group could be devised for national security policy, then Baruch hoped to see a similar one instituted for national economic policy. The nation needed a "priority committee" to adjudicate the economic demands of various groups. Thus, the priority concept of two world wars would be applied to the cold war, and policies would be publicized by blue-ribbon panels. It all came back to the WIB's proposed high court of commerce of 1919. It was not senility that caused Baruch to hearken back to that two-score-old nostrum. Ever abreast of events, Baruch saw it as the solution to the rail labor conflicts of the early 1960s. He urged a body similar to the National War Labor Board of 1918 upon Secretary of Labor Willard W. Wirtz in 1963, later admitting that Wirtz "did not seem to like the idea."[76] He never abandoned his belief that America needed a planning or a quasi-judicial body to effect peace and order in her markets.

In foreign markets, Baruch would have America stockpile raw materials through executive organizations such as those created in 1918 between Washington and the Allies. He hated to see America giving away its foodstuffs to underdeveloped countries that could trade their raw materials for food. Ever a believer in economic warfare, he denounced any trade with the communist bloc. ("We don't believe in starving our enemies to death," declared an Australian friend, W. S. Robinson, in defense of his nation's sale of wheat to China.) Conservation would allow America to "pace" itself for the long haul. "Our wheat, our stocks of food—there is a lever that, like that fellow, who was it—Archimedes —there is a lever that could move the world," Baruch expostulated in 1963. "Better than gold. We could use the threat of selling wheat below world prices to puncture Argentina for the way they are treating us on those oil contracts; we put a lot of money in and make something into a good business, and then they come along and take it away. Well, let's use our wheat to show them that they can't push us around."[77]

Domestic price stability always was his first preoccupation. Eisenhower had failed him by applying partial restraints upon prices, a move that Baruch considered ill advised. Steel price increases in 1957 demonstrated the need for controls or at least an investigation by Congress or the Federal Trade Commission, he told Eisenhower.[78] The Soviet launching of Sputnik in 1957 coincided with a downturn in the American economy, inspiring a major crisis of confidence as Americans bemoaned the apparent Russian advantage in missile technology, the inadequacy of Washington's defense preparations, and the stagnation of the Eisenhower economy. In early 1958, Democrats exploited these concerns with calls for vast federal expenditures on military and pump-priming projects. On 6 March every Senate Democrat except Harry Byrd endorsed Lyndon Johnson's resolution for stepped-up appropriations. Calling it "the greatest fiscal crisis in my 25 years in the Senate," Byrd pleaded for Baruch's help to stem the spending "hysteria."[79] Even at the age of eighty-seven, Baruch enjoyed this sort of fight. On 1 April he appeared before Chairman Byrd's Senate Finance Committee to testify on the financial condition of the United States; it was the last of many appearances before congressional committees in which he performed as an expert witness on America's political economy.

Baruch was an anachronism. At a time when the conventional wisdom called for fiscal adjustments to permit expansion (lower taxes and deficit spending), Baruch counseled a balanced federal budget and higher corporate taxes if necessary to achieve it. At a press conference, Eisenhower, no devotee of the new economics himself, would say only that he took Baruch's advice seriously, but that he would not necessarily endorse it. Privately, he informed Baruch that he considered antiinflation activity "a matter of public relations and persuasion rather governmental edict." The president knew well Baruch's predilection for coercive measures. "This voluntary talk about doing something about inflation reminds me of NRA days, but without any driving force—as yet," Baruch declared in early 1959. If only America had "an economic de Gaulle or someone similar to that"—a man whom it could trust to be the corporate "driving force" behind federal restraints upon profits and wages.[80]

A MOST ADMIRED MAN

As a very old man, Baruch was more trusted than ever. Politicians, it is said, become statesmen if they live long enough. Baruch never entered the public consciousness as a partisan figure, having astutely cultivated the image of a spokesman for the public interest. In his sixties he claimed the mantle of a statesman, and he had a long time yet to live. Power and influence with select people mattered very much to him, but, in the words of one publicist when Baruch was in his late eighties, "it's the awareness of the nation that you are around that counts, even though Washington has so stupidly detoured you." Publicists can be a fawning lot, especially around a notoriously vain and rich old man. Prone to hyperbole, which is part of their art, publicists considered Baruch a credible commodity. In his eighties he was tall, erect, handsome, clear minded, articulate, and a better public speaker than he had been at half his age. To anyone who met him or heard him, he was an interesting and impressive personage. Public attention pursued him. In an unstable world where the American dream was challenged by hostile ideologues and doubted by distant peoples discovering their own nationhood in the wake of colonialism, Baruch represented much that was right, wholesome, and enduring about the American way of life. "Americans will trust you, chief. Nobody else," publicist Tex McCrary told him when Baruch was already ninety. "They love Eisenhower. But they trust you."[81]

Even discounting some of the value of McCrary's words as obsequious hype, it remains true that Baruch was a man trusted by the public. Of course, trust and "greatness" are frequently a product of longevity. The United States Chamber of Commerce included Baruch on its list of five greatest living Americans in 1960, all of whom were past seventy.[82] In a more rational vein, a physician came up with his own list of "ten who know the secret of age," pointing out not only that these remarkable persons had accomplished much in their younger years, but also that they continued to be productive at an age when others entered their dotage. His accomplished elderly men possessed "a balance of egotism and sacrifice, a sense of humor and tragedy, . . . [and] undying curiosity." In justifying his inclusion of Baruch on the list, he wrote: "A tall man of amazing physical and mental capacity, [Baruch] has even transformed the use of a hearing aid into a symbol of elderly dignity and poised deportment."[83] Physicians, too, are given to ballyhoo.

All the same, much of the list-making hoopla is a confirmation of public perception (just as public perception is the confirmation of promotion). In late 1958 a sample of Americans was asked by the Gallup Poll, "What man that you have heard or read about, living today in any part of the world, do you admire the most?" Baruch was the ninth of the ten most frequently mentioned men and the eldest. It was not the first time he had made the Gallup Poll's "Most Admired Man" list, having done it before in 1949 and 1951.[84]

And that was not by happenstance. His chief publicist, Herbert Bayard Swope, labored hard to foster the public image of Baruch as sage and oracle. The "Most Admired Man" list was confirmation of their efforts. When Baruch failed to make the list, Swope was severely disappointed. But the Gallup Poll was hardly the sole measure of Baruch's fame. It also mattered that politicians and organizations pursued him for no other reason than to identify themselves with him publicly. When he was a mere septuagenarian his blessings and donations were sought after by the nascent Americans for Democratic Action, the Committee for the Marshall Plan, and the Atlantic Union Committee, among others. Senators and congressmen frequently made public his letters concerning an issue to enhance passage of a bill. A properly timed statement from Baruch was widely considered by Washington insiders an effective weapon in any crusade.[85]

Many editors and publishers in every section of the country still considered him a friend or an idol. There were also detractors—both right-wingers who considered him a threat to free enterprise and left-wingers who thought him the personification of reaction. He gloried in the simultaneous animosity of the *Chicago Tribune* and the *New York Post*. But most newspapers gave him their respectful attention, particularly his old friends at the *New York Times*, who scrupulously reported his travels at home and abroad. At one time or another its headlines informed readers, "First 'copter ride is taken by Baruch" or just "Baruch in Los Angeles." He was always news to the *Times*. And when he passed eighty a Baruch birthday was worth two days of stories, the first advising readers how he felt as it approached, the second noting how he spent it. As a *Times* editorial on his eightieth birthday declared, less than a month after he goaded the Congress to grant the Truman administration standby price controls it did not want, "Mr. Baruch has never been a more vital force in American affairs than he is at this very moment."[86]

Baruch remained prominent for the rest of his days. The Soviets believed in his importance, for seldom did Baruch miss being invited to a Soviet gathering in New York, and Andrei Gromyko assiduously maintained correspondence with him. Politicians always wanted him in their corner. He defended John Foster Dulles against charges of bigotry during his campaign against Herbert Lehman for the Senate in 1949. Against 1953 charges of corruption, Baruch defended incumbent New York Mayor Vincent Impellitteri during his race with Robert F. Wagner, Jr. He was eager to help Democrats at all levels in order to demonstrate an enduring commitment to the party following his endorsement of Eisenhower in 1952. In 1960, Eleanor Roosevelt advised John F. Kennedy that it would be useful to woo Baruch. Richard Nixon already had visited him. John Kenneth Galbraith served as Kennedy's emissary in September. Baruch enjoyed the attention, but he did not announce his vote in 1960. Nevertheless, the Kennedy administration paid considerable attention to this nonagenarian.[87]

Baruch had his own public "constituency." With the aid of Samuel Lubell and Herbert Bayard Swope, he developed and maintained his influence with various sectors of the electorate through contributions and contacts that identified him with those groups. A plea for and from the Young Christian Workers drew this advice from pollster-interviewer Lubell: "I suppose the question is whether you want to strengthen your hold on the labor-Catholic vote." Confounded by the fact that a man in his eighties wielded as much public influence as did Baruch, many observers attributed the phenomenon to Swope's efforts. They certainly were inseparable. Swope was a constant companion, adviser, and buffer. It was well known in New York and Washington that if an organization wanted to put Baruch on a committee, to get a contribution or a public endorsement from him, or even to honor him with an award or with the use of his name for a building, it had better see Swope first. Reporters seeking special interviews with Baruch found that his consent was more likely if they first used the Swope conduit. A senator once asked Swope to forward his regards to Baruch, a matter that caused the publicist to observe to Baruch, "Sometimes I wonder if my identification with you is not too complete. However, if either of us has a benefit thereby, I am satisfied to be offstage."[88] He wrote speeches for Baruch and participated in the composing of *My Own Story*—ghostwriting he characterized, with his usual penchant for coining words, as "largely Aaronic."*

The public image of Baruch was essentially Baruch's own creation. Swope knew of Baruch's independence. For years he had been counseling Baruch to increase his "Scarcity Value" by refraining from acts sure to get him newspaper space, such as visits to Roosevelt's White House. In 1950, Swope unburdened himself on Baruch's "tendency to appear too often in public [and] his unwillingness to see much of anyone who doesn't acquiesce in his views." To Swope's consternation, Baruch was very much his own man. In 1956, Swope wanted Baruch to issue a statement regarding Stevenson's position on abolishing nuclear weapons; but Lubell counseled silence and Swope was furious that his advice was again disregarded.[89]

Even so, Baruch missed him greatly after Swope's death in 1958. Baruch saw to it that he was memorialized as a racing buff, a liberal, and a journalist by Saratoga, Freedom House, and Columbia University School of Journalism respectively. However, even without his amanuensis, Baruch did not fall from public view.

"I am somewhat averse to having personal publicity which is of no value to the community," he once explained to a supplicant after Swope had passed on. He detested honorary committees. When he wanted plaudits, he could exercise considerable clout. Dean Acheson loved to repeat the tale of how Baruch got his bust in the National War College by persuading George Marshall that it should sit alongside of Napoleon, Alexander, and Caesar. Acheson neglected to say that Marshall considered it a cheap price to pay for Baruch's "very effective help" regarding appropriations. There were honors—galore: Baruch Park, named for his father at the corner of Baruch Place and Rivington Street on New York's lower East Side; the Theodore Roosevelt medal for distinguished service; the first annual award of the American Veterans Committee for contributions to Americanism; a gold plaque from the New York Board of Trade for preserving the heritage of America; a gold medal as citizen of the year by the United American Mechanics, Junior Order; and so on. Needless to say, the City of New York designated a Central Park bench as his alone, and his World War II "office" in Washington's Lafayette Park was commemorated. It was all publicity that had value to the community.[90]

For politicians in the know he was still a man worth knowing. Benton

---

*"Aaronic" was not an apt description of Swope's function for Baruch. Consider Exod. 4: 10–16: "And Moses said unto the Lord: '. . . I am slow of speech, and of a slow tongue.' . . . and He said: 'Is there not Aaron thy brother the Levite? I know he can speak well. . . . And he shall be thy spokesman unto the people . . . , that he shall be to thee a mouth.'"

and Bowles of Connecticut counted him as one of their financial angels. Albert Gore of Tennessee, both in the House and later in the Senate, arranged meetings with colleagues so that they could hear the Baruchian wisdom that had been dispensed to their predecessors over four decades. Embarking upon a Senate career, Stuart Symington proclaimed himself "devoted" to Baruch. Lyndon B. Johnson assured Baruch that he valued Baruch's counsel. Baruch was approaching the age of eighty-nine when Lewis L. Strauss, then embroiled in a tough fight for confirmation as secretary of commerce, appealed to Baruch to write in his behalf to Senators Gore and Fulbright of Arkansas; Strauss lost.[91]

Old friendships with the right people still contributed to the luster of his name. The "Greatest Englishman of the Twentieth Century"— Winston Churchill—could not visit the United States without being hosted in great style by his old comrade Baruch. "Churchill is here as Baruch's guest," proclaimed a front-page headline in 1952. He was once more prime minister, and his attachment to Baruch was undiminished. They disagreed on policy a great deal, but that could not disturb their mutually beneficial amity. Good friends are able to exploit each other without hard feelings.[92]

Eleanor Roosevelt—"The First Lady of the World," as the press then hailed her—also maintained an enduring tie with Baruch. "We shall always be friends—as I have enlisted with you," he had scrawled on a letter to her in 1939. He was true to his word. A frequent companion at lunch or dinner, an escort on numerous public occasions, Baruch was an intimate friend who advised her on personal matters and political economy. He was also a reliable contributor to her causes, most of which would never have seen a Baruch dime save for his trust in her humane judgment. Her friendship ennobled him, as his enriched her. More than any other person, Eleanor Roosevelt was responsible for keeping Democrats interested in Baruch following his breach with Truman and his endorsement of Eisenhower in 1952. She reminded the Fair Dealers that Baruch was a valuable man to have on the side of liberalism. She believed that Baruch was right on America's political economy. She linked Baruch to the modern liberal Democratic party that he despised and helped keep him a man worth knowing for those who would govern in the 1960s.[93]

INTO HISTORY AND OUT OF HISTORY

It was natural that Baruch in his very late years was concerned with how he would appear in history. He tried to influence old associates who were writing their memoirs to narrate his version of events, recounting for them the role he played in their lives. He was obsessed with moralizing on the lessons of Woodrow Wilson and securing Wilson's rightful place in history. He was also quite conscious that Baruch's place in history would be beside Wilson. As the centenary of Wilson's birth approached in 1956, Baruch focused more intently upon that golden period in his life. His biographer could not get answers to questions on Roosevelt and World War II because Baruch wanted only to discuss Wilson. He could be tiresome on any subject, but especially so on Wilson. "I note your quotations from Woodrow Wilson," Churchill once responded tartly. "I did not think he was a very good President, but certainly he seems to have said some pithy things." Baruch welcomed Herbert Hoover's *The Ordeal of Woodrow Wilson* in 1958, but he believed that only Baruch would have the definitive word on the Wilsonian legacy.[94]

Baruch always had been ambivalent concerning writings about himself. He never suffered from an excess of modesty that might compel him to understate his own role, but he constantly feared that overstatement of his prominence might depreciate the value of a history. Fearing a marbleizing of his image, Baruch encouraged magazine pieces that humanized him. A piece in *Collier's* told readers about Baruch's enjoyment of professional wrestling, horse racing, and conversation with young people. A three-part series of articles on Baruch in the *New Yorker* by John Hersey conveyed a sense of both intimacy and authenticity. Baruch must have known that Hersey would give the world a dependable perspective, for only six months before the articles appeared he had invested $3,000 in a magazine of which Hersey was a founder.[95]

Baruch held some definite ideas on biographies, having once declared that he wished Wilson's biography would be written "by some one who did not know" President Wilson as well as Ray Stannard Baker. An authorized work made its subject "a little too wise and a little too good." Carter Field's *Bernard Baruch: Park Bench Statesman* "disturbed" him, but Swope saw to it in 1946 that ten thousand libraries across the country received copies bought with Baruch's money. What bothered Baruch most about the Field book were the unauthorized quotations from Baruch's papers.[96] When W. L. White embarked upon his brief study of Baruch he had to promise to "submit the final text for your suggestion and corrections" and not publish material from Baruch's files without permission. Yet the book was White's and Baruch did not like it, asserting that it was full of errors and a vehicle for White's deprecations of Wilson, Roosevelt, and Truman.[97]

The White book appears to have galvanized the Baruch camp into thinking seriously about an appropriate biographer. In 1950, Claude G. Bowers reviewed a biography of John C. Calhoun by a young writer named Margaret L. Coit, and suggested to Baruch that she would be a good choice for a Baruch biography. After all, Calhoun was a South Carolinian and the book was written with great flair; when it won the Pulitzer Prize, that added frosting to the cake. Also, Coit was a southerner, intent upon writing next on Jefferson Davis, conservative in her political views, and admiring of Baruch—the "greatest living American." She was hired, and while she learned her way around Baruch's files, she performed some ghostwriting chores for him. Houghton Mifflin Company advanced her $12,000 for two years while she researched and wrote the book. Baruch admonished her that the product should not be a "monument or a tombstone." However, he introduced her to his friends and urged her to interview them. She worked hard on the book, and in a longer-than-expected course of its research and writing she suffered personal emotional difficulties. By 1955, Baruch had lost patience.[98]

In any case, Coit probably could never have satisfied Baruch or his coterie. An occurrence of 1954, about which she did not know, was a harbinger of trouble. Historian Gilbert C. Fite had written a study of George Peek and asked Baruch to read it. Baruch responded with encomiums, which Fite wanted to use for the book's dust jacket. Baruch agreed, but then reneged, explaining to Swope, "There were so many generous references to me in it that I suddenly realized that I was indulging in self-praise." As consolation for Fite, Baruch said that he would "try to get that book in every library everywhere."

In the early stages of her research, Coit was adulatory toward Baruch, taking him "at his own evaluation." Her letters to him were full of adoring comments. Baruch insisted that the book was hers alone, that he did not want to influence her. However, he admonished:

> You must be very careful in expressing opinions and drawing conclusions regarding my motives when you do not have the facts. I would not want to be put in a position where I would be compelled to protest against inaccurate and unjustified conclusions drawn by you regarding my motives or attitudes. . . . Several items in the material you showed me were wrong. You can say what you please, but you must be accurate. Work with facts, not your imagination.
>
> I can see no objection to my going over the quotations which you use in the completed manuscript. There is no point in publishing material which may needlessly hurt or embarrass an individual and which is of no public significance.

In particular, Baruch was perturbed by his 1935 opinion that any effort to alter race relations in America would result in another civil war; shortly following the Brown decision in 1954, he told Coit, "Of course I do not think that now."

> I am wondering if some time while writing the story you do not pick up things I wrote or said twenty odd years or more ago and use them in writing my opinion as it is today. At that time we did not have the unanimous Supreme Court Decision nor had the new Army regu-

lations been put into effect. And, perhaps we have advanced some in twenty years.

Coit then realized that this South Carolinian was no irreconcilable Calhoun. "My feeling is that the genius of Baruch," she responded, "is in knowing the difference between yesterday and today . . . and in adjusting to the difference." Her letters now assumed a respectful, correct tone; gone was her giddy admiration of a South Carolina hero. When the book was finally published more than three years later, she concluded that Baruch's weakness was his need to emerge on the winning side of an issue; "as has been said, flexibility has been one of Bernard Baruch's most useful secrets of survival." Later she told a Brown University audience, "Every writer has one book in him, . . . and mine is the story of a person fighting a last ditch fight hopelessly. Calhoun was my story. . . . Baruch was definitely not my story."[99] The story of Coit's *Mr. Baruch* had not reached its climax. Coit struggled through 1955, sometimes not in good health, emotionally upset, supported by fellowships, teaching, and writings after the advance money ran out.

Compounding her problems was the hostility of some of Baruch's closest associates, especially Swope. More than ever the life of Baruch was marketable to publishers, and his closest friend fretted that he would reap nothing from it—after being so much a part of that life. Baruch himself had tackled his memoirs in the mid-1930s when he employed Marquis James to write a manuscript that lay in Baruch's files, waiting to serve as the basis of a Baruch biography or an autobiography. In 1948, Swope had wanted to update and publish it, but Baruch scribbled on Swope's letter, "When I get old enough not to look to the future I will write of the past." Months later he informed Swope that his office staff was assembling his files for an undetermined person who would organize the material on his career. A young City College graduate, Harold Epstein, would be hired to serve as a personal historian and curator of his papers. Sam Lubell went through Baruch's public papers, contacted a publisher, and then proposed to Baruch a book of "selections of your best utterances over recent years." Baruch found that idea unacceptable. Then along came Coit. Although Baruch himself was always genial with her, his entourage treated her as an intruder; Swope, the man who knew him best, shunned Coit's quest for an interview until one very perfunctory, unrevealing sitting with her. Meanwhile the Baruch memoirs were revived, but, as Coit's project was delayed, so was Baruch. In February 1956 he urged Coit to finish her book, lest his own compete with hers for public attention.[100]

It was Coit's book, but Baruch still owned literary rights to his own papers; so she was obligated to seek his permission to use his private words. Baruch himself read part of her manuscript, then tired of it and warned her that he wanted to approve every quotation. He was holding up publication of his own memoirs to allow her book to precede his, but, at eighty-five, he feared that "his time is running out." Coit tried to explain the delays, declaring, "*You* came first, always." Baruch considered her excuses unjustifiable. Worse, he felt that her portrait of himself was distorted. In June, he told her:

> I am concerned by your lack of objectivity, by your tendency to romanticize and exaggerate. I appreciate, of course, the high regard you have for me and my work. But you should know that I am neither a superman nor a saint. I have, I think, previously cautioned you in this regard.
>
> In addition I have, in scanning your chapters, come across frequent factual errors, evidence of misunderstanding of events, imagined dialogue, etc.

He concluded, "I am very, very reluctant, on the basis of what I have seen to be quoted in the book." Coit, described by her editor as "in a rather exhausted and over-strained state of mind," denied that she had invented dialogue or failed to check her facts. "I, too, have a reputation to maintain," she declared. She conceded a tendency to romanticize her subject, calling it "both my strength and my weakness." After all, her romanticizing of Calhoun had attracted Baruch and won her the Pulitzer Prize. Now she endeavored to be objective: "I have never felt that you were a superman or a saint, but I have admired you greatly and felt that history should give you your just due. You will find, as the book goes on, that I am critical of some of your acts and judgments." Yet neither Baruch nor his office manager of many decades, Mary A. Boyle, a woman of inestimable influence over him, could see a way out of the dilemma short of disassociation from the book. "I am letting you know that I cannot permit any quotations from me," he told Coit on 19 June. "I cannot tell you how greatly I regret making this decision."[101] Direct contact between them ceased and the affair became principally an issue between his office and her publisher.

At whatever cost to Coit and Houghton Mifflin, the Baruch camp was determined to celebrate his eighty-seventh birthday with the publication of *My Own Story*. Republication rights in the *Saturday Evening Post* had been arranged, after Swope and Lubell argued with each other and Baruch over terms of serialization that could benefit them financially. (Lubell, who wrote the 1957 book, had negotiated the *Post* deal; Swope and Baruch's lawyer, Samuel Rosenman, renegotiated it to include nationwide newspaper syndication, which paid Swope $2,500; Lubell got $15,000.) As anticipated, the Baruch books were lucrative for all. The Book-of-the-Month Club made the Coit book a December selection. (Baruch, Coit later claimed, had hinted that she would get $20,000 for *not* publishing her book, but the Book-of-the-Month Club already had paid that much for it, and Baruch never raised the matter again.) Baruch's own book sold over one hundred thousand copies in the first few months and brought Baruch, Lubell, and Harold Epstein nearly $70,000 in a couple of years, Lubell and Epstein receiving 20 and 15 percent of the total respectively.[102]

The Coit episode did not end there. Baruch's prohibition on direct quotation boomeranged when Coit introduced her notes at the back of the book with a statement that included, "After I had been at this work for more than five years and had completed a preliminary draft of my manuscript, Mr. Baruch closed his papers to me and withheld permission to quote from his unpublished writings, including his letters and unpublished memoir." Her note conceded possible errors in the book, but it did not, as Baruch complained to her publisher, "hint at the keen disappointment I felt over how overworshipful and over-romantic her draft was in its treatment of me, and its inaccuracies." Certainly, Coit was not about to discuss that in public. However, it insinuated that Coit had uncovered something in Baruch's dark past that he wanted hidden. Far from being worshipful, the preface likewise suggested her knowledge of Baruch's lack of adherence to principles, reading in part: "What Calhoun represented met with defeat; what Baruch has represented, with victory. Calhoun fought the spirit of his time and lost; Baruch rode the mainstream and won. Calhoun saw the future and opposed it; Baruch saw the future and embraced it. Calhoun—a simple and intense man of thought —dealt with the America that was; Baruch—a complex and subtle man of action—dealt with the America that *is* today." It was nonsense, and had Baruch not been so anxious that his words of 1935 would reveal him as a racist and a bigot, Coit might not have written what she did. Yet the public ambiguity of their differences suggested more than the book revealed. Coit claimed that she really did not understand why Baruch took exception to the book, but she concluded that "perhaps I penetrated his own image of himself and came up with a portrait that he didn't want shown to the public." She would stick to writing about dead people after this experience.[103]

The Coit book was unfortunate for both. She was a young journalist who freely conceded that she knew nothing about economics, had never written a book on a twentieth-century topic, and agreed to write about Baruch only because she considered him the second greatest South Carolinian. Her most damaging criticism of Baruch was that he shirked responsibility in World War II by refusing the WPB and OES posts, a judgment suggested by Felix Frankfurter's interview with her. She considered biography "just as much a creative act as writing a poem or a novel, as long as your heart is in it." Baruch should have seen the problems that would develop, had he or his retainers given her Calhoun book a careful reading. He had a sincere commitment to facts, but he wanted to forget the ugly ones. He possessed a philosophy of history and an interpretation of his times, but he selected a biographer incapable of understanding them. He had been fair neither to her nor to himself, something he admitted to her: "Looking over the whole matter it may be that it was not entirely wise to write a biography of a person still living. Also, in writing about my career which has been so complex in government, economics, national and international affairs, a grasp of these subjects is as important perhaps as sheer writing ability. A proper evaluation may require time even for the best informed." A few years later he called her to say, "Margaret, you never wrote a dishonest word."[104]

Baruch's book was a best seller for many weeks in 1957–58 because it dealt primarily with his speculative career. As President Eisenhower observed, the critics "find all its dramatic interest in the makings of millions; I was more absorbed in those portions of your book that dealt with your family relationships." Ike notwithstanding, Baruch's fabled wealth sold his book. In the words of one reviewer, "Nothing bores the American public more than economics, and if Baruch has used his personality to keep before the public large economic issues he has performed a service by no means negligible."[105]

In his second volume, Baruch's purpose was greater than a mere recounting of his Washington activities from Wilson through Eisenhower days. It would describe and interpret his times, "what I was a part of," he told his publisher. "Why and what was done . . . and where we are today. Not what kind of man Baruch was but what took place of which he was a part." The events were paramount, and he was intent upon drawing lessons for the public from his activities. His central message was clear: laissez-faire was dead, but it had not yet been replaced by a dedication to self-discipline through planning and organization. Voluntary cooperation bred selfishness and chaos. Freedom was not incompatible with discipline; discipline secured liberty from the ravages of disorder. By no means was he prepared to embrace statism. Baruch's discipline would not be imposed by Washington, but must come from individuals; and here Americans confused self-discipline with nearly anarchic voluntary cooperation. It was a losing argument. He told "a plain unvarnished tale . . . of my failures as well as what little successes I have had."[106]

The *New York Times* had ever been Baruch's critical friend; even his obituary had long since been written with the editorial approval of Krock and Swope. Coit's book was reviewed there by Baruch's former retainer Adolf A. Berle, Jr., who praised it with quibbles concerning her interpretation of Wilson's New Freedom. *My Own Story* was reviewed by Krock, Baruch's publicist of nearly forty years. The daily critic of the *Times* devoted two columns to a joint review of the Coit and Baruch books, "the year's outstanding battle of the books." When *The Public Years* came out in 1960, the *Book Review* assigned Arthur M. Schlesinger, Jr., liberal chronicler of *The Age of Roosevelt*, to review it. In a review that had the sound of critical integrity, he pointed out mistakes and oversights in the book and labeled its predecessor "an amiable and diffuse . . . degeneration of the genre." Nevertheless, recognizing that *The Public Years* drew heavily upon Baruch's papers, Schlesinger hailed it as "on the whole . . . a valuable record of an impressive public career."[107]

In *The Public Years*, Baruch had the benefit of histories and memoirs written before his, and he consciously tried to support or refute what others had said where it was called for. In many ways, his book, researched and largely written by Epstein, was what Baruch thought Coit's book ought to have been: in fact, he omitted embarrassments he had feared she would reveal (though she did not). It was a solid memoir based upon sound research through a large portion of the extensive Baruch collection of papers.

The Baruch papers then attracted the attention of archivists and university presidents. Herman Kahn, director of the Franklin D. Roosevelt Library, had attempted to acquire them in 1949; Eleanor Roosevelt interceded in Kahn's behalf, but the effort was doomed. Baruch was conscious of whose papers were where—and he was not interested in sharing a library with Morgenthau, Winant, and Hopkins, least of all Hopkins. He was ever a Wilson man, and the Wilson papers were at the Library of Congress Manuscript Division. Through the 1950s his staff organized Baruch's papers, and in 1958, Baruch made a decision which he explained to the director of the Library of Congress:

> I have willed my papers to the Library of Congress which I think should have all papers. I do not think they should be used to establish memorials, or put in buildings that are difficult for historians to visit.
>
> I can see no reason, certainly not at the present time, for changing my plans.

The following year he reiterated his own "preference" for giving his papers to the Library of Congress; taking notice of Princeton University's quest to acquire the Woodrow Wilson papers, he told Wilson's widow that Princeton was entitled only to copies of the Wilson correspondence, not the letters themselves.[108] But very old men can easily forget and Baruch in his nineties found himself the object of blandishments and pleas for his papers from Columbia, Duke, and Yale universities. To all he stipulated that a governing factor in any irrevocable decision would be their holdings of other collections and use of research grants to encourage scholarly use. Through the efforts of New York banker Dean Mathey and others, including Krock, who considered himself a Princetonian because he had spent one semester there many years ago, Baruch began to change his mind concerning Princeton.

On 14 November 1963, David E. Lilienthal visited Baruch in New York and was told that Baruch's papers would be going to Princeton's proposed "Center for Studies in Twentieth Century American Statecraft and Public Policy." The Library of Congress was eager to have the papers but, Baruch said, "I didn't want them to be put in a mausoleum and that's what the Library of Congress is. I want the papers to be somewhere where they will be used by students so we put all that into the contract with Princeton." Six days later he wrote to President Robert F. Goheen of Princeton that he was donating his papers to the university because of "the use which it will make of these papers but, also, . . . the association which Princeton and I share with President Wilson." Yet it remained to be seen if Princeton could satisfy Baruch's conditions. The university envisioned Baruch's collection as a lure for acquiring other collections, and seemed unwilling to make the center more than a name on a door. In the end, Harold Epstein advised his ninety-three-year-old boss, it all came down to "the good faith and conscientiousness" of Princeton. Baruch brooded on it and finally agreed that his papers would go to Princeton. On 9 May 1964 his decision was announced. He hoped it would ensure his historical identification with Wilson.[109]

AMERICAN JEW

Baruch was identified as an American Jew—a fact of his existence that is central to his story and, because of his well-cultivated prominence, one that usually includes him in any history of the Jews in America. But Baruch's Judaism is something he lived with, rather than lived. He defined it, and like many aspects of his thinking, it emerged as a collage of contradictions. He was not religious; but almost nothing could interrupt his observance of Yom Kippur, the Day of Atonement. He lectured fellow Jews on the importance of being an American before being a Jew; yet he supported many Jewish causes and did nothing to detract from his reputation among both Gentiles and Jews as a representative Jewish leader. He denounced all forms of bigotry and intolerance, including anti-Semitism; still, some of his best friends were anti-Semites. He was an early contributor to Zionist groups and sought a homeland for Europe's homeless Jews; but if he had had his way, Palestine would never have become Israel and no Jewish state would exist. The "American Disraeli" was a Jew by birth and because it suited some of his purposes, but not because of his personal commitment. It was always important to Americans and to Baruch that he was a Jew, but during the destruction of European Jewry by the Nazis and the postwar drive for a Jewish homeland, his fellow Jews never could count upon the great Baruch to close ranks with them. "I know that [Baruch's] an upstanding Jew," Felix Frankfurter once told Swope, "but I sometimes wonder whether he isn't slightly kidding himself that he is in a different category, say, from Stephen Wise or Julian Mack. Have I ever told you the off-hand answer I made when Walter [Lippmann] and I had adjoining desks in Newton Baker's office, and Walter, resenting the charge that Baker was sur-rounded by Jews, asked 'What is a Jew anyhow?' 'Let me offer you this, Walter,' I replied, 'as a working definition: A Jew is a man whom non-Jews regard as a Jew.'" Baruch always brought out the self-righteousness in Frankfurter, but it was true enough that Baruch was a Jew because the world defined him as one and because he sometimes valued the heritage. He was a Jew when it suited him. In the words of one Jewish writer during the Holocaust, "From the Jewish point of view, Baruch has been what might be called a sleeper, not denying his Judaism, but making only glancing references to it."[110]

Baruch was religious only when it pleased others he wanted to please. It pleased his mother that he attended services on the High Holidays and did not do business. It pleased his wife that he allowed her to raise their children as Episcopalians. It pleased his public that he invoked godliness, religion, and spirituality as essential components of the American way of life. It pleased him to arrive late at High Holiday services at the West End Synagogue, a tall white-haired figure in command of the congregation's attention as he walked with dignity to his place of honor in the front row. Personally he distrusted religion. He regarded prayerful men in public life as untrustworthy. Baruch, who left instructions for his own cremation, was a Jewish agnostic.

He believed in the spirituality of enlightened secularism. Americanism and liberal capitalism were higher values than Judaism. Bigotry and intolerance would cease when people subscribed to the higher spirituality of the nation and the rules of the social system. Organized religion had its place when it reinforced secular spirituality and reinforced voluntary welfare activities, as opposed to government welfare activity. He con-tributed to the relief, education, and health activities of all the established religions—regardless of denomination.

Some of his most fervent defenses of Americanism and capitalism were delivered before Jewish or predominantly Jewish organizations. He was concerned with making Jews more American and diminishing their loyal-ties to Judaism. Although hesitant to identify himself too completely with the cause, Baruch used the launching of the United Jewish Appeal in 1946 as an occasion for lecturing Jews on why they ought to appreciate the United States in those early cold war years. Their country, he said, was confronted with "a great political and philosophical issue—statism versus individualism." Charity preserved "the system of personal initiative." Giving to great human welfare causes demonstrated that they lived by hard work and helpfulness—"that these are measures of social conscience." He conceded that capitalism "may not be the ultimate but it is the best thus far devised. . . . I believe in trying to better that system instead of tearing it down."[111]

It bothered him that so many Jews from eastern Europe were radicals. In the 1920s he had agreed with advocates of immigration restriction who sought to restrict the socialist Jews from Russia and Poland from American life. After World War II he was concerned with the communist threat and the fact that so many of America's communists and their "fellow travelers" were Jews. He followed Swope's counsel on which Jewish groups were "sometimes open to question" and supported only causes that demonstrated that he was, in Swope's words, "one of the Jewish faith, definitely opposed to the Reds." But as the anticommunist fervor reached a fever pitch during the McCarthyism of the 1950s, Baruch disregarded the liberal Swope and became a financial backer of the right-wing American Jewish Anti-Communist League. His contributions began in 1953 during the controversy over the pending execution of Julius and Ethel Rosenberg, and over the next decade he contributed at least $10,000 to the league's coffers, though he never allowed himself to be publicly affiliated with it. Obviously it lacked the liberal image he liked for himself, although its vigorous anticommunism was something that he believed American Jews ought to endorse.[112]

Baruch liked to remind people that his name meant "blessed" in Hebrew, which led some to conclude that he attended services only to hear his name mentioned frequently. He used his Jewishness to add to his fame and glory, making American Jews a special part of his "constituency." During World War I he had contributed to the American Jewish Relief Committee, and as his importance in the WIB grew, the estimable Jacob Schiff told him, "To me personally the lustre you are shedding upon our people is a source of special satisfaction." Jews were patriots and Jews admired Baruch as one of their kind who became a public leader and not merely a rich Jew. There were not many Jews then in public life with whom other Jews could identify. Harry Golden knew when he met Baruch in the early 1920s that he was "in the presence of a great Jew." His importance for American Jews grew with his prominence, something the Nazis and American Jew-haters added to by their attacks upon him as a representative Jew. For some haters the powerful Baruch was exempt: a North Carolina senator accused Jews of fomenting war with Hitler in 1939, but carefully sent word to Baruch via Jimmy Byrnes that he was not included in the accusation. Baruch's World War II reputation for sagacity blended well with his Jewishness. To one lady who urged President Truman to follow his advice he stood "like an ancient prophet of Israel"; a New York publisher found his ancient wisdom "Talmudic."[113] His public image flattered Jews. Gentiles and Jews both looked to him as a Jewish spokesman.

But when it came to Jewish causes, Baruch feared that he might be tabbed a "professional Jew," the term he and Swope used to brand those who identified themselves with peculiarly Jewish causes. He joined no Jewish organizations, and, even if he was one of the most famous Jews in America, no Jewish organization could make him an honorary chairman. He considered himself above special interests and concerned merely with the national interest. To identify with Jewish causes would be to abandon his pose as a "seemingly disinterested" sage and take on the role of "special pleader . . . a public advocate for a particular need." He did not object to accepting awards from Jewish organizations like the Zeta Beta Tau fraternity, which in 1950 hailed him as "the American who did the most for Jewry during the year," but he was selective and limited the number of awards. He contributed about $50,000 or more each year to Jewish philanthropies, more than he gave to other secular charities, thereby maintaining his Jewish identification on his terms. It always was on his terms. As he told a breakfast meeting of the Federation of Jewish Philanthropies in 1944, "I do not like classes or groups that come to-gether for special purposes, as opposed to the general good. I believe in the preservation of a broad front, without cleavages into special interests. But, charity is not special. Because, it is for another we give—not for ourselves, except for the joy of giving." Hailing him as "the leading Jew in America," Judge Joseph M. Proskauer appealed to Baruch a few years later on behalf of the federation; Baruch responded that he already had given, adding, "My contribution to Jewish charities is by no means my only contribution. I do what I can, and gladly, not as a Jew, but as an American citizen."[114]

Naturally, he was not a Zionist. Zionist and Israeli politicians usually sought him out, with decidedly mixed success. David Ben-Gurion once had the temerity to tell Baruch why he owed his support to the State of Israel and Baruch retorted that he was "more concerned with the stars and stripes than the Star of David." Likewise, he told Chaim Weizmann that he would not help Israel because "I do not think of myself as a Jew." (Weizmann responded, "Come Armageddon, you will be counted only as a Jew.")[115] But, since World War I, Baruch had supported Zionism with his money and his influence—on his terms, to be sure—and therefore Zionists never wrote him off as hostile.

Baruch felt compassion for the eastern European Jews victimized by pogroms or rendered homeless by the war in 1914–18 and gave gen-erously to the Zionist movement at that time. At the Paris Peace Confer-ence he told a Polish commissioner of his concern with "the Jewish question, and warned him to see that the Polish government should take some steps to stop the anti-Semitism." Perhaps, because his father came from Poland, he empathized with Polish Jewry. Like Jacob Schiff, he eschewed the anti-Zionism of some American Jews, countering it with a publicized $10,000 contribution to the Palestine Restoration Fund. When Albert Einstein came to America in 1921 to raise funds for Hebrew University in Jerusalem, Baruch was invited by the scientist to a meeting; responding that he had to be out of town on the day of the meeting, he inquired, "However, may I not come in some other time?"[116] He could not then be accused of shunning Zionist causes.

Even so, Baruch's aid to Zionism inspires cynicism. His cohorts from Wall Street were German Jews notoriously embarrassed by the wretched refuse from eastern Europe, their coreligionists who came by the millions between 1890 and 1920. As Eugene Meyer put it, until the Russian-Polish Jews came, "there never was a Jew in jail in New York State. Then there began to be criminals with this mass." In New York City's lower East Side, Meyer saw Jews who were only tradesmen, doing business with "somewhat less than what we consider good character." Baruch's New York and Washington friends had no wish to see any more of these Jews immigrating to the United States; they preferred an alternative refuge. That Baruch probably subscribed to this perspective is evidenced by his agreement with restrictionist views that would limit, if not shut off, the flow of Russian Jews into the United States during the 1920s.[117] He rejoiced in the British Balfour Declaration that promised a Jewish homeland in Palestine, but his later interests in refugee resettlement suggest something other than humanitarianism as a motivation.

The Nazi design to annihilate Europe's Jews in the late 1930s galvanized American Jews and Zionists. Baruch then dabbled heavily in foreign affairs, but his ideas on resettlement of refugees from the Nazis called for neither opening America's gates to Europe's persecuted Jews nor relocating them in Zion. As longtime Zionist Louis Brandeis commented, Baruch "would be more likely to consider colonization by Jews on some undiscovered planet than Palestine." He certainly was not about to add them to the rolls of America's unemployed during the depression. He helped a few Jews with professional talents find homes in America, and he gave aid to his father's family still living in Europe. However, he did not follow the advice of one man who had written Eleanor Roosevelt proposing the resettlement of European Jews in Montana. After all, in early 1937 it had appeared to Baruch that Hitler's only solution to the Jewish question was "to try to throw three million Jews out of Poland!" The magnitude of that project did not seem to necessitate an immediate American response. Although Roosevelt convened spring 1938 meetings in the White House with Baruch and others on the refugee question, nothing was forthcoming besides expressions of official concern. Jimmy Byrnes later urged the president to seek legislation to increase German immigration quotas as "the best evidence we could give to Hitler of our sincerity" in protesting his racial policies and giving Jews something more than "mere expressions of our sincerity." But Baruch himself kept aloof from protests and action that he feared would "only make things worse for Jews over there." He wanted to save the Jews of Europe, but he sought to avoid bringing them to his country. In that, he was not alone among prominent American Jews: presidential counsel Samuel Rosenman also urged Roosevelt not to create "a Jewish problem" in the United States by welcoming Hitler's victims.[118]

Never one for a small solution to a great conundrum, Baruch called for the creation of a "United States of Africa" as a haven for all of Europe's refugees. It would be a British protectorate, a responsibility London would be eager to have because the territory would consist of the Belgian Congo and Portuguese Angola, in addition to Kenya and Tanganyika; British imperial control of the dark continent would thereby be increased. Jews throughout the world would raise money for developing a modern capitalist society in the "United States of Africa." But Baruch did not advocate a Zionist homeland, for his pioneers in Africa would be "all kinds of people [and] not Jews alone," even if the bulk of Europe's current refugees were overwhelmingly Jewish. Baruch's non-Zionist sanctuary appealed to Rosenman, who did not want a "world ghetto" for Jews, and to GOP Representative Hamilton Fish, who publicly promoted it in 1939. Roosevelt was not about to endorse anything Fish crusaded for. Moreover, the Zionists among Jewish leaders were not about to pay for a British protectorate. World War II added urgency to the Zionist cause, but Baruch persisted in his African solution. Even after the war he hoped that it could be revived as an alternative to a Jewish homeland in Palestine.[119]

The Zionists saw it differently. In 1943, following Baruch's million dollar contribution to war relief, Rabbi Stephen Wise appealed to him to earmark some money for resettling Jewish refugees in Palestine. Baruch eventually gave Wise $1,000, but not before lecturing him on the importance of aiding refugees "who want to work out their destiny, not segregated, but alongside others working for civilization." The Zionists wanted Roosevelt to bring pressure upon the British to ease restriction upon Jewish immigration to Palestine, but the situation there was complicated by Arab resistance, British ambitions for Near Eastern oil, and U.S. State Department reluctance to incur Arab wrath by assisting Zionists. Roosevelt himself was unsympathetic. Before Roosevelt met with King Ibn Saud of Saudi Arabia in 1945, Baruch called Zionist publicist Ben Hecht and urged that he "call off further criticisms of President Roosevelt and his administration—until you hear from me again." He asserted that Roosevelt's forthcoming trip abroad "will settle the Jewish problems in the Near East to my satisfaction—and yours." Of course that was unlikely, and indeed, Roosevelt's statements following the Ibn

Saud meeting were favorable to the Arab perspective. Hecht then called Baruch to inform him that the moratorium on Zionist agitation was ended. As Hecht told it,* Baruch responded: "I have had a two-hour talk with President Roosevelt about the Jews and the Jewish problem. I have spoken also to Governor Dewey on the same subject. I can only tell you as a result of these talks that, despite my having been a lifelong Democrat, I would rather trust my American Jewishness in Mr. Dewey's hands than in Mr. Roosevelt's."[120]

Zionists knew that Baruch's Jewishness was not something they could trust. He kept his lines to the Zionists open, giving them enough encouragement to believe that his influence could be used for their cause. In early 1946 his sole acknowledgment of Europe's Jewish remnant was a declaration that "a place must be found for all displaced peoples of every religion and race who cry out from hunger and from despair of their future." But he did not then suggest a place—or agree with the Zionists on Palestine. Still, he could not ignore an idea that was making history without him. He told Zionist leader Abba Hillel Silver that if he wanted Washington's support for a homeland he would have to "get the Jews of Brooklyn and the Bronx muttering in their beards" against the Democratic administration that vacillated in its Near East policy. The 1946 Democratic setbacks, along with Zionist petitions in behalf of free Jewish migration to Palestine, provided sufficient "mutterings" to demonstrate that Jews were prepared to vote and fight for a homeland. Baruch was impressed. Once the Zionists had gone pleading to the great Baruch; now it was he who went to Ben Hecht to declare, "I'm on your side. . . . The only way the Jews will ever get anything is by fighting for it. I'd like you to think of me as one of your Jewish fighters in the tall grass with a long gun. I've always done my best work that way, out of sight."[121]

However, he did go public. "As an American and, after that, as a Jew—I have been shocked to the heart by the treatment accorded the pre-war and post-war refugees, particularly the Jews," he told an audience in late 1946. "I am not a political Zionist. But . . . I deplore and condemn the shilly-shallying and weathervaning of the British and, too, the American governments, regarding the right of haven that was to have been accorded these unfortunates under the Balfour Declaration." Baruch's outrage was sincere enough, as was his concern for refugees. But his public condemnation was mostly targeted against a Labour government in Britain that he despised. And his espousal of refugee havens,

---

*Baruch denied Hecht's account in a letter he did not send. "As you know, I never could have said any such thing to Hecht. Nor do I use that kind of language." But, he told Eleanor Roosevelt, FDR "told me of his great disappointment in not having been able to move Ibn Saud." Baruch also told Elliott Roosevelt that his father had agreed not to take any action adverse to Arab interests. Baruch to Mrs. Roosevelt, late July 1955 (not sent), Selected Correspondence, Baruch Papers; Elliott Roosevelt, *As He Saw It* (1946), p. 245.

whether in Zionist Palestine or his never wholly abandoned "United States of Africa," was also intended as a lure for "those left behind the Iron Curtain."[122]

When the United Nations partitioned Palestine and guaranteed there a Jewish state, Rabbi Silver was moved to acclaim Baruch one of "the leaders of American public opinion who have given their support to this noble cause." Increasingly, Baruch began to live up to Silver's praise. "I know the arguments, pro and con, for Palestine," he told Swope. "The arguments now are of no avail because the Rubicon has been crossed." He was moved by the Zionists' determination and ability to muster political support. He personally warned his friend Secretary of Defense Forrestal that the Democrats would lose politically if they played the British game of arming the Arabs to crush the Jews in Palestine. As he complained to Swope and Warren Austin, American policy on Palestine was "weathervaning" between the moral position of supporting the Jewish quest and the political one of backing the "Anglophiles" who wanted to protect British oil resources in the Near East. That policy, he told a Bronx audience, was "a mistake." Baruch used his influence with Secretary of State George C. Marshall to gain American backing for an extension of Israeli territory to the Negev Desert over British objections. So moved was Silver by Baruch's 1948 activities that he sought to make him the United Jewish Appeal's honorary chairman, but Baruch declined on the ostensible grounds that he could "be of more help on the outside."[123]

Relations between the Israelis and Baruch were never as warm as the former wished. He refused to serve as a congressional lobbyist for bills that would give aid to Israel. It was just another foreign government to him. His belated endorsement of the Zionist cause had been predicated upon humanitarian feelings for refugees and an expedient willingness to hector a British government he did not approve of. In the 1950s, however, he performed another *volte-face* and began to boast of his decades-old support of Zionist hopes. He praised Israel as "the greatest spiritual adventure for 2000 years." Swope diligently sought to embellish Baruch's public identification with the American Jewish community, although the Old Man restrained his publicist's more exuberant efforts. Disliking the sectarianism of Jews, he considered himself an enlightened universal humanist. At age eighty-six he told Henry Luce, "In no sense a deeply religious man, I have tried to remember what all religious teachers have preached—real understanding of our fellow man."[124]

Baruch's anxiety concerning the completion of his memoirs and the disposition of his papers was a sign that even he did not believe that Baruch could go on much longer. For over a year in 1956–57 he suffered from lack of appetite with consequent weight loss, and in 1957 he believed that his end was near. Inviting James B. Conant to visit soon, he urged, "And don't wait too long[,] Doc, for time is running out on me." The next day he told John Snyder that he hoped for a reconciliation with former President Truman: "I am 87 years of age and I do not want to go away and leave any unpleasantness behind me." It was not a face he showed the world. He was unafraid of death, but he did not like to betray doubts concerning his own prospects. By the end of that year, however, he was again reminding Churchill that the two of them still could solve most of the world's problems. In 1958 he became embroiled in a fight over the administration's fiscal policy. "Apparently you're as firm as a rock in Ability and in Work," Swope marveled. "Others are weakening. . . . But you're a Flaming Torch." On the other hand, Swope was depressed. He focused upon the illnesses of his wife and friends and talked of entering "the danger zone" and worrying all the time. Baruch was twelve years his senior and apparently indifferent to the perils of age. "I wish I had your imperturbability," Swope wrote him. "Did you notice the other day that the *New Republic* referred to me as 'the late HBS'?" Less than a month later someone in Baruch's office wrote at the bottom of that letter, "Herbert B. Swope died June 20, 1958." Swope's passing personally affected Baruch but in no way diminished his zest for participation in public affairs. In a few months he told Eisenhower that at eighty-eight years of age, "My thoughts are of the future."[125]

Although his health was beginning to deteriorate and the death of relatives and friends was an omnipresent fact of his life, he did not hesitate to make plans for himself. In his seventies he had retrenched a bit, selling his New York house and moving to a Fifth Avenue apartment. He remained quite active in the stock market. He had a passion for correspondence and, ever hating to be alone, often entertained at dinner in grand style—black tie and dinner jacket, attended by butler and another server. His women guests found such occasions quite memorable; he was handsome, charming, loquacious, and, as he discussed his famous friends past and present, an utterly romantic figure. Helen Lawrenson was served brandy after dinner from a bottle covered with dust and cobwebs and remarked that he should have the bottle dusted once in a while. "I see you're just as stupid as ever," he growled playfully. "You and Churchill are the only ones who have had this brandy." In his early nineties he was physically active. In South Carolina during the winter he hunted or at least shot every day and swam in the summer. South

Carolina without guests could be boring. Elizabeth Navarro, his nurse-companion from 1945 to his death, was with him always, amusing him with canasta when he could not sleep during the night hours. As he told Doris Fleeson, "The rest of the time I just sit and sit and sit and contemplate my navel. I should be glad to have you join me in any of these pastimes except the latter." He was an exhibitionist in the matter of his elderly vigor. Once when he was asked by reporters how he hurt his back, he answered, "Don't do a back flip from the high board." Judging by the many letters he wrote by hand, he had good control. "You thrill me by what you say of riding on horseback and on foot [sic] to shoot quail," Churchill wrote the eighty-five-year-old Baruch. Baruch traveled a great deal. At eighty-nine he did what he usually did in the summer: sailed for Britain for a six-week holiday that included a visit to Churchill.[126]

Still, his activity meant that there was much to ignore. Within two weeks of each other in 1953 his brothers Hartwig and Herman died. His third brother, Sailing, died in 1962. Baruch had become a survivor. Even a daughter, Belle, died in April 1964; she was sixty-four. When Churchill fell ill in 1958, Baruch readied a statement on his great friend's passing for the press, but Churchill recovered enfeebled. The day was approaching when nobody could reminisce with Baruch about how it was to run the war effort in 1917–18 and negotiate with the Allies and the Germans in 1919. John Foster Dulles died in 1959. A gaunt Baruch attended services for Herbert Hoover in October 1964; Baruch was the last Wilsonian.[127]

Into his early nineties, Baruch astonished everybody with his energy and outlook. At eighty-eight he wrote Lord Beaverbrook, "It is wonderful to have lived in the time which have been ours." At his eighty-ninth birthday newspaper interview, Baruch turned in a virtuoso performance; the *Times* man hailed him as radiating "charm and cordiality . . . [while] crotchety and obliging in masterly proportions." Asked to prescribe for the world, Baruch shrewdly answered, "Nothing is so terrible as a man who gets old and tries to tell everybody what to do." In 1960 he confessed that he was slowing down a bit. "I seldom get that second bird on the covey rise," he informed a former hunting companion. "I can't hit them so well, but I sure can scare them." He met reporters on the eve of his ninetieth birthday, declaring, "I feel wonderful. But I have done everything a man is not supposed to do." His only serious word on that occasion was a warning on inflation. A year later he informed the press that he had been swimming that morning and probably would swim again in the afternoon. "While I can't run 100 yards, or even ten yards," the ninety-one-year-old said, "I'm still breathing, as you can see." He obviously enjoyed talking with reporters. Several months later he responded to a question concerning President Kennedy's plan for medical aid for the elderly, "You'll have to ask someone older than I am." The phone also provided him with an instant audience: "David, this is Baruch calling from Kingstree. I have read your thing on disarmament..." Lilienthal noted that Baruch's voice was strong and firm at ninety-two, that he had not forgotten to ask about his son or about J. Robert Oppenheimer. His mind was clear and engrossed with individuals and events. At ninety-three he eschewed his usual birthday interview, if only because his views were "pretty well known." But he could not resist one affirmation: "I will say, however, that I still have faith in the future of this country, and confidence that we can solve the difficult problems besetting us if we use half the reason with which we are endowed." That summed him up quite well: nationalist, optimist, rationalist. "I noticed you cancelled your press conference this time," President Kennedy wrote Baruch. "I am sure you could handle mine tomorrow."[128]

But the years showed on his body, if not his mind. His hearing was the least of his problems. He had arthritic pains in his hips, legs, and ankles. Hospitalized for two months, he did not go to Europe as planned in 1962. Yet he roused himself to address an Electrical Workers convention at age ninety-three (on the subjects of inflation and self-discipline, of course). Always bantering and irascible with Helen Lawrenson, he responded to her question concerning a trip with "Listen, Madame Fathead, you don't have much fun when you're ninety-two." "How are you?" Dorothy Schiff asked when he called her after she appeared on a news broadcast; he said, "At ninety-three I can only look and admire you on television." He no longer hunted: "My eye and my hand haven't failed, but I find that my legs won't permit me to keep up with the dogs. Still I shouldn't complain, were it not for the pains of arthritis, I would feel like a boy of 70."[129]

He also suffered from the departure of friends. A Victorian affair came to an end when Eleanor Roosevelt died in November 1962. "Please always remember I have the highest regards and the deepest affection for you which has never lessened over the years," he had told her a couple of years before. When he could not keep an appointment in the last year of her life he wired, "I will be with you in spirit if not in flesh." Between them there was a warmth of mutual admiration that could only be suggested in his press statement that followed her passing: "Mrs. Roosevelt's death is a blow to me; we were friends for almost fifty years. I will miss her greatly as will all her friends and the millions of men and women in every country to whom she was the First Lady of the World. She was a rare combination of wisdom and goodness." When he was asked by Adlai Stevenson to serve on the board of directors of the Eleanor Roosevelt Foundation, the man who seldom accepted any such position responded, "I feel I cannot refuse this."

With physical deterioration and the passing of old comrades a commonplace in his existence, depression might have followed. But there is no outward evidence that Baruch had any mental problems. Lilienthal visited him in November 1963 and came away astounded by the alertness of "a mind that sorts out the important and the unimportant." Baruch at ninety-three seemed as forward-looking as a man of forty and possessing much more wisdom.[130]

Incredibly, the Old Man remained a political force. Nobody in public life who was just a little cognizant of his history and appreciative of his value as a publicist dared ignore him. Although Eisenhower disappointed him because his administration was "as inflationary as the others," their personal relationship was excellent. In the middle of the 1956 campaign, Eisenhower was able to call upon him for a public endorsement, even as Baruch aided the campaigns of Democratic senatorial candidates. He repeatedly clashed with both Eisenhower and the Senate Democratic leadership over fiscal policy. Even so, his calls were returned and his memoranda given recognition.[131]

He sat on the fence during the 1960 campaign, but that was not for lack of effort by Kennedy. The candidate assigned former OPA economist John Kenneth Galbraith, whom Baruch admired for his occasional espousal of price controls, to the task of securing Baruch's public endorsement. Baruch was doubtful of the ability of either Nixon or Kennedy to restrain inflation, but especially, he told Raymond Moley, he wanted "someone to whom I knew I would be able to talk." He did not want to see Galbraith only; he wanted accessibility to Kennedy.*
Kennedy's inaugural address, with its appeal for Americans to put country above themselves in a long struggle against communism, greatly impressed him. "If he had said that in the campaign, you and I would have been hustling for him," Baruch told Harry Byrd. Baruch knew few people in the new administration, but they soon made certain that they knew him. Assistant secretaries from the Treasury and Agriculture departments visited him in March 1961. The Kennedy people went out of their way to court this very special nonagenarian. Following his confirmation for the post of ambassador to India, Galbraith told Baruch that he had profited

---

*During the 1960 campaign, publicist Tex McCrary told Baruch, "*After* the Election, you will be the most important single man in the Free World. It doesn't matter whether Kennedy or Nixon wins, either will have to sit down with you and seek your guidance so that you can say to America: 'This young man will do his best for America. I shall try to help him.'" 18 October 1960, Selected Correspondence, Baruch Papers. As for the Kennedy motivation in seeking out Baruch's blessing during the 1960 campaign, Galbraith wrote me: "This had elements of ritual, although we were all, including Kennedy, disposed to be agreeable to a major figure, even one so skillfully self-enhanced. . . . There was a great effort to get Baruch to support Kennedy, and, indeed, I was the person designated for the effort. We did get a contribution of modest size, which, in Baruch's case, was an assurance that he would not endorse the other side." 31 August 1979.

National Kibitzer

from their recent exchange of ideas and added, "I am perhaps also indebted to you for the unanimous Senate vote in my behalf yesterday." Even if Baruch swung only one vote in the Senate, that made him important to a president who had won as narrowly as had Kennedy.[132] He had retained his accessibility to the White House.

Kennedy knew the value of Baruch, and the Old Man tried to speak only well of the young president. In the midst of the Berlin crisis of 1961, Baruch was invited to the White House to confer with the president on mobilization and other matters. Kennedy found their talk "charming," and Baruch was never too old to enjoy playing informal liaison. In October he had a routine conversation with Soviet Foreign Minister Andrei Gromyko, from which Baruch attempted to draw some significance. Baruch was more enthusiastic about Kennedy's policies than he had been about those of any president since Wilson: he cheered Kennedy's partial mobilization of armed forces, his antiinflation guidelines, and his call for a careful review of the nation's stockpile of strategic materials. He was visited by Undersecretary of the Treasury for Monetary Affairs Robert V. Roosa and Director of Emergency Planning Edward A. McDermott. Secretary of Defense Robert S. McNamara and his deputy, Roswell Gilpatric, were on their way to Baruch's apartment when they were summoned back to Washington at the outbreak of the Cuban missile crisis. It was Baruch who tipped off Walker Stone, editor-in-chief of Scripps-Howard newspapers, that Secretary of the Treasury C. Douglas Dillon would resign. In 1962, Baruch still provided "generous assistance" to Democratic senatorial candidates, as he had done for decades. The world had not forgotten him. Eric Sevareid trekked to Baruch's summer home on Long Island to interview him for "CBS Reports." He savored the briefings received from government officials. As much as ever, he was egotistical, telling Roosa, "If I were only eighty years old, and they would give me the job, I would give you a balanced budget by 1964 or eat the Washington Monument." Roosa and John J. McCloy took his ideas seriously. A McCloy memo asked, "Is not Baruch right when he says we have to establish priorities just as we did in the hot war?"[133]

Baruch was opinionated and unrestrained from taking his opinions to the White House. He objected to the administration's acquiescence when Canada sold wheat to China. The launching of two Russian cosmonauts into space brought disapproval of space programs in general: "The pity is all this human ingenuity and bravery and all this wealth which both we and the Soviet Union are devoting to the conquest of space couldn't be devoted to improving life on this planet." He predicted that England would have to be admitted to the Common Market. Test bans of nuclear weapons were ridiculed because he doubted their effectiveness in keeping further nations from acquiring such weapons. He never liked tax cuts because they were inflationary, as he reminded Galbraith in October 1963. "A President is likely to find himself differing at times from even his most respected and experienced advisers," President Kennedy wrote him. "I hope that even in the cases where we disagree, I will continue to have the benefit of your thoughts." He got them.[134]

Gracious deference to Baruch continued following the assassination of Kennedy. "How glad I am that you are already at work, as ever, in giving friendly counsel to our new boss," McGeorge Bundy wrote him. Lyndon B. Johnson was no stranger to Baruch. Within weeks of becoming president, Johnson entertained the ninety-three-year-old Baruch at the White House and followed that visit up with a note: "I have always regarded and shall continue to regard you as one of the finest minds in this country. Your advice and opinions mean a great deal to me. You would do me a great honor if, anytime you so desired, you would consider my White House office your park bench." Beneath his signature, Johnson added in pen, "Call National 8-1414 and ask for Jack Valenti when you wish to talk to me."[135] It was the right gesture to a Democratic talisman whom Johnson seldom heeded.

By early 1964, Baruch had troubles with his kidneys, and his dependence upon a catheter limited his public appearances. It constrained him. "I am not going to say anything publicly, politically or economically," he told Galbraith. "I feel that I have written all I can. Of course my mind and views are open to you." He would be quiet because it was all in the record. Perhaps most painful, he was out of touch with anything beyond what the newspapers told him. But he was irrepressible; in 1964 he wrote a letter to the *New York Times* espousing a high court of commerce to deal with labor-management conflicts. In August 1964, wearing a hat, topcoat, and silk scarf in a shirt-sleeved crowd, Baruch toured the New York World's Fair for two hours in an open taxi as the guest of Robert Moses. He smiled, shook the hands of other fair goers, made little quips, and told a young couple, "Don't ever grow old. Stay young always." He still retained some bravado, but sometimes the awful burden of time intruded. "Do you feel 94 years old today?" he was asked at his annual birthday press conference. "Yes, I do," he said. "I feel whatever it is." Two years before, he had gone bird hunting, but now he said, his fingers lacing as he spoke, "I can't keep up with the dogs, I can't keep up with the birds, and I can't keep up with the people." How did he spend his time? "I sit by and think and think and think," he said.[136]

He thought about many things current to the world, but he also gave death more consideration than before. He had his funeral instructions typed, read them, and then crossed out the lines "and that there should be no eulogy. Services are to be private." Then he wrote: "I wish my remains to be cremated. The ashes to be placed at the foot of my wife's grave." He still possessed intact his vanity and convictions. In his last

18. At 94 Baruch still makes his point. (Courtesy Seeley G. Mudd Manuscript Library, Princeton University)

year, while he was ill, Cardinal Spellman, a neighbor in their Fifth Avenue apartment building, dropped in and found him dozing. Thinking his end was near, the cardinal began to administer last rites to his Jewish friend. But the slumbering Baruch heard the ritual and, enraged by this affront to his conscience, ordered the cardinal from his apartment. "The old reaper is swinging his scythe and coming closer and closer but he hasn't hit me yet," he boasted to a newspaper friend.[137]

Baruch's mind was on political developments as well as on his impending demise. He contributed to 1964 Democratic campaigns for the Senate. He was inspired to praise Russell Baker of the *Times* for his incisive satire. Proposals for health insurance and medicare stirred him.* President Johnson's call for a voting rights act in March 1965 brought this telegram from Baruch, the old friend of racists: "As someone whose roots lie deep in the South I thought your speech historic. Everyone must have the right to vote." His temperament was that of the Baruch of forty years before. That same day he wired Jack Valenti, "Back from south for about ten days. Would like to get in touch with Ball of State and Connors of Commerce. May have some constructive suggestions." He cheered Johnson's escalation of the war in Vietnam, declaring that it would "reassure the world of your determination to meet American obligations and your dedication to achieving peace with honor and security." ("You and I both share the same purpose to make sure that freedom and decency and justice prevail and that communist subversion be turned back," Johnson answered.) Vietnam was the fifth American war of Baruch's lifetime. And three weeks before he died he was offering the administration his services as a publicist for the war.[138]

His death at the age of ninety-four, on 20 June 1965, of a heart attack, was duly reported on the front page of the *New York Times*. Jimmy Byrnes had been visiting him at the time and made the announcement, adding "He was my closest friend for forty years." New York City flew its flags at half-staff until after Baruch was interred. Three presidents of the United States—Johnson, Truman, and Eisenhower—paid tribute to him. Seven hundred people attended services for him at the former West End Synagogue, their numbers including a host of prominent Americans.

---

*Baruch congratulated Thomas Collins of the *Charlotte Observer* for his 4 February 1965 article on medicare, writing, "I thought your last two paragraphs were so good." They read: medicare "is one of the grave moral issues of our time. It is beyond the practical, and the economic. It gets into the realm of our religious beliefs, and what kind of people are we. Politics, the medical profession, and health insurance companies shouldn't decide it—our moral concepts should.

"Older people in this country are in urgent, painful need of better medical consideration than they are getting. Anybody who wants to dispute this will have to come up with something better than the 2,000 letters a month this column is getting from people who do the suffering."

Outside, another five hundred ordinary New Yorkers stood behind police barriers. Several of the other front-page stories in June 1965 reported the military and political developments in the Vietnam War, but there was practically nothing on stabilization policy.[139]

REPRISE AND CODA: "CIVILIZATION IS ORGANIZED SELF-RESTRAINT"

Before modern times, unemployment and inflation were considered polar conditions; planners could neutralize one by resorting to the other. Such a remedy—especially in moderate dosages—was considered salutary, as witness the early New Deal's administered inflation to conquer the plague of joblessness. Politicians and economists could take solace from the belief that *extreme* degrees of unemployment and inflation were simultaneously improbable. Thus, a conventional wisdom had grown that an economic wrong could correct another social wrong. Baruch tended to subscribe to older wisdoms, a fact that made him usually appear reactionary; following the Great Depression most Americans were convinced that the greater of social evils was unemployment, whereas Baruch still believed that the greater anathema was inflation. However, in 1958 it became apparent that the United States was experiencing immoderate increases in both unemployment and consumer prices. Still assuming a trade-off, Baruch gave inflation a higher priority among evils. This implausible condition ought to have suggested another: that Baruch could be concomitantly wrong on the dangers of unemployment and right on the nostrums for inflation.

Less than twenty years had passed since Americans had emerged from the Great Depression, and public opinion could be forgiven for nominating unemployment as the more traumatic of the economic bogeys confronting the country in 1958; but informed opinion, too, considered it the more cataclysmic of alternatives. The "new economics" of the time, a variety of Keynesianism Robert Lekachman calls commercial, took its cue from the *General Theory* of two score before and berated the Eisenhower administration for its apparent indifference to the jobless. John Kenneth Galbraith was one Keynesian inclined to balance the two evils, even if some of his best polemics castigated Republican deflationists as if every one of them wore a Hoover collar. Galbraith was an old warrior against inflation who believed that those who belabored the iniquities of higher prices were not necessarily Neanderthals: "Those who endorse an inflation of the modern sort are endorsing a policy of giving the most to the biggest and strongest and the least to the smallest and weakest. . . . The modern inflation is not neutral. Because of its inevitable identification with economic strength, it is inequitable, regressive, and reactionary." Galbraith earned Baruch's admiration and respect—approval

Baruch otherwise did not give the new economics. In turn, however, Galbraith was not inclined to consider Baruch anything more than "a man of self-inflicted self importance," and a friend of the Old Order who was useful to the New Frontier. Baruch, Galbraith would write after the Old Man's passing, was prominent on his list of "reliably hilarious [public] figures." "Magnificently fraudulent," in Galbraith's estimation, Baruch was "the most successful humbug since Henry Ward Beecher."[140]

In part these jibes stemmed from Baruch's reputation with some liberals as an influential ignoramus; of course, Baruch had intended his economic persuasion to reach the public as well as molders of public opinion. Informed opinion was academic and corporate; "Barney Baruch," Paul A. Samuelson has written, "was always, to insiders, a lightweight authority." Needless to say, Samuelson, a prize-winning academic of no small talents as a publicist himself, is unaware of the many insiders Baruch knew during his Washington career. In Samuelson's time, Baruch had become an outsider, and to certain adversaries, he was always a lightweight authority. To be sure, Baruch was not deeply intellectual. (Adlai E. Stevenson's spoken prose qualified him as a liberal intellectual in politics; ironically, we now know that this magnificent wordsmith was a more conservative man than most recognized and seldom read a book.) But, as Lekachman has written of Keynes, "It is possible to be an intellectual without being an economist and at least equally possible to be an economist without being an intellectual."[141] Baruch's talents as an economist went beyond the practical variety that any intelligent person might claim to possess. His analysis had insight and substance, his judgments were rational and sound, and he deserved the respectful hearing that informed and public opinion accorded him in his time.

In 1958, however, at a time when the jobless rolls were again lengthening, Baruch's focus on inflation seemed more of a monomania than a measured choice. But he had concluded that America's peace between Korea and Vietnam—in the midst of the trauma over Sputnik—required radical measures for stabilization. He knew that the national mood favored economic expansion, but he deeply believed that additional inflation was not in the national interest. "How much better off we would have been if only they had followed the stabilizers!" he had recently told the Korean War's stabilizer, Mike DiSalle. He did not prescribe comprehensive controls then, because, according to his diagnosis, Americans suffered more from the consequences of inflation than from inflation itself. Before Galbraith could warn informed opinion to "beware of the man who says, 'If you control anything, you must control everything,'" (who could he have meant?), Baruch was telling friends that under existing circumstances, "no over-all ceiling would do any good." Like Galbraith, Baruch espoused Washington's limited intervention in the price spiral through a strategy of "supervised self-regulation." In part this called for holding up to public contempt the malefactors of high prices. "The banks and the Federal Reserve System are now the most potent factors in the inflation," Baruch had advised Harry Byrd back in 1954; nearly three years later, Federal Reserve Chairman William McChesney Martin would concede that the lowering of the rediscount rate in 1954 had fomented inflationary psychology beyond what was warranted.[142]

Baruch's point was that inflation had its share of profiteers and victims; he would educate the latter, if he could, to understand how the former benefited at their expense. What disturbed him most was that big business preferred inflation's higher profits, regardless of the social consequences of inflation. In a concentrated corporate economy, what was good for the big banks, insurance companies, and steel producers was not good for unorganized white-collar workers, poor people, or pensioners—but nobody seemed to care. Baruch worried over his country's future because corporation executives worried only over their profits. "I do not think that big business men are showing any statesmanship in their eagerness to get greater profits which can only result in higher prices and less purchasing power, not alone for the average person but more particularly, the older people and those who have savings and pensions," he wrote. Insurance companies welcomed higher prices because they paid benefits in dollars cheaper than those they collected in premiums. Big steel companies and their unions knew that the costs of their higher prices and wages could be passed along to a vulnerable public, even if steel operated well below capacity. Baruch suggested a conspiracy of interest groups. Aside from the collaboration of big business and big labor to boost prices while they all subsidized unemployment, he was outraged by the indecent collusion between the Treasury and bankers to monetize the federal debt through the sale of short-term high-interest bonds that profited money changers at the expense of the public credit. It seemed to him that a consensus of interests had generated a psychology of mutual greed: "The various organizations like the Chambers of Commerce, the NAM and the Economic Development Committee [sic], are really nothing but pressure groups, aided and abetted by almost all the avenues of information."[143]

The consequences of this revolution in economic values and social attitudes staggered Baruch as he speculated on where they were heading the country. He remained quite firmly set in his Victorian attitudes. To him the modern lust for exorbitant profits amounted to an act of piracy against the national interest. "I have no patience with those who contend that any effort by the government to arrest inflation violates free enterprise," he told Eisenhower's secretary of defense. "Too often free enterprise is used as a cloak for free booting." Ever a staunch advocate of a stronger military, he could see the Pentagon's costs spiraling to the point where its preparedness would be jeopardized by prohibitive prices. He did not join business in blaming labor unions for higher costs. "It seems to me that the banking and business community," he told the chairman of the Guaranty Trust Company of New York, "as much as any other segment of our economy, has rejected the economic disciplines that sound money requires. . . . There is too much concern about the needs of business before the needs of government." He believed that this condition had incremental sources in World War II rather than in the current malaise. "The *Times* raising its Sunday Supplement [price] and you being forced to take ads," he told the publisher of the *Reader's Digest*, "the colleges to increase tuition—etc. are the results of our neglect and incompetence." He joined President Buell G. Gallagher of the tuition-free City College of New York in an effort to block Governor Nelson A. Rockefeller's effort to initiate tuition in 1959–61; the campaign to tax the poor for social services would have eventual success if inflation eroded government's ability to finance those services. He admonished an official of Blue Cross that his organization's indifference to inflation diminished the quality of health care for its subscribers. He sympathized with a proposed federal program that would subsidize health care for the elderly, he told its advocate in the Senate, but *"unless you stop inflation . . . , the aged and the crippled will never have the relief which you are interested in giving them."* The old patriot trembled at his nation's prospects when inflation would cause the dollar to "lose its position in the world."[144] His complaints had an antique quality to them—and yet they were eerily prophetic.

He knew that he was a public bore. As he commented to an old admirer late in 1958, his crusade against inflation "has not done me any good. A fellow writing me the other day said, 'You remind me of Cato. You always end up everything you say with some statement against inflation.'" It was true; he did. The habit alternately embarrassed and ennobled him. He yearned to be loved and admired by the public and he recognized that nobody loved a very old man who harped on the wrongs of youth. He wanted to be esteemed as a sage rather than deprecated as a fossil that had outlived his times. On the other hand, he retained values and knowledge that he considered timeless. He was enough of a rationalist to believe that basic laws of society and economics had not been made obsolete by contemporary conditions. "I have seen several versions of 'new economics' come and go in my life-time but none of these new theories have invalidated such fundamental laws as the law of supply and demand," he wrote. Even if excessive inflation and unemployment were now concurrent, the processes that brought them had not changed. (Or, as Galbraith put it, "We can't have a deficit in both depression and boom. Life is not yet that wonderful.")[145]

So he usually sounded his antiinflation refrain and let others wonder if he had entered his dotage. He did not espouse coercive action against prices unless the nation went to war. He did advocate informing the public of the looming dangers and mobilizing it against them. "After all, civilization is organized self-restraint," he said. In 1959 he would have organized the self-restraint of the community through the principle of "voluntary priority." He would have ended the collusion of the Treasury and the bankers by ending the sale of short-term government securities to the banks. He would have ended the collusion of big business and big labor through the establishment of a "priority committee" composed of government officials who represented the public interest in collective bargaining. However, he believed that no government body could repress inflation unless people appreciated that it was an ethical question. "It is this moral lethargy which has bred the atrocities of our time," he wrote Churchill. "We want moral valor. We have lost the sense of righteous indignation." He raged against the selfishness of producers and investors and against the indifference of politicians and other guardians of the public interest. Americans should, he averred, "think more of the de-cencies, duties and obligations of the country as a whole rather than . . . as groups and individuals."[146]

The first year of the Kennedy presidency renewed his optimism. He liked its move toward standby mobilization accompanied by price guide-lines for producers and workers. He urged administration officials not to be swayed by "critics constantly invoking free enterprise. What they really are interested in is freebooting, and the right to make excessive profits at the expense of the national interest." Any failures to curtail prices were not ascribed to Kennedy. Businessmen were "giving the Presi-dent lots of words but no deeds," Baruch told a friend. Bankers would not cooperate with Kennedy because they were too selfish. He preferred a Democrat in the White House if only because Democrats did not treat business institutions with such solemn approbation as did Republi-cans.[147] In 1964, Lyndon Johnson gave him high expectations that even then his own ego would be stroked no matter what economic policies were followed.

"Now the President has a terrific task before him," Baruch declared after the election. However, for the benefit of Johnson's majordomo, Jack Valenti, Baruch warned that "none of the President's goals will be achieved if we permit inflationary forces to break loose again." As it had been with Kennedy and Eisenhower, Baruch found it difficult to be dis-agreeable with a president who so graciously welcomed him to the White House. He endorsed Johnson's intervention in the Dominican Republic and the escalation in Vietnam, although he hoped that with the former the United States would "find a way to support legitimate reform move-ments and at the same time prevent the Communists from taking over" and that with the latter, Johnson would seek to "have a bill on the books to permit the President to put economic mobilization into effect." In this

respect, Baruch had been consistent and coherent in his recommendations. Now, about a month from his end, he responded to John Hay
Whitney's quest to raise funds for a medical research building. "I note
with regret, though not with surprise, that you have had to increase your
goal by five million dollars," Baruch wrote. "If any evidence were needed
to document the results of inflation, which I have been talking about for
more years than I care to remember, you have it here. The hospitals, the
colleges, and other institutions are all in the same boat, and yet I've seen
none of them try to make a fight."[148] Baruch had made the good fight
against inflation, and he had lost it. Yet time would tell how accurate
he had been as a speculator.

 NOTES

ABBREVIATIONS USED IN NOTES

BMB   Bernard M. Baruch
FDR   Franklin D. Roosevelt

From the Baruch Papers, Mudd Library, Princeton University:
SC   Selected Correspondence
GC   General Correspondence
PP   Public Papers
CND   Council of National Defense Papers
WIB   War Industries Board Papers
ACNP   American Commission to Negotiate Peace Papers
NIC   National Industrial Conference Papers
WF   Washington File, 1942–45
AE   United Nations Atomic Energy Commission Papers

From the Franklin D. Roosevelt Library, Hyde Park, New York:
OF   Official File, Franklin D. Roosevelt Papers
PPF   President's Personal Papers, Roosevelt Papers
ER   Eleanor Roosevelt Papers

COHC   Columbia University Oral History Collection

CITATION OF SOURCES

This book was planned and written to appeal to the general reader as well as the historian. Accordingly, the scholarly apparatus has been kept to a minimum, and the documentation is presented as simply as possible. To keep the text uncluttered, the sources for quotations and other items are often summarized in notes covering several paragraphs. Sources in each note are generally given in the order in which the information being documented appears in the text; by matching text and notes, the scholar should be able to discern reasonably readily the source for any particular item.

References to diaries are given usually by date or by date, volume, and page;

however, the Ickes Diary is cited by page number only, because the entries are weekly and a week tends to cover many pages.

The Morgenthau Diaries, so called, are actually a set of records kept by Henry Morgenthau, Jr., which are now located in the Franklin D. Roosevelt Library. Included are such matters as copies of letters and memoranda of meetings and telephone calls.

Citations to the Columbia Oral History Collection generally give just name and page number. References to the Henry A. Wallace project, however, sometimes includes dates identifying portions of Wallace's diary that have been incorporated into the record.

CHAPTER ONE

1. "Address delivered by invitation of the Legislature of the State of South Carolina at a Joint Session of the Legislature on April 7, 1931, at Columbia, S.C.," PP.
2. David E. Lilienthal, *The Journals of David E. Lilienthal: The TVA Years* (1964), p. 225.
3. Harry Golden, *The Right Time* (1969), p. 259.
4. Bernard Baruch, *My Own Story* (1957), pp. 32—35; BMB to James Forrestal, 23 August 1946, Forrestal Papers. (Unless otherwise cited, information in this chapter is taken from Baruch's memoir.)
5. Baruch, *My Own Story*, p. 24; Anderson Diary, 17 May 1918.
6. *New York Times*, 8 December 1912.
7. Baruch, *My Own Story*, p. 24; BMB to Edwin F. Gay, 21 March 1921, GC.
8. Baruch, *My Own Story*, p. 55.
9. Frances B. Sayre to BMB, 11 November, BMB to Sayre, 23 October 1956, SC; "Where the Frontier Still Lives, Address of Mr. Bernard M. Baruch," 8 October 1953, PP.
10. Baruch, *My Own Story*, p. 78.
11. Ibid., pp. ix, 55, 90—92.
12. Ibid., pp. 233—36; Richard Washburn Child, "Baruch and the Grim Job," *World's Work* 36 (June 1918): 187—88; James P. Warburg, COHC, p. 347.
13. Bernard Baruch, *The Public Years* (1960), pp. 26—31; Eugene Meyer, Jr., COHC, pp. 217—19.
14. Baruch, *My Own Story*, pp. 105, 84—85.
15. John Hersey, "The Old Man: A Day at Saratoga," *New Yorker*, 3 January 1948, p. 33; Robert Moses, *Public Works: A Dangerous Trade* (1970), p. 910; Emory S. Land, COHC, p. 190; statement of Donald R. McLennan, WIB.
16. Isador Lubin to FDR, 23 April 1941, Roosevelt Papers, OF 238, Box 1; BMB to Samuel Crowther, 13 March, 24 November 1920, GC; statement of William Denman, WIB; "Memo of a Conversation with Mr. Baruch, November 4, 1926," Edwin F. Gay Papers, Box 2; Hersey, "The Old Man," p. 33.
17. Gay Diary, 22 January 1919.
18. John Harriman, "The Inscrutable Mr. Baruch," *Atlantic Monthly*, February 1958, pp. 72—74; "Citizen Baruch," *Newsweek*, 30 November 1942, p. 42; Grosvenor Clarkson to BMB, 23 July 1919, GC, Council of National Defense folder; statement of C. M. Wooley, WIB; Samuel Lubell, "The Government's Unofficial Trouble Shooter," *Saturday Evening Post*, 10 June 1950, p. 151; Raymond Moley, "Baruch and Inflation," *Newsweek*, 2 October 1950, p. 92.

19. Orris C. Herfindahl, *Copper Costs and Prices: 1870–1957* (1959), pp. 80–83.
20. BMB to Jane Ickes, 6 June 1952, SC; Meyer, COHC, p. 93.
21. Baruch, *My Own Story*, pp. 180–90.
22. Ibid., pp. 307–8.
23. Ibid., p. 192.
24. Ibid., pp. 305–7.
25. Merlo J. Pusey, *Eugene Meyer* (1974), pp. 10–11, 17, 32, 36–37, 40–41, 56, 69–70, 74, 87, 94, 114, 126–29; Meyer, COHC, p. 93.
26. Copy of Harmon V. Swart to Eleanor Roosevelt, SC.
27. See BMB correspondence in John Skelton Williams Papers, Boxes 26 and 32; BMB to John Hersey, 10 July 1947, SC.
28. It is summarized in Margaret L. Coit, *Mr. Baruch* (1957), pp. 128–30.
29. BMB to Henry Evans, 6 January, to R. Lancaster Williams, 6 January, to C. E. ter Meulin, 8 April, to Frank J. Goold, 7 December 1915, GC.
30. *New York Times*, 10 November 1915.
31. Mary Jane Martz, *The Many Lives of Otto Kahn* (1963), p. 123.
32. Helen Lawrenson, *Stranger at the Party: A Memoir* (1975), p. 135.
33. For example, see Anderson Diary, 30 December 1917.
34. Statement of C. M. Wooley, WIB; BMB to Helen Bingaman, 29 March 1962, SC.
35. Statement of John M. Hancock, 23 February 1921, WIB; August Heckscher, "Public Servant without Office," *Saturday Review*, 15 October 1960, p. 28; "All Out," *Time*, 12 May 1941, p. 17.
36. Warburg, COHC, p. 347; Lawrenson, *Stranger at the Party*, p. 133; Jonathan Daniels, *White House Witness, 1942–1945* (1975), p. 1.
37. C. K. Leith to Edwin F. Gay, 24 March 1919, Gay Papers, Box 1; David E. Lilienthal, *The Journals of David E. Lilienthal: The Atomic Energy Years, 1946–1950* (1964), p. 195; "Old Independence," *Time*, 28 June 1943, p. 17.
38. Copy of the Diary of Colonel Edward M. House, 23 September 1917, SC; Child, "Baruch and the Grim Job," p. 189; Moses, *Public Works*, p. 911.
39. BMB to Gordon Abbott, 11 November 1915, GC; Churchill material for 1931, SC; Auchincloss Diary, 24 September 1918; Joseph P. Lash, *Eleanor: The Years Alone* (1972), p. 242.
40. BMB to R. W. Austin, 7 October 1916, GC.
41. New York contributors to campaign of 1912, Henry Morgenthau, Sr., Papers, Box 15.
42. John J. Broesamle, *William Gibbs McAdoo: A Passion for Change, 1863–1917* (1973), pp. 46–51, 69–74; Baruch, *The Public Years*, pp. 4–9; copy of House Diary, 12 October 1912, SC.
43. Baruch, *The Public Years*, p. 11.
44. Copy of House Diary, 19 December 1912, SC; Maurice F. Lyons, *William F. McCombs: The President Maker* (1922).
45. BMB to George H. Flint, 1 December 1909, GC.
46. Quoted in Introduction by William E. Leuchtenburg in Woodrow Wilson, *The New Freedom* (1961), p. 7.
47. See John Morton Blum, *Woodrow Wilson and the Politics of Morality* (1956).
48. Wilson, *The New Freedom*, pp. 22–23, 19, 32, 35, 30–31, 36, 40, 39. For the authentic version of Wilson's speeches in 1912, see Arthur S. Link, ed., *The Papers of Woodrow Wilson*, vols. 24 and 25 (1977, 1978).
49. Wilson, *The New Freedom*, pp. 109, 101–3, 52, 29.

50. Ibid., pp. 151–53, 87–99, 106–7.
51. Wilson, *The New Freedom*, pp. 112–13.
52. Robert H. Wiebe, *Businessmen and Reform: A Study of the Progressive Movement* (1962), pp. 127–56; Gabriel Kolko, *The Triumph of Conservatism: A Reinterpretation of American History, 1900–1916* (1967), pp. 190–305; Arthur S. Link, *Woodrow Wilson and the Progressive Era* (1954), pp. 1–80; Melvin I. Urofsky, *Big Steel and the Wilson Administration: A Study in Business-Government Relations* (1969), pp. 27–78; Broesamle, *William Gibbs McAdoo*, pp. 94–137; Kolko, *Railroads and Regulation, 1877–1916* (1970), pp. 208–30; Burton I. Kaufman, *Efficiency and Expansion: Foreign Trade Organization in the Wilson Administration, 1913–1921* (1974), pp. 63–90; James Weinstein, *The Corporate Ideal in the Liberal State, 1900–1918* (1968), pp. 62–91.
53. BMB to John Skelton Williams, 10, 13 November 1914, GC.
54. BMB to William G. McAdoo, 5 March 1915, GC; *New York Times*, 8 July 1915; McAdoo to BMB, 15 January 1916, SC; Broesamle, *William Gibbs McAdoo*, pp. 189–235.
55. Baruch, *My Own Story*, p. 308.
56. Meyer, COHC, p. 220.
57. Copy of House Diary, 7, 30 October, 3 November 1914, 13 April, 19 November 1915, 23 September, 28 October 1917, SC.
58. Isaac N. Seligman to BMB, 20 April, BMB to Seligman, 21 April, BMB to August Kohn, 19 October 1915, GC; Robert D. Ward, "The Origins and Activities of the National Security League, 1914–1919," *Mississippi Valley Historical Review* 47 (June 1950): 51–65; John Garry Clifford, *The Citizen Soldiers: The Plattsburgh Training Camp Movement, 1913–1920* (1972), p. 50; Baruch, *The Public Years*, p. 20; Robert D. Cuff, *The War Industries Board: Business-Government Relations during World War I* (1973), pp. 31–32; John Patrick Finnegan, *Against the Specter of a Dragon: The Campaign for American Military Preparedness* (1974), pp. 32, 63.
59. BMB to H. S. Callahan, 2 October, to W. B. Coster, 13 September 1915, GC; BMB quoted in Cuff, *The War Industries Board*, p. 33; copy of House Diary, 10 January 1917, SC.
60. Cuff, *The War Industries Board*, p. 32; Baruch, *The Public Years*, p. 23; *New York Times*, 9 September 1915; BMB to E. M. House, 25 October 1915, SC.
61. BMB to House, 24 April 1916, SC. On Coffin and other mobilization advocates, see Cuff, *The War Industries Board*, pp. 13–30; and Woodrow Wilson to BMB, 5 May 1916, SC.
62. Copy of House Diary, 23 June 1916, SC.
63. Copy of House Diary, 12 October 1916, SC; Baruch, *The Public Years*, p. 25.
64. Copy of BMB to House, November 1916, Sunday, SC; McAdoo to BMB, 2 February, BMB to McAdoo, 10 February 1917, GC.
65. BMB to W. H. Crocker, 10 March 1917, SC; BMB to W. S. Gifford, 12 January, Gifford to BMB, 15 January 1917, CND.
66. McAdoo to BMB, 9 February 1917, GC.
67. Cuff, *The War Industries Board*, pp. 46–56; Meyer, COHC, pp. 114–15, 227.
68. BMB to Wilson, 5 April 1917, CND.

CHAPTER TWO

1. Alfred D. Chandler, Jr., and Stephen S. Saulsbury, *Pierre S. du Pont and the Making of the Modern Corporation* (1971), p. 404.
2. Statements of C. M. Wooley, 31 December 1920, p. 304, and Donald R. McLennon, 11 December 1920, pp. 1–3, WIB.
3. For example, see GC for 1917–18 with Janet B. McDowell, J. C. Reynolds, R. C. Leffingwell, William Redfield, and James K. Vardaman; BMB to William G. McAdoo, 7 August 1917, GC; Anderson Diary, 1917–18, passim; BMB to Otto Kahn, 26 April 1917, WIB; and Gay Diary, 1918, passim.
4. BMB to E. M. House, 24 July 1918, WIB; Anderson Diary, 19 February 1918; Eugene Meyer, Jr., COHC, p. 260.
5. Newton D. Baker to Frank A. Scott, 8 January 1934, Scott Papers; Grosvenor B. Clarkson, *Industrial America in the World War* (1923), p. 51.
6. BMB to Donald Nelson, 7 September 1941, Nelson Papers, Box 2; Baker to Frank A. Scott, 8 January 1934, Scott Papers; H. R. Hatfield, "Experiences with the War Industries Board," Mark Sullivan to Edwin F. Gay, 20 December 1919, Gay Papers.
7. Herbert Hoover, *The Ordeal of Woodrow Wilson* (1958), p. 85.
8. Meyer, COHC, p. 255.
9. BMB to Gerald P. Nye, 22 March 1935, SC.
10. "Memo of Conversation with Mr. Brookings, November 17, 1926," Gay Papers, Box 2.
11. Bernard Baruch, *The Public Years* (1960), pp. 85–86; Anderson Diary, 20 March 1918; Robert D. Cuff, "We Band of Brothers—Woodrow Wilson's War Managers," *Canadian Review of American Studies* 5 (Fall 1974): 137.
12. Copy of House Diary, 8 April, BMB to Wilson, 25 September 1917, SC.
13. Hatfield, "Experiences with the War Industries Board," Gay Papers.
14. Mark Sullivan, *Our Times: The United States, 1900–1925: Over Here, 1914–1918*, 6 vols. (1933), 5:367, 379.
15. Daniel R. Beaver, *Newton D. Baker and the American War Effort, 1917–1919* (1966), p. 6; BMB to Henry S. New, 5 November 1920, GC; copy of House Diary, 27 May 1917 (emphasis added), SC.
16. Memo of conversation with George W. Goethals, 15 December 1926, Gay Papers, Box 2; Baruch, *The Public Years*, p. 55; Paul A. C. Koistinen, "The 'Industrial-Military Complex' in Historical Perspective: World War I," *Business History Review* 41 (Winter 1967): 388–91; Beaver, *Newton D. Baker*, pp. 71–72; E. David Cronon, ed., *The Cabinet Diaries of Josephus Daniels, 1913–1921* (1963), p. 148; Robert D. Cuff, *The War Industries Board: Business-Government Relations during World War I* (1973), pp. 99–103.
17. McAdoo to Woodrow Wilson, 10 July 1917, McAdoo Papers; BMB to Wilson, 11 July 1917, CND; Cuff, *The War Industries Board*, p. 110.
18. Cuff, *The War Industries Board*, pp. 104–15, 131–35; BMB to Frank A. Scott, 30 August 1917, CND.
19. BMB to C. H. Bentley, 13 October 1917, CND; Cronon, *Cabinet Diaries of Josephus Daniels*, p. 229; statement of Daniel Willard, 11 March 1921, pp. 42–49, WIB; "Diary 1918," 26 November 1917, WIB.
20. Cuff, *The War Industries Board*, pp. 135–41.
21. Cuff, "A 'Dollar-a-Year Man' in Government: George N. Peek and the War Industries Board," *Business History Review* 41 (Winter 1967): 410; Long Diary, 18 February 1918; "Diary 1918," 19 January 1918, WIB; State Department official quoted in Joseph Tulchin, *The Aftermath of War: World*

War I and U.S. Policy toward Latin America (1971), pp. 13–14.

22. Anderson Diary, 20, 22 December 1917, 2, 4 January 1918; Felix Frankfurter to Newton D. Baker, 4 January 1918, Baker Papers. Also see Frankfurter to House, 9 January 1918, Frankfurter Papers.

23. Copy of McAdoo to Wilson, 17 January 1918, SC; Anderson Diary, 22 January 1918; Cronon, *Cabinet Diaries of Josephus Daniels*, p. 271; Newton D. Baker to Wilson, 24 January 1918, Baker Papers; copy of House Diary, 28, 29 January 1918, SC; Auchincloss Diary, 29 January 1918.

24. Anderson Diary, 1 February 1918; Newton D. Baker to Wilson, 1 February 1918, Baker Papers; copy of Josephus Daniels to Wilson, 2 February 1918, SC; Wilson to Daniels, 4 February 1918, Daniels Papers.

25. Anderson Diary, 6–8, 21 February 1918; Meyer, COHC, p. 269; McAdoo to Wilson, 25 February, Wilson to McAdoo, 26 February 1918, McAdoo Papers; Cuff, *The War Industries Board*, pp. 141–47.

26. Statements of Charles A. McKinney, pp. 29–31, C. M. Wooley, pp. 3–4, Howard P. Ingels, pp. 1–8, Donald R. McLennan, pp. 1–4, and John M. Hancock, p. 35, WIB; Anderson Diary, 18 November, 4 December 1917.

27. Forrest Crissey, *Alexander Legge, 1866–1933* (1936), pp. 129, 130; Grosvenor Clarkson to BMB, 28 February 1918, WIB; George N. Peek to George T. Odell, 11 January 1919, Peek Papers.

28. Seward W. Livermore, *Politics Is Adjourned: Woodrow Wilson and the War Congress, 1916–1918* (1966).

29. James Kenney, *The Political Education of Woodrow Wilson* (1926), p. 396.

30. "Memo of Conversation with Walter S. Gifford, November 8, 1926," Gay Papers, Box 2.

31. Anderson Diary, 14 May, 19 February 1918; Herbert Heaton, *A Scholar in Action: Edwin F. Gay* (1952), pp. 110–11, 114, 124, 127.

32. Livermore, *Politics Is Adjourned*, pp. 51–52; Heaton, *A Scholar in Action*, p. 114; Long Diary, 23 February 1918; Herbert Hoover to BMB, 30 May, 4 June, 1 October, BMB to Hoover, 1 June, 4 October 1918, Food Administration Papers, WIB file. Also see Robert D. Cuff, "Herbert Hoover: The Ideology of Voluntarism and War Organization during the Great War," *Journal of American History* 64 (September 1977): 359–62, 365–68. And on the subject of bureaucratic recruit "poaching," see Wilson to H. A. Garfield, 8 May, Garfield to Wilson, 11, 20 May 1918, Garfield Papers, Box 92.

33. Cuff, "We Band of Brothers," pp. 138, 139, 147; copy of House Diary, 27, 28, 31 May 1917, SC; Anderson Diary, 10, 13, 27 June 1918.

34. McAdoo to Wilson, 27 February, 1, 6 March 1918, McAdoo Papers; copy of House Diary, 18 May 1918, SC; Auchincloss Diary, 20, 21 May 1918.

35. Wilson to BMB, 19 January 1918, SC.

36. BMB to Wilson, 18 January, copies of two handwritten notes, BMB to House, ca. May or June 1918, SC; BMB to House, 24 July 1918, WIB.

37. BMB to Jonathan Daniels, 1 July 1953, to Arthur Walworth, 9 January 1957, copy of House Diary, 14 May, 23 June, 19 November 1916, SC; W. H. Crocker to BMB, 14 March 1917, GC.

38. Melvin I. Urofsky, *Big Steel and the Wilson Administration: A Study in Business-Government Relations* (1969), pp. 117–51.

39. Cuff, *The War Industries Board*, pp. 58–60; Urofsky, *Big Steel*, pp. 37–116, passim; Cronon, *Cabinet Diaries of Josephus Daniels*, pp. 126, 129, 147–48; BMB to Josephus Daniels, 21 March, 13 April 1917, SC.

40. Josephus Daniels to BMB, 13 April, BMB to Daniels, 14 April, 16 May, Daniels to BMB, 1 June, BMB to Daniels, 14 June 1917, SC.

41. Josephus Daniels to BMB, 23 August, to Frank A. Scott, 23 August 1917, CND; Baruch, *The Public Years*, pp. 66–68; Robert D. Cuff and Melvin I. Urofsky, "The Steel Industry and Price-Fixing during World War I," *Business History Review* 44 (Autumn 1970): 295–305; BMB to Daniels, 24 August, Daniels to BMB, 27 August 1917, Daniels Papers; Cronon, *Cabinet Diaries of Josephus Daniels*, p. 339; J. Leonard Replogle to BMB, 12 April 1935, SC; statements of J. Leonard Replogle, pp. 8–13, and R. S. Lovett, pp. 5, 10–11, WIB.

42. Josephus Daniels to Wilson, 11 March 1918, Daniels Papers; meeting of the War Industries Board, 25 April 1918, p. 575, WIB; BMB to Daniels, 3 May 1918, SC; Urofsky, *Big Steel*, p. 177; statement of L. L. Summers, 2 February 1922, pp. 10–15, WIB.

43. Anderson Diary, 8 February 1918; statement of William Denman, pp. 18–19, WIB; Alvin Johnson, COHC, pp. 139–40; BMB to Arthur Krock, 29 August [1924] (handwritten), Krock Papers. Also see BMB to J. J. McSwain, 27 May 1924, SC; Meyer, COHC, p. 224; and Hurley Diary, 31 July 1918.

44. Baruch, *The Public Years*, pp. 68–69.

45. Cuff, *The War Industries Board*, pp. 220–40; Herman Hagedorn, *Brookings: A Biography* (1936), pp. 230–31, 240–41; Louis Galambos, *Competition and Cooperation: The Emergence of a National Trade Association* (1966), pp. 65–66; James Weinstein, *The Corporate Ideal in the Liberal State, 1900–1918* (1968), pp. 223–35.

46. Copy of House Diary, 24 September 1917, SC; Anderson Diary, 22, 25 January, 6, 15 March 1918; statement of Robert S. Brookings, p. 12, WIB; Hagedorn, *Brookings*, pp. 242–43.

47. Daniel Willard to Newton D. Baker, 31 March 1917, CND; BMB to Frank A. Scott, 4 May 1917, WIB; Benjamin Strong to McAdoo, 15 February 1918, McAdoo Papers; special meeting with representatives of Southern Pine Lumber Association, 9 July 1918, WIB.

48. Gass to Harry White, 30 June 1941, Morgenthau Diaries 415:337 (original emphasis).

49. Paul Willard Garrett, assisted by Isador Lubin and Stella Stewart, *History of Prices during the War: Government Control of Prices* (1920), p. 27.

50. Ibid., pp. 209–10, 284.

51. Joseph P. Cotton to BMB, 7 April 1917, GC; Benjamin Strong to McAdoo, 15 February 1918, McAdoo Papers; BMB to Wilson, 15 May 1917, CND; Galambos, *Competition and Cooperation*, pp. 53, 56–67, 74; Garrett, *History of Prices*, pp. 293–304; statements of Lincoln Cromwell, pp. 1–17, and Robert S. Lovett, pp. 13A, 18, WIB.

52. Robert D. Cuff, "Bernard Baruch: Symbol and Myth in Industrial Mobilization," *Business History Review* 43 (Summer 1969): 115–33.

53. Tulchin, *The Aftermath of War*, pp. 3–37; Burton I. Kaufman, *Efficiency and Expansion: Foreign Trade Organization in the Wilson Administration, 1913–1921* (1974), pp. 63–227; Weinstein, *The Corporate Ideal*, pp. 249–51; John J. Broesamle, *William Gibbs McAdoo: A Passion for Change, 1863–1917* (1973), pp. 188–231; Carl P. Parrini, *Heir to Empire: United States Economic Diplomacy, 1916–1923* (1969), pp. 15–71; Robert Neal Seidel, "Progressive Pan Americanism: Development and United States Policy toward South America, 1906–1931," doctoral dissertation, Cornell University, 1973, pp. 52–120.

54. Quoted in Hugh S. Johnson, *The Blue Eagle from Egg to Earth* (1935), p. 88.

55. Alex Legge to BMB, 19 February 1921, GC; lecture delivered before General

Staff, Army War College, 8 April 1922, pp. 4–5, PP.

56. BMB to Newton D. Baker, 13 July 1917, CND; H. A. Garfield to BMB, 7 March, meeting of the War Industries Board with representatives of the automobile industry, 7 May 1918, WIB; Cuff, *The War Industries Board*, pp. 193–203.

57. Quoted in Cuff, *The War Industries Board*, p. 204; BMB to James W. Wadsworth, Jr., 5 February 1923, SC; Meyer, COHC, p. 240; statement of William Denman, pp. 28–29, WIB.

58. Anderson Diary, 5 January 1918; Hurley Diary, 31 October 1917; statement of Charles H. McDowell, p. 18, WIB; memo of conversation with Felix Frankfurter, Gay Papers, Box 2; statement of Lincoln Cromwell, p. 23, WIB.

59. Peek to George B. Wells, 7 June 1940, Peek Papers; Baruch, *The Public Years*, p. 67; statement of Daniel Willard, pp. 41–42, WIB; Cronon, *Cabinet Diaries of Josephus Daniels*, p. 255; Hurley Diary, 31 July 1918; BMB to Wilson, 30 August 1918, SC; statement of John F. Wilkins, pp. 1 ff., WIB.

60. Hurley Diary, 14 August 1918; "Why McAdoo Really Resigned," folder 106–17, Lamont Papers.

61. Cuff, *The War Industries Board*, p. 203; meeting of the War Industries Board with representatives of the automobile industry, 7 May 1918, WIB; Wilson to Josephus Daniels, 24 July 1918, Daniels Papers; Urofsky, *Big Steel*, p. 177; BMB to Daniels, 3 May 1918, Daniels Papers; minutes, 18 June 1918 meeting, WIB; BMB to War Industries Board, 31 August 1917, CND; BMB to Herbert Hoover, 16 September, Hoover to BMB, 18 September, BMB to Hoover, 23 September 1918, Food Administration Papers, Box 178.

62. BMB to House, 24 July 1918, WIB; Chandler and Saulsbury, *Pierre S. du Pont*, p. 405; minutes, 9 April, 23 July, 25 July 1918 meetings, WIB; Anderson Diary, 7 January 1918.

63. Cuff, *The War Industries Board*, pp. 204–10; Anderson Diary, 5 January 1918; joint meeting of the Council of National Defense and Advisory Commission, 1 April 1918, CND; meeting of the War Industries Board with representatives of the automobile industry, 7 May 1918, WIB.

64. Meetings of the War Industries Board, 18 June, 2, 11, 16 July, 8 August 1918, WIB; Cuff, *The War Industries Board*, pp. 210–19.

65. Meeting with representatives of the National Federation of Building Industries, 22 August 1918, WIB; meetings of the War Industries Board, 21 May, 27 August, 1918, WIB; joint meeting of the Council of National Defense and Advisory Commission, 3 June 1918, CND.

66. Anderson Diary, 4 January 1918.

67. Meeting of the Advisory Commission, 1 August 1917, CND; meetings of the War Industries Board, 18, 25 July 1918, WIB.

68. Meetings of the Advisory Commission, 23, 26 April, 2 June, 1 August 1917, CND; meetings of the War Industries Board, 24, 29 October 1918, WIB; Hurley Diary, 29 September 1917.

69. Draft (1927) of statement to members of the War Industries Board, Alvin S. Johnson to BMB, 14 August 1957, SC; *Third Annual Report of the USCND* (1919), p. 28.

70. Edward S. Mason, *Economic Concentration and the Monopoly Problem* (1964), pp. 234–35; Clarkson, *Industrial America*, p. 387.

71. Mira Wilkins, *The Maturing of Multinational Enterprise: American Business Abroad from 1914 to 1970* (1974), p. 32.

72. Chandler and Saulsbury, *Pierre S. du Pont*, pp. 181–87, 205–206, 230–38, 377–78; Markos Mamalakis and Clark Winton Reynolds, *Essays on the*

Chilean Economy (1965), p. 215; Wilkins, *The Maturing of Multinational Enterprise*, pp. 10, 11.

73. Daniel Guggenheim to D. W. Morrow, 11 January, Eugene Meyer, Jr., to J. P. Morgan & Co., 1 March, Meyer to the Panyon Corporation, 2 March 1916, folder 87–6, Lamont Papers; *Government Control over Prices* (1920), pp. 338–39; Seidel, "Progressive Pan Americanism," pp. 320–33; Stephen Clissold, *Chilean Scrap-Book* (1952), pp. 29–30.

74. Clarkson, *Industrial America*, pp. 391–92; Bernard Baruch, *American Industry in the War: A Report of the War Industries Board* (1941), pp. 358–59; U.S. Department of State, *Papers Relating to the Foreign Relations of the United States, 1917: The World War*, [cited hereafter as *Foreign Relations, 1917*], supp. 2 (1932), 1:666–69.

75. *Foreign Relations, 1917*, supp. 2, 1:669–71; Conference on Nitrate Purchasing Executive in London, November 1917, WIB; Anderson Diary, 7, 8, 14 November 1917.

76. Anderson Diary, 7 December 1917.

77. *Foreign Relations, 1917*, supp. 2, 1:671–77, 681, 681 n; Anderson Diary, 8, 13, 22, 25, 28, 30 November, 5, 7 December 1917; L. L. Summers memo, 8 November 1917, WIB.

78. Anderson Diary, 23, 24 November, 4 December 1917, 2 January 1918, Chandler P. Anderson to BMB, 25 November 1917, Anderson Papers; Alfred B. Rollins, Jr., *Roosevelt and Howe* (1962), pp. 135–36.

79. *Foreign Relations, 1917*, supp. 2, 1:677–78; Anderson Diary, 15, 16, 18 December 1917, 21 February 1918; Clarkson, *Industrial America*, pp. 365–67; Baruch, *American Industry in the War*, pp. 97, 153–55.

80. Anderson Diary, 18, 14 December, 13 November 1917, 7–10 January 1920; *Foreign Relations, 1917*, supp. 2, 1:680–81; BMB to Daniel Willard, 22 November, BMB memo to Newton D. Baker, 19 December, BMB to Willard, 24 December 1917, "Diary, 1918," 26 November 1917, 3 January 1918, CND. The German government had built its nitrogen plants in 1914–15. See Gerd Hardach, *The First World War, 1914–1918* (1977), pp. 59–60.

81. Anderson Diary, 4 January, 27 February, 25 March 1918.

82. Ibid., 26, 28 January, 7, 21, 25 February, 14 June 1918; Tulchin, *The Aftermath of War*, pp. 28–29.

83. Anderson Diary, 11, 12 July 1918; copy of Lord Reading telegram to Winston Churchill, 12 July 1918, Anderson Papers.

84. Anderson Diary, 21 May, 18, 19, 26 July 1918; Clarkson, *Industrial America*, p. 266; Tulchin, *The Aftermath of War*, pp. 30–31; Hurley quoted in Kaufman, *Efficiency and Expansion*, p. 188. Also, see Robert Hardin Van Meter, Jr., "The United States and European Recovery, 1918–1923: A Study of Public Policy and Private Finance," doctoral dissertation, University of Wisconsin, 1971, pp. 11–22; and Michael J. Hogan, "The United States and the Problem of International Economic Control: American Attitudes toward European Reconstruction, 1918–1920," *Pacific Historical Review* 44 (February 1975): 87.

85. Anderson Diary, 11, 14, 28 June, 13, 18, 26 July 1918; Clarkson, *Industrial America*, pp. 262–64.

86. L. L. Summers to BMB, 18 August 1918, WIB.

87. Clarkson, *Industrial America*, pp. 263–69; Baruch, *American Industry in the War*, pp. 97–100; speech by Leland L. Summers, "Our Foreign Relations and the National Power of Retaliation," WIB dinner, 10 December 1920, GC; statement of L. L. Summers, pp. 32–44, WIB.

88. The price of rubber would be a source of contention until World War II. See pp. 390–95.
89. *Government Control over Prices*, pp. 292–93; James A. Field to Edwin F. Gay, 16 October 1918, Gay Papers; Auchincloss Diary, 12 September 1918; Clarkson, *Industrial America*, pp. 269–73; Baruch, *American Industry in the War*, p. 100; Summers quoted in Van Meter, "The United States and European Recovery," p. 14; meeting of the War Industries Board, 31 October 1918, p. 805, WIB.
90. Baruch quoted in Hogan, "The United States and the Problem of International Economic Control," p. 89; Laughlin to secretary of state, 8 November 1918, Daniels Papers, Box 65; Wilson to Edward N. Hurley, 9 September, Diary, 24, 28 October 1918, Hurley Papers, Box 101; Heaton, *A Scholar in Action* p. 122; minutes of Tonnage Conference, 2 October 1918, Gay Papers; William Diamond, *The Economic Thought of Woodrow Wilson* (1943), pp. 185, 186 n.
91. Auchincloss Diary, 16 September 1918; "By Bernard Baruch, Chairman, War Industries Board," marked "Personal," 4:248–49, CND; Hurley to Wilson, 27 February 1918, Hurley Papers, Box 101.
92. Clarkson, *Industrial America*, pp. 486, 487; Michael Abbot Goldman, "The War Finance Corporation in the Politics of War and Reconstruction, 1917–1923," doctoral dissertation, Rutgers University, 1971; Cuff, *The War Industries Board*, pp. 241–42, 243.
93. Baruch, *The Public Years*, p. 93; BMB to A. D. Noyes, 12 December 1917 (emphasis added), WIB; Walter Lippmann to Frankfurter, 5 November 1918, Frankfurter Papers; quoted in Cuff, *The War Industries Board*, p. 252.
94. Quoted in Cuff, *The War Industries Board*, pp. 251–52, 246; Heaton, *A Scholar in Action*, p. 129.
95. On small copper producers, see Key Pittman to A. H. Howe, 28 May, to A. C. Bachman, 23 May 1918, Pittman Papers, Box 128. On big finance, see Hamlin Diary, 18 November 1918. On big steel, see Cuff, *The War Industries Board*, pp. 251–52, 255; and Daniel C. Roper to Joseph P. Tumulty, 13 November 1918, WIB.
96. Wilson to Edward N. Hurley, 24 July 1918, Hurley Papers, Box 101; Wilson to Josephus Daniels, 24 July 1918, Daniels Papers.
97. Cronon, *Cabinet Diaries of Josephus Daniels*, p. 345; Anderson Diary, 16 October, 16 November 1918; meeting of the War Industries Board, 8 November 1918, WIB.
98. Newton D. Baker to Wilson, 8 November 1918, Baker Papers; Anderson Diary, 23 November 1918.
99. Cronon, *Cabinet Diaries of Josephus Daniels*, p. 350; Robert W. Woolley to Joseph P. Tumulty, 15 November 1918, Woolley Papers, Box 21; BMB to Wilson, 15 November 1918, WIB; Wilson to Josephus Daniels, 18 November, L. L. Summers message, Laughlin to Robert Lansing, 8 November 1918, Daniels Papers, Box 65; meeting of the War Industries Board, 3 December 1918, WIB.
100. BMB to Wilson, 27 November 1918, SC; Anderson Diary, 25 November 1918; Vance McCormick to Wilson, 29 November 1918, McCormick Papers; BMB to Newton D. Baker, 30 November, Baker to Wilson, 30 November 1918, Baker Papers (emphasis added); H. A. Garfield to Wilson, 1 December 1918, Garfield Papers, Box 93; *New York Times*, 3 December 1918; Cuff, *The War Industries Board*, pp. 259–61.
101. BMB to Wilson, 18 November 1918, "Service" file, "Related Material" folder, WIB.

102. Johnson, *The Blue Eagle*, p. 101; Meyer, COHC, p. 298; Baruch, *The Public Years*, pp. 91–92.
103. Anderson Diary, 12, 25 November, 13 December 1918; Albert C. Ritchie to BMB, 15 November 1918, GC; Baruch, *The Public Years*, pp. 139–40; copy of William H. King to Wilson, 25 November 1918, SC; BMB to Gavin McNab, 11 December 1918, WIB; BMB to James F. Bell, 14 December 1954, SC.

CHAPTER THREE

1. Bernard Baruch, *The Public Years* (1960), pp. 92–93.
2. BMB to Gavin McNab, 11 December 1918, WIB. Also see House Diary, 10 March 1924; and George A. Riddell, *Lord Riddell's Intimate Diary of the Peace Conference and After, 1918–1923* (1934), p. 13.
3. Anderson Diary, 23 November 1917.
4. Inga Floto, *Colonel House in Paris: A Study of American Policy at the Paris Peace Conference* (1973), pp. 94–95, 299.
5. H. A. Garfield to Woodrow Wilson, 2 December, Wilson to Garfield, 3 December 1918, Garfield Papers, Box 93; Floto, *Colonel House in Paris*, p. 95; Anderson Diary, 10, 13 December 1918; Auchincloss Diary, 17, 18 December 1918.
6. McCormick Diary, 9 June, 15 March 1919; C. K. Leith to Edwin F. Gay, 24 March 1919, James A. Field to Gay, 8 February 1919, Gay Papers, Box 1.
7. McCormick Diary, 13, 20 April 1919.
8. BMB to George N. Peek, 27 February 1919, Peek Papers; McCormick Diary, 30 March, 27 April 1919.
9. McCormick Diary, 21 April 1919; Auchincloss Diary, 16 April 1919.
10. Floto, *Colonel House in Paris*, p. 96.
11. Ibid., p. 65.
12. Anderson Diary, 30 November 1918; Auchincloss Diary, 3 August 1919. Also see Thomas W. Lamont, *Across World Frontiers* (1951), p. 172.
13. Walter Lippmann to Sidney E. Mezes, 5 September 1918, Mezes Papers; Floto, *Colonel House in Paris*, pp. 61–96, passim; Lawrence E. Gelfand, *The Inquiry: American Preparations for Peace, 1917–1919* (1963).
14. Floto, *Colonel House in Paris*, p. 98.
15. Auchincloss Diary, 17 December 1918.
16. C. K. Leith to Edwin F. Gay, 24 March 1919, Gay Papers, Box 1.
17. McCormick Diary, 6 May 1919; Cecil Diary, 30, 20 March, 8 May 1919; Floto, *Colonel House in Paris*, pp. 94–216.
18. Auchincloss Diary, 28 November, 14 December 1918, 4, 14, 20 January 1919; Hurley Diary, 29 November 1918; McCormick Diary, 13, 29 January, 1, 21 March 1919; Floto, *Colonel House in Paris*, p. 178.
19. Baruch, *The Public Years*, p. 95; Lamont, *Across World Frontiers*, p. 174; Hamlin Diary, 9 July 1919.
20. Anderson Diary, 13 December 1918; Clapper Diary, 14 December 1918. Also see Anderson Diary, 30 December 1918.
21. McCormick Diary, 11–14 January 1919; Cecil Diary, 14, 15 January 1919.
22. McCormick Diary, 18, 20 January 1919; Auchincloss Diary, 14, 15 January 1919.
23. Auchincloss Diary, 27 January 1919; McCormick Diary, 27, 30 January 1919.

24. House Diary, 11 February 1919; Cecil Diary, 25 February, 20 March 1919.
25. ACNP Diary, 9 May 1919; Cecil Diary, 10 May 1919.
26. Auchincloss Diary, 5 June 1919; Lamont Diary, 15, 20 February 1919; Hamlin Diary, 9 July 1919.
27. Cecil Diary, 30 March 1919; ACNP Diary, 10, 11 May, 4 June 1919; Auchincloss Diary, 5 June 1919; McCormick Diary, 5 June 1919.
28. BMB to Peek, 27 February 1919, Peek Papers.
29. Charles Seymour, *Letters from the Paris Peace Conference* (1965), p. 132; Riddell, *Intimate Diary*, pp. 12–13; Cecil Diary, 25 February, 8 May, 20 March, 29 April 1919.
30. Floto, *Colonel House in Paris*, pp. 178, 322, 205, 342, 97; BMB to Wilson, 14 April 1919, SC; Herbert Hoover, *The Ordeal of Woodrow Wilson* (1958), p. 239.
31. Arno J. Mayer, *Politics and Diplomacy of Peacemaking: Containment and Counterrevolution at Versailles, 1918–1919* (1967), pp. 799–802.
32. Seymour, *Letters*, p. 132; McCormick Diary, 14, 30 January 1919; Seth P. Tillman, *Anglo-American Relations at the Paris Peace Conference of 1919* (1961), pp. 229–32; John Foster Dulles to Edwin F. Gay, 29 January 1919, Dulles Papers; John Robinson Beal, *John Foster Dulles: 1888–1959* (1959), p. 63.
33. Tillman, *Anglo-American Relations*, pp. 232–35; Bliss Diary, 11 February 1919.
34. Lamont Diary, 15 February 1919; Cecil Diary, 15 February 1919.
35. Tillman, *Anglo-American Relations*, pp. 235–36; John Foster Dulles to Edwin F. Gay, 14 February 1919, Dulles Papers; McCormick Diary, 11, 16, 19 February 1919; Lamont Diary, 16 February 1919.
36. "Ammission" (Lansing, House, Baruch, Davis, McCormick) telegram to Wilson, 18 February 1919, Vance McCormick Papers, Box 3.
37. McCormick Diary, 21, 23, 25, 27 February 1919.
38. Ibid., 5, 20 March 1919; Lamont Diary, 18, 26, 22 March 1919; Tillman, *Anglo-American Relations*, pp. 236–44; Mayer, *Politics and Diplomacy of Peacemaking*, chaps. 18 and 19.
39. BMB to Simon Baruch, 10 March 1919, SC; Arthur Pound and Samuel Taylor Moore, eds., *More They Told Barron: The Notes of Clarence W. Barron* (1931), pp. 267–68; BMB to Norman Davis, 26 March 1919, GC; BMB to Wilson, 29 March 1919, SC; "Public Statement by Mr. Bernard M. Baruch in Paris," March or April 1919, ACNP.
40. Tillman, *Anglo-American Relations*, pp. 244–46; Lamont Diary, 31 March, 1 April 1919; McCormick Diary, 31 March, 1 April 1919 (emphases added); Auchincloss Diary, 16 April 1919.
41. Lamont Diary, 2, 3 April 1919; "Reparations: Memorandum of Conference held April 5 . . . ," pp. 69, 74, ACNP; McCormick Diary, 2–9 April 1919; Cecil Diary, 9 April 1919; Auchincloss Diary, 5 April 1919; Tillman, *Anglo-American Relations*, pp. 246–52. For a recent perspective on the reparations tangle, see Marc Trachtenberg, "Reparation at the Paris Peace Conference," *Journal of Modern History* 51 (March 1979): 24–55.
42. Hoover, *The Ordeal of Woodrow Wilson*, p. 85; Riddell, *Intimate Diary*, pp. 12–14; Cecil Diary, 3, 4 March 1919.
43. Anderson Diary, 16 October 1918; BMB to Wilson, 3 December 1918, WIB; William Diamond, *The Economic Thought of Woodrow Wilson* (1943), p. 186.
44. E. David Cronon, ed., *The Cabinet Diaries of Josephus Daniels, 1913–1921*

(1963), p. 347; BMB to Newton D. Baker, 30 November 1918, Baker Papers; "Personal by Bernard Baruch, Chairman, War Industries Board," CND.

45. Hurley Diary, 28 October, 15, 28 November, 24 October 1918; Edward N. Hurley to Wilson, 12 December 1918, Hurley Papers, Box 103.

46. Copy of E. M. House to Robert Lansing, 27 November 1918, Hurley Papers, Box 103; Mayer, *Politics and Diplomacy of Peacemaking*, pp. 266–69, 272–79; Robert Hardin Van Meter, Jr., "The United States and European Recovery, 1918–1923: A Study of Public Policy and Private Finance," doctoral dissertation, University of Wisconsin, 1971, pp. 25–30; McCormick Diary, 11 January 1919.

47. Riddell, *Intimate Diary*, pp. 12–13; Cecil Diary, 25 February 1919.

48. McCormick Diary, 21, 24 January 1919; Ray Stannard Baker, *Woodrow Wilson and World Settlement* (1922), pp. 328–30.

49. BMB to Wilson, 12 February 1919 (emphasis added), Wilson Papers (Library of Congress).

50. Bliss Diary, 11 February 1919; Wilson quoted in Van Meter, "The United States and European Recovery," p. 65.

51. McCormick Diary, 18 February, 2, 5 March 1919; Cecil Diary, 3, 4 March 1919.

52. McCormick Diary, 16, 17 March 1919; Joseph Tulchin, *The Aftermath of War: World War I and U.S. Policy toward Latin America* (1971), pp. 121–22; BMB to A. C. Bedford, 17 September 1920, GC; ACNP Diary, 12 April, 6, 28 May 1919; BMB to Josephus Daniels, 11 April 1919, Daniels Papers, Box 65; Van Meter, "The United States and European Recovery," pp. 70–71, 89, 100–101.

53. Cronon, *Cabinet Diaries of Josephus Daniels*, p. 385; BMB to Josephus Daniels, 11 April 1919, Daniels Papers, Box 65; Lamont Diary, 6 April 1919; Harold Sprout and Margaret Sprout, *Toward a New Order of Sea Power: American Naval Policy and the World Scene, 1918–1922* (1943), pp. 54–72; Tillman, *Anglo-American Relations*, pp. 287–94; Cecil Diary, 8 April 1919; Lord Robert Cecil to House, 8 April, House to Cecil, 9 April 1919, in Auchincloss Diary, 9, 10 April 1919.

54. McCormick Diary, 6 April 1919; "Memorandum of Conversation between President Wilson and Mr. Lloyd George . . . on Wednesday, April 23, [1919]," McCormick Papers.

55. Cecil Diary, 1, 8, 14, 31 March, 29 April 1919; BMB quoted in Diamond, *Economic Thought of Woodrow Wilson*, p. 186 n; BMB to Norman Davis, 26 March 1919, GC; Van Meter, "The United States and European Recovery," pp. 65–69.

56. McCormick Diary, 13 April 1919; Lamont Diary, 24, 25 April 1919.

57. C. K. Leith to Edwin F. Gay, 24 March 1919, Gay Papers, Box 1; Cecil Diary, 2 May 1919; BMB to Wilson, 7 May 1919 (emphasis added), WIB, reprinted in Baker, *Woodrow Wilson and World Settlement*, pp. 347–51; ACNP Diary, 18, 21 April 1919.

58. Michael Abbot Goldman, "The War Finance Corporation in the Politics of War and Reconstruction, 1917–1923," doctoral dissertation, Rutgers University, 1971, pp. 197–208; Eugene Meyer, Jr., COHC, p. 308; Merlo J. Pusey, *Eugene Meyer* (1974), pp. 167–68; Meyer Diary, 11 June 1919.

59. McCormick Diary, 9, 10 June 1919; Cecil Diary, 6 June 1919; ACNP Diary, 7 June 1919.

60. McCormick Diary, 13 June 1919; ACNP Diary, 13 June 1919; "American Economic Group, June 13, 1919," folder 164–8, Lamont Papers.

61. McCormick Diary, 22 June 1919; Lamont Diary, 22 June 1919. Also see Tillman, *Anglo-American Relations*, pp. 267–75.
62. Baker, *Woodrow Wilson and World Settlement*, pp. 376–81; BMB to House, 5 April 1919, SC; BMB to Norman Davis, 5 April 1919, GC.
63. ACNP Diary, 25, 30 April 1919.
64. Cecil Diary, 20 May 1919; ACNP Diary, 21, 22, 31 May 1919; Mayer, *Politics and Diplomacy of Peacemaking*, p. 802; McCormick Diary, 31 May 1919.
65. Baruch, *The Public Years*, pp. 119–21; ACNP Diary, 2, 3 June 1919; McCormick Diary, 2, 3 June 1919; Seymour, *Letters*, pp. 253–54.
66. Mayer, *Politics and Diplomacy of Peacemaking*, pp. 797–806; McCormick Diary, 7, 14 June 1919.
67. Sir James Headlam-Morley, *A Memoir of the Paris Peace Conference, 1919* (1972), pp. 7–8.
68. Mayer, *Politics and Diplomacy of Peacemaking*, p. 21.
69. ACNP Diary, 23 May 1919.
70. Cecil Diary, 9, 18 March 1919; Helen Lawrenson, *Stranger at the Party: A Memoir* (1975), pp. 145–46; ACNP Diary, 22 May 1919.
71. McCormick Diary, 19 February, 5, 8, 15, 24 March 1919; Riddell, *Intimate Diary*, p. 30.
72. Hurley Diary, 24 October 1918.
73. N. Gordon Levin, *Woodrow Wilson and World Politics* (1968), pp. 144, 147, 148, 150, 181.
74. McCormick Diary, 9, 10 April 1919; Harold Nicolson, *Peacemaking 1919* (1933), pp. 289, 362. For a British view that food and jobs would save Germany from Bolshevism, see Headlam-Morley, *A Memoir*, pp. 37–38, 163.
75. McCormick Diary, 9 June 1919; "American Economic Group, June 9, 1919" (emphasis added), folder 164–88, Lamont Papers. For another Hoover insight and advocacy, see Mayer, *Politics and Diplomacy of Peacemaking*, pp. 24–27.
76. ACNP Diary, 29 April, 2, 27, 28 May 1919; Riddell, *Intimate Diary*, p. 13.
77. Auchincloss Diary, 5 June 1919. Also see Cecil Diary, 21 April 1919.
78. Anderson Diary, 31 July, 1 August 1919; *New York Times*, 1–3 August 1919.
79. Anderson Diary, 19, 22, 27 August 1919.
80. Ibid., 17 October, 17 November 1919.
81. Ibid., 7–10 January 1920; Baruch, *The Public Years*, pp. 137–39; *New York Times*, 24 December 1919; BMB to Claude Swanson, 2 January 1920, SC.
82. C. S. Thomas to BMB, ca. February 1920, BMB to Frank W. Taussig, 19 March 1920, GC; John Morton Blum, *From the Morgenthau Diaries: Years of War, 1941–1945* (1967), p. 268; BMB to Winston Churchill, 10 November 1950, SC; Baruch, *The Public Years*, p. 124.
83. R. F. Harrod, *The Life of John Maynard Keynes* (1969), p. 282.
84. Ibid., p. 255; Baruch, *The Public Years*, p. 124.
85. John Maynard Keynes, *The Economic Consequences of the Peace* (Harper Torchbook ed., 1971), pp. 39, 41, 43–45, 274, 274 n. On Keynes, see Hoover, *The Ordeal of Woodrow Wilson*, pp. 234–35, 235 n.
86. BMB to Frank W. Taussig, 19 March 1920, GC; Baruch, *The Public Years*, p. 124.
87. Headlam-Morley, *A Memoir*, p. 142; Tillman, *Anglo-American Relations*, p. 269; McCormick Diary, 24, 25 April 1919; Lamont Diary, 25 April 1919.
88. Cecil Diary, 5, 13 May 1919; Keynes quoted in Harrod, *Life of John Maynard Keynes*, p. 250 (emphasis added).

89. Harrod, *Life of John Maynard Keynes*, pp. 249, 253; ACNP Diary, 27 May 1919.
90. Norman Davis to J. M. Keynes, 19 March, Keynes to Davis, 18 April 1920 (original emphasis), Davis Papers.
91. "LAC" to John Foster Dulles, 27 April, BMB to Dulles, 4 May, Dulles to BMB, 22 May 1920, Dulles Papers; Dulles telegram to BMB, 20 May 1920, GC; Ronald W. Pruessen, "John Foster Dulles and Reparations at the Paris Peace Conference: Early Patterns of a Life," *Perspectives in American History* 8 (1974): 385 n.
92. John Foster Dulles to Norman Davis, 11 June, to Vance McCormick, 12 June, to Bainbridge Colby, 16 June, to Thomas W. Lamont, 16 June, Fred K. Nielson to Dulles, 26 June 1920, Dulles Papers; Henry C. Breck memo to Davis, 18 June 1920, Davis Papers.
93. Bernard Baruch, *The Making of the Reparation and Economic Sections of the Treaty* (1920), pp. 8, 19–20, 24–32, 51, 53, 54–55; Baruch, *The Public Years*, p. 104; *The Collected Writings of John Maynard Keynes*, vol. 17, *Activities, 1920–1922: Treaty Revision and Reconstruction* (1977), pp. 91–98.
94. Mark Sullivan to BMB, 18 October 1921, BMB to Louis Loucheur, 4 November 1920, to J. J. Jusserand, 9 April 1923, to R. W. Bingham, 18 October 1920, to Sullivan, 25 October 1925, GC.

CHAPTER FOUR

1. *New York Times*, 8 December 1912, 23 July, 28 March, 1 January 1911, 4 September 1910, 13 August, 20, 28 September, 9 December 1913, 18, 20 March, 28 September, 19 December 1916.
2. Ibid., 15 November 1908, 19, 26 June, 4 July 1917, 15 June, 14 July 1918.
3. Ibid., 10 February 1914, 14 February 1915, 12 July 1914.
4. Ibid., 4, 11, 18 July, 29 August 1915.
5. Ibid., 4 February 1924.
6. Memo, "About November 8 or November 9, 1918," and memo, "Subsequent to Armistice Day, November 11, 1918," Homer Cummings Papers, Box 68.
7. Cummings Diary, 31 May 1920.
8. "Memorandum of Interview with Woodrow Wilson June 28, 1922 . . . ," Cummings Papers, Box 68. Also see Davis Diary, 10 March 1921.
9. BMB to William Allen White, 8 September 1920, GC; BMB to Wilson, 16 December 1920, SC; *New York Times*, 23 June 1919; BMB to Albert C. Ritchie, 5 April 1921, GC.
10. BMB to Albert C. Ritchie, 5 April 1921, GC; BMB to W. J. Bryan, 21 November 1919, SC.
11. BMB to Lincoln Colcord, 5 April 1921, to William Allen White, 8 September, to H. B. Brougham, 12 July 1920, GC; quoted in E. David Cronon, ed., *The Cabinet Diaries of Josephus Daniels, 1913–1921* (1963), p. 528.
12. BMB to Frank Kent, 15 May 1929, SC; BMB to Kent, 17 October 1927, Kent Papers, Box 5. Also see Norman Davis to Cordell Hull, 2 January 1924, Davis Papers.
13. Christopher Lasch, *The New Radicalism in America* (1967), p. 227; BMB to M. A. Boyle, 19 February 1918, GC; *New York Times*, 19 July 1919; BMB to Cary T. Grayson, 1 December 1919, GC.
14. *New York Times*, 26 May 1920; BMB to William Clark, 24 November 1920, GC; BMB to William S. Kenyon, 23 May 1921 (original emphasis), SC.
15. BMB to Mark Sullivan, 13 October 1921, GC; BMB to Sullivan, 11

November 1922, SC; *New York Times*, 16 November 1924, 13 April, 25 May 1928; BMB to John Morron, 1 July 1925, SC.

16. Bernard Baruch, *My Own Story* (1957), pp. 240-41; BMB to John J. Pershing, 3 March 1927, SC.

17. *New York Times*, 22 November 1967; Daniel Willard to BMB, 8 May 1928, 6 December 1930, 10 March 1931, 20 January, 18 April, 18 October 1930, 4 October 1932, 23 October 1935, BMB to Willard, 6 June 1928, 18 January 1930, 25 May 1931, 5 October 1932, GC.

18. BMB to Cary T. Grayson, 20 March 1922, 3 January 1925, William G. McAdoo to BMB, 30 December 1919, Matthew Woll to BMB, 15 November, 15 December 1921, GC; *New York Times*, 8 July 1925.

19. Bernard Baruch, *The Public Years* (1960), pp. 139-40; Margaret L. Coit, *Mr. Baruch* (1957), p. 456.

20. Helen Lawrenson, *Stranger at the Party: A Memoir* (1975), p. 153; Coit, *Mr. Baruch*, p. 457; Anderson Diary, 30 December 1917, 3 January 1918.

21. Lawrenson, *Stranger at the Party*, pp. 135-36; BMB to Arthur Krock, ca. August-September 1925, Krock Papers.

22. Stephen Shadegg, *Clare Boothe Luce: A Biography* (1970), pp. 67-68, 76, 95; Lawrenson, *Stranger at the Party*, pp. 106-9; Jonathan Daniels, *White House Witness, 1942-1945* (1975), p. 49.

23. Cronon, *Cabinet Diaries of Josephus Daniels*, p. 131; Joseph P. Lash, *Eleanor and Franklin* (1971), pp. 535-36, 295; Lincoln Colcord to Nan Colcord, 3 December 1917, Colcord Papers.

24. Baruch, *The Public Years*, p. 172; "Items for Mr. Baruch in the Library of Congress," from Arthur Walworth, 24 September 1957, SC; *New York Times*, 6 September, 24 November 1919; Hamlin Diary, 17, 19, 23 November 1919; Anderson Diary, 19 February 1920; BMB to Cary T. Grayson, 1 December 1919, GC.

25. *New York Times*, 25 May, 3 June 1920, 22, 23 February, 2 March, 1 June 1921.

26. Ibid., 28 October 1920; BMB to Grosvenor Clarkson, 30 October 1920, S. M. Reynolds to BMB, 10 February 1921, GC.

27. BMB to Grosvenor Clarkson, 3 December 1920, GC.

28. Mark Sullivan to BMB, 28 September, BMB to Sullivan, 28 September, 20 December 1923, SC.

29. BMB to Mark Sullivan, 22 September, to McAdoo, 18 May 1922, to O. E. Bradfute, 9 November 1923, SC.

30. BMB to J. J. Donovan, 29 January 1920, GC.

31. Cummings Diary, 27 November 1916; Anderson Diary, 2 January, 8 February, 26 May, 13, 14 June, 25 November 1918.

32. Long Diary, 14 November 1918; Clapper Diary, 22 November 1918, "Why McAdoo Really Resigned," folder 106-17, Thomas Lamont Papers.

33. McCormick Diary, 14 January 1919; Wesley M. Bagby, *The Road to Normalcy: The Presidential Campaign and Election of 1920* (1962), pp. 54-55; Henry Morgenthau, Sr., Diary, 26 March, 23 May 1919; Auchincloss Diary, 3 August 1919.

34. McAdoo to BMB, 28 October 1919, personal correspondence, WIB; Anderson Diary, 7-10 January 1920; BMB to J. J. Donovan, 29 January 1920, GC.

35. Bagby, *The Road to Normalcy*, p. 60; *New York Times*, 10 February, 26, 29 May 1920; BMB to C. S. Thomas, 13 May, to Robert W. Woolley, 24 May 1920, GC.

36. Bagby, *The Road to Normalcy*, pp. 60-71; Anderson Diary, 21 June 1920.

37. BMB to Martin H. Glynn, 12 July 1920, GC; Cummings Diary, 29 July 1920.

38. BMB to M. A. Gunst, 14 August, to Vance McCormick, 4 November 1920, GC; BMB to Wilson, ca. 6 November 1920, SC.
39. Long Diary, 14 November 1920; Homer S. Cummings to J. Bruce Kremer, 25 February 1921, Cummings Papers, Box 52; Robert W. Woolley to Thomas B. Love, 12 March 1921, Woolley Papers, Box 11; Cummings to C. Rentz Rees, 26 May, Frank Pace to Cummings, 3 November 1921, Cummings Papers, Box 50; *New York Times*, 12 February 1921; BMB to James M. Cox, 10 February, Cox to BMB, 12 March, BMB to Cox, 7 April, Cox to BMB, 9 April, BMB to Cox, 10, 18 August, to Joseph P. Tumulty, 2 September 1921, GC; BMB to Carter Glass, 22 September, 17 November, Glass to BMB, 23 September, Woolley to Glass, 7 September 1921, Glass Papers, Box 165.
40. BMB to McAdoo, 18 May, to Mark Sullivan, 2, 22 September 1922, SC; Robert W. Woolley to Daniel C. Roper, 7 August 1922, Woolley Papers, Box 18; BMB to McAdoo, 30 September 1922, SC.
41. BMB to C. S. Thomas, 6 December, to McAdoo, 10 April, McAdoo to BMB, 31 December 1923, SC.
42. Robert K. Murray, *The 103rd Ballot* (1976), pp. 45–48; Baruch, *The Public Years*, pp. 180–82; Lee N. Allen, "The McAdoo Campaign for the Presidential Nomination in 1924," *Journal of Southern History* 29 (May 1963): 220–21.
43. BMB to McAdoo, 27 February, 12 April 1924, SC; Long quoted in Burl Noggle, *Teapot Dome: Oil and Politics in the 1920's* (1965), pp. 114 n, 137.
44. BMB to Pat Harrison, 16 April, to Albert C. Ritchie, 31 May 1924, SC.
45. *New York Times*, 5 July 1924.
46. Baruch, *The Public Years*, p. 184.
47. On loans to McAdoo, see Baruch-McAdoo correspondence, 1924–26, GC; McAdoo to BMB, 21 November 1928, SC.
48. McAdoo to BMB, 26 March 1927, GC; BMB to McAdoo, 10 January, 29 March, 16, 30 May, to Albert C. Ritchie, 7 March 1927, SC.
49. James Benesch Levin, "Albert C. Ritchie: A Political Biography," doctoral dissertation, City University of New York, 1970, pp. 58–64, 75, 104–6, 175, 427–30; Ritchie speech, 12 May 1926, GC; Auchincloss Diary, 17 September 1918.
50. Albert C. Ritchie to BMB, 15 August, 7, 19 October 1919, 29 January 1920, GC; *New York Times*, 21 November 1923; Levin, "Albert C. Ritchie," pp. 213–39, passim; BMB to Ritchie, 31 May 1924, SC.
51. BMB to Pat Harrison, 16 April, to Mark Sullivan, 10 May 1924, SC; Norman Davis to Cordell Hull, 2 May, Hull to Davis, 3 May 1924, Davis Papers; "Preconvention Plan," 1924, GC.
52. BMB to Krock, 24 August [1924] (handwritten), Krock Papers; BMB to George N. Peek, 29 September 1924, SC.
53. Jesse H. Jones to BMB, 1 October, BMB to Jones, 10 October 1924, GC; BMB to George C. Jewett, 10 October 1924, SC; Bascom N. Timmons, *Jesse H. Jones* (1956), p. 137; Baruch, *The Public Years*, pp. 183–84.
54. Norman Davis to BMB, 24 July, BMB to Davis, 26 July 1920, GC.
55. Hamlin Diary, 14 December 1924; *New York Times*, 2, 18 July 1926; Claude Swanson to BMB, 23 October 1925, BMB correspondence with Thomas F. Bayard, 5 February, 23 June, 23 July, 27 August, 22, 28 September, 16 October 1926, SC; R. W. Bingham to BMB, 10 March, 10 October 1926, BMB to Bingham, 7 October, 14 November 1926, Bingham Papers, Box 6; BMB to Key Pittman, 14 October, Pittman to BMB, 7 December 1926, Pittman Papers, Box 11; Alben W. Barkley to BMB, 27 November 1926, SC.
56. BMB to Krock, 28 May 1920, GC; BMB to Mark Sullivan, 27 October 1926,

to John Francis Neylan, 22 February 1945, to Albert Gore, 23 February 1956, SC.

57. BMB to Joe T. Robinson, 16 May 1924, SC.
58. See Joe T. Robinson-Baruch correspondence for 1922–29, especially Robinson to BMB, 13 February 1926, 29 November 1927, GC; BMB to Robinson, 11 April 1927, SC; and BMB to Krock, 18 August [1926], Krock Papers.
59. Cordell Hull to BMB, 13 October 1925, SC.
60. For Baruch's version of his relationship with the Senate, see *The Public Years*, pp. 203–6.
61. BMB to Lincoln Colcord, 5 January 1927, SC; Baruch, *The Public Years*, p. 207.
62. Norman Davis to Cordell Hull, 3, 8, 17, 25 January, Hull to Davis, 16 March 1927, Davis Papers; BMB to Peek, 21 November 1927, SC.
63. BMB to R. W. Bingham, 4 November, to James M. Cox, 6 November 1926, SC.
64. BMB to Mark Sullivan, 7 March, 11 May, to Joe T. Robinson, 5 April, to Alben W. Barkley, 29 November 1927, SC.
65. BMB to Albert C. Ritchie, 7 March, 6 April 1927, SC; Levin, "Albert C. Ritchie," pp. 300–309.
66. David Lawrence to BMB, 24 March 1928, SC; *New York Times*, 26 March 1928; BMB to George Fort Milton, 23 March 1928, SC.
67. BMB to Richard I. Manning, 9 April, to George Fort Milton, 23 March 1928, SC; Claude Bowers, *My Life: The Memoirs of Claude Bowers* (1962), p. 186; BMB to Milton, 30 April, 2 May 1928, SC.
68. BMB to William Jennings Bryan, 24 August 1920, SC; "Elections in 1926," 23 November 1925, in BMB Special File, GC; BMB to McAdoo, 30 May 1927, to H. A. Garfield, 2 July 1928, SC.
69. Baruch, *The Public Years*, p. 210; "Proposed Plan of Organization, Democratic Campaign 1928," dated 3 July 1928, GC; *New York Times*, 30 June, 5 July 1928.
70. Telegrams, John J. Raskob to BMB, 19 July, BMB to Raskob, 20 July 1928, Raskob Papers, file 602; *New York Times*, 5 July, 21 August 1928; Baruch, *The Public Years*, pp. 210–12.
71. BMB to Winston Churchill, 6 September, to Carter Glass, 2 July, to Walter F. George, 23 August 1928, SC.
72. BMB to George Fort Milton, 10, 21 September 1928, SC; Milton quoted in Lawrence H. Fuchs, "Election of 1928," in Arthur M. Schlesinger, Jr., ed., *American Presidential Elections* (1971), p. 2599; BMB to McAdoo, 24 October 1928, SC.
73. Baruch, *The Public Years*, p. 213; McAdoo to Jesse H. Jones, 5 October 1928, McAdoo Papers; McAdoo to BMB, 15 October 1928, SC.
74. John J. Raskob to BMB, 17 October 1928, Raskob Papers, file 602.
75. On the sociology of journalism in the 1920s, see Walter B. Pitkin and Robert F. Harrel, *Vocational Studies in Journalism* (1931), pp. 101, 103, 116–18, 123–26, 137–38, 147–48; on the economic history of journalism, see Frank Luther Mott, *American Journalism* (1941), pp. 593, 597, 609, 635.
76. BMB to E. M. House, 18 June, to W. C. Rieck, 12 July, Wilson to BMB, 19 January 1918, WIB.
77. Craig Lloyd, *Aggressive Introvert: Herbert Hoover and Public Relations Management, 1912–1932* (1972), pp. 82–83, 94; Herbert Heaton, *A Scholar in Action: Edwin F. Gay* (1952), pp. 140, 143–44.
78. Wilson to BMB, 19 January 1918, WIB; Raymond Swing, "*Good Evening!*":

A Professional Memoir (1964), pp. 126–28; Lincoln Colcord to BMB, 27 February 1918, WIB. On the House-Colcord relationship, see Lasch, *The New Radicalism in America*, pp. 224–28, 234–50; on Colcord, see "Lincoln Ross Colcord," *Dictionary of American Biography*, supp. 4, pp. 171–73.

79. Auchincloss Diary, 21 April, 12 September 1918; Emil M. Schulz to BMB, 14 May, BMB to House, 18 June, 24 July 1918, WIB; Heaton, *A Scholar in Action*, pp. 143, 149; Lincoln Colcord to BMB, 9 November 1918, WIB; Auchincloss Diary, 21 January, 19 February, 9 March 1919.

80. Herbert Bayard Swope to BMB, 13 November 1919, GC; Krock to BMB, 13 November 1920, 4 May, 11 September 1922, Krock Papers, Box 17; Bruce Bliven to BMB, 31 January, 9 February, 18 March 1921, GC; Robert W. Woolley to Thomas B. Love, 10, 12 March 1921, Woolley Papers, Box 11; Vance McCormick to BMB, 8 December 1920, Lincoln Colcord to BMB, 31 March, BMB to Colcord, 5 April, to Mark Sullivan, 28 May, 13 October 1921, GC.

81. J. O. H. Congrave to BMB, 1 August 1921, 18 October 1920, Bruce Bliven to BMB, 2 August 1921, BMB to Herbert S. Houston, 26 September 1922, M. Lincoln Schuster to BMB, 15 October 1923 (in Swope file), BMB to David Lawrence, 19 February 1926, Condé Nast letters for 1933–34, GC; Josephus Daniels to BMB, 18 January 1932, BMB to Daniels, 23 January 1934, Daniels Papers, Box 65.

82. Leo Rosten, *The Washington Correspondent* (1937), pp. 15, 18, 85, 104–6, 139–42, 174–75, 264.

83. Ibid., pp. 106–7, 111.

84. Ibid., pp. 30, 159–65, 193. For an interesting 1920s critique of journalists as publicists, see Silas Bent, *Ballyhoo: The Voice of the Press* (1927).

85. BMB to Kenneth McKellar, 19 June 1918, WIB. On Hoover as a publicist, see Lloyd, *Aggressive Introvert*, pp. 37–152, passim; for a description of Baruch's journalistic qualities, see Clarkson interview of William Denman, p. 15, WIB.

86. Bess Furman, *Washington By-Line* (1949), pp. 209–10, 216.

87. Rosten, *The Washington Correspondent*, pp. 94–95, 170–72, 194–99.

88. BMB to David Lawrence, 19 February 1926, GC; BMB to Lawrence, 13 March 1933, SC.

89. Krock to Swope, 21 May 1920, Krock Papers; Krock to BMB, 1 July 1924, BMB to Raymond P. Brandt, ca. 1946, SC; Krock to BMB, 13 January 1923 (handwritten), BMB to Krock, ca. 1932, Krock Papers, Box 17; Arthur Krock, *Memoirs: Sixty Years on the Firing Line* (1968), pp. 3–78, passim; Gay Talese, *The Kingdom and the Power* (1970), p. 22; Rosten, *The Washington Correspondent*, p. 138.

90. BMB to Cary T. Grayson, 1 December 1919, Grosvenor Clarkson to A. W. Shaw, 18 June 1923, John E. Nevin to BMB, 22 December 1919, 13 May, 22 July 1920, S. M. Reynolds to BMB, 12 January 1920, GC. See correspondence with Theodore M. Knappen and Samuel Crowther, 1920–22, GC; and Ishbel Ross, *Power with Grace* (1975), p. 291.

91. *New York Times*, 14 October 1921, 16 July 1922, 24 July 1924, 13 December 1922, 17 April 1925, 5 June 1927, 30 January 1928.

92. "Proposed Plan of Organization, Democratic Campaign, 1928," 3 July 1928, GC. For examples of a Baruch dinner list, see "Guests at Dinner Given by Mr. B. M. Baruch on Thursday Evening, March 6, 1924," Peek Papers; and Bowers, *My Life*, pp. 215–16, 222.

93. Hoover quoted in Lloyd, *Aggressive Introvert*, pp. 70, 33. See examples of

Hoover propaganda techniques in ibid., pp. 59—154, passim; see also BMB to Joe T. Robinson, 17 September 1929, SC.

94. Quotation from Introduction by James Boylan in Boylan, ed., *The World and the Twenties: The Golden Years of New York's Legendary Newspaper* (1973), p. 3.

95. Quotations from Introduction by John K. Hutchens in Hutchens and George Oppenheimer, eds., *The Best in the World* (1973), pp. xxi—xxii.

96. Swope quoted in E. J. Kahn, Jr., *The World of Swope* (1965), p. 51. For another biography of Swope, see Alfred Allan Lewis, *Man of the World* (1978).

97. Kahn, *The World of Swope*, pp. 11, 188—89, 200, 203—5; BMB to Henry W. Williams, 22 September 1917, WIB; memos, BMB to Swope and Swope to BMB, ca. February 1918, WIB.

98. Swope and friend quoted in Kahn, *The World of Swope*, pp. 204, 212—13, 200, 219.

99. Auchincloss Diary, 24 August 1918; Grosvenor Clarkson to BMB, 23 December 1918, WIB.

100. Swope to BMB, 13 November 1919, GC.

101. Kahn, *The World of Swope*, pp. 391—92.

102. Krock, *Memoirs*, p. 53; Swope quoted in Kahn, *The World of Swope*, p. 276.

103. Kahn, *The World of Swope*, pp. 391—92, 396—97; Krock to Swope, 27 August 1957, Krock Papers; BMB to Swope, 4 December 1921, GC; BMB quoted in Lawrenson, *Stranger at the Party*, p. 149.

104. BMB quoted in Kahn, *The World of Swope*, p. 395; "Notes re Swope," 1958, SC; Dwight D. Eisenhower to Arthur Krock, 11 October, Krock to Eisenhower, 14 October 1968, Krock Papers.

105. Swope quoted in Kahn, *The World of Swope*, p. 393.

106. Swope to BMB, 24 March 1921, BMB to Swope, 23 September 1931, GC.

107. Moley Diary, 25 March 1933; Swope to BMB, 13 January, 12 September, Swope telegram to BMB, 6 December 1933, SC; Kahn, *The World of Swope*, p. 408.

CHAPTER FIVE

1. Robert D. Cuff, "A 'Dollar-a-Year Man' in Government: George N. Peek and the War Industries Board," *Business History Review* 41 (Winter 1967): 404—20; Robert F. Himmelberg, "Business, Antitrust Policy, and the Industrial Board of the Department of Commerce, 1919," *Business History Review* 42 (Spring 1968): 4—6; George N. Peek to M. J. Healey, 11 January, to S. P. Bush, 24 January 1919, Peek Papers.

2. BMB quoted in Himmelberg, "Business, Antitrust Policy, and the Industrial Board," p. 8.

3. Gay Diary, 1 February 1919; Alex Legge to Peek, 7 February, A. G. Jensen telegram to Peek, 12 February, Legge to Peek, 13 February, Peek to D. R. McLennan, 25 February, BMB to Peek, 27 February 1919, Peek Papers.

4. Himmelberg, "Business, Antitrust Policy, and the Industrial Board," pp. 12—13; Melvin I. Urofsky, *Big Steel and the Wilson Administration: A Study in Business-Government Relations* (1969), pp. 311—16; "Weekly Report to the President, March 24, 1919," p. 9, Central Bureau of Planning and Statistics, Vance McCormick Papers, Box 9; Peek telegram to BMB, 24 March 1919, Peek Papers.

5. Peek telegram to BMB, 26 March, Peek to BMB, 26 March, Peek telegram to BMB, 27 March, William Redfield telegram to Woodrow Wilson, 27 March 1919, Peek Papers.
6. Wilson to BMB, 1 April 1919, WIB; William Redfield to A. Mitchell Palmer, undated, Peek Papers; Himmelberg, "Business, Antitrust Policy, and the Industrial Board," pp. 18–21. For War Trade Board support of the Industrial Board, see Robert W. Woolley's remarks in Phillips telegram to Vance McCormick, 29 March 1919, McCormick Papers.
7. *New York Times*, 3 April 1919; Peek to BMB, 5 April, BMB to Peek, 7, 8 April, Alex Legge to Peek, 8 April 1919, Peek Papers. Also see Peek to BMB, 8, 22 April 1919, Peek Papers.
8. Peek to Alex Legge, 15 April 1919, Peek Papers; Urofsky, *Big Steel*, pp. 321–22; Himmelberg, "Business, Antitrust Policy, and the Industrial Board," pp. 21–22; *New York Times*, 28 February 1920.
9. See E. Jay Howenstine, Jr., "The Industrial Board, Precursor of the N.R.A.: The Price Reduction Movement after World War I," *Journal of Political Economy* 51 (June 1943): 235–50.
10. Wilson to BMB, 8 August 1919, WIB; David Brody, *Labor in Crisis: The Steel Strike of 1919* (1965), pp. 103–4; telegrams, Cary T. Grayson to BMB, 5 September, BMB to Grayson, 8 September 1919, GC; Wilson telegram to BMB, 17 September 1919, WIB.
11. Urofsky, pp. 324–31; Bernard Baruch, *The Public Years* (1960), pp. 150–51; *New York Times*, 29 January 1920.
12. See Edward N. Hurley autobiography, chap. 11, pp. 6–8, Hurley Papers.
13. BMB, "Address at Industrial Preparedness Meeting of the American Society of Mechanical Engineers in Cleveland, May 28, 1924," p. 11, PP.
14. BMB to Mark Sullivan, 10 November 1921, Edwin B. Parker to BMB, 31 August 1920, GC.
15. BMB to H. B. Brougham, 17 September 1920, GC.
16. BMB quoted in Brody, *Labor in Crisis*, p. 128; BMB to George R. James, 3 January 1927, SC.
17. Alex Legge to BMB, 13 November 1919, Ira Bennett to BMB, 14 May 1920, GC.
18. BMB telegram to Carter Glass, 25 June (emphasis added), to James M. Cox, 30 July 1920 (emphasis added), GC.
19. BMB to Herbert Hoover, 27 April 1921, GC; "A Plan to Promote the Public Welfare by More Effective Cooperation between the Government of the United States and Industry," 26 February 1919, H. A. Garfield to Wilson, 4, 27 March, 6 April 1919, Garfield Papers, Box 93. Also see Robert D. Cuff, "Harry Garfield, the Fuel Administration, and the Search for a Cooperative Order during World War I," *American Quarterly* 30 (Spring 1978): 49–52.
20. Grace Whalen for Peek to BMB, 10 November, BMB to Peek, 18 November 1920, Peek to BMB, 13 April 1921, GC; BMB, War Industries Board reunion address, 11 November 1924, PP; *New York Times* 12 November 1924, 2 May 1930.
21. BMB to Carter Glass, 15 February 1929 ("not sent"), SC; clipping from *Washington Post*, 16 June 1929, "Special Memoranda," Miscellaneous 1929 folder, SC.
22. BMB memo to Hugh Johnson, 22 November 1933, "Special Memoranda," Miscellaneous 1929 folder, SC; Hugh S. Johnson, *The Blue Eagle from Egg to Earth* (1935), pp. 153–57, 271; BMB to Charles E. Wilson, 2 January 1946, to Irving Ives, 13 June 1952, SC.
23. Bernard Baruch, "The Consequences of the War to Industry," *Current His-*

tory 29 (November 1928): 189–96; BMB to Mark Sullivan, 21 June 1926, SC.

24. BMB to Alex Legge, 7 March, to Mark Sullivan, 28 May, to Hoover, 27 April 1921, GC; Anderson Diary, 7–10 January 1920.

25. BMB to Frank W. Taussig, 27 October 1920, Hoover to BMB, 1 June, BMB to Hoover, 6 June, to Grosvenor Clarkson, 3 June 1921, GC. Also see *New York Times*, 12 June 1921, sec. 7.

26. Craig Lloyd, *Aggressive Introvert: Herbert Hoover and Public Relations Management, 1912–1932* (1973); Ellis W. Hawley, "Herbert Hoover and the Expansion of the Commerce Department: The Anti-Bureaucrat as Bureaucratic Empire-Builder," paper delivered at the Organization of American Historians convention, April 1970; Richard Hofstadter, *The American Political Tradition* (1948), p. 293.

27. Quoted in Joan Hoff Wilson, "Hoover's Agricultural Policies, 1921–1928," *Agricultural History* 51 (April 1977): 355.

28. Ellis W. Hawley, "Herbert Hoover, the Commerce Secretariat, and the Vision of an 'Associative State,' 1921–1928," *Journal of American History* 61 (June 1974): 117, 121, 124.

29. Ibid., p. 139.

30. Ibid., pp. 139–40.

31. Long Diary, 7 February 1920; "Tuesday, February 10, 1920, Additional Memorandum," and untitled memo, 11 April 1920, Homer Cummings Papers, Box 68.

32. Hofstadter, *The American Political Tradition*, p. 286; Cecil Diary, 3 April 1923.

33. BMB to A. W. Shaw, 3 December 1925, to Hoover, 16 October, to William G. McAdoo, 24 October 1928, SC.

34. Quoted in David Alan Horowitz, "Visions of Harmonious Abundance: Corporate Ideology in the 1920's," doctoral dissertation, University of Minnesota, 1971, pp. 36–37 (emphasis added).

35. Baruch, *The Public Years*, pp. 153–55; *New York Times*, 4 September 1920; "Notes on Baruch Enterprise," undated, W. Jett Lauck Papers, Box 53, BMB to E. T. Meredith, 8 October, Meredith to BMB, 18 October, BMB to Henry A. Wallace, 18 November 1920, GC.

36. E. David Cronon, ed., *The Cabinet Diaries of Josephus Daniels, 1913–1921* (1963), pp. 335, 342; Auchincloss Diary, 3 October, 12 September 1918; BMB to George R. James, 8 November 1920, to Grosvenor Clarkson, 5 April 1921, GC; BMB to H. A. Garfield, 1 November 1927, SC.

37. BMB to Henry S. Berry, 6 November 1919, NIC; BMB to Arthur Capper, 3 January 1920, GC.

38. BMB to J. C. Mohler, 3 December 1920, SC.

39. Copy of Aaron Sapiro to Arthur Capper, 3 January, Theo D. Hammett to BMB, 5 May 1921, GC.

40. James H. Shideler, *Farm Crisis, 1919–1923* (1957), pp. 98, 104–8; *New York Times*, 16, 17 February 1921; James Gray, *Business without Boundary: The Story of General Mills* (1954), p. 86.

41. Shideler, *Farm Crisis*, pp. 108–11; *New York Times*, 2 June 1921; BMB to A. A. Elmore, 4 February, to Mark Sullivan, 21 May, to Herbert S. Houston, 30 May, to Clifford Thorne, 31 May, 3 June, Alex Legge to BMB, 4 June, BMB to Legge, 11 August, Legge to BMB, 13 August, BMB to Thorne, 19 August, 13 September 1921, GC.

42. BMB to Hoover, 2 November 1921, GC.

43. *New York Times*, 22 January 1921; R. W. Bingham to BMB, 25 May 1921, GC; Arthur Krock, *Memoirs: Sixty Years on the Firing Line* (1968), p. 28; Arthur Krock to Herbert Bayard Swope, 7 September 1921, Krock Papers.
44. BMB to Harold C. Booker, 26 January, BMB telegrams to R. A. Cooper, 10 February, 9 March, cotton memo, 22 March 1921, GC.
45. BMB to Hoover, 14 June 1921, GC; Edward C. Blackorby, *Prairie Rebel: The Public Life of William Lemke* (1963), pp. 131, 132, 138, 197; H. B. Brougham to BMB, 17 November, BMB to Brougham, 22 November 1920, George C. Jewett to BMB, 19 September 1924, GC. For more on Baruch's activities in financing farmers in the 1920s, see his correspondence with Eugene Meyer, Jr., John Morron, and Thomas Chadbourne, GC.
46. BMB to William Eckhardt, 14 June, to Carl Gustafson, 14 June 1921, GC; Gary H. Koerselman, "Secretary Hoover and National Farm Policy: Problems of Leadership," *Agricultural History* 51 (April 1977): 383–84.
47. Koerselman, "Secretary Hoover," pp. 381–87; BMB to Eugene Meyer, Jr., 10 August 1921, SC; BMB to Ellery Sedgewick, 10 August, to Alex Legge, 11 August, Theodore M. Knappen to BMB, 8 September, BMB to Knappen, 9 September 1921, GC.
48. BMB to Ellery Sedgewick, 7 April 1921, GC; Theodore M. Knappen, "Looking at the Farmer's Side," *World's Work* 43 (March 1922): 474–80.
49. Bernard Baruch, "Some Aspects of the Farmers' Problems," *Atlantic Monthly*, July 1921, pp. 111–20.
50. C. H. MacDowell to BMB, 2 April, BMB to MacDowell, 5 April 1921, GC: BMB to Mark Sullivan, 9 January 1922, SC; BMB to William S. Kenyon, 9 January 1922, GC.
51. Shideler, *Farm Crisis*, pp. 107–11; William Eckhardt telegram to BMB, 29 March, Carl Gustafson to BMB, 7 April, BMB to Gustafson, 13 March 1922, to E. T. Meredith, 14 December 1921, GC.
52. Gilbert C. Fite, *George N. Peek and the Fight for Farm Parity* (1954), pp. 38–202, passim.
53. Chester C. Davis, COHC, pp. 189–91.
54. BMB to Henry C. Wallace, 1 March, to Arthur Capper, 14 April, 25, 29 May 1922, to William S. Kenyon, 23 January 1923, to Mark Sullivan, 11 November 1922, SC; BMB to R. W. Bingham, 26 June 1923, Bingham Papers; BMB to C. H. MacDowell, 15 October, to J. A. H. Hopkins, 16 October 1923, SC.
55. "Guests at Dinner Given by Mr. B. M. Baruch on Thursday Evening, March 6, 1924," Peek Papers; Peek to BMB, 11 March 1924, GC; BMB to Alex Legge, 19 March 1924, SC; BMB to Otto Kahn, 1 May 1924 (emphasis added), Kahn Papers; George C. Jewett to BMB, 2 May, BMB to Thomas J. Walsh, 14 May 1924, SC.
56. BMB to Peek, 27 April, 12 October 1925 (emphasis added), Peek Papers.
57. BMB to Pat Harrison, 1 May, to Peek, 13 May 1926, SC; Peek to BMB, 17 May 1926, GC; *New York Times*, 14 June, 17, 11 October 1926; Aaron Sapiro to R. W. Bingham, 7 January 1927, Bingham Papers, Box 29; BMB to Joe T. Robinson, 16 February 1927, SC; Fite, *George N. Peek*, pp. 151–84.
58. Fite, *George N. Peek*, pp. 185–220; BMB to Peek, 5, 19 November 1927, 22 December 1928, Peek Papers; BMB to Burton F. Peek, 5 June 1929, 15 January 1930, GC; William T. Hutchinson, *Lowden of Illinois: The Life of Frank O. Lowden* (1957), pp. 626–27.
59. R. A. Cooper to BMB, 13 October 1923, Hugh Johnson memo to BMB, February 1928, BMB to Peek, 31 May 1927, GC; R. W. Bingham to BMB, 29

November 1924, Bingham Papers, Box 4; Eugene Meyer, Jr., to Silas Bent, 16 August 1923, Meyer Papers, Box 151; BMB to George C. Jewett, 30 September 1924, SC.

60. BMB to Alex Legge, 19 March 1924, SC.

61. BMB to Alex Legge, 10 June 1929, to Arthur Capper, 1 April 1927, SC.

62. *New York Times* (from *Forbes Magazine*), 15 April 1927; June 1926 memo attached to BMB to Calvin Coolidge, 22 January 1926 (emphasis added), SC.

63. June 1926 memo attached to BMB to Calvin Coolidge, 22 January 1926, SC; Fite, *George N. Peek*, p. 222 (emphasis added); Herbert Hoover, *Memoirs: The Cabinet and the Presidency* (1952), p. 174.

64. Harry Stuart quoted in Meyer Diary, 19 May 1919.

65. BMB to Frank A. Munsey, 8 June 1925, to Joe T. Robinson, 16 May 1924, SC.

66. "Special Memoranda," Miscellaneous 1919, 1920 folder, 1918–23 box, SC; ACNP Diary, 14 May 1919; BMB to McAdoo, 10 April 1923, memo, June 1923, SC; War Industries Board reunion address, 11 November 1924, PP; memo, 1927, SC. See BMB correspondence with McAdoo, 1924–26, GC; and Baruch, "The Consequences of the War to Industry," p. 193.

67. Preston J. Hubbard, *Origins of the TVA: The Muscle Shoals Controversy, 1920–1932* (1968), pp. 9–10, 82; *New York Times*, 11 January 1920, 27 January 1923; L. L. Summers to BMB, 13 December 1922, BMB to Gray Silver, 25 January 1923, GC; BMB to C. H. MacDowell, 9 January 1923, "Memorandum of Long-Distance Telephone Conversation Between B. M. Baruch and C. H. MacDowell concerning Muscle Shoals Plant," 1923, BMB to Gray Silver, 8 May, to Pat Harrison, 8 May 1924, SC.

68. See Charles S. Maier, *Recasting Bourgeois Europe: Stabilization in France, Germany, and Italy in the Decade after World War I* (1975).

69. C. K. Leith to Edwin F. Gay, 24 March 1919, Gay Papers, Box 1; Norman Davis to Cordell Hull, 9 January 1926, Hull Papers; BMB to Wilson, 3 December 1918, WIB; BMB to J. A. H. Hopkins, 16 October 1923, BMB telegram to George C. Jewett, 21 June 1924, BMB to Peek, 13 May 1926, to Thomas J. Walsh, 14 May 1924, SC.

70. BMB telegram to George C. Jewett, 21 June 1924, BMB to Arthur Capper, 28 September 1922, to Pat Harrison, 1 May 1926, SC.

71. Wilson to Vance McCormick, 8 August 1919, McCormick Papers, Box 3; Meyer Diary, 9 May 1919; Michael Abbott Goldman, "The War Finance Corporation in the Politics of War and Reconstruction, 1917–1923," doctoral dissertation, Rutgers University, 1971; Norman Davis to McAdoo, 25 April 1922, Davis Papers; BMB to Alex Legge, 11 August 1921, copy of Eugene Meyer, Jr., to William S. Benson, 2 May, Meyer to BMB, 5 May 1920, Meyer, "Financing Foreign Trade," speech to American Bankers Association, 10 October 1920, GC.

72. Copy of Otto Kahn, "America and the League of Nations: A Letter to Senator Poindexter," 29 November 1919, reprinted by the American Committee of Businessmen, GC; Cecil Diary, 3 April 1923.

73. *New York Times*, 2 August 1919, 18 July 1921, 10 August 1926; BMB to Mark Sullivan, 27 September 1922, SC; BMB to Sullivan, 7 March 1921, GC; BMB to McAdoo, 18 May 1922, "Confidential Document," 1924, BMB to Mark Sullivan, 7 October, 11 November 1922, SC; BMB to J. J. Jusserand, 9 April 1923, GC; BMB to William S. Kenyon, 9 April 1923, SC; BMB to M. A. Gunst, 3 January 1921, GC; BMB to Frank Kent, 8 April 1929, Kent Papers.

74. See L. L. Summers, "Political Control of Raw Materials in War and Peace," *Proceedings of the Academy of Political Science* 12 (July 1926): 197–203; and Norman Davis to James M. Cox, 17 September 1920, Davis Papers.
75. *New York Times*, 23 June, 2 August 1919, 11 December 1920; Meyer Diary, 14 August 1919; Keith L. Nelson, *Victors Divided: America and the Allies in Germany, 1918–1923* (1975), pp. 102–3; Cronon, *Cabinet Diaries of Josephus Daniels*, pp. 573–74.
76. H. C. B. [Henry C. Breck] memo to Norman Davis, 18 June 1920, attached to galleys, Davis Papers; Fred K. Nielson to John Foster Dulles, 26 June 1920, Dulles Papers.
77. BMB to Louis Loucheur, 24 May, to Grosvenor Clarkson, 17 September 1921, GC; BMB to Carter Glass, 22 September 1921, Glass Papers, Box 165; BMB to Richard H. Edmonds, 28 September, 17 October, to Daniel C. Roper, 4 November 1921, GC; War Industries Board reunion address, 10 December 1920, PP; *New York Times*, 19 December 1920, 13 February, 9 April 1921.
78. Memo, 20 March 1922, GC; Bernard Baruch, "Popular Fallacies about Reparations," *World's Work* 44 (July 1922): 324–27; *New York Times*, 14 December 1922; BMB to Seeley W. Mudd, 23 October 1922, GC; *New York Times*, 8 March 1925; "For the New York Herald Tribune, January, 1928," GC.
79. *New York Times*, 13 May 1923; BMB to J. J. Jusserand, 9 April 1923, GC; BMB to Wheeler Sammons, 19 April 1923, to Pat Harrison, 16 April 1924; memo to Andrew W. Mellon, 1925, SC.
80. BMB to Thomas J. Walsh, 8 February, to Joe T. Robinson, 19 February 1926, SC; *New York Times*, 21 December 1926, 3 August 1927; BMB to Carter Glass, 17 October 1927, Glass Papers, Box 1.
81. Anderson Diary, 23 November 1917; Marquis W. Childs, *I Write from Washington* (1942), p. 152; *New York Times*, 16 July 1922, 18, 31 July 1921, 3 August 1927, 25 November 1929, 13 December 1922.

CHAPTER SIX

1. "'Practical Economist,'" *Time*, 14 March 1938, p. 13; BMB to Brendan Bracken, 15 January 1954, SC; Felix Frankfurter to Eugene Meyer, Jr., 5 June 1935, Frankfurter Papers; Helen Lawrenson, *Stranger at the Party: A Memoir* (1975), p. 142.
2. Jordan A. Schwarz, *The Interregnum of Despair: Hoover, Congress, and the Depression* (1970), pp. 69–70; "Baruch, Enthusiastic Democrat, Helps Hoover in Emergency," *Business Week*, 23 December 1931, pp. 20–21; Agnes E. Meyer Diary, 11 February 1932, in Eugene Meyer, Jr., COHC, p. A23.
3. E. A. Halsey to BMB, 18 September, 11, 29 October, Millard Tydings to BMB, 16 September, 8 November 1930, SC; *New York Times*, 18 June 1931; Frank Kent to BMB, 28 May 1930, SC.
4. For instance, see BMB telegram to Joe T. Robinson, 18 February, BMB to Robinson, 7 June 1932, GC.
5. BMB to George N. Peek, 22 December 1928, Peek Papers; BMB to Joe T. Robinson, 27 March, 25 April 1929, SC.
6. Joe T. Robinson to BMB, 29 November 1930, SC; BMB to Carter Glass, 28 September, Glass to BMB, 1 October 1931, Glass Papers, Box 280; BMB to

Thomas J. Walsh, 10 October 1931, Walsh Papers; BMB to M. M. Neeley, 10 November, to Key Pittman, 11 November 1930, SC; BMB to Glass, 23 May 1930, Glass Papers, Box 280.

7. BMB to John Morron, 7 November 1929, Eugene Meyer, Jr., to BMB, 1 May 1950, SC; *New York Times*, 18 October 1930; BMB to William G. McAdoo, 27 April 1931, GC.

8. BMB to Frank Kent, 1 June 1931, Kent Papers, Box 5; Raymond Moley, *The First New Deal* (1966), p. 388; Daniel Willard to BMB, 4 October, BMB to Willard, 5 October 1932, GC.

9. Hugh Johnson to BMB, 7 July 1930, Johnson memos to M. A. Boyle, 10 February, 27 July, Johnson telegram to Boyle, 29 July 1931, GC; Peek to BMB, 1 June 1932, Peek to Frank O. Lowden, 9 October 1931, Peek Papers.

10. BMB to René de Rougemont, 29 October 1931, GC; Pat Harrison to BMB, 18 December 1931, Harrison Papers; *Congressional Record*, 72d Cong., 1st sess., p. 6357; BMB telegram to Henry T. Rainey, 5 January, Hugh Johnson to BMB, 2 February 1932, SC; BMB to Josephus Daniels, 31 March 1932, Daniels Papers, Box 65.

11. BMB to Herbert Hoover, 10 May, Hoover to BMB, 13 May, BMB to Hoover, 18 May, Hoover to BMB, 23 May 1932, Hoover Presidential Papers; Hugh Johnson to BMB, 3 August, BMB to Joe T. Robinson, 11 December 1931, Arthur Krock telegrams to BMB, 8 March, 17 May 1932, Robinson telegram to BMB, 16 May 1932, SC; Mark Sullivan to Larry Richey, 26 May 1932, Sullivan folder, Richey Papers, Box 26; Schwarz, *The Interregnum of Despair*, pp. 142–73.

12. Key Pittman to BMB, 3 March 1930, Pittman Papers, Box 11; "Special Memoranda," 6 June 1929, Miscellaneous 1929 folder, GC. On European corporatism in the 1920s, see Charles S. Maier, *Recasting Bourgeois Europe: Stabilization in France, Germany, and Italy in the Decade after World War I* (1975).

13. "Special Memoranda," 15 September 1930, Miscellaneous 1930 folder, "Special Memoranda," 12 June 1931, Miscellaneous 1931 folder, GC.

14. *New York Times*, 11 September, 1, 4, 6 October, 13, 21, 22 November 1931, 13, 22 January 1932; BMB telegram to Eugene Meyer, Jr., 22 January 1932, Meyer Papers, Box 5; Agnes E. Meyer Diary, 11 February 1932, in Meyer, COHC, p. A23; Schwarz, *The Interregnum of Despair*, pp. 88–98; James Stuart Olson, *Herbert Hoover and the Reconstruction Finance Corporation, 1931–1933* (1977), pp. 24–44.

15. Report of the National Transportation Committee, New York, 13 February 1933, pp. 45, 4, 6, 11 (emphasis added), PP; BMB to Daniel Willard, 18 January, Willard to BMB, 20 January, 18 April, 18 October 1930, GC; Beatrice Bishop Berle and Travis Beal Jacobs, eds., *Navigating the Rapids, 1918–1971: From the Papers of Adolf A. Berle* (1973), pp. 61–62, 74; *New York Times*, 28 September 1932, 1 January 1931; BMB to Willard, 27 December 1932, GC; Bernard Baruch, *The Public Years* (1960), pp. 193–94.

16. Report of the National Transportation Committee, pp. 17–19, 42–44, 37–39, PP; Robert Moses, *Public Works: A Dangerous Trade* (1970), pp. 317–18, 321, 698, 699.

17. Beatrice B. Berle Diary, 6 October 1932, in Berle and Jacobs, *Navigating the Rapids*, p. 71.

18. Norman Davis to BMB, 24 July, BMB to Davis, 26 July 1920, GC; BMB to Frank Kent, 15 May 1929, SC; Arthur M. Schlesinger, Jr., *The Crisis of the Old Order, 1919–1933* (1957), p. 275.

19. Baruch quoted in Schlesinger, *Crisis of the Old Order*, p. 288; *New York Times*, 12 November 1931; John J. Raskob to Albert C. Ritchie, 5 November 1931, Raskob Papers, file 1966.
20. BMB to Carter Glass, 14 November 1931, Glass Papers, Box 280; Elliott Roosevelt, *F.D.R.: His Personal Letters* (1948), p. 244; Lela Stiles, *The Man behind Roosevelt* (1954), p. 145; BMB to Frank Kent, 1 June 1931, Kent Papers, Box 5; BMB to McAdoo, 27 June 1931, GC; Schlesinger, *Crisis of the Old Order*, p. 288; James F. Byrnes, *All in One Lifetime* (1958), pp. 63–64.
21. Schlesinger, *Crisis of the Old Order*, pp. 404–5; Raymond Moley, *After Seven Years* (1939), pp. 31–32; Rexford Guy Tugwell, *The Brains Trust* (1968), pp. 273–74; *New York Times*, 19 July, 6 September 1932.
22. Tugwell, *The Brains Trust*, p. 274.
23. "Chicago Convention, June 27, 1932," GC; *New York Times*, 27 June, 28 August 1932; "Federal Taxes Can Be Cut a Billion," from *Nation's Business*, September 1932, PP.
24. Berle and Jacobs, *Navigating the Rapids*, pp. 51–54.
25. Tugwell, *The Brains Trust*, p. 346; Schlesinger, *Crisis of the Old Order*, p. 433; Rexford Guy Tugwell, *In Search of Roosevelt* (1972), p. 172.
26. BMB to John J. Raskob, 30 April 1929, SC; Raskob to BMB, 13 November 1929, Raskob Papers, file 158; Moley, *The First New Deal* (1966), p. 388; Frank Freidel, *Launching the New Deal* (1973), p. 142; Elliot A. Rosen, *Hoover, Roosevelt, and the Brains Trust* (1977), pp. 311–13; Harold Ickes, *The Inside Struggle, 1936–1939* (1954), p. 328; Schlesinger, *Crisis of the Old Order*, p. 421.
27. Glass quoted in Lawrenson, *Stranger at the Party*, p. 143; Berle and Jacobs, *Navigating the Rapids*, p. 51; George F. Sparks, ed., *A Many-Colored Toga: The Diary of Henry Fountain Ashurst* (1962), p. 324; Freidel, *Launching the New Deal*, p. 167; Tugwell, *In Search of Roosevelt*, p. 141; BMB to Pat Harrison, 11 January, to Louis [*sic*] Douglas, 22 April, to James M. Cox, 28 April, to FDR, 11 April 1933 ("not sent"), SC; BMB to R. W. Bingham, 20 January 1933, Bingham Papers, Box 7.
28. "Investigations of Economic Problems," Hearings before the Senate Committee on Finance, 72d Cong., 2d sess., 13, 14 February 1933, pp. 1–67; "Fundamentals of Recovery," 13 February 1933, PP; "Leaning on Government," an address before Johns Hopkins University, 22 February 1933, PP; *New York Times*, 25 January, 16 February 1933.
29. BMB to Lord Beaverbrook, 6 April 1956, SC; Cummings Diary, 8–11 December 1932; BMB to McAdoo, 9 February 1933, SC.
30. *New York Times*, 10 November 1932; Berle and Jacobs, *Navigating the Rapids*, p. 75; Moley, *The First New Deal*, pp. 389–90; Moley Diary, 28 January 1933; Cummings Diary, 8–11 December 1932; Freidel, *Launching the New Deal*, p. 142; Moley Diary, 30 January 1933.
31. Tugwell, *In Search of Roosevelt*, p. 243; Tugwell, *The Brains Trust*, p. xxviii; Cummings Diary, 11 January 1933, 23, 8–11 December 1932; Moley Diary, 28 January 1933.
32. BMB to R. W. Bingham, 20 January 1933, Bingham Papers, Box 7; Cummings Diary, 15 January 1933; Freidel, *Launching the New Deal*, pp. 145, 147–49; BMB to McAdoo, 9 February 1933, SC; Joseph P. Lash, *From the Diaries of Felix Frankfurter* (1975), p. 135; Moley Diary, 12, 14 February 1933; Moley, *After Seven Years*, pp. 118–23.
33. Bingham Diary, 5 March 1933; Tugwell, *The Brains Trust*, p. xxviii. Also see Henry A. Wallace, COHC, pp. 149–51.

34. William E. Leuchtenburg, *Franklin D. Roosevelt and the New Deal* (1963), p. 45.
35. Cummings Diary, 15 January 1933; Moley Diary, 22, 28, 30 January, undated [ca. February], 10 February, 7 March 1933; Tugwell Diary, 23 January, 10, 12, 13, 15, 26 February 1933.
36. Herbert Feis to Frankfurter, 23 February, BMB to Feis, 8 March 1933, Feis Papers, Boxes 33 and 11; Bingham Diary, 5 March 1933.
37. The best account of the issues and personalities involved in the conference is Herbert Feis, *1933: Characters in Crisis* (1966). For a study of its international significance, see James Ray Moore, "A History of the World Economic Conference, London, 1933," doctoral dissertation, State University of New York at Stony Brook, 1972.
38. James P. Warburg, COHC, pp. 347, 413, 676; Bingham Diary, 12 July 1933; David E. Koskoff, *Joseph P. Kennedy* (1974), pp. 48–49; Moore, "History of the World Economic Conference," pp. 194, 321; Arthur M. Schlesinger, Jr., *The Coming of the New Deal* (1958), pp. 201–2.
39. Cummings Diary, 15 January 1933.
40. Warburg, COHC, p. 819; James M. Cox, *Journey through My Years* (1946), pp. 356–57; Lash, *From the Diaries of Felix Frankfurter*, pp. 134–35; Frankfurter to Raymond Moley, 12 April 1933, Moley Papers.
41. Moley Diary, 16 May 1933; Feis, *1933*, pp. 198–99; Warburg, COHC, pp. 978, 1038; Moley, *The First New Deal*, p. 436; *New York Times*, 20, 22, 23, 24 June 1933.
42. Feis, *1933*, pp. 201, 190, 195; Warburg, COHC, p. 1068; Bingham Diary, 30, 29 June 1933.
43. Edgar B. Nixon, ed., *Franklin D. Roosevelt and Foreign Affairs*, 3 vols. (1969), 1:143; BMB telegram to Herbert Bayard Swope, 27 June 1933, SC; George Foster Peabody to FDR, 27 February 1933, PPF 660.
44. Moley Diary, 30 June 1933.
45. Ibid., 1 July 1933; Feis, *1933*, pp. 202–58.
46. Moley, *The First New Deal*, p. 387; Cummings Diary, 3 July 1933; Bingham Diary, 13 July 1933; Clapper Diary, 8 September 1933; Swope to Frankfurter, 8 July 1933, Frankfurter Papers; E. J. Kahn, Jr., *The World of Swope* (1965), pp. 381–85; *New York Times*, 21, 27 July 1933.
47. *Baltimore Sun*, quoted in *New York Times*, 25 June 1933, sec. 4; T. R. B., "Washington Notes," *New Republic*, 5 July 1933, p. 207.
48. Henry A. Wallace to Gilbert Fite, 18 June 1953, Wallace Papers; Wallace, COHC, pp. 162, 2400, 1889, 292, 163.
49. Peek to BMB, 29 October, Peek to Wallace, 29 October 1931, Peek Papers; Wallace to BMB, 2 March 1932, Wallace Papers; Gilbert C. Fite, *George N. Peek and the Fight for Farm Parity* (1954), pp. 237–39; Wallace to BMB, 9, 19 November, BMB to Wallace, 21 November 1932, Wallace Papers.
50. Freidel, *Launching the New Deal*, pp. 307–19; BMB to Peek, 19 November, copy of Wallace to FDR, 17 November 1932, Peek Papers; Fite, *George N. Peek*, pp. 241–42, 248; Peek Diary, 4 March 1933; Wallace, COHC, p. 231.
51. BMB to Gilbert Fite, 19 January 1954, SC; Schlesinger, *Coming of the New Deal*, p. 46; Baruch, *The Public Years*, p. 251; BMB to Wallace, 3 April 1935, SC; Wallace, COHC, p. 226; William T. Hutchinson, *Lowden of Illinois: The Life of Frank O. Lowden* (1957), p. 669; BMB telegram to Wallace, 20 March 1933, SC; Peek Diary, 18, 20, 11 March, 4, 5 April 1933.
52. Tugwell Diary, 3 April 1933.
53. Tugwell, *The Brains Trust*, pp. 454–57, 477; Rexford Guy Tugwell,

Roosevelt's Revolution: The First Year–A Personal Perspective (1977), pp. 107, 84; James Gray, *Business without Boundary: The Story of General Mills* (1954), p. 193; BMB to Alex Legge, 19 March 1924, SC; Peek Diary, 16, 17, 21, 24–28 March 1933; Freidel, *Launching the New Deal*, p. 314.

54. Peek to S. P. Bush, 25 May 1932, Peek Papers; Moley Diary, 5 January 1933; *New York Times*, 1 October, 23 November 1931; BMB to Josephus Daniels, 31 March 1932, Daniels Papers, Box 65; BMB to Wallace, 21 November 1932, Wallace Papers; "Fundamentals of Recovery," 13 February 1933, pp. 25–27, 33–34, PP; Peek Diary, 23 February 1933.

55. Peek to S. P. Bush, 25 May 1932, Diary, 29 January, 14, 15 March 1933, Peek Papers; Gray, *Business without Boundary*, p. 194; Wallace, COHC, p. 231.

56. Peek Diary, 16, 18, 22, 25, 26, 28–31 March, 1, 2 April 1933.

57. Ibid., 25, 29, 31 March, 2, 4, 5, 7 April 1933; Tugwell Diary, 3 April 1933; Fite, *George N. Peek*, pp. 251–53, 256; Freidel, *Launching the New Deal*, pp. 316–19.

58. BMB to FDR, 10 April ("not sent"), to Amon G. Carter, 29 June, to Joe T. Robinson, 11 December 1933, SC.

59. Fite, *George N. Peek*, pp. 253–66; Tugwell, *Roosevelt's Revolution*, pp. 193–99; Schlesinger, *Coming of the New Deal*, pp. 57–59, 74–75.

60. Cummings Diary, 8 December 1933.

61. John Kennedy Ohl, "Tales Told by a New Dealer," *Montana: The Magazine of Western History* 25 (Autumn 1975): 68; Frances Perkins, COHC, 5:112.

62. Clapper Diary, 13 July 1933; Fite, *George N. Peek*, pp. 72–76; Hugh S. Johnson, *The Blue Eagle from Egg to Earth* (1935), pp. 103–8, 115–16; John Kennedy Ohl, "'Old Iron Pants': The Wartime Career of General Hugh S. Johnson, 1917–1918," doctoral dissertation, University of Cincinnati, 1971; BMB to Cary T. Grayson, 13 February 1920, Hugh Johnson to BMB, ca. February 1930, GC.

63. Tugwell, *In Search of Roosevelt*, pp. 135–36; Moley, *After Seven Years*, pp. 43–44, 184–88; Moses, *Public Works*, pp. 698–99; Moley Diary, 5 January 1933; Peek Diary, 14–16, 20, 27 March, 13 April 1933; Johnson, *The Blue Eagle*, pp. 191–92; Hugh Johnson memo to Louis Howe, 24 March, FDR to Johnson, 31 March 1933, PPF 702.

64. Tugwell Diary, 30 May 1933; Johnson, *The Blue Eagle*, pp. 207–8.

65. Perkins, COHC, 5:94–104; Frances Perkins, *The Roosevelt I Knew* (1964 ed.), pp. 200–201.

66. Johnson, *The Blue Eagle*, pp. 152–57, 250–51, 271–72, 262–65; Louis Galambos, *Competition and Cooperation: The Emergence of a National Trade Association* (1966), pp. 209–14, 228 n, 234–38; Ellis W. Hawley, *The New Deal and the Problem of Monopoly* (1966), pp. 35–71; Schlesinger, *Coming of the New Deal*, pp. 87–151.

67. BMB telegrams and letters to Hugh Johnson, 1933, SC and GC; BMB to Johnson, 8 February 1934, SC.

68. BMB to H. G. Moulton, 24 March 1933, SC; BMB quoted in Johnson, *The Blue Eagle*, pp. 279, 154–55 (emphasis added).

69. BMB telegram to McAdoo, 3 June 1933, SC.

70. See marked copy of Johnson's St. Louis speech, GC; Johnson, *The Blue Eagle*, pp. 262–65; *New York Times*, 3 November 1933; memo to Hugh Johnson, 1 November 1933, GC; BMB to Johnson, 4 November 1933, SC; and Schlesinger, *Coming of the New Deal*, p. 121.

71. "Special Memoranda" to Hugh Johnson, 22 November 1933, untitled, 25 June 1934, GC.

72. Tugwell, *Roosevelt's Revolution*, pp. 80–82, 146–47, 233–45 (quotation from p. 244); BMB to Hugh Johnson, 8 June 1934, SC.
73. Clapper Diary, 13, 17 July 1933; Peek Diary, 27 September 1933.
74. *New York Times*, 1, 2 January 1934; Harold L. Ickes, *The First Thousand Days, 1933–1936* (1953), pp. 147–48, 173; copy of Hugh Johnson to FDR, 20 August, Johnson telegram to BMB, 19 August 1934, SC.
75. Donald R. Richberg, *My Hero: The Indiscreet Memoirs of an Eventful but Unheroic Life* (1954), p. 176; Perkins, COHC, 5:109–12, 544–45; *New York Times*, 24, 25 September 1934; Schlesinger, *Coming of the New Deal*, pp. 152–57; Hawley, *The New Deal and the Problem of Monopoly*, pp. 91–146; BMB-Peek telephone conversation, 17 November 1934, Peek Papers.
76. Memo from Stephen Early, 8 October 1934, PPF 88; BMB-Peek telephone conversation, 17 November 1934, Peek Papers; "Rabbit" to Louis Howe, ca. 1935, Presidential Secretary File, Roosevelt Papers, Box 7; BMB to FDR, 20 December 1935, SC.
77. "(Continuation of General Journal for the middle of October, 1936)," Moley Papers, Box 1; Ickes, *The Inside Struggle*, p. 7. See Hugh Johnson correspondence for 1941–42, GC.
78. BMB to Bernard M. Baruch, Jr., 30 March 1932, to Henry Morgenthau, Jr., 30 December 1937, 13 January 1938, GC; Moley Diary, 19 February 1933; Freidel, *Launching the New Deal*, pp. 320–36.
79. Perkins, COHC, 5:101–5.
80. "Investigation of Economic Problems," Hearings before the Senate Committee on Finance, 72d Cong., 2d. sess., 1933, pt. 1, pp. 30, 33.
81. BMB to James F. Byrnes, 22 April 1933 ("not sent"), to Joe T. Robinson, 17 January 1934, SC; Swope to BMB, 24 November 1933, GC; BMB to Winston Churchill, 17 November 1933, SC; Cummings Diary, 16 November 1933; Schlesinger, *Coming of the New Deal*, pp. 238–47; Merlo J. Pusey, *Eugene Meyer* (1974), p. 87.
82. BMB to Marguerite LeHand, 8 May, LeHand to BMB, 14 May 1934, OF 197-A, Box 2; BMB memo to FDR, 11 October, BMB memo on silver, 15 October 1934, PPF 1820, Box 1.
83. Baruch, *The Public Years*, pp. 222–23; Bernard Baruch, *My Own Story* (1957), pp. 229–30; "Alaska Juneau Gold Mining Company, 1930–1937" file, Ogden L. Mills, Jr., Papers, Box 89; BMB correspondence with Ogden L. Mills, Jr., 1935–36; Joe T. Robinson to BMB, 25 April 1936, GC.
84. BMB to William E. Borah, 8 October 1934, SC.
85. BMB to Joe T. Robinson, 17 January 1934, SC.
86. BMB to H. A. Garfield, 5 June 1933, GC; BMB telegram to FDR, 6 March 1933, SC; Peek Diary, 7 April 1933; BMB to FDR, 10 April 1933 ("not sent"), SC; "The World You Enter," Oglethorpe University commencement address, 28 May 1933, PP.
87. *New York Times*, 10 September 1933; Bernard Baruch, "The Dangers of Inflation," *Saturday Evening Post*, 25 November 1933, pp. 5–7, 84–87; BMB to FDR, 6 November ("not sent"), to Louis Howe, 18 November 1933, SC; Key Pittman to FDR, 23 November 1933, OF 229, Box 15.
88. BMB to Churchill, 17 November 1933, SC; memo, "Setting Class vs. Class," 14 November 1933, "The 1934th Psalm," GC; Schwarz, *The Interregnum of Despair*, p. 174.
89. BMB to Joe T. Robinson, 17 January 1934, SC; untitled memo, 14 February 1934, GC.

90. Untitled memo, 14 February 1934, GC; BMB to L. du Pont, 1 October 1934, SC.
91. BMB to Christie Benet, 18 December 1935, SC.
92. BMB to James F. Byrnes, 5 November 1936, to J. J. McSwain, 16 December 1935, SC.
93. BMB to Wallace, 6 July 1937, Wallace Papers.
94. Alfred P. Sloan, Jr., to BMB, 12 May, BMB to Sloan, 25 May, Sloan to BMB, 2 June, BMB to Sloan, 17 June, Sloan to BMB, 27 June, Krock to BMB, 13 June 1938, SC; Paul Conkin, *The New Deal* (1967), p. 74.
95. "Retirement: Baruch Decides to Quit Business and Write," *Newsweek*, 30 June 1934, pp. 24–25; *New York Times*, 22 December 1934.
96. Marquis James to BMB, 5 March 1934, 10 February 1936, ca. March 1936, BMB to W. F. Clark, 26 June 1934, GC; BMB to Churchill, 12 May 1935, SC.
97. BMB to Frank W. Taussig, 12 May 1937, GC.
98. Swope to Frankfurter, 5 December 1933, Frankfurter Papers, Oxford file; Wallace, COHC, p. 1679.
99. Jeffrey Potter, *Men, Money and Magic: The Story of Dorothy Schiff* (1976), p. 262; BMB to FDR, 8 July, FDR to BMB, 21 July, BMB to FDR, 30 December 1937, to Samuel I. Rosenman, 6 January 1959, SC; Unofficial Observer [John Franklin Carter], *The New Dealers* (1934), p. 338.
100. Samuel I. Rosenman, *Working with Roosevelt* (1952), p. 335; Perkins, COHC, 5:427.
101. BMB to Eleanor Roosevelt, 5 April 1955, SC; Stephen Early memo, 8 October 1934, PPF 88; BMB to Marguerite LeHand, 18 February 1935, SC; BMB to Louis Howe, 23 November 1933, GC; articles dated 17 December 1935, Edwin Watson Papers, Box 15; Harry B. Hawes to Stephen Early, 5 March 1940, Early Papers, Box 1; BMB to FDR, 14 November 1934, SC; Koskoff, *Joseph P. Kennedy*, p. 55; Krock to Frank Kent, 7 May 1937, Kent Papers, Box 6.
102. Warburg, COHC, p. 347; Robert E. Sherwood, *Roosevelt and Hopkins* (1948), p. 98; Matthew Josephson, *Infidel in the Temple* (1967), p. 259; Herbert Feis to Frankfurter, 23 February 1933, Feis Papers. Box 33.
103. Tom Corcoran and Ben Cohen to Frankfurter, 18 June 1934, Frankfurter Papers.
104. Joseph P. Lash, *Eleanor and Franklin* (1971), p. 536.
105. Eleanor Roosevelt quoted in Joseph P. Lash, *Eleanor: The Years Alone* (1972), pp. 211–12, and in Lash, *Eleanor and Franklin*, pp. 572–73, 546.
106. Lawrenson, *Stranger at the Party*, p. 137, 136; Eleanor Roosevelt quoted in Margaret L. Coit, *Mr. Baruch* (1957), p. 451; BMB quoted in Lash, *Eleanor and Franklin*, p. 538; BMB to Eleanor Roosevelt, 28 May 1935, ER, Box 1328. For more on the Baruch-Mrs. Roosevelt friendship, see their sizable correspondence, SC, GC, and ER.
107. John A. Salmond, "Aubrey Williams: Atypical New Dealer," in John Braeman, Robert H. Bremner, and David Brody, eds., *The New Deal: The National Level* (1975), p. 236; Elliott Roosevelt and James Brough, *A Rendezvous with Destiny: The Roosevelts of the White House* (1975), p. 95; James Roosevelt with Bill Libby, *My Parents: A Differing View* (1976), p. 177.
108. Bess Furman, *Washington By-Line* (1949), pp. 209–10; *New York Times*, 29 January 1935; Lash, *Eleanor and Franklin*, p. 529; BMB to Eleanor Roosevelt, 26 January 1935, ER, Box 1328.

109. Lash, *Eleanor and Franklin*, pp. 536–38, 543–47; BMB to Eleanor Roosevelt, 26 January 1935, 16 April 1936, ca. 1941, ER, Boxes 1328, 1365, and 1588. Also see BMB to Wallace, 6 July 1937, Wallace Papers; and Coit, *Mr. Baruch*, pp. 451–54. For a good history of Arthurdale, see Thomas H. Coode and Dennis E. Fabbri, "The New Deal's Arthurdale Project in West Virginia," *West Virginia History* 36 (July 1975): 291–308.
110. Journal, 3 March 1936, Moley Papers.
111. BMB to Frank Kent, 13 March, to Ogden L. Mills, Jr., 13 March, to Josephus Daniels, 12 March 1936, SC.
112. *New York Times*, 6 May 1936; BMB to Eugene Meyer, Jr., 20 May 1936, SC; Pusey, *Eugene Meyer*, pp. 272–74; Stephen Early to FDR, 22 May 1936, PPF 88.
113. BMB to Frank Kent, 17 March 1936, SC; Stephen Early to FDR, 22 May 1936, PPF 88; *New York Times*, 25, 30 June 1936.
114. BMB to Frank Kent, 17 March 1936, SC; "(Continuation of General Journal for middle of October, 1936)," Moley Papers, Box 1; Frank Kent telegram to BMB, 4 November 1936, SC.
115. Thomas Corcoran and Benjamin Cohen to Frankfurter, 18 June 1934, Frankfurter Papers; Hawley, *The New Deal and the Problem of Monopoly*, pp. 344–50; Arthur M. Schlesinger, Jr., *The Politics of Upheaval* (1960), pp. 325–34; Leuchtenburg, *Franklin D. Roosevelt*, pp. 153–54; Herbert Stein, *The Fiscal Revolution in America* (1969), p. 83.
116. Stein, *The Fiscal Revolution in America*, pp. 85–90; Randolph E. Paul, *Taxation in the United States* (1954), pp. 189–99; Hawley, *The New Deal and the Problem of Monopoly*, pp. 350–57; Walter Kraft Lambert, "New Deal Revenue Acts: The Politics of Taxation," doctoral dissertation, University of Texas at Austin, 1970, pp. 266–356, 409–21.
117. Schwarz, *The Interregnum of Despair*, pp. 213–16; BMB to Raymond G. Carroll, 20 November 1934, SC.
118. BMB to John J. Pershing, 11 March 1935, to Churchill, 22 November 1934, to Joe T. Robinson, 18 June, to Frank Kent, 17 October 1935, SC.
119. Morgenthau Diary, 11 December 1935; BMB to FDR, 19 December 1935, SC.
120. BMB to Frank Kent, 18 March, to Josephus Daniels, 12, 16 March 1936, SC; Joe T. Robinson to BMB, 12 April 1936, GC.
121. BMB to Joe T. Robinson, 18 April, to FDR, 30 April (emphasis added), to Key Pittman, 12 June 1936, SC; Stein, *The Fiscal Revolution in America*, p. 89.
122. Leuchtenburg, *Franklin D. Roosevelt*, pp. 231–38; BMB to Eleanor Roosevelt, 7 February, to FDR, 30 April, to Joe T. Robinson, 19 April, Robinson to BMB, 12 July 1937, SC.
123. Ickes, *The Inside Struggle*, pp. 161–62; *New York Times*, 15 July 1937.
124. See correspondence with E. A. Halsey, 1937–38, GC; Krock, *New York Times*, 29 April 1937; Daniel Willard to BMB, 10 July, BMB to Joe Guffey, 22 June, James F. Byrnes to BMB, 30 June, 7 October 1937, SC; Ickes, *The Inside Struggle*, pp. 154–55, 164.
125. BMB to Harry L. Hopkins, 28 September, to Wallace, 18 October, to Leon Henderson, 18 October 1937, SC; James F. Byrnes to R. G. Elbert, 20 October 1937, Byrnes Papers; Stein, *The Fiscal Revolution in America*, p. 115.
126. Pat Harrison, "Our Tax Problem," *Vital Speeches*, 15 December 1937, pp. 138–40; Lambert, "New Deal Revenue Acts," pp. 422, 428–33, 448.
127. Morgenthau Diaries, 11 December 1935; testimony of BMB before the Spe-

cial Committee of the U.S. Senate to Investigate Unemployment and Relief, 28 February, 1 March 1938, PP; *New York Times*, 1, 2 March 1938. See BMB's handwritten notes re taxes on Hotel Carlton stationery, 1937, SC; and Lambert, "New Deal Revenue Acts," pp. 451–52.

128. John Morton Blum, *From the Morgenthau Diaries: Years of Crisis, 1928–1938* (1959), p. 443; Ickes, *The Inside Struggle*, p. 428; Krock, *New York Times*, 3 March 1938.

129. Krock, *New York Times*, 3 March 1938; BMB to E. A. Halsey, 3 March, to James F. Byrnes, 4 March, Byrnes to BMB, 7 March 1938, SC; Lambert, "New Deal Revenue Acts," pp. 464–66, 484–94; Krock, *New York Times*, 20, 22 April 1938 (original emphasis); BMB to Byrnes, 30 April 1938, SC; Paul, *Taxation in the United States*, pp. 208–18.

130. *New York Times*, 30 May 1938.

131. Wallace, COHC, pp. 528–29; Leuchtenburg, *Franklin D. Roosevelt*, pp. 266–67; James T. Patterson, *Congressional Conservatism and the New Deal: The Growth of the Conservative Coalition in Congress, 1933–1939* (1967), pp. 272–73.

132. BMB telegram to Alben W. Barkley, 9 June 1933, SC; anonymous assessment of Kentucky race, clipping from *New York Times*, 11 July 1938, Homer Cummings Papers, Box 78; Ickes, *The Inside Struggle*, p. 328; BMB to Barkley, 6 January 1953, 8 June 1954, SC; Baruch, *The Public Years*, pp. 258–59.

133. BMB to James F. Byrnes, 30 April, Byrnes to BMB, 5 May 1938, SC; "Baruch Case" folder in miscellaneous 1937 file, Byrnes to BMB, 16 August, Byrnes to M. A. Boyle, 17 August 1938, file 21, Byrnes Papers; Jack Irby Hayes, Jr., "South Carolina and the New Deal, 1932–1938," doctoral dissertation, University of South Carolina, 1972, pp. 517–18; Winfred Bobo Moore, Jr., "New South Statesman: The Political Career of James Francis Byrnes, 1911–1941," doctoral dissertation, Duke University, 1976, p. 173.

134. James F. Byrnes to BMB, 28 September 1938, Byrnes Papers; Byrnes to BMB, 8, 14 October 1938, SC; E. A. Halsey to BMB, 26 October 1938, GC.

135. *New York Times*, 15 June 1937; Roosevelt quoted in Stein, *The Fiscal Revolution in America*, pp. 103–4 (emphasis added); Hawley, *The New Deal and the Problem of Monopoly*, pp. 391–98, 412; BMB to James F. Byrnes, 30 April 1938, SC.

136. Stein, *The Fiscal Revolution in America*, pp. 108–12, 116–17; Hawley, *The New Deal and the Problem of Monopoly*, pp. 408–10; Frank Kent to Joseph P. Kennedy, 12 April 1938, Kent Papers, Box 6; BMB to James F. Byrnes, 30 April, 30 May 1938, SC.

CHAPTER SEVEN

1. *New York Times*, 7, 12 September 1937; BMB to FDR, 2 June 1938, SC.

2. FDR memo, 1938, copy of original with Harold Epstein explanatory note, 14 November 1952, BMB telegram to FDR, 3 September 1938, SC; dispatch, 15 September 1938, Louis Johnson Papers, Box 2; BMB to Winston Churchill, 22 July 1947, SC; *New York Times*, 20 September 1938; clipping, *Washington Star*, 20 September 1938, and editorial summary, Johnson Papers, Box 2.

3. Eliot Janeway, *The Struggle for Survival: A Chronicle of Economic Mobilization in World War II* (1951), pp. 24–25; Harold Ickes, *The Inside Struggle*,

1936–1939 (1954), pp. 474–75, 470; Harold Ickes, *The Lowering Clouds, 1939–1941* (1955), p. 438; *New York Times*, 24 September 1938.

4. Hugh Johnson to BMB, 28 November 1919, BMB to Grosvenor Clarkson, 3 September, 5 December 1920, copies of Henry M. Channing to Clarkson, 5 April, and Clarkson to Channing, 7 April 1921, GC; Anderson Diary, 28 October 1921; BMB to Herbert Bayard Swope, 4 December 1921, Mark Sullivan to BMB, 18 April 1923, GC; BMB to John W. Weeks, 22 January 1923, SC.

5. BMB to Mark Sullivan, 20 December 1921, GC; Harry B. Yoshpe, "Bernard M. Baruch: Civilian Godfather of the Military M-Day Plan," *Military Affairs* 29 (Spring 1965): 1–15.

6. Robert D. Ward, "Against the Tide: The Preparedness Movement of 1923–1924," *Military Affairs* 38 (April 1974): 59–61.

7. BMB to Sidney Ballou, 11 May 1926, to James H. Wadsworth, Jr., 5 February 1923, SC; BMB to Arthur Krock, 29 August [1924] (handwritten), Krock Papers.

8. BMB to C. H. McDowell, 6 January, to John W. Weeks, 22 January, Alex Legge to BMB, 9 February, BMB to Dwight F. Davis, 6 March, 18 June, 30 October, to John J. Pershing, 1 June, Davis to BMB, 20 August 1923, SC.

9. Dwight F. Davis to John J. Pershing, 4 June 1924, Pershing Papers.

10. "Paper on price-fixing used in making War College address, December 2, 1925," SC; BMB, speech to convention of Reserve Officers Association, Indianapolis, 22 April 1929, BMB, Army War College speeches, 12 February 1924, 15 January 1925, PP; Yoshpe, "Bernard M. Baruch," 3–11.

11. Dwight D. Eisenhower, *At Ease: Stories I Tell to Friends* (1967), pp. 210–12; D. Clayton James, *The Years of MacArthur, 1880–1941* (1970), pp. 462–63; Steve Neal, *The Eisenhowers: Reluctant Dynasty* (1978), p. 78.

12. "Taking the Profit out of War: Suggested Policies," 6 March 1931, PP; *New York Times*, 7, 10, 12 March, 15, 22, 23 May 1931; Yoshpe, "Bernard M. Baruch," 11–12; Albert A. Blum, "Birth and Death of the M-Day Plan," in Harold Stein, *American Civil-Military Decisions* (1963), pp. 65–67; James, *The Years of MacArthur*, pp. 463–64; Bernard Baruch, *The Public Years* (1960), pp. 264–65.

13. BMB to Krock, 29 August [1924] (handwritten), Krock Papers; BMB to John J. Pershing, 1 February 1935, GC; Forrest C. Pogue, *George C. Marshall: Education of a General, 1880–1939* (1963), p. 224; Emory S. Land, COHC, p. 190.

14. Eisenhower, *At Ease*, p. 211; BMB to Frank A. Scott, 4 March 1926, GC.

15. Edgar B. Nixon, ed., *Franklin D. Roosevelt and Foreign Affairs*, 3 vols. (1969), 2:311–13, *New York Times*, 13, 16 December 1934; John E. Wiltz, *In Search of Peace: The Senate Munitions Inquiry, 1934–1936* (1963), pp. 119–22, 131–32; Wayne S. Cole, *Senator Gerald P. Nye and American Foreign Relations* (1962), pp. 82–83.

16. Baruch had been articulating the theme "taking the profit out of war" since at least 1922 and had published an article summarizing his proposals. See Bernard Baruch, "Taking the Profit out of War," *Atlantic Monthly*, January 1926, pp. 23–29; also see Baruch memo, 11 December 1934, OF 178, Box 1.

17. Wiltz, *In Search of Peace*, pp. 132–37; Paul A. C. Koistinen, "The 'Industrial-Military Complex' in Historical Perspective: The Interwar Years," *Journal of American History* 56 (March 1970): 834–35.

18. Gerald P. Nye to BMB, 8 March 1935, SC; "Munitions Industry," Senate Special Committee Hearings, 74th Cong., 1st sess., 1935, pp. 6261–62; An-

derson Diary, 5 December 1917; E. J. Kahn, Jr., *The World of Swope* (1965), pp. 397–98; James F. Byrnes, *All in One Lifetime* (1958), p. 90.

19. BMB to J. J. McSwain, 18 February, McSwain to BMB, 19 February 1935, SC; "Munitions Industry," pp. 6278–79, 6270–72, 6633–48; BMB to Churchill, 12 May, to C. H. McDowell, 8 April 1935, SC; *New York Times*, 28–30 March, 16 April 1935.

20. Wiltz, *In Search of Peace*, pp. 137–40; *New York Times*, 17 April 1935; Arthur H. Vandenberg to BMB, 23 April, BMB to Swope, 18 April 1935, GC; BMB to Frank Kent, 8 May, to Pat Harrison, 18 June, to Vandenberg, 22 April 1935, SC.

21. BMB to Pat Harrison, 18 June, to J. J. McSwain, 13 June, to Joe T. Robinson, 18 June, to Arthur H. Vandenberg, 13 December 1935, SC.

22. *New York Times*, 3 October 1935 (emphasis added).

23. BMB to Louis Loucheur, 4 November 1920, to J. R. Howard, 9 September 1921, GC; Anderson Diary, 13 June 1921.

24. BMB-Peek telephone conversation, 17 November 1934, Peek Papers; BMB to Daniel Willard, 11 September, 1940, SC.

25. Bernard Baruch, "Cash and Carry," *Today*, 2 November 1935, pp. 6–7.

26. E. A. Halsey to BMB, 2 January 1936, GC; *New York Times*, 11, 20 January 1936; BMB to Joe T. Robinson, 25 January 1936, SC; Robert A. Divine, *The Illusion of Neutrality: Franklin D. Roosevelt and the Struggle over the Arms Embargo* (1962), pp. 139–61.

27. Bernard Baruch, "'Neutrality,'" *Current History* 44 (June 1936): 32–44; *New York Times*, 3 May, 14, 24 August 1936.

28. State Department memo quoted in Divine, *The Illusion of Neutrality*, p. 166; conversation of Peek and Raymond Moley, 27 November 1935, Peek Papers; *New York Times*, 3 January 1937, sec. 4.

29. Pittman quoted in Divine, *The Illusion of Neutrality*, p. 185; Key Pittman to BMB, 5 June 1937, GC; William E. Borah to BMB, 6 January, BMB to Borah, 18 January 1937, SC; *New York Times*, 29 January, 5 February 1937; Bernard Baruch, "Neutrality and Common Sense," *Atlantic Monthly*, March 1937, pp. 368–72 (emphasis added).

30. Bernard Baruch, "Neutrality—An Uncharted Sea," *Vital Speeches*, 15 June 1937, pp. 535–38.

31. Helen Lawrenson, *Stranger at the Party: A Memoir* (1975), pp. 143–44; BMB to Brendan Bracken, 21 March, to Josephus Daniels, 28 June 1938, SC; Divine, *The Illusion of Neutrality*, pp. 168–72, 223–27; BMB to the editor, *Tablet*, Brooklyn, 5 October 1938, GC.

32. Divine, *The Illusion of Neutrality*, pp. 236–51; *New York Times*, 8 March, 6, 7, 9 April 1939; "Neutrality, Peace Legislation, and Our Foreign Policy," Hearings before the Senate Committee on Foreign Relations, 76th Cong., 1st sess., 5, 6 April 1939; "Neutrality, Peace Legislation, and Our Foreign Policy," Testimony of Bernard M. Baruch before the United States Senate Committee on Foreign Relations, 6 April 1939, PP.

33. Key Pittman to BMB, 24 April 1939, GC; Divine, *The Illusion of Neutrality*, pp. 257–85.

34. *New York Times*, 8 November 1935.

35. See, for instance, lecture to the Army War College, 6 March 1930, PP.

36. BMB-Peek telephone conversation, 17 November 1934, Peek Papers.

37. Peek-Cordell Hull telephone conversation, 16 June, Peek-BMB telephone conversation, 16 June, conversation of GNP with BMB, 8 January 1934, Peek to Charles Stephenson Smith, 7 June 1940, Peek Papers. Also see Lloyd C.

Gardner, *Economic Aspects of New Deal Diplomacy* (1964), pp. 98–104.

38. Joseph P. Kennedy to BMB, 28 March 1938, SC (also, for nearly identical content, see Kennedy to Krock, 28 March 1938, Krock Papers); *New York Times*, 14 August 1936.

39. *New York Times*, 24, 28, 30 August 1936.

40. Cordell Hull to BMB, 27 February, BMB to Hull, 9 March, Hull to BMB, 13 March, BMB to Hull, 30 April, BMB to FDR, 30 April 1937, SC.

41. BMB to Churchill, 20 September 1937, SC. Also see BMB to Brendan Bracken, 24 December 1937, SC.

42. Joseph P. Kennedy to BMB, 28 March, 14 April, 3, 17, 31 May 1938, SC.

43. James F. Byrnes to BMB, 17 October, BMB to Byrnes, 18 October, to Josephus Daniels, 11 April, 28 June, to Cordell Hull, 16 October 1938, SC; copy of BMB memo to the White House, 27 June 1938, Johnson Papers, Box 2; BMB to Josephus Daniels, 28 June 1938, GC; Joseph S. Tulchin, *The Aftermath of War: World War I and U.S. Policy toward Latin America* (1971), p. 74; David E. Koskoff, *Joseph P. Kennedy* (1974), pp. 195–98; Gardner, *Economic Aspects of New Deal Diplomacy*, pp. 106–7.

44. BMB to E. M. Watson, 19 July 1939, Watson Papers, Box 10; Long Diary, 17 January 1939; BMB to Cordell Hull, 30 August 1939, SC; *New York Times*, 8 February 1939; "Neutrality, Peace Legislation and Our Foreign Policy," Testimony of Bernard M. Baruch before the United States Senate Committee on Foreign Relations, 6 April 1939, p. 7, PP; BMB to Eugene G. Grace, 31 October 1939, SC.

45. BMB to FDR, 31 July, FDR to BMB, 5 August 1939, SC.

46. Blum, "Birth and Death of the M-Day Plan," pp. 66–72.

47. Louis Johnson to BMB, 19 August, BMB to Johnson, 20 September (2), Johnson to BMB, 5 October, BMB to Johnson, 7 October, Johnson to BMB, 20 October 1937, SC; "Personnel Suggested for Membership on 'Advisory Board for Industrial Mobilization,'" FDR memo to Louis Johnson, 26 November 1937, Johnson Papers, Box 84.

48. Blum, "Birth and Death of the M-Day Plan," p. 79.

49. BMB to Louis Johnson, 24 December, Johnson to BMB, 29 December 1937, BMB to James F. Byrnes, 14 May, BMB to Johnson, 7, 24 May, Johnson to BMB, 1 June 1938, SC; copy of BMB memo to FDR, 29 April, BMB to Marguerite LeHand, 29 April, FDR memo to Johnson, 13 May, Johnson Memo to FDR, 18 May 1938, Johnson Papers, Box 2; Janeway, *The Struggle for Survival*, pp. 28–30; Henry A. Wallace, COHC, p. 528.

50. Blum, "Birth and Death of the M-Day Plan," p. 73; Yoshpe, "Bernard M. Baruch," pp. 12–13.

51. Keith D. McFarland, *Harry H. Woodring* (1975), p. 172; Robert Greenhalgh Albion and Robert Howe Connery, *Forrestal and the Navy* (1962), pp. 71–72; Blum, "Birth and Death of the M-Day Plan," pp. 74–78; "Joint Release, August 9, 1939," Johnson Papers, Box 84; John J. Pershing to BMB, 26 August 1939, SC; Janeway, *The Struggle for Survival*, pp. 53–58; *Washington News*, 11 August 1939; Charles M. Wiltse memo to James W. Fesler re interview with H. G. Moulton, 19 July 1946, RG 179/011.2, War Production Board (WPB) Papers.

52. For New Dealer reaction to the WRB, see E. M. Watson memo to FDR, 30 August 1939, Watson Papers, Box 10; Ickes, *The Inside Struggle* (1954), pp. 710, 716, 719, 721; Smith Diary, 2, 4 September 1939; Blum, "Birth and Death of the M-Day Plan," pp. 76–77; Charles M. Wiltse memo to James W. Fesler, 19 July 1946, RG 179/011.2, WPB Papers.

53. Memo, "Re: War Industries [Resources] Board," 1939, PPF 702; "Joint Press Release, August 9, 1939," Johnson Papers, Box 84.
54. Janeway, *The Struggle for Survival*, pp. 62, 66; Memo, "Re: War Industries [Resources] Board," 1939, PPF 702; Ickes, *The Inside Struggle*, p. 687; BMB to Benjamin Cohen, 23 August (draft), to James F. Byrnes, 12 September 1939, SC; BMB to Krock, 4 April 1950, Krock Papers, Box 17; Swope to Felix Frankfurter, 30 September 1940, Frankfurter Papers. Also see Ickes, *The Lowering Clouds*, p. 614; Marquis W. Childs, *I Write from Washington* (1942), p. 162; and letter to Albert A. Blum, 15 October 1954 (draft), initialed H.E., SC.
55. BMB to Edward R. Stettinius, Jr., 30 August 1939, SC.
56. Ibid.; BMB to Oscar Chapman, 20 November 1950, GC.
57. Louis Brownlow, *A Passion for Anonymity* (1958), pp. 424–27; Smith Diary, 29, 30 August, 4, 5, 7 September 1939; BMB to James F. Byrnes, 12 September 1939, SC.
58. Clipping from *Wall Street Journal*, 27 September 1939, Johnson Papers, Box 61; *New York Times*, 28 September 1939; Charles M. Wiltse memo to James W. Fesler, 19 July 1946, RG 179/011.2, WPB Papers; Koistinen, "The 'Industrial-Military Complex': The Interwar Years," p. 839; Blum, "Birth and Death of the M-Day Plan," p. 89; Blum, "Roosevelt, The M-Day Plans, and the Military-Industrial Complex," *Military Affairs* 36 (April 1972): 46.
59. BMB to James F. Byrnes, ca. December 1939 (handwritten), Byrnes Papers, Baruch folder; BMB to Christie Benet, 24 July 1940, SC; Joseph P. Lash, *Roosevelt and Churchill, 1939–1941* (1976), p. 238.
60. Joseph P. Kennedy to Krock, 22 April 1940, Krock Papers; BMB to Robert F. Wagner, 10 June 1940 (emphasis added), SC.
61. *New York Times*, 15, 17 September 1939; BMB to James F. Byrnes, 1 February, 4 April 1940, SC.
62. George C. Marshall telegram to BMB, 25 March, Marshall to BMB, 29 March, 3 April, BMB to Marshall, 5 April, to E. M. Watson, 5 April 1940, SC; Forrest C. Pogue, *George C. Marshall: Ordeal and Hope, 1939–1942* (1965), pp. 26–28.
63. Smith Diary, 13, 14, 22 May 1940; *New York Times*, 19 May 1940.
64. Beatrice Bishop Berle and Travis Jacobs, eds., *Navigating the Rapids, 1918–1971: From the Papers of Adolph A. Berle* (1973), p. 316; Smith Diary, 25, 30 May 1939; Brownlow, *A Passion for Anonymity*, pp. 429–32; Marvin A. Kreidberg and Merton G. Henry, *History of Military Mobilization in the United States Army, 1775–1945* (1955), pp. 683–84.
65. BMB to E. M. Watson, 23 May 1940, Watson Papers, Box 9; BMB to James F. Byrnes, 23 May 1940, Byrnes Papers, file 21; BMB memo, 18 June 1940, OF 335, Box 4; John Morton Blum, *From the Morgenthau Diaries: Years of Urgency, 1938–1941* (1965), p. 168; BMB to Harry F. Byrd, 14 September 1950, SC; Stimson Diary, 22 August 1940, 30:112.
66. Ickes, *The Inside Struggle*, p. 687; Baruch, *The Public Years*, pp. 281–82; Swope to FDR, 15 May, FDR memo to E. M. Watson, 18 May, Watson to Swope, 22 May 1940, Watson Papers.
67. BMB to Joseph Guffey, 17 January 1940, SC; Gilbert C. Fite, *George N. Peek and the Fight for Farm Parity* (1954), pp. 295–96; BMB to George N. Peek, 2 August 1940, Peek Papers; James F. Byrnes to Frank Hogan, 16 August 1940, Byrnes Papers, "Personal 1936–1940" file; Byrnes, *All In One Lifetime*, p. 101; David E. Lilienthal, *The Journals of David E. Lilienthal: The TVA Years* (1964), p. 225; Frank Kent to BMB, 14 September 1940, SC.

68. Lilienthal, *Journals: The TVA Years*, p. 225.
69. BMB to Marquis James, 5 August 1940, SC; Swope to Frankfurter, 30 September 1940, Frankfurter Papers; *New York Times*, 22 December 1940, sec. 4.
70. BMB to James F. Byrnes, 7 May, to Leon Henderson, 1 June 1940, SC; diaries, 27 August 1940, Henderson Papers, Box 36; "Notes on Mr. Baruch's Discussion with Defense Commission, 13 November 1940," RG 179/012.61, WPB Papers.
71. *New York Times*, 24 December 1940; E. M. W[atson] memo to FDR, 19 December 1940, Watson Papers, Box 11; BMB telegram to Frank Knox, 20 December, Knox to Baruch, 21 December 1940, SC.
72. *New York Times*, 14 February 1941.
73. Ibid., 11 January, 21 February, 12, 13 March 1941.
74. James L. Tyson, "The War Industries Board," *Fortune*, September 1940, supp.; Bernard Baruch, "Problems of Industrial Mobilization," *National Industrial Conference Board Report*, 16 January 1941; Bernard Baruch, "Priorities: The Synchronizing Force," *Harvard Business Review*, Spring 1941, pp. 261−70; Bernard Baruch, *American Industry in the War* (1941).
75. BMB to Donald Nelson, 23 July 1940, GC; "Notes on Mr. Baruch's Discussion with Defense Commission, 13 November 1940," RG 179/012.61, WPB Papers. On the steel industry's resistance to capacity expansion in 1941, see Krug Papers; Robert P. Patterson memo to H. K. Rutherford, 10 July 1941, F. Eberstadt to Patterson, 25 January 1942, and memo, "Conversion of Automobile Industry," Patterson Papers, Box 117.
76. Second meeting of Economic Defense Board, 20 August 1941, Patterson Papers, Box 131−32; Leon Henderson memo to FDR, 19 July 1941, Samuel I. Rosenman Papers, Box 5; James Forrestal to W. Averell Harriman, 7 July 1941, Forrestal Papers; random notes, 1941, Henderson Papers.
77. Ickes Diary, p. 5433; Krock, *New York Times*, 13 March 1941; Kent, *Baltimore Sun*, 15 March, 14 April 1941; "All Out," *Time*, 12 May 1941, pp. 16−19. Also see Henderson file, GC.
78. Lilienthal, *Journals: The TVA Years*, pp. 316−18; Ickes Diary, pp. 5578−79, 5622−23, 5635−36, 5670, 5717; E. M. W[atson] memo to FDR, 14 May 1941, Watson Papers, Box 11.
79. David Ginsburg, chronological statement of the priorities problem for Samuel I. Rosenman, 8 August 1941, Ginsburg memo to Rosenman, 3 August 1941, William S. Knudsen to FDR, 4 June 1941, Rosenman Papers, Box 5; U.S. Bureau of the Budget, *The United States at War* (1946), pp. 51−53, 57; Donald Nelson, *Arsenal of Democracy* (1946), pp. 145−46.
80. Wayne Coy memo to E. M. Watson, 2 June 1941, OF 327, Box 3; Harold Smith memo to FDR, 15 May 1941, Smith Papers; Bernard L. Gladieux memo to FDR, 12 August 1941, Rosenman Papers, Box 5; U.S. Bureau of the Budget, *The United States at War*, pp. 73−76.
81. For instance, see Pierrepont Noyes memo on War Industries Board priorities approach to Edward R. Stettinius, Jr., 18 March 1941, RG 179/141.1, WPB Papers; and John Lord O'Brien, COHC, p. 487. Also see M. L. Harrison memo to Mr. Tupper, "The informational basis of priority decisions during the first World War," 23 December 1940, RG 179/002, WPB Papers.
82. Ickes Diary, pp. 5869−70, 5880−81; clipping from *Labor*, September 1941, Special 1941, GC.
83. *New York Times*, 5 September 1941; clipping from *Washington Star*, 4 September 1941, Watson Papers, Box 5.

84. *New York Times*, 5 (Krock), 6 September 1941; BMB to E. M. Watson, 10 September, E. M. W[atson] memo to FDR, 11 September 1941, Watson Papers, Box 11; BMB to Donald Nelson, 7 September, Nelson to BMB, 13 September 1941, Nelson Papers, Box 2.
85. BMB to Krock, 5 September 1941, Krock Papers; Fred L. Israel, ed., *The War Diary of Breckenridge Long* (1965), p. 217.
86. *New York Times*, 5 September 1940.
87. Isador Lubin to BMB, 21 February 1940, 31 October 1941, BMB memo to James Forrestal, 23 July, BMB to H. G. Moulton, 9 October 1940, SC.
88. BMB to Frank Knox, 20 February 1941, GC; U. S. Bureau of the Budget, *The United States at War*, p. 237.
89. Wayne Coy memo to FDR, 23 May 1941, OF 327, Box 3; David Ginsburg to BMB, 15 December 1948, BMB to E. D. Coblentz, 1 August 1941, SC.
90. BMB memo to Hugh Johnson, 17 September 1941, SC; *New York Times*, 29 July 1941; Donald Nelson to BMB, 11 September 1941, Nelson Papers, Box 2; BMB to James F. Byrnes, 22 September 1941, Byrnes Papers, file 109.
91. Price control bill, Hearings before the House Committee on Banking and Currency, 77th Cong., 1st sess., 1941, passim; *New York Times*, 6 August, 20, 21, 23 September 1941; R. Elberton Smith, *The Army and Economic Mobilization* (1959), pp. 397–98.
92. *New York Times*, 23 September, 6, 8 October, 10, 16, 20, 22 November 1941; price control bill hearings, pp. 1029–30; BMB to Frank Kent, 29 October, Samuel Lubell to BMB, 17 October, ca. October 1941, 5 December 1941, SC.
93. BMB to Carter Glass, 6 December 1941, SC; U.S. Bureau of the Budget, *The United States at War*, p. 239.
94. BMB to Richard Hooker, 25 September 1940, SC.
95. BMB to Bennett C. Clark, 19 June 1941, SC; Wallace, COHC, p. 948; diaries, 25 September 1940, Henderson Papers, Box 36; Lilienthal, *Journals: The TVA Years*, p. 209; BMB memo to FDR, 1 August 1940, Watson Papers, Box 11.
96. Baruch, *American Industry in the War*, p. vi; BMB to James Forrestal, 23 January 1941, Forrestal Papers; BMB to William S. Knudsen, 6 March 1941, SC; Bernard Baruch, "Can Inflation Be Prevented by the Administration's Bill for the Control of Prices?" *Congressional Digest* 20 (October 1941): 246–47.
97. BMB to Albert Gore, 18 November 1941, SC.
98. *Wall Street Journal*, 27 September 1939; David Ginsburg memo to Samuel I. Rosenman, 8 August 1941 (original emphasis), Rosenman Papers, Box 5.
99. F. Eberstadt to James Forrestal, 21 January, 14 February 1941, Forrestal Papers.
100. David Ginsburg memo to Samuel I. Rosenman, 8 August 1941, Rosenman Papers, Box 5; Forrestal to W. Averell Harriman, 7 July 1941, Forrestal Papers; Ickes Diary, p. 5903.

CHAPTER EIGHT

1. Bernard Baruch, *The Public Years* (1960), pp. 294, 298–99; Levin H. Campbell, Jr., *The Industry Ordnance Team* (1946), pp. 3, 5, 10; *New York Times*, 31 May 1942.
2. The seven mentioned ahead of Baruch were Douglas MacArthur, Wendell

Willkie, Henry Ford, Thomas E. Dewey, Herbert Hoover, Fiorello La Guardia, and Charles Lindbergh. Hadley Cantril, ed., *Public Opinion, 1935–1946* (1951), p. 558.

3. *New York Times*, 7 August 1942; FDR to BMB, 6 August 1942, SC.

4. Gibson Bell Smith, "Rubber for Americans: The Search for an Adequate Supply of Rubber and the Politics of Strategic Materials, 1934–1942," doctoral dissertation, Bryn Mawr College, 1972, pp. 32, 46–48, 92–102, 148–54, 159, 162–63, 169–73, 181–87; Herbert Feis, *Three International Episodes: Seen from E. A.* (1946), pp. 36–44.

5. Smith, "Rubber for Americans," pp. 193–97, 213–49, passim; Feis, *Three International Episodes*, pp. 55–87, passim; Jesse H. Jones with Edward Angly, *Fifty Billion Dollars: My Thirteen Years with the RFC* (1951), pp. 396–430; Frank A. Howard, *Buna Rubber: The Birth of an Industry* (1947), pp. 124–62; BMB to James F. Byrnes, 18 May 1941, SC.

6. Smith, "Rubber for Americans," p. 250; Henry A. Wallace, COHC, pp. 94, 1167; BMB to Jesse Jones, 18 July 1941, SC.

7. Roosevelt quoted in Smith, "Rubber for Americans," pp. 255–56; Truman committee quoted in Roland Young, *Congressional Politics in the Second World War* (1956), p. 38; Murray quoted in *New York Times*, 10 April 1942; John Morton Blum, *The Price of Vision: The Diary of Henry A. Wallace, 1942–1946* (1973), pp. 71, 76, 82, 93; Civilian Production Administration (CPA), *Industrial Mobilization for War: History of the War Production Board and Predecessor Agencies* (1947), pp. 377–78.

8. Conference with FDR, 5 June 1942, Harold Smith Papers.

9. Stephen Early memo to FDR, 6 June 1942 ("very confidential"), Early Papers, Box 1.

10. James MacGregor Burns, *Roosevelt: The Soldier of Freedom* (1970), pp. 258–59; Smith, "Rubber for Americans," p. 257; U.S. Bureau of the Budget, *The United States at War* (1946), p. 293.

11. Ickes Diary, pp. 6868–70, 6886, 6895; Drew Pearson, *Diaries, 1949–1959* (1974), p. 37; FDR to BMB, 4 August 1942, SC.

12. Report of the rubber survey committee, 10 September 1942, PP; BMB to Donald Nelson, 6 July 1942, Nelson Papers, Box 2.

13. *New York Times*, 12, 14 September 1942.

14. Ibid., 14 September 1942; Weizmann quoted in Blum, *The Price of Vision*, pp. 188–89; Wallace, COHC, p. 2337; Ickes Diary, p. 6981.

15. V. O. Key, Jr., *Public Opinion and American Democracy* (1964), p. 426; Cantril, *Public Opinion*, p. 865; *New York Times*, 2 October, 19 September 1942; Henry A. Wallace to FDR, 12 July 1943, Wallace Papers.

16. BMB to Felix Frankfurter, 21 September 1942, SC.

17. Memos, 11, 29 August, 6, 7 September 1942, SC; report of the Rubber Survey Committee, 10 September 1942, p. 48, PP.

18. Bernard Baruch, *American Industry in the War* (1941), pp. 65–68.

19. Ibid., pp. 383, 269–71; Robert D. Cuff, *The War Industries Board: Business-Government Relations during World War I* (1973), pp. 235–38; Grosvenor B. Clarkson, *Industrial America in the World War* (1923), pp. 224, 435–36.

20. Baruch, *American Industry in the War*, p. 71; *New York Times*, 29 April 1920.

21. Baruch quoted in Cuff, *The War Industries Board*, p. 237. Also see ibid., pp. 233, 235.

22. BMB to Albert Gore, 18 November 1941, SC.

23. Samuel I. Rosenman, *The Public Papers and Addresses of Franklin D. Roosevelt, 1942*, pp. 223, 224.
24. BMB to Donald Nelson, 6 July 1942, Nelson Papers, Box 2; BMB to Leon Henderson, 6 July 1942, SC.
25. "Proposal for an Economic Policy Council," 8 August 1942, Samuel I. Rosenman Papers, Box 6; *New York Times*, 17 September 1942.
26. BMB memo to FDR, 7 November 1942, SC; BMB memo to James F. Byrnes, 17 September 1943, WF, Box 31; BMB memo to FDR, 16 September, FDR memo to Byrnes, 28 September 1943, OF 327, Box 4.
27. Nelson quoted in *New York Times*, 22 January 1943; CPA, *Minutes of the War Production Board* (1946), pp. 236, 285, 301; meeting of the War Production Board, 27 July 1943, Nelson Papers; CPA, *Industrial Mobilization for War*, p. 650.
28. Jordan A. Schwarz, *The Interregnum of Despair: Hoover, Congress, and the Depression* (1970), p. 217; Stephen W. Baskerville, "Frankfurter, Keynes and the Fight for Public Works, 1932–1935," *Maryland Historian* 19 (Spring 1978): 1–16.
29. Herbert Stein, *The Fiscal Revolution in America* (1969), pp. 131–68; Alan Sweezy, "The Keynesians and Government Policy, 1933–1939," *American Economic Review* 62 (May 1972): 116–23; Robert Lekachman, *The Age of Keynes*, pp. 58–143, passim.
30. John Maynard Keynes, *How to Pay for the War* (1940), pp. 4–5, 2 (emphasis added).
31. Ibid., pp. 8–12, 21, 25–34, 37–38, 51–57, 74.
32. Alvin H. Hansen, "Defense Spending and Inflation Potentialities," *Review of Economic Statistics* 23 (February 1941): 3, 6–7; J. K. Galbraith, "The Selection and Timing of Inflation Controls," ibid., p. 83.
33. Alvin H. Hansen, "Some Additional Comments on the Inflation Symposium," ibid., p. 93.
34. J. M. Clark, "Further Remarks on Defense Financing and Inflation," ibid., p. 112.
35. BMB to David Lawrence, 22 April 1940, SC.
36. Byrd L. Jones, "The Role of Keynesians in Wartime Policy and Postwar Planning, 1940–1946," *American Economic Review* 62 (May 1972): 127–28.
37. Keynes, *How to Pay for the War*, pp. 17, 19.
38. Untitled, 5 June 1941, Leon Henderson Papers, Box 6; Mr. Gass to Harry Dexter White, 13 June 1941, Morgenthau Diaries, 415: 336–39. For an OPM view of WIB priorities, see M. L. Harrison memo to Mr. Tupper, 23 December 1940, entitled "The informational basis of priority decisions during the First World War" (original emphasis), RG 179/002, War Production Board (WPB) Papers.
39. Harold Smith memo to FDR, 23 July 1941, Smith Papers.
40. David Ginsburg memo to Samuel I. Rosenman, 8 August 1941, Rosenman Papers, Box 5.
41. Leon Henderson to BMB, 19 January 1942, GC; BMB to Isadore Lubin, 21 February 1942, SC; U.S. Bureau of the Budget, *The United States at War*, p. 237.
42. U.S. Bureau of the Budget, *The United States at War*, pp. 239–51; Rosenman, *Public Papers, 1942*, p. 19; memo to FDR, 16 March, conferences with FDR, 25 March, 1, 4, 8 April 1942, Smith Papers; *New York Times*, 14 April 1942.
43. Fred L. Israel, ed., *The War Diary of Breckenridge Long* (1965), p. 263; *New York Times*, 10 April 1942; John Kenneth Galbraith to Jordan A. Schwarz,

31 August 1979, author's possession.

44. Paul R. Porter memo to Wendell Lund, 25 May 1942, Nelson Papers; Kathryn Smul Arnow, "The Attack on the Cost of Living Index," in Harold Stein, ed., *Public Administration and Policy Development* (1952), pp. 781–86.

45. *New York Times*, 23 August 1942; John Morton Blum, *V Was for Victory* (1976), pp. 133–36.

46. U.S. Bureau of the Budget, *The United States at War*, pp. 265–71; "A Proposal for the Creation of an Economic Stabilization Authority," Wayne Coy memo to Samuel I. Rosenman, 3 August, Department of Justice, "The War Powers of the President," 25 August (inflation folder), "Proposal for Economic Policy Council," 8 August 1942, Rosenman Papers, Box 6.

47. Baruch, *The Public Years*, pp. 308–9; "Memo to an Inquiring Senator," 1958, SC; "Aide Memoir," BMB Special 1945 folder, GC; Ickes Diary, pp. 7050–51, 7056–57, 7060, 7175; John Morton Blum, *From the Morgenthau Diaries: Years of War, 1941–1945* (1967), pp. 69–70.

48. Ickes Diary, p. 7060; "Memo to an Inquiring Senator," 1958, SC; John Morton Blum, *From the Morgenthau Diaries: Years of Urgency, 1938–1941* (1965), pp. 20–21.

49. Smith Diary, 12 June 1939; Robert M. Collins, "The Committee for Economic Development and the Keynesian Revolution, 1942–1964: A Case Study in American Corporatism," paper given at American Historical Association meeting, December 1977; Robert M. Collins, "Positive Business Responses to the New Deal: The Roots of the Committee for Economic Development, 1933–1942," *Business History Review* 52 (Autumn 1978): 369–91; Stein, *The Fiscal Revolution in America*, pp. 102–3, 184–86.

50. Joseph J. O'Connell, Jr., to Henry Morgenthau, Jr., 8 October 1941, Morgenthau Diaries, 449:76–88; John Kenneth Galbraith to Jordan A. Schwarz, 9 April 1976, author's possession.

51. Memos to FDR, 23 June 1941, 16 March 1942, Smith Papers; Morgenthau quoted in Blum, *Morgenthau: Years of War*, pp. 37–38.

52. Conferences with FDR, 4, 8, April 1942, "Anti-inflation meeting, April 10, 1942," Smith Papers, Blum, *Morgenthau: Years of War*, p. 38.

53. Randolph E. Paul, *Taxation in the United States* (1954), pp. 301, 322; Israel, *War Diary of Breckenridge Long*, pp. 263–64; BMB to Walter F. George, 16 March 1942, SC; BMB to Henry Ittleson, 8 August 1942, GC; Morgenthau-BMB telephone conversation, 15 December 1952, Morgenthau Diaries, 599:179–80; Herbert Bayard Swope to BMB, 16 December 1942, SC; *New York Times*, 24 December 1942.

54. Robert Wayne Carlson, "The Revenue Act of 1942: A Case Study in the Financing of the Corporate State," master's thesis, Northern Illinois University, 1975, passim; Paul, *Taxation in the United States*, pp. 328–32; R. Paul, "Draft of tax section for Judge Rosenman," 18 August 1942, Rosenman Papers, Box 6; Lester V. Chandler, *Inflation in the United States, 1940–1948* (1951), p. 85.

55. Conference with FDR, 3 June 1943, Smith Papers.

56. James Forrestal to Arthur Krock, 4 December 1943, Forrestal Papers.

57. Keynes, *How to Pay for the War*, pp. 6, 9–11; FDR to BMB, 17 September 1942, Morgenthau Diaries, 570:90; Carlson, "The Revenue Act of 1942," pp. 96, 112, 71, 73, 76, 77–81, 83–93.

58. Conference with FDR, 30 October 1944, Smith Papers.

59. Ickes Diary, pp. 5578–79; Joseph P. Lash, *Roosevelt and Churchill, 1939–1941* (1976), p. 478.

60. "Old Independence," *Time*, 28 June 1943, p. 19; *New York Journal-American*, 6 October 1941; Jeffrey Potter, *Men, Money and Magic: The Story of Dorothy Schiff* (1976), p. 166; William Hassett memo to Stephen Early, 5 October, Early memo to Hassett, 6 October 1941, PPF 88; Baruch, *The Public Years*, p. 286.

61. Samuel I. Rosenman, *Working with Roosevelt* (1952), pp. 335–36; Arthur Krock, *The Consent of the Governed* (1971), pp. 142, 145; Burns, *Roosevelt*, p. 352; Baruch, *The Public Years*, p. 279; Jonathan Daniels, *White House Witness, 1942–1945* (1975), p. 49; Potter, *Men, Money and Magic*, p. 166; Helen Lawrenson, *Stranger at the Party: A Memoir* (1975), p. 150; James Roosevelt with Bill Libby, *My Parents: A Differing View* (1976), pp. 178, 109, 102–3; Elliott Roosevelt and James Brough, *A Rendezvous with Destiny: The Roosevelts of the White House* (1975), p. 371.

62. Lash, *Roosevelt and Churchill*, p. 484; John Toland, *The Rising Sun: The Decline and Fall of the Japanese Empire* (1971), p. 213; Baruch, *The Public Years*, pp. 288–91. See Mrs. Edwin M. Watson file, 1952, Watson Papers.

63. On Baruch and executive war personnel, see correspondence with D. R. McLennan, Robert P. Patterson, and James Forrestal, 1941–42, SC; BMB telegram to FDR, 9 April, and FDR memo to Frank Knox, 11 April 1941, OF 18, Box 8.

64. Leon Henderson to BMB, 19 January 1942, GC; FDR memo to E. M. Watson, 13 February 1940, Box 13, memo to Watson, 23 April 1941, Box 4, Watson Papers; untitled, 5 June 1941, Henderson Papers, Box 36; BMB to Watson, 16 March, Watson memo to FDR, 19 March, FDR memo to the acting secretary of the Treasury, 21 March 1942, OF 48-H, Box 25.

65. Ickes Diary, pp. 7329–30, 7343; Wallace, COHC, p. 2100; Henry H. Adams, *Harry Hopkins* (1977), pp. 302–3.

66. Harold L. Ickes to FDR, 11 December 1941, PPF 8.

67. Ickes Diary, pp. 5719, 6403; Lawrenson, *Stranger at the Party*, p. 150.

68. Wallace, COHC, pp. 2890–91.

69. See David E. Lilienthal, *The Journals of David E. Lilienthal: The TVA Years* (1964), pp. 317–18; Joseph P. Lash, *Eleanor Roosevelt: A Friend's Memoir* (1964), pp. 215–16.

70. Roosevelt and Brough, *A Rendezvous with Destiny*, pp. 95, 48–49; Roosevelt with Libby, *My Parents*, p. 177; Frances Perkins, COHC, pp. 422, 105.

71. Ray F. Harvey et al., *The Politics of This War* (1944), p. 85; Hearst columnist quoted in Davis R. B. Ross, *Preparing for Ulysses: Politics and Veterans during World War II* (1969), p. 127; clipping with BMB to N. G. Henthorne, 16 November 1944, WF, Box 29.

72. Gay Talese, *The Kingdom and the Power* (1969), p. 232; "New York *Times* of October 1, 1940, Statements in Krock's column, from 'thoroughly reliable source,'" Robert P. Patterson Papers, Box 155; Arthur Krock, *Memoirs: Sixty Years on the Firing Line* (1968), pp. 192, 202; Krock, *The Consent of the Governed*, p. 47. On their friendship, see BMB to Krock, 30 December 1936 (handwritten), Krock Papers.

73. "Aide Memoir," BMB Special 1945 folder, GC; Winfred Bobo Moore, Jr., "New South Statesman: The Political Career of James Francis Byrnes, 1911–1941," doctoral dissertation, Duke University, 1976, pp. 354–59; Raymond G. Carroll to BMB, 2 October 1939, SC; James F. Byrnes to BMB, 7 December 1939, file 21, Byrnes to John N. Garner, 23 June 1941, Personal 1936–40 folder, Byrnes Papers.

74. Stimson Diary, 14 December 1940, 32:27–29.
75. Lilienthal, *Journals: The TVA Years*, p. 318; BMB telegram to James S. Knowlson, 20 July 1942, GC; Emory S. Land, COHC, p. 188.
76. Joseph P. Lash, *From the Diaries of Felix Frankfurter* (1975), p. 166; Harold Smith memo to FDR, 15 May 1941, Smith Papers.
77. Bradley Dewey review of Carter Field, *Park Bench Statesman*, in *Chemical and Metallurgical Engineering*, December 1944, p. 219; Rosenman, *Working with Roosevelt*, p. 335.
78. Arthur Krock, COHC, pp. 83–84; BMB to C. W. Carroll, 3 April, BMB telegram to Donald Nelson, 16 March 1942, SC.
79. Daniels, *White House Witness*, p. 154.
80. John F. Fennelly, *Memoirs of a Bureaucrat: A Personal Story of the War Production Board* (1965), passim.
81. BMB to Donald Nelson, 9 September 1941, Nelson Papers, Box 2; BMB to Robert P. Patterson, 18 December (copy in Forrestal Papers), to Milo Perkins, 5 December, to William S. Knudsen, 18 December 1941, GC; BMB memo, September 1941, OF 285-C, Box 11; BMB telegram to Nelson, 9 March 1942, SC; John Lord O'Brian, COHC, p. 504.
82. BMB telegram to Donald Nelson, 17 September 1942, Nelson Papers, Box 2; BMB to James F. Bell, 5 November, F. Eberstadt memo to Nelson, 5 December 1942, WF; James F. Byrnes to FDR, 10 January 1944, Byrnes Papers, file 70. For additional insights on the antitrust question in World War II, see Blum, *V Was for Victory*, pp. 131–40; and Richard Polenberg, *War and Society* (1972), pp. 77–78.
83. Baruch, *The Public Years*, p. 294; "1940–1941 Diaries," Henderson Papers, Box 36; conference with FDR, 13 January 1942, Smith Papers.
84. Lash, *From the Diaries of Felix Frankfurter*, p. 167; James Knowlson quoted in CPA, *Industrial Mobilization for War*, p. 210.
85. Stimson Diary, 14 December 1940, 32:28; BMB to Robert P. Patterson, 6 January 1942, GC; CPA, *Industrial Mobilization for War*, p. 212; BMB to Krock, ca. 1942 (handwritten), Krock Papers.
86. BMB telegram to Donald Nelson, 16 March, Nelson memo to James S. Knowlson, 20 March 1942, Nelson Papers, Box 2.
87. BMB to Garet Garrett, 31 January 1942, GC; BMB to C. W. Carroll, 3 April to James M. Cox, 8 June, to David Lawrence, 16 July 1942, SC; Ickes Diary, p. 6656.
88. Book outline in Cass Canfield folder, 1946, Forrestal Papers; interviews with F. Eberstadt by Calvin Christman, Eberstadt Papers; Calvin Lee Christman, "Ferdinand Eberstadt and Economic Mobilization for War, 1941–1943," doctoral dissertation, Ohio State University, 1971, pp. 11–42, 59–65.
89. Christman, "Ferdinand Eberstadt," pp. 43–48; Lash, *From the Diaries of Felix Frankfurter*, p. 166; BMB telegram to James Forrestal, 7 February 1942, SC.
90. Wallace, COHC, p. 1885.
91. Christman, "Ferdinand Eberstadt," pp. 69–100, 141–52, 180–81, 205–6; Lincoln Gordon, "An Official Appraisal of the War Economy and Its Administration," *Review of Economic Statistics* 29 (August 1947): 185–86.
92. Christman, "Ferdinand Eberstadt," pp. 103–8, 116–21; CPA, *Industrial Mobilization for War*, pp. 307–24.
93. Christman, "Ferdinand Eberstadt," pp. 180–83, 187–89, 192–201; Thomas C. Blaisdell, Jr., "Concurring Opinion in re Planning Committee Recommendation No. 17," Nelson Papers, Box 11; John E. Brigante, "Determination of

War Production Objectives for 1942 and 1943," in Lester V. Chandler and Donald H. Wallace, eds., *Economic Mobilization and Stabilization* (1951), pp. 78–91; R. Elberton Smith, *The Army and Economic Mobilization* (1959), pp. 555–63; CPA, *Industrial Mobilization for War*, pp. 474–85.

94. F. Eberstadt telegrams to BMB, 12, 19 September 1942, SC.

95. R. Elberton Smith, *The Army and Economic Mobilization*, p. 567.

96. CPA, *Industrial Mobilization for War*, pp. 505–7; John E. Brigante, *The Feasibility Dispute* (1945), pp. 61–69.

97. CPA, *Industrial Mobilization for War*, pp. 508, 518–19, 509–14; *New York Times*, 18 September 1942; Christman, "Ferdinand Eberstadt," pp. 280–82. Also see F. Eberstadt's reflections to BMB, 6 June 1958, SC.

98. CPA, *Industrial Mobilization for War*, pp. 514–16; Blum, *The Price of Vision*, pp. 119, 120–21; "Submitted by Ezekiel, Nov. 23," Wallace Papers; Wallace, COHC, p. 1987; Stimson Diary, 6 February 1943, 42:28.

99. Christman, "Ferdinand Eberstadt," pp. 289–91; CPA, *Industrial Mobilization for War*, pp. 578–80.

100. Lash, *From the Diaries of Felix Frankfurter*, p. 192; BMB to Frankfurter, 21 September 1942, SC.

101. BMB to Brehon B. Somervell, 24 December 1942, SC. Also see Robert P. Patterson to Eugene Meyer, Jr., 21 December 1942, Patterson Papers; and "Memo for Historians of WPB," Nelson Papers, Box 4.

102. William D. Leahy, *I Was There* (1950), pp. 130–31; Stimson Diary, 25 November 1942, 41:63–64.

103. Lash, *From the Diaries of Felix Frankfurter*, pp. 143–44.

104. Stimson Diary, 9 January 1943, 41:157–58; Lash, *From the Diaries of Felix Frankfurter*, pp. 166, 178.

105. James F. Byrnes, *All in One Lifetime* (1958), pp. 171–72; p. 293; "Aide Memoir," BMB Special 1945 folder, GC; Byrnes to FDR, 5 February 1943, Byrnes Papers, file 75.

106. I. F. Stone, "The Charming Mr. Baruch," *Nation*, 27 February 1943, p. 298; Byrnes, *All in One Lifetime*, pp. 172–74; Baruch, *The Public Years*, p. 316; "February 5, 1943—Senator Pepper—Baruch," Wallace, COHC, p. 2301; F. Eberstadt to BMB, 6 June 1958, BMB to Samuel Lubell, 17 May 1950, SC; Christman, "Ferdinand Eberstadt," pp. 293, 297; Stimson Diary, 6 February 1943, 42:28; Lash, *From the Diaries of Felix Frankfurter*, pp. 185–86.

107. BMB to Swope, 11 November 1943, WF; John M. Hancock to BMB, 7 June 1943, SC; Daniels, *White House Witness*, p. 158.

108. Christman, "Ferdinand Eberstadt," pp. 298–307; Ickes Diary, pp. 7485–86; BMB to Drew Pearson, November 1947 ("draft, not sent"), SC; Lash, *From the Diaries of Felix Frankfurter*, pp. 186, 189; Daniels, *White House Witness*, pp. 154–55; telephone conversation with FDR, 15 February 1943, Smith Papers; Blum, *The Price of Vision*, p. 193; O'Brian, COHC, pp. 571–78.

109. Stimson Diary, 18 February 1943, 42:64; Ickes Diary, p. 7495; memo to FDR, 19 February 1943, Smith Papers; Wallace, COHC, p. 2400; Lash, *From the Diaries of Felix Frankfurter*, pp. 191–92.

110. Stimson Diary, 22, 24 February 1943, 42:71, 78. Also see Wallace, COHC, p. 2387.

111. Stone, "The Charming Mr. Baruch," pp. 298–99.

112. Wallace, COHC, pp. 2387, 2400; Ickes Diary, pp. 7796–97; Lash, *From the Diaries of Felix Frankfurter*, p. 247.

113. For the story of the Coit biography and the Frankfurter thesis, see pp. 552–57.
114. "Aide Memoir," BMB Special 1945 folder, GC; John M. Hancock memo, untitled, 28 May 1943, GC; *New York Times*, 9 June 1943.
115. BMB to Donald Nelson, 23 May 1943, Nelson Papers, Box 2; BMB to Harry F. Byrd, 1 June, to James F. Byrnes, 13 June, to Herbert Hoover, 14 June, Hoover to BMB, 19 June 1943, SC; *New York Times*, 30 May 1943; Lash, *From the Diaries of Felix Frankfurter*, p. 204; conference with FDR, 3 June, memo to FDR, 3 June 1943, Smith Papers.
116. BMB memo to Walter F. George, 25 June 1943 (emphasis added), WF.
117. *New York Times*, 29 May 1943; Herman Miles Somers, *Presidential Agency: The Office of War Mobilization and Reconversion* (1950), pp. 47–51, 54, 56–75; Ickes Diary, p. 7807.
118. Ickes Diary, p. 7428; Byrnes, *All in One Lifetime*, p. 174.
119. Ickes Diary, p. 7625; BMB telegrams to James F. Byrnes, 16, 18 March 1943, SC; Daniels, *White House Witness*, pp. 156–58; Byrnes memo, 19 April 1943, file 71, BMB to Byrnes, Wednesday, ca. 1943, Miscellaneous 1935–47 file, Byrnes Papers.
120. Stimson Diary, 15 June 1943, 43:116; Krock, *New York Times*, 9, 10, 20 June 1943; BMB telegram to James F. Byrnes, 14 June 1943, SC; BMB memos to Byrnes, 16, 29 June, 9, 18, 23 July, John M. Hancock memos to Byrnes, 25, 30 June 1943, WF; Somers, *Presidential Agency*, p. 55.
121. *New York Times*, 4 July 1943; "Aide Memoir," BMB Special 1945 folder, GC; Wallace, COHC, pp. 4013–14; Ickes Diary, pp. 9586, 9644, 9831.

CHAPTER NINE

1. Bernard Baruch, *The Public Years* (1960), p. 321; U.S. Bureau of the Budget, *The United States at War* (1946), p. 431.
2. BMB memo to FDR, 7 November, FDR memo to BMB, James F. Byrnes, and Samuel I. Rosenman, 11 November 1942, SC; Samuel I. Rosenman, *Working with Roosevelt* (1952), pp. 419–20; Civilian Production Administration (CPA), *Minutes of the War Production Board* (1946), p. 270.
3. Conference with FDR, 14 June 1941, Smith Papers; Stimson Diary, 21 October, 40:168, 11 November 1942, 41:37; Henry A. Wallace, COHC, p. 2387; James F. Byrnes, *All in One Lifetime* (1958), pp. 175–76; Joseph P. Lash, *From the Diaries of Felix Frankfurter* (1975), p. 205; Byron Fairchild and Jonathan Grossman, *The Army and Industrial Manpower* (1959), p. 52.
4. Memo, 16 June 1943, WF.
5. Herman Miles Somers, *Presidential Agency: The Office of War Mobilization and Reconversion* (1950), pp. 138–52; U.S. Bureau of the Budget, *The United States at War*, pp. 435–44; Paul A. C. Koistinen, "Mobilizing the World War II Economy: Labor and the Industrial-Military Alliance," *Pacific Historical Review* 42 (November 1973): 451–56; Fairchild and Grossman, *The Army and Industrial Manpower*, pp. 145–47; CPA, *Industrial Mobilization for War: History of the War Production Board and Predecessor Agencies* (1947), p. 702; CPA, *Minutes of the War Production Board*, p. 293.
6. Henry L. Stimson to BMB, 28 September, Grenville Clark to BMB, undated and 19 August, BMB to Clark, 11 August, Herbert Bayard Swope to BMB, 20 August 1943, WF; Fairchild and Grossman, *The Army and Industrial Manpower*, p. 227.

7. Samuel Lubell draft, "Objections to the National Service Act," 4 September 1943, WF; *New York Times*, 22 January 1941; Rosenman, *Working with Roosevelt*, p. 421; Richard Polenberg, *War and Society: The United States, 1941–1945* (1972), pp. 171–72; Smith Diary, 9 November 1943; James F. Byrnes on railroad strikes, 20 December 1943, OF 56–B, Box 8; Byrnes to Josiah W. Bailey, 22 December 1943, Byrnes Papers, file 107; BMB telegram to E. M. Watson, 26 December 1943, OF 4226.

8. Conference with FDR, 7 January, memo for FDR, "National Service Legislation," 9 January 1944, Harold Smith Papers; Stimson Diary, 3 January, 17 April 1944, 46:6, 183; BMB memo to James F. Byrnes, 15 January 1944 ("was not sent but keep"), SC.

9. U.S. Bureau of the Budget, *The United States at War*, pp. 187–89, 450–55; Roland Young, *Congressional Politics in the Second World War* (1956), pp. 76–82; Baruch, *The Public Years*, pp. 327–28; untitled, 19 January 1945, WF; BMB to Samuel I. Rosenman, 21 September 1949, SC.

10. Robert P. Patterson to George W. Healy, Jr., 10 September 1946, Patterson Papers; J. A. Krug to Donald Nelson, 19 April, to J. L. Weiner, 12 April, to August Richard, 28 April 1943, Krug Papers; W. F. Tompkins memo to E. S. Greenbaum, 19 August 1943, Samuel I. Rosenman Papers, Box 4.

11. Isador Lubin memo to Samuel I. Rosenman and James F. Byrnes, 18 October 1943, Rosenman Papers, Box 4; Barton J. Bernstein, "The Debate on Industrial Reconversion: The Protection of Oligopoly and Military Control of the Economy," *American Journal of Economics and Sociology* 26 (1967): 160–61; U.S. Bureau of the Budget, *The United States at War*, p. 463; Jack W. Peltason, "The Reconversion Controversy," in Harold W. Stein, ed., *Public Administration and Policy Development* (1952), pp. 226–27, 234; John Lord O'Brian, COHC, pp. 585–87.

12. Ernest Kanzler, "Economic Demobilization and Reconversion," 21 June 1943, RG 179/965R, War Production Board (WPB) Papers; J. Carlyle Sitterson, *Development of the Reconversion Policies of the War Production Board: April 1943 to January 1945* (1945); Historical Reports on War Administration, James W. Fesler, WPB historian, pp. 1, 3–8; Peltason, "The Reconversion Controversy," pp. 224–26, 228; Alonzo L. Hamby, "Sixty Million Jobs and the People's Revolution: The Liberals, the New Deal, and World War II," *Historian* 30 (1968–69): 586–87; Robert R. Nathan, *Mobilizing for Abundance* (1944).

13. Conference with FDR, Thursday, 31 August 1943, Smith Papers; R. E. McConnell to Henry Morgenthau, Jr., 18 August, Milton Handler to Samuel I. Rosenman, 23 August, Alfred E. Davidson to Handler, 14 August 1943, Rosenman Papers, Box 4.

14. Sitterson, *Development of the Reconversion Policies*, pp. 19–20; R. Elberton Smith, *The Army and Economic Mobilization* (1959), pp. 625–27; Peltason, "The Reconversion Controversy," p. 229; U.S. Bureau of the Budget, *The United States at War*, p. 464.

15. Somers, *Presidential Agency*, pp. 175–76; James F. Byrnes to BMB, 16 August 1957, Byrnes Papers, file 886; Byrnes, *All in One Lifetime*, p. 207; memos, BMB to Byrnes, 4 November, Byrnes to BMB, 5 November 1943, SC; Smith Diary, 29 October 1943.

16. Donald Nelson to Stuart Chase, 30 October 1946, Nelson Papers, Box 4; Simon Kuznets memo on reconversion problems and the WPB to Stacy May, 9 November 1943, WPB Papers, RG 179/960R.

17. *New York Times*, 11, 12, 19, 20 November 1943; two BMB letters to Donald

Nelson, 16 November 1943, Nelson Papers, Box 2; Ickes Diary, p. 8386; BMB to Leon Henderson, 30 November 1943, GC.

18. Gene Duffield to James Forrestal, ca. spring 1943, Forrestal Papers; Stimson Diary, 2 August 1944, 48:23; BMB to Donald Nelson, 16 November 1943, Nelson Papers, Box 2; F. Eberstadt to James Forrestal, 23 September 1946, Forrestal Papers; BMB to Charles E. Wilson, 26 October 1948, SC.

19. CPA, *Minutes of the War Production Board*, p. 293; Sitterson, *Development of the Reconversion Policies*, p. 2; Peltason, "The Reconversion Controversy," pp. 229–30; Bernstein, "The Debate on Industrial Reconversion," p. 162; Wallace, COHC, p. 2931.

20. "Notes on talk with Nelson and Wilson," 22 December, Donald Nelson to BMB, 29 December 1943, BMB to Nelson, 7 January 1944, WF.

21. Stimson Diary, 3 January 1944, 46:5–6; James Forrestal to Harry L. Hopkins, 2 January 1944, Hopkins Papers, Box 153; CPA, *Minutes of the War Production Board*, 11 January 1944, pp. 299–301; Peltason, "The Reconversion Controversy," pp. 231–33.

22. BMB to George N. Peek, 21 November 1943, Peek Papers; BMB to David Sarnoff, 15 December 1943, WF; BMB to Henry Morgenthau, Jr., 12 November 1943, 676:238, "Committee Representation," Treasury Department conference, 12 November 1943, 675:161–66, Morgenthau Diaries; Smith Diary, Tuesday, 16 November 1943.

23. BMB to Peek, 21 November 1943, Peek Papers; F. Eberstadt to James Forrestal, 11 January 1941, Forrestal Papers; "Byrnes on Railroad Strike," 20 December 1943, OF 56-B, Box 8; conference with FDR, 7 January 1944, Smith Papers; Byrnes to FDR, 26 January, file 69, copy of Morris L. Cooke to FDR, 2 March, file 73, FDR to Byrnes, 3 March 1944, file 73, Byrnes Papers; William L. Clayton, COHC, pp. 103, 108–10; David E. Lilienthal, *The Journals of David Lilienthal: The TVA Years* (1964), pp. 632–33.

24. Ickes Diary, pp. 8664–65, 8901; Joseph P. Lash, *Eleanor and Franklin* (1971), p. 904; Sitterson, *Development of the Reconversion Policies*, pp. 27–31.

25. I. F. Stone, "Millionaires' Beveridge Plan," *Nation*, 25 March 1944, p. 354; "The Baruch Plan" and "Baruch Report (Cont'd)," *New Republic*, 28 February, 6 March 1944, pp. 263–64, 304; Max Lerner, *Public Journal: Marginal Notes on Wartime America* (1945), p. 363; J. Donald Kingsley, "Hell-Bent for Chaos," *New Republic*, 24 April 1944, pp. 554–56.

26. "Baruch Program," *Time*, 28 February 1944, p. 82; clipping from *San Francisco Call-Bulletin*, 21 February 1944, GC.

27. Stone, "Millionaires' Beveridge Plan," p. 355; Davis R. B. Ross, *Preparing for Ulysses: Politics and Veterans during World War II* (1969), pp. 130–31; BMB to Marquis Childs, 9 March, to William Jeffers, 10 August 1944, SC.

28. Byrnes, *All in One Lifetime*, pp. 208–9; James F. Byrnes to FDR, 16 February 1944, Byrnes Papers, file 69; Lerner, *Public Journal*, p. 366; Allen Drury, *A Senate Journal, 1943–1945* (1963), pp. 82–83; "Aims of Baruch-Hancock Report Meet with Approval of Majority," *Newsweek*, 28 February 1944, p. 60; Stephen Kemp Bailey, *Congress Makes a Law* (1964), p. 32.

29. Young, *Congressional Politics*, pp. 207, 202; untitled memo, 30 August 1944, WF.

30. "Statement by James F. Byrnes, Director of War Mobilization, on George-Murray Bill . . . June 12, 1944," memo to James F. Byrnes, 8 September 1944, GC; BMB to Byrnes, 27 June, to Marquis Childs, 27 June, to Marriner S. Eccles, 3 August, John M. Hancock memo, 28 April 1944, SC; BMB to Robert

Hannegan, 21 December 1945 [*sic*], GC.
31. "Mr. DuBois re Reconversion, December 24, 1944," Morgenthau Diaries, 805:64–76; BMB to George C. Marshall, 3 July 1944, SC; F. Eberstadt to James Forrestal, 18 July 1944, Forrestal Papers; Donald Nelson to BMB, 25 May, BMB to Nelson, 1 June 1944, Nelson Papers, Box 2.
32. Unsigned to Donald Nelson, 5 July 1944, memo, "Initial Steps in the Approach to Reconversion," Nelson Papers, Box 12; F. Eberstadt to James Forrestal, 18 July 1944, Forrestal Papers; Nelson to Charles E. Wilson, 15, 29 July 1944, Byrnes Papers, file 75; "Statement and directive issues today by Director of Mobilization James F. Byrnes to provide adequate manpower for essential war production," 4 August 1944, SC; conference with FDR, 13 July 1944, Smith Papers; Jonathan Daniels, *White House Witness, 1942–1945* (1975), p. 242; Bernstein, "The Debate on Industrial Reconversion," 163–72.
33. Undated notes on Donald Nelson's book *Arsenal of Democracy* (1946), Patterson Papers, Box 94; James Forrestal to W. Y. Elliot, 8 May, to Charles R. Hook, 5 September, to W. Averell Harriman, 3 October 1944, Forrestal Papers; Philip Murray to James F. Byrnes, 16 September, A. D. Searles memo to Byrnes, "Program for Newspaper Publicity Concerning Industrial and Military Demobilization," 22 September 1944, Patterson Papers, Box 130; J. A. Krug to R. S. Reynolds, 11 October, to George Meader, 14 October, to Donald D. Davis, 21 October 1944, Krug Papers, Box 2; Patterson to BMB, 14 November 1944, GC.
34. Roosevelt quoted in conference with FDR, 31 August 1944, Smith Papers; George C. Marshall to BMB, 7 July 1944, SC.
35. Memos to FDR, 31 August, 13 September, FDR to Harold Smith, 18 September 1944, Diary, 21 December 1944, Smith Papers; U.S. Bureau of the Budget, *The United States at War*, p. 488.
36. Norman D. Markowitz, *The Rise and Fall of the People's Century: Henry A. Wallace and American Liberalism, 1941–1948* (1973), p. 141.
37. *New York Times*, 5 April 1945; "Reporter, Spare My Quotes," *Time*, 16 April 1945, p. 73; BMB to Walter F. George, 17 March 1945, SC.
38. Harold Smith memos to Samuel I. Rosenman, 23 December 1944, 14 March 1945, Robert F. Wagner to Harold Smith, 3 March 1945, Diary, 18, 26 April 1945, Smith Papers (Truman Library). On the Bureau of the Budget and the full employment bill, see Bailey, *Congress Makes a Law*, p. 25.
39. BMB to Levin H. Campbell, 24 August, to Claude Pepper, 5 July, to Guy M. Gillette, 15 May, to Albert Gore, 24 January 1945, SC; *New York Times*, 13 May 1945; BMB memo, 10 May 1945, WF.
40. *New York Times*, 19 August 1945.
41. Walter Millis, ed., *The Forrestal Diaries* (1951), p. 100; J. A. Krug to BMB, 24 October, BMB telegram to Krug, 25 October, Krug to BMB, 27 October, BMB to Krug, 30 October 1944, SC.
42. Eleanor Roosevelt quoted in Lash, *Eleanor and Franklin*, p. 904; "Bretton Woods," Treasury Department conference, 16 February 1945, Morgenthau Diaries, 820:29–30.
43. Robert P. Patterson to BMB, 25 December 1945, GC; Patterson to BMB, 4 April, Robert A. Lovett memo to Patterson, April 1941, Charles C. Segrist memo to H. M. Exton, 29 April 1946, Patterson memo to Mr. Peterson, 15 December 1945, Swope folder, Patterson Papers.
44. Baruch quoted in Helen Lawrenson, *Stranger at the Party: A Memoir* (1975), p. 131; 1940–41 diaries, Leon Henderson Papers, Box 36; "Baruch's Visit,"

13 March 1945, Morgenthau Diaries, 827:161; BMB to Brendan Bracken, 16 July 1943, SC. For Baruch on Henderson, see Daniels, *White House Witness*, p. 158.

45. Wallace, COHC, p. 2891; Ickes Diary, pp. 8014, 8362–63; Wallace, COHC, p. 4011; "Visit from Baruch," 21 April 1945, Morgenthau Diaries, 839:149–50. For Wallace's reaction to Baruch's dislike of Jones, see Wallace, COHC, pp. 1360, 1679.

46. Baruch quoted in Treasury Department conference, 21 April 1945, Morgenthau Diaries, 839:106; Ickes Diary, p. 8106.

47. *New York Times*, 5, 6 April 1945; BMB telegram to Jonathan Daniels, 16 April 1945, PPF 8113.

48. James F. Byrnes news conference, 21 February 1944, pp. 5, 9, "Aide Memoir," BMB Special 1945 folder, GC; Ickes Diary, pp. 9505, 9586–87; *New York Times*, 3 March 1945; BMB to Arthur Krock, 18 March 1945 ("not sent but keep in files temp"), SC.

49. BMB to James F. Byrnes, 2 October 1944, file 71, to Byrnes, Monday, ca. March–April 1945, Miscellaneous 1943–47 file, Byrnes Papers; Ickes Diary, pp. 9831, 9874, 9969; Wallace, COHC, 19 July 1945, pp. 4009–14; BMB to Fred Searls, 13 March 1946, memo to Harold Epstein, December 1958, SC.

50. Ickes Diary, pp. 7181, 8080, 8101, 8103, 8622–23, 8846; BMB telegram to Thomas E. Dewey, 4 November 1942, WF; Edwin C. Johnson to BMB, 5 January 1943, SC; Wallace, COHC, p. 3315.

51. BMB to G. B. Parker, 21 July, to Dave McGill, 21 July, to Harold Ickes, 28 July 1944, SC; Frank Kent to Harry Byrd, 14 December 1950, Kent Papers, Box 5; BMB to Thomas E. Dewey, 5 July 1944, "The Washington Merry-Go-Round, for release Saturday, August 12, 1944 and thereafter," SC.

52. BMB to Eleanor Roosevelt, November 1944 (handwritten), ER, Box 1706.

53. Ickes Diary, p. 8216; Lilienthal, *Journals: The TVA Years*, p. 625; Thomas E. Hachey, *Confidential Dispatches: Analyses of America by the British Ambassador, 1939–1945* (1973), p. 121; Hearst columnist quoted in Ross, *Preparing for Ulysses*, p. 127; "Baruch's Visit," 13 March 1945, Morgenthau Diaries, 827:165; George H. Gallup, *The Gallup Poll: Public Opinion, 1935–1971* (1972), p. 550. Also named in the poll were MacArthur (by 26% of the respondents), Eisenhower (24%), Kaiser (8%), Ford (2%), Eleanor Roosevelt (2%), and others (36%).

54. Keith Hutchinson, "Mr. Baruch Muddies the Waters," *Nation*, 17 November 1945, p. 523; Felix Frankfurter to Walter Lippmann, 16 November 1945, Frankfurter Papers; "Recollections of the Interment Train, April 14–15, 1945," Henry A. Wallace Papers.

55. On the gasoline situation, see correspondence in OF 56, Box 4, and OF 56-B, Box 8. See also BMB memo, 23 July 1943, WF; and *New York Times*, 17 January 1946.

56. Lawrenson, *Stranger at the Party*, p. 132; Rosenman, *Working with Roosevelt*, p. 336; copy of Swope to Drew Pearson, 7 November 1947, SC; Samuel Lubell to Mary Lou Simon, 22 July 1944, to M. A. Boyle, 7 July, John M. Hancock to BMB, 2 January 1945, GC.

57. Robert P. Patterson to David Ginsburg, 10 September, Ginsburg to Patterson, 24 September 1946, Patterson Papers; Vannevar Bush to BMB, 24 October, Karl T. Compton to BMB, 20 October, Bradley Dewey to BMB, 31 July 1945, SC.

58. Wallace, COHC, p. 4009; Millis, *The Forrestal Diaries*, p. 100.

59. On the Morgenthau Plan controversy, see John Morton Blum, *From The*

Morgenthau Diaries: Years of War, 1941–1945 (1967), pp. 327–464; David Rees, *Harry Dexter White: A Study in Paradox* (1973), pp. 239–322; Lloyd C. Gardner, *Architects of Illusion: Men and Ideas in American Foreign Policy, 1941–1949* (1970), pp. 233–34; Lloyd C. Gardner, "America and the German 'Problem,' 1945–1949," in Barton J. Bernstein, ed., *Politics and Policies of the Truman Administration* (1970), pp. 114–17; John H. Backer, *Priming the German Economy: American Occupational Policies, 1945–1948* (1971), pp. 7–30; John H. Backer, *The Decision to Divide Germany: American Foreign Policy in Transition* (1978), pp. 32–43, 82–84; Warren F. Kimball, *Swords for Ploughshares: The Morgenthau Plan for Defeated Nazi Germany, 1943–1946* (1976); Bruce Kuklick, *American Policy and the Division of Germany: The Clash over Reparations* (1972), pp. 47–73; John Lewis Gaddis, *The United States and the Origins of the Cold War, 1941–1947* (1972), pp. 117–25; and Meredith Lentz Adams, "The Morgenthau Plan: A Study in Bureaucratic Depravity," doctoral dissertation, University of Texas at Austin, 1971.

60. Blum, *Morgenthau: Years of War*, p. 343; Henry Morgenthau, Jr.-BMB telephone conversation, 18 October 1944, 783:13, BMB memo, 14 November 1944, 805:273, Morgenthau Diaries; BMB to Milo Perkins, 18 November 1944, to E. D. Coblentz, 23 March 1945, SC.

61. Stimson Diary, Sunday, 11 March 1945, 50:178; Thomas M. Campbell and George Herring, ed., *The Diaries of Edward M. Stettinius, Jr., 1943–1946* (1975), p. 298; "F.D.R.—March 13, 1945," Henderson Papers, Box 36. Also see Blum, *Morgenthau: Years of War*, p. 403.

62. John Foster Dulles to BMB, 19 March, Samuel Lubell memos on Yalta discussions, ca. March 1945, "Outlining Reparations Problem," 13 March 1945, SC; "Baruch's Visit," 13 March 1945, 827:161, Du Bose memo for the files, 16 March 1945, 829:232–33, telephone conversation, 16 March 1945, 828:352, Morgenthau Diaries.

63. Samuel Lubell memo to BMB, 25 March 1945, SC; *New York Times*, 17, 30 March, 5, 6, 12 April 1945; Lubell memos to BMB, ca. 31 March, 1, 14 April Treasury Department conference, 21 April 1945, 839:106–7, "Visit from Baruch, April 21, 1945," 839:149–50, Morgenthau Diaries; J. M. Keynes to R. H. Brand, 6 April 1945, Brand Papers, file 198.

64. BMB to Dwight D. Eisenhower, 17 April, Eisenhower to BMB, 28 April 1945, SC; Treasury Department conference, 21 April 1945, 839:106, "Visit from Baruch, April 21, 1945," 839:149–50, telephone conversation, 24 April 1945, 839:219, Morgenthau Diaries; BMB to Harry S. Truman, 20 April, Truman to BMB, 3 May 1945, SC; *New York Times*, 25 May (Krock), 1 June 1945.

65. *New York Times*, 23 June 1945; Testimony of BMB, "Elimination of German Resources for War," Hearings before a Subcommittee of the Senate Committee on Military Affairs, 79th Cong., 1st sess., 1945, PP.

66. "Mr. Baruch Has a Plan," *Economist*, 9 June 1945, p. 770, copy in WF; Blum, *Morgenthau: Years of War*, p. 464.

67. BMB to Thomas W. Lamont, 9 November 1948, to Eliot Janeway, 29 October 1951, to Winston Churchill, 24 September 1957, to Lord Beaverbrook, 15 December 1961, SC; Baruch, *The Public Years*, pp. 408–9.

68. BMB to Brendan Bracken, 16 July, to R. C. Leffingwell, 20 May, to John Francis Neylan, 20 May 1943, to Henry Morgenthau, Jr., 27 October, memo to Edward R. Stettinius, Jr., 1 December 1944, SC. Also see Morgenthau Diaries, 805:261–64, 267–69, 272, for December 1944 exchanges; Daniels,

White House Witness, p. 158, for Baruch's antipathy to Keynes; BMB to James F. Byrnes, 1 December 1944, Byrnes Papers, file 92, for a summary of Baruch's arguments; Keynes to Brand, 6 April 1945, Brand Papers, file 198.

69. BMB to Henry Morgenthau, Jr., 28 February 1945, WF; "Baruch's Visit," 13 March 1945, 827:163, BMB to Morgenthau, 22 March 1945, 836:176–77, Morgenthau to Gaston, 8 April 1945, 836:173, Morgenthau Diaries.

70. BMB to Truman, 20 April 1945, SC; Baruch, *The Public Years*, pp. 357–58.

71. "Visit from Baruch, April 21, 1945," Morgenthau Diaries, 839:149–50; BMB to Tom Stewart, 1 August 1945, GC. Also see BMB to Claude Pepper, 5 July 1945, SC.

72. W. L. Clayton to R. E. Wood, 17 November 1945, Clayton Papers; Smith Diary, 19 December 1945 (Appleby notes).

73. BMB to Albert Gore, 17 January, 19 February, Henry A. Wallace to BMB, 5 February, BMB to Michael L. Hoffman, 18 February, to Ralph Coghlan, 1 April 1946, SC.

74. Gardner, *Architects of Illusion*, p. 125; copies of Eleanor Roosevelt to Truman, 20 November, Truman to Mrs. Roosevelt, 26 November, W. L. Clayton to BMB, 8 October, BMB to Clayton, 20 October, 19 November, R. H. Brand to BMB, 23 November 1945, SC; BMB to James F. Byrnes, 13 March 1946, Byrnes Papers, file 632; R. H. Brand memo to Lord Halifax, 19 December, Brand to Halifax, 20 December, to J. M. Keynes, 14 December 1944, 10 January 1945, Brand Papers, file 197. Also see BMB to Churchill, 28 July 1949, SC.

75. Memo to W. L. Clayton, 17 April, Clayton to BMB, 26 April, BMB to Clayton, 29 April 1946, SC.

76. *New York Times*, 23 June, 5, 8 November 1945; Wallace, COHC, 19 July 1945, pp. 4012–13; Treasury Department conference, 21 April 1945, Morgenthau Diaries, 839:108–9. Also see "Draft—April 5, 1945 Re: Russia," Nelson Papers, Box 3.

77. BMB to Woodrow Wilson, 13 July 1918, SC; ACNP Diary, 22, 23 May 1919; Baruch, *The Public Years*, p. 195; *New York Times*, 11 April 1920; Swope to BMB, 12 September 1923, SC; BMB to John Spargo, 5 January 1921, GC.

78. *New York Times*, 11 April 1920; BMB to John Spargo, 5 January 1921, to Louis Loucheur, 11 November 1920, to J. R. Howard, 9 September 1921, GC; *New York Times*, 1 January 1925.

79. Baruch, *The Public Years*, pp. 196–98; BMB to William Reswick, 3 June 1947, SC.

80. René de Rougemont to BMB, 11 November 1936, SC; *New York Times*, 13 August 1933, 15 September 1936; BMB to Churchill, 12 May 1935, SC; BMB to E. M. Watson, 1 August 1940, Watson Papers, Box 11; BMB memo to Harry L. Hopkins, 13 October 1943, WF; Lawrenson, *Stranger at the Party*, p. 147.

81. D. F. Fleming, *The Cold War and Its Origins*, 2 vols. (1961).

82. BMB to FDR, 15 February, to Truman, 21 April 1945, SC; BMB to D. F. Fleming, 25 June, 20 October 1945, GC; M. A. Boyle to Fleming, 3 May, BMB telegram to Fleming, 24 January, Fleming to BMB, 14 March 1945, Fleming, "The Dangers of a New Balance of Power," "Why Are the Russians Slow to Trust the Western Powers?" "Whither Russia?" "The War with Japan," "A United States of Europe," SC.

83. "Elimination of German Resources for War," 22 June 1945, PP.

84. BMB to Tom Stewart, 18 July 1945, GC.

85. BMB to Truman, 21 April, 10 May 1945, SC; James F. Byrnes to FDR, 22

January 1945 ("secret"), Byrnes Papers, file 71; BMB to Swope, 2 March 1946, to Harry F. Byrd, 2 March 1950, SC.

86. ACNP Diary, 22, 23 May 1919; Lawrenson, *Stranger at the Party*, pp. 145–47; BMB to Brendan Bracken, 24 August, to D. F. Fleming, 24, 26 December 1945, to Herbert Hoover, 13 February 1946, SC; *New York Times*, 18 February 1946; Gaddis, *The United States and the Origins of the Cold War*, pp. 307–8. For Hoover's view of the Russians, see 1945 Hoover memo, SC.

87. Richard G. Hewlett and Oscar E. Anderson, Jr., *The New World, 1939–1946: A History of the United States Atomic Energy Commission*, 2 vols. (1962), 1:556; BMB to E. D. Coblentz, 7 April 1946, SC.

88. For Truman's troubles with Congress regarding atomic energy, see Smith Diary, 5 October 1945; Hewlett and Anderson, *The New World*, pp. 428–530, passim; Wallace, COHC, 20 December 1945, p. 4556; and memo to James F. Byrnes, 8 March 1946, Forrestal Papers.

89. David E. Lilienthal, *The Journals of David E. Lilienthal: The Atomic Energy Years, 1946–1950* (1964), p. 32.

90. BMB to James F. Byrnes, 13 March 1946, AE; Lilienthal, *Journals: The Atomic Energy Years*, pp. 49–50.

91. Dean Acheson to David E. Lilienthal, 16 January 1946, Lilienthal Papers; Hewlett and Anderson, *The New World*, pp. 539–40; Eberstadt Diary, 25 March 1946; Swope to Frankfurter, 2 April 1946, Frankfurter Papers; Campbell and Herring, *Diaries of Edward M. Stettinius*, p. 459; Lilienthal, *Journals: The Atomic Energy Years*, pp. 33, 131; Wallace, COHC, 20 February 1946, p. 4556.

92. Dean Acheson, *Present at the Creation: My Years in the State Department* (1969), pp. 154, 156; BMB to Dean Acheson, 21 August, Acheson to BMB, 23 August 1946, AE. For Frankfurter's perspective, see Frankfurter to John J. McCloy, 5 April 1946, Frankfurter Papers; and Lilienthal, *Journals: The Atomic Energy Years*, p. 30.

93. Lilienthal, *Journals: The Atomic Energy Years*, pp. 31–32, 43–44, 70–71; Acheson, *Present at the Creation*, p. 154.

94. Hewlett and Anderson, *The New World*, pp. 557–58; Baruch, *The Public Years*, pp. 361–63; Joseph I. Lieberman, *The Scorpion and the Tarantula: The Struggle to Control Atomic Weapons, 1945–1949* (1970), pp. 267–68.

95. Lilienthal, *Journals: The Atomic Energy Years*, pp. 39–40; Hewlett and Anderson, *The New World*, pp. 559–61; James F. Byrnes to BMB, 19 April, John M. Hancock memo for the Atomic Energy file, 19 April 1946, AE; BMB to Eugene Meyer, Jr., 29 April 1946, SC.

96. Lilienthal, *Journals: The Atomic Energy Years*, pp. 41–47; Dean Acheson telegram to Lilienthal, 9 May 1946, Lilienthal Papers; Acheson, *Present at the Creation*, pp. 154–55.

97. Hewlett and Anderson, *The New World*, pp. 564–66; Lilienthal, *Journals: The Atomic Energy Years*, pp. 131, 49–50; Acheson, *Present at the Creation*, p. 155; Lieberman, *The Scorpion and the Tarantula*, pp. 281–83.

98. Lilienthal, *Journals: The Atomic Energy Years*, pp. 51–54.

99. BMB to Lilienthal, 27 May, Lilienthal to J. Robert Oppenheimer, 28 May 1946, Lilienthal Papers; Lilienthal, *Journals: The Atomic Energy Years*, p. 55; folder, "requests for adoption of Acheson-Lilienthal report," June, John M. Hancock memo to James F. Byrnes, 1 June, "BMB Phone Conversation with JFB," 6 June 1946, "BMB Memorandum of Meeting on June 7, 1946, with the President and J. F. Byrnes," AE; E. J. Kahn, Jr., *The World of Swope*

(1965), p. 400; Hewlett and Anderson, *The New World*, pp. 567–74.

100. "BMB Phone Conversation with JFB," 6 June 1946, AE; Hewlett and Anderson, *The New World*, p. 576; Byrnes quoted in Lilienthal, *Journals: The Atomic Energy Years*, p. 59.

101. John M. Hancock memo to James F. Byrnes, 1 June 1946, BMB memo of meeting on 7 June 1946 with Truman and James F. Byrnes, AE.

102. Swope to Robert P. Patterson, 21 June 1946, Patterson Papers; Kahn, *The World of Swope*, pp. 400–401; Baruch, "Atomic Energy Control," *Vital Speeches of the Day*, 1 July 1946, p. 546; Hewlett and Anderson, *The New World*, pp. 576–79.

103. See folders on press reaction and radio opinion in AE, Box 64; BMB to Dean Acheson, 23 June, 9 July 1946, AE; "The Bomb: The U.S. Will Yield Its Secret—If," *Newsweek*, 24 June 1946, pp. 23–24; Kahn, *The World of Swope*, p. 401; *New Republic*, 17 June 1946, pp. 851–52.

104. Frankfurter to Swope, 18 June 1946, Frankfurter Papers; Harry Winne to Lilienthal, 18 June, Carroll L. Wilson to Lilienthal, 25 June, Chester I. Barnard to Walter Lippmann, 20, 24 June, Lippmann to Barnard, 25 June, Barnard to Lippmann, 27 June 1946, Lilienthal Papers; Lilienthal, *Journals: The Atomic Energy Years*, p. 60; Dean Acheson memo to Truman, 27 June 1946, Truman Papers, Official File 430.

105. Andrei A. Gromyko, "Control of Atom Bomb," *Vital Speeches of the Day*, 1 July 1946, pp. 551–53; Hewlett and Anderson, *The New World*, pp. 583–91; BMB draft of U.S. position, 11 July 1946, AE; Lilienthal to Chester I. Barnard, 24 July 1946, Lilienthal Papers; Lilienthal, *Journals: The Atomic Energy Years*, pp. 69–77, 81–82. Baruch expected that the international authority's leadership would be American and wanted Lilienthal there to satisfy the American left. Ibid., p. 75. But although Baruch spoke favorably of Lilienthal with the president, his later recommendations did not include Lilienthal's name. See "M. J. C." memo to Clark Clifford, 9 October 1946, Clifford Papers.

106. "Notes on Staff Conference, Thursday Morning," 1 August, John M. Hancock to Dean Acheson, 15 August, memo from BMB, 3 September, Franklin Lindsay memo to BMB, 11 September 1946, AE; Hewlett and Anderson, *The New World*, pp. 591–97.

107. The text of the letter can be found in John Morton Blum, ed., *The Price of Vision: The Diary of Henry A. Wallace, 1942–1946* (1973), pp. 589–601. See also Hewlett and Anderson, *The New World*, pp. 599–602; Joseph P. Lash, *Eleanor: The Years Alone* (1972), pp. 89–90; BMB to David Ginsburg, 20 September 1946, SC; "Wallace Episode Chronology," 1946, T. F. Farrell memo to John M. Hancock, 18 September, "LG" memo to BMB, 18 September, Hancock memo for file, 19 September 1946 AE; James F. Byrnes to James Forrestal, 28 September 1946, Forrestal Papers; and Wallace, COHC, pp. 5020–21.

108. Wallace, COHC, p. 5021; "R. G. Arneson's Notes of Meeting with Mr. Wallace . . . September 27, 1946," AE; Hewlett and Anderson, *The New World*, pp. 602–3. When *The New World* was published in 1962, Wallace became embittered against Hauser and wondered if he were "fearful . . . of Baruch's long arm." Wallace to Don Murphy, 8 April 1962, Wallace Papers. Also see Wallace to Philip M. Hauser, 8 April, 15 June 1962, Wallace Papers. Hauser, after a quick reading of *The New World*, observed, "It seems likely that we were not entirely up to date on the status of negotiations being conducted by Mr. Baruch." Hauser to Wallace, 22 August 1962, Wallace Pa-

pers. Six years after it erupted, Wallace erroneously attributed the controversy to Baruch's personal feeling that Wallace's letter "reflected on him." Wallace to Curtis MacDougall, 21 August 1952, Wallace Papers.

109. Hewlett and Anderson, *The New World*, pp. 603–5; F. Eberstadt, "Memo re My Discussions with Wallace and Hauser by Telephone," 8 October, John M. Hancock memo of 1 October, "Notes on Press Conference Held in Mr. Hancock's Office," 2 October, "Text of Wallace's Reply to Baruch Charges over U. S. Atomic Policy," 4 October, Albin E. Johnson memo, "Public Reaction to Baruch-Wallace Controversy," 28 October 1946, AE; *Time*, 14 October 1946, p. 24.

110. Swope to James F. Byrnes, 10 October 1946, Byrnes Papers, file 492; Bernard Baruch, "Atom Plan Stands Despite Intrigue," *Vital Speeches of the Day*, 1 November 1946, pp. 59–61.

111. Joseph Chase memo to Franklin Lindsay, "Views of United Nations members on Veto . . . November 5," Lindsay memo to BMB on Gallup Poll, 25 November, BMB-Dean Acheson telephone conversation, 26 November, 1946, AE.

112. John M. Hancock memo on White House meeting for Atomic Energy file, 19 April, BMB memo of meeting on 7 June 1946 with Truman and James F. Byrnes, AE; Lilienthal, *Journals: The Atomic Energy Years*, p. 123; "Telephone Conversation with Bernard M. Baruch, December 16, 1946, 3:00 P.M.," Lilienthal Papers; BMB to Lord Beaverbrook, 25 August 1953, SC; Hewlett and Anderson, *The New World*, p. 618. The British, regardless of political party or ideological persuasion, did not forgive the Americans for refusing to share atomic energy secrets on development, because it meant "losing several years and spending a lot." Brendan Bracken to BMB, 29 August 1954, SC.

113. Lilienthal, *Journals: The Atomic Energy Years*, pp. 124–25, 130–32; "The Inflexibles," *Time*, 30 December 1946, p. 20; "United Nations: Either-Or," *Newsweek*, 6 January 1947, pp. 32–33; BMB to Dean Acheson, 18 January 1947, and Franklin A. Lindsay file, Box 62, AE.

114. Frederick Kuh, "USSR Fears U.S. Atom Plan as Wedge in Its Economy," *PM*, 30 September 1946, Franklin Lindsay memo to BMB on Sobolev meeting, 21 October 1946, AE.

115. Hewlett and Anderson, *The New World*, p. 608; BMB to Dean Acheson, 23 June, Acheson to BMB, 1 July, BMB to Acheson, 9 July, John M. Hancock memo to T. F. Farrell, 15 August ("Bomb Manufacture" folder), Franklin Lindsay, "Comments," October, Lindsay memo to BMB on Sobolev meeting, 21 October 1946, AE.

116. BMB to Dean Acheson, 2 November, to Warren Austin, 2 November, Franklin Lindsay confidential memo to the staff, 12 November, John M. Hancock memo to the staff, 21 November ("Bomb Manufacture" folder), Lindsay memo on Gallup Poll, 25 November 1946, AE; Millis, *The Forrestal Diaries*, p. 217; Walter Lippmann-James Forrestal telephone conversation, 29 November 1946, Forrestal Papers.

117. BMB memo to James F. Byrnes. 8 December 1946, AE; John Foster Dulles to BMB, 6 January 1947, Dulles Papers; Chester I. Barnard to Lilienthal, 6, 20 January 1947, Lilienthal Papers; Millis, *The Forrestal Diaries*, p. 241.

118. Speech at Churchman Dinner for Eisenhower, 3 December 1946, PP.

CHAPTER TEN

1. Telegram to Truman, 13 February 1946, SC.
2. Harold Smith to Elmer Davis, 20 August 1943, Smith Papers; Chester Bowles to Henry A. Wallace, 15 February, 3 May, to James F. Byrnes, 25 February, to Donald Nelson, 10 March 1944, Bowles Papers.
3. BMB to James F. Byrnes, 27 June 1944, Byrnes Papers, file 71; memo to Byrnes, 8 September 1944, memo, "Price Control during the Transition from War to Peace," ca. late 1944, GC; BMB memo, "Little Steel Formula," 15 November 1944, OF 98, Box 4.
4. Bob Brooks memo to Chester Bowles, 28 July, Bowles to Samuel I. Rosenman, 23 August, to James Brownlee, 26 October 1945, Bowles Papers; Seymour E. Harris memo to A. C. C. Hill, Jr., "Reconversion Pricing Policy," 31 August 1945, RG 179/035.005, War Production Board (WPB) Papers; Chester Bowles, *Promises to Keep: My Years in Public Life, 1941–1969* (1971), pp. 127, 133–34; Bowles to Rosenman, 29 October, Box 4, to Harry S. Truman, 2 November 1945, Rosenman Papers, Truman Library, Box 8; Bowles to John Kenneth Galbraith, 18 December 1945, Bowles Papers.
5. Bowles, *Promises to Keep*, pp. 140–42; clipping, Marquis Childs, "The Search for a Wage-Price Formula," ca. January 1946, BMB to John W. Snyder, 14 January, BMB memo to Truman, 20 January, Truman to BMB, 24 January, Chester Bowles to BMB, 24 January 1946, SC; Robert J. Donovan, *Conflict and Crisis: The Presidency of Harry S. Truman, 1945–1948* (1977), pp. 166–68; James Forrestal to F. Eberstadt, 24 January, Eberstadt to Forrestal, 4 February 1946, Forrestal Papers; BMB to Truman, 1 February 1946, SC; *Wall Street Journal* and BMB quoted in Randolph E. Paul, *Taxation in the United States* (1954), pp. 481–82.
6. BMB telegrams to Chester Bowles, 12 February, to John W. Snyder, 12 February, to Truman, 13 February, Truman to BMB, 15 February 1946, SC.
7. BMB to Albert Gore, 19 February, to Truman, 26 February 1946, SC. For samples of citizen support for BMB's antiinflation statement, see Oliver Reagan telegram to Truman, 25 March, Richard Rand to Truman, 28 March 1946, Truman Papers, Official File 430; Chester Bowles memo to James Brownlee and Henry Hart, 1 April, Brownlee to Bowles, 1 April 1946, Bowles Papers; "The Shape of Things," *Nation*, 6 April 1946, p. 386; Ralph Robey, "Mr. Baruch on the Extension of OPA," *Newsweek*, 8 April 1946, p. 74; Bowles to BMB, 25 April, and BMB telegram to Bowles, 30 April 1946, SC.
8. On inflation during 1946–47, see Bowles, *Promises to Keep*, pp. 143–57; Crauford D. Goodwin, ed., *Exhortation and Controls: The Search for a Wage-Price Policy, 1945–1971* (1975), pp. 25–48; Barton J. Bernstein, "Economic Policies," in Richard S. Kirkendall, ed., *The Truman Period as a Research Field* (1967), pp. 99–108; Lester V. Chandler, *Inflation in the United States, 1940–1948* (1951), pp. 216–396, passim; Allen J. Matusow, *Farm Policies and Politics in the Truman Years* (1967), pp. 20–62, 154–63.
9. BMB to Olin D. Johnston, 17 February 1947, SC; Council of Economic Advisers to Truman, 7 April 1947, Truman Papers, Official File 985; Goodwin, *Exhortation and Controls*, pp. 39–41; clipping, Raymond Moley, "Baruch vs. Truman," 24 April 1947, SC; "The Shape of Things," *Nation*, 26 April 1947, pp. 466–67.
10. BMB memo to John W. Snyder, 21 August, BMB to James F. Byrnes, 23 April, to Winston Churchill, 2 November, to Philip Murray, 19 June (draft; "B phoned M"), 12 August, 26 November, to John L. Lewis, 12 August 1947, 20

May, 16 November 1948, to Walter Reuther, 3 September 1948, SC.
11. Copies of John M. Hancock to E. C. Stevens, 23 May, Hancock memo to the Partners, 26 September 1947, Alfred P. Sloan, Jr., to BMB, 29 July 1948, BMB to Ralph Coghlan, 17 February 1946, to Richard B. Russell, 8 December, to Harry F. Byrd, 29 May 1947, to Paul Hoffman, 21 June, to Joseph O'Mahoney, 3 December 1948, SC.
12. BMB to Arthur H. Vandenberg, 10 February 1947, SC.
13. David E. Lilienthal, *The Journals of David E. Lilienthal: The Atomic Energy Years, 1946–1950* (1964), pp. 163–64.
14. Ibid., p. 162.
15. "Long-distance telephone conversation with Bernard M. Baruch at 4 P.M., March 25, 1947," Arthur Krock Papers; Arthur Krock, *Memoirs: Sixty Years on the Firing Line* (1968), p. 266; BMB to Harry F. Byrd, 23 April 1947, SC.
16. BMB to Herman B. Baruch, 1 April 1946, to Arthur H. Vandenberg, 14 May, to Harry F. Byrd, 14 May, BMB memo to George C. Marshall, 19 May, Marshall to BMB, 22 May 1947, SC; "Telephone conversation with Mr. Baruch, May 27, 1947—David E. Lilienthal," Lilienthal Papers; Lilienthal, *Journals: The Atomic Energy Years*, p. 184. Also see BMB to Brendan Bracken, 22 July, to R. P. Brandt, 30 June 1947, SC.
17. Frederick J. Dobney, ed., *Selected Papers of Will Clayton* (1971), p. 203; W. L. Clayton to BMB, 30 May, George C. Marshall to BMB, 21 July 1947, SC.
18. BMB to Sailing W. Baruch, 30 September, to W. Averell Harriman, 2 July 1947, to Ralph Coghlan, 26 January 1948, SC; Lilienthal, *Journals: The Atomic Energy Years*, p. 195; BMB telegram to Krock, 25 January 1948, Krock Papers.
19. James Forrestal-F. Eberstadt telephone conversation, 10 June 1947, Forrestal Papers; BMB memo to George C. Marshall, 23 June 1947, SC; Lilienthal, *Journals: The Atomic Energy Years*, p. 236; copy of John M. Hancock memo to the Partners, "Meetings of Business Advisory Council . . . September 23rd and 24th, September 26, 1947," SC.
20. Copy of "American Interest in European Reconstruction," speech by Winthrop W. Aldrich to American Bar Association, 30 September 1947, R. C. Leffingwell to BMB, 30 January, Robert P. Patterson to BMB, 20 February 1948, SC; Walter Millis, ed., *The Forrestal Diaries* (1951), pp. 310–11; Drew Pearson, *Diaries, 1949–1959* (1974), p. 83; George C. Marshall to BMB, 19 November, BMB to Albert Gore, 20 December 1947, C. B. Ormerod to BMB, 14 January 1948, SC.
21. *New York Times*, 20, 22, 23 January 1948; Bernard Baruch, "A Peace Waging Program," *Vital Speeches*, 1 February 1948, pp. 234–38; BMB to Harry F. Byrd, 25 January, 18 March, to Krock, 25 January 1948, SC; memo, 26 January, private memo, 7 April 1948, Krock Papers; Krock, *Memoirs*, p. 267.
22. "Baruch Takes a Look at ERP," *Newsweek*, 26 January 1948, p. 17; James Reston, *New York Times*, 20 January 1948; BMB to James Reston, 10 April 1949, SC.
23. BMB to Brendan Bracken, 6 February, to James Forrestal, 7 February, to Harry F. Byrd, 11 February, 18 March, to Herbert Bayard Swope, 25 February 1948, SC. For a dissent on a military alliance with Europe, see R. C. Leffingwell to BMB, 30 January 1948, SC.
24. Robert P. Patterson to James F. Byrnes, 11 February, James Forrestal to Patterson, 21 August 1947, Patterson Papers; Millis, *The Forrestal Diaries*, p. 291; F. Eberstadt to Forrestal, 2 October, 6 November 1947, Eberstadt-Forrestal telephone conversation, 9 October 1947, Forrestal Papers. On the

NSRB, see Thomas H. Etzold, "American Organization for National Security, 1945–1950," in Thomas H. Etzold and John Lewis Gaddis, eds., *Containment: Documents on American Policy and Strategy, 1945–1950* (1978), pp. 8–10.

25. Arthur M. Hill to BMB, 6 February, BMB to Hill, 5 April 1948, SC; private memo, 7 April 1948, Krock Papers; "Report of telephone conversation, Mr. Baruch with Arthur M. Hill and Ferdinand Eberstadt, April 23, 1948, 11:15 A.M.," SC; Charles H. Kendall memo to the chairman, "Baruch's Speech," 29 June 1949, Charles G. Ross Papers.

26. BMB to Arthur M. Hill, 1, 3 May, to F. Eberstadt, 28 April, to Owen Bewster, 1 May 1948, SC; James Forrestal-James F. Byrnes telephone conversation, 28 April 1948, Forrestal Papers; Millis, *The Forrestal Diaries*, p. 428; Eberstadt to BMB, 13 May, BMB to John W. Snyder, 18 May, copy of John R. Steelman to Hill, 3 June, BMB to Hill, 31 August, to George C. Marshall, 12 August 1948, SC; Charles H. Kendall memo to the chairman, "Baruch's Speech," 29 June 1949, Ross Papers. On the Truman antiinflation program of 1947–48, see Goodwin, *Exhortation and Controls*, pp. 45–60.

27. Katie Louchheim, *By the Political Sea* (1970), p. 113; Krock to BMB, 1 April 1950, Krock Papers.

28. BMB to Albert Gore, 19 February, to Marquis Childs, 18 February, to Ralph Coghlan, 8 March, to Truman, 26 February, Truman to BMB, 1 March, Herman B. Baruch ("Tot") to BMB, 4 February, 6, 21 March 1946, SC; BMB to James F. Byrnes, 22 March 1947, Byrnes Papers, Miscellaneous 1935–47 folder.

29. Harry H. Vaughn to Doris Fleeson, 5 February 1947, Truman Papers, Official File 491; BMB to Eleanor Roosevelt, 10 July 1947, ER, Box 3746; Lilienthal, *Journals: The Atomic Energy Years*, p. 163; BMB to Arthur H. Vandenberg, 10 February 1947, SC; BMB to Krock, 7 November 1947, Krock Papers; E. J. Kahn, Jr., *The World of Swope* (1965), p. 402; Swope to BMB, 21 November 1947, SC.

30. *New York Times*, 24 January 1948; BMB to Harry F. Byrd, 25 January, to Truman, 25 January, to Krock, 25 January, Truman to BMB, 18 February 1948, SC; private memo, 7 April 1948, Krock Papers.

31. BMB to Truman, 30 April, Truman to BMB, 5 May, BMB to Truman, 12 May, Truman to BMB, 12 May 1948, SC.

32. Truman to BMB, 19 August, BMB to Truman, 27 August, Truman to BMB, 31 August, BMB to Truman, 2 September 1948 ("not sent"), SC; Helen Lawrenson, *Stranger at the Party: A Memoir* (1972), p. 155. Baruch omitted mention of his brother in his own reproduction of the correspondence in *The Public Years* (1960), p. 399.

33. Leon Henderson to BMB, 16 June 1948, BMB to Jonathan Daniels, 2 October ("draft not sent"), to Truman, 2 October 1950 ("draft not sent"), to Louis Johnson, 17 September, to James F. Byrnes, 29 September, to Leslie L. Biffle, 30 September 1948, SC; Baruch, *The Public Years*, pp. 394–400; Samuel Lubell, *The Future of American Politics* (1965 ed.), pp. 32–33; Julius Abels, *Out of the Jaws of Victory* (1959), pp. 123, 164; Pearson, *Diaries, 1949–1959*, p. 83.

34. Lilienthal, *Journals: The Atomic Energy Years*, pp. 621–22; BMB telegram and letter to Thomas E. Dewey, 29 June 1948, SC.

35. BMB to Eleanor Roosevelt, 15 October 1948, to Churchill, 2 February, to John Foster Dulles, 13 June 1955, statement given wire services, 4 November 1948, BMB special file, BMB to Alben W. Barkley, 5 November, to Chester

Bowles, 19 November 1948, to Scott W. Lucas, 11 June, to Bennett C. Clark, 25 August, to Stephen Early, 20 December 1949, to Leslie L. Biffle, 6 January, to Harold L. Ickes, 17 January, to John R. Lord, 2 August 1950, to Herman B. Baruch, 19 February 1949, SC; Lilienthal, *Journals: The Atomic Energy Years*, p. 543.

36. Clipping from *Washington Times-Herald*, 30 June 1949, Truman Papers, Official File 491; Charles H. Kendall memo to the chairman, "Baruch's Speech," 29 June 1949, Ross Papers; Pearson, *Diaries, 1949–1959*, p. 61; BMB to Louis Johnson, 23 August 1949, SC; Krock to F. Eberstadt, 2 July 1949, Krock Papers.

37. J. A. Krug to BMB, 17 November, BMB to Krug, 18 November 1949, SC.

38. BMB to Krock, 6 October 1949, Krock Papers; BMB to Clare Boothe Luce, 22 September 1949, to Gordon Gray, 20 November, to William Benton, 9 November, BMB to Truman, 3 July 1950 ("did not send"), SC.

39. Kahn, *The World of Swope*, p. 403; Pearson, *Diaries, 1949–1959*, p. 84.

40. Churchill to BMB, 28 April, Churchill telegram to BMB, 15 November, BMB telegram to Churchill, 16 November 1949, BMB to Harry F. Byrd, 14 January, to Paul Hoffman, 16 January, to Roy W. Howard, 11 February 1950, SC; address at National War College, 22 March 1950, PP. Also see BMB to Krock, 4 April 1950, Krock Papers; and BMB to Hoffman, 2 May 1950, SC.

41. Address to the United States Conference of Mayors, 21 March 1949, PP; Bernard Baruch, "What of Our Future?" *Saturday Evening Post*, 23 April 1949, pp. 19–21.

42. BMB to Louis Johnson, 22 April, Johnson to BMB, 3 May 1949, Johnson Papers, Box 102; BMB to David Lawrence, 30 July 1949, to Ralph Coghlan, 6 December 1948, to Harry F. Byrd, 17 May, to Paul Douglas, 17 May, to Coghlan, 13 June 1949, to Hedda Hopper, 2 March 1950, SC. On economic policy in 1948–50, see William O. Wagnon, Jr., "The Truman Administration, the 1949 Recession, and the Problem of Growth," paper delivered at Organization of American Historians session, 6 April 1972, Washington, D.C.; Goodwin, *Exhortation and Controls*, pp. 60–69; Alonzo L. Hamby, *Beyond the New Deal: Harry S. Truman and American Liberalism* (1973), pp. 297–303; and Herbert Stein, *The Fiscal Revolution in America* (1969), pp. 233–40.

43. Address at Washington University, 6 June 1950, PP.

44. Goodwin, *Exhortation and Controls*, pp. 69–70; "Report of several off the record meetings in July, 1950," Leon H. Keyserling to Krock, 14, 19 July 1950, Krock Papers.

45. *New York Times*, 27 July 1950.

46. Ibid.; James W. Gerard telegram to Charles Ross, 26 July, Truman to Gerard, 27 July 1950, Truman Papers, Official File 491.

47. For 1950 letters or telegrams to Truman concerning inflation, see, in the Truman Papers, Official File 2855, those of David French (28 July), Mrs. Florence R. Long (27 July), Dr. R. L. Sanders (31 July), Jim Sweeney (26 July), Rebecca A. Robinson (30 July), Benjamin J. Mobley (27 July), Mary E. Lezotte (3 August), George Savage King (30 July), Sam Duke (28 July), A. N. Abbott (28 July), David Abrahams (27 July), and Margaret Kent (28 July).

48. *New York Times*, 29, 30 July, 1 August 1950; Senate committee report quoted in Maeva Marcus, *Truman and the Steel Seizure Case: The Limits of Presidential Power* (1977), p. 8; Matusow, *Farm Policies and Politics*, p. 224; Goodwin, *Exhortation and Controls*, p. 70; Harry F. Byrd to BMB, 10 Au-

gust, BMB to Paul Douglas, 15 August, to Burnet R. Maybank, 18 August, to Edwin C. Johnson, 2 August 1950, SC; Raymond Moley, "Baruch and Inflation," *Newsweek*, 2 October 1950, p. 92.

49. Keyserling quoted in Goodwin, *Exhortation and Controls*, p. 73; *New York Times*, 22 August, 20 October 1950; Bernard Baruch, "A Test of Democracy—Inflation," *Vital Speeches of the Day*, 1 November 1950, pp. 47–51; BMB to Robert A. Lovett, 10 November, to Ralph E. Flanders, 21 November, to Lyndon B. Johnson, 16 November, to John W. Snyder, 17 November, to W. Stuart Symington, 21 November 1950, SC.

50. BMB to W. Stuart Symington, 5 December, to Bradley Dewey, 5 December, BMB telegrams to Paul Douglas, Burnet R. Maybank, and John W. Bricker, 6 December 1950, Hubert H. Humphrey to BMB, 10 January, 16 February, BMB to Humphrey, 9 March, John M. Hancock to BMB, 7, 26 February, BMB to David Ginsburg, 1 May, Michael V. DiSalle to BMB, 1 May, Albert Gore to BMB, 16 March, BMB to Blair Moody, 6 June, BMB telegram to Maybank and Brent Spence, 28 June, John F. Kennedy to BMB, 17 July 1951, SC; *New York Times*, 9 December 1950, 8 June 1951; Goodwin, *Exhortation and Controls*, pp. 76–82; Albert P. Morano to Truman, 11 January 1951, Truman Papers, Official File 491.

51. Swope to Stephen Early, 7 December 1950, Early Papers, Box 19; BMB to Harry F. Byrd, 12 January, Truman to BMB, 23 May, BMB to Truman, 1 June, to Frank Kent, 5 June 1951, to Estes Kefauver, 22 January 1952, SC; *New York Times*, 26 June, 3 August 1951; Baruch, *The Public Years*, p. 401.

52. BMB to Roy W. Howard, 13 September, to Michael V. DiSalle, 31 October, to Charles E. Wilson, 4 October, to Alben W. Barkley, 21 September 1951, SC.

53. Goodwin, *Exhortation and Controls*, pp. 82–89.

54. BMB to Harry F. Byrd, 12 January, 12, 25 September, to Joseph O'Mahoney, 13 January, 30 October, to Hubert H. Humphrey, 20 September, to Alben W. Barkley, 21 September, to Bradley Dewey, 13 September, to Eliot Janeway, 29 October 1951, copy of "Third Quarterly Report to the President" by Director of Defense Mobilization C. E. Wilson, p. 3, SC. Also see speech to officers and noncommissioned officers, headquarters, First Army, Governors Island, 28 September, and speech to Association of American Universities, New Haven, 23 October 1951, PP.

55. Dwight D. Eisenhower to BMB, 30 June 1952, BMB to Eisenhower, 27 October 1961, SC; Eisenhower to Krock, 10 December 1947, Krock Papers.

56. Frank Kent memo, 11 December, Eisenhower to Krock, 10 December 1947, Krock Papers; BMB to Eisenhower, 1 October 1957, 22 June 1949, SC.

57. Eisenhower to BMB, 31 July, 16 September 1950, Marquis Childs to BMB, 8 August, BMB to Eisenhower, 8 August, to Harry F. Byrd, 3 August 1951, SC; *New York Times*, 3 August, 5 November 1951.

58. BMB to the editor, *Financial World*, 15 May, to Robert W. Johnson, 12 June, to Joe Kotcka, 16 June, 11 August, to James F. Byrnes, 14 August, to Robert F. Wagner, Jr., 17 September, to Walter Reuther, 22 October, to James F. Bell, 7 November, to Sinclair Weeks, 3 December 1952, SC.

59. BMB to Harold R. Moskovit, 27 June, to Brendan Bracken, 29 August, to Albert Gore, 7, 16 October, 7 November 1952, BMB to Alben W. Barkley, 6 January 1953, statement, 9 October 1952, SC; Joseph P. Lash, *Eleanor: The Years Alone* (1972), pp. 211–12; Krock to Swope, 10 October 1952, Krock Papers.

60. Eisenhower to BMB, 30 June, "copy of letter sent by Mr. Baruch to General

Eisenhower via Tex McCrary," 4 July, Eisenhower to BMB, 6 August, Robert A. Taft to BMB, 20 December, Harry F. Byrd to BMB, 18 December 1952, Eisenhower to BMB, 12 January 1953, SC; *New York Times*, 6–9 January 1953; H. Scott Gordon, "The Eisenhower Administration: The Doctrine of Shared Responsibility," in Goodwin, *Exhortation and Controls*, pp. 97, 109–10.

61. Eisenhower to BMB, 10 March 1953, SC.

62. *New York Times*, 24, 25 March, 4 April 1953; Bernard Baruch, "Views on Temporary Controls Bill," *Congressional Digest* 32 (June 1953): 182, 184, 186, 188, 190.

63. *New York Times*, 4 April, 8 May 1953; BMB to Homer Capehart, 19 March, Capehart to BMB, 10 April, BMB to Joseph Pulitzer, 7 April, to James F. Bell, 24 February, 2 April, to Lyndon B. Johnson, 1 July 1953, SC.

64. BMB to Burton K. Wheeler, 12 November, to Swope, 11 December 1953, to Hedda Hopper, 19 January 1954, to Eisenhower, 29 October, to Doris Fleeson, 25 May, to John Foster Dulles, 19 November 1953, SC; BMB to Frank Kent, 5 February 1954 (handwritten), Kent Papers, Box 5; *New York Times*, 23 May, 23 June, 24 November 1953.

65. BMB to Frank Kent, 5 February 1954 (handwritten), Kent Papers, Box 5; BMB to Harry F. Byrd, 5 February, to Brendan Bracken, January 1954 ("not sent"), to Omar Bradley, 22 January, to Marquis Childs, 22 February, to Harry F. Byrd, 22 February, 1 March, to W. Stuart Symington, 15 March 1954, SC; *New York Times*, 18 May, 23 July 1954, 30 March 1956.

66. BMB to Churchill, 14 December 1954, SC; to Eleanor Roosevelt, 5 December 1954 (handwritten), ER, Box 4138.

67. Wallace to Cyril Clemens, 3 July 1965, Henry A. Wallace Papers.

68. BMB to Christie Benet, 16 January 1950, to Albert Gore, 7 November 1952, to Eleanor Roosevelt, 19 September 1952, 29 November 1955, SC.

69. BMB to Swope, 23 January, Swope to BMB, 27 January, BMB to Harold Epstein, 20 January 1954, to John W. Bricker, 13 January 1955, SC.

70. Address at Washington University, St. Louis, 6 June 1950, PP; BMB to George C. Marshall, 10 April 1949, to William E. Jenner, 12 May, to Irving R. Kaufman, 5 January 1953, to J. Edgar Hoover, 19 February, to Francis E. Walter testimonial committee, 28 February, to Barry Goldwater, 14 November 1958, to Curtis E. LeMay, 13 February 1965, Harry F. Byrd to BMB, 15 June 1951, Carl Hayden to BMB, 16 September, BMB to James R. Lord, 8 June, to Mike Monroney, 25 August, to Leslie L. Biffle, 27 August, to Hayden, 17 August, to Philip L. Graham, 2 December 1953, to Hedda Hopper, 19 January, to W. Stuart Symington, 24 March, to Swope, 9 April, to Walker Stone, 15 March 1954, BMB Special, 22 March 1954, SC; *New York Times*, 10 March, 17 August 1954, 17 August 1955; "Bernard M. Baruch, RIP," *National Review* 17 (13 July 1965): 582.

71. BMB to Lord Beaverbrook, 16 September 1953, to Louis Bromfield, 25 June 1951, SC.

72. Speech to Medical Society of New York, 19 November 1947, PP; lobbyist quoted in Monte M. Poen, *Harry S. Truman versus the Medical Lobby: The Genesis of Medicare* (1979), pp. 118–19, 227.

73. BMB to Paul Douglas, 29 January, Douglas telegram to BMB, 20 July 1961, BMB to Douglas, 12 January 1962, SC; *New York Times*, 24 July 1961.

74. BMB to James F. Byrnes, 7 July 1961, to Swope, 8 December 1954, to John Harriman, 1 April 1955, to William Benton, 28 March 1950, to Billy Rose, 20 January 1955, SC; Bernard Baruch, *My Own Story* (1957), pp. 242–45.

75. BMB to Eleanor Roosevelt, 1 December 1956, ER, Box 4211; untitled, 27 March 1956, SC.
76. BMB to Churchill, 27 July 1955, to Dean Acheson, 25 September 1950, to Herbert Hoover, 19 January 1954, untitled, 6 February 1959, BMB to Willard W. Wirtz, 20 January 1963, SC; *New York Times*, 4 December 1964. Also see John M. Hancock to Joseph Pulitzer, 28 February 1951, and John J. McCloy to Robert V. Roosa, 27 August 1962, SC.
77. BMB to Churchill, 10 November 1950, to Marquis Childs, 15 April, to Burnet R. Maybank, 10 October 1949, W. S. Robinson to BMB, 6 December 1962, BMB to Krock, 20 September 1960, SC; BMB quoted in David E. Lilienthal, *The Journals of David E. Lilienthal: The Harvest Years, 1959–1963* (1971), p. 519.
78. BMB to Gordon Gray, 7 February, Eisenhower to BMB, 3 July 1957, SC; Eisenhower to Krock, 21 February 1957, Krock Papers; Gordon, "The Eisenhower Administration," pp. 129–30.
79. Harry F. Byrd to BMB, 7, 13, 19, 27 March 1958, SC.
80. "Investigation of the Financial Condition of the United States," Hearings before the Senate Committee on Finance, 85th Cong., 2d sess., 1, 2 April 1958, pp. 1633–89; *New York Times*, 2 April 1958; Eisenhower to BMB, 17 June 1958, BMB to W. S. Robinson, 21 January, to Albert Gore, 30 March 1959, SC.
81. A. R. Pinci to BMB, 23 November 1958, Tex McCrary to BMB, 18 October 1960, SC.
82. *New York Times*, 20 April 1950, 3 May 1960. The others were Learned Hand, Clarence Randall, Carl Sandburg, and Herbert Hoover.
83. Martin Gumpert, "Ten Who Know the Secret of Age," *New York Times Magazine*, 27 December 1953, pp. 10–11. The others were Frank Lloyd Wright, W. Somerset Maugham, Learned Hand, Konrad Adenauer, Abraham Flexner, Winston Churchill, Bernard Berenson, Arturo Toscanini, and Bertrand Russell.
84. George H. Gallup, *The Gallup Poll: Public Opinion, 1935–1971* (1972), pp. 875, 963, 1584.
85. Swope to BMB, 30 December 1948, David Ginsburg to BMB, 8 May 1947, Leon Henderson to BMB, 16 June, Robert P. Patterson to BMB, 20 February, John Ferguson to Swope, 25 February 1948, W. L. Clayton to BMB, 16 May 1949, BMB to Scott W. Lucas, 3 May 1947, Harry F. Byrd to BMB, 29 May, BMB to Swope, 15 January 1958, SC; Patterson to Ginsburg, 10 September 1946, Patterson Papers; Arthur Krock to Swope, 6 February 1950, Krock Papers.
86. BMB to Leon Henderson, 14 February 1947, BMB to Swope, 26 January 1948, BMB to Sylvia Porter, 12 December 1953, SC; *New York Times*, 18 August 1954, 6 September 1948, 19 August 1950.
87. *New York Times*, 6 October 1957, 6 October 1951, 3 October 1962, 27 October 1949, 28 October 1953; Lash, *Eleanor: The Years Alone*, pp. 262, 299; BMB to Eleanor Roosevelt, 23 October 1956, Richard Nixon to BMB, 22 June, Hubert H. Humphrey to BMB, 31 August, John Kenneth Galbraith to BMB, 2 September, BMB to Galbraith, 7 September, to Krock, 20 September, to John F. Kennedy, 11 October, to Thomas Corcoran, 15 December 1960, to Galbraith, 28 March 1961, SC.
88. Samuel Lubell to BMB, 8 April 1958, BMB to Swope, 30 January 1950, Swope to BMB, 15 December 1952, 28 May 1957, SC; Swope to Felix Frankfurter, 28 August 1953, Frankfurter Papers.

89. Kahn, *The World of Swope*, p. 396; Krock to Swope, 15 June, Swope to Krock, 20 June, Krock to Swope, 22 June 1950, Krock Papers; Swope to Frankfurter, 8 July 1954, Frankfurter Papers; Swope to BMB, 19 October 1956, SC.

90. BMB to Iphigenia Ochs Sulzberger, 26 January 1959, to Swope, 17 April 1949, Swope to BMB, 4 December, to W. L. Clayton, 20 June, George C. Marshall to BMB, 21 July 1947, SC; Krock to Mrs. Arthur Hays Sulzberger, 30 November 1943, Krock Papers; Lilienthal, *Journals: The Atomic Energy Years*, pp. 201, 257–58; Dean Acheson, *Present at the Creation: My Years in the State Department* (1969), p. 216; *New York Times*, 1 November 1948, 28 October 1950, 17 May, 15 October 1952, 18 June 1953, 20 October 1958, 17 August 1950.

91. W. Stuart Symington to BMB, 19 May 1952, Lyndon B. Johnson to BMB, 8 January 1951, Lewis L. Strauss to BMB, 25 May, 2 June 1959, SC.

92. *New York Times*, 10 January 1952; Lord Moran, *Churchill* (1966), pp. 384–85, 493.

93. BMB to Eleanor Roosevelt, 14 December 1939, ER, Box 1485; Lash, *Eleanor: The Years Alone*, pp. 146–47, 211–12, 242, 216–17, 262–63, 299.

94. BMB memo to George C. Marshall, 14 May 1947, to James H. Duff, 9 November 1950, Margaret Coit to BMB, 12 January, BMB to Coit, 20 January 1955, Churchill to BMB, 15 April 1956, BMB to James F. Bell, 11 July, to Herbert Hoover, 13 November 1958, SC; *New York Times*, 28 December 1954, 28 April 1955; Bernard Baruch, "Woodrow Wilson's Claim to Greatness," *Vital Speeches*, 15 December 1947, pp. 158–60; Bernard Baruch, "The Wilsonian Legacy for Us," *New York Times Magazine*, 23 December 1956, pp. 12, 18.

95. Virginia Leigh, "The Private Life of Bernard Baruch," *Collier's*, 27 November 1948, pp. 13, 70–71; John Hersey, "The Old Man," *New Yorker*, 3 January, pp. 28–34, 10 January, pp. 30–34, 17 January 1948, pp. 30–34; BMB to John Hersey, 10 July 1947, SC.

96. Hamlin Diary, 2 December 1924; BMB to R. H. Hipplehauser, 20 February 1939, GC; BMB to N. G. Henthouse, 16 November 1944, WF; Kahn, *The World of Swope*, p. 406. See McGraw-Hill invoice, 28 March 1946, Swope file, SC.

97. W. L. White to BMB, 25 October 1949, BMB to Paul Douglas, 27 September 1950, SC; Marquis James, "Baruch: An Interpretation," *New York Times Book Review*, 17 September 1950, pp. 6, 31.

98. Jordan A. Schwarz interview with Margaret Coit, June 1978. See Margaret L. Coit folder, 1950, Houghton Mifflin Co. to BMB, 31 October, BMB to Houghton Mifflin Co., 13 November 1950, SC; and Kahn, *The World of Swope*, pp. 409–10.

99. BMB to Swope, 16 January, to Gilbert Fite, 19 January, to Margaret Coit, 23 March, Coit to BMB, 24 May, BMB to Coit, 28 May, Coit to BMB, 31 May 1954, clipping from *Providence Journal*, 5 May 1958, SC; Margaret L. Coit, *Mr. Baruch* (1957), pp. 694–95.

100. Marquis James file, 1934–36, GC; Swope to BMB, 16 June 1948, BMB to Swope, 17 April, Samuel Lubell memo to BMB on Bobbs-Merrill book, 30 August 1949, BMB to Margaret Coit, 11 February 1956, SC; Kahn, *The World of Swope*, p. 409; Coit interview.

101. BMB to Margaret Coit, 20 February, Coit to M. A. Boyle, 11 April, Boyle to Coit, 20 April, Coit to BMB, 7 May, Coit to Boyle, 23 May, BMB to Coit, 7 June, Craig Wylie to Boyle, 8 June, Coit to BMB, 11 June, Boyle to Wylie, 29

May, BMB to Coit, 19 June, BMB Special, memo about Coit on Hotel Drake letterhead, August 1956, SC.

102. Harold Epstein to Craig Wylie, 21 August 1956, Samuel Lubell to BMB, 6 February, BMB to Henry Laughlin, 22 March, BMB telegram to M. A. Boyle, 13 March, Swope to BMB, 28 May, Lubell to BMB, 15 June, Benn Hibbs to BMB, 17, 25 September, Lubell to BMB, 24 August, Henry Holt and Co. file, 1957, SC; Kahn, *The World of Swope*, pp. 409–10; Coit interview.

103. BMB to Craig Wylie, 3 September, Harold Epstein to Wylie, 1 October 1957, clipping from *Providence Journal*, 5 May 1958, SC; Coit, *Mr. Baruch*, pp. 699, vi. Also see *New York Times Book Review*, 24 November 1957, p. 8.

104. Coit interview; clipping from *Providence Journal*, 5 May 1958, BMB to Coit, 4 September 1957, SC.

105. Eisenhower to BMB, 3 September 1957, SC; Paul Bickrel, "Bernard Baruch, Texas, and Some Lesser Subjects," *Harper's*, December 1957, p. 86.

106. BMB to William F. Buckley, 19 December 1957, "BMB Plan Re. Vol. II," 1958 BMB special, untitled Samuel Lubell memo [1957], BMB to Eugene W. Castle, 20 March, to Samuel I. Rosenman, 13 February 1958, SC; BMB to Raymond Moley, 13 September 1957, Moley Papers, Box 69.

107. Krock to Swope, 26 October 1948, Krock Papers; *New York Times Book Review*, 24 November, pp. 6, 18, 18 August 1957, pp. 1, 25, 16 October 1960, pp. 6, 18; *New York Times*, 21, 23 November 1957, 11 October 1960; Krock to BMB, 1 July 1957, SC.

108. Herman Kahn to BMB, 4 November, Kahn to Eleanor Roosevelt, 4 November, Mrs. Roosevelt to BMB, 14 November, BMB to Mrs. Roosevelt, Christmas 1949, ER, Box 3746; BMB to David C. Mearns, 24 February 1958, to Mrs. Woodrow Wilson, 2 September 1959, SC.

109. Lilienthal, *Journals: The Harvest Years*, p. 519; BMB to Robert F. Goheen, 20 November, Goheen to BMB, 22 November 1963, 21 February 1964, BMB to Goheen, 7 March, Goheen to BMB, 13 March, Harold Epstein memo to BMB, 1 April, BMB to Goheen, 20 April 1964, SC; *New York Times*, 10 May 1964.

110. Frankfurter to Swope, 6 May 1938, Frankfurter Papers; Harry Salpeter, "A Life of Bernard Baruch," clipping with BMB to Swope on Hotel Carlton notepaper, 20 February 1945, SC.

111. "Address at Launching of UJA," 24 February 1946, PP.

112. Swope to BMB, 10 February 1942, 15 February 1940, GC; Swope to BMB, 18 October 1950, SC; M. A. Boyle to Rabbi Benjamin Schultz, 4 September, 15 December, BMB to Alfred Kohlberg, 21 December 1953, contributions to American Jewish League against Communism in BMB special 1964 file, George E. Sokolsky to BMB, 30 July, 5 September 1956, SC.

113. BMB to Jacob H. Schiff, 5 January 1916, GC; Schiff to BMB, 6 March 1918, WIB; Harry Golden, *The Right Time* (1969), p. 90; House Diary, 25 March 1920; James F. Byrnes to BMB, 27 March 1939, SC; Florence R. Long to Truman, 27 July 1950, Truman Papers, Official File 2855; M. Lincoln Schuster to BMB, 18 April 1957, SC.

114. Swope to BMB, 12 March, BMB to Swope, 14 March 1958, SC; Kahn, *The World of Swope*, p. 437; *New York Times*, 13 May 1950; speech to "Federation Day" breakfast meeting, Federation of Jewish Philanthropies, Hotel Astor, 12 December 1944, PP; Joseph M. Proskauer to BMB, 28 December 1948, BMB to Proskauer, 7 January 1949, SC.

115. BMB to Clare Boothe Luce, 19 January 1963, SC; Alfred Allan Lewis, *Man of the World* (1978), p. 278.
116. BMB to Leo Lerner, 12 June 1918, WIB; ACNP Diary, 14 June 1919; *New York Times*, 12 September 1918; Albert Einstein to BMB, 6 May, BMB to Einstein, 13 May 1921, GC.
117. Eugene Meyer, Jr., COHC, pp. 74-75; Mark Sullivan to BMB, 25 September, BMB to Sullivan, 28 September 1923, SC.
118. Alpheus Thomas Mason, *Brandeis: A Free Man's Life* (1956), p. 635; Frank W. Taussig to BMB, 7 January, BMB to Taussig, 19 January 1937, SC; copy of Frank A. Hazelbaker to Eleanor Roosevelt, 1 August 1938, GC; FDR telegram to BMB, 8 April, James F. Byrnes to BMB, 21 November, Byrnes telegram to FDR, 16 November 1938, SC; BMB quoted in Lawrenson, *Stranger at the Party*, p. 147; Saul S. Friedman, *No Haven for the Oppressed: United States Policy toward Jewish Refugees, 1938–1945* (1973), p. 91 n. For a Gallup Poll on U.S. anti-Semitism in 1938, see Swope to BMB, 31 March 1939, SC.
119. BMB to Rex Benson, 24 January, to Lewis L. Strauss, 31 January, Hamilton Fish to BMB, 28 February 1939, SC; Henry L. Feingold, *The Politics of Rescue: The Roosevelt Administration and the Holocaust, 1938–1945* (1970), pp. 102-4; Henry A. Wallace, COHC, p. 3151; BMB to Julius Hirsch, 20, 30 October 1945, GC.
120. Stephen S. Wise to BMB, 4 January, BMB to Wise, 9 January, 10 May 1943, SC; Ben Hecht, *A Child of the Century* (1954), p. 580.
121. Abba Hillel Silver to BMB, 21 September, 6 November 1945, 21 March, 7 November 1946, SC; address at launching of United Jewish Appeal, 24 February 1946, PP; Hecht, *A Child of the Century*, pp. 617-18.
122. Speech at Cardinal Spellman's dinner, 16 October 1946, PP; BMB to Churchill, 22 July 1947, SC.
123. Abba Hillel Silver to BMB, 12 December 1947, BMB to Swope, 14 May, Swope to BMB, 26, 29 January, BMB to Warren Austin, 5 April 1948, SC; Millis, *The Forrestal Diaries*, p. 364; speech at James Monroe High School, 20 April 1948, PP; Lash, *Eleanor: The Years Alone*, p. 135; BMB to Eleanor Roosevelt, 15 October 1948, Robert A. Lovett to BMB, 5 January 1949, copy of Silver to Swope, 24 December, BMB to Swope, 27 December 1948, SC.
124. Abba Eban to BMB, 2 May 1951, 12 March 1956, Eban telegram to BMB, 1 January 1957, BMB to Eliahu Elath, 26 February 1961, BMB to Swope, 18 February 1954, 7 January 1955, Swope to BMB, 19 October 1956, 12 March 1958, BMB to Swope, 14 March 1958, BMB to Henry R. Luce, 23 February 1957, SC.
125. BMB to George C. Marshall, 13 May, to James B. Conant, 29 August, to John W. Snyder, 30 August, to Churchill, 6 December 1957, Swope to BMB, 20 January, 18 April, 23 May 1958, SC. On Truman see Roy W. Howard to BMB, 16 December, and BMB to Eisenhower, 21 August 1958, SC.
126. BMB to Hartwig N. Baruch, 6 May 1947, to Doris Fleeson, 9 February 1954, Churchill to BMB, 6 March 1956, SC; Jeffrey Potter, *Men, Money and Magic: The Story of Dorothy Schiff* (1976), p. 234; Lawrenson, *Stranger at the Party*, pp. 160-61; *New York Times*, 14 July 1955, 24 June, 29 November 1958.
127. *New York Times*, 2, 16 March 1953, 15 June 1962, 26 April, 23 October 1964; statement draft, 21 February 1958, BMB to Robert Anderson, 24 May 1959, SC.

128. BMB to Lord Beaverbrook, 15 May 1959, to Marshall Carter, 4 April 1960, John F. Kennedy to BMB, 19 August 1963, SC; *New York Times*, 19 August 1959, 19 August 1960, 19 August 1961, 22 May 1962, 19 August 1963; Lilienthal, *Journals: The Harvest Years*, p. 440.

129. BMB to Dr. L. Zukschwendt, 31 July 1962, to Mrs. Rex Benson, 18 September 1964, SC; *New York Times*, 30 October 1963; Lawrenson, *Stranger at the Party*, p. 161; Potter, *Men, Money and Magic*, p. 268.

130. BMB to Eleanor Roosevelt, 25 February 1960, BMB telegram to Mrs. Roosevelt, 29 May 1962, press statement, 8 November 1962, BMB to Adlai E. Stevenson, 16 February 1963, SC; Lilienthal, *Journals: The Harvest Years*, p. 519; Lilienthal to F. Eberstadt, 15 November 1963, Lilienthal Papers.

131. Emmet John Hughes, *The Ordeal of Power* (1964 ed.), p. 33; BMB to Harry F. Byrd, 21 January, Lewis L. Strauss telegrams to BMB, 23, 25 October 1956, George Smathers to BMB, 8 February 1957, SC.

132. John Kenneth Galbraith to BMB, 2 September, BMB to Galbraith, 7 September, to John F. Kennedy, 11 October, to Raymond Moley, 14 December 1960, to Galbraith, January 1961 (draft), to Harry F. Byrd, 21 January 1961, to John J. McCloy, 13 December 1960, to Galbraith, 28 March, to Orville Freeman, 27 March, Galbraith to BMB, 29 March 1961, SC.

133. BMB to John F. Kennedy, 22 June, John Kenneth Galbraith to BMB, 22 November, McGeorge Bundy to BMB, 11 September 1961, "October 4, 1961 at Gromyko's Office," BMB to Hedda Hopper, 4 December 1961, to Kennedy, 10 February, Walker Stone to BMB, 8 May, George Smathers to BMB, 28 March, BMB telegrams to Kennedy, 1 October, 11 December, BMB to Robert V. Roosa, 13 December, copy of John J. McCloy to Roosa, 27 August 1962, Roosa to BMB, 15 April 1963, SC.

134. BMB to John Fitzgerald Kennedy, 13 October 1961, "Probably given on tape at birthday press conference, August 18, 1962," BMB to Lord Beaverbrook, 27 April, to Krock, 27 July, Kennedy to BMB, 31 October, BMB to Kennedy, 8 November 1963, SC.

135. McGeorge Bundy to BMB, 15 December, Lyndon B. Johnson to BMB, 17 December 1963, SC.

136. BMB to John Kenneth Galbraith, 15 June, to Emory S. Land, 15 June 1964, SC; *New York Times*, 4 December, 1, 19, August 1964.

137. BMB special, 29 October 1964, correspondence with Flushing, N. Y., cemetery, October and November 1964, BMB to Hedda Hopper, 30 January 1965, SC.

138. Mike Monroney to BMB, 3 December 1964, BMB to Russell Baker, 13 February, BMB telegrams to Lyndon B. Johnson and Jack Valenti, 17 March, BMB to Johnson, 9 April, Johnson to BMB, 21 May, BMB to Robert V. Roosa, 28 May 1965, SC.

139. *New York Times*, 21, 22, 24 June 1965.

140. John Kenneth Galbraith, *The Liberal Hour* (1960), p. 62; John Kenneth Galbraith to Jordan A. Schwarz, 9 April 1976; John Kenneth Galbraith, *Economics, Peace and Laughter* (1971), pp. xii, 270-71.

141. Paul A. Samuelson, "A Burns Depression," *Newsweek*, 3 March 1975, p. 63; Robert Lekachman, *The Age of Keynes* (1966), p. 56. For pejorative comment on Baruch as an economist, see R. H. Brand memo to Lord Halifax, 19 December 1944, Brand to J. M. Keynes, 10 January 1945, Brand Papers, files 197 and 198.

142. BMB to Michael V. DiSalle, 30 August, to Leslie R. Groves, 5 September

1957, to Harry F. Byrd, 20 December 1954, SC; Stein, *The Fiscal Revolution in America*, pp. 344, 503.

143. BMB to Harry F. Byrd, 27 October, to George D. Bjurman, 13 April 1955, to John J. McCloy, 4 December 1958, to Clinton P. Anderson, 20 January 1959, "Memo to an inquiring Senator," 1958, BMB to J. Luther Cleveland, 29 July, to Robert Anderson, 16 September, to Julian Braden Baird, 15 October, to Eleanor Roosevelt, 2 December 1958, SC; BMB to Mrs. Roosevelt, 6 January 1959, ER, Box 4344; BMB to Byrd, 23 January 1958, SC.

144. BMB to Neil H. McElroy, 28 August, to Lyndon B. Johnson, 17 April, to J. Luther Cleveland, 29 July 1958, to DeWitt Wallace, 28 January 1955, to Buell G. Gallagher, 27 May 1959, Gallagher to BMB, 28 March 1961, BMB to Frank Van Dyk, 11 July, to Eleanor Roosevelt, 2 December 1958, to Charles S. Silver, 2 February 1959, to Pat M. McNamara, 23 March 1960, 1 June 1962 (original emphasis), to Harry F. Byrd, 3 September 1950, SC.

145. BMB to F. Eberstadt, 13 December, to the editor, *Memphis Commercial Appeal*, 9 May 1958, SC; Galbraith quoted in Stein, *The Fiscal Revolution in America*, p. 501.

146. Speech to Dr. Simon Baruch Chapter, American Veterans' Committee, 31 October 1948, PP; untitled, 5 February 1959, BMB to Julian Braden Baird, 6 November 1959 (not sent), to Churchill, 9 April 1956, to Jim Bishop, 20 April, to William Benton, 20 April 1959, SC.

147. BMB to McGeorge Bundy, 27 July 1961, to W. S. Robinson, 30 July 1962, BMB to Robert V. Roosa, 29 April 1963, SC; Harry Hamilton, "An Ounce of Prevention," *America* 105 (30 September 1961): 819.

148. BMB to Harry F. Byrd, 6 November, to Jack Valenti, 9 November 1964, 18 May 1965, to John Hay Whitney, 18 May 1965, SC.

BIBLIOGRAPHY OF
UNPUBLISHED SOURCES

MANUSCRIPT COLLECTIONS

Chandler P. Anderson Papers, Diary, Library of Congress, Washington, D.C.
Gordon Auchincloss Papers, Diary, Yale University Library, New Haven, Conn.
Newton D. Baker Papers, Library of Congress.
Bernard M. Baruch Papers, Seeley G. Mudd Manuscript Library, Princeton
    University, Princeton, N.J.
Robert W. Bingham Papers, Diary, Library of Congress.
Tasker Bliss Papers, Diary, Library of Congress.
Chester Bowles Papers, Yale University Library.
Robert H. Brand Papers, Bodleian Library, Oxford University, England.
James F. Byrnes Papers, Clemson University Library, Clemson, S.C.
Lord Robert Cecil Papers, Diary, British Museum, London.
Raymond Clapper Papers, Diary, Library of Congress.
William L. Clayton Papers, Harry S. Truman Library, Independence, Mo.
Clark Clifford Papers, Harry S. Truman Library.
Lincoln Colcord Papers, Mr. Brooks Colcord, Yarmouth, Maine.
Homer Cummings Papers, Diary, University of Virginia Library, Charlottesville,
    Va.
Josephus L. Daniels Papers, Library of Congress.
Norman H. Davis Papers, Diary, Library of Congress.
John Foster Dulles Papers, Firestone Library, Princeton University.
Stephen Early Papers, Franklin D. Roosevelt Library, Hyde Park, N.Y.
Ferdinand Eberstadt Papers, Diary, Mudd Library, Princeton University.
Herbert Feis Papers, Library of Congress.
Food Administration Papers, Hoover Institution, Stanford University, Stanford,
    Calif.
Foreign Office Papers, Public Record Office, Kew, England.
James V. Forrestal Papers, Mudd Library, Princeton University.
Jerome Frank Papers, Yale University Library.
Felix Frankfurter Papers, Library of Congress.
Harry A. Garfield Papers, Library of Congress.
Edwin F. Gay Papers, Diary, Hoover Institution, Stanford University.
Carter Glass Papers, University of Virginia Library.
Charles S. Hamlin Papers, Diary, Library of Congress.

Byron "Pat" Harrison Papers, University of Mississippi Library, University, Miss.
Leon Henderson Papers, Franklin D. Roosevelt Library.
Herbert Hoover Papers, Herbert Hoover Presidential Library, West Branch, Iowa.
Harry Hopkins Papers, Franklin D. Roosevelt Library.
Edward M. House Papers, Diary, Yale University Library.
Cordell Hull Papers, Library of Congress.
Edward N. Hurley Papers, Diary, University of Notre Dame Library, Notre Dame, Ind.
Harold L. Ickes Papers, Diary, Library of Congress.
Louis Johnson Papers, University of Virginia Library.
Otto Kahn Papers, Mudd Library, Princeton University.
Frank A. Kent Papers, Maryland Historical Society, Baltimore.
Arthur Krock Papers, Mudd Library, Princeton University.
Julius A. Krug Papers, Library of Congress.
Thomas Lamont Papers, Diary, Baker Library, Harvard University, Cambridge, Mass.
W. Jett Lauck Papers, Maryland Historical Society.
David E. Lilienthal Papers, Mudd Library, Princeton University.
Breckenridge Long Papers, Diary, Library of Congress.
William Gibbs McAdoo Papers, Library of Congress.
Vance McCormick Papers, Diary, Yale University Library.
Eugene Meyer, Jr., Papers, Diary, Library of Congress.
Sidney E. Mezes Papers, Columbia University Library, New York, N.Y.
Ogden L. Mills, Jr., Papers, Library of Congress.
Raymond Moley Papers, Diary, Hoover Institution, Stanford University.
Henry Morgenthau, Jr., Papers, Diary, Franklin D. Roosevelt Library.
Henry Morgenthau, Sr., Papers, Diary, Library of Congress.
Donald Nelson Papers, Henry E. Huntington Library and Art Collection, San Marino, Calif.
Office of War Mobilization and Reconversion Papers, National Archives, Washington, D.C.
Robert P. Patterson Papers, Library of Congress.
George N. Peek Papers, Diary, Western Historical Collections, University of Missouri Library, Columbia, Mo.
John J. Pershing Papers, Library of Congress.
Key Pittman Papers, Library of Congress.
John J. Raskob Papers, Eleutherian Mills Library, Wilmington, Del.
Larry Richey Papers, Herbert Hoover Presidential Library.
Eleanor Roosevelt Papers, Franklin D. Roosevelt Library.
Franklin D. Roosevelt Papers, Franklin D. Roosevelt Library.
Samuel I. Rosenman Papers, Franklin D. Roosevelt Library. Citations to the Rosenman Papers are to this collection.
————, Harry S. Truman Library.
Charles G. Ross Papers, Harry S. Truman Library.
Frank A. Scott Papers, Mudd Library, Princeton University.
Harold Smith Papers, Diary, Franklin D. Roosevelt Library. Unless otherwise indicated, citations to the Smith Papers are to this collection.
————, Harry S. Truman Library.
Henry F. Stimson Papers, Diary, Yale University Library.
Treasury Papers, Public Record Office, Kew, England.
Harry S. Truman Papers, Harry S. Truman Library.
Rexford Guy Tugwell Papers, Diary, Franklin D. Roosevelt Library.

Henry A. Wallace Papers, University of Iowa Library, Iowa City, Iowa.
Thomas J. Walsh Papers, Library of Congress.
War Production Board Papers, National Archives.
Edwin "Pa" Watson Papers, University of Virginia Library.
John Skelton Williams Papers, University of Virginia Library.
Woodrow Wilson Papers, Library of Congress.
————, Firestone Library, Princeton University.
Robert W. Woolley Papers, Library of Congress.

COLUMBIA UNIVERSITY ORAL HISTORY COLLECTION,
NEW YORK, N.Y.

William L. Clayton   Eugene Meyer, Jr.
Chester C. Davis   John Lord O'Brian
Alvin Johnson   Frances Perkins
Arthur Krock   Henry A. Wallace
Emory S. Land   James P. Warburg

UNPUBLISHED DOCTORAL DISSERTATIONS

Meredith Lentz Adams. "The Morgenthau Plan: A Study in Bureaucratic
    Depravity." University of Texas at Austin, 1971.
Jack Stokes Ballard. "The Shock of Peace: Military and Economic Demobiliza-
    tion after World War II." University of California, Los Angeles, 1974.
Calvin Lee Christman. "Ferdinand Eberstadt and Economic Mobilization for
    War, 1941–1943." Ohio State University, 1971.
Lawrence Hopkins Curry, Jr. "Southern Senators and Their Roll-Call Votes in
    Congress, 1941–1944." Duke University, 1971.
Robert Charles Erhart. "The Politics of Military Rearmament, 1935–1940: The
    President, the Congress, and the United States Army." University of Texas at
    Austin, 1975.
Michael Abbot Goldman. "The War Finance Corporation in the Politics of War
    and Reconstruction, 1917–1923." Rutgers University, 1971.
Jack Irby Hayes, Jr. "South Carolina and the New Deal, 1932–1938." University
    of South Carolina, 1972.
Gregory Franklin Herken. "American Diplomacy and the Atomic Bomb, 1945–
    1947." Princeton University, 1974.
David Alan Horowitz. "Visions of Harmonious Abundance: Corporate Ideology
    in the 1920's." University of Minnesota, 1971.
Theodore Philip Kovaleff. "Business and Government in the Eisenhower Era."
    New York University, 1972.
Walter Kraft Lambert. "New Deal Revenue Acts: The Politics of Taxation."
    University of Texas at Austin, 1970.
James Benesch Levin. "Albert C. Ritchie: A Political Biography." City University
    of New York, 1970.
Evan Bowen Metcalf. "Economic Stabilization by American Business in the
    Twentieth Century." University of Wisconsin, 1972.
James Ray Moore. "A History of the World Economic Conference, London,
    1933." State University of New York at Stony Brook, 1972.
Winfred Bobo Moore, Jr. "New South Statesman: The Political Career of James

Francis Byrnes, 1911–1941." Duke University, 1976.
John Kennedy Ohl. "'Old Iron Pants': The Wartime Career of General Hugh S. Johnson, 1917–1918." University of Cincinnati, 1971.
Thomas Ross Runfola. "Herbert C. Hoover as Secretary of Commerce, 1921–1923: Domestic Economic Planning in the Harding Years." State University of New York at Buffalo, 1973.
James Allen Sayler. "Window on an Age: Arthur Krock and the New Deal Era, 1929–1941." Rutgers University, 1978.
Robert Neal Seidel. "Progressive Pan Americanism: Development and United States Policy toward South America, 1906–1931." Cornell University, 1973.
Dale Norman Shook. "William G. McAdoo and the Development of National Economic Policy, 1913–1918." University of Cincinnati, 1975.
Gibson Bell Smith. "Rubber for Americans: The Search for an Adequate Supply of Rubber and the Politics of Strategic Materials, 1934–1942." Bryn Mawr College, 1972.
Robert Hardin Van Meter, Jr. "The United States and European Recovery, 1918–1923: A Study of Public Policy and Private Finance." University of Wisconsin, 1971.

UNPUBLISHED MASTER'S THESIS

Robert Wayne Carlson. "The Revenue Act of 1942: A Case Study in the Financing of the Corporate State." Northern Illinois University, 1975.

INDEX

"Court-packing," 318–19
Covenant, peace treaty, 152, 496
Cox, James M., 177, 178, 216, 278, 313, 472
Coy, Wayne, 378, 410, 411, 439
Crash of 1929. See Depression: Great
Credit, 219; expansion of, as goal of Wilson, 40, 41; and international trade after World War I, 99, 129, 134, 135–36, 138–39, 140, 150, 200, 242, 250, 251, 277; and agriculture, 229, 234, 239, 311; expansion of, in Depression, 259, 260, 263; restriction of, after World War II, 512, 529, 544. See also Investment
Crillon Hotel, 112, 113, 116, 117, 129
Crop reduction, 281, 284, See also Agriculture: and Depression
Crowder, Gen. Enoch, 286
Crowther, Samuel, 200
Cuban missile crisis, 571
Cuevas, Enrique, 92
Cuff, Robert D., 57
Cummings, Homer, 178, 225–26, 273, 274, 275
Current History, 346
Currie, Lauchlin, 359, 402
Curtis, Charles, 187
Cycles, business, 17, 18, 26, 207, 217, 333
Czechoslovakia, 200, 251, 329, 330, 348, 357, 363, 520

Daniels, Jonathan, 33, 457
Daniels, Josephus, 45, 57, 61, 62, 63, 67, 70–72, 83, 132, 172, 196, 266
Darling, Jay N. "Ding," 424
Davies, Joe, 273
Davis, Chester C., 236, 285, 366
Davis, Dwight, 336
Davis, John W., 164, 178, 181, 183, 184, 189, 200, 272
Davis, Norman H., 116, 119, 120, 121, 123, 124, 128, 129, 130, 135, 136, 139, 140, 141, 142, 143, 156, 157, 158, 183, 189, 222, 246, 272
Dawes Plan, 251, 485
Dearborn Independent, 174
Debt: private, in Depression, 272, 300; public 512, 516, 577. See also Balanced budget; Deficit spending; War debts
Decentralization, 224, 370
Decontrol, 101, 104. See also Readjustment
Deere and Company, 208
Defense Acts: of 1916, 366; of 1920, 358
Defense Commission, 369
"Defense Coordination Board," 330, 331, 358
Defense Day, 335
Defense Department, 520, 528, 577

Defense Plants Corporation, 386, 469
Defense preparations. See Mobilization
Defense Production Act (1950), 530
Deferments, military, 450
Deficit spending, 271, 402, 547. See also Government, spending by
Deflation, 210, 227, 404; and Depression, 260, 261, 270, 285, 290; after World War II, 527, 533, 539, 575. See also Baruch, Bernard M.: as deflationist
Deindustrialization, German, 476, 478, 487
Demand, consumer, 104, 333, 402; in wartime, 79, 103, 377, 396–98, 399, 400, 401, 403, 405, 407, 412, 414, 427, 432, 434, 443; for automobiles, 84, 86; for rubber, 392; after World War II, 508, 509, 516, 527, 534. See also Production, civilian; Supply and demand
Demobilization. See Readjustment
Democracy, 213, 228, 305, 383, 387, 416, 434, 544; European, 112, 349, 350; Wilsonian emphasis on, 164–65; and taxation, 315–16, 317; and war, 332–33, 398, 403, 427. See also Liberalism; Wilsonism
Democratic party: and Baruch, 3, 4, 35–36, 37, 47, 52, 59, 62, 173, 174, 175–89, 215, 230, 243, 244, 245, 250–64 passim, 269–70, 298–99, 305, 314, 318, 320, 322, 323–25, 367, 368, 417, 467, 471–72, 473, 490, 522, 523, 524, 524, 525, 529, 536, 541, 549, 551, 570, 571, 574; after World War I, 152, 164, 165, 166–67, 175–82, 184, 185, 189–99 passim, 203, 224, 225, 237, 238, 251; and Depression crisis, 256–70 passim, 274, 282, 283, 298, 299, 300, 304, 305, 307, 312–25 passim; and mobilization for World War II, 367, 380, 414; after World War II, 524, 546, 551, 566, 579. See also Congress, U.S.: Baruch's influence in
Denmark, 363
Depression, 26, 207, 213, 326, 352, 402, 476, 533; Great, 4, 5, 6, 7, 8, 18, 169, 252, 254, 255–328, 333, 344, 406, 431, 563, 575; of 1890s, 16, 17, 18; of 1914, 41; of 1921, 427, 398; of 1937–38, 318, 320–21, 325, 354, 356
Dern, George H., 338
de Rougement, Count René, 122
Determinism, economic, 332, 342
Developing nations, 131, 149, 244, 245, 546, 547. See also Small nations
Dewey, Thomas E., 471, 472, 524, 565, 620 (n. 2)
Dillon, C. Douglas, 571
Dillon Read, 360, 430
Diplomacy. See Baruch, Bernard M.: as

546. *See also* Agriculture, and foreign trade; Raw materials

Investment, 333, 385, 485; agricultural, 229–30; private, during Depression, 259, 268, 270–71, 295, 318, 321; public, 271, 383; and mobilization, 341, 402, 412. *See also* Credit; Baruch, Bernard M.: as speculator; Government, spending by; Speculation

"Iron Curtain," 56; speech, 489, 490

Isolationism, 141, 151, 154, 157, 233, 245–46, 247, 250, 251, 260, 272, 343, 346, 349, 350, 351, 417, 480, 481, 517

Israel, 562, 566. *See also* Zionism

Italy, 140, 482, 518; and approach of World War II, 329, 342, 343, 345, 346, 347, 350, 354, 355

Jackson, Robert, 327

James, Marquis, 304, 554

Janeway, Eliot, 534

Japan, 92, 160, 343, 345, 349, 350, 355, 356, 364, 381, 384, 389, 392, 427, 476, 479, 481, 482, 497, 516, 518, 534

Jeffers, William, 461

Jeffersonian, Hoover as, 224, 225

Jenner, William E., 543

Jewett, George, 239

Jewishness, Baruch's. *See* Baruch, Bernard M.: as Jew

Johns Hopkins University, 170

Johnson, Alvin S., 88

Johnson, Edwin C., 472

Johnson, Hugh S., 170, 192, 235, 237, 255, 259, 260, 261, 262, 265, 268, 269, 270, 280, 283, 284, 304, 307; and NRA, 5, 266, 286–98 passim; and mobilization for World War II, 331, 338, 339, 356, 357, 358, 359, 360

Johnson, Louis, 356, 358, 359, 360, 367, 369, 525, 527, 528

Johnson, Lyndon B., 7, 539, 546, 551, 572, 574, 579

Johnston, Olin, 325

Jones, Jesse, 183–84, 188, 321, 386, 391–92, 395, 425, 446, 469, 484, 523

Josephson, Matthew, 307

Journalists: at Paris Peace Conference, 111, 114–15, 116; and Baruch, 168, 173–74, 193–206, 237, 248, 249, 250, 251, 253, 255, 256, 304, 307, 311, 320, 323, 330, 341, 346, 369, 373, 381, 405, 415, 422–24, 425, 430, 437, 440, 466, 470, 471, 472, 475, 477, 485, 486, 490, 491, 498, 503, 505, 526, 527, 535, 536, 537, 541, 547, 548, 549, 568, 569, 572, 574. *See also* Krock, Arthur; Press; Public opinion; Swope, Herbert Bayard

Justice Department, 428

"Just punishment," 142–43. *See also* Reparations

Kahn, Herman, 558

Kahn, Otto, 31, 179, 237, 246

Kaiser, Henry, 630 (n. 53)

Kansas, agricultural problems of, 228–30, 232

Kanzler report, 453

Kaufman, Irving R., 543

Keene, James R., 23

Kelly, Ed, 473

Kennan, George, 518

Kennedy, John F., 532, 549, 568, 569, 570, 571, 572, 579

Kennedy, Joseph P., 20, 275, 307, 321, 327, 351–52, 354, 364, 365

Kent, Frank R., 166, 183, 198, 256, 258, 313, 314, 317, 320, 327, 368, 373, 472

Kenyon, William S., 237, 247

Keynes, John Maynard, 7, 255, 321, 402–8, 413, 415, 469, 480, 576; and Paris Peace Conference, 111, 124, 144, 153–60

Keynesians, 404, 406, 412, 413, 447, 541, 575

Keyserling, Leon, 528, 530

Klotz, Louis-Lucien, 145

Knappen, Theodore M., 200

Knox, Frank, 367, 369, 378, 434, 444

Knox, Philander C., 151

Knudsen, William S., 366, 369, 372, 374, 375, 469

Kohn, Julius A., 15

Kolchak, Adm. Alexander, 145

Korea, 518

Korean War, 7, 218, 526, 528, 529, 530, 531, 532, 533, 534, 536, 537, 576

Krassin, Leonid, 485

Krock, Arthur, 196, 198, 199, 204, 205, 304, 319–20, 322, 323, 338–39, 360, 369, 370, 373, 376, 422–23, 440, 445, 470, 478, 504n, 520, 521, 522, 525, 537, 557, 558–59

Krug, Julius A. "Cap," 463, 467–68, 525

Kuhn, Loeb, 31

Ku Klux Klan, Baruch's view of, 174, 175

Kun, Bela, 145

Kurusu, Soburo, 418

Labor, 384, 385, 478; as concern of Wilsonians, 148, 149, 164–66, 211–12; as participant in economic planning, 211, 455; and Baruch, 218, 228, 258–59, 291, 302–3; organized, 221, 263, 292, 359, 360, 366, 367, 369, 370, 372, 373, 378, 381, 387, 403, 410, 414, 450, 451,

Racism, 192; imputed to Baruch, 542, 553–54, 556, 574; of Nazis, 564. *See also* Blacks

Radicalism, 166, 339, 341, 399, 511, 526, 561; Wilsonian, 148, 149, 166; imputed to farmers, 228, 232, 236; of Baruch's associates, 255, 281, 307, 489; of Keynes, 403. *See also* Bolshevism

Railroad Administration, 68, 99, 107, 176, 209, 210, 242

Railroads, 225, 242, 243, 425, 546; Baruch's interest in, 3, 15, 25–26, 27, 28, 30–31, 168, 169, 175, 240, 265, 275; and McAdoo's mobilization efforts, 68, 99, 107, 175, 176; and steel prices, 210; in Depression period, 258, 260, 264–66. *See also* Transportation

Raleigh News and Observer, 196

Rainey, Henry T., 261

Raskob, John J., 265, 267, 270

Rationing, 79, 87, 374, 392, 393, 395, 396, 399, 404, 408, 410, 413, 414, 511, 529. *See also* Gasoline: rationing of

Raw materials, 332; Baruch's speculation in, 3, 19, 25, 27–28, 30, 31, 36, 40–41; and mobilization for World War I, 4, 52, 68, 71, 89–98, 227, 266, 306; after World War I, 99, 103, 104, 110, 131, 132, 136, 139, 207, 211, 218, 229, 241, 243, 245; and German reparations issue, 129, 134, 249; during Depression, 258, 291; and mobilization for World War II, 333, 334, 350, 351, 354, 357–58, 364, 368, 374, 377, 384, 386, 390, 394, 400, 401, 403, 424, 432, 433, 434, 436, 442, 452, 457; after World War II, 457, 516, 518, 520, 521, 533, 534, 546, 571

"Reactionaries," 145, 148, 164, 166, 303, 320, 335, 460, 461, 465, 485, 536, 539, 542, 548, 575. *See also* Conservatism

Reader's Digest, 578

Reading, Lord, 97

Readjustment: after World War I, 5, 7, 98–107, 150, 207–12, 227, 333, 399; after World War II, 453–89 passim, 509, 510, 520. *See also* Production, civilian

Rearmament: European, 342, 354

Recession, after World War II, 526, 527. *See also* Depression

Reconstruction. *See* Europe, stabilization of: after World War I; Europe, stabilization of, after World War II; Readjustment

Reconstruction Finance Corporation (RFC), 169, 264, 270, 275, 386, 391, 425, 446, 469

Reconversion. *See* Postwar economy; Readjustment

Redfield, William C., 62, 173, 208, 209, 210, 219

Reed, David, 257

Reed, James, 191

Reedsville (West Virginia), 309, 311, 312

Reform. *See* Liberalism; Progressivism; New Deal

Refugees: European, 174; Jewish, 563–64, 565, 566. *See also* Immigration

Relief: European, 134; domestic, 300, 301. *See also* Agriculture: and Depression; Paris Peace Conference; Public works

Religion, as political issue, 189–90, 191, 192. *See also* Anti-Catholicism; Anti-Semitism

Reparation Commission, 249

Reparations: following World War I, 113–58 passim, 244–45, 247–48, 249, 250, 251; following World War II, 475, 476, 477, 478, 484

Reparations Committee (Paris Peace Conference), 118, 119, 120, 124, 125, 126, 158

Replogle, J. Leonard, 331, 431

Republican party: and peace treaty, 149, 151, 152; as offering contrast to Wilsonism, 166–67; after World War I, 177, 184, 188, 189, 191, 194, 216, 219, 250, 253, 256, 257, 264; and Hoover, 224, 225, 226, 239; and farm issues, 237, 238; and Depression crisis, 256–57, 258, 261, 267, 268, 271, 272, 295, 312, 313, 325; in World War II period, 334, 341, 362, 367, 368, 370, 451, 471, 472, 473; after World War II, 514, 522, 524, 532, 533, 536, 537, 538, 539, 564, 575, 579

Reservationists, 151, 152, 153, 272

Resettlement Administration, 312

Resources. *See* Raw materials

Reston, James, 519

Restraint of trade, 208, 215

Reuter's (news agency), 195

Reuther, Walter, 513

Revenue Act (1942), 414

Revolution: Russian, 88, 144; perceived as threat by Wilson and Wilsonians, 164–66. *See also* Bolshevism; Communism

Reynolds, S. M., 200

RFC. *See* Reconstruction Finance Corporation

Rich. *See* Baruch, Bernard M.: and wealth; Class, economic; "Economic royalists"

Richberg, Donald, 293, 294

Riddell, Lord George, 122, 134

Right wing. *See* Conservatism

Ritchie, Albert Cabell, 107, 180, 182–83,

498, 499, 501, 503, 508n, 509n, 523,
526, 548, 549–62 passim, 566, 567
Swope, Mrs. Herbert Bayard, 204
Symington, W. Stuart, 528, 530, 532, 551
Synthetics: rubber, 390–91, 392, 393, 394,
469, 486; nitrates, 390–91

Taft, Robert A., 535, 537
Taft, William Howard, 35
Talese, Gay, 422
Tammany Hall, 190, 191, 192
Tardieu, André, 122, 144, 170, 251, 545
Tariff, 18, 41, 132, 217, 238, 245, 257,
263, 351, 352. *See also* Trade barriers,
international
Taxation: as war measure, 79, 332–33,
336, 339, 340, 341, 366, 377, 380, 381,
384, 403, 404, 407, 408, 411–15, 441,
442, 443, 458; in Depression, 261, 301,
305, 314–18, 320–23; after World War
II, 511, 516, 528, 529, 530, 534, 538,
547
Taxes, 186, 271, 285, 359; progressive,
149, 315, 321; consumer, 261, 315, 385,
411, 413, 414; on liquor, 261, 268, 274;
on automotive transportation, 265–66;
capital gains, 298, 314, 317, 321, 322,
323; undistributed profits, 298, 314, 315,
321, 322, 323; regressive, 315, 385, 412,
443, 514; excess profits, 333, 334, 412,
415, 511, 532; income, 412, 413, 414;
gift, 413–14; withholding, 414, 415;
Victory, 415; proposed cuts in, 509, 511,
512, 514, 519, 571
Teague, Charles C., 282
Teapot Dome, 179
Temporary National Economic Committee,
327
Tennessee Valley Authority (TVA), 373,
425, 458, 492, 493
Texas Gulf Sulphur, 169
Textile industry, 77–78, 87, 227, 294, 401.
See also Clothing industry
Thomas, Charles A., 492n
Thomas, C. S. 185
Thomas, Elbert, 348, 349, 478
Thomas, Elmer, 184
Thomas Amendment, 299
Time, 373, 460, 505
Tin, 93, 96, 354, 358
Tires. *See* Rubber
Tobacco: market, 24; production of, 170,
231
Today, 345
Tolman, Richard, 495
Totalitarianism. *See* Communism; Fascism
"Totalization," 482, 483, 485, 488. *See also*

Nationalization; Socialism
Trade. *See* Demand, consumer; Interna-
tional trade; Production, civilian
Trade associations, 77, 213, 214, 221, 223,
242, 253, 284, 290, 326
Trade barriers, international, 134, 135,
138, 245, 352, 353, 355, 385. *See also*
Embargo; Tariff
Trade war. *See* Economic warfare
Transportation: and mobilization, 68, 81,
176; and question of governmental control, 242–43, 265–66. *See also* Railroads
Transportation Act (1920), 242
Treasury Department: Baruch, as potential
secretary of, 107–8, 109–10, 120, 173,
187; and Depression, 269, 274, 315, 321,
322, 323; and mobilization for World
War II, 406, 408, 411, 412, 413, 414,
415, 442, 454, 468; after World War II,
476, 477, 479, 482, 570, 577, 579
Treaty, atomic energy, 496. *See also* Sanctions, atomic treaty
Treaty, peace, 149–153, 157, 158, 160,
173, 177, 246, 250, 272
Truman, Harry, 5, 7, 218, 368, 370, 437,
458, 465, 471–543 passim, 549, 552,
561, 567, 574. *See also* Baruch, Bernard
M.: and Truman
Truman committee, 392, 422, 441, 454,
458, 463
Truman Doctrine, 514, 516, 522
Trusts, Wilson's opposition to, 36–37, 38,
39. *See also* Antitrust measures
"Truth-in-lending" bill, 544
Tugwell, Rexford, 239n, 268, 269, 274,
275, 283, 284, 285, 288, 292, 305, 311
Tumulty, Joe, 62, 153, 168, 173, 179
Tungsten, 340, 358
Turkey, 514, 515, 518
TVA. *See* Tennessee Valley Authority
Tydings, Millard, 313, 318, 325

UNAEC. *See* United Nations Atomic
Energy Commission
Underdeveloped nations. *See* Developing
nations
Underproduction, 216
Underwood, Oscar, 183
Underwood Tariff, 41
Unemployment, 385, 404, 407, 432; and
inflation, 7, 208, 387, 575, 577, 578; in
Depression, 258, 259, 260, 264, 271,
287, 302, 303, 317, 318, 320, 322, 327,
402, 405; after World War II, 454, 459,
460, 462, 463, 465, 509
Unilateralism, American, 130–41
Unions. *See* Labor: organized

Union Tobacco, 24
United Jewish Appeal, 560, 566
United Nations, 487, 490, 492, 494, 496,
498, 500, 502, 505, 506, 511, 514, 522,
532, 566; Security Council, 495, 498,
501
United Nations Atomic Energy Commission
(UNAEC), 5, 490–91, 493, 495, 498,
500, 501, 502, 504, 505, 512, 634 (n.
105)
United States Atomic Energy Commission
(USAEC), 494n, 495, 501
United States at War, 523
United States Chamber of Commerce, 292,
380, 548
United States Daily, 198
United States News, 198
"United States of Africa," 564
Universal Military Training Law, 520
Uranium, 495
USAEC. See United States Atomic Energy
Commission
U.S. News and World Report, 198
U.S. Steel, 40, 41, 71, 72, 82, 84, 535
Utilities, in World War I, 82, 83
Utopianism, Hoover's, 223, 224

Valenti, Jack, 572, 574, 579
Vandenburg, Arthur, 312, 341, 409, 514,
518
Vanderbilt group, 25
Vanderbilt University, 486
Vanity Fair, 196
Veterans, 466, 470, 477, 509. See also GI
Bill of Rights
Veto power, and atomic energy, 495, 496,
498, 500, 501, 504, 505, 507
Vietnam war, 7, 574, 575, 576, 579
Villard, Oswald Garrison, 195
Vinson, Fred M., 444, 452, 479
Vogue, 196
Voluntarism, 260; Baruch's view of, 7, 9,
234, 291, 520, 532, 534, 535, 547, 557,
560, 578; in relation to Hoover's, 221,
232, 235. See also Cooperation: volun-
tary
"Voluntary priority," 579

Wabash Railroad, 30–31, 40
Wadsworth, James W., 186, 451
Wages, 209, 211, 218, 398, 476; in World
War I, 52, 87; in Depression, 259, 327;
minimum, 290, 291, 292, 323; and
mobilization for World War II, 352, 377,
378, 380, 381, 387, 403, 405, 408, 409,
442, 443, 449, 450, 451, 452; after
World War II, 482, 510, 511, 512, 513,

514, 530, 535, 536, 539, 547, 577. See
also Labor
Wagner, Robert F., 186, 364
Wagner, Robert F., Jr., 549
Wagner Act, 303, 318
Waldorf-Astoria, 23
Wallace, Henry A., 228, 281–83, 284, 293,
302, 305, 321, 323, 338, 358, 359, 375,
392, 396, 420, 421, 425, 431, 436, 438,
453, 456, 465, 469, 471, 473, 475, 480,
483, 502, 503, 504, 542, 634 (n. 108)
Wallace, Henry C., 220, 232, 241, 281
Wall Street. See Baruch, Bernard M.: as
speculator; Market, stock; Speculation
Wall Street Journal, 362, 385, 511
Walsh, Thomas J., 191, 237
War: economic effects of, 42, 43, 44, 51,
61, 73; and prosperity, 42, 43, 44, 218,
227; causes of, 332, 342. See also
Mobilization
Warburg, James P., 33, 275, 276, 277, 307
"War cabinet," 361; Wilson's 57–58,
65–69, 72, 81, 82, 83, 84, 85, 97, 99,
104, 105–6, 110, 116, 117, 119,
130–31, 147, 214; in World War II, 444,
449
War College. See Army War College
War Contracts Act, 462
War costs, 250; as issue at Paris Peace Conference, 126–27, 128, 129, 134, 158. See
also Reparations
War debts: of Allies, 126, 129, 134, 138,
156, 158, 245, 247–48, 250, 260, 272,
273, 274, 276, 277, 353, 386, 431;
domestic, 333, 415; German, after World
War II, 479
War Department, 51, 59, 60, 260, 334, 335,
336, 337, 356, 358, 359, 364, 369, 371,
372, 373, 380, 387, 388, 389, 391, 408,
416, 419, 424, 426, 431, 432, 434, 435,
436, 437, 439, 440, 444, 445, 451,
452, 453, 454, 456, 457, 463, 467, 475,
476, 477, 479, 482. See also Defense
Department; Mobilization
War Finance Corporation, 63, 99, 100, 139,
227, 232, 246
War Industries Board, 4, 51–108 passim,
110, 122, 151, 167, 169, 171, 176, 182,
187, 188, 195, 200, 203, 226, 230, 266,
334, 335, 336, 350, 427, 431, 439, 458,
546, 561; and economic policy of 1920s,
207–21 passim, 230, 234, 235; and Depression policy, 259, 267, 283, 284, 285,
286, 287, 289, 290, 291, 306, 326, 357,
359, 360, 361; as influence on mobilization policy for World War II, 329, 331,
356, 366, 367, 370, 371, 375, 376, 397,